*Paul and the Gentile Problem*

# PAUL AND THE GENTILE PROBLEM

MATTHEW THIESSEN

OXFORD
UNIVERSITY PRESS

# OXFORD
UNIVERSITY PRESS

Oxford University Press is a department of the University of Oxford. It furthers
the University's objective of excellence in research, scholarship, and education
by publishing worldwide. Oxford is a registered trade mark of Oxford University
Press in the UK and in certain other countries

Published in the United States of America by Oxford University Press
198 Madison Avenue, New York, NY 10016, United States of America

© Oxford University Press 2016

First issued as an Oxford University Press paperback, 2018

Library of Congress Cataloging-in-Publication Data
Thiessen, Matthew, 1977–
Paul and the gentile problem/Matthew Thiessen.
pages cm
Includes bibliographical references and indexes.
ISBN 978–0–19–027175–6 (hardcover)—ISBN 978–0–19–027176–3 (ebook)
ISBN 978–0–19–088918–0 (paperback)
1. Bible. Epistles of Paul—Criticism, interpretation, etc. 2. Jews in the New
Testament. 3. Gentiles in the New Testament. I. Title.
BS2655.J4T547 2015
227'.06—dc23
2015017723

*For Jennifer*

# *Contents*

# *Acknowledgments*

THIS BOOK HAS travelled with me as I moved from Durham, North Carolina, to Saskatoon, Saskatchewan, and finally to St. Louis, Missouri. Along the way, I have incurred debts to numerous people and institutions.

Durham: I began formulating the argument of this book while still a doctoral student at Duke University. It brings to bear some of the arguments of my dissertation, now published as *Contesting Conversion: Genealogy, Circumcision, and Conversion in Ancient Judaism and Christianity* (OUP, 2011), on the writings of the apostle Paul. My dissertation advisor, Joel Marcus, remains a model of emulation for me—always available to talk and to offer thoughtful criticism, sage advice, and hearty encouragement. Further, I am indebted to the multiple conversations which I have had with former fellow students at Duke: Hans Arneson, Lori Baron, Nathan Eubank, Jill Hicks-Keeton, T. J. Lang, Colin Miller, David Moffitt, and Isaac Villegas. The communal nature of the Graduate Program in Religion that made Duke such a wonderful place to pursue a Ph.D. continues long after most of us have dispersed.

Saskatoon: Although I was reluctant to face the harsh winters of the Canadian prairies, the opportunity to take up a two-year position at the College of Emmanuel and St. Chad was an absolute godsend at a time when the academic job market was at its lowest point. The cold winters were moderated by the warm welcome provided to me by the faculty, staff, and students of the Saskatoon Theological Union—most of all Bill Richards and Walter Hannam, who made for stimulating conversation partners for this project as well as guides to me as I entered into the vocation of teaching. During my time in Saskatoon I was able to present pieces of Chapters 2 and 3, and received helpful criticism from the participants in the Pauline Epistles Section of the Annual Meeting of the Society of Biblical Literature, San Francisco, 2011, and the New Testament Section of the Canadian Society of Biblical Studies Annual Meeting, Fredericton, New Brunswick, 2011. Concurrent with my appointment at the College of Emmanuel and St. Chad, I received generous financial support in the form of a postdoctoral fellowship from the Social Sciences and Humanities Research Council of Canada. Terry Donaldson, whose numerous writings on the apostle Paul and gentiles have shaped much of my own thinking, kindly agreed to supervise this research and provided incisive comments on early drafts of Chapters 1 and 2.

St. Louis: The majority of this book was written during my time at Saint Louis University. SLU has provided a fruitful context within which to teach, research, and write. I am grateful to a number of my colleagues—especially Geoff Miller,

Daniel Smith, and Jeffrey Wickes—for their insightful remarks made on my work. Additionally, I am thankful to Joshua Jipp, Benjamin White, and Stephen Young for helpful feedback on parts of this book, and particularly Rafael Rodríguez and Matthew Novenson, who both graciously agreed to read an earlier draft of the entire book. The Mellon Foundation provided a generous summer research grant that enabled me to focus on completing this project. Parts of Chapters 4 and 5 were presented to the Scripture in Early Judaism and Christianity section of the Annual Meeting of the Society of Biblical Literature, Baltimore, 2013, the colloquium for the Manfred Lautenschlaeger Award for Theological Promise 2014, and the Pauline Epistles section of the Annual Meeting of the Society of Biblical Literature, San Diego, 2014. I am also grateful to Brill for permitting me to publish here (part of Chapter 2) material it has published in a somewhat different form as "Paul's Argument against Gentile Circumcision in Romans 2:17–29," *Novum Testamentum* 56 (2014): 373–91.

Steve Wiggins, my editor at Oxford University Press, has been a model of patience and wisdom in bringing this manuscript to press. I am grateful for his encouragement, knowledge, and support throughout the process.

The one constant throughout all of these long-distance moves has been my partner, Jennifer Coon. Being married to an academic means having to suffer the consequences of one's spouse's dubious vocational choice. Even when one is fortunate enough to find gainful employment (no small boon!), this "terrible life choice," as Marge Simpson puts it, permits very little flexibility as to where one will live, yet she has joyfully adapted to the many changes of our life together.

# Note on Sources

QUOTATIONS FROM NON-JEWISH Greco-Roman sources come from the Loeb Classical Library. Unless otherwise noted, all other translations are my own.

# Introduction

GAUTAM MALKANI'S NOVEL, *Londonstani*, follows four teenagers, Hardjit, Amit, Ravi, and Jas, who live in the London borough of Hounslow. Surrounded by the dominant British culture, they have grown deeply antagonistic toward *goras*, that is, Caucasian people. In their eyes, their hardworking parents, with their proper British accents, are *gorafied* Indians—they have assimilated to British culture. They call any Indian who takes school seriously, goes to university, holds down a steady job, or, worst of all, listens to mainstream British music a "coconut"—such people look Indian on the outside but are white at heart. In contrast, they perceive themselves to be true *desis*, that is, "natives."

The story is told from the perspective of Jas, who acknowledges with a great deal of shame that he was at one point a coconut himself, dressing and talking like a *gora*, reading books, and applying himself to his studies. Only after Hardjit takes him under his wing does he learn how to behave like a proper *desi*. Nonetheless, when it comes to being a *desi* he admits that "Ravi an the others are better at being it than I am." Throughout, Jas struggles to fit in with those around him, never quite seeming to be comfortable in his own skin or fully accepted by those whom he tries to emulate.[1]

*Londonstani* provides a powerful portrayal of the modern intersection of ethnicity, religion, and identity construction. Who is Indian? How does one remain true to one's "Indianness" while living in London? Can people lose their Indian identity, becoming "gorafied" or turning into "coconuts"? How does one go about establishing borders around Indian identity? Who gets to define authentic Indian behavior? And, once it is defined, how does one police these borders?

The identity issues that Malkani raises parallel many of the same sorts of questions that the apostle Paul faced. Like *Londonstani*, Paul's letters deal with questions of ethnic and religious identity, albeit in the first-century CE Greco-Roman world. The letters to Rome and Galatia, in particular, focus on matters surrounding the observance of the Jewish law, as well as questions pertaining to descent from Abraham. In short, Jews, non-Jews, and their respective identities and practices are central to Paul's writings.[2] Jewish identity has never been something fixed or stable, but it was particularly in the Greco-Roman period that such identity construction was contested. Like other subjugated ethnicities, Jews in the first century CE faced the question of what it meant to be Jewish living within the cultural environment of the Greco-Roman world. (Of course, Greeks and Romans were likewise involved in the complex task of identity construction.[3]) Yet, just as *Londonstani* portrays the disdain of these teenagers toward the "gorafication" of

Indians, some Jews lamented what they perceived to be the "Greekification" of their compatriots. For instance, the author of 2 Maccabees bemoaned the hellenization and "foreignization" (*allophylismos*) of Jews in the days of the wicked and false high priest Jason (4:13). It should not be surprising, then, that Jews provided numerous different answers to the problem of identity construction in the Greco-Roman world.[4] Many interpreters of Paul conclude, based on passages such as Rom 2:28–29, in which Paul seems to redefine Jewishness as something internal, and Gal 6:16, where Paul appears to redefine Israel as the Christian Church, that he too was involved in the process of Jewish identity construction, radically redefining Jewishness so as to include gentiles who believe in Christ and exclude Jews who do not.[5]

## *Reading as the Creation of Coherence*

But it is the ending of *Londonstani* that I believe nicely exemplifies the problem facing modern interpreters of Paul's letters. In the final pages of the book, Malkani surprises his readers who have, to this point, constructed a particular image of Jas in their minds. The narrative comes to a close with Jas's estranged parents trying to figure out why their son bears them so much animosity. Jas's father asks him, "What's wrong with us, son? What's wrong with us that you spend more time with Hardjit's father and mother than you do with your own father and mother?" Not getting a response, his father again prods him, "I don't even know why we agree to use this Jas nonsense nickname of yours anyway, I mean what kind of a name is that, Jason? You hear what your mother and I are trying to say to you, Jason?" This question jars readers, who until now have likely thought that Jas was a shortened form of Jaswinder, not Jason—an oddly western name for someone of Indian descent. His father pushes his point yet again: "What nonsense is this you don't even respond to your own name? Jason Bartholomew-Cliveden, do you hear what I'm saying?" Now readers have been entirely thrown—Bartholomew-Cliveden is surely not an Indian surname. Still not getting any response, his father grabs Jas's medical chart and shoves it in his son's face: "Look, he says.—It says your name here on your medical chart: Jason Bartholomew-Cliveden, aged nineteen, white, male."[6]

And the shoe finally drops. Jas is not an Indian named Jaswinder, but a Caucasian male named Jason Bartholomew-Cliveden. For over three hundred pages readers have constructed a particular portrait of Jas in their minds: he is a male teenager of Indian descent. As a result, they unconsciously but systematically interpret statements and incidents within the narrative based on the notion that Jas is Indian. On the whole, this interpretation, even though it turns out to be wrong, appears both coherent and compelling. Most of the data fit with readers' assumptions that Jas is Indian, and those details that do not are easy to miss. Because of the coherence of this interpretation, they never suspect that the main character is something quite different from how he presents himself. Of course, readers do not see what characters within the novel would see—Jas's appearance would presumably give his non-Indian identity away. Instead, because Jas is so ashamed of his ethnicity, he hides this from readers, never telling us his full name. Only when his father forces him to confront these facts do readers realize that their (generally unrecognized as such) interpretation, while cogent, is actually incorrect. Wolfgang Iser has argued that "Consistency-building is the indispens-able basis for all acts of comprehension, and this in its turn is dependent upon processes of selection. This basic structure is exploited by literary texts in such a way that the reader's imagination can be manipulated and even reoriented."[7] The narrative of *Londonstani* manipulates its readers in precisely this way.

Just like readers of *Londonstani*, readers of Paul make numerous interpretive decisions, many of which go unrecognized. The act of reading requires inter-pretation, which is, most basically, a matter of attempting to create coherence or meaning out of a given set of information. When it comes to Paul's letters, the hard work of interpretation is made all the more difficult by a number of facts. First, interpreters of Paul are not reading a single work—a novel or a gos-pel or a monograph. Instead, they need to deal with the evidence of seven let-ters (or possibly a few more, depending on one's stance on the six disputed letters of Ephesians, Colossians, 2 Thessalonians, 1–2 Timothy, and Titus).[8] For example, while the task of providing a coherent reading of Paul's view of the law in Galatians is difficult, the quest for coherence across all of Paul's writings becomes exponentially more so. Second, Paul's letters are occasional, directed to specific people, living in particular places, at specific times, facing peculiar issues. Although careful historical work can help modern interpreters, we know with certainty neither the identity of those people to whom Paul wrote nor the exact issues that occasioned his letter writing. Paul's initial readers had one important advantage over every subsequent reader: they knew what Paul was responding to and to whom he was writing. In this sense, they are like the char-acters within Malkani's novel who can see Jas and thus are unable to fall into the same interpretive traps that the reader does with regard to Jas's ethnicity. If Paul's initial readers parallel characters within *Londonstani*, then modern read-ers of Paul parallel readers of *Londonstani*, who are not privy to all the informa-tion that Malkani's literary characters would have had. While scholars frequently provide accounts of what issues Paul's assemblies (*ekklēsiai*) faced,[9] much of this work occurs through what John M. G. Barclay calls "mirror-reading," that is, arguing that Paul's statements within his letters reflect direct responses to the teachings or beliefs of a group of people whom Paul opposes.[10] This scholarly attempt to reconstruct both the identity and the message of Paul's opponents from the evidence of Paul's letters is akin to the reader's attempt to provide a construction of Jas's identity based upon what he and others say because they cannot actually see Jas. While interpreters must provide some reconstruction of the issue to which Paul responds, I am convinced that most have inaccurately identified this issue. This error, consequently, leads them to seemingly coherent, albeit incorrect, accounts of Paul's thinking.

While making their way through the narrative of *Londonstani*, readers attribute Jas's inability to fit in with his peers to his awkwardness and lack of self-confidence. But upon discovering that he is Caucasian, they find that numerous details within the preceding narrative take on new meaning. Surely one cause of Jas's insecurity is the fact that he is a Caucasian male who has adopted the speech and customs of one particular Indian subculture. Previously, when Jas says to himself, "Let's face it, Mum an Dad weren't gonna do any a the Diwali dusting," readers think either that his parents are lazy or that they have assimilated to such a degree that they no longer celebrate this five-day festival. Now readers realize that, not being Indian, they never celebrated Diwali. When Jas compares his mother's behavior to the way that the mother of his friend Arun has been acting in preparation for a wedding, he states without explanation that Arun did not think this comparison worked "cos apparently that's different." We now realize that Arun rejected this comparison because Jas's mother was Caucasian, while his own mother was Indian. When Jas interferes in the wedding planning and tells Arun to stand up to his mother, Arun's mother asks him why he is speaking, claiming, "You don't understand such things" about "our proper style" of weddings. At first, readers think that the mother criticizes Jas for being too young to appreciate his own culture's traditions. Now we realize that she is angry with him because he is, in fact, an outsider who has criticized Indian traditions.[11] The words remain the same, yet their meaning changes.

Just as the significance of these statements is transformed in light of the reader's realization that Jas is Caucasian and not Indian, so too does the meaning of Paul's statements depend upon the conjectured historical context within which modern scholarship sets them. Anticipating the argument below, if scholars assume that Paul attacks the religion of Judaism in defense of Christianity, one will find the evidence for such an attack within his letters, while relegating data that do not fit this interpretive model to a lesser role within Paul's thinking. But if one conceives of another occasion for Paul's letters, one might find that these statements suggest something quite different and that other previously underappreciated aspects of Paul's writings make far greater sense.

## Judaism and the Quagmire of Pauline Studies

Any attempt to provide a coherent account of Paul's thinking must consider the predominance of his quotations and echoes of Jewish scriptures,[12] his references to biblical characters and events, his discussions of Jewish rituals, such as circumcision and dietary laws, as well as Jewish beliefs, such as the division of humanity into the categories of Jew and gentile.[13] In light of this evidence, it is understandable that so many scholars have concluded that Paul writes to communities of Jews, or at least to mixed communities of Jews and gentiles, to warn them of the dangers of the Jewish law or the religion of Judaism.

But why, according to such accounts, does Paul warn his readers against Judaism? This question has led to considerable debate in the last few decades. As noted above, it is no small task to provide a coherent account of Paul's thinking by examining multiple letters that were addressed to different people in different places at different times in Paul's life. Inexorably, then, modern Pauline interpreters have found themselves at odds with one another in their efforts to provide a coherent reading of Paul's thinking, especially with regard to the Jewish law. While this fact should not elicit surprise, it has led a few scholars to conclude that the very existence of these competing readings of Paul highlights the fact that such coherence-creating accounts fail because Paul's own thinking was self-contradictory. For instance, Heikki Räisänen avers that "contradictions and tensions have to be *accepted* as *constant* features of Paul's theology of the law."[14] Although it is possible that Paul was, in the end, fundamentally confused and thus incoherent in his views of the Jewish law, interpreters must exhaust all other possibilities before coming to this conclusion. The reader's first task is to attempt to provide a coherent reading of a work (or, in this case, Paul's letters) that takes into account all or as much of the evidence as possible. With regard to claims that Paul's view of the Jewish law is fundamentally incoherent, John G. Gager rightly cautions, "The danger that must be overcome is cultural myopia, the all-too-familiar tendency to label something as inconsistent or irrational simply because it fails to follow our way of thinking or because we have not plunged deeply enough into the circumstances surrounding the original author and readers."[15]

Scholarly literature on Paul and the Jewish law is voluminous, yet the majority of Pauline interpreters locate most coherence-creating attempts within one of two camps, an anti-legalistic Paul, often referred to as the "Lutheran reading," and an anti-ethnocentric Paul, often referred to as the "new perspective" on Paul.[16] Those holding to an anti-legalistic reading of Paul often assert that Judaism required people to keep the Jewish law in order to participate in Israel's salvation.[17] At the same time, such interpreters generally maintain that the Jewish law was impossible to keep perfectly.[18] Despite this fact, there were some Jews who wrongly convinced themselves of their ability to keep the law and thus became guilty of self-deluded pride. In contrast, there were other Jews who were more honest with their own shortcomings and saw that they did not, and could not, keep the law. For such Jews, the result was despair. Rudolf Bultmann, for instance, claims that to take the Jewish law "seriously meant making life an intolerable burden. It was almost impossible to *know* the rules, let alone put them into practice." In this coherence-creating reading, Paul's problem with Judaism was that it required people to earn their salvation through good works. In contrast, Paul preached a gospel of faith in Christ Jesus, apart from works. As Martin Luther asserted, Paul "shuts out the Jews, and all such as will work for their salvation."[19] Most scholars within this stream of Pauline interpretation believe that Judaism, or at least Judaism as Paul understood it,[20] was a religion of "works-righteousness" that required perfect obedience to the Jewish law for one to be saved. Thus Paul vehemently fought against this religion (and, by extension, all other religions), which inescapably led either to anguish or arrogance, in order to proclaim that God had provided a way of salvation in Christ that was unrelated to human effort, and therefore free from both self-despair and self-reliance. In short, such readings of Paul's letters contrast Pauline Christianity, a religion emphasizing human faith and divine grace, to Judaism, a legalistic religion stressing human works and divine judgment.

At the beginning of the twentieth century, a few biblical scholars began to question the way in which previous scholarship had used Judaism as a foil for Christianity. George Foot Moore, for instance, demonstrated that Christian polemical and apologetic concerns, not attention to historical accuracy, too often dictated how scholars portrayed early Judaism.[21] A growing aspiration to understand Jewish thinking on its own terms, combined with the horrors of the Holocaust, motivated many biblical scholars to reconsider the ways in which they depicted ancient Judaism. Markus Barth and Krister Stendahl called for a new reading of Paul in relation to the Judaism of his day, a call that E. P. Sanders's *Paul and Palestinian Judaism* answered most proficiently.[22] In this work, Sanders made the case that Judaism was neither a religion that was concerned with the question "How might a person be saved?" nor a system of works-righteousness that promised salvation only to those who had achieved perfect obedience to the Jewish law. Most important for Sanders was the fact that the Jewish law contained within itself the means of recourse for when Jews broke it. That is to say, built into the Jewish law was the knowledge that people would keep it imperfectly. Instead of condemning people for this inability, the law provided them a way to remedy the situation: repentance and the temple cult. According to Sanders, the sacrificial system demonstrates that Judaism was a religion of grace: "covenantal nomism [the dominant form of Jewish thinking, according to Sanders] is the view that one's place in God's plan is established on the basis of the covenant and the covenant requires as the proper response of man his obedience to its commandments, while providing means of atonement for transgression."[23] Any sympathetic reading of Jewish scriptures and early Jewish literature cannot fail to observe the dense connections between divine grace and human deeds. Paul himself could hardly have ignored this fact. Consequently, as George Howard asserts, "For Paul to have argued that the law demanded absolute obedience and that one legal infraction brought with it unpardonable doom, would have been for him to deny what all the world knew, namely, that the Jerusalem Temple stood as a monument to the belief that Yahweh was a forgiving God who pardoned his people when they sinned."[24]

While not belonging to the anti-ethnocentric reading of Paul tradition, Sanders's account of early Judaism functions as the basis for this line of interpretation.[25] Those scholars who accept Sanders's assessment of the significance of grace and election in the Judaism of Paul's day, most notably N. T. Wright and James D. G. Dunn, argue that Paul did not think that Judaism was legalistic.[26] Furthermore, as Dunn rightly notes, the role that good works play in the apostle Paul's writings makes it difficult to distinguish early Judaism from Pauline Christianity on the basis of human works versus divine work: "If it is indeed fair to characterise [and condemn] Jewish soteriology as synergistic, should we not in fairness read the exhortations in passages like Rom. 12.9–21, Gal. 6.1–5 and Col. 3.5—4.1 in a similar way? Was Paul's 'works of faith and labour of love' (1 Thess. 1.3) or his 'faith working through love' (Gal. 5.6) or his 'obedience of faith' (Rom. 1.5) as synergistic in its own way as Judaism's covenantal nomism?"[27] Attempts to create coherence out of Paul's statements on the Jewish law by distinguishing between a works-righteousness in Judaism and a work-free Pauline gospel falter on the evidence of Paul's own letters, which contain an ethical code that is at least as demanding as those that are found in other forms of early Judaism.[28]

Instead, both Dunn and Wright argue that one of Paul's primary problems with Judaism was that it was ethnocentric and exclusivistic. While Jews did not think that they needed to keep the law perfectly, they did believe that God had elected them and had given them the law in order to set them apart from the other nations. Consequently, the observance of the Jewish law, particularly circumcision, Sabbath, and dietary laws, functioned as an identity badge that distinguished Jews from non-Jews. In the readings of Dunn and Wright, Judaism insisted that gentiles could only enjoy the covenantal benefits that Jews possessed by undergoing circumcision and adoption of the Jewish law. That is to say, gentiles needed to become Jews. It was this ethnocentricity, according to Dunn and Wright, that Paul resisted, preaching a gospel that was free from the observance of such distinctively Jewish rites.

Yet this portrayal of Paul's problem with Judaism is not without its own set of issues. For instance, Gager criticizes Dunn for continuing to caricature Judaism negatively: "His emphasis on Jewish ethnic pride reverts to the outmoded, unhistorical dichotomy between Jewish particularism and Christian universalism."[29]

Although Dunn has taken issue with this charge in the 2008 introduction to his collected essays on Paul, it is difficult not to see a caricatured portrait of early Judaism, since he implicitly compares early Jewish ethnocentrism to modern ethnic conflicts such as apartheid in South Africa, segregation in the United States, and the Rwandan genocide, concluding of early Jewish ethnocentrism:

> It is a kind of fundamentalism which can only safeguard the correctness of its belief by persecuting those who disagree or by seeking to eliminate (through conversion or otherwise) those who hold divergent views. That sort of exclusivism can produce a complete spectrum of violence, from the most subtle of social pressure to outright force. It was that sort of "attitude to the law" which Paul came to abhor.[30]

Further, Paul's own letters contain considerable evidence of how deeply ethnocentric his own thinking was, stressing, for instance, that the gospel was for the Jew first, and then for the Greek (e.g., Rom 1:16). Even something as basic as Paul's frequent use of the term "gentile" to refer to all non-Jews demonstrates the ethnocentric nature of his thought—dissolving all non-Jewish ethnicities and cultures into one catch-all word.[31] Paul appears to be at least as indebted to an ideology that divides humans into two categories—Jews and non-Jews—as any of his Jewish contemporaries. In fact, Ishay Rosen-Zvi and Adi Ophir argue, in contrast to the majority of Pauline interpreters, that, "if there is a consistent effort in his letters, it is to erect 'the dividing wall' between Jews and non-Jews."[32]

In assessing the claims of the anti-ethnocentric reading of Paul, it might be helpful to briefly map Paul's thinking in terms of modern ethnographic theory. Following the work of Fredrik Barth, most ethnographers distinguish between primordialist and constructivist conceptions of ethnicity.[33] In brief, the former conception understands ethnicity to be an essence inherent to human beings, while the latter understands ethnicity to be a social construction that has no objective basis in reality. Some Pauline scholars have attempted to bring such ethnographic theory to bear on Paul's thinking, implying that Paul is self-consciously a constructivist—Paul redefines Jewishness in order to include gentiles in the people of God. But, as R. Barry Matlock argues, Paul, like most, if not all, of his Jewish contemporaries, understood Jewishness and gentileness in essentialist terms—these were divinely instituted identities.[34] Like most people throughout history, Paul was what ethnographers call a primordialist. As we shall see in Chapter 4, even when Paul portrays the incorporation of gentiles into the "domesticated olive tree" (Romans 11), he continues to distinguish between Jewish and gentile identity because he thinks that these are God-ordained natures.[35] In other words, contrary to the anti-ethnocentric reading of Paul, Paul's worldview was no less ethnocentric than that of his Jewish contemporaries.

## *A New Argument for the Coherence of Paul*

Although the debate between anti-legalist and anti-ethnocentric readers of Paul continues to rage, they agree on two essential issues. First, they agree that Paul wrote Galatians and Romans, the letters in which Paul has the most to say about the Jewish law, to communities that contained both Jewish and gentile Christ-followers and that he meant such remarks to address both groups. Second, in light of their shared assumption that Paul intended to address both Jews and gentiles, these scholars believe that Paul's letters contain substantial criticisms of Judaism. I disagree with both of these assumptions and am convinced that both readings misunderstand Paul in the same way that assuming Jas is Indian inevitably leads readers to misunderstand *Londonstani*.

For too long, interpreters have read Paul's letters under the—on this point at least—negative influence of early Christian writers who allowed their own efforts to create a Christian identity distinct from Jewish identity to color their understanding of Paul. Paul's statements on the Jewish law provided the perfect fodder for early Christian writers, such as Justin, Jerome, and Chrysostom, who opposed Christians who were attracted to Judaism.[36] Yet numerous scholars have argued that terms such as "Judaism" and "Christianity" are anachronisms that unavoidably distort first-century CE realities.[37] To be sure, such anti-Jewish interpretations of Paul's letters have a degree of cogency to them. There remain, however, a few troublesome details that threaten the coherence of this reading.[38]

In the following pages I will argue for a thoroughgoing consistency to Paul's statements about the law and its relationship to his gospel. This consistency arises out of Paul's claim that Jewish scriptures previously preached his circumcision-free gospel for gentiles to Abraham: "Scripture foreseeing that God would justify the gentiles through faith, prepreached the gospel to Abraham, saying 'In you will all the gentiles be blessed'" (Gal 3:8). Paul therefore implies that a proper understanding of the Abraham Narrative (Gen 12:1—25:11) enables one to comprehend more fully his own thinking on circumcision, the Jewish law, and the gospel to gentiles. For this reason, I focus on Paul's understanding of the rite of circumcision and the Abraham Narrative in his letters to the Romans and the Galatians. Although my argument fits neither the anti-legalist nor the anti-ethnocentric understanding of Paul, it draws on insights from both.

My starting point for Paul's understanding of the Jewish law may seem an unlikely one, but I believe it is the internal key to interpreting Paul's view of the law. In writing to Christ followers in the city of Corinth, Paul advises those who are uncircumcised to remain uncircumcised and those who are circumcised to remain circumcised.[39] He then provides his rationale for this admonition: "Circumcision is nothing and uncircumcision [literally, "foreskin"] is nothing, but (what matters is) keeping the commandments of God" (ἡ περιτομὴ οὐδέν ἐστιν καὶ ἡ ἀκροβυστία οὐδέν ἐστιν, ἀλλὰ τήρησις ἐντολῶν θεοῦ, 1 Cor 7:19; cf. the similar slogan in Gal 5:6; 6:15). As Sanders exclaims, this is "one of the most amazing sentences [Paul] ever wrote."[40] How can Paul say that circumcision is nothing in one breath and, then, in the next breath, insist upon the importance of keeping God's commandments? To any person who viewed the Pentateuch as the oracles of God (cf. Rom 3:2), how could it make sense to distinguish between circumcision and the commandments of God? After all, Jewish scriptures explicitly state that God commanded the rite of circumcision (Genesis 17; Lev 12:3). Trying to make sense of this conundrum, numerous Christian interpreters argue that Paul contrasts the commandments of God as they are found in discipleship to Christ to the commandments of the written code of the Jewish law. C. K. Barrett's remarks are representative: "That *we keep God's commandments* means an obedience to the will of God as disclosed in his Son far more radical than the observance of any code, whether ceremonial or moral, could be."[41] But this interpretation is unconvincing since Paul does not state that these commandments of God are christologically focused. For that matter, it is not clear why a radical obedience to the will of God as it is disclosed in Christ necessarily precludes the observance of circumcision. Only a reader who comes to the text with later Christian assumptions about the irrelevance of circumcision could find such an interpretation compelling. In fact, Paul's use of the verb "to keep" (τηρέω) with the noun "commandment" (ἐντολή), a construction that other Jews used to signify faithful observance of the Jewish law (cf. Sir 32:23; *T. Dan.* 5.1; Josephus, *Ant.* 8.120; Matt 19:17–19; Rev 12:17; 14:12), suggests that Paul signals the abiding relevance of law observance.[42]

The answer to the riddle which 1 Cor 7:19 poses comes from the realization that Paul frequently uses the words "circumcision" and "uncircumcision" to refer to Jews and gentiles, respectively. Most explicitly, in portraying his discussion with the leaders of the Jerusalem assembly of Christ followers, Paul tells the Galatians that these leaders saw that God had entrusted him with the gospel of the uncircumcision (τὸ εὐαγγέλιον τῆς ἀκροβυστίας) and Peter with the gospel of the circumcision ([τὸ εὐαγγέλιον] τῆς περιτομῆς, Gal 2:7). Paul makes it clear that the term "uncircumcision" stands for the gentiles, since he states in the next sentence that God appointed him to be the apostle "to the gentiles" (εἰς τὰ ἔθνη, 2:8). His claim that God entrusted Peter with the gospel of the circumcision implies that Peter was ordained to be the apostle to the Jews. The letter to the Ephesians also demonstrates this usage, since the author claims that gentiles were "called 'the uncircumcision' by what is called 'the circumcision' [i.e., the Jews]" (οἱ λεγόμενοι ἀκροβυστία ὑπὸ τῆς λεγομένης περιτομῆς, 2:11). As Joel Marcus argues, this verse, as well as the evidence of Galatians and Romans, indicates that people within Pauline assemblies used "circumcision" and "uncircumcision" as epithets to refer to Jews and gentiles.[43]

Paul's statement that neither circumcision nor uncircumcision matters now makes better sense. Paul does not contrast the rite of circumcision to the commandments of God; rather, he claims that being Jewish (circumcision) or being gentile (uncircumcision) does not matter—only keeping the commandments that God requires of each group of people.[44] Paul's discussion of circumcision and uncircumcision occurs within a broader context in which Paul stresses that people should not seek another form of life; rather, they should lead the life that God has assigned to them: the married should remain married, the single should remain single, and the slave should remain a slave.

In support of this interpretation, Niko Huttunen has demonstrated that this passage contains significant parallels to the later teachings of the Stoic philosopher Epictetus, who likewise argues that external things such as status and position are matters of indifference.[45] To the question "What is the law of God?" Epictetus answers, "To guard what is his own, not to lay claim to what is not his own, but to make use of what is given him, and not to yearn for what has not been given" (τίς δ'ὁ νόμος ὁ θεῖος; τὰ ἴδια τηρεῖν, τῶν ἀλλοτρίων μὴ ἀντιποιεῖσθαι, ἀλλὰ διδομένοις μὲν χρῆσθαι, μὴ διδόμενα δὲ μὴ ποθεῖν, *Discourses* 2.16.28). For Epictetus, one's position is indifferent; God's law is to keep (τηρεῖν; cf. 1 Cor 7:19) those things (what Epictetus elsewhere refers to as "the commandments and ordinances" [ἐντολὰς καὶ τὰ προστάγματα], 3.23.113–114; cf. 1 Cor 7:19) that pertain to one's position or calling, which comes from God. What matters is fidelity to the summons or calling of God (τὴν κλῆσιν ἣν κέκληκεν, 1.29.49; cf. 1 Cor 7:17). When Paul talks about neither circumcision nor uncircumcision mattering, then, he refers to the status or position associated with being circumcised or uncircumcised, that is, with being Jewish or gentile. Speaking of a similar phrase in Gal 5:6, Barclay helpfully asks, if "the issue here were justification by good works (the Lutheran reading), the inclusion of uncircumcision would be incomprehensible: circumcision is a work, but how is leaving oneself uncircumcised a work? Yet Paul equally discounts *both* circumcision *and* uncircumcision. And if the issue at stake were national restriction or exclusion (as in 'the new perspective'), why is uncircumcision—a mark of non-particularity—also here devalued?"[46] These statements apply equally well to 1 Cor 7:19. Paul argues that his readers should not worry themselves about their position, only about the commandments that pertain to that position: "Paul's exhortation proves that God's distributive activity is not just an option which people are allowed to accept or repudiate. What God has given is in fact an assignment."[47]

Paul claims that he teaches this same rule in all of his assemblies (καὶ οὕτως ἐν ταῖς ἐκκλησίαις πάσαις διατάσσομαι, 1 Cor 7:17). Consequently, William S. Campbell concludes that "it must have operated as an important element in Paul's formation of his communities and their ongoing identity construction."[48] Like a number of other interpreters, therefore, I believe that this passage serves as a hermeneutical clue for how to understand Paul's teaching about the Jewish law in general: this passage acts as a baseline of coherence regardless of the various contingencies of Paul's letters. He argues that Jews should keep the laws that God gave to them, while gentiles should be satisfied with the laws that God has laid upon them, not coveting those laws that God has given to Jews alone. Pamela Eisenbaum puts it well:

> God did indeed command Abraham to be circumcised and to circumcise all the male members of his family. This biblical event becomes known later in Jewish tradition as the *berit milah*, the covenant of circumcision, and it is indeed regarded as one of God's most important commandments for most any Jew of Paul's time. But it is understood as a marker of Jewish identity and incumbent on Jewish males *only*. In other words, the commandment to circumcise applies specifically and exclusively to Jewish males, meaning it is not appropriate to circumcise Gentiles, for God did not and does not command Gentiles to be circumcised. When Paul says, "Circumcision is nothing and uncircumcision is nothing; but obeying the commandments of God is everything," he is not therefore claiming that circumcision is a meaningless ritual that can be ignored. Rather, Paul's point is that God does not require the same things of all people at all times. Priests, for example, had to obey a set of purity laws that did not apply to Israelites in general. Since only Jews are commanded to be circumcised, Gentiles are following the will of God by not being circumcised.[49]

Eisenbaum's remarks fit within what some scholars refer to as the "radical new perspective" on Paul, a reading that understands him to be speaking predominantly to gentiles, not Jews.[50] This book aligns most closely with this interpretation of Paul, which attempts to do justice to Paul's repeated claims that he is an apostle to non-Jews. Following the lead of a number of recent scholars, though, I think it more appropriate to refer to this stream of scholarship not as a "radical new perspective," but as the *Paul within Judaism* perspective, a designation that rightly stresses its difference from both the anti-legalistic and anti-ethnocentric readings of Paul, both of which, for different reasons, set Paul in *opposition to* Judaism.[51]

If Paul holds that both Jewish and gentile Christ followers need to keep the commandments of God, but that these commandments differ for the two groups, then it is imperative that interpreters correctly identify whom Paul intends to address in his letters (or specific passages within his letters). This question is distinct from the question of the actual initial audience of Paul's letter. Two thousand years of intervening history have made it difficult for modern readers of Paul to determine his original readership. We do not and cannot know with any certainty the precise makeup of the assemblies in Rome, Galatia, Corinth, or Philippi. All we have are the arguments of Paul's letters and the evidence contained therein that might help us reconstruct whom Paul intended to address when he wrote these individual letters. Any attempt to understand Paul's letters, consequently, must begin with his oft-repeated assertions that God called him and set him apart as his agent to preach the gospel of Christ to the gentiles (e.g., Rom 1:5; 11:13; 15:16; Galatians 2; cf. Eph 3:6–8). These claims to having divine authority to preach to gentiles suggest that he wrote primarily, perhaps even exclusively, for gentiles-in-Christ. Therefore, when Paul quotes Jewish scriptures or comments on the Jewish law, he does so in relation to his mission to non-Jews.

As a number of scholars have previously argued, at virtually every point modern readers need to interpret Paul's letters in light of this intended gentile audience.[52] By reading his letters as though he intends to speak to Jews, Christ followers or otherwise, and against Judaism, interpreters universalize Paul's arguments in ways that he never intended, and in so doing commit a reading error analogous to the mistake readers of *Londonstani* make in thinking that Jas is Indian. Such readings account for much of the material within Paul's letters, yet they nonetheless fundamentally misunderstand them. Later Christians needed this universalization of Paul's letters in order to distinguish Christianity from Judaism and to protect against Christian attraction to Judaism. In his extant letters, though, Paul rarely intends his remarks to address Jews directly. In his mind, only the gentiles fall under his purview and authority. To be sure—and here I part ways with some proponents of the Paul-within-Judaism perspective—Paul stresses that the gospel is for the Jew first, then for the Greek (Rom 1:16), but this claim does not necessitate that he directed his own preaching toward Jews first and then to gentiles. Just prior to this sentiment, Paul states that he is God's ordained apostle to the gentiles (Rom 1:5, 1:13–15). Romans 1:16, therefore, provides no evidence of his own missionary practices; rather, the verse encapsulates the two-pronged mission of the early Jesus movement that he mentions in Galatians 2—his gospel was divinely given for gentiles, while Peter's gospel was divinely given for Jews (Gal 2:7–9).[53] Based on his own explicit claims that he is the apostle to the gentiles, it is historically more accurate to read his letters as addressing gentiles, and thus considerably more helpful in our quest for providing a coherent account of Paul's thinking. This assumption, together with Paul's remarks in 1 Cor 7:19, provides the hermeneutical key to reading Paul's letters.

# *Outline of* Paul and the Gentile Problem

This book consists of two major sections. Part 1 remaps Paul's thinking in relation to Jewish ideologies of gentiles and then reexamines two key texts for my claim that Paul does not attack Judaism or the Jewish law: Rom 2:17–29 and Gal 4:21–31. These texts are central to both anti-legalist and anti-ethnocentric readings of Paul, and potentially problematic for reading Paul within Judaism, purportedly demonstrating Paul's opposition to and redefinition of the Jewish rite of circumcision. In Part 2, I will provide an account of Paul's own solution to what he believes to be the gentile problem.

## Part 1: Jewish Universalism and the Gentile Problem

Modern interpreters must understand Paul's statements about law observance, and circumcision in particular, within an entirely different context than a conflict between two different systems of religion—a law-observant Judaism and a law-free Christianity. Since Paul intends to write to gentiles about the way that God is now including them in Israel's story, one must read his letters within contemporary Jewish debates over the way in which gentiles relate to Israel and Israel's God. To be sure, it is improbable that all Jews in Paul's day concerned themselves with this issue, but since it is clear that Paul and other early Christ followers found themselves wrestling with the implications of the Christ event for gentiles, they likely depended, in part, upon preexisting resources within Jewish thinking to answer this question. For this reason, Part 1 of this book first surveys the different answers some Jews gave to the gentile problem and then resituates Paul within, not against, these debates.

In his classic study on conversion, A. D. Nock states, "Judaism said in effect to a [gentile] who was thinking of becoming a proselyte: 'You are in your sins. Make a new start, put aside idolatry and the immoral practices which go with it, become a naturalized member of the Chosen People by a threefold rite of baptism, circumcision, and offering, live as God's Law commands, and you will have every hope of a share in the life of the world to come.' "[54] For many years, Nock's study on conversion in antiquity has shaped the way in which scholars have thought about early Jewish approaches to gentiles. Nonetheless, his portrayal of Judaism is problematic. Most importantly, Nock's statement assumes that Judaism was a monolithic system of belief and practice and, therefore, that there was one single and universal Jewish solution to the gentile problem—proselytizing. Modern scholarship has made it abundantly clear that these remarks do not fit the evidence of early Judaism. Paula Fredriksen puts it well: "Judaism, of course, did not have views of Gentiles; Jews did. Their encounter with other nations, across cultures and centuries, resulted in a jumble of perceptions, prejudices, optative descriptions, social arrangements, and daily accommodations that we can reconstruct from the various literary and epigraphical evidence only with difficulty."[55] For instance, Josephus mentions three sects, the Sadducees, the Pharisees, and the Essenes, each with their own distinctive practices and beliefs,[56] while the Palestinian Talmud claims that there were as many as twenty-four different sects flourishing at the time of the Jerusalem Temple's destruction (*y. Sanh.* 10.6). Whatever the precise number of distinctive Jewish groups in the first-century CE, we should not be surprised that Jews put forward numerous proposed solutions to the problem gentiles faced.[57] Second, this portrayal of Judaism as a missionary religion goes well beyond the evidence of Second Temple Jewish literature, unwittingly fashioning Judaism in the image of Christianity.

Returning briefly to *Londonstani*, Jas's Caucasian ethnicity raises questions about other aspects of the narrative. Jas learns to speak, dress, and act like his peers. He even adopts numerous ethno-religious customs, such as Diwali and proper funeral observances. How do people of Indian descent view such behavior? Are they honored that he would try to imitate them? Or are they insulted because he has co-opted their cultural distinctives? Of course, the possibility exists that some Indians would be honored and others insulted, or even that some would be honored with regard to certain aspects of this imitation but insulted by other aspects. Such questions, I believe, are of tremendous import for understanding Paul's letters. As Alan F. Segal observes, in modern scholarship on early Judaism and Paul, a "strong argument rages over whether or to what extent Jews proselytized. Few fully recognize or analyze the obvious fact that different Jews and different Jewish sects reached different opinions about proselytism and behaved accordingly. Attitudes range from a total denial of a mission to the gentiles to an extreme interest in one."[58]

Chapter 1, then, begins with a survey of the variety of attempts some early Jews made to relate gentiles to Israel's God. Terence L. Donaldson has recently organized the literary evidence of Jewish openness to gentiles into one of four basic categories: sympathization, ethical monotheism, eschatological pilgrimage, and conversion.[59] Given his emphasis on patterns of universalism in early Jewish thinking, it is understandable that Donaldson focuses only on strategies of openness. This focus, though, could unintentionally lead to the inaccurate conclusion that Second Temple Jews were universally interested in answering the question of how to relate gentiles to Israel and Israel's God and always did so with openness. It is therefore important to note both that many Jews likely gave little thought to this question, and that some of those who did answered the question in non-universalistic ways. Some Jews, as I have argued elsewhere, and as I will discuss in Chapter 1, thought gentiles were excluded from any positive connection to Israel and Israel's God.[60] Reading Paul's letters in light of these disagreements enables modern readers to relate both Paul's own approach to gentiles and that of his opponents to preexisting Jewish patterns. Paul's letters and the controversies that occasioned them serve as a distinctive continuation of a debate that had been going on, and would continue to do so, within Jewish circles for centuries. Paul's opponents, like some Jews in the late Second Temple period, believed gentiles could and should undergo circumcision and adopt the Jewish law, that is, they should convert to Judaism. I will outline indirect evidence from Paul's letters for this position, filling out this evidence with details from early Jewish literature on the possibility and value of gentile conversion to Judaism.

Paul's mission to the gentiles, therefore, faced a persistent challenge: his gentile communities were encouraged to judaize. Paul's opponents preached that gentiles-in-Christ needed to adopt the Jewish law. Scholarly and popular interpretations (the anti-legalist reading) of Paul's letters have predominantly understood this challenge and Paul's vehement reaction to it as a condemnation of the works-righteousness inherent in the religious system of Judaism, or, more recently in the anti-ethnocentric reading, as a condemnation of the ethnic or nationalistic exclusivity of Judaism. In contrast, in Chapters 2 and 3, I argue that Paul opposes gentile circumcision and adoption of the Jewish law, not because he thought Judaism was a religion of works-righteousness or because the ethnocentricity of Judaism repulsed him, but because he rejects one particular Jewish solution to the gentile problem—conversion. Paul does not concern himself with Judaism as a religion distinct from the religion that he now practices, since there had not yet been a parting of the ways between two distinct entities that fit the modern religious traditions known as Christianity and Judaism.[61] Further, Paul does not concern himself greatly (at least in his extant writings) with the general plight of humanity, but with the specific plight of gentiles. Romans 9–11 constitutes Paul's only sustained discussion of the problem facing Jews who do not believe that Jesus was the Messiah, but even here his solution remains to focus on his gentile mission.[62]

In contrast to virtually all scholarship, and on the basis of both the circumcision legislation of Jewish scriptures, which required covenantal circumcision to take place on the eighth day after birth (Gen 17:9–14, Lev 12:3), and the way in which some early Jews such as the author of *Jubilees* interpreted Genesis 17, I contend that Paul not only thought that gentiles *did not need to* or *should not* convert to Judaism to be acceptable to God, but that they *could not* convert to Judaism. Here I make an argument about Paul's view of the Jewish law that is as essential as it is unique: Paul did not think that gentiles could become Jews (i.e., convert to Judaism).[63] Although Paul may have originally thought that gentiles should adopt the Jewish law, after his encounter with the risen Christ, he underwent a change of mind (Gal 1:13–14). In light of this encounter, as Sanders has argued, Paul's thinking moved from the solution that God provided in Christ to a new understanding of the plight gentiles faced.[64] Paul was not burdened by a sense of the helpless and hopeless plight facing humanity, which drove him to recognize his need for Christ. Rather, when God revealed his son to him, Paul became convinced that the Jewish law was the wrong solution to the gentile problem because his understanding of the gentile problem had been inaccurate. If Christ provides the solution to the gentile problem, then other attempted solutions inadequately address the gentile problem—that, or Christ died in vain (Gal 2:21).

Paul's arguments against circumcision and the law in Romans 2 (Chapter 2) and his reading of Genesis 16–21 in Gal 4:21–31 (Chapter 3) become significantly more persuasive once readers recognize that they belong within a stream of Jewish thinking that rejected the possibility that gentiles could undergo circumcision and adopt the Jewish law, thereby becoming Jews. Using the Abraham Narrative as his scriptural basis, Paul outlines two proposed solutions to the gentile problem: works of the law (the solution of his opponents) or the cross of Christ (his own solution). While Paul may have formerly believed that gentile adoption of works of the law solved the problem, and his opponents continued to hold this view, the death and resurrection of God's son demonstrated to Paul that the gentile problem ran much deeper than he previously had thought.[65] Now he believes that gentiles are irremediably gentiles and no amount of Jewish law observance can alter this fact.

Paul opposes a nomistic solution to the gentile problem because he thinks that it seriously misunderstands how essentially hopeless the gentile situation is outside of Christ. Consequently, Paul chastises the gentile who adopts the Jewish law, thinks that he has become a Jew, and now believes himself to be in an enviable position vis-à-vis other gentiles (Romans 2). In his reading of the Abraham Narrative in Gal 4:21–31, Paul stresses that not all circumcisions result in one becoming an heir to the promise God gave to Abraham. Paul resists those who teach gentiles to adopt Jewish customs and to become Jews because, in effect, he believes that they misconstrue the gentile problem. Ironically, given modern apologetic portrayals of Paul that contrast his supposed universalism to Jewish particularism, one might be tempted to conclude that Paul is convinced that his opponents' gospel is too inclusivistic, too open, too lax. Their solution does not fit the problem, thus leaving gentiles even more enslaved than they were previously, for they now think that they have adequately addressed their gentileness when, in fact, they have only disguised it with what Paul considers an ineffectual solution. Given the frequency with which Christian interpreters negatively portray Judaism as particularistic and exclusivistic, I use these terms polemically here.[66] If particularlism and exclusivism are inherently negative, surely Paul must be censured as well. By adopting the Jewish law, and consequently considering themselves to be Jews, gentiles fall away from Paul's gospel because they fail to realize the truth about their identity and therefore deprive themselves of the only sufficient remedy for their situation—entrance into Christ.

## Part 2: Abraham's Seed and the Gentile Solution

In Part 2, I move from Paul's arguments against his opponents to his own positive account of the way in which his gospel for the gentiles relates to the Abraham Narrative. Building on the important work of Caroline Johnson Hodge,[67] I argue in Chapter 4 that Paul does not deny the importance of genealogical descent. Rather, the gentile problem is so deeply rooted that the adoption of the Jewish law cannot overcome it. Instead of rejecting the supposition that gentiles must become sons of Abraham, though, Paul reasserts this claim in Galatians 3 and Romans 4. He agrees, then, with his opponents who argue that gentiles need to become related to and descended from Abraham. His detailed arguments about Abraham in these chapters are compelling evidence that Paul thinks it imperative that gentiles become Abrahamic seed. Consequently, Paul's gospel remains just as ethnocentric as the thinking of his opponents.

For Paul, gentile circumcision does not result in gentiles becoming Abrahamic seed (or, as we shall see in Gal 4:21–31, the right kind of Abrahamic sons). Instead, Paul argues that God provides a way for gentiles to become descended from Abraham apart from circumcision. Although Romans 4 does not contain an explanation for the way in which faith makes one a son of Abraham, Galatians 3 makes it clear that faith leads to the reception of Christ's *pneuma*. Having received the *pneuma* of Christ, gentiles are incorporated into Christ Jesus, who is the singular seed of Abraham. For Paul, the reception of Christ's *pneuma* materially relates gentiles to Abraham. To use a modern medical analogy, to Paul's mind gentile circumcision is mere cosmetic surgery compared to the holistic remedy of gene therapy that the infusion of Christ's *pneuma* into gentile flesh provides.

The argument of Chapter 4 raises an important question: Why could Paul not have opted for a simple version of ethical monotheism or eschatological participation, strategies of gentile inclusion that, as we shall see, already existed within Jewish thought?[68] As Donaldson recognizes, there are important structural similarities between Paul's previous and current views of gentiles:

> The effect of his Damascus experience was to alter some of the convictional substance of his previous approach to the *ethnē*, but not its structure. That is, he continued to believe that for non-Jews to have a portion in the age to come they needed to become full members of Abraham's *sperma* in the present, and that this opportunity would come to an end with the redemption of "all Israel." However, Christ had come to replace Torah as the means by which non-Jews could become incorporated into Abraham's *sperma*.[69]

Why is it so important for Paul that gentiles become Abraham's seed? Is God not able to save gentiles as gentiles without their becoming related to Abraham?

In Chapter 5, then, I address the question of what benefit accrues to gentiles-in-Christ now that they have become pneumatic sons and seed of Abraham. I argue that Paul thinks that God had made certain promises to Abraham that only those who are his seed could enjoy. In particular, Paul believes, on the basis of a common Jewish interpretation of the promises of Gen 15:5 and 22:17, that God had promised Abraham and his seed that he would make them like the stars, that is, participants in God's *pneuma*. The reception of the *pneuma* makes gentiles into sons of God. Since God gave these promises to Abraham and to his seed, Paul believes that gentiles must become the seed of Abraham in order to become sons of God. Paul is convinced that his gospel addresses the gentile genealogical problem—that gentiles-in-Christ have become sons of Abraham, which simultaneously enables them to receive God's promised *pneuma*. Consequently, God's *pneuma* addresses two additional problems that the gentiles face—a morality and a mortality problem. Having received God's own *pneuma*, all those who are seed of Abraham enjoy God's power in the present to live righteously in ways that the Jewish law could never, and never was meant to, enable. Having been given the ability to live virtuous lives, the gentiles have the additional hope that they can now partake in the world to come. The *pneuma* of God functions, then, to ensure that gentiles will overcome their corruptible bodies, inheriting the kosmos and enjoying an indestructible life in the future.

# PART 1

# Jewish Universalism
# and the Gentile Problem

# *I*

# *Jewish Solutions to the Gentile Problem*

PAUL'S LETTERS REPEATEDLY portray his opponents in a negative light. For instance, on the basis of Romans 2, it appears that they are self-righteous hypocrites who condemn others for not observing the Jewish law, but fail to see the ways in which they also do not keep it. In Galatians, Paul implies that his opponents seek only to please other people, not God (Gal 1:10), and preach circumcision to gentiles in order to avoid being persecuted themselves, even though they do not keep the law perfectly (6:12–13). And in Philippians, Paul calls his opponents "dogs," "evil workers," and "the mutilation," people who put their confidence in the flesh, not in God (Phil 3:2).

The polemical nature of Paul's letters has enabled later Christians to deploy his writings as scriptural ammunition to combat those with whom they disagree. Generally speaking, many readers of Paul's letters have neither worried greatly about understanding the precise rationale of Paul's opponents, nor attempted to comprehend sympathetically their motivations. Rather, these faceless opponents stand in for both the Judaism from which Paul broke away and the contemporary threats that face Paul's theological descendants, be they early Christians, the Reformers, or modern Christian groups. Even among biblical scholars, as John M. G. Barclay notes,

> There is a particular danger in the temptation to dress up Paul's opponents with the clothes of one's own theological foes. I suspect this is why, in Protestant circles, Paul's opponents have so often been described as legalistic and mean-minded Jewish Christians, with a streak of fundamentalist biblicism: in exegeting and supporting Paul one can thereby hit out at Jews, Catholics and fundamentalists all at once![1]

Especially since the Holocaust, though, New Testament scholarship has begun to make a concerted effort to understand both Paul's opponents and early Judaism historically and sympathetically.[2] Yet many Pauline interpreters still persist in using both Judaism and Paul's opponents as foils for Paul's message of grace and inclusion, a message free of legalism and ethnocentricity. While a considerable body of scholarship on Paul, especially that within the anti-ethnocentric reading of Paul portrays Second Temple Judaism as particularistic and exclusivistic, such a characterization fails to account for the numerous ways in which many Jews in this period thought that gentiles could relate to Israel and its God.

# The Diversity of Jewish Thought on the Gentile Problem

In a comprehensive survey and synthesis of the evidence, Terence L. Donaldson demonstrates that early Jewish literature reflects a variety of views on gentiles, who were frequently portrayed as idolatrous and immoral people, existing outside the providential care of the one true God.[3] Donaldson outlines four broad patterns of the ways in which Jews thought gentiles could relate to Judaism: sympathizing with Judaism, being ethical monotheists, participating in eschatological salvation, or converting to Judaism. Each of these strategies provides positive ways that gentiles can relate to Jews and their God. This rich diversity of Jewish thought helps us situate Paul's opponents and Paul's own beliefs, both prior to and after his calling (as I will show in the next two chapters), about the way in which God deals with gentiles.

## Sympathization

A number of early Jewish works portray gentiles who sympathize with Judaism, but who neither adopt Jewish practices nor identify themselves as Jews. For instance, some sources portray foreign rulers who provide support for the Jerusalem Temple (Cyrus in Ezra 1:1–4; Xerxes in Josephus, *Ant.* 11.120–132; Seleucus in 2 Macc 3:1–3; Antiochus Eusebes in Josephus, *Ant.* 13.242–244; Caesar Augustus in Philo, *Embassy* 309–310), although these acts of benefaction likely had more to do with political diplomacy than personal piety. Nonetheless, according to the author of 2 Maccabees, this esteem for the temple was not limited to rulers, since it was "honored throughout the entire world" (3:12).

Similarly, some Jewish authors mention gentile respect for the Jewish law and customs. The *Letter of Aristeas*, for example, portrays the Egyptian king Ptolemy II Philadelphus (283–247 BCE) honoring the Jewish law and giving thanks to the God who pronounced these oracles (*Aristeas* 177). Throughout the work, the author presents the king as a gentile who sympathizes with the content of the Jewish law without supposing that he ought to adopt the entirety of it. Similarly, Philo claims that Ptolemy II's desire to translate the Jewish law was the result of his zeal and longing for it (*Moses* 2.31; cf. Josephus, *Apion* 2.45). Likewise, according to Philo, Petronius, the governor of Syria under Emperor Gaius, sympathized with Jewish philosophy and piety (*Embassy* 245). Again, Philo states that this respect for the law was not limited to rulers: "Almost every other people, particularly those who take more account of virtue, have so far grown in holiness as to value and honor our laws" (*Moses* 2.17; cf. Josephus, *Apion* 2.282).

Although many of these portrayals occur in accounts of suspect historical value, the fact that gentile writers such as Seneca mention and lament gentile attraction to Judaism further confirms the existence of gentile sympathizers with Judaism. As Donaldson concludes, "Gentile sympathizers existed throughout the areas represented by these texts in sufficient numbers that the phenomenon was widely recognized not only by Jews themselves but also by outsiders."[4] Such gentiles did not necessarily abandon their ancestral customs and gods, although they might have adopted some Jewish customs or shared beliefs in common with Jews.[5]

## Ethical Monotheism

While some Jews caricatured gentiles as immoral idol worshipers, others portrayed a small number of gentiles worshiping one supreme god and living a moral life, apart from any knowledge of Israel's God and Jewish law and customs. The *Letter of Aristeas*, for example, depicts Aristeas informing Ptolemy II that Jews "worship God, the overseer and creator of all" and claiming that this is the same god who others call Zeus or Dis (*Aristeas* 16). This worship of one supreme god who benevolently rules over the world was one point of contact between Judaism and many gentiles.[6] Philo can even assert that "all Greeks and barbarians unanimously acknowledge" the existence of "the supreme Father of gods and men and the Maker of the whole universe" (*Special Laws* 2.165). Josephus also states that some Greek philosophers, such as Pythagoras, Anaxagoras, Plato, and the Stoic philosophers, held to a conception of God that Moses taught to the Jews (*Apion* 2.168; cf. Aristobulus, fragment 4). Likewise, Book Three of the *Sibylline Oracles* expects gentiles to give up idolatry and to worship the one true God (3.546–554), living morally by honoring righteousness, not oppressing others (630), avoiding sexual immorality, and not killing one's children (764–765). Similarly, Philo claims that there are a small number of people sprinkled throughout the world who have wisdom and a concern for virtue (*Special Laws* 2.47).

These examples demonstrate that some Jews believed that gentiles could worship God properly without having to adopt or even know of the Jewish law. Instead, God had established a law, sometimes equated with a Noahide law, for gentiles to keep. For instance, the book of *Jubilees* depicts Noah commanding his sons, and by extension all of their descendants, to bless the one who created them (i.e., monotheism), do justice, honor their parents, love their neighbors, and abstain from sexual immorality and pollution (*Jub.* 7.20; cf. 1QapGen 6.6–9). This Noahide law became an important component in later rabbinic attitudes toward gentiles (e.g., *t. Avodah Zarah* 8.4; *b. Sanh.* 56a–b).[7]

Those Jews whose thinking fits the pattern of what Donaldson calls ethical monotheism acknowledge a universal law that coexists with the Jewish law. God intended all of humanity to observe the former law and only Jews to observe the latter law. Both laws require the worship of the one true God and appropriate morality, particularly as it relates to sexual morals and acts of violence, but the Jewish law is much more extensive in what it requires and prohibits. Again, within this paradigm, gentiles remain gentiles and need not adopt Jewish practices to be obedient and pleasing to God.

## Eschatological Participation

Other works portray the eschatological participation of the gentiles in Israel's restoration. One key text for such a view of gentile inclusion is Deutero-Isaiah, which pictures Israel's eschatological restoration as the time at which the gentiles will stream to Jerusalem and to Israel's God: "Gentiles who have not known you will call upon you, and peoples who have not known you will flee to you, for the sake of your God, the Holy One of Israel" (Isa 55:5 LXX).[8] Similarly, the book of Tobit states that when God restores Israel, "the gentiles will genuinely turn to fear the Lord God, and they will bury their idols, and all the gentiles will bless the Lord" (14:6). The hopes presented here make no mention, whether positive or negative, of the possibility that gentiles might turn to God before God's eschatological deliverance of Israel. The implication may be that one cannot expect or bring about the repentance of the gentiles in the here-and-now; rather, God will directly bring about this change in gentiles when he rectifies Israel's situation.

Within this pattern there exists an important disagreement over the relationship between gentiles and the Jewish law. Some authors envisage gentiles adopting the entirety of the Jewish law as their way of life at the eschaton. For instance, Isa 2:2–4 portrays the gentiles streaming to Jerusalem in order to undergo instruction in the law, presumably in order for them to practice it.[9] Similarly, Philo depicts the gentiles abandoning their own customs and honoring Jewish laws alone when Israel experiences restoration (*Moses* 2.44).[10] In contrast, other authors perceive gentile participation in God's eschatological deliverance in terms of an influx of gentiles who worship the one true God, but do so as gentiles. The second-century BCE *Animal Apocalypse* provides a striking example of this pattern: at the eschaton, God transforms the gentiles, who are portrayed as unclean animals, into white bulls, that is, clean animals (1 *Enoch* 90.37–38). This transformation restores the gentiles to the status with which God originally created humanity. Yet they remain distinct from Jews, whom the author depicts as a different species of clean animal—sheep. That is to say, although the gentiles undergo a remarkable transformation from unclean to clean animals, God does not transform them into Jews (sheep). They remain gentiles, but have now undergone a miraculous genealogical purification that makes them acceptable to God.[11]

In light of this disagreement, the paradigm of eschatological participation is somewhat harder to categorize. It appears that such a pattern assumes that, at best, most gentiles in the present era do not relate positively to Israel's God, but that God will remedy the gentile problem in the future. What these writers disagree on is whether such a remedy requires an eschatological conversion to Judaism or merely an eschatological return to worshiping the true God as gentiles. While some works make this explicit, it is often unclear in writings that preserve this pattern how one ought to classify these gentiles who participate in God's rectification program at the eschaton. Even if some writers envisage gentiles becoming Jews at the eschaton, it would be wrong to equate this pattern in general with conversion. Consequently, Paula Fredriksen rightly laments the fact that "interpreters routinely slip from seeing the eschatological *inclusion* of Gentiles as meaning eschatological *conversion*," concluding: "This is a category error. Saved Gentiles are *not* Jews. They are Gentiles; they just do not worship idols any more."[12]

## Conversion

Best known of Jewish strategies for dealing with gentiles is the belief that gentiles can, and perhaps must, convert to Judaism.[13] In conversion gentiles no longer merely sympathize with Jewish customs and beliefs; instead, they identify them-selves with the Jewish people and undergo incorporation into the community. The book of Judith contains one of the earliest examples of this belief, portraying an Ammonite named Achior who circumcises the flesh of his foreskin and joins the house of Israel in response to God's miraculous deliverance of the Jews from the hand of Holofernes and the Assyrians (14:10). That the author identifies Achior as an Ammonite is all the more striking since Deuteronomy explicitly forbids Ammonites from joining the congregation of Israel (Deut 23:3).[14] Whereas Achior is a fictional character within the book of Judith, the actions of the Hasmoneans, in incorporating Idumeans and Itureans into the Jewish community via circum-cision, demonstrate that something akin to conversion did occur in the second century BCE.[15] Further, Izates, a first-century CE king of Adiabene, also converted to Judaism, undergoing circumcision at the behest of a Galilean named Eleazar (Josephus, *Ant.* 20.17–47).

Of the four patterns Donaldson discusses, conversion is the only one in which gentiles cease to be gentiles. That is to say, those Jews who advocated this solution to the gentile problem believed that through conversion gentiles receive a new identity—they become Jews. According to those who held this view, gentiles could and should become Jews, joining Israel in its worship of the one true God and adopting the entirety of the Jewish law as one's way of life. It is this solution to the gentile problem that proponents of an anti-ethnocentric reading of Paul have labeled ethnocentric and exclusivistic. Yet, contrary to this understanding, even the belief that gentiles should convert to Judaism is inclusivistic. As Donaldson states,

> While conversion is not generally seen as a form of universalism in con-temporary discourse, our interest here is the world of late antiquity, a world in which proselytism represented a striking step in a universalistic direc-tion. In a world where religion had traditionally been embedded in the constitutive domains of a tribe or a people, the idea that religious identity was something that could be adopted was a significant innovation.[16]

## Exclusion

These patterns are not exhaustive: all early Jews did not fit neatly into one of these four paradigms. Some Jews may have never concerned themselves with trying to answer such a problem. Nonetheless, Donaldson's patterns remain helpful in that they organize what evidence we do have of Jewish thinking about gentiles who existed outside of God's covenant with Israel. But because Donaldson's focus lies on the forms of Jewish universalism in antiquity he does not discuss one further Jewish answer to the gentile problem—the total exclusion of gentiles.[17] Some Second Temple period Jews believed that gentiles simply could not relate positively to Israel and to Israel's God. One sees this perspective throughout Ezra-Nehemiah, which portrays the expulsion of the foreign wives of Jewish men, as well as the offspring of such marriages, from the Jewish community. Without any discussion of or apparent concern over the question of whether these wives and their children worship Israel's God, Ezra commands the men to cast out the foreign women and the offspring of mixed ethnic descent.[18] The work assumes that gentiles can never become part of the Jewish community, regardless of their desire to worship YHWH. Integral to this strategy is the belief that there is an onto-logical and irremediable difference between Jews and gentiles: the former are holy seed (Ezra 9:2); the latter, Ezra implies, are profane seed. Since Lev 19:19 commands, "You shall not sow your field with two kinds of seed," to mix two kinds of human seed, holy and profane, together is to flaunt God's statutes, which require the separation of the holy and the profane (Lev 10:10). The mixing of different seed, whether plant, animal, or human, is contrary to the will of God. Some centuries later, Josephus expounds upon the importance of keeping seed distinct: "The seeds should be pure and unmixed; and do not sow two or three kinds together, for nature does not rejoice in association of dissimilar things. As to animals, do not lead those that are not of similar species. For from this there is fear that the dishonor for that which is of the same kind may pass over even to human practices, having taken its beginning from the previous treatment of small and trivial things" (*Ant.* 4.228–229; trans. Feldman).

The second-century BCE book of *Jubilees* provides a similar answer to the gentile question. In this rewriting of Genesis and the first twelve chapters of Exodus, the author portrays God's election of the seed of Jacob alone to celebrate the Sabbath and practice the rite of eighth-day circumcision.[19] Like Ezra-Nehemiah, the author deploys seed imagery in order to stress the genealogical difference between Israel and the nations. Using the story of the rape of Dinah and subsequent slaughter of the Shechemites (Genesis 34), the author forbids Jewish fathers from giving their daughters in marriage to gentile seed and Jewish men from taking gentile women as wives (30.7). Intermarriage defiles the holy seed of Jacob (30.9–10).[20]

Although Ezra-Nehemiah and *Jubilees* are perhaps the most explicit in their strategy of exclusion, they are not alone. Christine E. Hayes argues that 4QMMT's reference to the pollution of the holy seed with women whom they were forbidden to marry is also a condemnation of the marriage of Jews to gentiles (Lines B75–82), specifically "intermarriage between Jews and *converted* Gentiles—those persons of profane seed who are assimilated through circumcision and inter-marriage."[21] Likewise, the *Testament of Levi* condemns priests who "take wives from the daughters of the gentiles, purifying them with an unlawful purification" (14.6; cf. 9.9–10). The author appears to condemn those who believe that gentile women can become Jews through a purification process, perhaps a proselyte baptism.[22] Such "converted gentiles," in the author's mind, remain gentiles, and thus marriage to them constitutes an illicit marriage camouflaged by an unlawful purification process. Similarly, the *Animal Apocalypse* categorically excludes gentiles from Israel. Through his systematic use of animal imagery, the author portrays the genealogical distinction between Jews and gentiles as equivalent to the genealogical difference that exists between clean and unclean species of animals: Jews are sheep, while gentiles are a variety of unclean animals. Just as one cannot make an unclean animal, such as a wolf or lion, into a clean animal, one cannot make gentiles into Jews. Intermarriage between Jews and gentiles is akin to cross-breeding clean and unclean species of animals. This difference between Jew and gentile in the *Animal Apocalypse* is ontological and seemingly permanent. Even at the eschaton, gentiles become bulls (righteous gentiles), not sheep (Jews).

## Combinations of These Paradigms

The *Animal Apocalypse* illustrates a caveat to the preceding discussion: the five paradigms discussed above, sympathization, ethical monotheism, eschatological participation, conversion, and exclusion, are not mutually exclusive. Donaldson's treatment of these patterns makes this fact clear, since he first examines and categorizes individual passages within each Jewish work and only then moves forward to synthesizing general patterns.[23] The author of the work provides little hope that gentiles might sympathize with Judaism or even fit within the pattern of ethical monotheism. Further, it excludes the possibility that they could convert to Judaism: gentile identity is genealogical and irreparable. Yet, as noted above, the author portrays God remedying the gentile problem at the eschaton, transforming gentiles into a clean and unified species again. Here quotidian exclusion and eschatological participation coexist.[24] Jews could hold together almost any combination of these paradigms. In fact, only the strategies of conversion and exclusion could not be held together. If gentiles and Jews were thought to be ontologically distinct, and if genealogical difference could not be overcome, then there simply was no opportunity for gentiles to convert and become Jews. The only ways in which such gentiles could seemingly relate positively to God, if at all, were through ethical monotheism, sympathization, or eschatological participation (as gentiles).

Many NT scholars portray conversion as the most exclusionary of Jewish options, since sympathization, ethical monotheism, and eschatological participation seem, at first glance, to be more open and welcoming. Perhaps some Jews thought that gentiles could convert but that they did not need to do so in order to become acceptable to God. On the other hand, another possibility exists: perhaps some Jews thought that gentiles could not convert to Judaism, but that they could relate to God positively through sympathization, ethical monotheism, or eschatological participation. That is to say, in this latter case, exclusion coexists with sympathization, ethical monotheism, or eschatological participation. Just as the *Animal Apocalypse* combines present-day exclusion with eschatological participation, is it likewise possible that some Jews thought that it was impossible for gentiles to become Jews (i.e., conversion), but that they could nonetheless sympathize with Judaism or be ethical monotheists in the present? If so, then those ideologies that emphasized gentile sympathization, ethical monotheism, and eschatological participation might be, in one sense, even more exclusionary than an ideology that promoted the belief that gentiles could and should convert.[25]

It is this typology, slightly modified from the one Donaldson proposes, that provides the historical context in which modern scholars need to situate both Paul's apostleship and the competing Christ-believing mission to the gentiles. While many Jews may not have concerned themselves with the question of gentiles, Paul and his opponents did, and in fact actively promoted what they believed to be the divine remedy to the gentile problem. The question of the gentile problem was no academic question for Paul; rather, it was constitutive both for Paul's self-understanding and for his vocation, as the self-proclaimed apostle to the gentiles. Consequently, examining the various preexisting solutions to this problem helps us more accurately contextualize and understand both Paul and those he opposed. Before turning to a discussion of Paul's opponents, it is important to stress that each of these solutions to the gentile problem could find support in Jewish scriptures. There was no monolithic Jewish solution to the gentile problem, not merely because of the diversity of early Jewish movements, but also because those asking how one should deal with the gentile problem found in Jewish scriptures multiple answers.

## Paul's Opponents, Abraham, and Gentile Conversion

The task of reconstructing the identity of Paul's opponents and the content of their message is fraught with danger, but it remains necessary for understanding what issues Paul addresses in his letters. Fortunately, his letter to the Galatians provides some relatively secure information about their message. Paul's chief concern in this letter is that some unidentified people are encouraging the Galatians, who are gentiles, to undergo circumcision and adopt the Jewish law (e.g., Gal 4:10; 5:11–12; 6:12–13). While the majority of scholars claim that these opponents are Jews, whether Christ followers or not,[26] some scholars argue that they are gentiles, perhaps even some of the Galatians, who have adopted the Jewish law and now advocate the adoption of the law by other gentiles.[27] Although I tentatively agree with those who think that Paul's opponents are non-Jews who have adopted Jewish practices, their precise identification does not greatly impinge upon the arguments of this book.

Paul casts aspersions on the motives of these people, claiming that they only compel the Galatians to undergo circumcision in order to escape persecution. Nonetheless, we must always keep in mind that Paul's portrayal of them is polemical—he hardly intends to do justice to their thinking as he writes. It is unlikely, therefore, that the motivations which Paul attributes to them, such as a desire to avoid persecution (Gal 6:12) or a desire to boast (4:17; 6:13), are the sole factors which drove them to preach circumcision to the Galatians.[28] It is, in fact, probable that these missionaries had coherent and rational reasons for preaching that gentiles needed to undergo circumcision and adopt the Jewish law.

Barclay has observed the difficulties of distinguishing between Paul's ideological construction of his opponents to serve his own rhetorical purposes and the historical realities that occasioned Paul's writing to the Galatians.[29] Nonetheless, a few facts about their teaching appear unassailable. It seems that these teachers preached something about Jesus since Paul refers to their teaching as a gospel (1:7–9). Second, they preached that gentiles-in-Christ needed to observe the Jewish law, perhaps emphasizing most of all the rite of circumcision as the entryway into Jewish life (5:11–12; 6:12–13).[30] Third, given Paul's attention to the question of the identity of the sons of Abraham (3:6–29; 4:21–31), it appears that these teachers preached that it was necessary for gentiles to become sons of Abraham through circumcision and law observance. In other words, they preached that gentiles-in-Christ needed to convert and become Jews. The fact that Paul addresses both Abraham and circumcision in his letter to the Romans suggests that his concerns there are similar to those he addresses in Galatia. As noted above, the belief that gentiles could and perhaps should convert to Judaism was one available strategy for relating gentiles to Judaism and to Israel's God. It is thus historically plausible that some teachers might offer to Paul's assemblies a message that required gentiles to become Jews and pointed to Abraham as scriptural evidence for their claim. In this sense, then, Paul's opponents shared this belief with some Jews of the late Second Temple period. (As we shall see, Paul's own solution was also related to one available strategy for relating gentiles to Israel and God.) Consequently, it will be instructive to outline early Jewish portrayals of Abraham and how some Jews related Abraham to contemporary gentiles.

## *Jewish Scriptures and Gentile Conversion*

Of all the gentiles who turn to the one true God in Jewish scriptures, Abraham holds the place of preeminence.[31] According to the narrative of Genesis, God called Abraham, the son of Terah, to leave his family and to go to a land that God would show him (Gen 12:1–3). Early Jewish interpreters took these details to demonstrate that Abraham was a Chaldean who worshipped numerous false gods. The book of *Jubilees*, for instance, portrays his family both fashioning and worshiping idols:

> *Ur*, Kesed's son, built the city of Ara of the Chaldeans. He named it after himself and his father. They made molten images for themselves. Each one would worship the idol which he had made as his own molten image. They began to make statues, images, and unclean things; the spirits of the savage ones were helping and misleading (them) so that they would commit sins, impurities, and transgression. Prince Mastema was exerting his power in effecting all these actions and, by means of the spirits, he was sending to those who were placed under his control (the ability) to commit every (kind of) error and sin and every (kind of) transgression; to corrupt, to destroy, and to shed blood on the earth. (*Jub.* 11.3–5; trans. VanderKam)

It is within this setting that Abraham was born. Significantly, the Abraham Narrative of Genesis makes no mention of the idolatry of Abraham's family. Such a tradition arises not out of Genesis but out of the words of Joshua, who reminds Israel, "Your fathers lived on the other side of the river from of old, Terah, the father of Abraham, and the father of Nahor. And they served other gods" (Josh 24:2). In fact, the belief that they not only worshipped idols but were also involved in their production stems from this verse as well. The Hebrew text states that "they served (יעבדו) other gods," which, as Ben Begleiter notes, contains "a bilingual pun."[32] Although in Hebrew עבד means "to serve/worship," in Aramaic the word can also mean "to make." With the rise of Aramaic in the Second Temple period, many readers, evidently the author of *Jubilees* among them, read Josh 24:2 as evidence that Abraham's family was involved in the idol-making industry. While Joshua says nothing of Abraham's own idolatry, the author of *Jubilees* portrays a precocious fourteen-year-old realizing the errors of his family and separating himself from his father: "[Abraham] began to pray to the creator of all that he would save him from the errors of mankind and that it might not fall to his share to go astray after impurity and wickedness" (11.17; trans. VanderKam). In response to this prayer, God calls Abraham to leave his family and land, promising to make his name great (12.23).[33]

In *On Abraham*, Philo also portrays Abraham as growing up in the idolatry of his father. In contrast to *Jubilees*, Philo does not portray Abraham as being guilty of the gross error of worshipping idols made by human hands; like all Chaldeans he was devoted to astronomy, believing the kosmos to be God. In *On the Decalogue*, Philo claims of those who worship the sun, stars, and moon (i.e., the kosmos):

> Their offence is less than that of the others who have given shape to wood and stones and silver and gold and similar materials each according to their fancy and then filled the habitable world with images and wooden figures and the other works of human hands fashioned by the craftsmanship of painting and sculpture, arts which have caused great mischief in the life of humanity. (66; slightly modified from LCL)

Philo depends here upon Deut 4:15–23, which condemns idolatry but states that God had given the sun, moon, and stars for the gentiles to worship. Thus, one can see in Philo's portrayal of Abraham a softening of his idolatrous origins: although guilty of worshipping astral beings, at least he did not descend to the crass worship of terrestrial beings or inanimate objects.[34] In contrast to *Jubilees*, though, Philo portrays Abraham remaining in this idolatrous state for many years: "In this creed Abraham had been reared, and for a long time remained a Chaldean" (*On Abraham* 70), before awakening to the truth that the created was not the Creator.

In the late first century CE, Josephus claims that Abraham began to have greater notions of virtue and was the first to recognize that there was one supreme God who ruled over all (*Ant.* 1.155–157). Similarly, the late first- or early second-century CE *Apocalypse of Abraham* portrays Abraham involved in the idol-making business of his father Terah, but conflicted by the observation that these idols were unable to save themselves from harm. Thinking of his father's activities, Abraham asks himself, "Is it not [my father] who is god for his gods, because they come into being from his sculpting, his planing, and his skill? They ought to honor my father because they are his work" (3.3–4; trans. Rubinkiewicz [*OTP*]). After recounting Abraham's many musings in *Apoc. Abr.* 1–6, the narrator depicts him finally forsaking the worship of both handmade idols and the celestial bodies in order to seek the one true God (7.1–12). At this point, God appears to him and calls him to leave his father and home (8.3–4; cf. Genesis 12).

Similarly, rabbinic traditions about Abraham acknowledge that his father Terah was a manufacturer of idols and that he enlisted Abraham's help in his trade (*Gen. Rab.* 38.13). Nonetheless, the rabbis stress that Abraham was a poor salesman of idols, asking one would-be customer why he, a fifty-year-old, would worship something that was only a day old, and mocking another person's sacrifice to these idols. Terah's shocked response to this behavior implies that, to this point, Abraham had been properly reverential toward the idols that his father built. This implication finds confirmation in another rabbinic tradition about Abraham. *Genesis Rabbah* preserves numerous observations on the fact that God twice commands Abraham to go (לֶךְ לְךָ) from his father's house (*Gen. Rab.* 39.8; cf. Gen 12:1).[35] One rabbinic explanation for this grammatical construction and apparent redundancy is that Abraham "was afraid and said to himself, 'Perhaps I bear guilt for having worshipped idols all these years.'"[36] Thus God must repeat his desire that Abraham leave his family in order to demonstrate that he had forgiven him for his many years of idolatrous worship.

While the narrative details of these various accounts about Abraham differ, they all acknowledge his idolatrous roots. Surrounded by idolatry, and perhaps raised in a home devoted to the very production of idols, Abraham was himself guilty of this grave error. Further, being a Chaldean by birth, Abraham belonged to the nations. That is to say, Abraham was a gentile. Consequently, to any Jews who thought about the question of how gentiles ought to relate to Israel's God, Abraham's story could be of considerable relevance. For instance, Philo begins his work *On Abraham* by asserting that the stories of such people as Abraham "stand permanently recorded in the most holy scriptures, not merely to sound their praises but for the instruction of the reader and as an inducement to him to aspire to the same" (4). Just as Abraham left behind such idolatrous behavior and came to worship the one true God, so too can contemporary gentiles. If God forgave Abraham his idolatry and called him to a new life, it is conceivable that he would do so for other idolaters who had come to acknowledge him as the one supreme God. We see this use of Abraham elsewhere in the works of Philo. For instance, in *On the Virtues*, Philo says of him, "He is the standard of nobility for all foreigners/proselytes (ἐπηλύταις),[37] who, abandoning the ignobility of strange laws and monstrous customs which assigned divine honors to wood and stones and soulless things in general, have come to settle in a better land, in a commonwealth full of true life and vitality, with truth as its director and president" (219; slightly modified from LCL).

If Abraham functions as a paradigm for gentiles who have come to abandon their idols and false gods, then, it could follow, his circumcision in Genesis 17 might function similarly. As later rabbis observed, Genesis 17 links circumcision to God's covenant with Abraham in an unparalleled way by mentioning ברית thirteen times in connection with the institution of circumcision (*m. Ned.* 3.11). By undergoing circumcision, Abraham was transformed from a gentile into the father of Isaac, and the grandfather of Jacob. In effect, Abraham became a proto-Jew, a transformation of identity that the Priestly writer signifies through his name change: Genesis 17 "heralds the 'divine birth' by changing Abram's name to Abraham."[38] Those who wanted to convince gentiles of the value of undergoing circumcision could point to Abraham and the narrative of Genesis 17 as a fitting paradigm: undergo circumcision and be transformed from a gentile into a son of Abraham. *Mekhilta de-Rabbi Ishmael*, an early rabbinic commentary on Exodus, provides such a reading:

> Beloved are the proselytes (הגרים). It was for their sake that our father Abraham was not circumcised until he was ninety-nine years old. Had he been circumcised at twenty or at thirty years of age, only those under the age of thirty could have become proselytes (להתגייר). Therefore God bore with Abraham until he reached ninety-nine years of age, so as not to close the door to future proselytes. (*Nezikin* 18 [trans. Lauterbach, slightly modified]; cf. *Gen. Rab.* 46.2; *Pss. Mid.*, Addendum to Psalm 17.12)[39]

This rabbinic tradition makes the argument that, since Abraham underwent circumcision so late in life, gentiles too could undergo circumcision (cf. Gen 17:1; 24).

Abraham underwent a deathbed circumcision, so to speak; consequently, it is never too late for a gentile to undergo circumcision. The fact that God commanded Abraham to be circumcised at the age of ninety-nine demonstrates divine forbearance and grace not only to Abraham, but also to all subsequent gentiles whom God is willing to receive. This interpretation of the rite of circumcision is remarkably open and welcoming: the rabbis emphasize God's patience in waiting for gentiles to receive the Jewish law. In rabbinic thinking, then, Abraham functions as the "father of proselytes" (see the discussions of *y. Bikk.* 1.4; *Midrash Tanhuma* B, *Lekh-Lekha* 3.6).[40] Modern scholarship almost universally follows this rabbinic interpretation of Genesis 17. For instance, Paul R. Williamson claims that, according to Genesis 17, "circumcision was a mechanism through which non-Israelites could become part of the covenant community."[41] In this reading, Abraham functions as the first of the proselytes (*b. Hag.* 3a).

Admittedly, no extant Jewish work from the Second Temple period makes such a clear statement about Abraham's circumcision. Further, we have no clear way to date the interpretation preserved in the *Mekhilta*. Even on a maximalist reading, which believes that the saying goes back to Rabbi Ishmael (ca. 90–135 CE), this interpretation postdates Paul by over fifty years. Given Paul's concern in Romans 4 and Galatians 3 to combat the belief that Abraham's circumcision must be paradigmatic for gentiles-in-Christ, it is clear that an interpretation similar to this must have existed in Paul's day. While it is possible that it was within the early movement of Christ followers that such an interpretation arose, and only later that others Jews also came to this understanding of Genesis 17, it seems more plausible to assume that such a reading already existed in early Judaism prior to Paul's day, and that both some early Christ followers and some early rabbis continued to read the passage in this way. In fact, the book of Judith hints at the existence of just such a reading, for, in portraying the circumcision of Achior the Ammonite, the author paints him in the same language that Genesis uses of Abraham. Like Abraham, Achior believed in God (ἐπίστευσεν τῷ θεῷ σφόδρα) and then subsequently was circumcised in the flesh of his foreskin (περιετέμετο τὴν σάρκα τῆς ἀκροβυστίας αὐτοῦ, Judith 14:10; cf. Gen 15:6; 17:24 LXX).

Through circumcision, gentiles not only imitated Abraham, they also addressed a central concern in the Greco-Roman world: the passions.[42] Numerous Jewish works conceive of the Jewish law as the divinely ordained way in which one could gain mastery over desire, avoid immorality, and cultivate virtue.[43] The Jewish law thus distinguished Jews from gentiles because it served to discipline them into a virtuous life. Consequently, one could conclude that any gentile who wanted to gain self-mastery needed to adopt the Jewish law. We see such thinking in the writings of Philo. For instance, he claims that gentiles who come to worship God properly undergo a change in behavior. They move "from ignorance to knowledge of things which it is disgraceful not to know, from senselessness to good sense, from lack of self-mastery to self-mastery (ἐξ ἀκρατείας εἰς ἐγκράτειαν), from injustice to justice (ἐξ ἀδικίας εἰς δικαιοσύνην), from timidity to boldness" (*On the Virtues* 180, slightly modified from LCL). Shortly after making this statement, he avers,

> [Upon adopting the Jewish law], foreigners/proselytes (οἱ ἐπηλύται) become at once temperate, self-mastered (ἐγκρατεῖς), modest, gentle, kind, humane, serious, just (δίκαιοι), high-minded, truth-lovers, superior to wealth and

pleasure, just as conversely the rebels from the holy laws are seen to be incontinent, shameless, unjust, frivolous, petty-minded, quarrelsome, friends of falsehood and perjury, who have sold their freedom for dainties and strong liquor and delicacies and the enjoyment of another's beauty, thus ministering to the delights of the belly and the organs below it—delights which end in the gravest injuries to body and soul. (*On the Virtues* 182, slightly modified from LCL)

The use of holy laws makes formerly immoderate and vice-ridden gentiles into virtuous people. As Walter T. Wilson states, "The amended life that non-Jews attain through admission to the Mosaic polity encompasses a whole spectrum of the sorts of virtues to which people in the Greco-Roman world aspired generally."[44] For Philo, the Mosaic law functioned as a distinctively Jewish therapy for gentile desire, one that transcended all other competing therapies: Jews "live under exceptional laws which are necessarily grave and severe, because they inculcate the highest standard of virtue (πρὸς τὴν ἄκραν ἀρετὴν)" (*Special Laws* 4.179). Elsewhere he argues that the rite of circumcision is significant for numerous reasons, not least of which is the vital role it plays in the process of self-mastery:

(Circumcision [περιτομή] is the symbol of) the excision (ἐκτομή) of pleasures which bewitch the mind. For since among the delights of pleasure the highest is held by the mating of man and woman, the legislators thought good to cut the organ which ministers to such intercourse; thus making circumcision the figure of the excision of excessive and superfluous pleasure, not only of one pleasure but of all the other pleasures signified by one, and that the strongest. (*Special Laws* 1.9 [slightly modified from LCL]; cf. Philo, *QG* 3.47–48)[45]

Philo here relies on the common Greco-Roman belief that the genital organs were the seat of human passion, a belief found as early as Plato, who states, "In men the nature of the genital organs is disobedient and self-willed, like a creature that is deaf to reason, and it attempts to dominate all because of its frenzied lusts" (*Timaeus* 91B). Through undergoing the rite of circumcision, a person is able to master both sexual desire, the strongest of desires, and all other forms of desire as well. For Philo, then, the Jewish law functions as God's remedy for one of the worst plagues facing humanity: desire. No wonder that so many gentiles, who generally did not practice circumcision, were, in the minds of many Jews, enslaved to the passions.

While we do not know for certain the claims of Paul's opponents, I think it likely that they also argued for the virtue-inducing power of circumcision (and the Jewish law more generally) by pointing to the connection that Gen 17:1 makes between wholeness and circumcision.[46] According to Genesis 17, "When Abraham was ninety-nine years old YHWH appeared to Abraham, and said to him, 'I am El-Shaddai; walk before me, and be complete (תמים). And I will make my covenant between me and you, and will multiply you greatly'" (Gen 17:1–2). According to the LXX translation of Gen 17:1, God commanded Abraham, "Be pleasing before me and be blameless" (ἄμεμπτος). The earliest evidence that links circumcision and wholeness can be found in the comments of Rabbi Yehudah ha-Nasi, who, according to *m. Ned.* 3.11, claimed, "Great is circumcision, for, despite all the commandments which our father Abraham did, he was not called whole until he underwent circumcision. As it is said, 'Walk before me and be complete.'" Later rabbinic interpretations of Genesis 17 also discuss this connection between circumcision and wholeness. Most expansively, *Genesis Rabbah* states, "So did God say to Abraham: 'There is nothing unworthy in you except your foreskin: remove it and the blemish ceases': hence, walk before me, and be whole" (46.1). Building on this claim, it portrays Rabbi Levi comparing God's commandment in Gen 17:1 to the words of a king to a noble lady:

> This may be illustrated by a noble lady whom the king commanded, "Walk before me." She walked before him and her face went pale, for, thought she, who knows but that some defect may have been found in me? Said the king to her, "Thou hast no defect, but that the nail of thy little finger is slightly too long; pare it and the defect will be gone." Similarly, God said to Abraham, "Thou hast no other defect but this foreskin: remove it and the defect will be gone." Hence, WALK BEFORE ME, AND BE THOU WHOLE. (46.4)

According to Rabbi Levi, the rite of circumcision is not meant to be a particularly onerous commandment: its fulfillment is likened to the shortening of a long fingernail.

The missionaries who were in competition with Paul possibly viewed gentiles-in-Christ as being in the same situation that Abraham was in Genesis 12–16. Like Abraham, who left his land and family in order to obey God's original calling (Gen 12:1–3), these gentiles had abandoned their ancestral practices, no doubt leading to some degree of familial and social ostracism. But God was not content to leave Abraham as he was. God had originally called Abraham, apart from any reference to law observance, but in Genesis 17, God called him again, this time specifying the need to practice circumcision. The missionaries who came to Paul's gentile assemblies could point to Abraham as the biblical parallel and paradigm for them.

The fact that Abraham figures prominently in both Galatians and Romans, Paul's two letters that are most concerned about the possibility of gentiles adopting the Jewish law and the rite of circumcision, suggests that he was responding to a message that pointed to Abraham and his circumcision as a model for gentiles-in-Christ.[47] J. Louis Martyn, in an imaginative reconstruction, depicts the teachers' message in the following way: "Pay attention to these things: Abraham was the first proselyte. As we have said, he discerned the one true God and turned to him. God's blessing took the form, therefore, of an unshakable covenant with Abraham, and God defined the covenant as the commandment of circumcision."[48] James D. G. Dunn argues that this interpretation of Genesis 17 is "the plainest possible teaching of scripture."[49] In light of the way in which Second Temple Jewish texts portray Abraham as an idolatrous gentile who came to worship the one true God and the way in which later rabbinic literature explicitly interprets Genesis 17 as a model for gentile conversion to Judaism, it is probable that Paul's opponents believed that gentiles-in-Christ needed to imitate Abraham's circumcision in Genesis 17. Undergoing circumcision and adoption of the Jewish law would make gentiles into Jews, or sons of Abraham (cf. Galatians 3–4).

## *A Preexisting Jewish Mission to the Gentiles?*

As I outlined above, early Judaism was marked by considerable differences of opinion with regard to the way in which gentiles could relate to Israel's God. In promoting circumcision and adoption of the Jewish law among gentiles, Paul's opponents belonged within a stream of Judaism that thought gentiles could and should convert to Judaism. But to say that some Second Temple Jews thought gentiles could and should convert to Judaism does not necessarily imply that there was a concerted effort, even within this stream of Jewish thinking, to proselytize gentiles in a manner akin to modern Christian missionary movements. Some gentiles did convert to Judaism in the Second Temple period, but it remains a matter of debate whether one can describe any group within early Judaism as missionizing prior to the Jesus movement.

In contrast to a number of scholars who maintain that Judaism actively sought out converts from the gentiles,[50] Martin Goodman and Scot McKnight have argued that while some Jews were open to gentile conversion to Judaism they did not actively encourage gentiles to do so.[51] If they are correct, Paul's opponents had no precedents within other forms of Second Temple Judaism in their efforts to actively encourage gentile adoption of the Jewish law. Were their missionizing activities new developments within first-century Judaism? In what ways was the early Christ-believing movement unique in its desire and endeavors to convert the gentiles?

The strongest evidence that some Jews were not only open to gentile conversion but also made missionizing efforts relates to the Pharisees, but even this evidence, as we shall see, is not without problems. The clearest example of both conversion to Judaism and Jewish proselytism of gentiles comes from Josephus's account of the conversion of Izates, an early first-century CE king of Adiabene (*Ant.* 20.17–47).[52] According to Josephus, Ananias, a Jewish merchant, instructed the royal house of Adiabene in Jewish customs, but dissuaded Izates from undergoing circumcision. Nonetheless, at a later date a Galilean by the name of Eleazar learned that Izates was not circumcised, and chastised him for reading the laws but not obeying them. In response, Izates underwent circumcision in order to become, in Josephus's words, "a genuine Jew" (εἶναι βεβαίως Ἰουδαῖος, *Ant.* 20.38).

Josephus depicts Eleazar as one who was thought to be very precise with regard to the ancestral customs of the Jews (περὶ τὰ πάτρια δοκῶν ἀκριβὴς εἶναι, *Ant.* 20.43).[53] This description of Eleazar suggests that he belonged to the party of the Pharisees, since elsewhere Josephus mentions a Pharisee by the name of Simon claiming that the Pharisees were thought to be the most precise in the knowledge of the ancestral laws (οἳ περὶ τὰ πάτρια νόμιμα δοκοῦσιν τῶν ἄλλων ἀκριβείᾳ διαφέρειν, *Life* 191). Likewise, in the *Jewish War*, Josephus describes the Pharisees as a sect that was thought to be more pious than others and more precise in the interpretation of the laws (δοκοῦν εὐσεβέστερον εἶναι τῶν ἄλλων καὶ τοὺς νόμους ἀκριβέστερον ἀφηγεῖσθαι, 1.110). These Pharisees attached themselves to Queen Alexandra (167–141 BCE), who was especially precise in her own observance of the ancestral law (ἠκρίβου γὰρ δὴ μάλιστα τοῦ νόμου τὰ πάτρια, 1.108). Finally, Josephus relates that near the end of Herod's life two men who were thought to be exceedingly precise with regard to the ancestral customs (μάλιστα τοῦ νόμου τὰ πάτρια) encouraged several young men to remove a golden eagle that Herod had erected over a temple gate (*War* 1.648–650; cf. *Ant.*

17.149–167). Scholars generally identify these two men as Pharisees, in part, as E. P. Sanders notes, because ἀκριβής "is the word that most often occurs when the Pharisees are discussed."[54]

Josephus's portrayal of the Pharisees as precise interpreters of the law finds additional support in the book of Acts. There Luke claims that Paul was educated at the feet of the Pharisee Gamaliel "with preciseness in the ancestral laws" (πεπαιδευμένος κατὰ ἀκρίβειαν τοῦ πατρῴου νόμου; Acts 22:3). Thus, in light of the fact that Josephus describes Eleazar as one who was thought to be precise in regard to the interpretation of the law, it is likely that he was a Pharisee who, in the early- to mid-first century CE, encouraged Izates to undergo circumcision and adopt the Jewish law in its entirety.

The story of Izates demonstrates two things. First, it provides evidence that Jews disagreed over the way in which gentiles should relate to the Jewish law: Ananias's teachings fit the pattern of ethical monotheism, while Eleazar's teachings fit the pattern of conversion. Second, it suggests that at least one Pharisee demanded that a gentile convert to Judaism. While Josephus does not portray Eleazar as though he were involved in a larger proselytizing mission akin to that of Paul and his competitors, he also does not portray him in a way that would suggest his missionizing was entirely unique and therefore worthy of explanation.

The late first-century CE gospel of Matthew may provide further evidence that some first-century Pharisees were open to gentile conversion to Judaism, and in fact may have sought it. In a series of woe-oracles against them, Jesus states, "Woe to you, scribes and Pharisees—hypocrites—for you cross sea and land to make one proselyte (ποιῆσαι ἕνα προσήλυτον), and you make him become twice as much a son of gehenna as yourselves" (23:15). Most interpreters have taken this statement as evidence that some Pharisees actively sought gentile converts to Judaism,[55] but others have suggested that the saying alludes to the Pharisees' attempt to persuade Jewish people to join their sect, not gentiles to become Jews.[56] Matthew's use of the infrequently attested word προσήλυτος, which has often been thought to mean "convert" or "proselyte" to Judaism, complicates matters. In contrast to the assumptions of most scholars, the term προσήλυτος did not originally mean "proselyte"; rather, it referred to a resident alien, as shown in two recent articles on the topic.[57] Nonetheless, Matthew clearly knows of a later technical use of προσήλυτος to mean a gentile convert to Judaism and uses it here either to refer to gentile converts to Judaism or to refer to Jewish people "converting" to a distinct form of Jewish life. If the verse refers to the attempt of some Pharisees to convert gentiles to Judaism, this provides us with a second piece of evidence, albeit post-Pauline evidence (unless one believes that the saying goes back to either the historical Jesus or a pre-Pauline follower of Jesus), that some Pharisees were both open to and actively sought out gentile converts to Judaism.

Additionally, Luke portrays at least one group of Pharisees in a way that suggests that they believed gentiles could and should convert to Judaism. As the early Jesus movement began to spread out to gentiles, controversy arose over how to incorporate them into this new community. According to Luke, at the Jerusalem Council some Christ-following Pharisees argued that the Jewish believers in Jesus should require these gentiles to observe the Jewish law: "It is necessary to circumcise them and to instruct them to keep the law of Moses" (δεῖ περιτέμνειν αὐτοὺς παραγγέλλειν τε τηρεῖν τὸν νόμον Μωϋσέως, Acts 15:5). This is not to assert that Luke's account is historical, only that Luke thought it historically plausible to portray, and thereby provides indirect evidence to the existence of, first-century Pharisees wanting gentiles to undergo conversion to Judaism.

This late Second Temple and early post-70 CE evidence fits well with later rabbinic literature, which contains various degrees of openness to conversion. While one must be careful not to make a facile identification of the Pharisees with later rabbis, numerous similarities exist between their halakhic reasoning.[58] The earliest evidence with regard to rabbinic thinking about conversion comes from the Mishnah, which mentions an Ammonite named Judah who asks to enter into Israel. Although Rabbi Gamaliel forbids it due to the scriptural prohibition against an Ammonite entering into the congregation of Israel (Deut 23:3: "No Ammonite or Moabite shall enter the assembly of YHWH, even to the tenth generation none of them shall enter into the assembly of YHWH forever"), Rabbi Joshua permits it, citing Isa 10:13 ("I have removed the boundaries of the peoples") as evidence that the Ammonites as a distinct people no longer existed. In the end, the Mishnah concludes, "And they permitted [Judah the Ammonite] to come into the congregation" (*m. Yad.* 4.4; cf. *t. Yad.* 2.17–18; *b. Ber.* 28a). The fact that this passage ends with the conclusion that an Ammonite convert may enter into the congregation of Israel, and the fact that it works to find a way around the clear prohibition of Deuteronomy 23 (i.e., "he's not really an Ammonite after all!"), demonstrate the remarkable openness to gentile conversion to Judaism in early rabbinic thinking.

Similarly, the Babylonian Talmud contains a series of stories about would-be proselytes and their interactions with Shammai and Hillel, two of the leading Pharisees in the late first century BCE and early first century CE (*b. Shabb.* 31a). In the first incident, a gentile approaches Shammai to ask him how many laws he observes. Shammai responds by saying that there are two—the written and the oral law. The gentile claims that he would like Shammai to make him a proselyte on the condition that he only require him to keep the written law, a request which Shammai vehemently rejects. The gentile proceeds to ask the same thing of Hillel, who patiently instructs him in the significance and authority of the oral law. In the second incident, a gentile states that he is willing to become a proselyte on the condition that Shammai and Hillel recite the law while standing on one foot. Shammai again dismisses the man, but Hillel summarizes the law as the love of neighbor, describing the rest as commentary on that one commandment. In the final story, a gentile approaches both Shammai and Hillel, stating that he would become a proselyte on the condition that they appoint him the Jewish high priest. Again, Shammai chases the man off, but Hillel makes him a proselyte and then instructs him to learn the Jewish laws pertaining to high priesthood that preclude him from ever becoming the high priest.

These three stories portray the figure of Hillel welcoming gentiles who desire to convert to Judaism. In contrast, one can interpret Shammai's actions in one of two ways. On the one hand, it is possible that, although he also believes that gentiles can and should convert to Judaism, Shammai's temperament discourages them from doing so. On the other hand, given the connections between the halakhah of the school of Shammai and Sadducean halakhah,[59] one could conclude from these stories that Shammai, like many Sadducees, was deeply suspicious of, or even downright hostile toward, the idea that gentiles could become Jews. If the latter is the case, it is clear that the editors of this series of stories have sided with the position and approach of Hillel. Gentiles can convert to Judaism, and Jews should graciously welcome them into the community.

Such rabbinic evidence fits with the inclusive reading of Genesis 17 preserved in *Mekhilta de-Rabbi Ishmael, Nezikin* 18, which portrays Abraham's circumcision at the age of ninety-nine. Such a late circumcision, according to the *Mekhilta*, provides proof that God welcomes gentiles who convert no matter how late in life they do so. Thus later rabbis provided scriptural justification for their belief that gentiles could undergo conversion to Judaism and did so, in part, on the basis of the figure of Abraham.

These various pieces of information, from diverse sources and time periods, suggest that at least some Pharisees (and later some rabbis) belonged to one strand of early Judaism that was open to the possibility of gentiles becoming Jews. Connected to this evidence is the frequent rabbinic claim that Abraham not only served as the father of proselytes, but also proselytized others. For instance, the rabbis interpret the statement that Abraham and Sarah took with them all the people that they had gotten (עשו) in Haran (Gen 12:5) as confirmation that Abraham converted numerous people while in Haran. Surprised at the occurrence of the verb עשה ("to make"), Rabbi Eleazar in the name of Rabbi Jose b. Zimra expounded the text as follows: "If all the nations assembled to create one insect, they could not endow it with life, yet you say, '*And the souls that they had made in Haran!*' It refers, however, to the proselytes. Then let it say, 'That they had converted': why, 'Which they had made'? That is to teach you that if one brings a proselyte near [to God] it is as though he created him" (*Gen. Rab.* 84.4; cf. *Gen. Rab.* 39.14). In light of this evidence, Goodman concludes, "By the third century CE, the patriarch Abraham was described as being so good a proselytizer that he caused God to be known as king of earth as well as heaven, and this prowess in winning proselytes was one of the main features of the career of Abraham singled out for praise in later rabbinic writings."[60] Admittedly, these claims do not demonstrate that the rabbis themselves pursued a mission to gentiles. Nonetheless, it remains conceivable that some rabbis imitated Abraham the missionary on some level, even if they did not set off to foreign lands in order to do so.

This evidence suggests, then, that some Jews in the Second Temple period were open to and even could encourage gentiles to adopt the Jewish law, although one should note, in the words of Fredriksen, "the improvisational character of 'Jewish outreach.' "[61] The goal of such Jews in encouraging law observance was to incorporate gentiles into the people of Israel. Although these passages at times link this belief to Pharisees or early rabbis, some rabbis remained troubled by the reality that these converts were originally of non-Jewish ethnic descent, prohibiting them from claiming Israel's fathers as their own (e.g., *m. Bikk.* 1.4; cf. *b. Qidd.* 70b).[62] As noted above, the rabbinic portrayals of Hillel and Shammai suggest, at the least, differing degrees of openness. Knowing the human proclivity to remind others of their past errors, *t. Baba Metsia* states, "[If] one saw a proselyte [coming] to study Torah, he should not say to him, 'Look who's coming to study Torah—this one who ate carrion and *teref*-meat, abominations and creeping things!' " (3.25; trans. Neusner). Clearly, tensions remained within rabbinic thinking about gentiles who adopted Jewish law.[63] Such tensions were, as Avi Sagi and Zvi Zohar argue, a result of the fact that Jewishness was fundamentally a genealogically derived identity:

According to halakha, a person's Jewishness is an unalterable fact. A Jew who renounces Judaism or who joins another religion, remains a Jew nevertheless, in the eyes of halakha. Moreover, if a Jewess converted out of the faith, and then conceived and gave birth, her offspring, and all subsequent generations through the female line, are Jews. In other words, being a Jew is not at all dependent upon personal consciousness or commitment, i.e., whether a person regards herself as Jewish or observes the Jewish religion.

Indeed, the converse is also true: if a non-Jew acknowledges the Sinaitic revelation and observes the Jewish religion, he is not thereby considered a Jew according to halakha. It is thus apparent that the halakhic concern for Jewishness is one of kinship: any person whose mother was Jewish is once and for all a Jew.

Following this logic, it would appear reasonable to assume that any person whose mother is not Jewish is once and for all a Gentile. In other words, conversion to Judaism should be impossible. In fact, of course, this is not so; it is quite possible for a non-Jew to become Jewish, through a ritual outlined in halakhic sources. After conversion, such a person is irrevocably Jewish, however she subsequently conducts herself.[64]

Although the extant literature frequently links gentile conversion to the activities of the Pharisees, some non-Pharisaic Jews also believed that gentiles could and should convert, as such works as Judith, which portrays Achior the Ammonite believing in God, undergoing circumcision, and joining the house of Israel (14:10),[65] and *Joseph and Aseneth*, which dramatically portrays the Egyptian Aseneth's transformation into a Jew,[66] demonstrate. Consequently, the proselytizing mission of Paul's opponents, while perhaps novel in its motivations and deliberateness, fits with the preexisting positive perspective that some Jews had regarding the possibility of gentile conversion, as well as with the infrequent and unsystematic proselytizing actions of some Second Temple period Jews.

## Paul the Pharisee and Circumcision of the Gentiles

The connections some Second Temple writers make between proselytism and certain Pharisees is of further significance for situating Paul within early Judaism precisely because Paul claims that, prior to his calling, he was himself a Pharisee (Phil 3:5) who followed the traditions of the ancestors (Gal 1:14). Luke also asserts that Paul was (and continued to be) a Pharisee (Acts 23:6; 26:5), adding that Paul was educated at the feet of Rabbi Gamaliel, a leading Pharisee of the first-century CE (Acts 22:3; cf. 5:34).[67] In light of this biographical information, it is possible that Paul, too, was open to gentiles becoming Jews. In fact, Paul alludes to his own proselytizing efforts in the past: "Brothers, if I still preach circumcision, why am I still being persecuted?" (ἐγὼ δέ, ἀδελφοί, εἰ περιτομὴν ἔτι κηρύσσω, τί ἔτι διώκομαι; Gal 5:11).[68] Since Paul intends this statement to dissuade his gentile readers from undergoing circumcision and adopting Jewish practices, it must refer to the fact that he once preached that gentiles needed to undergo circumcision.[69] As Donaldson and others have argued, Paul, most likely prior to his calling, preached the value of undergoing circumcision to gentiles.[70] In this regard, then, Paul must

have originally preached a message similar to those unnamed people Luke portrays as teaching gentiles: "Unless you are circumcised according to the custom of
Moses, you cannot be saved" (Acts 15:1). At the time of his writing to the Galatians,
though, Paul has abandoned this teaching, and the fact that he is currently enduring persecution should demonstrate to his readers this considerable change in his
message.[71]

Galatians 5:11 sheds light on Paul's earlier remarks on his prior persecution of
the Jesus movement: "For you have heard of my former way of life in *ioudaismos*,
that with excess I was persecuting the assembly of God and was destroying it, and
I was advancing in *ioudaismos* beyond many contemporaries among my people,
being exceedingly zealous for the traditions of my ancestors" (Gal 1:13–14).[72] I leave
untranslated here the Greek word *ioudaismos*, which scholars almost universally
render as "Judaism," because this translational decision too frequently leads interpreters to conclude that Paul has abandoned Judaism for Christianity, converting
from one religion to another. For instance, Hans Dieter Betz claims that the term
*ioudaismos* "describes the Jewish religion and way of life as a whole as it is distinct
from that of other religions." Similarly, Martyn states, "Galatians is thus the letter in which Paul speaks directly and explicitly and repeatedly about Judaism as a
*religion*." In light of this reading, even Sanders asks, "Does he not reveal here that
there is a sense in which he is no longer fully described by the appellation 'Jew'
or 'Israelite'?"[73]

But, as Steve Mason observes, the term that Paul uses twice to describe his
former life, *ioudaismos*, is rare in early Jewish and Christian literature, and nonexistent outside of it. Apart from this passage, Paul never uses the term. While the
author of 2 Maccabees uses the word four times, clearly in contrast to the helleniz-
ing program (*hellenismos*) of the Seleucids, and, following 2 Maccabees, the author
of 4 Maccabees uses *ioudaismos* once (cf. 2 Macc 2:21; 8:1; 14:38; 4 Macc 4:26),
the word does not occur elsewhere in the LXX, NT, Josephus, Philo, or the Greek
Pseudepigrapha. Nor, for that matter, do we know of a corresponding Hebrew
word in the Second Temple period.

In light of its infrequency, the question of the term's meaning merits careful
attention. As Mason notes, "The Greek –ισμός noun represents in nominal form
the ongoing action of the cognate verb in –ίζω."[74] Thus *ioudaismos* is related to
the verb *ioudaïzein* ("to judaize"). In a groundbreaking essay on *ioudaïzein*, Shaye
J. D. Cohen argues that there are three basic valences to any –*izein* verb in Greek:

(1)  providing political support to a group
(2)  adopting the customs of that group
(3)  speaking that group's language.

In all verbs of this group, "the noun stem is the name of a region or an *ethnos*." Most importantly, Cohen stresses that, "when describing political or cultural behavior, the verbs generally have as their subjects people from whom such
behavior would not be expected: Medes do not medize, Greeks do. Spartans do
not lakonize, non-Spartans do. The verbs refer not to a change of essence but to a
change of behavior, not 'to be' but 'to be like.' " In contrast to much of NT scholarship, which describes early Jewish Christ followers who keep the Jewish law as
"Judaizers," Jews cannot judaize, only non-Jews can.

Further, Cohen stresses that *–izein* verbs generally "have a negative valence. Since they describe behavior that is unexpected or paradoxical, they have a nasty or a comic edge; they frequently appear in comedy." In other words, those who medize act in a way which is contrary to what they actually are: they act contrary to nature (φύσις). Because this behavior diverges from both expectation and reality, people looked upon it negatively. Being a Mede is not a bad thing; rather, it is bad for a Greek, for example, to act like a Mede. Similarly, to refer to judaizing negatively is not to suggest that being a Jew is a bad thing, but to be a non-Jew who adopts Jewish customs is. As Cohen observes, to use the word "judaizing" suggests that a person is "being like," but not actually "becoming," a Jew. It is this discrepancy between the exterior and the interior that leads to the word's negative meaning. Cohen cites Suetonius's description of the insulting character of *–izein* verbs: "Many insults in the form of verbs have been made from the names of nations, cities, and demes. From the names of nations: for example, 'to Cilicize . . ., to Egyptiaze, to Cretize (*On Insults*).'[75] In modern parlance, one might say that such a person is a poseur (akin to Jas in *Londonstani*).

In fact, one can see this usage of the verb as early as Esth 8:17 LXX, which claims that, after Esther saved the Jews from Haman's murderous plotting, "many of the gentiles were circumcised and judaized (καὶ πολλοὶ τῶν ἐθνῶν περιετέμοντο καὶ ιουδάιζον) out of fear of the Jews." This is an interpretive expansion on the Hebrew *Vorlage*, which states only that "many gentiles professed to be Jews (מתיהדים) out of fear of the Jews." Although some interpreters have understood the Hebrew version of Esther to portray positively the actions of these gentiles as converting to Judaism, the *hithpael* form of יהד can, and in this case should, be understood to signify that these gentiles pretended to be Jews in order to avoid the royally sanctioned revenge against the enemies of the Jews (cf. Esth 8:11). As Jon D. Levenson notes, this is an ironic turning of the tables: "Whereas the Jews were once threatened and trying to pass as non-Jews, now the Gentiles, feeling endangered by the unexpected consequences of the anti-Semitism in their midst, are passing as Jews, perhaps permanently."[76]

Another clear instance where the verb "to judaize" refers to gentiles who adopt Jewish customs and manners can be found in Josephus's *Jewish War*. In his account of the buildup to the Jewish Revolt against Rome, Josephus narrates the rising tensions between Jews and Syrians. A direct consequence of this tension and physical violence was the suspicion cast upon a group whom Josephus refers to as the judaizers (ιουδαΐζοντας, *War* 2.462–463). Josephus distinguishes this group from the Jews (Ἰουδαῖοι); they are in fact Syrians who sympathize and side with the Jews, and who are also adherents to Jewish practices, since he makes clear elsewhere that many Syrians not only sympathized with Jews, but also adopted Jewish customs (*War* 2.560). Similarly, in narrating the massacre of the Roman garrison stationed in Jerusalem, Josephus claims that Metilius, the commander of the garrison, survived only because he vowed to judaize to the point of circumcision (μέχρι περιτομῆς ιουδαΐσειν, *War* 2.454). Again, Josephus provides evidence that gentiles judaized, and that there were gradations of judaizing, with circumcision (i.e., conversion) being one of the fullest forms of the process. This passage suggests that we cannot too easily distinguish between "full conversion" to Judaism and gentile judaizing. At least for some Jews, and perhaps for some non-Jews, judaizing included not only gentiles who adopted some Jewish customs, but also the phenomenon of gentiles who underwent circumcision, adopted the Jewish law, and entered into the Jewish community. In other words, although some Jews welcomed a gentile who underwent circumcision and adopted the entire Jewish law as his way of life, considering such a process something akin to "conversion," others would have viewed this same process negatively as judaizing—a mere pretension to be something one was not.

Paul himself uses the verb in this negative way in Gal 2:14. In his response to Peter at Antioch, he asks, "If you, a Jew, are living like a gentile, and not living like a Jew, how can you compel the gentiles to judaize" (εἰ σὺ Ἰουδαῖος ὑπάρχων ἐθνικῶς καὶ οὐχὶ Ἰουδαϊκῶς ζῇς, πῶς τὰ ἔθνη ἀναγκάζεις ἰουδαΐζειν)? Just as Peter's living like a gentile (ἐθνικῶς), whatever Paul precisely means by this statement, does not make him a gentile, so too a gentile living like a Jew (Ἰουδαϊκῶς), or judaizing (ἰουδαΐζειν), does not become a Jew: "Paul does not speak of *becoming* a gentile, but of the possibility of *living* or *acting like* a gentile."[77] Peter remains a Jew, regardless of his "gentile" behavior; a gentile remains a gentile regardless of his or her judaizing behavior. For Paul as well, then, Cohen's distinction between "acting like" and "being" holds true. The man who formerly preached circumcision to gentiles—i.e., conversion—now regards this message negatively. Paul now thinks of gentiles who judaize with the same suspicion as other Greco-Roman writers viewed one ethnic group taking up the customs of a different ethnic group. In light of this suspicion toward judaizing, it becomes clear, as I will argue more fully in Chapters 2 and 3, that Paul is not fundamentally concerned with Jewish practices per se, but rather with gentiles who adopt Jewish practices.

The meaning of the verb *ioudaïzein* sheds light on Paul's use of the noun *ioudaismos* in his letter to the Galatians. As Mason states, "Paul's only employment of Ἰουδαϊσμός, in two contiguous sentences, comes in a letter devoted to the *problem* of Judaizing."[78] Given the meaning of *ioudaïzein* and its relation to *ioudaismos*, it is possible that Paul refers in Gal 1:13–14 to his former inclination to promote judaizing behavior among gentiles. This suggestion departs from Matthew V. Novenson, who argues that *ioudaismos* in 2 and 4 Maccabees refers to the commitment to Jewish laws and customs among those of Jewish descent. While my suggested reading of Gal 1:13–14 may not, at first glance, fit with the use of *ioudaismos* in 2 and 4 Maccabees, where it contrasts with *hellenismos*, it nevertheless works well with both the customary meaning of *–izein* verbs and Paul's claim that he formerly preached circumcision in Gal 5:11. Additionally, it is possible that the references to *ioudaismos* in Maccabean literature include Hasmonean efforts to encourage or force non-Jews within the boundaries of Judea to undergo circumcision and law adoption: after all, the *ioudaismos* which the Hasmoneans promote leads to their compelling the Idumeans and Itureans to judaize (Josephus, *Ant.* 13.258, 318–319), as well as to their forcible circumcision of "all the uncircumcised children that they found within the borders of Israel" (1 Macc 2:46).[79] The fact that the author describes this circumcision as forced suggests that he believed both Jews and gentiles were circumcised. In other words, even in the Maccabean literature, *ioudaismos* likely refers, at least in part, to encouraging or enforcing gentile judaizing.

Contrary to the common interpretation of Gal 1:13–14, then, Paul does not indicate that he has abandoned one religion, Judaism, for another, Christianity. Paul did not cease to self-identify as a Jew. After all, in Gal 2:15, Paul can say to Peter that they are by nature Jews (φύσει Ἰουδαῖοι), and not gentile sinners (ἐξ ἐθνῶν ἁμαρτωλοί).

In Romans, Paul speaks of his fellow Israelites and calls himself an Israelite of the tribe of Benjamin (Rom 9:2; 11:1). In Philippians, Paul refers to himself as being of the *genos* of Israel, from the tribe of Benjamin, and a Hebrew born to Hebrews (3:5). And in 2 Corinthians, he asserts that he is a Hebrew, an Israelite, and a seed of Abraham (2 Cor 11:22). Rather, Paul has abandoned one message directed toward gentiles, judaization, for another message also directed toward gentiles, a circumcision-free gospel of Jesus Christ.

Galatians 1:13–14 and 5:11, therefore, suggest that Paul at one point in his past preached circumcision and the necessity of conversion to gentiles. Presumably his message shared some commonalities with the message that his opponents later preached in Galatia. But Paul states that he has broken with this past. He no longer preaches circumcision, he no longer persecutes the Christ movement, and he no longer practices his former way of calling gentiles to convert to Judaism, something he now calls *ioudaismos*, precisely because he no longer views gentile adoption of the Jewish law as conversion, but rather as judaizing—mere playacting and pretension. Although in the past Paul had been extremely zealous for this way of life, God revealed his son to him, causing a dramatic change in Paul's life. Now he preaches Christ to the gentiles (Gal 1:15–16).

This negative understanding of gentile judaizing provides a somewhat different answer to the question of why Paul no longer preaches circumcision. According to the anti-legalist reading of Paul, Paul's encounter with the risen Christ made it clear to him that one cannot become righteous through human effort and work, that is, through observance of the law. Since one has become righteous through faith in Christ, undergoing circumcision and law observance demonstrates a lack of faith in Christ's death and resurrection. According to the anti-ethnocentric reading of Paul, the Christ event opens up God's grace beyond the boundaries of the Jewish community. To require gentiles to undergo circumcision is to undermine the radical inclusivity of the gospel. It is the argument of Chapters 2 and 3 that, although he originally thought that circumcision and adoption of the Jewish law solved the gentile problem, Paul later changed his mind.[80] In response to his encounter with Christ and subsequent reflection on the Christ event, Paul concluded that the Jewish law did not actually address the gentile problem effectively. In this regard, he did not break with "Judaism," as is usually thought; rather, his negative assessment of gentiles who undergo judaizing coincides with the perspective of some other early Jews who also viewed gentile judaizing negatively. Paul's most stringent criticisms of circumcision—Rom 2:17–29 and Gal 4:21–31—must not be understood as a universal condemnation of the rite; rather, we must interpret Paul's letters in light of his intended readers: gentiles who believed in Christ. These passages demonstrate that Paul thought that a solution to the gentile problem that posited the need for gentile circumcision and adoption of the Jewish law was deeply flawed, not because it was legalistic or ethnocentric, but because it did not actually remedy the problem of gentile identity.

# The Gentile Identity
## of the "So-Called" Jew in Romans

ACCORDING TO ANTI-LEGALIST readings of Paul, in Rom 2:17–29 Paul denigrates the practice of genital circumcision and attacks ethnic Jews for their inability to keep the Jewish law. Anti-ethnocentric readings of Paul agree that he attacks ethnic Jews and genital circumcision, but claim that he does so because he rejects the ethno-centrism inherent in such practices as circumcision. But, before interpreters can begin to understand Paul's rhetorical purpose in this passage, they must properly situate it within the larger diatribe to which it belongs.[1] Precisely because of the anonymity of the interlocutor in the diatribe, though, interpreters have debated the identity of the person Paul's argument in Romans 2 aims to address. For instance, F. C. Baur argued that Paul writes Romans not "in opposition to Jewish Christian errors, but merely in opposition to Judaism."[2] Many interpreters, on the other hand, believe that in Rom 2:17–29 Paul addresses Jewish followers of Christ who preach that gentiles-in-Christ need to undergo circumcision and adopt the Jewish law.[3]

In contrast, building upon the important but neglected work of Runar M. Thorsteinsson, I will argue in this chapter that Paul's literary interlocutor is a judaizing gentile. To be sure, some readers will find speculative this identification of the interlocutor; but, in light of Paul's rhetorical coyness, any attempt to identify him remains inexorably uncertain. Nonetheless, correct identification of this interlocutor is essential in order to understand what Paul says about circumcision and why he says it. Returning briefly to the Introduction of this book, it is here where proponents of both anti-legalist and anti-ethnocentric accounts of Paul, who have identified the interlocutor as a Jew (whether believer in Christ or otherwise), have fallen into a trap similar to the one that Gautam Malkani sets for readers of *Londonstani*. They have misidentified the interlocutor and, therefore, have misdiagnosed the problem Paul addresses. Paul does not concern himself with Judaism as such. He attacks neither some supposed works-righteousness inherent in Judaism nor the exclusivity and particularism of Judaism.[4]

While this argument can only remain inconclusive, Thorsteinsson's work on the role of interlocutors in ancient letters demonstrates that it is less speculative than the claims of those who think that Paul addresses a Jew. After examining the epistolary evidence, Thorsteinsson concludes:

> in accord with the dialogical nature of the epistolary medium, conversational partners are widely employed in ancient letters. Moreover, the

sources available give ample support to the general principle of identity, viz. that, unless otherwise stated or implied, the epistolary interlocutor represents or speaks for the letter's recipient(s), thus functioning as an object of identification for the latter.[5]

Since, as we shall see shortly, the evidence of Romans repeatedly indicates that Paul intends to address gentile followers of Christ, some of whom both know and are attracted to Jewish law observance (cf. Rom 7:1), the most probable identification of the interlocutor in Paul's diatribe is a gentile who wants to or has already adopted the Jewish law and believes himself to be superior to and a teacher of his fellow gentiles who have not adopted Jewish practices.

Paul's attack, therefore, is not against Judaism as a religion or the Jewish law in itself; rather, he attacks the practice of gentile judaizing and the belief that gentiles can become Jews through observance of the Jewish law. In order to demonstrate this contention, I begin by briefly examining the evidence of Romans in order to determine the identity of Paul's intended readers. This question of the identity of the encoded reader is distinct from the question of the identity of his actual readers. It is quite possible, for instance, that he addresses his words to a certain group of people, but that others to whom Paul does not mean to speak also read his letter.[6]

## *The Gentile Audience of Paul's Letter to the Romans*

Paul's letter to the Romans contains numerous quotations and allusions to the Jewish scriptures.[7] He talks about Christ, the seed of David (Rom 1:3), the Jewish law and circumcision (Romans 2), the patriarch Abraham (Romans 4), and Jewish unbelief and final redemption (Romans 9–11). He even claims that he writes to those who know the Jewish law (Rom 7:1). This material suggests that his readers would have been interested in and knowledgeable about these topics. Consequently, the position of most scholars, that Paul addresses an audience consisting of at least some Jews, is not farfetched.[8] Nonetheless, evidence within Romans indicates that he predominantly, if not exclusively, intends to address gentiles throughout his letter.

First, to an assembly of Christ followers that he did not found and whose members he did not, as a rule, know personally, Paul introduces himself explicitly as having divine authority as an apostle to the gentiles: "we received grace and apostleship for the obedience of faith among all the gentiles for the sake of his name" (εἰς ὑπακοὴν πίστεως ἐν πᾶσιν τοῖς ἔθνεσιν, 1:5).[9] This definition of his apostleship stresses Paul's target: all the gentiles and only the gentiles.[10] As Robert Jewett has argued, the contents of Rom 1:13–7 "fit exactly into the style of a cautiously diplomatic letter that introduces an ambassador with proper protocol before carefully setting forth the mission to be accomplished."[11] Thus Paul's introduction of himself to a group of Christ followers that does not know him personally establishes the extent of his ambassadorial authority over all gentiles, including those whom he addresses in Rome (1:6).[12]

Further, in Rom 1:13–15 Paul informs his readers that he has often hoped to visit them in order that he might reap a harvest among them just as he has among the rest of the gentiles (καθὼς καὶ ἐν τοῖς λοιποῖς ἔθνεσιν). Paul again asserts that he is obligated to the entire gentile world, to the Greek and to the barbarian, to the wise and the foolish (1:14).[13] The phrases "to the Greek and to the barbarian" and "to the wise and the foolish" serve to define the phrase "the rest of the gentiles," and thereby stress the universality of Paul's mission to all non-Jewish nations.[14] Romans 1:13–15 explicitly identifies Paul's readers in Rome as those falling under his apostleship, presumably because they are themselves gentiles: "Paul's commission to bring about the obedience of faith of the gentiles therefore serves as the warrant for his writing to those in Rome. Far from a mere parenthetical comment, the identification of the audience as gentile grounds Paul's rationale for writing."[15]

Additionally, in Rom 6:17 Paul claims that his readers were previously slaves of sin but have now become obedient (ὑπηκούσατε) to the gospel. Just as they previously had presented their body parts as slaves to impurity and lawlessness, so now they are to present them as slaves to righteousness (6:19). Such language hardly corresponds to Paul's description of his fellow Jews, even those who do not believe in Christ, since he elsewhere describes them as being zealous for God and seeking to establish their own righteousness (Rom 10:1–3). Further, his claim that his readers now obey (ὑπακούω; cf. 16.19) matches the response that he believes his apostleship was ordained to engender among gentiles—obedience (ὑπακοή, 1:5; 15:18; 16:26).

Again, in Rom 11:13, Paul explicitly refers to his readers as gentiles—"But I say to you gentiles (ὑμῖν δὲ λέγω τοῖς ἔθνεσιν)," arguing that the unbelief of many of his fellow Jews has not resulted in their divine abandonment. The conjunction δέ in v. 13 should be read as a development of his argument in Romans 11, since nothing preceding the verse addresses Jewish readers.[16] Paul repeatedly refers to Jews with third-person plural nouns and verbs: "They are Israelites. To them belong the adoption, the glory, the covenants, the giving of the law, the [cultic] service, and the promises. And to them belong the patriarchs and from them Christ" (Rom 9:4–5). He claims that Jews "have stumbled over the stumbling block [Christ]" (9:32), but that this stumbling will not cause their ultimate downfall (11:11–12). Rather, through this stumbling, God will bring about salvation among the gentiles. The fact that Paul points not to any Jews among his intended audience but only to himself as evidence that God has not abandoned Israel confirms that he does not address Romans 9–11 to Jews or to a mixed audience.[17] Clearly, he does not envisage himself speaking to Jews exclusively or even to a mixture of Jews and gentiles; rather, he speaks about the cause and consequences of Jewish unbelief, which prompts him in Rom 11:13 to address his gentile readership, who themselves are in danger: "From [Rom] 9:1 onward Paul has focused upon his non-Christ believing kinsmen, who are definitely not among the audience, whereas Paul's readers have mainly stood in the background. In Rom 11:13, however, he turns directly to his audience and explains to them their status with respect to these kinsmen."[18] Here too he stresses that he speaks authoritatively to those in Rome, inasmuch as he is the apostle to the gentiles.

Finally, in Rom 15:14–32, Paul again emphasizes his authority with reference to the gentiles, asserting that he can write boldly to those in Rome because he is a minister of Christ Jesus to the gentiles (εἰς τὰ ἔθνη) in order to make the offering of the gentiles acceptable (15:16).[19] In fact, he claims to speak of nothing else but what God has done through him to bring about the obedience of the gentiles (εἰς ὑπακοὴν ἐθνῶν, 15:18). Significantly, Jeffrey A. D. Weima observes that Rom 1:5–15 and 15:14–32 form a thematic *inclusio* around the body of Paul's letter to the Romans, signifying to the ancient reader the reason why he thinks he can authoritatively address a community of Christ-following gentiles in Rome with which he has formerly had no connection.[20]

This evidence should signify to the modern reader that Paul intended his letter to address gentiles in Rome—that segment of humanity to which God had sent him (cf. Gal 1:16; 2:2, 7–9; and the deutero-Pauline evidence of Eph 3:8; 1 Tim 2:7; and 2 Tim 4:17 as well as non-Pauline evidence such as Acts 13:47; 1 *Clement* 5.7; *Acts of Paul* 11.3). As Benjamin L. White has documented, "The most dominant and unifying aspect of the early layer of the Pauline tradition appears to have been that Paul engaged in a wide and far-flung mission to the Gentiles."[21] Paul's repeated statements about his apostleship and calling to the gentiles, then, suggest that his encoded readers were gentiles. While this evidence does not prove the actual ethnic makeup of his first readers in Rome, Paul's repeated references to his divinely ordained authority in relation to gentiles would allow any Jews in his audience to point to such claims to demonstrate that what he said did not apply to them.

In spite of the clear assertions of Rom 1:5–15 and 15:14–32, however, numerous scholars persist in the belief that Paul addresses not only gentiles in Rome, but also Jews. In support of this contention, Richard B. Hays, for instance, contends that Romans 16 contains "some of the strongest evidence for the mixed Jewish-gentile composition of the Christian community at Rome" because it contains numerous Jewish names in the greetings of Rom 16:3–15.[22] Yet Thorsteinsson rightly notes that these verses consist of second-person addresses. Paul himself does not greet these people; rather, he calls his readers to greet those he names, likely in order to help establish his credentials with a group of people who do not know him personally, but do know the people he mentions here. Consequently, "the greetings in Romans 16 say nothing conclusive about the identity of Paul's intended audience."[23]

As Thorsteinsson concludes, "According to Paul's presentation, he is a divinely appointed apostle, assigned by God to carry on a mission towards a certain group of people, and the letter's recipients are explicitly addressed as belonging to this particular group." But if those interpreters, such as Stanley K. Stowers, Thorsteinsson, and A. Andrew Das, are correct in arguing that Paul addresses gentiles, why would Paul belabor topics so evidently Jewish in nature? Why discuss circumcision (Romans 2), Abraham (Romans 4), and the Jewish law (Romans 7)? Why quote and allude to Jewish scriptures so frequently? Why address the question of Israel's election (Romans 9–11)? The answers to these questions lie in rethinking the purpose of Romans 1–2. Following Thorsteinsson, "the letter's original setting, its intended audience, and specific literary traits" should guide interpreters in determining both "the function and identity of Paul's interlocutor(s)."[24] Given the fact that Paul intended to address gentiles in Rome, it is probable that his literary interlocutor throughout the letter is also gentile—one who has adopted the Jewish law. If so, Rom 2:17–29 can no longer be read as an attack against Judaism or the Jewish law; instead, in these verses Paul seeks to undermine the judaizing efforts of his gentile interlocutor. Before turning to this passage, though, we must briefly consider the way in which the diatribe of Rom 1:18—2:16 builds up to and prepares for Paul's argument in these verses.

## Gentile Idolatry and the Gentile
## Moral Problem (Rom 1:18–32)

Many interpreters understand Rom 1:18–32 to indict all of humanity for abandoning God and descending into gross immorality. The NRSV is representative in sub-
titling this section "The Guilt of Humankind,"[25] but Paul's target in Rom 1:18–32 is
the pagan gentile world alone. Throughout this passage, Paul emphasizes the otherness of the people he describes. As Douglas A. Campbell notes, "The short passage sounds the note 'they,' 'their,' or 'them' no fewer than twenty-seven times!"[26]

In conjunction with this language of otherness, Paul's portrayal of these people fits the gentile world best. Romans 1:18–20 depicts the gentile problem as origi-
nating in their rejection of the knowledge of God that the divinely created order
afforded to them. Such a refusal to acknowledge God leaves these people without
excuse (ἀναπολόγητος). Although one could understand these statements as a universal indictment of all humanity, Israel had not only the created order but also the
Jewish scriptures to point it to God: the Jews had been entrusted with the oracles
of God (3:2). They had no need for the limited revelatory power of creation to direct
them to God, nor would Paul need the evidence of creation to make the claim that
Jews are without excuse: being entrusted with divine oracles, yet being faithless in
regard to them, would be a more powerful piece of evidence of any Jewish guilt,
as Rom 3:3 demonstrates.[27]

Further, by characterizing these people as rejecting the incorruptible God in
order to worship corruptible created things, such as humans, birds, four-footed
animals, and reptiles (1:21–23; cf. Deut 4:16–18), he again signals that he is portraying the gentile world, not all of humanity. Paul's fellow Jews believed that they
worshiped the true God and that the majority of gentiles worshiped idols (e.g.,
*Letter of Aristeas* 137; Philo, *Special Laws* 2.166). This idolatry was the fundamental
sin of the gentiles and the root of the gentile problem. To be sure, some Israelites
had fallen into idolatry from time to time throughout Israel's history (cf. 1 Cor
10:7–10, in which Paul states four times that *some* of the Israelites [τινες αὐτῶν]
were guilty of idolatry). Further, the language which he uses here ("to exchange
the glory of the incorruptible God" [ἤλλαξαν τὴν δόξαν τοῦ ἀφθάρτου θεοῦ] for images
of created things) might remind the reader of Psalm 105:20 LXX, which speaks of
Israel exchanging their glory (ἠλλάξαντο τὴν δόξαν αὐτῶν) for the image of an ox (cf.
Jer 2:11). Nonetheless, it is important to note the difference in whose glory is being
exchanged—God's or Israel's. Some scholars argue that the calf incident to which
Psalm 105 LXX refers shows that Israel was included in the denunciation of Rom
1:18–32, but any allusion seems quite weak.[28] And even though Israelites had in
the past fallen into idolatry, Paul speaks of his contemporary Jews in much different terms: far from being idolatrous and enslaved to desire, they are zealous for
God and vigorously pursue righteousness (Rom 10:2–3). For that matter, he also
claims that even now the glory belongs to Israel, suggesting that he does not think
contemporary Jews have exchanged or lost it (Rom 9:4).

Additionally, according to the decline narrative of Romans 1, this people's idolatry leads God to hand over their women to unnatural relations. Likewise, the men
also give up natural relations, having unnatural sex with one another (1:24–27).
In the words of Pelagius, "Those who turned against God turned everything on

its head: for those who forsook the author of nature also could not keep to the order of nature" (*Commentary on Romans* 1.26).[29] This connection between idolatry and sexual immorality, homoeroticism specifically (at least with regard to the men), identifies this group as gentiles alone.[30] Paul's contemporary Jews believed strongly that gentiles were almost universally guilty of homoerotic activity and that this behavior distinguished them from Jews, who abstained from such actions. For instance, the *Letter of Aristeas* claims that most other nations commit egregious sexual sins, men having intercourse not only with other men, but also with their mothers and daughters. In contrast, "We [Jews] are separated from these things" (152). Likewise, Book 3 of the *Sibylline Oracles* claims that Jews have kept themselves from impure intercourse with male children/slaves (πρὸς ἀρσενικοὺς παῖδας μίγνυνται ἀνάγνως), unlike the Phoenicians, Egyptians, Latins, Greeks, and many other nations (3.596–600; cf. Josephus, *Apion* 2.199). Second Temple Jews characterized gentiles as being enslaved to impure desires, committing sexual transgressions unheard of among Jews. Paul himself makes it clear that he intends only gentiles here, since he refers to "*their* women," not women in general.[31]

Further, Rom 1:18–32 is remarkably similar to the indictment of the gentile world found in the Wisdom of Solomon. Although Paul does not explicitly identify the people of Rom 1:18 as gentiles, this does not suggest that he intends to condemn all of humanity: "He does not target 'the impiety and injustice of all people,' but 'all the impiety and injustice of persons who unjustly subvert the truth.' 'All' describes the impiety, not the people."[32] Even Wisdom 13:1, which condemns "all people" (πάντες ἄνθρωποι), nonetheless refers only to the gentile world. Wisdom claims that God disciplines Israel in mercy, but he judges the impious (ἀσεβεῖς) in wrath (μετ' ὀργῆς, 11:9), denoting gentiles only. So too Rom 1:18 speaks of impious and unjust (ἀσέβεια καὶ ἀδικία) people who merit God's wrath (ὀργὴ θεοῦ). The author of Wisdom describes the idolatry of the gentiles, who should have seen the greatness and beauty of creation and recognized the creator (13:5), and asks how it was possible that these people were unable to find God through investigation of his created world (13:9). Instead, the gentiles were ignorant of God and were unable from the good things of creation to recognize the one who created them (13:1), something that was inexcusable (οὐδ' αὐτοὶ συγγνωστοί, 13:8). Similarly Rom 1:20 avers that the gentiles are without excuse (ἀναπολόγητος), since what was known of God is manifest to them in the things that have been made (1:19–20). George H. van Kooten argues that in making such arguments, Paul and Wisdom fit within a larger Greco-Roman stream of natural theology: "Both Paul and the author of the Wisdom of Solomon appear to be well-versed in the Greek, mainly Platonic and Stoic discussions of 'intelligent design,' in which the existence of the one God is deduced from physical reality."[33] One example of this notion of intelligent design can be found in Cicero's portrayal of the Stoic Lucilius, who states: "When we gaze upward to the sky and contemplate the heavenly bodies, what can be so obvious and so manifest as that there must exist some power possessing transcendent intelligence by whom these things are ruled" (*Nature of the Gods* 2.2.4; cf. *On Divination* 2.148).

Both Wisdom and Rom 1:18–32 claim that the gentiles, in foolish thinking, abandoned worship of God for worship of created things (Wis 11:15–16; Rom 1:23). Such idolatry led the gentiles into a whole host of vices, including sexual sins and murder (Wis 14:24–29; Rom 1:26–32). In Rom 1:18–32, Paul outlines the way in which gentile impiety and injustice lead to God's wrath. Because they exchanged the glory of the incorruptible God for corruptible creatures, God gave them over to impurity and the dishonoring of their own bodies. Because they exchanged the truth of God for a lie, God gave them over to dishonorable passions. Because they did not think God worthy of honor, God gave them over to a worthless mind. Just as Paul depicts the decline of the gentiles as beginning with idolatry and then progressing to sexual transgression, so does Wisdom, which, in speaking of the idols of the gentiles, claims that their invention was the beginning of sexual immorality (14:12). In fact, the worship of idols is the beginning, cause, and end of all evil, leading to violence, unfaithfulness, false oaths, and sexual misconduct (14:25–26).

In addition to the fact that Paul's argument fits well with Jewish depictions of the gentile world,[34] particularly the portrayal of Wisdom of Solomon 13–14, it also coincides with Roman portrayals of the origins of Roman cultic practices and Greco-Roman understandings of the distinction between popular non-Jewish practices and Jewish practices.[35] According to Augustine, the first-century BCE Roman writer Varro bemoans the decline of Roman cultic practices from aniconic to iconic worship. Varro laments, "If this practice [aniconism] had remained down to the present day . . . the gods would have been worshipped with greater purity" (as found in Augustine, *City of God* 4.31; trans. Dyson). Likewise, the first-century CE Roman philosopher Plutarch claims that Roman piety was, under the influence of Pythagoras, originally aniconic, but eventually incorporated the use of images in worship: "And in like manner Numa forbade the Romans to revere an image of God which had the form of man or beast . . . while for the first hundred and seventy years they were continually building temples and establishing sacred shrines, they made no statues in bodily form for them, convinced that it was impious to liken higher things to lower, and that it was impossible to apprehend deity except by the intellect" (*Life of Numa* 8.8; cf. Plutarch, Fragment 158).[36] In other words, two Roman writers present the history of Roman worship in the same way that Paul portrays this unnamed people's abandonment of the worship of one, invisible God for the worship of multiple idols. Those recipients of Paul's letter who were familiar with such accounts of the devolution of Roman practices would, therefore, naturally connect Rom 1:18–32 to Roman worship specifically.[37]

What is more, Varro explicitly contrasts this Roman decline into iconic worship to Jewish practices which remain aniconic (as found in Augustine, *City of God* 4.31). Indeed, diverse non-Jewish writers in antiquity demonstrate knowledge of the fact that Jews used no images in their worship. For instance, the fourth-century BCE philosopher Hecataeus of Abdera states, "[Moses] had no images whatsoever of the gods made for them, being of the opinion that God is not in human form" (in Diodorus of Sicily 40.3.1–4). In the late first century BCE or early first century CE, Strabo claims that Moses taught that "the Egyptians were mistaken in representing the Divine Being by the images of beasts and cattle, as were also the Libyans; and that the Greeks were also wrong in modeling gods in human form" (*Geography* 16.2.35; slightly modified from LCL). His contemporary, Livy, makes similar claims: "[The Jews] do not state to which deity pertains the temple at Jerusalem, nor is any image found there, since they do not think the God partakes of any figure" (*Scholia in Lucanum* 2.593 [=Stern 133]). In the early second century CE, Tacitus notes that "the Jews conceive of one god only, and that with the mind alone: they regard as impious those who make from perishable materials representations of gods in man's image; that supreme and eternal being is to them incapable of representation and without end" (*Histories* 5.5.4). Finally, in the second century CE, the Roman historian Dio Cassius says that the Jews "never had any statue [of their god] even in Jerusalem itself, but believing him to be unnamable and invisible, they worship him in the most extravagant fashion on earth" (*Roman History* 37.17.2). Non-Jews knew that Jewish worship was aniconic and that, in this regard, they differed considerably from the non-Jewish world—a fact that has gone virtually unremarked upon with reference to Romans 1. Given this awareness, it is highly improbable that any gentile reader of Rom 1:18–32 would conclude that Paul, a Jew, intends to implicate both gentiles and Jews in this indictment. In other words, both Jewish and non-Jewish literature demonstrate a nearly ubiquitous awareness that Jewish cultic practices were aniconic, while non-Jewish practices were predominantly iconic. Paul's presentation of a descent into iconic worship of numerous idols fits all perspectives on non-Jewish worship.

Finally, the reception history of Rom 1:18–32 demonstrates that Paul's earliest readers universally understood his words to indict gentiles, not Jews.[38] Most significantly, one of Paul's first interpreters, the author of the letter to the Ephesians, portrays gentiles in some of the same terms that Paul uses for the unnamed people of Rom 1:18–32. Speaking to gentile Christ followers, the author exhorts them to a lifestyle distinct from their former ways:

> You must no longer walk as the gentiles walk in the futility of their minds (ἐν ματαιότητι τοῦ νοὸς αὐτῶν). They are darkened in their understanding (ἐσκοτωμένοι τῇ διανοίᾳ ὄντες), estranged from the life of God because of the ignorance that is in them on account of the hardness of their heart. Having become unfeeling, they have given themselves over in licentiousness to the work of every impurity in greed (ἑαυτοὺς παρέδωκαν τῇ ἀσελγείᾳ εἰς ἐργασίαν ἀκαθαρσίας πάσης ἐν πλεονεξίᾳ). (Eph 4:17–19)

Just as Ephesians depicts gentiles as walking in the futility of their minds, Paul claims in Rom 1:21 that the people he portrays "became futile in their thinking" (ἐματαιώθησαν ἐν τοῖς διαλογισμοῖς αὐτῶν). Whereas Ephesians describes gentiles as having darkened understanding, Paul says of these people that "their senseless heart has been darkened" (ἐσκοτίσθη ἡ ἀσύνετος αὐτῶν καρδία, Rom 1:21). Finally, like Ephesians, which states that gentiles gave themselves over to every impurity, and did so in greed or lust, Paul claims that God gave these people over, in the desires of their hearts, to impurity (παρέδωκεν αὐτοὺς ὁ θεὸς ἐν ταῖς ἐπιθυμίαις τῶν καρδιῶν αὐτῶν εἰς ἀκαθαρσίαν, Rom 1:24), and that, as a result, they had been filled with all kinds of vices, including greed or lust (πλεονεξία, 1:29). Since many scholars do not believe that Paul wrote Ephesians, this passage confirms that a relatively early disciple of Paul thought it consonant with Paul's thinking to portray gentiles, and only gentiles, in this way.[39] In fact, these verbal correspondences between Rom 1:18–32 and Eph 4:17–19, I would argue, demonstrate that the author of Ephesians reads Rom 1:18–32 specifically as a reference to gentiles.

In the late second century CE, Tatian addresses the men of Greece, citing Rom 1:20 as the reason why he and other Christians refuse to follow the Greeks in the worship of creation (*Oration against the Greeks* 4.2). Likewise, Irenaeus claims that Paul's reference to those who "worship and serve the creature rather than the creator" (Rom 1:25) are gentiles (*Against Heresies* 4.33.1). Clement of Alexandria also claims that in Rom 1:18–32 Paul made accusations against the Greeks (*Exhortation to the Greeks* 8). Similarly, on the basis of Paul's claim that though they knew God through his creation they did not honor him as God (1:19–20), Origen concludes that Paul describes gentiles alone: "For there is a difference between knowing God and knowing God's will. God could be known even by the Gentiles 'from the creation of the world through the things that have been made, and through his external power and deity.' His will, however, is not known except from the law and the prophets" (*Commentary on Romans* 2.7.1; trans. Scheck; cf. *Against Celsus* 3.47). In a similar way, he understands Paul's statement that these people did not honor God (Rom 1:21) to refer to gentiles: "The Apostle seems to condemn the Gentiles because, though they knew God by natural understanding, they did not honor him as God" (*Commentary on Romans* 2.7.6; trans. Scheck). Again, Origen understands Rom 1:22–24 to refer only to gentiles: "Therefore he accused certain Greeks, i.e., the Gentiles, of being under sin when he says, 'For claiming to be wise, they became fools and exchanged the glory of the incorruptible God for the likeness of the image of corruptible man and birds and four-footed animals and reptiles. Therefore God handed them over to a base mind,' and so forth" (*Commentary on Romans* 3.2.3; trans. Scheck; cf. *Against Celsus* 4.30).

In the fourth century, Athanasius composed a two volume work, *Against the Pagans* and *On the Incarnation*, in which he depicts the vices of the non-Jewish Greco-Roman world. Such people, he claims, "glorified creation instead of the creator (τὴν κρίσιν παρὰ τὸν κτίσαντα δοξάζοντες)," a reference to Rom 1:25 (*Against the Pagans* 8.29–30; cf. 47.18–19; *On the Incarnation* 11.26–27). He quotes Rom 1:21–24 as evidence of the idolatrous practices of the gentile world (*Against the Pagans* 19.11–17). Citing Rom 1:26–27, he argues that, as a result of worshipping idols, the gentile world descended into sexual immorality, their women giving themselves over to cultic prostitution, while their men preferred the role of women (*Against the Pagans* 26.1–11; cf. *On the Incarnation* 5.28–34). Six times, then, his depiction cites verses from Rom 1:18–32, showing that he believes that in these verses Paul characterized the gentile world.

Another of Paul's earliest commentators, Pelagius, notes that Paul had only gentiles in mind in Rom 1:18: "He begins [to address] the case [of the Gentiles, and he says that the wrath of God is revealed through the Gospel, or else through the testimony of nature]" (*Commentary on Romans* 1.18; trans. de Bruyn [material within brackets is lacking from some manuscripts]). The *Primum Quaeritur*, a prologue to Paul's letters most likely composed by Rufinus of Syria in the late fourth century CE, claims that Paul wrote Romans 1 to remind his readers "of their prior vices as gentiles."⁴⁰ This example is of particular significance in that it understands Romans 1 to be about gentiles and assumes that Paul intended to address the entirety of the letter only to gentile readers. Similarly, in his *Homilies on Romans*, Chrysostom repeatedly claims that Paul directs the accusations of Rom 1:18–32 against Greeks (i.e., gentiles; cf. especially *Homily* 3). In fact, in *Homily* 5, Chrysostom links Rom 1:28 to Paul's negative comments about gentiles in 1 Thess 4:5, concluding that "here too he shows that it was to them [i.e., the gentiles] the sins belonged." Theodoret of Cyrus claims that at Rom 1:18, Paul begins to accuse all non-Jews of "fearlessly breaking the law placed in nature by the creator," arguing that it is only at 2:10 that he "intends now to introduce the accusation against

Jews" (*Commentary on Romans* to 1:17 and 2:10; trans. Hill). Likewise, Ambrosiaster argues that Paul describes gentiles in Rom 1:24–28 (*Commentary on Romans* 1.24–28; trans. Bray). Finally, Augustine, too, believes that Paul intends Rom 1:21–23 to describe gentiles, who "knew [the Creator] but did not give thanks and, claiming to be wise, actually became fools and fell into idolatry" (*Propositions from the Epistles to the Romans* 3.2; trans. Fredriksen Landes). And, even though Paul does not explicitly state whose impiety (ἀσέβεια) incurs the wrath of God in Rom 1:18, Augustine links this *impietas* to gentiles alone (3.5). It is only at Rom 2:1 that Augustine believes that Paul introduces (*subintrat*) an indictment of Jews (7–8.2).

Finally, although difficult to date, the *Euthalian Apparatus*, which is attributed to Euthalius who was bishop of Alexandria at some time between the fourth and seventh centuries, provided interpretive guides to, among other things, Paul's letters. The author begins his treatment of Romans by stating that Paul "accuses first the Greeks," citing Rom 1:20–23 as proof. Further, the heading he provides for Rom 1:18–2:11 states that this section "concerns the judgment against the gentiles who do not keep the natural (laws)."[41]

Our earliest extant interpreters of Paul and commentators on his letter to the Romans unanimously agree that Rom 1:18–32 addresses the gentile world, not all of humanity, and this despite their varied degrees of animosity toward Jews.

To summarize: the internal evidence of Rom 1:18–32 points to a gentile target, something confirmed by the parallel argument found in Wisdom of Solomon 13–14, which explicitly identifies its target as gentiles. Paul's argument looks like a stock Jewish criticism of the gentile world. Further, Paul's portrayal of a decline from aniconic to iconic practices fits with Roman perceptions of the development of the Roman cult. In fact, his portrayal of this descent provides quite the contrast to both Jewish and gentile perceptions of the aniconic and monotheistic nature of Jewish worship. Finally, the unanimous interpretation of Paul's earliest extant commentators provides strong evidence that Paul's first readers would also have understood Rom 1:18–32 to be an attack on the gentile world alone.

## *The Virtuous Gentile (Rom 2:1–16)*

While many interpreters recognize that the target of Rom 1:18–32 is the gentile world, some try to absolve Paul of such ethnic stereotyping, arguing that he does not agree with this depiction; rather, he puts these words into the mouth of his interlocutor, whom scholars almost always identify as an ethnic Jew, only to turn this portrayal on its head in Rom 2:1–3 in order to condemn those Jews who arrogantly consider themselves to be not only ethnically, but also ethically, distinct from gentiles: "Therefore you have no excuse, oh person who judges! For in judging the other, you condemn yourself! For the one judging does the same things." Again, Paul does not explicitly identify his target in Rom 2:1–3, but interpreters since Augustine have frequently concluded that Paul targets Jews who condemn the gentiles of gross immorality but who are themselves guilty of such sins.[42] For instance, in light of this identification, John M. G. Barclay argues that "Paul is out to destabilize a Jewish sense of confidence that Jews were in a different category from Gentiles in their obedience to the law, or at the least in their possession of it."[43]

Yet the fact that Paul begins Rom 2:1–16 with the inferential conjunction διό suggests that what he is about to say draws a conclusion from the preceding verses which have encapsulated the wickedness of the gentiles.[44] Further, Stowers rightly argues, to conclude that the one who judges is a Jew is to apply later Christian portrayals of Jews to Paul:

> No evidence exists to show that the character of the hypocritical and arrogant judge was ever applied to Jews until after Paul's time, and then by Christians. . . . There is absolutely no justification for reading 2:1–5 as Paul's attack on "the hypocrisy of the Jew." No one in the first century would have identified the *ho alazôn* [i.e. the pretentious person; cf. Rom 1:30] with Judaism. That popular interpretation depends upon anachronistically reading later Christian characterizations of Jews as "hypocritical Pharisees." . . . The text simply lacks anything to indicate that the person is a Jew.[45]

These efforts to distance Paul from such Jewish views about gentiles fail when one takes into consideration Paul's statements about gentiles elsewhere. For instance, in writing to the gentile Thessalonians, Paul connects gentile ethnicity to both ignorance of God and immorality: "For this is the will of God, your sanctification: that you abstain from sexual immorality; that each one of you know how to take his own vessel in holiness and honor, not in the passion of lust like those gentiles who do not know God" (1 Thess 4:3–5). Similarly, in writing to the Corinthians, Paul describes the former status of some of his gentile recipients as immoral idolaters (1 Cor 6:9–10; cf. 1 Cor 6:18). Although later than Paul, 1 Peter confirms that early Jewish believers in Christ continued to view the gentile world in such terms: "Let the time that is past be enough for doing what the gentiles like to do, living in wantonness, desires, drunkenness, revels, carousing, and lawless idolatries" (1 Peter 4:3). Consequently, Thorsteinsson concludes, "There is little doubt that for Paul and his audience the people described in Romans 1:18–32 belonged to the non-Jewish world."[46] However Rom 2:1–16 functions, one simply cannot read it in a way that absolves Paul of holding such negative perceptions of gentiles.

At this point, the reader only knows that the one who judges wrongly believes himself to be distinct from traditional Jewish characterizations of the gentile world. In this regard, Paul's criticism of this person fits Greco-Roman criticisms of the pretentious person. For instance, Aristotle's student Theophrastus vilifies the pretentious person as the one who claims to own "nonexistent goods" (*Characters* 23.1). Similarly, Xenophon, a student of Socrates, portrays Cyrus claiming that "the name 'pretender' (ἀλαζών) seems to apply to those who pretend that they are richer than they are or braver than they are, and to those who promise to do what they cannot do, and that, too, when it is evident that they do this only for the sake of getting something or making some gain" (*Cyropaedia* 2.2.12, slightly modified from LCL). Such texts demonstrate that the "pretentious person is above all a boaster and someone who pretends to be what he is not. This person strives for the external trappings of wealth, honor, power, or virtue rather than really possessing them."[47]

Instead of an attack on Jewish ethnocentricity, then, it is more likely that Paul undermines one of two Greco-Roman discourses. Either Paul undermines the discourse, noted above, of philosophers like Varro, who lament their compatriots' turn to iconic worship and present their own aniconic worship as exemplary (and resulting in a superior morality),[48] or he undermines a discourse which distinguished cultured, virtuous Greeks from uncultured, vice-ridden barbarians (e.g., Plutarch, *Fortune of Alexander* 329C–D), something Paul already hints at in Rom 1:13–14 where he proclaims that his gospel is for all gentiles, Greeks and barbarians alike. As Stowers notes, "In Greek constructions of the ethnic other, as in Jewish constructions of the gentile, barbarians often lack self-control because of either innate weaknesses or inferior laws and constitutions."[49] Paul provides his readers with very little information about this person who judges in Rom 2:1–16, yet I believe that Stowers and Thorsteinsson correctly argue that Paul continues to address gentiles in Rom 2:1–16—not the immoral and incontinent gentile, but a gentile who condemns such behavior among his fellows. This gentile appears to be one who attempts to live a virtuous life.[50] Consequently, in Rom 1:18–32 Paul condemns the vice-ridden gentile world—a condemnation with which his judaizing gentile interlocutor agrees, while in Rom 2:1–16, Paul condemns gentiles who believe that they have attained a virtuous life (however achieved). And in Rom 2:17–29 Paul directs his attention to the interlocutor, condemning judaizing gentiles.

## *The So-Called Jew as Judaizing Gentile (Rom 2:17–29)*

In his reading of Rom 2:17–29, Origen cautions, "So then, as in the prophetic writings, the person who wants to understand what is written must direct attention carefully in order to ascertain the *personae*, i.e., who is speaking, to whom the words are addressed, or about whom the discourse is being made. So also, it seems to me, one must now do here in the Epistle to the Romans" (*Commentary on Romans* 2.11.3; trans. Scheck).[51] In Rom 2:17–20, Paul provides his readers with information that might help to clarify the identity of the interlocutor with whom he engages in 2:17–29. Unfortunately, here too interpreters—both anti-legalist and anti-ethnocentric readers of Paul—have misunderstood Paul. Brendan Byrne, for instance, argues that Paul's question in Rom 2:17 ("If you call yourself a Jew. . . .") shows that the entire chapter functions "as a continual diatribal accusation against the Jew who defines himself or herself in terms of possession of the law and (falsely in Paul's eyes) rests confidence therein."[52] Possible confirmation of this identification might be found in the numerous ways in which Paul describes this person's view of himself: he relies upon the law, boasts in God, knows the divine will, approves what is important, is instructed in the law, is convinced that he is a guide to the blind, a light to those in darkness, an instructor of the foolish, a teacher of children, and one who has the outward form of knowledge and truth in the law (2:17–20). Jewett argues that these are "typical examples of Jewish self-identity,"[53] and concludes that Paul's depiction of the Jew here is meant to trap a gentile audience that exhibits similar pretensions. Even Stowers, who has done so much in drawing attention to the fact that Paul's interlocutor to this point in the letter is a gentile, believes that Paul moves from engaging a gentile in 2:1–16 to debating with a Jew, albeit a Jewish missionary, in 2:17–29: "Verses 17–29 depict a Jewish teacher of gentiles, but the portrait is even more specific: The discourse of 2:17–29 suggests a polemical construction of 'missionary' opponents. This Jew is one of Paul's competitors for gentiles."[54]

Yet there are a number of problems with the claim that the interlocutor is a Jew. First, as Jewett points out, "Paul's target is ostensibly far from his audience,"[55] which consists predominantly, if not exclusively, of gentiles. Why would Paul turn in Rom 2:17–29 to address a Jewish teacher, if his encoded readers are gentiles? Again, it is important to recall that the interlocutor in epistolary contexts, as Thorsteinsson has argued, functions to represent the intended audience of the letter.[56]

Second, and more significantly, this reading of Rom 2:17–29 creates a considerable conflict between this passage and the remainder of Paul's writings. This tension arises out of the belief that in Rom 2:17–29 Paul redefines Jewishness. Standard interpretations run roughly as follows: in vv. 17–20, Paul echoes this Jewish person's lofty description of himself; in vv. 21–27, he demonstrates that this Jewish person has no right to boast in his law observance and circumcision because he does not keep the entirety of the Jewish law perfectly, resulting in his being reckoned as uncircumcised; and, in vv. 28–29, he comes to the conclusion that true Jewishness and true circumcision are hidden and unrelated to ethnic descent and genital circumcision.[57] In short, then, most scholars believe that in Rom 2:17–29 Paul rejects the common definition of Jewishness in his day, including those marks of identity like circumcision that were thought to distinguish Jews from non-Jews. In the words of N. T. Wright, "The covenant God has not given up on the category of 'circumcision', on the idea of there being an elect people; he has merely redefined it."[58]

Such a redefinition of Jewishness does not fall outside the bounds of possibility in the first century CE. For instance, according to Philo, there were some Jews in Alexandria who allegorized the Jewish law to the point that, once one understood their deeper meaning, the observance of the literal laws became unnecessary (*Migration* 89–93).[59] Philo does not say so explicitly, but it is possible that such people redefined Jewishness in terms of these larger principles, abandoning the practice of the literal rites.[60] Yet Jewish tradition had long been able to understand circumcision metaphorically, while still practicing the physical rite. For example, Leviticus demands physical eighth-day circumcision, but also describes disobedience to the law as uncircumcision of the heart (Lev 12:3; 26:41).[61] Jeremiah distinguishes between the physical circumcision Israel practiced and the physical circumcision its neighbors practiced, while speaking of circumcision of the heart (Jer 4:4; 9:26). The author of *Jubilees* uses the phrase "circumcision of the heart," while stressing the importance of the appropriate observance of physical circumcision (*Jub.* 1.23; 15.11–33).[62] Philo himself interprets circumcision allegorically, but he does not think that this allegorical meaning implies the irrelevance of the physical rite (*Migration* 92).[63] Circumcision of the heart does not necessarily preclude the observance or diminish the importance of genital circumcision.[64] For Philo, "Allegory explains circumcision, but does not explain it away." But Barclay concludes that Paul takes the step that Philo was unable to: in Rom 2:25–29, Paul "thoroughly redefines the term 'Jew' and 'circumcision' in a way which preserves their honorific status but cancels their normal denotation."[65]

It is here where the traditional interpretation of Rom 2:17–29 results in the creation of a tension within Paul's letters: outside of this passage, Paul always uses *Ioudaios* ("Jew") to refer to those who were ethnically Jewish. Apart from Romans, there are fourteen occurrences of the word *Ioudaios* in the undisputed Pauline letters. The word occurs eight times within 1 Corinthians, including four times where Paul contrasts *Ioudaios* to Greeks (1:22, 24; 10:32; 12:13) and once to gentiles (1:23). Additionally, in discussing his mission strategy of becoming a slave to all, Paul claims that to Jews he became as a Jew in order to win the Jews (9:20). The first five references clearly use *Ioudaios* in an ethnic sense, since he opposes Greeks and gentiles to the category of Jews. The three occurrences in 1 Cor 9:20 likewise appear to refer to ethnic Jews. In 2 Cor 11:24, he claims that the Jews gave him thirty-nine lashes on five different occasions. Since this punishment is based upon Jewish scriptures (Deut 25:3; cf. Josephus, *Ant.* 4.238, 248), again the *Ioudaioi* here are ethnic Jews.

Likewise, Paul uses the appellation *Ioudaios* four times in Galatians. The word occurs twice within two verses, in addition to the related adverb Ἰουδαϊκῶς ("Jewishly") and verb ἰουδαΐζειν ("to judaize," 2:13–15). Significantly, in these verses Paul claims that Peter and other Jews acted with hypocrisy: while a Jew, Peter lives like a gentile and not like a Jew, yet he requires gentiles to judaize. The dispute does not revolve around Peter's Jewish identity, or the identity of those from James, but rather over the fact that Peter's behavior forces gentiles to act like Jews. This passage uses *Ioudaios*, therefore, in a way that contrasts it to the category of the gentile. A similar opposition is found in Gal 3:28, where Paul says that in Christ there is neither Jew nor Greek. Thus, in Galatians, Paul uses the word *Ioudaios* in its customary ethnic sense.

In 1 Thess 2:14, Paul claims that the assemblies of Christ followers in Judea suffered at the hands of the Jews, in much the same way that the Thessalonians are suffering at the hands of their own compatriots. The fact that he compares the suffering of the Thessalonian Christ-following assembly at the hands of their fellow countrymen to the sufferings of the Christ-following assemblies in Judea at the hands of the Jews suggests that he uses the word to refer to a group who shared the same ethnicity with those in the Judean assemblies; that is to say, Paul again uses the term to refer to an ethnic group.[66] Finally, the letter to the Colossians uses *Ioudaios*, contrasting the term again with the Greek (3:11). Although the authorship of Colossians is a matter of scholarly dispute, this contrast between Greek and Jew is clearly ethnic and parallels Paul's remarks in Gal 3:28.

The evidence of Romans is especially problematic for the belief that Paul redefines Jewishness in Rom 2:17–29: the three occurrences of *Ioudaios* that precede Rom 2:17–29 contrast the *Ioudaios* to the Greek (1:16, 2:9, 10). These verses indicate that Paul divides the world into two groups—Jews and non-Jews (here referred to as Greeks). Immediately after Rom 2:17–29, Paul, or possibly his interlocutor, asks what advantage the *Ioudaios* has (3:1). Given that this question is followed by another question pertaining to the benefits of circumcision, clearly *Ioudaios* signifies ethnic Jews. Confirming this interpretation, in Rom 3:9 Paul twice uses *Ioudaios* and contrasts the term again to Greeks. This ethnic definition of Jewishness is found in the three remaining occurrences of the term, which contrast Jews to gentiles (3:29; 9:24) and Greeks (10:24). In fact, Rom 3:29 is particularly embarrassing on this reading, since, if Paul redefines Jewishness so that Christ-following gentiles are now Jews, then the answer to the question "Is God the God of Jews alone?" is actually a resounding "yes." Even in Romans, then,

Paul consistently uses *Ioudaios* to refer to ethnic Jews, and he does so both before and after Rom 2:17–29. No scholar questions this interpretation of the data. But this evidence should then give pause to anyone who believes that Rom 2:17–29 redefines Jewishness, undermining its ethnic meaning and constructing a spiritualized meaning that includes only Jews and gentiles who believe in Jesus.[67] For instance, Philip F. Esler acknowledges the tension between this reading of Rom 2:17–29 and Rom 3:1–8: "Realizing that these statements [i.e., Rom 2:17–29] may appear to have erased the reality of the divine election of Israel, Paul draws back a little to reassert the existence of [Jewish] privileges (Rom. 3:1–8)." Similarly, after arguing that Paul redefines Jewishness in Rom 2:17–29, C. E. B. Cranfield admits that Rom 3:1–4, in addition to what Paul says of the abiding benefits to ethnic Israel in Rom 9:1—11:36, seriously undermines his interpretation of Rom 2:28–29.[68]

This tension, consequently, should lead interpreters to reconsider their rendering of the Greek of Rom 2:28–29, which states:

οὐ γὰρ ὁ ἐν τῷ φανερῷ Ἰουδαῖός ἐστιν οὐδὲ ἡ ἐν τῷ φανερῷ ἐν σαρκὶ περιτομή, ἀλλ᾽ ὁ ἐν τῷ κρυπτῷ Ἰουδαῖος, καὶ περιτομὴ καρδίας ἐν πνεύματι οὐ γράμματι, οὗ ὁ ἔπαινος οὐκ ἐξ ἀνθρώπων ἀλλ᾽ ἐκ τοῦ θεοῦ.

The NRSV, typical of most modern translations, renders these verses in the following manner:

For a person is not a Jew who is one outwardly, nor is true circumcision something external and physical. Rather, a person is a Jew who is one inwardly, and real circumcision is a matter of the heart—it is spiritual and not literal. Such a person receives praise not from others but from God.[69]

According to this reading, there is a true Jewishness that has nothing to do with genital circumcision and, presumably, other traditional cultural signifiers of Jewish identity. The true Jew is the spiritual Jew. This supposed redefinition swings open the doors of Jewish identity so that gentiles can become Jews without undergoing circumcision and the adoption of Jewish customs. At the same time, it excludes all those of Jewish descent who are not also circumcised of heart. For instance Jewett interprets these verses in the following way: "The Jew with a circumcised heart, whether of Jewish or Gentile lineage, performs the law out of a transformed heart, without regard to reputation."[70] Unfortunately, what Jewett means by the phrase "performs the law" is unclear.

To translate the passage in this way, though, interpreters must make a number of additions to Paul's Greek. Illustrative of this tendency, Cranfield provides the Greek of Rom 2:28–29 with his additions in parentheses:

οὐ γὰρ ὁ ἐν τῷ φανερῷ (Ἰουδαῖος) Ἰουδαῖός ἐστιν οὐδὲ ἡ ἐν τῷ φανερῷ ἐν σαρκὶ (περιτομή) περιτομή (ἐστιν), ἀλλ᾽ ὁ ἐν τῷ κρυπτῷ Ἰουδαῖος (Ἰουδαῖος ἐστιν), καὶ περιτομὴ καρδίας ἐν πνεύματι οὐ γράμματι (περιτομή ἐστιν), οὗ ὁ ἔπαινος οὐκ ἐξ ἀνθρώπων (ἐστιν) ἀλλ᾽ ἐκ τοῦ θεοῦ.[71]

Greek often requires English readers to supply words, especially verbs such as "to be" (εἰμί). Nonetheless, as Barclay argues, "given the dangers of interpretative paraphrase, it is as well to use as few additions as possible." Stowers also notes the dangers associated with supplying additions to these verses: "The highly elliptical language of 2:28–29 makes it easy to read and translate, as traditional Christian treatments have, in a manner that spiritualizes circumcision and Judaism to the point that they vanish."[72] In light of these potential dangers, would not a reading of these verses that makes sense of the passage and keeps paraphrasing to a minimum be preferable?

Hans K. Arneson helpfully suggests that a more accurate translation of these two verses should read as follows:

> For it is not the external Jew, nor the external circumcision in the flesh,[73] but the internal Jew, and the circumcision of the heart in spirit and not in letter, whose praise [is] not from humans but from God.[74]

The strength of Arneson's proposal is that, while it also adds the verb "to be" (ἐστιν), it does not require adding "Jew" (Ἰουδαῖος) and "circumcision" (περιτομή) twice, as does Cranfield's translation. Additionally, this rendering does not import the word ἀληθινός, "true" (NRSV) or "real" (RSV). Since Paul does not use the word ἀληθινός, supplying it might mean one inadvertently imports into the text a conclusion foreign to Paul. Finally, this translation takes into account the final clause of v. 29, the relevance of which, as both Barclay and Jewett recognize, has puzzled scholars.[75] The central focus of Rom 2:28–29 is the praise of God, not defining true Jewishness or true circumcision.[76] That is to say, according to these verses, ethnic Jewishness and genital circumcision do not in and of themselves guarantee that God will be pleased with someone, a statement that, as we shall see shortly, has strong scriptural support and would therefore be uncontroversial.

Further, Arneson's argument that Paul's emphasis is on the praise of God lessens the problem created by Rom 3:1, where Paul (following Campbell) or his interlocutor (following Neil Elliott, Stowers, and Thorsteinsson) raises the question of what benefit results from being a Jew.[77] If Paul redefines Jewishness, then there is great benefit to being a true Jew and Rom 3:1–9 should make this clear. But Rom 3:1–9 reverts back to discussing the benefit of being ethnic Jews and observing the rite of genital circumcision as though Paul had not redefined Jewishness and circumcision.[78] In contrast, if Paul intends to demonstrate that not all Jews have God's praise, and that not all genital circumcisions result in obedience, then the question naturally arises, "What is the point of being a Jew or of being circumcised?" Paul's answer, "Much in every way," makes sense because he notes that Jews, whether they have God's praise or not, are entrusted with God's words. And, as Rom 9:1–4 demonstrates, Paul thinks ethnic Jews continue to have considerable advantages.[79]

Contrary to virtually every interpreter of Romans, Paul does not redefine Jewishness in Rom 2:28–29. This conclusion leads us back then to the identity of the interlocutor in Rom 2:17: "But if you call yourself a Jew and rely upon the law and boast in God . . . (Εἰ δὲ σὺ Ἰουδαῖος ἐπονομάζῃ καὶ ἐπαναπαύῃ νόμῳ καὶ καυχᾶσαι ἐν θεῷ)."[80] Paul portrays the interlocutor as one who calls himself a Jew, a claim that Paul clearly regards with some suspicion. As Origen states of the significance of the verb ἐπονομάζω: "But now let us see what the Apostle says to him who is called a Jew. First of all it must be observed that he has not said of him, 'But if you are a Jew (*Iudaeus es*),' but rather, 'if you call yourself a Jew (*Iudaeus cognominaris*).' This is because to be a Jew and to be called a Jew are not the same thing (*non idem est esse Iudaeum et cognominari Iudaeum*)" (*Commentary on Romans* 2.11.4; trans. Scheck).[81] Like Origen, Thorsteinsson argues that "Paul does not actually state that the person addressed in 2:17 *is* a Jew. Rather, this person is depicted as someone who wants to be *called* a Jew." Supporting this understanding of Rom 2:17, he points to 1 Cor 5:11, where Paul refers to someone who calls himself a brother, but lives in such a way that belies this title: "I wrote to you not to associate with anyone who calls himself (ὀνομαζόμενος) 'brother' if he is sexually immoral, or greedy, or idolatrous, or a slanderer, or a drunkard, or a thief—do not even eat with such a person." But if Paul does not redefine Jewishness in Rom 2:17–29, why will he not concede that his interlocutor is Jewish? The answer to this question, and the key to understanding the argument of Rom 2:17–29, lies in recognizing that Paul's interlocutor is someone of non-Jewish descent who believes that he has become a Jew—that is, a gentile who has adopted the Jewish law, including circumcision. In Rom 1:18—2:29, then, Paul works to trap the entire gentile world, even a gentile who has undergone circumcision and adopted the Jewish law. Paul's interlocutor thought that he was a Jew and therefore "took for granted that he no longer belonged to the group of people once 'handed over' by God to an existence filled with vicious deeds. Paul sweeps away this false belief" in Rom 2:17–29.[82] Thorsteinsson argues for this identification, but, I think, fails to offer a compelling explanation for the way in which verses 21–29 function to demonstrate that this gentile interlocutor's claim to Jewishness, to Paul's mind, is vacuous.[83] The remainder of this chapter will provide a reading of Rom 2:21–29 in light of the belief that Paul addresses a gentile who has judaized.

## The One Who Does Not Practice What He Preaches (Rom 2:21–23)

In order to understand the purpose of Rom 2:17–29, one must first determine the rhetorical function of Rom 2:21–23, in which Paul mentions several vices—theft, adultery, and the combination of idolatry and temple robbery/sacrilege: "The one who teaches another, do you not teach yourself? The one preaching, 'Do not steal (κλέπτειν),' do you steal? The one saying, 'Do not commit adultery (μοιχεύειν),' do you commit adultery? The one who abhors idols (ὁ βδελυσσόμενος τὰ εἴδωλα), do you commit sacrilege (ἱεροσυλεῖς)?"[84]

These accusations against the anonymous teacher, frequently identified as a "typical" or "representative" Jew, have stirred the imaginations of numerous Christian interpreters. For instance, Cranfield argues that Rom 2:21–22 reveals the hypocritical behavior of Paul's Jewish contemporaries, who were actually involved in stealing, adultery, and robbing temples.[85] Similarly, C. H. Dodd believes that Romans 2 provides "evidence enough of the terrible degradation of Jewish morals in the period preceding the Destruction of the Temple."[86] To be sure, it is unlikely that all Jews in Paul's day were paragons of virtue, but this observation is a far cry from the implied or explicit claim that all Jews in the first century were involved in one or all of these immoral activities. Neither Cranfield nor Dodd cites convincing evidence for this portrayal of the immorality of Jews en masse in the first century CE.[87]

Instead, they permit Paul's rhetoric in this passage, along with their belief that Paul engages a Jewish interlocutor, to dictate their portrayals of early Judaism.

At worst, Paul might be making the uncontroversial claim that some of his contemporary Jews failed to lead exemplary moral lives. In a vast improvement upon the suggestion that Jews as an ethnic group were universally implicated in degraded morals, a number of scholars, following Francis Watson, argue that Paul has a specific historical incident in mind. This episode, which Josephus mentions, involved a few Jewish men who defrauded a Roman noblewoman named Fulvia of her donation to the Jerusalem Temple (*Ant.* 18.81–84).[88] Yet the supposed connection to Rom 2:21–22 is unconvincing, for it fails to explain Paul's reference to adultery. Additionally, even if Paul's readers knew of this incident, there would be little reason for them to associate any Jewish teachers in their midst with the actions of a few rogues some thirty years prior. Again, only a few Jews were involved in these actions; presumably the majority of Jews were not guilty of such misdeeds. Consequently, Paul's interlocutor, or a reader of Paul's letter to the Romans, need only demonstrate the existence of innumerable exceptions to this rule in order to unravel Paul's supposed argument. As Timothy W. Berkley asks, "How is the interlocutor or someone identified with the interlocutor as a Jew, in Ernst Käsemann's words, 'trapped' by accusations that have no application to most individual Jews?"[89]

To answer the question of how this section of Paul's argument functions, it is necessary to note that these three vices were a common trope in hellenistic moral philosophy. For instance, in his discussion of just and unjust actions, Aristotle argues that such classification occurs on the basis of one of two laws: the particular law of each community and the universal law that is Nature. He provides a list of such unjust actions, including theft (κλέψαι), adultery (μοιχεῦσαι), and temple robbery (ἱεροσυλῆσαι, *Rhetoric* 1.13). Writing in Latin, the first-century CE philosopher Seneca laments the argument that good can come out of evil, claiming that such a belief leads to the conclusion that various vices are actually good: "We have, to be sure, actually convinced the world that sacrilege, theft, and adultery (*sacrilegium, furtum, adulterium*) are to be regarded as among the goods. How many men there are who do not blush at theft, how many who boast of having committed adultery! For petty sacrilege is punished, but sacrilege on a grand scale is honoured by a triumphal procession" (*Moral Letters* 87.23). In fact, in the third century CE, the biographer Diogenes Laertius claims that the philosopher Theodorus (340–250 BCE) argued that theft, adultery, and temple robbery (κλέψειν τε καὶ μοιχεύσειν καὶ ἱεροσυλήσειν, *Lives of the Philosophers* 2.99) were not in themselves wrong.

Likewise, Philo refers to people who swear oaths to commit acts of theft and temple robbery (κλοπὰς καὶ ἱεροσυλίας), or depravity and adultery (φθορὰς καὶ μοιχείας), or assaults and murders, or other such evil deeds in order then to claim that they must fulfill the oath that they have made. He derides such arguments, contending that God would prefer justice and virtue (*Special Laws* 2.13). In the same work he warns of the danger of desire (ἐπιθυμία): "If the desire is directed to money, it makes men thieves (κλέπτας) and cut-purses, footpads, burglars, guilty of defaulting to their creditors, repudiating deposits, receiving bribes, robbing temples (ἱεροσυλίαις) and of all similar actions. . . . If the object is bodily beauty they are seducers, adulterers (μοιχούς), pederasts, cultivators of incontinence and lewdness, as though these worst of evils were the best of blessings" (4.87, 89). In his discussion of the patriarch Joseph, Philo asserts that jail keepers dwell among thieves (κλέπταις) and robbers, burglars, insolent persons, the violent, corruptors, murderers, adulterers (μοιχοῖς), and temple robbers (ἱεροσύλοις), and as a result pick up these various vices from those whom they guard. In contrast, Joseph was unaffected by the vices of his fellow prisoners. Instead, by his teaching and life of temperance and virtue, he changed those who seemed incurable, healing the diseases of the soul (*On Joseph* 84–87). Yet one more time, Philo connects these three vices, arguing that "only one who is utterly incurable would not pray for obstacles to keep himself from thieving (κλέπτειν), adultery (μοιχεύειν), murder, temple robbery (ἱεροσυλεῖν), and other such things. To be given free reign is to suffer harsh judgment. The one not restrained is given over to the greatest disease, injustice" (*Confusion of Tongues* 162–163).

These various authors demonstrate that theft, adultery, and temple robbery often occurred in ancient vice lists from Aristotle onward. But the Wisdom of Solomon provides the closest parallel to Paul's statements in Romans 2. As numerous scholars have shown, the decline narrative of Rom 1:18–32 corresponds most closely to Wisdom of Solomon 13–14, which depicts the depravity of the gentile world. Yet no scholar to my knowledge has noted that this description of the gentile world also contains a passage that corresponds strikingly to the three actions Paul notes in Rom 2:21–22. In a lengthy portrayal of the vices of the gentile world, the author states:

> For whether killing children in initiations, or in secret mysteries, or celebrating the frantic carousing of strange rites, neither lives nor marriages did they keep pure, but they either treacherously kill one another, or hurt one another by adultery (νοθεύω). And all was blood and murder, theft (κλοπή) and deceit, corruption, faithlessness, tumult, false oath, confusion of the good, forgetfulness of favors, pollution of souls, changing of birth, disorder of marriage, adultery (μοιχεία), and sensuality. For the worship of unnamed idols (εἰδώλων θρησκεία) is the beginning and cause and end of all evil. (14:23–27)

This passage contains the same collocation of theft, adultery, and idol worship that Paul refers to in Romans 2. For Wisdom, numerous vices characterize the gentile world and all of them spring from the initial mistake of abandoning the worship of the true god for the worship of idols. For that matter, it is possible that Philo also views these vices as particular to gentiles. After all, in *Confusion of Tongues*, it is pre-Israel, pre-law humanity that God abandons to unfettered license, with the consequence that they might give in to theft, adultery, temple robbery, and other such. Likewise, in *On Joseph*, Joseph dwells among the most depraved elements of Egyptian society, including those given over to theft, adultery, and temple robbery. That Joseph resists temptation, and in fact provides a beneficial influence through his teaching and life, could suggest that Jews are particularly well-suited to a life of virtue.

Wisdom of Solomon and Philo, then, portray these three vices as distinctly gentile, springing out of gentile idolatry. Such a depiction fits well with Paul's own views, since in Romans 1 he claims that gentile idolatry led to gentile descent into a whole host of vices. In fact, Paul elsewhere links the vices of adultery, thievery, and idolatry to gentile behavior: "Do you not know that the unjust will not inherit the kingdom of God? Do not be deceived; neither the immoral, nor idolaters (εἰδωλολάτραι), nor adulterers (μοιχοί), . . . nor thieves (κλέπται), . . . will inherit the kingdom of God. And such were some of you. But you were washed, you were sanctified, you were made righteous in the name of the Lord Jesus Christ and in the *pneuma* of our God" (1 Cor 6:9–11). Interestingly, in light of the larger argument that Paul intends to address a judaizing gentile here, Peter J. Tomson makes the observation that these three examples are drawn from the Noahide Law—laws that in Jewish tradition apply to all humans, Jews and gentiles alike.[90]

Admittedly, it is not as though all gentiles committed each of these crimes, as Paul himself acknowledges in 1 Cor 6:11: "such were some of you." It is doubtful, therefore, that readers of Romans would agree with Paul were they to think that he was claiming that all gentiles were adulterers, thieves, and temple robbers. This unlikelihood becomes all the greater in view of the fact that Paul addresses a gentile who describes himself in the glowing terms of Rom 2:17–20, that is, someone who claims to know God's will, approves what is excellent, and is instructed from the law. It is improbable that a gentile who had gone to any lengths in judaizing would be guilty of such vices. In other words, if Paul intends to show that his gentile interlocutor is guilty of these specific sins, it is unlikely that he could convince his readers that such accusations had any real foundation.[91]

By focusing on historical examples of these three vices, interpreters have lost sight of Paul's larger point in the passage. The entire diatribe has been moving to demonstrate that the interlocutor, who claims to be a Jew and is preaching law observance to his fellow gentiles, is no better off than the gentile pagan world that he condemns. Paul intends to create the pattern of someone who preaches one thing but does the opposite: "The one, therefore, who teaches another, do you teach yourself?" The target of Paul's attack is the hypocrite. This coincides with Theophrastus's description of the pretentious person, which I noted above: "You can be sure fraudulence will seem to be a pretence of nonexistent goods" (ἀμέλει δὲ ἡ ἀλαζονεία δόξει εἶναι προσποίησίς τις ἀγαθῶν οὐκ ὄντων; *Characters* 23.1). As a comical example of such fraudulence, Theophrastus depicts a person who not only rents a luxurious house, pretending to own it, but then also has the audacity to claim that he is considering selling it because it has become too small.

This understanding of the pretentious person fits Rom 2:21–22. The one who preaches against theft commits theft. The one who speaks against adultery commits it. The one who abhors idols robs their temples. Paul may have chosen these particular actions out of the panoply of gentile vices because of a specific similarity: in each, the person benefits from what does not belong to him. The thief steals possessions that belong to another. The adulterer has intercourse with another man's wife. Given that the preceding two illustrations demonstrate hypocrisy, it appears that Paul envisages in the final question someone who claims to abhor idols, but then desires and steals the valuable objects which are used in cultic worship of these idols. Presumably, Paul thought that these objects should be abhorred and avoided, not stolen, on the basis of the law which prohibits not only idolatry, but also the coveting (ἐπιθυμήσεις) and taking of the materials that make up such idols (Deut 7:25 LXX). While appearing to be a just and virtuous person, this teacher secretly reaps the unjust benefits of the very vices against which he rails.

Romans 2:23 confirms that Paul's concern relates less to these individual vices than to the pattern his examples establish: "You who boast in the law, through disobedience to the law do you dishonor God?" This verse makes explicit Paul's point—the one who boasts in the law breaks it. But here too interpreters frequently miss Paul's intention, arguing that he demands perfect obedience to the entire Jewish law of the one who boasts in it.[92] In fact, they seem to read Paul under the influence of the epistle of James, which states, "For whoever keeps the whole law but falls in one [thing] (ὅλον τὸν νόμον τηρήσῃ πταίσῃ δὲ ἐν ἑνί) becomes guilty of all. For the one who said, 'Do not commit adultery' also said, 'Do not murder.' And if you do not commit adultery but you murder, you are a transgressor of the law (γέγονας παραβάτης νόμου)" (2:10–11). James argues that if one obeys one aspect of the law, by not committing adultery, but does not obey another aspect, by committing murder, one has not kept the whole law. But if Paul were making a claim akin to the one James makes, he would need to argue similarly: those who preach against adultery, do you steal? Those who preach against stealing, do you commit adultery? Paul's point is entirely different. The one preaching against stealing commits theft. The one preaching against adultery commits adultery. Romans 2:21–22 illustrates the absurdity of the person who preaches one thing, but does the exact opposite.[93] Paul does not accuse anyone of breaking the entire law because they fail to keep it at one point. Theft, adultery, and temple robbery serve as three examples of this principle of preaching one thing and doing another.

## Blasphemed Among the Gentiles (Rom 2:24)

In support of his claim that the one who boasts in the law actually transgresses it, Paul refers to Isa 52:5b LXX: "Thus says the Lord, because of you, my name is continuously being blasphemed among the gentiles" (δι᾽ ὑμᾶς διὰ παντὸς τὸ ὄνομά μου βλασφημεῖται ἐν τοῖς ἔθνεσιν). The LXX appears to have added the phrases "through you" (δι᾽ ὑμᾶς) and "among the gentiles" (ἐν τοῖς ἔθνεσιν) to the underlying Hebrew *Vorlage*, which states, "And continuously all day, my name is despised." On the basis of the LXX rendering of this verse, Paul argues that because this person boasts in the law, but transgresses this very law, he causes God's name to be blasphemed among the gentiles (v. 24). This quotation from Isa 52:5 justifiably surprises those scholars who identify the interlocutor as a Jew, since in the context of Isaiah 52 it is the gentile subjection of Israel that leads to God's name being despised. According to standard interpretations of this verse, Paul flips Isaiah 52 on its head, using it to accuse Israel (i.e., ethnic Jews) of living in such a way that they cause gentiles to blaspheme God's name. In light of this reading, Hays concludes that Paul's use of this verse is "not only a low blow but also . . . a stunning misreading of the text."[94] While Paul and his readers did not practice modern critical exegesis, such a misuse of Isaiah 52 would presumably have been obvious to many of them and would have, therefore, undermined his argument. Further, if Paul were looking for a scriptural passage that implicated Jews in leading the gentiles to blaspheme God, much better texts exist (e.g., Jer 34:16; Ezek 20:39; 36:20–23; 39:7; Amos 2:7). Consequently, Thorsteinsson asks, "Why would Paul have chosen an indirect accusation against *gentiles* to [prove] his case against a *Jewish* interlocutor?"[95] But if the interlocutor is a gentile, then Paul can no longer be accused of misreading the text: it is gentile misbehavior, that is, gentiles who act like Jews, which causes other gentiles to blaspheme Israel's God. In contrast, Paul's circumcision-free gospel leads gentiles to glorify God (Rom 15:9).

Returning to the three examples Paul provides of the one who teaches others but not himself, if theft, adultery, and temple robbery function as illustrations of a broader principle, what precise law is his interlocutor guilty of preaching but not keeping? The answer, as Rom 2:25–27 makes clear, is the rite of circumcision. Thus, in contrast to Campbell, who states that "whereas Paul is concerned in 2:17–24 primarily with the law, he clearly turns his attention in vv. 25–29 to circumcision,"[96] vv. 17–24 prepare the ground for the specific accusation of vv. 25–27. Romans 2:21–22 sets the trap for the interlocutor: of course he would condemn the person who does the precise thing against which he preaches. Romans 2:23 leads to the principle that Paul and his interlocutor will agree upon—the one who breaks the very law in which he boasts dishonors God. The trap then ensnares the judaizing gentile interlocutor, who boasts in and preaches circumcision, but, as Paul argues in Rom 2:25–27, does not actually keep the law of circumcision.[97]

## Proper Observance of the Law of Circumcision (Rom 2:25–27)

In Rom 2:25 Paul begins to address his central concern—circumcision—in engaging his gentile interlocutor:

> For circumcision benefits, if you keep the law. But if you are a transgressor of the law, your circumcision has become uncircumcision. So, if a man who is uncircumcised keeps the precepts of the law, will not his uncircumcision be reckoned as circumcision? Then those who are uncircumcised by nature but keep the law will condemn you, a transgressor of the law, through the letter and circumcision.

> περιτομὴ μὲν γὰρ ὠφελεῖ ἐὰν νόμον πράσσῃς· ἐὰν δὲ παραβάτης νόμου ᾖς, ἡ περιτομή σου ἀκροβυστία γέγονεν. ἐὰν οὖν ἡ ἀκροβυστία τὰ δικαιώματα τοῦ νόμου φυλάσσῃ, οὐχ ἡ ἀκροβυστία αὐτοῦ εἰς περιτομὴν λογισθήσεται; καὶ κρινεῖ ἡ ἐκ φύσεως ἀκροβυστία τὸν νόμον τελοῦσα σὲ τὸν διὰ γράμματος καὶ περιτομῆς παραβάτην νόμου. (2:25–27)

Paul claims that circumcision profits if one keeps the law. But if one transgresses the law, one's circumcision becomes uncircumcision. Again, most interpreters understand these statements to signify that failure in law observance in one area leads God to reckon one a lawbreaker in every area. And since no one can keep the Jewish law perfectly, why keep any aspect of it? While some modern interpreters of Paul might find such logic compelling, Paul's contemporaries would not have. Based on this interpretation, most scholars have argued that Paul thought circumcision was of no value, for no one could keep the law perfectly. Yet when his interlocutor asks the question, "What is the value of circumcision?" Paul's response is not that it is of no value, but that it is of much value in every way (3:1–2). Did the slightest transgression of the law really render circumcision null and void? In other words, did Paul actually believe that there was no room for grace in God's covenant with Israel? To avoid this absurd conclusion, Jewett claims that "to fall into the status of a παραβάτης νόμου ('transgressor of law') requires that the violations be more than occasional or accidental."⁹⁸ This interpretation finds a parallel in a statement which *Genesis Rabbah* attributes to Rabbi Levi: "In the Hereafter Abraham will sit at the entrance to Gehenna and permit no circumcised man of Israel to descend therein. What then will he do to those who have sinned too much? He will remove the foreskin from babes who died before circumcision and set it upon them [the sinners], and then let them descend into Gehenna" (48.8). In contrast to Rabbi Levi, Paul does not actually say that this person sins too much—Jewett supplies this meaning in order to make this reading of Paul's statement more theologically palatable.

More to the point, even James, who uses similar logic, does not conclude that one should abandon law observance. It is simply implausible that James would argue that since people sin, they may as well give up trying to keep any and all aspects of law observance. Instead, James's rhetorical point is that his readers, while priding themselves on their sexual purity, treat the poor with contempt, thereby endangering their lives and incurring guilt (James 5:1–6). Again, interpreters should follow the logic of Paul's examples of the one who preaches against theft but then steals, and the one who preaches against adultery but then commits it. Following this established pattern, Paul's statement that circumcision is of value only if one keeps the law refers not to the entirety of the Jewish law, but specifically to the law of circumcision: circumcision is of value, if one follows the entirety of the law which pertains to circumcision.

The second-century BCE book of *Jubilees* provides a helpful parallel in its lengthy discussion of the rite of circumcision. According to the author, when God instituted the practice of circumcision, he said to Abraham: "I am now telling you that the Israelites will prove false to this ordinance. They will not circumcise their sons in accord with this entire law because they will leave some of the flesh of their circumcision when they circumcise their sons" (*Jub.* 15.33; trans. VanderKam). The author refers here to the practice of *periah*, in which the entirety of the foreskin is removed in the process of circumcision.⁹⁹ The author considers physical circumcision that does not include *periah* to be a circumcision that is not in accord with "this entire law." And failure to keep this entire law is nothing less than proving "false to this ordinance." In discussing what invalidates a circumcision, the Mishnah contains a similar sentiment: if one does not properly circumcise, "[it is as if] one did not circumcise" (*m. Shabb.* 19.6; cf. *b. Shabb.* 137b).

In fact, Rom 2:27 confirms that Paul's point pertains specifically to the legislation of circumcision. Here Paul makes the startling claim that the uncircumcised person of v. 26 will judge the circumcised person of v. 25 who transgresses the law.¹⁰⁰ Yet v. 27 contains a phrase that complicates this assertion: the prepositional clause διὰ γράμματος καὶ περιτομῆς. This phrase further describes the one who is a transgressor of the law, although, as Jewett notes, "the precise meaning of the phrase διὰ γράμματος καὶ περιτομῆς ('by/through letter and circumcision') remains a matter of debate."¹⁰¹ Of the 197 occurrences in Paul of the preposition διά when it takes the genitive, the vast majority indisputably mean "through," whether in the sense of agency, means, or movement through space or time.¹⁰² Yet interpreters almost universally render διά with the genitive here as "in spite of" or "while."¹⁰³ In support of this translation, they posit the infrequently attested use of διά with the genitive to indicate attendant circumstances, because "it is difficult to see how γράμμα καὶ περιτομή can constitute the means by which the interlocutor transgresses the Law."[104] Most interpreters rely upon the standard New Testament Greek Grammar (Blass-Debrunner-Funk [BDF]), which notes two other Pauline passages (Rom 14:20 and Gal 4:13) where it detects such a function (§223.3) as evidence that διά with the genitive can have this meaning. Unfortunately, the latter of these two passages provides no evidence of this usage since the preposition διά takes here an object in the accusative (δι᾽ ἀσθένειαν). Thus, on the basis of Rom 14:20 alone, which Jewett refers to as an "unusual, virtually untranslatable combination [of words],"[105] BDF suggests that the διά construction of Rom 2:27 signifies attendant circumstance: "you who, while you have the writings and circumcision. . . ." This translation requires the addition of the phrase "you have," making γράμματος καὶ περιτομῆς the direct object of this paraphrastic addition. Such a translation might be permissible, but again, would it not be preferable to translate it in a way that adds as little as possible to the Greek while still making sense? If we can provide an interpretation of this passage that makes sense of this phrase functioning instrumentally, we should prefer it to the attendant circumstance interpretation, since the preponderance of such phrases mean "through."

A few scholars have argued that διά functions instrumentally. For instance, Gottlob Schrenk argues that "it is precisely through what is written and through circumcision that the Jew is a transgressor," since possession of the letter and circumcision do not lead the Jew to fulfilling the law because they do not lead him to action. Yet this remark suggests only that the letter and circumcision do not help this person keep all the various requirements of the law. Schrenk does not explain how the letter and circumcision prove instrumental in making this person a transgressor of the law. More recently, Stanley E. Porter also claims that in Rom 2:27 διά functions instrumentally, but unfortunately provides no argumentation to support this interpretation. James D. G. Dunn likewise interprets the prepositional phrase in an instrumental sense. Unlike Schrenk and Porter, Dunn provides one possible, although ultimately improbable, way in which the letter and circumcision function to make this person, who Dunn believes is an ethnic Jew, a transgressor of the law. He avers, "To continue to identify the point of the law with Israel as a national entity (clearly distinguished from the other nations by circumcision) was actually to prevent God's purpose in the law attaining fulfillment."[106] For Dunn, at least since the advent of Christ, any use of the law to distinguish ethnic Jews from non-Jews is a misuse of the law. By their use of scriptures/law and by pointing to circumcision as a necessary marker of Jewish identity, Jews now become transgressors of the law. For Dunn, the transgression of the law is ethnocentrism and the use of ethnic identity markers. Such a fundamental criticism of this role of circumcision undermines the way in which it functions in Genesis 17 to distinguish Abraham's seed through Isaac from all other nations. While it is possible that such ethnocentrism troubled Paul and led him to undermine traditional Jewish understandings of the rite—even scriptural accounts of it like Genesis 17—such concerns seem more modern than ancient. Paul himself repeatedly distinguishes between Jew and gentile (e.g., Rom 3:1–8; Romans 9–11; Galatians 2), even as he asserts that such categories no longer exist in Christ (Gal 3:28). Consequently, interpreters need to provide a more satisfactory explanation for Rom 2:27 in light of the argument that the phrase διὰ γράμματος καὶ περιτομῆς means "by/through the letter and circumcision."

If Thorsteinsson correctly argues that in Rom 2:17–29 Paul continues his diatribe with a gentile interlocutor, the way in which this person could be circumcised and yet a law transgressor by means of circumcision and the letter becomes apparent. Careful attention to the circumcision legislation of Jewish scriptures once again enables the reader to make sense of Paul's seemingly nonsensical claim that one can be circumcised and yet be considered a transgressor of the law with regard to circumcision. According to the legislation of Gen 17:12 and Lev 12:3, Jewish circumcision is distinct from the circumcision of other nations in that it occurs on the eighth day after birth. Covenantal circumcision is not just any form of circumcision, but circumcision on the eighth day after birth. In fact, Gen 17:14 LXX, supported by both *Jubilees* and the Samaritan Pentateuch, states that the person not circumcised on the eighth day after birth is cut off from the covenant people.[107] As Genesis 17 shows, and as I will discuss at greater length in the next chapter, Ishmael undergoes circumcision at the age of thirteen, but falls outside the covenant that God made with Abraham. In Genesis 21 Abraham circumcises Isaac on the eighth day after his birth and, consequently, he alone is the covenantal seed. Ishmael's circumcision is not in accord with the law of circumcision and therefore has no covenantal value. His circumcision is treated as uncircumcision with regard to the covenant. According to Gen 17:9–14, God's command to circumcise refers only to Abraham's sons and to the slaves of his household. What is more, in order to distinguish Israel's covenantal circumcision from the circumcision practiced by many of the surrounding nations, Genesis 17 insists that circumcision must take place on the eighth day after birth and that any male not circumcised on the eighth day after birth must be cut off from his people. Any adult gentile male undergoing circumcision fails to keep the law because he does not do so on the eighth day after he was born. Just as significantly, such an adult gentile breaks the law because he is neither Abraham's son nor his slave.[108]

This interpretation finds support in the earliest extant commentary written on Romans. In his discussion of Romans 2, Origen provides an allegorical interpretation of circumcision, but then pauses to examine the literal meaning of the scriptural commandments regarding the rite:

> Indeed, [God] openly declares that he wants even those born of foreign parents to be circumcised, that is to say, those who by no means are regarded as Abraham's stock. . . . [Yet] on no occasion has he mentioned the proselyte, i.e., the foreigner, but he certainly orders the indigenous slave to be circumcised, whether born at home in that nation or even the one bought at a price. He does not bind the freedman, the guest, or the foreigner to be circumcised. (*Commentary on Romans* 2.13.11; trans. Scheck)

He proceeds to make a similar point in his discussion of the commandment to circumcise in Lev 12:3:

> Notice here as well how Moses is commanded to speak only to the sons of Israel [see Lev 12:1] concerning the law of circumcision; there is no mention of those born in a foreign land. For if we believe that what is entered in

the law has been written through the divine Spirit, then assuredly nothing can be considered either to have been added or kept silent to no purpose. For this reason it is absolutely critical to observe the distinctions. (2.13.12; trans. Scheck)

Origen thus concludes that any gentile who undergoes physical circumcision fails to keep the commandment precisely because he fails "to observe the distinctions" that God has created between Jews and gentiles. It is for this reason that he believes that one must interpret the commandment of circumcision allegorically, as he believes Paul goes on to do in Rom 2:17–29, so that it can be of continuing relevance to gentile Christians.

A gentile undergoing circumcision in order to become a Jew fails to keep the law of circumcision in the very act of being circumcised. He is circumcised and yet becomes a transgressor of the law of circumcision through the letter, *gramma* (understood as the detail or prescription of the law), and through the rite of circumcision.[109] His circumcision becomes uncircumcision (ἡ περιτομή σου ἀκροβυστία γέγονεν; cf. Rom 2:25).

## Paul's Reading of Jer 9:24–25 LXX (Rom 2:28–29)

Significantly, this very way of characterizing circumcised gentiles occurs in Jer 9:24–25 LXX, where the prophet condemns Israel along with numerous other circumcised peoples:

> Behold, the days are coming, says the Lord, when I will visit upon all the circumcised their foreskins (ἐπὶ πάντας περιτετμημένους ἀκροβυστίας αὐτῶν). On Egypt, and on Idumea, and on Edom, and on the sons of Ammon, and on the sons of Moab, and on everyone who shaves his face round about, that is, those dwelling in the wilderness—for all the gentiles are uncircumcised in flesh (πάντα τὰ ἔθνη ἀπερίτμητα σαρκί), and all of the house of Israel are uncircumcised in their heart (ἀπερίτμητοι καρδίας αὐτῶν).

Jeremiah first describes all of these nations as circumcised, but then goes on to distinguish Israel, who is uncircumcised in heart, from these nations, who are uncircumcised in their flesh.[110] These gentiles are paradoxically physically circumcised yet reckoned as uncircumcised in the flesh, precisely the condition Paul discusses in Rom 2:25. Berkley also notes that Paul alludes to Jer 9:24–25 LXX in Rom 2:25–29, but his interpretation undermines Jeremiah's logic and the way in which it supports Paul's argument: "The reason that those who are physically circumcised are considered uncircumcised in Jer 9:26 is that they are not circumcised inwardly or spiritually: 'all the house of Israel is uncircumcised in their hearts' (ἀπερίτμητοι καρδίας αὐτῶν). This is also the case implied in Rom 2:25, where the circumcision of those who break the law becomes uncircumcision."[111] Berkley fails to recognize that Jeremiah's accusation against the gentile nations that practice genital circumcision is not that they are uncircumcised in heart; rather, and the LXX translator makes this distinction even more apparent than the MT, Jeremiah claims that, although circumcised, these gentiles are uncircumcised in their flesh.

Such a seemingly contradictory accusation (these gentile nations are physically circumcised and yet somehow physically uncircumcised) has caused confusion among interpreters of Jeremiah. Richard C. Steiner provides one potential solution to this problem, arguing that Egyptian circumcision allowed for the retention of the foreskin, while Israelite circumcision included *periah*, which amputated the entirety of the foreskin from the penis.[112] Thus, to the Israelite eye, the Egyptians (and by extension the other nations mentioned here) retained their foreskin in spite of their circumcision. They were circumcised, yet uncircumcised. Steiner's interpretation rightly emphasizes that physical circumcision remained important for Jeremiah. Interestingly, as noted above, the author of *Jubilees* makes a similar claim with regard to the current practice of circumcision among his contemporary Jews. In his description of Israel's future failure to observe properly the rite of circumcision, the author mentions that some Jews will not circumcise their sons and that other Jews will, but will not remove the entirety of the foreskin, claiming that in doing so they fail to keep circumcision according to "all of this law" (*Jub.* 15.33).

But it is also possible that the difference Jeremiah perceives between Israelite circumcision and the circumcision of other nations lies in the timing of the rite. Genesis 17 distinguishes between Ishmael and Isaac based on the timing of their circumcisions. Whereas Israel circumcised its males on the eighth day after birth, the Egyptians and Arabs circumcised males at a much later date.[113] While the timing of circumcision among Edomites, Ammonites, and Moabites is uncertain, under the influence of the Arabs and Egyptians, they too likely circumcised adult males, not infants. How does one distinguish between the numerous nations who practiced circumcision? It is possible that Jeremiah uses the difference in the timing of circumcision to create a boundary between Israel/Judah and other circumcised nations. It is on the basis of this difference in timing between Israelite and non-Israelite circumcision, therefore, that Jeremiah can claim that Egypt, Edom, Ammon, Moab, and the Arabs are circumcised and yet foreskinned. Such an interpretation of Jer 9:24–25 LXX coincides with Paul's allusion to the passage in Rom 2:25–29. Just as Jeremiah claims that gentile circumcision is no different from uncircumcision—and does so via the mechanics of gentile circumcision (whether that be in relation to the timing or the rite of *periah*), which differ from Israelite circumcision—so too Paul can claim that gentiles who undergo circumcision are truly uncircumcised and are transgressors of the very law that they are trying to keep—on the basis of the timing of their circumcision.

What is more, Paul then uses Jeremiah's depiction of the house of Judah who is physically circumcised, yet uncircumcised of heart, to his advantage. Jeremiah does not suggest that physical circumcision is unimportant for Judah; rather, he stresses that it is insufficient. In addition to practicing physical circumcision, Judah needs to be circumcised of heart. While they are physically circumcised, they are uncircumcised of heart and are, therefore, not pleasing to God. These claims do not suggest that Jeremiah thinks that physically circumcised Jews who are uncircumcised of heart are not real Jews or that physical circumcision is not real circumcision. Rather, they are real Jews who displease God. Likewise, in Rom 2:28–29 Paul attempts to convince his gentile readers that although they are unable to keep the law of circumcision, they do not need to do so to be pleasing to God. Just as physically circumcised Jews are pleasing to God when they are also circumcised of heart, physically uncircumcised gentiles can be pleasing to God through heart circumcision and the *pneuma*. Both Paul and Jeremiah make the uncontroversial claim that physical circumcision and Jewish descent alone do not make a Jew pleasing to God; rather, a circumcised Jew's circumcised heart pleases God. Paul, though, extrapolates from this observation to convince his gentile readers that, although he has demonstrated that they cannot undergo the rite of circumcision correctly, they can still please God by having a circumcised heart.

## *Conclusion*

While virtually every scholar, whether endorsing the anti-legalist or anti-ethnocentric reading of Paul, has concluded that in Rom 2:17–29 Paul criticizes an interlocutor of Jewish descent who insists on the importance of law observance, Thorsteinsson has rightly called this interpretation into question. The Jew of this passage is only a so-called Jew. He thinks of himself as a Jew, but Paul disagrees. And Paul disagrees, not because he has redefined Jewishness, but because he does not believe that a gentile can actually become a Jew: for Paul *nomos* does not overcome *physis* or *genos*. Paul rejects the belief, held by some of his contemporary Jews (Christ followers and otherwise), that gentiles needed to or even could become Jews. For Paul, as for a number of other Second Temple Jews, most notably the author of *Jubilees*, gentiles profited nothing from the adoption of the Jewish law.[114] Paul alludes to the details of the law of circumcision in Genesis 17, as well as to the prophet Jeremiah, to bolster his claim that undergoing circumcision does not make gentiles into Jews. In fact, their non-scriptural circumcision confirms their identity as transgressors of the very law that they try to keep and in which they boast. In this regard, Paul's criticism parallels that of the author of the *Testament of Levi*, who condemns priests for taking gentile wives after "purifying them with an unlawful purification" (14:6). Just as the author of the *Testament of Levi* does not condemn all purification rites in this passage, only a purification rite applied to gentile women, so too Paul's words against genital circumcision in Rom 2:17–29 need to be understood as directed at gentile circumcision alone. Paul believes that undergoing circumcision and adopting the Jewish law leave gentiles in the same predicament facing non-judaizing gentiles (Rom 1:18—2:16). In contrast, Paul preaches that the God of Israel has dealt with the gentile problem in Christ, a belief that he meticulously unpacks in Rom 3:21—8:39.[115]

Paul's statements regarding circumcision in Romans 2 become both considerably more coherent and rhetorically more convincing if one identifies the interlocutor as being a gentile who has adopted the Jewish law. This gentile believes himself to be a Jew, but Paul denies him this identity, showing the interlocutor the way in which his circumcision is in reality uncircumcision. Any reading of Romans 2 contains within it a degree of uncertainty because Paul does not explicitly identify his interlocutor. But such uncertainty disappears once one reads the letter to the Galatians, since interpreters of that letter are certain that Paul's primary readers were gentiles-in-Christ. Modern readers know that what he says in Galatians about the Jewish law and circumcision arises out of his concern that some gentiles-in-Christ in Galatia want to undergo circumcision and adopt the Jewish law. Further, his understanding of the legislation of Genesis 17 and his larger interpretation of the Abraham Narrative lie beneath the surface of his argument in Rom 2:17–29. In contrast, Gal 4:21–31 contains an explicit discussion of the Abraham Narrative. Paul's argument against circumcision in his letter to the gentile Galatians, therefore, corroborates the argument of this chapter.

# 3

# "Do You Not Hear the Law?"

AS IN ROMANS, Paul reminds his readers in Galatia that God has ordained him to preach the gospel to gentiles (1:16; 2:2–9). In this letter he addresses gentiles to whom he had preached this gospel of Christ crucified, but who are now being taught that they need to undergo circumcision and adoption of the Jewish law. Throughout Galatians 3–4 Paul responds to this other gospel in an effort to convince the Galatians that they need not, and in fact cannot, become Jews in order to become sons of Abraham. In Gal 4:21–31, Paul turns to the Abraham Narrative to prove his point:

> Tell me, those who desire to be under the law, do you not hear the law? For it is written that Abraham had two sons, one out of the slave woman and one out of the free woman. But the one who is out of the slave woman was born according to the flesh, and the one who is out of the free woman was born through the promise. These things are spoken allegorically. For they are two covenants, one from Mount Sinai giving birth into slavery—this is Hagar. For Hagar, Mount Sinai, is in Arabia and it stands for the present Jerusalem.[1] For she is enslaved with her children. But the Jerusalem above is free—this is our mother. For it is written, "Rejoice, O barren one who does not give birth; break out and shout, you who are not in labor; for the children of the barren one are many more than the children of the one who has a husband" (Isa 54:1). And you, brothers, like Isaac, are children of the promise. But just as then the one born according to the flesh persecuted the one born according to the *pneuma*, so also now. But what does the scripture say? "Cast out the slave woman and her son, for the son of the slave woman will not inherit with the son" (Gen 21:10) of the free woman. Wherefore, brothers, we are not children of the slave woman, but of the free woman.

In an allusive manner, Paul directs his readers to Genesis 16–21, beginning by referring to Abraham's two sons and their mothers, and ending with Sarah's command to Abraham to cast out Hagar and her son. Paul intends his readers to identify these references to Hagar and Ishmael (Genesis 16) and Sarah and Isaac (Genesis 21) and to view them as bookends to the passage of the law (Genesis 16–21) that he desires them to hear more fully: "Those who desire to be under the law, do you not hear the law?" (Gal 4:21). His reading of Genesis 16–21 forms one component, then, of his larger argument that the Galatians must not undergo circumcision.

But, since Genesis 17 portrays the circumcision of Abraham and commands Israel to circumcise the males of its household, modern readers frequently accuse Paul of gross misinterpretation. Although Richard B. Hays otherwise makes a compelling case that Paul was a thoughtful interpreter of Jewish scriptures, he concedes that "we see Paul in Gal. 4:21–31 practicing hermeneutical jujitsu." Hays's colorful description of Paul's reading of Genesis seems, therefore, to admit that here Paul strays from his usual, and usually defensible, method of interpretation. Hays concludes:

> The claim that Torah, rightly read, warrants the *rejection* of lawkeeping is, on its face, outrageous. No sane reader could appeal, without some flicker of irony, to the Law in order to nullify circumcision as the definitive sign of covenant relation with God. Unless we suppose that Paul was an insane (or duplicitous) reader, we must credit him with some ironic sensibility as he flips the story on its back.[2]

Interpreters usually opt for the conclusion that Paul was somewhat duplicitous, albeit cloaking this assessment in more generous terms. For instance, R. P. C. Hanson claims that Paul uses typology here, but that it has "been strained and distorted in an unconvincing but highly Rabbinic fashion into allegory." Bruce W. Longenecker argues that "the voice of scripture that Paul wants his audience to hear speaks in concert with his gospel only by removing it from its original narrative context." Likewise, Frank J. Matera states that "even the general reader immediately notices that Paul's allegorical interpretation goes against the plain and literal sense of the Book of Genesis," which "neglects the fact that the eternal covenant which God established with Abraham was a covenant of circumcision." Has Paul neglected, distorted, or strained Jewish scriptures, willfully or otherwise? If knowingly, did he really think that such a tendentious interpretation of Genesis would persuade his readers of the validity of his statements regarding circumcision and the law? Based on this understanding, W. M. Ramsay concludes that Gal 4:21–31 is "weak as an argument, and not likely to advance [Paul's] purpose."[3]

According to these interpreters, proponents of both the anti-legalist and anti-ethnocentric readings of Paul, the Abraham Narrative simply does not support Paul's circumcision-free gospel to the gentiles. Consequently, the fact that he refers to this passage at all suggests that he must have been compelled to do so. That is to say, Paul discusses Genesis only because his opponents have marshaled it in support of their gospel and now he must counter their arguments. In the words of C. K. Barrett: "This is a part of the Old Testament that Paul would have been unlikely to introduce of his own accord; its value from his point of view is anything but obvious, and the method of interpretation is unusual with him. . . . It stands in the epistle because his opponents had used it and he could not escape it."[4] For most interpreters, then, Paul's reading of Genesis 16–21 in Gal 4:21–31 is explicable only as a last resort. The teachers have backed Paul into a corner by arguing from Jewish scriptures that gentiles need to undergo circumcision in order to become sons of Abraham. As Matera concludes, "On face value, the agitators had a strong scriptural argument that Paul could not counter with a literal reading of the Genesis text. Consequently, he appeals to an allegorical interpretation."[5] Confronted with this seemingly undeniable reading of Genesis 17, Paul must resort to allegory to defend his non-legalistic gospel, according to anti-legalist interpreters, or to defend his non-ethnocentric gospel, according to anti-ethnocentric interpreters. What all of these interpreters implicitly concede, then, is that their construals—anti-legalist or anti-ethnocentric—of Paul's gospel cannot be reconciled with their understanding of the Abraham Narrative.[6]

This chapter contests these readings, providing an interpretation of both Genesis 16–21 and Paul's argument that could plausibly convince Paul's readers, and can, therefore, avoid caricatures of early Judaism. As Francis Watson puts it:

> When [Paul] asks his readers, "Tell me, you who wish to be under law, do you not hear the law?" (Gal. 4.21), he is inviting them to participate with him in a responsible interpretation of this text. He does not regard the text as a pretext for a free interpretative fantasia. He does not draw from it cheap debating points, in the hope of persuading impressionable readers to return to a gospel that is in principle independent of the scriptural texts to which appeal is made.[7]

Both anti-legalist and anti-ethnocentric proponents have universalized Gal 4:21–31, a universalization that unavoidably leads to the conclusion that Paul has misused Genesis 16–21. Again, we shall see that the key to understanding Paul's interpretation of Genesis 16–21 lies in recognizing that Paul provides a reading of this text in response to gentile judaizing—most especially, gentiles undergoing circumcision.

## *The Missionaries' Reading of Genesis 17*

Paul begins his reading of Genesis 16–21 without mentioning the names of either the mothers or their respective children, referring to Abraham's wives as the free woman and the slave woman (Gal 4:22–23). Only at the end of Gal 4:24 does Paul first note that the name of the slave woman is Hagar. And, while Paul eventual names the son of the free woman, he only identifies him as Isaac in Gal 4:28. Even more, Paul fails to mention that the free woman is Sarah and that the child of the slave woman is Ishmael. It appears, then, that Paul assumes that his readers would be familiar with the narrative details of Genesis 16–21. This fact suggests to most interpreters that Paul's opponents have used the Abraham Narrative and Genesis 17 to convince the Galatians that they needed to undergo circumcision and law observance in order to become sons of Abraham.[8] Although I agree with the conclusion that these missionaries used Genesis 17, as the next chapters demonstrate, the Abraham Narrative already constituted a significant component of Paul's preaching and shaped his understanding of his gospel prior to this controversy.

Paul demonizes these competing missionaries throughout his letter. Whoever has preached this gospel to the Galatians, which in Paul's mind is no gospel at all (1:6–9), has really only bewitched them (3:1). They are zealous on behalf of the Galatians, but for no good purpose; they are in fact trying to exclude the Galatians in order to make the Galatians jealous of them (4:17).[9] He further claims that the missionaries want the Galatians to undergo circumcision because they wish to avoid persecution (6:12). All of these assertions cast the missionaries in a rather negative light. Yet, as John M. G. Barclay reminds us, modern interpreters need to employ caution when using Paul's statements to reconstruct the thinking and motivations of his opponents. Paul engages in polemics throughout his letter in order to dissuade his readers from listening to this other gospel.[10] While he disagrees with this gospel, presumably his competitors sincerely believed that it was divinely inspired. Additionally, the very fact that their teachings elicit Paul's response in the form of a letter indicates that at least some Galatians found their gospel both attractive and convincing. Alan F. Segal observes that modern interpreters of Paul "often assume that arcane and punctilious Jewish ceremonial food laws and observances can scarcely have been attractive to anyone. But Paul's ferocity belies this error."[11]

In Chapter 1, I outlined the sorts of claims that these missionaries in Galatia and elsewhere may have made about Abraham to gentiles. In brief, it is likely that they preached that just as Abraham, who was of gentile origin, heard God's call, left his family, and later underwent circumcision, so too should gentiles in Galatia. They had come to the Galatians with a gospel about Jesus that included the necessity of undergoing circumcision and observing the law.[12] By becoming Jews through circumcision and adoption of the law, the Galatians could rid themselves of their gentile identity and enter into full covenant with the God of Israel on par with ethnic Jews. Modern interpreters frequently characterize these missionaries as ethnocentric and exclusivistic, harshly requiring gentiles to undergo circumcision and conversion.[13] But, as Terence L. Donaldson argues,

> [W]hile conversion is not generally seen as a form of universalism in contemporary discourse, our interest here is the world of late antiquity, a world in which proselytism represented a striking step in a universalistic direction. In a world where religion had traditionally been embedded in the constitutive domains of a tribe or a people, the idea that religious identity was something that could be adopted was a significant innovation.[14]

The missionaries' gospel assumed that any gentile was able and welcome to become a Jew and would thereby gain access to all the privileges of God's covenant with Abraham. Their message was one of hope, promising salvation from fleshly impulses, as well as from the powers of the age that enslaved the gentiles (cf. Gal 1:4; 4:8–9).[15] Viewed from this perspective, the gospel of these missionaries was universalistic. Why would the Galatians not want to heed this good news, undergoing minor surgery in order to gain so much? After all, these missionaries seemed to have Jewish scriptures on their side. In response to Paul's gospel, the assemblies in Galatia had already entered into a fundamentally Jewish world, with distinctive Jewish beliefs (e.g., worship of Israel's God) and practices (e.g., distinctive sexual practices)—why not enter all the way by adopting circumcision and other Jewish practices such as dietary laws and Sabbath observance?[16]

Paul's use of Abraham in Galatians confirms that his opponents referred to Abraham in their own preaching. Although it appears that nothing in the preceding context prepares readers for the introduction of Abraham in Gal 3:6, Paul's question in Gal 3:3 likely alludes to the missionaries' teaching: "Having begun in the *pneuma*, are you now making yourselves complete in the flesh?" (ἐναρξάμενοι πνεύματι νῦν σαρκὶ ἐπιτελεῖσθε). On the basis of Genesis 17, the missionaries may have preached that the gentiles could be made whole through the rite of circumcision just as Abraham had been made whole: "When Abraham was ninety-nine years old, ʏʜᴡʜ appeared to Abraham and said, 'I am El Shaddai. Walk before me and be whole (*tamim*/ἄμεμπτος)'" (Gen 17:1).[17] As I mentioned in Chapter 1, the rabbis connected this command to be whole to God's commandment that Abraham undergo circumcision. Admittedly, the verb Paul uses for completion or perfection (ἐπιτελέω) is not a cognate of ἄμεμπτος ("blameless"), the word which most LXX manuscripts of Gen 17:1 have in place of the Hebrew word *tamim*. But some textual witnesses to Gen 17:1 LXX do translate *tamim* as τέλειος, as does Aquila's translation of the Hebrew Bible (cf. Philo, *That God Is Unchangeable* 4). Arguably, τέλειος better captures the positive sense of *tamim*, stressing wholeness, completion, and perfection, whereas ἄμεμπτος stresses the lack of something—it is without blame.[18] Additionally, ἄμεμπτος has no verbal form (only the antonym μεμφόμαι exists). Thus, Paul's use of the verb ἐπιτελέω, particularly in reference to the flesh (σάρξ), both evokes this stream of Jewish interpretation of God's covenant of circumcision with Abraham and prepares his readers for his explicit introduction of Abraham in Gal 3:6–9. Interestingly, Paul's question in Gal 3:3 finds a close verbal parallel in *Targum Pseudo-Jonathan*'s paraphrase of Gen 17:1: "When Abraham was ninety-nine years old the Lord appeared to Abraham and said to him: '. . . be complete in your flesh (הוי שלים בבישרך).'" Although neither the MT nor the LXX contains the words "in your flesh," the targum makes explicit that the perfection or wholeness envisaged here relates to circumcision. *Targum Pseudo-Jonathan*, then, contains an Aramaic phrase equivalent to Paul's Greek phrase σαρκὶ ἐπιτελεῖσθε.[19]

Paul rejects this interpretation of the significance of Genesis 17, claiming that Abraham had already been declared righteous prior to his circumcision (Gal 3:6; cf. Gen 15:6).[20] Thus, Genesis 15, not Genesis 17, shows the way in which Abraham functions paradigmatically for the Galatians. Yet if Paul concurs with the presupposition that Abraham is an example for his gentile readers, how can he persuade them that his opponents wrongly apply Abraham's actions in Genesis 17 to the Galatian situation? The answer to this question comes from recognizing the way in which he moves the discussion from Abraham to Abrahamic sonship. In Gal 3:6—4:10, he discusses Abrahamic sonship and *pneuma* in light of Genesis 15 and other scriptural passages (an argument that we shall examine more fully in Chapters 4 and 5). After a brief treatment of his relationship to the Galatians (Gal 4:11–19), Paul attempts to undermine his competitors' understanding of the relevance of Genesis 17.

## *Covenantal Circumcision in Genesis 17*

In response to his opponents' gospel, Paul claims in Gal 4:21 that his audience wants to be under the law but does not hear it correctly. Apparently, as E. P. Sanders points out, the fact that his readers are trying to hear and follow the law does not concern him; rather, the fact that they are hearing and following it wrongly bothers him. "The debate about Abraham is conducted on the assumption that the law reveals the true way to righteousness, and thus God's own intention. This assumption characterizes not only Gal. 3:6–18, but also 4:21–31, where Paul cites 'the law' to prove his own case."[21] In Gal 4:21–31, he brings his readers back to the story of Israel's beginnings. Following Paul's advice, I suggest that modern interpreters need to reread and rethink Genesis 16–21 in order to understand the way in which he could use this narrative to justify his claim that the Galatians must not undergo circumcision.

Genesis 16 portrays Abraham and Sarah, old and childless, despite God's repeated promises that he would provide Abraham with an heir (cf. Gen 12:7; 13:15–16; 15:4–5, 13, 18). Having inferred that God has prevented her from bearing Abraham a child, Sarah offers him her Egyptian maidservant Hagar in order to sire a child through her. Abraham successfully impregnates Hagar, possibly leading the reader to conclude that God has finally fulfilled his promise of a son to Abraham (16:1–4). When Hagar runs away due to Sarah's mistreatment of her, the angel of the Lord commands her to return, pronounces the name of Hagar's son, and promises that he will multiply Hagar's offspring (16:9–15). Uninitiated readers can hardly be faulted for assuming that God has sent Hagar back to Abraham's household because he approves of Ishmael as Abraham's promised heir—he does, after all, come out of Abraham's loins, as God promised in Gen 15:4. It is this narrative that precedes the establishment of the covenant of circumcision.

In Genesis 17, God commands Abraham to circumcise all the males of his household, sons and slaves. Consequently, almost every modern scholar concludes that Genesis 17 demonstrates the porous nature of the boundaries around God's covenant with Abraham. For instance, on the basis of Genesis 17, Paul Williamson avers that "circumcision was a mechanism through which non-Israelites could become part of the covenant community," and concludes:

> Clearly this covenant cannot be viewed in an exclusively nationalistic sense. Rather than envisaging the inclusion of just one nation, the covenant in Genesis 17 encompasses those from other nations also. It is not just the physical descendants of Abraham who will be incorporated within this covenant, but all to whom the sign of the covenant is applied. . . ; the numerical increase will apparently come about through all who will align themselves with Abraham by submitting to the conditions of the covenant, primarily expressed through circumcision."

Similarly, despite the lack of evidence until the second century BCE, Torsten Löfstedt claims: "Ever since Abraham's day, Jewish boys and male converts to Judaism have been circumcised."[22]

As I argued in Chapter 1, some of Paul's Jewish contemporaries could and did read Genesis 17 as a conversion narrative that confirmed that gentiles could undergo circumcision and become Jews. Such an interpretation is preserved in the *Mekhilta de-Rabbi Ishmael*, an early rabbinic work, which says of Genesis 17:

> Beloved are the proselytes (*gerim*). It was for their sake that our father Abraham was not circumcised until he was ninety-nine years old. Had he been circumcised at twenty or at thirty years of age, only those under the age of thirty could have become proselytes. Therefore God bore with

Abraham until he reached ninety-nine years of age, so as not to close the door to future proselytes. (*Nezikin* 18 [trans. Lauterbach, slightly modified]; cf. *Gen. Rab.* 46.2; *Psalms Midrash*, Addendum to Psalm 17.12)

Although this interpretation is one way in which readers can understand Genesis 17, it is not the only way. In fact, there are a number of potential problems for this reading of the passage. First, if the Priestly writer of Genesis 17 believes that circumcision functioned as a rite of conversion to Israelite identity, why does he portray the circumcision of Ishmael in Gen 17:25–26? After all, the narrative makes clear that Ishmael, although circumcised, falls outside the covenant that God makes with Abraham (17:18–21).[23] Additionally, Genesis 17 mentions the circumcision of Abraham's slaves. Are readers to assume that they have become Israelites? If so, why is the subsequent narrative silent about their fate? They certainly have not become Abrahamic sons, since otherwise God would not refer to Isaac as Abraham's only son (Gen 22:2). And they are not his covenantal seed, since it is only through Isaac that Abraham's seed would be called (21:12; cf. 17:12). To be sure, Abram the gentile becomes Abraham the grandfather of Israel through the rite of circumcision. But circumcision has no apparent impact on the identity of Ishmael, whose name remains the same, or that of Abraham's nameless slaves.[24] In light of this tension, Roger Syrén concludes, "The inclusion of Ishmael in vv. 23 and 26 cannot in any way be reconciled with the previous verses." Similarly, Hermann Gunkel claims that the Priestly writer "made the error of having Ishmael circumcised," while Carl Steuernagel attributes this discrepancy to the composite nature of the chapter.[25] But is it really conceivable that the Priestly writer, who labors in Genesis 17 to connect the rite of circumcision to the covenant (recall that he uses the word "covenant" thirteen times in this chapter alone), could include Ishmael's circumcision without realizing the way in which it undermines this connection?

By means of the details of the narrative, the Priestly writer signals to readers the reason why Ishmael, despite being circumcised, falls outside the covenant that God made with Abraham.[26] Repeatedly in this chapter he makes references to chronology. Abraham is ninety-nine years old at the inception of the covenant of circumcision (17:1) and Sarah is ninety years of age (17:17). Again in Gen 17:24 the writer reminds us that Abraham is ninety-nine years old when he undergoes circumcision. And in Gen 17:25, he states that Abraham circumcised Ishmael at the age of thirteen. J. P. Fokkelman has shown that temporal references occur frequently in the Abraham Narrative, so it is unsurprising to find this emphasis in Genesis 17 as well.[27] Nonetheless, these temporal indicators take on considerable significance in juxtaposition with the detailed legislation pertaining to circumcision:

> You shall keep my covenant, you and your seed after you in their generations. This is my covenant which you shall keep between me and between you and between your seed after you: to circumcise every male among you. And you shall circumcise the flesh of your foreskin and it shall be for a sign of the covenant between me and between you. And the eight-day-old child shall be circumcised, every male among you throughout your generations, the one born in your house and the one purchased from any foreigner who

does not belong to your seed. Surely the one born in your house and the one purchased shall be circumcised, and my covenant shall be in your flesh for an eternal covenant. And any uncircumcised male, who is not circumcised in the flesh of his foreskin on the eighth day, his life shall be cut off from his people; he has broken my covenant. (Gen 17:9–14)

According to Gen 17:12, God commands Abraham to circumcise the males of his household on the eighth day after their birth. Leviticus 12:3, another Priestly text, contains this same temporal requirement. Genesis 17:14, which according to the LXX states that one who is not circumcised on the eighth day is to be cut off from the people, makes clear the consequences of failing to circumcise an infant on the eighth day after birth. Although the MT does not contain this stipulation, the book of *Jubilees*, the Samaritan Pentateuch, and the Old Latin do. I have argued elsewhere that the LXX and Samaritan Pentateuch preserve the earliest inferable form of Gen 17:14.[28] Whether or not one is persuaded by that argument, Paul used the LXX, and since Paul's readers in Galatia would have known the LXX version of Genesis, they would have heard, upon rereading the narrative, that covenantal circumcision occurs only on the eighth day after birth.

The Priestly writer provides few details regarding the mechanics of circumcision: the rite is to take place only on the males, slave and son, of Abraham's household, and in their foreskins. Apart from these details he mentions only one other stipulation—the timing of circumcision. Consequently, it appears that the timing of the rite was of central importance to the Priestly writer. As David A. Bernat argues, priestly literature "is replete with explicit detail pertaining to ritual performance. Any divergence from the prescriptions has dire consequences."[29] In light of this temporal stipulation, then, the fact that Ishmael did not undergo circumcision on the eighth day after his birth suggests that he exists outside of the covenant, at least in part, because of the fact that he was not circumcised at the right time. In contrast, the Priestly writer stresses that Isaac, the son of Sarah, undergoes covenantal circumcision: "And Abraham circumcised Isaac on the eighth day, just as God had commanded him" (Gen 21:4).

# Jubilees' *Reading of Genesis 17*

The problems listed above demonstrate that one need not read Genesis 17 as evidence that circumcision functioned as a rite of conversion. In fact, reading it in this way runs aground on Ishmael's presence in the narrative—although circumcised, God explicitly excludes him from the covenant. Ishmael provides scriptural proof that not all circumcisions are of covenantal value. In contrast, the reading outlined above suggests that the Priestly writer has portrayed Ishmael's circumcision at the age of thirteen years in order to demonstrate that not all circumcised people groups who claimed descent from Abraham were his covenantal descendants. The Priestly writer's account of circumcision stresses the timing of the rite: only eighth-day circumcision was covenantal. The descendants of Abraham through Isaac and Jacob practiced infant circumcision, demonstrating that they alone were and are the rightful heirs of God's promises to Abraham.

The book of *Jubilees* demonstrates not only that Paul's near contemporaries could read Genesis 17 in this way, but also that some in fact did so.[30] Like Gen 17:12–14, *Jubilees* emphasizes that covenantal circumcision occurs on the eighth day after birth. While Gen 17:9–14 contains two references to the eighth day, *Jub.* 15.12–14 faithfully contains these same occurrences, but then, in an exegetical expansion, adds this stipulation two more times:

> This law is (valid) for all history forever. There is no circumcision of days, nor omitting any day of the eight days because it is an eternal ordinance ordained and written on the heavenly tablets. Anyone who is born, the flesh of whose private parts has not been circumcised by the eighth day does not belong to the people of the pact which the Lord made with Abraham but to the people (meant for) destruction. Moreover, there is no sign on him that he belongs to the Lord, but (he is meant) for destruction, for being destroyed from the earth, and for being uprooted from the earth because he has violated the covenant of the Lord our God. . . . For the Lord did not draw near to himself either Ishmael, his sons, his brothers or Esau. He did not choose them (simply) because they were among Abraham's children, for he knew them. But he chose Israel to be his people. He sanctified them and gathered (them) from all mankind. For there are many nations and many peoples and all belong to him. He made spirits rule over all in order to lead them astray from following him. But over Israel he made no angel or spirit rule because he alone is their ruler. (15.25–26, 30–32a; trans. VanderKam)

The author of *Jubilees* stresses that circumcision cannot take place prior to the eighth day: there "is no circumcising of days, nor omitting any day of the eight days because it is an eternal ordinance." He also emphasizes that circumcision cannot take place after the eighth day, since those who are not circumcised by the eighth day do not belong to God but are meant for destruction (vv. 25–26). Thus, *Jub.* 15.25–26 functions as the author's interpretive expansion of Gen 17:14, which states that circumcision must take place upon the eighth day after birth. As Fergus Millar notes, *Jubilees* emphasizes "that the Covenant was to be solely for those circumcised at eight days, and categorically excludes Ishmael and his descendants."[31]

The requirement of eighth-day circumcision closely intertwines genealogical descent (*genos* and *physis*) with law observance (*nomos*), for only those born to Jewish parents would undergo circumcision on the eighth day after birth. The author of *Jubilees* does not appear to consider the possibility that gentiles who have adopted Jewish customs might choose to circumcise their sons on the eighth day. For the author, God categorically distinguishes between Jacob's seed and all other nations, including even those who traced their lineage back to Abraham. Thus, being born to a Jew (i.e., being born to someone who, like Isaac, underwent circumcision on the eighth day) and then being circumcised on the eighth day (like Jacob) distinguishes Jacob's seed from all others.

Through the emphasis this passage places upon the rite of eighth-day circumcision, the author also addresses the fact that Ishmael and Esau and their descendants claim Abraham as their ancestor. While Abraham already has a son in Ishmael, the fact that he was circumcised at the age of thirteen suggests that God's covenant of circumcision actually excludes him from Abraham's covenantal family. *Jubilees* makes this exclusion more forcefully than does the Priestly writer of Genesis 17: "Anyone who is born, the flesh of whose private parts has not been circumcised by the eighth day does not belong to the people of the pact which the Lord made with Abraham but to the people (meant for) destruction" (15.26). Although God makes the covenant with Abraham, only his descendants who are circumcised on the eighth day belong to this covenanted people. Significantly, in his rewriting of Gen 21:4, the author of *Jubilees* states that only Isaac's circumcision has covenantal value: "Abraham circumcised [Isaac] when he was eight days old. He was the first to be circumcised according to the covenant which was ordained forever" (16.14; trans. VanderKam).[32]

## Excursus: Why Did Abraham Undergo Belated Circumcision?

Surprisingly, the implication that Abraham's circumcision at the age of ninety-nine was not according to the covenant does not appear to disturb the author of *Jubilees*. Nor did such a conclusion seem to bother the Priestly writer of Genesis 17. Of course, neither the Priestly writer nor the author of *Jubilees* had any doubts about Abraham's connection to God's covenant. After all, God had explicitly made several covenants with Abraham and given him numerous promises. The question facing these authors and their respective audiences was not about Abraham's relationship to the covenant, but the relationship of Abraham's various descendants to the covenant. Because no one questioned Abraham's covenantal status, neither Genesis nor *Jubilees* appears to worry about the fact that Abraham underwent circumcision at the age of ninety-nine instead of on the eighth day as God commanded.

Like the Priestly writer and the author of *Jubilees*, Paul believes that gentile circumcision serves no positive purpose. But if Abraham's circumcision does not function as a model for contemporary gentiles, then why did Abraham undergo circumcision? Similarly, if God reckoned Abraham to be righteous in Genesis 15, why did he then command him to be circumcised in Genesis 17? Does the Abraham Narrative not suggest that Abraham lacked something if God gave him the covenant of circumcision after the declaration of Gen 15:6? And if Paul parallels the uncircumcised and trusting Abraham to gentiles-in-Christ, then does the Abraham Narrative not suggest that gentiles subsequently need to undergo circumcision? If gentiles-in-Christ do not need to undergo circumcision, why was Abraham commanded to do so? As Bradley R. Trick notes, Paul's readers or opponents "could fully endorse Paul's position and use it to their advantage: yes, Abraham was justified by faith, but he was then subsequently circumcised, just as you Galatians should also be. Paul could hardly have made a worse argument against a subsequent circumcision."[33]

Paul does not address these questions in Galatians 3–4, in part, because he changes the discussion from Abraham to Abrahamic sons, focusing on Isaac and Ishmael as paradigmatic figures. Nonetheless, he does address these questions in Rom 4:11–12, verses which occur within a larger passage in which Paul argues that his readers are not sons of Abraham via the flesh (Rom 4:1), that is, through circumcision,[34] but through faith. This argument, like Galatians 3–4, implicitly raises the question of Abraham's own circumcision at the age of ninety-nine. In responding to this issue, Paul claims:

> [Abraham] received the sign of circumcision as a seal of the righteousness of faith which he had in a state of uncircumcision, in order to be through uncircumcision[35] the father of all who believe, in order that righteousness might be reckoned to them (εἰς τὸ εἶναι αὐτὸν πατέρα πάντων τῶν πιστευόντων δι᾽ ἀκροβυστίας, εἰς τὸ λογισθῆναι καὶ αὐτοῖς τὴν δικαιοσύνην), and the father of the circumcision, to those who are not out of circumcision alone but who also walk in the faith of our father Abraham, which he had in an uncircumcised state. (4:11–12)

As interpreters note, because Abraham was justified while in a state of uncircumcision, he can be the father of uncircumcised gentiles who are justified, yet this claim does not explain why Abraham subsequently underwent the rite of circumcision. In response to the natural question of why Abraham was circumcised if he was already reckoned as righteous when he was uncircumcised, Paul implies that he needed to become circumcised in order to be the father of both uncircumcised gentiles who believe and circumcised Jews who have Abraham's faith. Romans 4:11–12 suggests that, for Paul, if Abraham had not undergone circumcision, he would only have become the father of believing gentiles. Through uncircumcision and then the subsequent reception of the sign of circumcision, Abraham could become the father of both the uncircumcised and the circumcised, gentiles and Jews. This understanding of circumcision is surprising in that it suggests that Abraham was first the father of believing gentiles and that an additional covenant and sign, circumcision, was necessary for him to become the father of Jews.[36] Origen provides early support for this reading:

> Yet because [Abraham] received circumcision after he had faith, a faith which occurred during his uncircumcision, [Paul] consequently sets forth the reason circumcision would have been given to him: It was to be a sign of his faith which he had while uncircumcised, so that through this he might become the father also of those who are born into circumcision, but only if they should attain to that faith which justifies Abraham while he was uncircumcised. Through faith he is a father of those who are uncircumcised; through the flesh, of those who are circumcised. (*Commentary on Romans* 4.2.3; trans. Scheck, slightly modified)

Through the confidence in God that he manifested in his uncircumcised state, Abraham becomes father of uncircumcised gentiles who believe. Through his circumcision, which is a sign of the faith which he had when uncircumcised, he becomes the father of Jews. This parallels the thinking of later rabbis, who claim that Abraham underwent circumcision at the age of ninety-nine so "that Isaac might issue from a holy source" (*Gen. Rab.* 46.2). Abraham's belated circumcision still matters: even though it is not strictly covenantal, it has value in distinguishing Jews from non-Jews. Ishmael was the offspring of Abram's uncircumcision, while Isaac was the offspring of Abraham's circumcision.

In Rom 4:11–12 Paul provides a rationale for Abraham's subsequent circumcision that, while showing its irrelevance for gentiles, does not denigrate its abiding importance for Jews. Paul states that circumcision was a sign of Abraham's righteousness, but implies that God gave it to him in order that he might be the father of the circumcised, that is, the Jews. In other words, had he not undergone circumcision, he would only have been able to be the father of uncircumcised gentiles who believe. Now he can be father to both, since he was reckoned righteous while uncircumcised, and continued to be reckoned as righteous after undergoing circumcision. Circumcision is thus unnecessary for gentiles and unnecessary for being reckoned righteous, but it continues to function for Paul as an important component of identity for male Jews. Abraham needs to be circumcised in order to be the father of Jews, a fact that suggests that Paul believed the rite to be of abiding significance for Jewish identity—even for those who are in Christ.[37] Again, Origen rightly states, "After all, that is the reason Abraham is justified by faith earlier, while he was still uncircumcised, and afterwards is circumcised, so that he might first be shown as one who was going to be the father of many nations and afterwards of those who were going to believe from the circumcision" (*Commentary on Romans* 4.2.8; trans. Scheck).[38]

## *The Function of Allegory in Paul's Thought*

Before reexamining Paul's interpretation of Genesis 16–21, it is important to reconsider Paul's use of ἀλληγορέω in Gal 4:24, a verb that Richard Longenecker argues can mean "to speak or write allegorically" or "to explain or interpret allegorically." That is to say, when Paul uses ἀλληγορέω, he might be claiming that Jewish scriptures themselves speak allegorically of something, or he might be acknowledging that in his letter to the Galatians he interprets the text allegorically, not literally.[39] Although Gal 4:24 is ambiguous with regard to the question of whom Paul thinks is doing the allegorizing, Longenecker points out that elsewhere Paul's statements demonstrate that at least at times he thinks that the scripture writers themselves allegorize. For instance, in 1 Cor 9:9–11 Paul cites the demand of the law of Moses that Israel not muzzle an ox while it treads grain (cf. Deut 25:4), but then asserts that the law speaks for the sake of Paul and his readers. Although he does not use the verb ἀλληγορέω in the passage, clearly this is how Paul understands the law to function. Paul uses the narratives of Israel's wilderness period in an analogous manner (1 Cor 10:1–11): stories of Israel in the wilderness were meant as examples or warnings (τύποι) for Paul and his contemporaries (1 Cor 10:6). Consequently, Longenecker acknowledges that it is possible "that this is what Paul meant with regard to the biblical accounts of Hagar and Sarah: the story was originally given as an allegory and meant by its original authors to be treated as such."[40] If Paul intends his readers to conclude that Jewish scriptures speak allegorically, then Hans Joachim Schoeps is incorrect to claim that "Gal. 4:21–31 is an utter violation of the basic rule of rabbinical hermeneutics: 'No word of scripture must ever lose its original sense' [*b. Shabb.* 63a]."[41] For Paul, Genesis 16–21 itself originally spoke and continues to speak allegorically. By understanding it allegorically, Paul is being faithful to what he believes is the original sense.

Supporting this interpretation of Paul's use of ἀλληγορέω, Steven Di Mattei argues that scholarly understandings of later Christian allegorization have unduly influenced modern treatments of Paul's intentions in Gal 4:21–31.[42] He focuses attention on the rhetorical trope of *allegoria* in Greco-Roman sources, two of which bear mentioning here since they come from the first centuries BCE or CE. The Alexandrian grammarian Tryphon states that "*allegoria* is an enunciation which, while signifying one thing literally, brings forth the thought of something else" (*On Tropes* 1.1, translation slighted adapted from Di Mattei). Likewise, in his commentary on and defense of Homer, Heraclitus states that *allegoria* is "the trope which says one thing but signifies something other than what it says" (*Homeric Allegories* 5.2; trans. Russell and Konstan).[43] Repeatedly, Heraclitus makes it clear that the problems that Plato and the Stoics have had with Homer's writings are due to the fact that they do not realize that Homer originally intended much that he said to be understood allegorically: "some ignorant people fail to recognize Homeric allegory" (δ᾽ ἀμαθεῖς τινες ἄνθρωποι τὴν Ὁμηρικὴν ἀλληγορίαν ἀγνοοῦσιν), thereby attributing great impiety to him (3.2; cf., for example, 1.1, 3; 5.13; 22.1; 29.4; 41.12). In fact, he can even claim that the entirety of the *Odyssey* is "full of allegory" (75.12; cf. 70.1). Both Heraclitus and Tryphon, therefore, use the word to signify a literary device that an author uses *within* a text, not to denote a hermeneutical strategy used by a reader *on* a text.

Noting, along with Longenecker, that the verb can signify "to speak/write allegorically" or "to interpret/explain allegorically," Di Mattei argues that, apart from Philo, first-century writers always use the verb to reflect that it is "the author or the personified text itself [that is, not the interpreter] which speaks allegorically."[44] In fact, both Philo and Josephus describe the law in these terms. Philo, for instance, makes the generalization that "broadly speaking, all or most of the law-book is an allegory" (τὰ πάντα ἢ τὰ πλεῖστα τῆς νομοθεσίας ἀλληγορεῖται, *On Joseph* 28). Similarly, Josephus avers that Moses sets forth things about God at times in enigmas and at other times in reverent allegory (ἀλληγοροῦντος μετὰ σεμνότητος, *Ant.* 1.24). Further, David Dawson points out that, although they do not use the terminology of allegory, both Aristobulus and Aristeas, second-century BCE Jewish authors, "do not read the Pentateuch 'creatively' or 'imaginatively'; instead, they read the text allegorically in order to retrieve Moses' deliberately hidden message."[45] Like Heraclitus and Tryphon, then, Jewish writers from the second century BCE to the first century CE thought that scripture/Moses spoke allegorically, not that one should interpret a literal text in an allegorical manner.

Commenting on Gal 4:28–31, Di Mattei observes that Paul believed "Scripture, in speaking of the events of then (τότε), discloses, allegorically, the events which are now (νῦν) currently being revealed. . . . It is God who, in speaking of the events of then, discloses the mysteries of what shall befall those living in the final generation."[46] Elsewhere, on the basis of Paul's claim that the events of Israel's history happened as a warning to the Israelites, but were written for the admonition of those upon whom the end of the ages had come (e.g., 1 Cor 10:11), Di Mattei concludes that Paul thought that the "biblical narratives speak of what will happen in the final generation."[47] In this regard, Paul's use of Jewish scriptures parallels the Qumran Community, which understood scriptures to refer to events in their own time (e.g., 1QpHab 7.1).[48] Following Longenecker and Di Mattei, I believe that Paul was convinced that Jewish scriptures, and the Abraham Narrative specifically, were written allegorically. While the narrative portrays the figures of Abraham, Hagar, Ishmael, Sarah, and Isaac, it also speaks about and directly to Paul's communities in his own day.

Interestingly, many modern interpreters conclude that the narratives of Genesis were constructed not as a historical record of the birth of the people of Israel, but as narratives intended to guide Persian-period readers in their own circumstances. For instance, R. Christopher Heard details the similarities between the narrative of Genesis 16–21 and Ezra-Nehemiah's concern about Jewish intermarriage with non-Jewish women and the birth of mixed offspring. Heard argues that Hagar stands for or allegorically represents the foreign wives which Jewish men had taken, while Ishmael represents the mixed offspring of those intermarriages. Just as Ezra calls for Jewish men to separate themselves from their foreign wives and mixed offspring (Ezra 10:2–4, 11), so too Sarah calls for Abraham to expel Hagar and Ishmael from their household and finds divine sanction for her wishes (Genesis 21). That is, Heard and others argue that the Persian-period editors of Genesis 16–21 crafted this section of the Abraham Narrative to function allegorically: the narrative speaks about one thing (Abraham, Hagar, Ishmael, Sarah, and Isaac), but refers to another—the problem of intermarriage and inheritance in Persian-period Judea.[49]

Additionally, it is important to stress the way in which the author of *Jubilees* also extrapolates from the narrative of Genesis 17 to make broader statements about the relationship of Israel to the nations in his own day. In his rewriting of Genesis 17, the author builds upon the distinction between Isaac and Ishmael in the narrative (*Jub.* 15.30, τότε), and then explicitly states that this difference holds throughout history: God has separated Jacob's seed from all the nations (*Jub.* 15.31–32, νῦν). Therefore, Hays suggests that the "interpretation offered in Jubilees is allegorical, with its symbolic identification of Ishmael and Isaac as representatives of Gentiles and Jews."[50] It should be emphasized, however, that *Jubilees'* interpretation is not so much allegorical, as it is, in fact, an extension and contemporization of the original allegorical intentions of the Priestly writer of Genesis 17.

Returning to Galatia, it is also imperative to recognize that the missionaries themselves understand Genesis 17 allegorically, for, on its surface, Genesis 17 discusses Abraham's circumcision and the subsequent circumcision of his household, not the circumcision of gentiles who want to enter into the Jewish people. A literal reading of Genesis 17 contains no reference to gentiles who want to convert to Judaism or become sons of Abraham: the only people who undergo circumcision in Genesis 17 are Abraham, Ishmael, and Abraham's slaves. Consequently, interpreters wrongly characterize the missionaries' conversion-narrative interpretation of Genesis 16–21 as a literal or plain-sense reading of the narrative in contrast to Paul's fanciful, non-literal, and allegorical reading. Both Paul and the missionaries he so vehemently opposes contemporize a passage about figures from the ancient past in order to guide the gentile Galatians in the present. And neither contemporization of Genesis 17 is entirely fanciful: one focuses on Abraham as the positive paradigm for gentiles who undergo circumcision, the other focuses on Ishmael as the negative paradigm for gentiles who undergo circumcision.

Nonetheless, I am convinced that, like *Jubilees*, Paul's reading of Genesis 16–21 functions in the same exclusionary way that the Priestly writer intended the narrative to function for his Persian-period audience. On the basis of this understanding of allegory, then, Paul's belief that Genesis itself speaks of Abraham, Isaac, Ishmael, Sarah, and Hagar then (τότε), but refers to two sorts of missions to the gentiles now (νῦν) corresponds to the editors' intent in crafting a narrative about Abraham's day (τότε), that addressed Persian-period issues (νῦν).

As noted in the preceding chapter, Origen long ago realized that a reading of Genesis 17 that concludes that gentiles should undergo circumcision and convert to Judaism was a non-literal reading: "On no occasion has [Moses] mentioned the proselyte, i.e., the foreigner, but he certainly orders the indigenous slave to be circumcised, whether born at home in that nation or even the one bought at a price. He does not bind the freedman, the guest, or the foreigner to be circumcised" (*Commentary on Romans* 2.13.11; trans. Scheck). Of Lev 12:3, he states, "Notice here as well how Moses is commanded to speak only to the sons of Israel concerning the law of circumcision; there is no mention of those born in a foreign land" (2.13.12; trans. Scheck). Origen claims that a literal reading of Genesis 17 and Lev 12:3 does not promote proselyte circumcision. His conclusion, based on a more literal reading of both of these passages than many modern commentators offer, is that "we should also understand the things said about circumcision, whether in what has been said to Abraham or in what is contained in Leviticus: no one is bound to the law of circumcision unless he derives his lineage from Abraham or is their indigenous slave or a purchased slave" (2.13.13; trans. Scheck). It is this understanding of the exclusionary role of circumcision in Genesis 17 that leads Paul to distinguish between two types of Abrahamic sons: slaves and heirs.

## Two Types of Abrahamic Sonship and Two Gentile Missions

In contrast to both anti-legalist and anti-ethnocentric readings of Gal 4:21–31, Paul neither attacks Judaism or Jews in this allegory, nor denigrates circumcision or the Jewish law.[51] In fact, the preceding reading of Genesis, supported by *Jubilees'* treatment of the rite of circumcision, should demonstrate that Paul's use of the passage to argue against gentile circumcision is neither as unprecedented nor as unjustifiable as many scholars think. Significantly, Paul's interpretation of Genesis 16–21 focuses on the question of Abrahamic sonship, not on the question of imitating Abraham himself. For Paul, the Galatians are to imitate Abraham's faithful response to the God who called him out of Chaldea, but not his circumcision (Gal 3:6–9; Gen 15:6; cf. Romans 4). In other words, Paul does not think that Abraham's circumcision in Genesis 17 is of contemporary relevance to his Galatian readers. In fact, Paul's argument in Galatians 3–4 repeatedly redirects his readers from Abraham to Abraham's sons. In Gal 4:21–31 Paul focuses explicitly on Ishmael and Isaac, yet many interpreters of Paul fail to notice that Ishmael himself underwent circumcision. For instance, Philip F. Esler summarizes the significance of Genesis 17 in the following way: "Sarah's male line were circumcised (Gen. 17.9–14) and were blessed (Gen. 17.16–19), while Hagar's were gentiles and were expelled from the family of Abraham at Sarah's instigation." He concludes that "the respective destinies of Sarah and Hagar sharply highlighted the benefits of being circumcised and joining the descendants of Abraham through Sarah."[52] The discrepancy between these two statements is stunning in that the latter takes no account of Ishmael's circumcision. Hagar's male line underwent circumcision, so why was it not blessed? If there are benefits to all who undergo circumcision, why is Ishmael's destiny so different from the destiny of Isaac?

Even those interpreters who recognize that Ishmael also underwent circumcision fail to see the way in which Paul could deploy him as evidence that not all circumcisions are of covenantal value. For instance, Hays states that the "teachers in Galatia would have insisted that the Gentile Galatians be circumcised in order to legitimize themselves and to regularize their status as recipients of salvation. After all, even Ishmael was circumcised when he was thirteen years old (Gen. 17:25)."[53] But Genesis 17 portrays Ishmael undergoing circumcision with no benefit accruing to him, thereby opening up the possibility that not all circumcisions have covenantal implications. Consequently, Paul could use this passage and the figure of Ishmael to call into question his opponents' claim that if the Galatians undergo circumcision they would become covenantal heirs. Despite Ishmael's circumcision, God informs Abraham that his seed would be called only in Isaac (Gen 21:12; cf. *Jub.* 17.6; Rom 9:7). Contrary to the majority of interpretations of Gal 4:21–31, then, Genesis 17 actually supports Paul's argument against gentile circumcision.

Paul's reading of Genesis insists that there are two types of Abrahamic sons—those born according to the flesh into slavery, and those born through the promise into freedom (Gal 4:22–26). Close consideration of the Abraham Narrative bears this out. As a result of their inability to have children, Sarah determines that she will provide a solution:

> Now Sarah, the wife of Abraham, did not bear [a child] to him. And she had an Egyptian slave woman, and her name was Hagar. And Sarah said to Abraham, "Behold, the Lord has kept me from bearing; go in to my slave woman, so that you might make children out of her." And Abraham listened to the voice of Sarah (ὑπήκουσεν δὲ Αβραμ τῆς φωνῆς Σαρας). And Sarah, the wife of Abraham, took (λαβοῦσα) Hagar the Egyptian, her slave woman ... and she gave her to Abraham her husband (καὶ ἔδωκεν αὐτὴν Αβραμ τῷ ἀνδρὶ αὐτῆς) as a wife. And he went in to Hagar, and she conceived. (Gen 16:1–4)

The narrative of Genesis 16 emphasizes human activity: Sarah speaks to Abraham, Abraham listens to her, and Sarah takes her slave Hagar and gives her to her husband, who goes into her. Her actions lead to the conception and the birth of Ishmael, suggesting that he is born according to the flesh (i.e., in the normal manner) to a slave woman, and thus born into slavery, just as Paul claims in Gal 4:24–25. Claus Westermann argues that the narrator perceives nothing to be amiss with regard to Sarah's proposal, since it was the customary ancient Near Eastern method for dealing with infertility issues. On the other hand, Gerhard von Rad concludes that the author disapproves, precisely because Sarah's actions were in keeping with local custom.[54]

Werner Berg makes the convincing case that the broader narrative context of Genesis confirms that the author or editor of Genesis 16 viewed the actions of Sarah and Abraham negatively, since the passage evokes the actions of Eve and Adam in Genesis 3:[55]

And the woman saw that the tree was good for food, and that it was a delight to the eyes, and that the tree was to be desired to give understanding, and taking (λαβοῦσα) of its fruit she ate. And she also gave [it] to her husband (καὶ ἔδωκεν καὶ τῷ ἀνδρὶ αὐτῆς) who was with her, and they ate. . . . And to Adam [God] said, "Because you listened to the voice of your wife (ὅτι ἤκουσας τῆς φωνῆς τῆς γυναικός σου), and ate from the tree of which I commanded you, 'This one alone you shall not eat from,' cursed is the ground in your works; in pain you shall eat of it all the days of your life." (3:6, 17)

Both Eve and Sarah take (λαμβάνω) and give (δίδωμι) (fruit or another woman) to their respective husbands (ἀνήρ). Additionally, in Genesis 3 God punishes Adam because he listened ([ὑπ]ἀκούω) to the voice (φωνή) of his wife, something the narrator says that Abraham does in Genesis 16. In both stories we see an emphasis upon human activity. In the case of Genesis 16, Sarah speaks to Abraham, and he listens to her. Sarah takes Hagar and gives her to her husband. And Abraham goes into Hagar, who conceives and gives birth to Ishmael. Ishmael is born, then, according to the flesh, just as Paul characterizes his birth in Galatians 4.

In contrast, the narrative of the birth of Isaac stresses divine activity: "The Lord visited (ἐπεσκέψατο) Sarah just as he had said (καθὰ εἶπεν), and the Lord did (ἐποίησεν) to Sarah just as he had said (καθὰ ἐλάλησεν). And Sarah conceived, and bore Abraham a son in his old age at the time of which God had spoken to him" (καθὰ ἐλάλησεν, 21:1–2). The birth of Isaac is, from first to last, the result of divine action and prerogative, or, as Paul would say, through divine promise (δι᾿ ἐπαγγελίας, Gal 4:23) and according to the *pneuma* (κατὰ πνεῦμα, 4:29).[56]

Paul claims that the events surrounding the motherhoods of Hagar and Sarah stand for two distinct and competing missions to the gentiles: the missionaries' gospel and his gospel. The machinations of Sarah and Abraham in Genesis 16 correspond, for Paul, to the missionaries' gospel. Paul equates gentile believers who undergo circumcision and judaize with Ishmael and his opponents with Hagar.[57] His opponents' call to the gentiles to judaize is tantamount to the actions surrounding Hagar's motherhood in Genesis 16. They too are attempting to help God fulfill his promises to Abraham that he would be the father of a multitude of nations. They believe that for this promise to be fulfilled, gentiles must become Jews. And, just as the actions of Abraham and Sarah evidence their vain belief that they can create an heir to God's promises, so too for Paul, the missionaries' goal of creating sons for Abraham through the rite of circumcision is ultimately determined by the vain belief that they can create new heirs and descendants of Abraham, instead of trusting God to create new heirs. As Scott W. Hahn argues, "Both [efforts] represent attempts to produce heirs from Abraham by human (natural or 'fleshly') means—Ishmael through concubinage, the Gentiles through circumcision."[58] This mission remains unaware of the implications of Isaac's birth for the way in which God intends gentiles to become Abrahamic sons: "Rejoice, O barren one who does not give birth; break out and shout, you who are not in labor; for the children of the barren one are many more than the children of the one who has a husband" (Gal 4:27; Isa 54:1).[59] God was the one who enlivened Sarah's dead womb. God was and is the one who brings into existence that which did not exist—a legitimate heir to the promise (cf. Rom 4:19–20).

Presumably Paul's opponents had a very different perspective on their actions. For instance, in certain streams of later rabbinic thought, conversion through the rite of *giyyur* (circumcision and baptism) resulted in the shedding of gentile identity and transformation of the convert into a Jew, so that the rabbis could liken the convert to a newborn Jew (e.g., *b. Yeb.* 22a). Perhaps of significance for understanding the theological hope that motivated these missionaries, the rabbis wondered how Gen 12:5 could speak of the lives or souls that Abraham and Sarah made (עשׂה; LXX reads κτάομαι ["to acquire"]) in Haran: "R. Eleazar observed in the name of R. Jose b. Zimra: If all the nations assembled to create one insect, they could not endow it with life, yet you say, '*And the souls that they had made in Haran!*' It refers, however, to the proselytes. Then let it say, 'That they had converted': why, 'Which they had made'? That is to teach you that if one brings a proselyte near [to God] it is as though he created him" (*Gen. Rab.* 84.4; cf. *Gen. Rab.* 39.14; *Targum Pseudo-Jonathan* to Gen 12:5). From this perspective, the transformation of identity occasioned by gentile circumcision and adoption of the Jewish law is nothing short of miraculous and presumably of divine origin.[60]

It is in this way that Hagar stands for the mission of Paul's opponents,[61] while Sarah stands for Paul's mission. The actions leading to Hagar's motherhood demonstrate a lack of confidence in God's promise, just as the actions of Paul's opponents do. Ishmael's circumcision left unaddressed the fact that he was non-covenantal seed and the son of a slave woman. Likewise, the circumcision of the Galatians would leave them separated from the covenant and reenslaved to the *stoicheia* of the kosmos (thus the frequent slavery language throughout Galatians 4). For Paul, God's creation of Isaac out of nothing prefigures Paul's mission to the gentiles. Just as Isaac, the heir of the promise, came out of nothing, so too do Paul's assemblies—children of the promise arising out of the gentiles—a no-people, those who were not God's children (cf. Rom 10:19). God is the one who enlivens Sarah's dead womb. God is the one who brings into existence that which did not exist—a legitimate heir to the promise.

As Daniel Boyarin suggests, this calling into existence may well have occurred through divine conception:

> It should be noted that in the biblical text, it is not stated that Abraham "knew Sarah his wife" after the "annunciation." There may have even been, then, a tradition that the conception of Isaac was entirely by means of the promise. The birth of Isaac would be, then, an even more exact type of Jesus' birth. This would also explain Paul's application of Isaiah 54:1, in which Hagar is called "she who has a husband," to whom Sarah is contrasted. The point would be that Hagar had sex with a man in order to conceive, but Sarah did not!

Similarly, Schoeps suggests that belief in Isaac's divine birth goes back to Hellenistic rabbis and that Paul inherited it from them, but unfortunately provides no evidence. One potential piece of evidence comes from Philo's *Questions and Answers on Genesis*, in which he asks of Gen 16:1: why does Genesis speak of Sarah's barrenness? His answer: "First of all, in order that the seed of offspring may appear more wonderful and miraculous. Second, in order that the conceiving and bearing might be not so much through union with a man as through the providence of God. For when a barren woman gives birth, it is not by way of generation but the work of the divine power" (3.18). The birth of Isaac, according to Philo, can only be attributed to divine intervention, not to traditional means of conception. Even those interpreters who believed that Abraham had sexual intercourse with Sarah leading to the birth of Isaac could view the results as nothing less than divinely wrought. According to the medieval rabbi David Kimchi, Isaac was born after Abraham was circumcised in order to demonstrate the miraculous fact that Abraham could have a child through his wounded organ. The nineteenth-century rabbi Malbim also notes that Abraham gave birth to Isaac at the age of 100 and after he underwent circumcision, facts that emphasize the miraculous nature of his birth.[62] Isaac's birth was thoroughly miraculous, distinguishing him from Ishmael.

Not only do the methods of birth differ, but so too do the sources of these births. Ishmael was fathered by the uncircumcised gentile *Abram* and born to an Egyptian slave woman, while Isaac was fathered by the circumcised grandfather of Israel, *Abraham,* and born to Sarah. According to *Genesis Rabbah,* in answer to the question as to why Abraham was circumcised at the age of ninety-nine, the rabbis claimed: "In order that Isaac might issue from a holy source" (46.2)—a significant implication of this statement being that Ishmael does not. As Phyllis Trible states, "Placed after the birth of Ishmael (Gen. 16) and before the birth of Isaac (Gen. 21), Abraham's circumcision in Gen. 17 makes a difference for his two sons. Ishmael (who himself is circumcised at the age of thirteen, Gen. 17:25) is conceived and born outside the circumcised covenant, and Isaac, within it. Abraham's circumcision would appear to introduce, if not induce, the fertility of Sarah, who will bear the child of the covenant."[63] *Pirqe de Rabbi Eliezer* contains a similar interpretation, connecting it to the reason why it was Isaac, not Ishmael, whom Abraham offered to God: "So with our father Abraham; before he was circumcised, the fruit which he produced was not good [in its effects, and was disqualified from the altar; but when he had been circumcised, the fruit which he produced was good in its effects, and his wine] was chosen to be put upon the altar like wine for a libation" (29; trans. Friedlander [bracketed material lacking in some manuscripts]). One can thus read Genesis 16–21 as a story that demonstrates that God, not humanity, is ultimately the source of new life for Abraham's seed. Such a reading coincides with the broader themes of Jewish scriptures which consistently depict God as the one who opens and closes the womb (cf. Gen 25:21; 29:31; 30:2, 22; 49:25; Deut 28:11; 1 Sam 1:5–6; Ps 113:9) and the one who gives and takes away life (Deut 32:39; 2 Kgs 5:7). In light of this evidence, Seth Daniel Kunin concludes that "circumcision might be seen as a symbolic form of castration, the ultimate denial of human fruitfulness. Indeed, only after Abraham is circumcised and human fruitfulness denied can divine fruitfulness come to the fore in Isaac's birth."[64]

## *Anyone Undergoing Circumcision Needs to Keep the Whole Law (Gal 5:3)*

Paul believes that the circumcision of the Galatians models the circumcision of Ishmael, not that of Isaac, since if they undergo circumcision it will not be done at the age of eight days. And, as the law makes clear, one not circumcised on the eighth day after birth cannot be part of the covenant of Genesis 17. Regrettably, most Pauline interpreters refer to a version of Gen 17:14 which omits the temporal stipulation pertaining to circumcision, and thereby fail to do justice to Paul's understanding of Genesis 17 and the rite of circumcision.[65] Elsewhere, Paul stresses that he himself is, with regard to circumcision, an "eighth-dayer" (περιτομῇ ὀκταήμερος, Phil 3:5), implying that any other form of circumcision was of lesser, if any, value. Noting the covenantal importance of eighth-day circumcision for such Jews as the author of *Jubilees*, Segal argues, "In Phil. 3:4–8 [Paul] tells us that he was circumcised properly."[66] Those desiring to undergo circumcision have not heard the full witness of the law. Given the temporal stipulation connected to the rite of circumcision, any Galatian man (or gentile man more broadly) who undergoes circumcision fails to keep even this law in its entirety. This may be what Paul implies immediately after outlining his reading of Genesis 16–21: any person who undergoes circumcision is required to do the whole law (ὀφειλέτης ἐστὶν ὅλον τὸν νόμον ποιῆσαι, 5:3).[67]

Unfortunately, scholars frequently interpret this remark as signifying that if a man undergoes circumcision, then he also needs to keep the other various laws that make up the entirety of the Jewish law. In his *Commentary on Galatians*, Augustine states of Gal 5:3: "[Paul] says this so that at least from the terror of such countless observances as are recorded among the works of the law, the Galatians might avoid being forced to fulfil them all and be kept away from the things his opponents wanted to use to subjugate them" (trans. Plumer).[68] Augustine's interpretation suggests that the Galatians do not realize the massive set of obligations for which they sign up if they undergo circumcision. They fail to see that as attractive as circumcision might appear, it entails an overwhelming host of other commandments that, to Augustine's mind at least, should elicit terror. In a similar vein, Rudolf Bultmann claims that following the Jewish law "meant making life an intolerable burden. It was almost impossible to *know* the rules, let alone put them into practice."[69] Further, the fact that Paul needs to make this statement has led a number of scholars to suggest that the missionaries have preached circumcision somewhat disingenuously, not informing the Galatians of the roughly six hundred attendant laws that they would need to adopt after being circumcised.

This interpretation fails for a number of reasons. First, it is apparent that the Galatians have been instructed in at least some other Jewish laws, such as days, months, and years (Gal 4:10).[70] Second, and most problematic for this line of reasoning, it seems unlikely that missionaries would begin with requiring that gentiles observe circumcision, instead of what would presumably be less daunting commandments such as Sabbath, dietary laws, and so forth. Surely, as James D. G. Dunn notes, it is improbable that circumcision would be the first step in the process of judaizing: "a policy of 'gradualism' would usually have worked up to circumcision as the most challenging demand (for a Greek) rather than taking it as a starting point."[71] In fact, the late first- and early-second century CE Roman poet Juvenal mentions the trend of Roman fathers who begin by observing the Sabbath, and end with leading their children to reject pig meat and adopt circumcision (*Satires* 14.96–106). Similarly, Josephus describes the slaughter of Roman soldiers in Judea, mentioning that only one person, Metilius, was spared because he swore to judaize to the point of circumcision (*War* 2.454). That is, Metilius was willing to go to great lengths in judaizing to avoid being put to death.

Other interpreters believe that Paul claims in Gal 5:3 that the Jewish law is impossible to keep in its entirety. Any failure in one aspect of keeping the law is like breaking the entire law, and so attempts to keep it are futile. To be sure, later rabbinic literature stresses that gentiles who convert to Judaism must be willing to adopt the entire law: "A proselyte who took upon himself all the obligations of the Torah except for one item—they do not accept him. R. Yosé the son of R. Judah says, 'Even [if it be] a minor item from among the stipulations of the scribes'" (*t. Demai* 2:4–5; trans. Neusner).[72] Yet, as Sanders rightly argues, the rabbis emphasize the need for acceptance of the entirety of the law, not perfect obedience to it.[73] That is to say, someone who is contemplating converting to Judaism cannot pick and choose what he or she will and will not observe. Further, F. F. Bruce rightly criticizes this interpretation, since Paul elsewhere describes his obedience to the law as blameless (κατὰ δικαιοσύνην τὴν ἐν νόμῳ γενόμενος ἄμεμπτος, Phil 3:6). Paul, even from his post-Christ vantage point, does not appear to have suffered the debilitating guilt of one who felt that his imperfect obedience to the Jewish law rendered all his other observant actions superfluous.[74]

In contrast, it is possible that, in a way that parallels his argument in Rom 2:17–29 (see the preceding chapter), Paul makes the claim that any Galatian man who undergoes circumcision has already, in the very act of undergoing circumcision, failed to keep the entire law pertaining to circumcision. That is to say, Paul may intend the phrase ὅλος ὁ νόμος to refer to the entirety of the law of circumcision, not the entirety of the Jewish law.

Significantly, the author of *Jubilees* uses a similar phrase with reference to the commandment of circumcision. In his discussion of Israel's future, the author predicts that some Jews would not circumcise their sons, while others would not remove the entirety of the foreskin, claiming, therefore, that they would fail to keep circumcision according to "all of this law" (*Jub.* 15.33). The Mishnah contains a similar assessment, claiming that if one does not properly circumcise, "[it is as if] one did not circumcise" (*m. Shabb.* 19.6).

Additionally, although in Jewish scriptures the phrase "the whole law" frequently refers to the entirety of the Jewish law, there is one clear instance where it means the entirety of one specific commandment. The LXX translation of Deut 24:8–9 refers to the law on *lepra* (often erroneously translated as "leprosy"), commanding that Israel "be very careful to do according to all the law (φυλάξῃ σφόδρα ποιεῖν κατὰ πάντα τὸν νόμον)."[75] This verse demonstrates that one can talk about all the requirements of one particular law using a phrase (πάντα τὸν νόμον) synonymous with the phrase Paul uses in Gal 5:3 (ὅλον τὸν νόμον). Paul might be suggesting, in a way that is similar to *Jubilees* 15 and worded like Deut 24:8–9 LXX, that, unless one performs the entirety of the law of circumcision, one has in fact not kept that law. John Chrysostom recognized this possibility, as seen in his *Homilies on Galatians*:

> The law (ὁ νόμος) introduces many things even through the one commandment (διὰ τῆς μιᾶς ἐντολῆς). Accordingly, if you are circumcised (περιτμηθῇς), but not on the eighth day (μὴ ἐν τῇ ὀγδόῃ δὲ ἡμέρᾳ), or on the eighth day, but no sacrifice is offered, or a sacrifice is offered, but not in the required place, or in the required place, but not the required objects, or if the required objects, but you are impure, or if pure yet not purified by appropriate rules,

all is undone (πάντα οἴχεται ἐκεῖνα). Consequently, [Paul] says, "that he is a debtor to the whole law." (*Homilies on Galatians* 5.3)[76]

Like the author of *Jubilees*, Chrysostom understood the rite of circumcision to imply numerous attendant commandments. Failure to comply with the whole complex of stipulations relating to the rite of circumcision signifies failure in completing that rite. One can see the seriousness with which the complex of circumcision legislation was taken within an anecdote that the *Tosefta* preserves:

> Rabbi Nathan said, "When I was in Mazaca of Cappadocia, there was a woman who would give birth to male infants and they would be circumcised and die. She circumcised the first and he died, the second and he died, the third and she brought him to me. I saw that he was green. I examined him and I did not find the blood of the covenant in him. They asked me, 'Are we to circumcise him?' I said to them, 'Wait until blood enters him.' They waited and circumcised him and he lived." (*t. Shabb.* 15.8; trans. Neusner)

This story demonstrates that Jews were earnest in their efforts to circumcise their infants on the eighth day after birth: the woman circumcised two of her infants on the eighth day, even though it led to their deaths. Only after this tragedy occurred twice, did she consider seeking permission to delay the circumcision of her third son. In fact, Samaritan halakhah demonstrates the continuing commitment to eighth-day circumcision, regardless of the threat to human life.[77]

On the other hand, one could also read the claim of Gal 5:3 in light of the preceding use of the word "law" in Galatians. Galatians 5:3 comes immediately after Paul's discussion of Genesis 16–21, an exegetical discussion of the law. In fact, Paul refers to this section of scripture explicitly as the law in Gal 4:21: "Those who desire to be under the law do you not hear the law?" As Jerome argues, "One should note that the historical narrative of Genesis is here called 'law.' It refers not, as is popularly thought, to what is to be done or what is to be avoided, but everything that is composed concerning Abraham and his wives and children is called 'law'" (*Commentary on Galatians* to 4:21; trans. Scheck). If the Galatians want to listen to and obey the law of circumcision as it is found in Genesis 17, then they need to listen to the rest of the story—that is, the law of Genesis 16–21.[78] If they undergo circumcision as non-infants, they will become modern-day Ishmaels. And if they become modern-day Ishmaels, as Paul argues in Gal 4:22–29, then they need to obey the rest of the passage, particularly God's law, through the voice of Sarah (Gen 21:10), that Paul quotes: "Cast out the slave woman with her son, for the son of the slave woman shall not inherit with the son of the free woman" (Gal 4:30). In other words, if the Galatians take Genesis 17 as a commandment to undergo circumcision, then they also need to obey the commandment of Gen 21:10, which requires their expulsion from the community of Christ that inherits the Abrahamic promise. This interpretation provides a cogent account for the presence of the word πάλιν ("again") in Gal 5:3. Paul may refer back to the argument of Gal 4:21–31, which to his mind demonstrates the necessity of keeping the entirety of the law (whether that be the law of circumcision itself, or the larger narrative of Genesis 16–21), and thus undermines the conclusion that the Galatians benefit from undergoing circumcision. This reading also provides an explanation for Paul's assertion that those who desire to be under the law and undergo circumcision will gain no benefit from Christ and, in fact, are cut off from him (Gal 5:2, 4). In becoming modern-day Ishmaels, they suffer the ban of Gen 21:10 and are no longer counted among Abraham's seed.

The Priestly writer of Genesis 17, the author of *Jubilees*, and Paul believe that the Abraham Narrative gives no hope to the proselyte—neither Ishmael nor any slave within Abraham's household ever enters into the covenant that God makes with Abraham.[79] Non-eighth day circumcision was not a sign of the covenant.

## Those Undergoing Circumcision Do Not Keep the Law (Gal 6:13)

This interpretation of Paul's reading of Genesis 16–21 and his understanding of circumcision also provides a coherent explanation for Paul's claim that those circumcising themselves do not keep the law (οὐδὲ γὰρ οἱ περιτεμνόμενοι αὐτοὶ νόμον φυλάσσουσιν, Gal 6:13).[80] Scholars have interpreted this statement in one of two ways. As in Gal 5:3, the majority of interpreters understand Paul to be making the (uncontroversial) claim that Jews, who had previously undergone circumcision, were unable to fulfill perfectly all the requirements of the Jewish law. The observation that Jews did not keep the law without any fault (and by extension, that no human could) supposedly leads to the realization that there is no point in trying to keep the law. Again, this logic requires doggedly ignoring the fact that the Jewish law contained within itself the means for addressing human failure and sin through atonement and repentance. Or, if interpreters admit this fact, it requires that we believe that Paul ignored or rejected this built-in means for forgiveness.

A variation of this reading, as mentioned above, suggests that the missionaries have only preached the necessity of circumcision, remaining silent about the other commandments. Hans Dieter Betz, for instance, asks, "Paul's flat statement that the circumcised do not themselves keep the Torah is strange. If this is not merely polemic but is indeed fact, we would want to know why they were not observing the Torah. Were they libertines, or were they interested only in circumcision as a magical ritual? Did they keep only part of the Torah, or a special Torah?"[81] As I argued earlier, this possibility seems unlikely.

Another interpretation, placing weight on the fact that the participle περιτεμνόμενοι is in the present tense,[82] argues that Paul has in mind those who have quite recently undergone the rite of circumcision. Paul's statement would then pertain to gentile believers who have judaized by undergoing circumcision. For instance, A. E. Harvey argues that "none of the evasive tactics adopted by commentators can really mitigate the force of this present participle. Those who are troubling (ταράσσων [Gal 5:10]) the [Galatian assemblies] are not Jews by birth, but Gentiles who have only recently become Jewish proselytes, or who are still contemplating doing so."[83]

While one cannot rule out this interpretation (and this identification of the missionaries in Galatia fits well with the reading of Rom 2:17–29 outlined in the preceding chapter), this discussion of the present tense participle in Gal 6:13 needs to be informed by recent discussions of verbal aspect theory. A writer may use a verb in the present tense without intending it to refer to present time. Here the present tense form of φυλάσσω does not necessitate a temporal reference to the present. That grammatical tense should not be confused with time is even more the case with participles, and especially substantival participles. As Daniel B. Wallace argues, "When a participle is *substantival*, its aspectual force is more susceptible to reduction in force." Substantival participles, and particularly substantival present participles, can function as generic utterances: the present tense is often used "in proverbial statements or general maxims about what occurs at *all* times."[84] Does Paul intend to indict all of humanity in the claim that they cannot keep the entirety of the Jewish law perfectly? Or does this maxim have a more limited target? In other words, does Paul make a specific claim applicable only to the person who has himself circumcised? While most scholars apply the pronoun αὐτοί to φυλάσσουσιν, thus taking it to refer to keeping the law ("those undergoing circumcision do not themselves keep the law"), it is possible and, in fact, grammatically preferable to apply αὐτοί to περιτεμνόμενοι. The verse should then be translated in the following way: "For those who circumcise themselves do not keep the law." Consequently, Paul uses the plural pronoun to indicate to his readers that they should interpret the participle as a reflexive middle, not as a passive. These men have not merely been circumcised, they have sought to have themselves circumcised. The people whom Paul has in mind are not those who are passively circumcised as infants—Jewish males, but those who actively choose to undergo circumcision—adult gentile males.

In support of this argument, elsewhere Paul uses different constructions to indicate Jews, ἡ περιτομή or οἱ ἐκ τῆς περιτομῆς (cf. Gal 2:7–9, 12).[85] Paul argues neither that Jews fail to keep the law, a rather uncontroversial claim if one understands it to mean that Jews did not keep the law perfectly, nor that these teachers only advocate circumcision, forgetting or ignoring other aspects of the Jewish law. Paul's point is that those who willingly undergo circumcision do not keep the law, an assertion evidenced by the fact that one key aspect to the specific law that they think they are in the process of keeping, the timing of the rite, is being broken at the very instant that they undergo circumcision. The use of the participle in the present tense does not necessitate that this action has happened just prior to or simultaneous with Paul's writing of the letter. Rather, the present participle indicates that the act of circumcising is taking place concurrently with the main verb: that is, the breaking of the law. Their supposed act of lawkeeping is, to Paul, at the very same time a transgression of the law.

## Paul, the Galatians, and Gentile Judaizing

Returning again to Gal 4:21–31, in Paul's mind, by attempting to create more heirs of the promise through circumcision, the missionaries have displayed a stunning ignorance of what the law says, an ignorance that the Galatians have inherited. It is for this reason that he calls them back to Jewish scriptures, focusing on aspects of the story that the missionaries had neglected in their haste to produce heirs for Abraham. How was Ishmael born? Just as Ishmael was born of the scheming of Sarah, those gentile believers who succumb to pressure to undergo circumcision are born of the scheming of these missionaries. The actions of Abraham in siring a child through Hagar, at the behest of Sarah, signify the human effort to produce sons in order to fulfill God's promise. In the same way, the actions of the missionaries and the response of the Galatians appear to Paul to be human effort. They believe that, through requiring gentiles to undergo circumcision, that is, converting gentiles into Jews, they can fulfill God's promise to produce children. The thinking behind such actions, to Paul's mind, remains oblivious to the fact that God alone is the one who is faithful and able to produce children of the promise. It is God who creates children for Abraham, not humans. As Paul says in Rom 4:17, Abraham believed in God "who gives life to the dead and calls into existence the things that do not exist." The birthing of descendants of Abraham—both Isaac and now gentile believers—echoes God's resurrection of Christ Jesus from the dead.

It is in this way, then, that Hagar stands for the mission of Paul's opponents, while Sarah stands for Paul's mission. In Genesis 16, Abraham, Sarah, and Hagar demonstrate a lack of confidence in God's promise and an attempt to force God's hand, just as Paul's opponents do. Ishmael's circumcision left unaddressed the fact that he was non-covenantal seed and the son of a slave woman. Likewise, the circumcision of the Galatians would leave them separated from the covenant and enslaved to the elements of the kosmos. As we observed above, God's creating Isaac out of nothing prefigures Paul's mission to the gentiles. Just as Isaac came out of nothing, so too did Paul's assemblies (cf. Deut 32:21, Hosea 1:10; 2:23, Rom 9:25–26). In the words of another early Christ follower, Paul's gospel attests to the belief that "God is able from these stones to raise up children to Abraham" (Matt 3:9; cf. Luke 3:8). By being misunderstood and misused by the missionaries and erroneously applied to the gentiles, the law has created offspring through Hagar, gentiles who are now circumcised but who are, like Ishmael, slaves, not heirs. It is in this way that the law, Sinai, has found itself on the side of slavery.

In Gal 4:21 Paul introduces his reading of Genesis with a question: "Tell me, those who desire to be under law, do you not hear the law" (Λέγετέ μοι, οἱ ὑπὸ νόμον θέλοντες εἶναι, τὸν νόμον οὐκ ἀκούτε)? Paul's description of his readers as those who desire to be under the law confirms that gentile judaizing, not Judaism, is his primary concern, since the only other occurrence of the term "desiring to be under the law" is found in Josephus's *Against Apion* to describe gentiles who wish to adopt the Jewish law: "To all who desire to come and live under the same laws with us (θέλουσιν ὑπὸ τοὺς αὐτοὺς ἡμῖν νόμους ζῆν), [Moses] gives a gracious welcome, holding that it is not family ties alone which constitute relationship, but agreement in the principles of conduct. On the other hand, it was not his pleasure that casual visitors should be admitted to the intimacies of our daily life" (*Apion* 2.210).[86]

Yet Paul does not link the rite of circumcision in general to being the product of the flesh—as traditional Christian interpretation would have it. Rather, Paul demonstrates that the Galatians are in peril of becoming contemporary Ishmaels because their observance of circumcision dangerously replicates the fundamental problems surrounding Ishmael's birth. In other words, Paul rejects the belief that gentiles can become heirs of Abraham through circumcision and adoption of the Jewish law.

As I discussed in Chapter 1, and as Shaye J. D. Cohen and Michele Murray argue more fully, ancient writers frequently depicted gentile judaizing in negative terms, not because it was considered bad to be a Jew, but because judaizing involved the pretension to be something that one was not.[87] For instance, in Esth

8:17 LXX, many gentiles judaized and underwent circumcision in order to avoid the wrath and violence of the Jews. They playacted to save themselves. At Antioch, Paul angrily chastises Peter for compelling those who are gentile sinners by nature to judaize, forcing them to be something that they were not (Gal 2:14–15). This statement shows Paul's disdain for the idea that gentiles can benefit from the process of judaizing. As Pheme Perkins notes: "Paul is as intolerant of the Gentile who assimilates to Jewish habits and religious practices as the sharp-tongued Roman satirists who make fun of such Judaizing."[88]

Paul's concluding remarks about Genesis highlight yet again correspondences between the Abraham Narrative and the situation in Galatia. Genesis 21:9–10 states, "But Sarah saw the son of Hagar the Egyptian, whom she had borne to Abraham, playing (מְצַחֵק) [LXX adds 'with Isaac her son']. So she said to Abraham, 'Drive out this slave woman with her son—for the son of this slave woman shall not inherit (לֹא יִירַשׁ/οὐ κληρονομήσει) with my son Isaac (יִצְחָק).'" Interpreters through the centuries have debated what wrong Ishmael committed according to this passage. In Paul's day, Philo states, "We find Ishmael banished with his mother, because he, the illegitimate son (νόθος), claimed to play (ἐν παιδιαῖς) on equal terms (ἰσότης) with the true-born (γνήσιος)" (Sobriety 8). Josephus, too, connects the verse to Hagar's presumptuous belief that Ishmael would inherit Abraham's dominion (ἡγεμονίας, Ant. 1.188). Similarly, the Tosefta, after giving various interpretations to the verb "playing" (מְצַחֵק), including idolatry (cf. Exod 32:6), sex (cf. Gen 39:17), and murder (cf. 2 Sam 2:14–16), claims that the first-century CE rabbi, Simeon ben Yoḥai, stated:

> But playing which is stated here refers only to the matter of inheritance (יְרוּשָׁה). For when our father Isaac was born to our father Abraham everyone rejoiced and said, "A son has been born to Abraham! A son has been born to Abraham! He will inherit the world and take two shares." But Ishmael played (מְצַחֵק) with the thought, saying "Don't be fools! Don't be fools! I am first-born and I am going to take two portions." For in the reply to the matter you learn: For the son of this slave woman shall not be heir (לֹא יִירַשׁ) along with my son Isaac. (t. Sotah 6.6, slightly adapted from Neusner; cf. Sifre Deuteronomy, Piska 31; Ephrem, Commentary on Genesis 13.2)

These traditions, both contemporary to and later than Paul, identify Ishmael's playing as his attempt to usurp Isaac's place as Abraham's covenantal heir. One can see how easily such an interpretation of Ishmael's actions lends itself to the conclusion, which Paul makes, that Ishmael persecuted Isaac.

The play on words, as Robert Alter observes, between Isaac's name (יִצְחָק) and the verb "to play" (מְצַחֵק) supports this interpretation: "Given the fact, moreover, that [Sarah] is concerned lest Ishmael encroach on her son's inheritance, and given the inscription of her son's name in this crucial verb, we may also be invited to construe it as 'Isaac-ing-it'—that is, Sarah sees Ishmael presuming to play the role of Isaac, child of laughter, presuming to be the legitimate heir."[89] Just as Sarah is bothered by Ishmael's pretension to be something which he is not—Isaac, Abraham's covenantal heir—so too Paul is angered by gentiles who judaize, pretending, in his mind, to be Jews in the hopes of gaining a portion in the inheritance (κληρονομία; cf. Gal 3:18, 29; 4:1, 7; 5:21). Both Sarah and Paul demand that those guilty of such pretension be removed from Abraham's household in order to avoid any confusion over who will inherit.

Related to this issue of inheritance, the Aramaic paraphrase of Gen 22:1 contained in *Targum Pseudo-Jonathan* portrays Ishmael and Isaac arguing over who would inherit from Abraham:

> After these events, after Isaac and Ishmael had quarreled, Ishmael said, "It is right that I should be my father's heir, since I am his first-born son." But Isaac said, "It is right that I should be my father's heir, because I am the son of Sarah his wife, while you are the son of Hagar, my mother's maidservant." Ishmael answered and said, "I am more worthy than you, because I was circumcised at the age of thirteen. And if I had wished to refuse, I would not have handed myself over to be circumcised. But you were circumcised at the age of eight days. If you had been aware, perhaps you would not have handed yourself over to be circumcised." Isaac answered and said, "Behold, today I am thirty seven years old, and if the Holy One, blessed be He, were to ask all my members I would not refuse." These words were immediately heard before the Lord of the world, and at once the Memra of the Lord tested Abraham. (*Targum Pseudo-Jonathan* Gen 22:1; cf. *Gen. Rab.* 55 4; *b. Sanh.* 89b)[90]

This story provides an explanation for why God would ask Abraham to sacrifice his son Isaac and illustrates one of the central problems with the narrative of Genesis 16–21. Not only does Ishmael undergo circumcision, but he also presumably submits to this circumcision in a way that Isaac, as an eight-day-old child, never could. Should not such a decision to undergo this painful rite at the age of thirteen be rewarded accordingly? How can it be that someone who was circumcised entirely apart from his own decision stands to inherit? Building on the possibility that the missionaries in Galatia are gentiles who have themselves judaized and now encourage other gentiles to do so, Lloyd Gaston states, Ishmael "was circumcised as a young adult, and this provided the basis for his boasting of his righteousness. If the troublemakers in Galatia were not only boastful but specifically were boasting of being circumcised as adults (Gal 6:12–13), then Paul must have immediately thought about Ishmael when he heard of them." Gaston concludes that in Galatia the modern-day Ishmaels "are those who undergo voluntary circumcision as adults (6:13) and urge it on others (5:2; 6:12) as an achievement and a boast. Paul's argument is not against circumcision (or Judaism) as such, but for adult Gentiles to circumcise themselves would mean seeking to earn something and thus deny God's grace."[91] Again, while my own interpretation does not require that the missionaries be gentiles who have judaized and are now preaching judaizing to other gentiles, I believe that Gaston's hypothesis fits well with the arguments presented here.

## *Conclusion*

Two important conclusions follow from my interpretation of both Rom 2:17–29 and Gal 4:21–31. First, at least on the issue of circumcision, the early Jesus movement did not differ greatly from certain contemporary streams of Jewish thought. Just as Philo and later rabbinic literature could point to Abraham as an example of the ideal convert to Judaism, who underwent circumcision and law observance, so too did the missionaries who visited the Galatians. For this strand of thinking, Jewish identity was permeable. Non-Jews could become Jews through circumcision. On the other hand, just as the author of *Jubilees* could use the Abraham Narrative to exclude the possibility of conversion through emphasizing eighth-day circumcision, so Paul could use Ishmael to show that gentile circumcision resulted in slavery, not covenantal sonship. Paul, then, like the author of *Jubilees*, thought that gentiles gained no benefit from circumcision and law observance. For this strand of thinking, Jewishness was inherent, genealogical, and impermeable to penetration by non-Jews. This statement, as the next chapter will argue, needs slight qualification when considering Paul's own thinking on the issue. Paul did not think that gentiles could adopt the Jewish law in order to become Jews, but he did think that God could rewrite gentile genealogy in order to make them Abraham's sons and seed—something he was now accomplishing through Paul's mission. Paul's letter to the Galatians demonstrates that early Jesus believers argued over the proper way to "give birth" to children of Abraham. How were they to go about making gentiles into Abraham's seed?

Second, too often interpreters, both anti-legalist and anti-ethnocentric readers, have read Galatians as though Paul contrasts Jews and Christians, and, consequently, two distinct religious systems—Judaism and Christianity. According to these interpretations, all of Paul's statements about the works of the law and circumcision demonstrate his rejection of the religion of Judaism for the superior faith of Christianity. In light of this interpretation of Galatians, Betz concludes that Gal 4:21–31 "is one of Paul's sharpest attacks upon the Jews," and that, according to Paul, "Judaism is excluded from salvation altogether, so that the Galatians have to choose between Paul and Judaism."[92] Yet, as most scholars now realize, it is anachronistic to portray Christianity and Judaism as two distinct religions in the first century CE.[93] Further, as Barclay and J. Louis Martyn among others have argued, Paul did not attack Judaism or Jews as such, but a group of Christ-missionaries who preached that gentile Christ followers needed to undergo circumcision and adoption of the Jewish law.[94] The anti-legalistic interpretation of Paul's writings fails to account for the exclusively gentile audience of the letter to the Galatians. Paul does not attack the Jewish law and Judaism, but the misapplication of the Jewish law to gentiles.[95] The anti-ethnocentric reading of Paul's writings, while cognizant of the importance of the Jew/gentile distinction, misunderstands Paul's criticism of the Jewish law to be that it divided Jew and gentile, a division that Paul's gospel sought to overcome. Paul continued to hold to a strict distinction between Jew and gentile (Gal 3:28 notwithstanding), and thus condemned gentile judaizing, not Jews who continued to observe the Jewish law.

Given that Paul attacked gentile judaizing, specifically gentiles in Galatia adopting circumcision and the law, one must be careful to take neither his letter as a whole, nor the individual statements within it, out of the specific historical context in which they originated. As Murray states, "Whereas Paul's negative statements about certain aspects of the Jewish law have been understood by later generations of Christians and scholars to target Jews, Jewish Christians, or Judaism, in the original context of the letter they were meant to correct the practices of *Gentile*

Christians."⁹⁶ Paul did not reject the rite of circumcision or the law in general. He rejected their application to gentiles. It is in fact a misapplication of the law to apply it to gentiles, akin to applying the laws of *shehitah* (kosher slaughtering) to a pig and thinking that the resulting meat will not be pork. Just as no amount of legal rigor can transform a pig into an edible animal, so too no amount of law observance can transform a gentile into a Jew. For Paul, the gentile problem was too deeply rooted to be addressed through what he perceived to be human action unsanctioned by God.⁹⁷ He believed that in the crucified and resurrected Christ God had intervened in the world to address gentiles, saving them from what he referred to as this present evil age and from the elements of the kosmos that enslaved them.

In the second part of this book, I turn to Paul's constructive use of the Abraham Narrative to explain the way in which Israel's God has provided this deliverance to gentiles-in-Christ, the seed of Abraham. As we shall see, contrary to Boyarin's claim that Paul's reading of Genesis 16–21 must "reverse the terms of that constitutive biblical text and uproot any genealogical significance of the Promise," Paul's gospel remained fundamentally genealogical and was rooted in his reading of the biblical text, especially the Abraham Narrative.⁹⁸

# PART 2

# Abraham's Seed and the Gentile Solution

# 4

# *Gentile Sons and Seed of Abraham*

IN THE PRECEDING chapter, I argued that Paul's reading of the Abraham Narrative in Gal 4:21–31 undermines the claims of his competitors, who insist that gentiles-in-Christ need to undergo circumcision and adoption of the Jewish law in order to become sons of Abraham.[1] This circumcision-encouraging gospel makes gentiles into slaves, not inheriting sons of Abraham. Circumcision and adoption of the Jewish law are a dead end for gentiles because God did not intend for the Jewish law to make gentiles into sons of Abraham. For that matter, as Pamela Eisenbaum observes, the Jewish law did not even make Jews into sons of Abraham:

> Torah did not create Jewish patrilineal privilege; neither does the obser-
> vance of all the Torah's precepts ("works of the law") maintain it. The privi-
> lege came through being divinely ordained descendants of Abraham. Torah
> observance, therefore, is largely irrelevant for Gentiles. What Gentiles need
> is not Torah but reception into the lineage of Abraham.[2]

While he rejects the belief that law observance enables gentiles to become Abraham's heirs, Paul agrees with his competitors that gentiles must somehow become genealogically descended from Abraham. He makes his own case for gentile Abrahamic descent in Romans 4 and Galatians 3–4, where he provides a close reading of the Abraham Narrative, particularly Genesis 15 and 17. In both passages, Paul argues, on the basis of Gen 15:6 (LXX: "and Abraham trusted in God and it was reckoned to him as righteousness"), that it is *pistis*—trust or faithfulness—which makes Abraham righteous and thus it is *pistis* that makes both gentiles and Jews righteous.[3] In contrast to the slave-producing gospel of his competitors, Paul argues in Romans 4 and Galatians 3–4 that his gospel gives birth to free sons and heirs of Abraham. In these texts Paul stresses the impor-tance of *pistis*, an emphasis that has led many interpreters to conclude that he contrasts *pistis* to descent, belief to genealogy.[4]

Building on the important work of Caroline Johnson Hodge, I will focus in this chapter on Paul's argument about Abraham and Abrahamic sonship in Galatians 3 in order to explicate the way in which Paul argues for the conclusion that those who are of faith are sons of Abraham (Gal 3:6–7). Paul makes it clear that it is not faith as such that makes one a son of Abraham; rather, faith brings the *pneuma*. Since those who are out of faith receive the *pneuma* of Abraham's seed, Christ, they too become Abraham's seed. The reception of the *pneuma* thus provides gen-tiles with a new genealogy so that they become truly descended from Abraham, not through the flesh, but through the *pneuma*. Paul does not reject genealogical descent; instead, he envisages a newly possible pneumatic form of such descent. This chapter therefore gives an account of an aspect of Paul's argument for which neither the anti-legalist nor the anti-ethnocentric readers of Paul can provide an adequate explanation—the continuing centrality of genealogical descent from Abraham for Paul's gospel.

## Paul's Gospel: Gentiles Blessed in Abraham (Gal 3:8)

Paul claims that "the scripture, foreseeing that God would justify the gentiles out of faith, prepreached the gospel (προευηγγελίσατο) to Abraham, stating, 'All the gentiles will be blessed in you'" (ἐνευλογηθήσονται ἐν σοὶ πάντα τὰ ἔθνη, Gal 3:8). This statement is illuminating for a number of reasons.

First, it demonstrates that Paul's main concern in writing Galatians 3–4 is to give an account not of the justification of all people, but of the gentiles specifically. Whatever the precise meaning of the various assertions that Paul makes in Galatians 3–4, they must be understood in relation to God's dealings with gentiles, not Jews: "God's dealings with Israel are not in question in this letter, and Paul has no reason to deny their importance; the issue that separates Paul from those who are agitating the Galatians is the way in which God's salvation comes to gentile[s]."[5] Although beyond the scope of the argument of this chapter, Gal 3:8 demonstrates that what Paul says about the Jewish law in Gal 3:10–14 (which also ends with an explicit reference to gentiles) relates not to all humanity, but to gentiles alone.[6] Thus, the curse of the law rests not upon Jews because they cannot or did not keep the entirety of the law, an ahistorical and derogatory understanding of the function of the Jewish law,[7] but upon gentiles who attempt to keep it. As Lloyd Gaston observes, "Since the ones 'Christ has redeemed from the curse of the law' are explicitly called Gentiles in verse 14, the curse of verse 10 must also be one which lay upon Gentiles."[8]

Second, Paul claims that the gospel that he preaches is the same gospel that Jewish scriptures preached to Abraham. He makes a similar claim about the scriptural basis of the gospel he preaches in Rom 1:2, asserting that it was promised beforehand (προεπηγγείλατο) in the prophets and holy scriptures. Rarely do scholars take Paul seriously here, essentially agreeing with the sentiments of William Wrede that, while he may have convinced himself that he found the gospel in Jewish scriptures, Paul "generally extracts from scripture only that which he has himself read into it."[9] In contrast, Gaston asks, "What if Paul's claim that 'his' gospel is already proclaimed in the Old Testament (Gal 3:8; Rom 1:2, etc.) and [his claim] that he interprets current events through Scripture and not the other way around were taken seriously?" While modern readers might find Paul's scriptural justifications for his gospel unconvincing, presumably he believed that they were persuasive enough to marshal in his effort to dissuade his contemporaries from the alternative gospel being preached in Galatia.[10]

Finally, Gal 3:8 demonstrates that Paul does not merely think of Abraham as an exemplar for the gentiles to whom he preaches; rather, gentiles will be blessed in (ἐν) Abraham: "The importance of Abrahamic descent in Paul's argument throughout Gal 3–4 implies that Abraham plays a more integral role in securing

the blessing for Christian believers than simply serving as a convenient example of justification by faith."[11] While Paul alludes to a promise that God made to
Abraham, his quotation matches no specific text from Genesis. Instead, it is similar to Gen 12:3 (ἐνευλογηθήσονται ἐν σοὶ πᾶσαι αἱ φυλαὶ τῆς γῆς), 18:18 (ἐνευλογηθήσονται
ἐν αὐτῷ πάντα τὰ ἔθνη τῆς γῆς), and 22:18 (ἐνευλογηθήσονται ἐν τῷ σπέρματί σου πάντα
τὰ ἔθνη τῆς γῆς), possibly being an amalgamation of all three.[12] Paul's use of this
thrice-repeated promise demonstrates that his gospel requires gentiles not only
to imitate Abraham, but also somehow to become incorporated into Abraham.[13]

G. Walter Hansen argues that Paul's opponents also "interpreted this promise
of blessing for Gentiles in Abraham (ἐν σοί) to mean that Gentiles will be incorporated among the descendants of Abraham by circumcision and the observance of
the Mosaic law, and so receive the blessing."[14] If they did hold this view, again, we
see that they fit within a larger trend of early Judaism in which gentiles could and
should convert to Judaism, and that, in doing so, they become related to Abraham.
For Paul, as I have argued in Chapters 2 and 3, circumcision and adoption of the
Jewish law failed to accomplish this incorporation because the Jewish law was not
intended for gentiles and because Jewish identity was impermeable to penetration
via law observance. Paul's own thinking also corresponds to a larger trend within
early Judaism that rejected the view that gentiles could convert to Judaism via circumcision and adoption of the law. But, because Jewish scriptures predict it, Paul's
gospel requires that gentiles enter into Abraham in order to access God's blessing.
In light of this verse, Johnson Hodge contends that "Paul envisions the *ethnē* 'in
Christ' as descendants of a common ancestor, Abraham. The scriptural citation of
Galatians 3:8—'All the gentiles will be blessed in you'—serves as the foundation
for this argument: the gentiles are 'in' Abraham the same way that descendants
are 'in' their ancestors. The 'in' language of Genesis 12:3 and 18:18 supports this
patrilineal argument beautifully."[15] If circumcision and observance of the Jewish
law do not incorporate gentiles into Abraham, what does? As the verses surrounding Gal 3:8 suggest, gentiles who are "out of faith" are both Abraham's sons (3:7)
and blessed with Abraham (3:9).[16]

The answer to the question of how faith makes one a son of Abraham lies
in the fact that Paul brackets this discussion of Abraham, faith, and Abraham's
sons with numerous references to the Galatians' reception of the *pneuma*. After
almost two chapters of laying out his own autobiography, Paul turns to the specific situation in Galatia, asking the Galatians how they received the *pneuma*—out
of works of the law or out of the hearing of faith (Gal 3:1–5). The implication
is clear that the Galatians received the *pneuma* upon the hearing of faith, not
through works of the law such as circumcision. Similarly, Paul concludes in Gal
3:14 that Christ came

> so that into gentiles the blessing of Abraham might come in Christ,
> so that we might receive the promise of the *pneuma* through faith.

Francis Watson observes that the "second purpose clause [ἵνα τὴν ἐπαγγελίαν τοῦ
πνεύματος λάβωμεν διὰ τῆς πίστεως] appears to be in apposition to the first [ἵνα εἰς τὰ
ἔθνη ἡ εὐλογία τοῦ Ἀβραὰμ γένηται ἐν Χριστῷ Ἰησοῦ], and the blessing of Abraham
would then be identified with the promise of the Spirit, received by faith." What
this observation suggests, although Watson does not draw this conclusion, is that

Gaston is correct in maintaining that Paul identifies the "we" of the second purpose clause with "the gentiles" of the first clause.[17]

The fact that Paul begins with a discussion of the reception of the *pneuma*
from the hearing of faith (Gal 3:1–5), then turns to Abrahamic sonship (3:6–9), and
then returns to faith and the *pneuma*, demonstrates that Abrahamic sonship and
the reception of the *pneuma* are intertwined in Paul's thought. But how does this
connection between faith and the reception of the *pneuma* relate to the question
of Abrahamic sonship?

## Confidence in God and the Reception
### of the Pneuma (Gal 3:1–6)

In Rom 4:23–24, Paul claims that the words of Gen 15:6 were not written with
regard to Abraham alone but for all who trust in the one who raised Jesus from
the dead. That is to say, Gen 15:6 does not merely describe something that happened long ago; rather, Gen 15:6 textualizes the principle that God followed with
Abraham and continues to follow in Paul's day: God reckons trust in him as righteousness. Paul concludes that Abraham is the father of all who are out of faith
(οἱ ἐκ πίστεως, Rom 4:16). Although in Romans 4 Paul does not elucidate the way
in which this trust enables a gentile to become a son of Abraham, he provides this
explanation in Galatians 3. There, too, he portrays Abraham as the father of "those
who are out of faith" (οἱ ἐκ πίστεως), and begins with a discussion of the same principle and verse he cites in Rom 4:22–23: "Abraham trusted God and it was reckoned to him as righteousness" (Gal 3:6). Paul concludes: "You know, therefore,
that those who are out of faith, these are the sons of Abraham" (οἱ ἐκ πίστεως, οὗτοι
υἱοί εἰσιν Ἀβραάμ, 3:7). Based on this passage, Jan Lambrecht claims, "According to
Paul faith is so important that it constitutes the basis for a connection between
Abraham and the others, a connection so strong that the believing Galatians can
be called children of Abraham."[18] This remark may be true as far as it goes, but it
fails to explain the way in which faith forges this genealogical connection between
gentiles and Abraham. For that matter, as Bradley R. Trick argues,

> The view that Gal 3:6–7 identifies gentiles as Abraham's sons based solely
> on their faith also goes against the Genesis context of Paul's cited text (Gen
> 15:6). In the first place, Abraham's frustration at his lack of a biological
> heir forms the starting point for the whole discussion in Gen 15; it would
> be exceedingly ironic if Paul were to use Abraham's subsequent belief in
> God's promise of incalculable physical descendants (Gen 15:2–3) essen-
> tially to disinherit those very biological descendants in favor of "adopted"
> children.[19]

In light of Abraham's concerns for a son in Genesis 15, were Paul to use Gen 15:6
to argue against the importance of genealogical descent, he would have a difficult
time convincing his readers.

Admittedly, Paul does not explain how the hearing of faith, or faith, brings
about the reception of the *pneuma*. Attempting to elucidate Paul's logic at this
point, Troy W. Martin examines Greco-Roman medical texts relating to *pneuma*,

concluding that it was generally thought that *pneuma* entered the body in one of three ways: through oro-nasal cavities, through the pores of the skin, or through the digestive system. Although Martin acknowledges that what Paul and these medical writers mean by *pneuma* differs, he suggests that when Paul emphasizes receiving the *pneuma* from the hearing of faith (Gal 3:2, 5), this language "may reflect the entrance of the Spirit through the oro-nasal passages." Luke provides a narratival portrayal of the gentiles receiving the *pneuma* in Acts 10:44: "While Peter was still speaking these words, the holy *pneuma* fell upon all who were hearing the word." The *pneuma* accompanies the message of Christ crucified and raised and penetrates those who hear it.[20]

As tantalizing as Martin's suggestion is, it remains conjectural—unfortunately Paul does not provide us with a discussion of the mechanics of *pneuma* reception. Yet Paul was not the only ancient Jew to see a relationship between *pistis* and the *pneuma/ruaḥ*, and so perhaps felt no need to explain this connection. For instance, on the basis of Gen 15:6, Philo claims that Abraham was the first person to trust in God (πιστεῦσαι . . . τῷ θεῷ πρῶτος). Having acquired this confidence in God, the most certain of the virtues, he possessed all other virtues (*On the Virtues* 216). Philo connects this trust to Abraham's reception of the divine *pneuma*, which breathed upon (καταπνευσθέν) him from above and entered into his soul (εἰσῴκίσατο τῇ ψυχῇ, 217). Despite the fact that the Abraham Narrative makes no mention of the divine *pneuma* indwelling Abraham, Philo believes that Abraham's trust in God led directly to his reception of divine *pneuma*.

Although later than Paul, the *Mekhilta de-Rabbi Ishmael* contains similar connections between faith and the reception of the *ruaḥ*. In commenting on Exod 14:31 ("[Israel] trusted [ויאמינו] in YHWH and in his servant Moses"), the *Mekhilta* states, "Great indeed is faith (אמנה) before Him who spoke and the world came into being. For as a wage for the faith with which Israel trusted in God, the holy *ruaḥ* rested upon them and they uttered the Song of the Sea" (*Mekhilta de-Rabbi Ishmael, Beshallaḥ* 7; trans. Lauterbach, slightly modified; cf. *Exod. Rab.* 22.3). Rabbi Nehemiah extrapolates from this verse to conclude that the person who accepts even a single commandment in faith (אמנה) merits the indwelling of the holy *ruaḥ* as a wage (שכר), since it was the case that Israel's fathers merited (זכו) the holy *ruaḥ* resting upon them because of their faith. The verb זכי/זכה, which can also mean "to be acquitted, be right," shares the same root as the noun זכי which the Targumim use to translate the Hebrew word צדקה ("righteousness") in Gen 15:6, so it is unsurprising that the *Mekhilta* ties these remarks about faith in Exod 14:31 to Gen 15:6 and the statement that Abraham trusted God. Thus, *Mekhilta de-Rabbi Ishmael* connects righteousness, faith, Abraham, and the reception of the *pneuma*, just as Paul does in Galatians 3. Further, this passage, with its depiction of God as "the one who spoke and the world came into being" provides yet another parallel to Paul's own portrayal in Romans 4 of Abraham trusting in "the one who calls the things that do not exist as existing (καλοῦντος τὰ μὴ ὄντα ὡς ὄντα, Rom 4:17).[21]

Consequently, Paul argues for a connection between faith and the *pneuma* based not only upon the Galatians' experience (Gal 3:1–5), but also upon a common tradition in Jewish thinking, preserved in both Philo and rabbinic literature, that faith enables or merits the reception of the *pneuma*. Granting the presupposition that Paul's readers would understand this connection between faith and the reception of the *pneuma*, how does the reception of the *pneuma* through faith make gentiles into sons of Abraham?

## *Those Born out of Faith*

To answer this question, we must first reexamine Paul's claim that it is "those out of faith" (οἱ ἐκ πίστεως) who are sons of Abraham. Scholars frequently translate this phrase in a way similar to the NRSV's "those who believe."[22] To be sure, the absence of a verb permits interpreters to render it any number of ways, yet, as Richard B. Hays argues, although it is common to translate it as equivalent to "those who believe," the unusual construction suggests that Paul means something else. Hays concludes that the phrase refers to those who are justified out of Christ's faith and is an allusion to Hab 2:4 ("the righteous one will live out of faith" [ὁ δίκαιος ἐκ πίστεως ζήσεται]), which Paul will subsequently quote in Gal 3:11.[23]

While this interpretation is possible, Johnson Hodge provides a compelling argument that writers often used the preposition ἐκ "in contexts of descent and kinship where it describes the relationship between offspring and parents."[24] The Greek manuscripts of 1 Enoch provide a clear example of this genealogical use of ἐκ, portraying Noah's father Lamech claiming that Noah was not his child, but the offspring of an angel: "He is not out of me, but out of an angel (οὐκ ἔστιν ἐξ ἐμοῦ ἀλλὰ ἐξ ἀγγέλου)" (106.6). Toward the end of the first century CE, Plutarch claims that Pericles instituted a new law that required that Athenian citizens come out of two Athenian parents (εἶναι τοὺς ἐκ δυεῖν Ἀθηναίων, *Pericles* 37.3). Similarly, in the third century CE, Plotinus claims that "all individual things come into being according to their own natures, a horse because it comes from a horse, and a human from a human (κατὰ τὰ αὐτῶν φύσεις, ἵππος μέν, ὅτι ἐξ ἵππου, καὶ ἄνθρωπος, ὅτι ἐξ ἀνθρώπου)" (*Enneads* 3.1.6.1–3; LCL slightly adapted). Paul also uses ἐκ in this genealogical sense in a number of places (e.g., Gal 1:15; 4:4; Rom 1:3; 9:5–6, 10; 11:1; Phil 3:5). In fact, Johnson Hodge observes that the Abraham Narrative contains an important use of this construction, since God promises Abraham, "The one who comes out of you, this one will inherit you" (ὃς ἐξελεύσεται ἐκ σοῦ, οὗτος κληρονομήσει σε, Gen 15:4 LXX; cf. Gen 17:16; 49:10). If Paul has this text in mind, as his discussion of Abraham, Abraham's seed, and inheritance would suggest, then Paul may use the phrase to mean "those who are born out of faith." Paul contrasts those who are born out of faith and are Abraham's sons to those gentiles who wish to be born Abraham's sons through the observance of the Jewish law (ὅσοι ἐξ ἔργων νόμου, Gal 3:10; οἱ ἐκ νόμου, Rom 4:14).

Similar constructions from Paul's reading of the Abraham Narrative confirm that this translation is not only viable, but also preferable. In Gal 4:21–31 Paul discusses two types of Abrahamic sons: the one who is out of the slave woman (ἕνα ἐκ τῆς παιδίσκης) and the one who is out of the free woman (ἕνα ἐκ τῆς ἐλευθέρας) (4:22). Paul claims that the former son has been born according to the flesh (ὁ ἐκ τῆς παιδίσκης κατὰ σάρκα γεγέννηται), while the latter has been born through the promise (ὁ ἐκ τῆς ἐλευθέρας δι' ἐπαγγελίας [γεγέννηται], 4:23). The construction ὁ ἐκ here explicitly refers to the birthing process. Since Paul identifies the slave woman with the law, the ones born of the slave woman must be gentiles who attempt to become sons of Abraham through observance of the Jewish law: they are οἱ ἐκ νόμου. In contrast, the ones born to the free woman are those born through the promise and according to the *pneuma*. Given what Paul has said about the promise and reception of the *pneuma* in Galatians 3, it is likely that he would describe these sons as those who are born out of faith. Galatians 4:21–31, therefore, provides confirmation that Paul intends the phrase οἱ ἐκ πίστεως to mean those "born out of faith." The one born out of faith is the one who is born through the reception of the *pneuma*. But how does the reception of the *pneuma* bear sons for Abraham?

## *Pneumatic Entrance into Christ*

Paul claims in Gal 3:1–5 and 3:14 that gentiles have received the *pneuma*. He explains what this reception entails in Gal 4:6: "God sent the *pneuma* of his son into our hearts" (ἐξαπέστειλεν ὁ θεὸς τὸ πνεῦμα τοῦ υἱοῦ αὐτοῦ εἰς τὰς καρδίας ἡμῶν). Paul's language suggests that the *pneuma* dwells within the very being of believers. The author of Ephesians, an early interpreter of Paul's thought, expands upon this idea, expressing his desire that his gentile readers might be strengthened by God's *pneuma* "into the inner person (εἰς τὸν ἔσω ἄνθρωπον, 3:16) so that Christ would dwell in your hearts through faith" (κατοικῆσαι τὸν Χριστὸν διὰ τῆς πίστεως ἐν ταῖς καρδίαις ὑμων, 3:17). The *pneuma* of Christ resides within those who are born out of faith.

At the same time, Paul also claims that those who "have been baptized into Christ have been clothed in Christ" (ὅσοι γὰρ εἰς Χριστὸν ἐβαπτίσθητε, Χριστὸν ἐνεδύσασθε, Gal 3:27; cf. Rom 13:12–14). This language of being clothed in Christ, within a context stressing the promised *pneuma*, suggests that the Galatians have been pneumatically placed into Christ (3:26). Although Gal 3:26–29 lacks any explicit reference to the *pneuma*, the language of "enclothing" (ἐνδύω) often occurs in pneumatic contexts. For instance, Judg 6:34 states that the *pneuma* of God enclothed Gideon, empowering him to defend the nation of Israel. Likewise, 1 Chron 12:19 LXX states that the *pneuma* enclothed Amasai, leading to his verbal commitment to David, while 2 Chron 24:20 portrays the *pneuma* of God enclothing Zechariah, enabling him to prophesy against the sins of Judah and Jerusalem. Closer to Paul's time, the speaker of the Qumran scroll known as "Bless O My Soul" states, "[God has] clothed me in the *ruaḥ* of salvation" (4Q438 frag. 4 ii.5). Writing after Paul, Luke portrays the risen Jesus saying to his disciples: "And behold, I am sending the promise of my Father upon you; but stay in the city, until you are clothed (ἐνδύσησθε) in power from on high" (Luke 24:49).[25] This latter passage, with its connections between the *pneuma*, the promise, and being enclothed, closely parallels Paul's argument in Gal 3:14–29. David John Lull observes, "When Paul first speaks of the Spirit in 3:1–5, where he refers to the Galatians' receiving of the initial gift of the Spirit, he mentions neither baptism nor 'sonship.' In 3:26–28, where he does mention baptism and 'sonship,' he does not mention the Spirit."[26] This shift from discussing the *pneuma* to baptism and "sonship/adoption" suggests that Paul equates baptism and sonship/adoption with the reception of the *pneuma*.

To receive the *pneuma* is to be enclothed in Christ because the *pneuma* is the *pneuma* of God's son, who is Christ (Gal 2:20; 4:6; cf. Rom 8:9; Phil 1:19). In the words of Johnson Hodge, "Baptism ushers gentiles 'into' Christ; it forges a kinship relationship between them and Christ. In the same way that descendants share the same 'stuff' as ancestors, gentiles are 'of Christ'—they have taken in his pneuma."[27] The Galatians envelop Christ—Christ's *pneuma* is in them (3:13; 4:6), and are simultaneously enveloped by Christ—they put on Christ (3:26–28). This mutual enveloping occurs also in Pseudo-Philo, which asserts that Kenaz was able to defeat Israel's enemies because he "was clothed in" (*indutus est*) a *spiritus* of power, while having this same *spiritus* inhabit (*habitans in*) him (*L.A.B.* 27.10, 28.6; cf. Judg 10:3). Such mutual interpenetration recalls ancient debates about mixtures, a question that ancient philosophers spent considerable time discussing. Richard Sharvy helpfully summarizes the problem as Aristotle lays it out in *On Generation and Corruption* 1.10.327a30–1.10.327b7:

> Aristotle begins his discussion by asking whether mixture (*mixis*) is even possible, for "as some say": (i) if the ingredients continue to exist in the supposed mixture and are not altered, then they are not really mixed; (ii) if one ingredient is destroyed, then the ingredients have not been mixed, but one ingredient has being and the other does not, whereas what has been mixed should still be what it was before; (iii) if both ingredients are destroyed, then they are not mixed since they do not even still exist.[28]

In partial response to this longstanding philosophical puzzle, the early Stoic philosopher Chrysippus, according to Diogenes Laertius (*Lives of the Philosophers* 7.151 [=*SVF* 2.479]; cf. Plutarch, *Moralia* 1078E [=*SVF* 2.480]), discussed mixtures in his *Physics*. He and later Stoics argued that there were three possible types of mixture: juxtaposition (παράθεσις), in which two substances are mixed together but retain their separate identities and adjacent space (much like beans and wheat grains mixed into a bowl), total fusion (σύγχυσις), in which two substances are mixed together to become a new substance (much like the combination of two chemicals which are themselves destroyed in the process of creating a third chemical), and blending (κρᾶσις), in which the "complete interpenetration of all the components takes place, and any volume of the mixture, down to the smallest parts, is jointly occupied by all the components in the same proportion, each component preserving its own properties under any circumstances, irrespective of the ratio of its share in the mixture."[29] The third-century CE philosopher Alexander of Aphrodisias cites the example of the soul and body: for Stoics, *krasis* is demonstrated by "the fact that the soul which has its own substantiality [*hypostasis*], just like the body that receives it, pervades the whole of the body while preserving its own substantiality in the mixture with it (for there is nothing in the body possessing the soul that does not partake of the soul)" (δι' ὅλου τοῦ σώματος διήκειν ἐν τῇ μίξει τῇ πρὸς αὐτὸ σώζουσαν τὴν οἰκείαν οὐσίαν οὐδὲν γὰρ ψυχῆς ἄμοιρον τοῦ τὴν ψυχὴν ἔχοντος σώματος, *Mix.* 217.32; cf. 216.14). This discussion of *krasis*, as Robert B. Todd argues, "is closely related to the Stoic theory of pneuma."[30] Being an extremely fine and rarified material substance in Stoic thinking, *pneuma* can interpenetrate other, coarser substances without either altering them or being altered by them.

It is this peculiar sort of mixture that shapes Paul's thinking about the reception of the *pneuma* into human bodies:[31] God pours the *pneuma* of his son into the hearts of people, thereby effecting a substantive, real change. In fact, Paul's language of being clothed in Christ, particularly within the context of the reception of the *pneuma*, is similar to the language of fully blended bodies, as Gitte Buch-Hansen notes: "Blended bodies may also be said to 'indwell' or 'envelop one another.'"[32] In ridiculing the Stoics, Plutarch says of the theory of *krasis*, "If blending occurs in the way [the Stoics] require, however, it is necessary that the things being mixed get into each other and the same thing be at once encompassed by being in the other and encompass it by being its receptacle [καὶ ταὐτὸν ὁμοῦ τῷ ἐνυπάρχειν περιέχεσθαι καὶ τῷ δέχεσθαι περιέχειν θάτερον]" (*Against the Stoics* 1078B–C). Although Plutarch's terminology differs from Paul's, one can see the similarity between the way in which Paul envisages what happens to gentiles-in-Christ and the way in which Plutarch describes the Stoic theory of *krasis*.

Likewise, in Romans 8 Paul claims that readers are in the *pneuma*, since the *pneuma* of God dwells in them (ὑμεῖς . . . ἐστὲ . . . ἐν πνεύματι, εἴπερ πνεῦμα θεοῦ οἰκεῖ ἐν ὑμῖν, 8:9). As in Galatians 3, but much more succinctly, Paul describes believers as simultaneously existing in the *pneuma* and having the *pneuma* exist within them.[33] He proceeds to identify this *pneuma* with the *pneuma* of Christ, claiming that the one who does not have Christ's *pneuma* is not of Christ (εἰ δέ τις πνεῦμα Χριστοῦ οὐκ ἔχει, οὗτος ἔστιν αὐτου, 8:9; cf. Rom 12:4–5) because he identifies the *pneuma* with Christ. Just as the *pneuma* of God dwells in Paul's readers (8:9, 11), so too does Christ (εἰ δὲ Χριστὸς ἐν ὑμῖν, 8:10) or the *pneuma* of Christ (8:9).[34] The thought is quite similar to Galatians 3, even though Paul does not discuss Abrahamic sonship in Romans 8.[35]

Further, the implication that the person who has the *pneuma* of Christ is "of him" (ἔστιν αὐτου) parallels Paul's statement in Gal 3:29 that the Galatians are "of Christ" (ὑμεῖς Χριστοῦ; cf. 1 Cor 3:23): "Those in Christ are members of him. The relation is like the relation of the arm to the rest of the body. The same stuff makes Christ and believers contiguous."[36] This body imagery arises briefly in Rom 12:4–5, but it is in 1 Corinthians where Paul expands upon his belief that those in Christ form his body. Through the reception of the *pneuma*—in baptism and possibly communion (1 Cor 12:13, 27),[37] Jews and gentiles enter into Christ and become his body parts. In his important study on the body in Paul's letters to the Corinthians, Dale B. Martin concludes, "The pneumatic union between the body of the [Christ follower] and the body of Christ (6:17) is what identifies the [Christ follower]. The man's body and Christ's body share the same pneuma; the man's body is therefore an appendage of Christ's body, totally dependent on the pneumatic life-force of the larger body for its existence."[38] It is this belief to which Paul alludes when he states that gentile believers are "of Christ."

An illuminating parallel to Paul's thinking occurs in Epictetus: "But if our souls are so bound up with God and joined together with Him (ἐνδεδεμέναι καὶ συναφεῖς τῷ θεῷ), as being parts and portions of His being, does not God perceive their every motion as being a motion of that which is His own and of one body (συμφυοῦς) with Himself?" (*Discourses* 1.14.6). Just as for Epictetus a person can share God's substance, so too for Paul do believers partake in Christ: "For if we have been united (σύμφυτοι) in the likeness of [Christ's] death, so too will we be united in his resurrection" (Rom 6:5). Again, in light of such texts, it becomes apparent that Paul holds both to a theory of *krasis* and to a conception of the *pneuma* that are similar to Stoic thinking. To be clear, Paul's understanding of the *pneuma* was also indebted to Jewish scriptures. Nonetheless, Paul and his contemporaries would have read Jewish scriptures and thought about the *pneuma* in light of certain Stoic assumptions which were broadly disseminated in the first century Greco-Roman world. N. T. Wright correctly observes that

> when we ask what Paul might have supposed his hearers would be thinking when he spoke or wrote about a being he referred to as *theos*, about a powerful *pneuma* through which this "god" might perform new deeds in his people, about the creation and recreation of the cosmos, and many other things besides, we must assume, and we must assume that he assumed, that the default mode for their thinking would be somewhere in the region of the Stoic development of Plato's thought.[39]

The very fact that we can assume this, though, suggests that Paul himself had no problem with this understanding of both God and the *pneuma*. If Paul expected that his readers would understand *pneuma* in a broadly Stoic way, and had a problem with this understanding, he presumably would have gone out of his way to correct any such misunderstandings. In contrast, Paul consistently portrays the reception of the *pneuma* in ways that coincide quite closely with Stoic conceptions of both *pneuma* and *krasis*. Speaking of *krasis*, Buch-Hansen observes, "In the case where κρᾶσις concerned solids, the Stoic spoke of 'unified bodies' (τὰ ἡμωμένα σώματα), in the case of living things, they spoke of bodies that had grown together (σύμφυσις)."[40] Paul's ethical vision for Christ followers, which he outlines in Romans 6, is predicated upon his belief that Christ and the believer are two living beings whose bodies grow together (σύμφυτοι, Rom 6:5), enabling the believer to participate organically in Christ's death and resurrection. The presence of the *pneuma* means that believers share the very substance of Christ and therefore share the shape of his life, death, and resurrection. It is for this reason that Paul believes that the joining together of a believer with a prostitute constitutes such a troublesome transgression (1 Cor 6:15–16): by joining one member of Christ's body to a prostitute, one not only joins one's own body, but also Christ's body, to the prostitute.

In claiming that Paul's conception of the entrance of the *pneuma* into the bodies of gentile believers in Christ is similar to Stoic thinking on mixtures, I am indebted to the arguments of Johnson Hodge and Stanley K. Stowers. The theory of *krasis* helps account for the way in which the *pneuma* provides a new genealogy for gentiles-in-Christ. Since *krasis* permits the perfect mixture of two substances, while allowing those two substances to retain their own distinctive aspects, Paul's gentiles-in-Christ both remain gentiles, and yet are distinguished from gentiles who are not in Christ.[41] That is to say, gentile believers are both fully flesh-and-blood gentile bodies, and fully infused with the *pneuma* of Christ. Since Christ is the seed of Abraham (Gal 3:16), the infusion of his *pneuma* into gentiles forges a pneumatic connection between Abraham and gentiles-in-Christ. As Paul concludes in Gal 3:29, "If you are of Christ, then you are Abraham's seed (εἰ δὲ ὑμεῖς Χριστοῦ, ἄρα τοῦ Ἀβραὰμ σπέρμα ἐστε)." Reception of Christ's *pneuma* genealogically relates gentiles to Abraham. Through faith, gentiles have received the *pneuma* of Abraham's seed, making them not only sons of Abraham (3:7), but also the very seed of Abraham. Receiving the *pneuma* of Christ, the son of God and the promised seed of Abraham, solves the gentile problem of being unrelated to Abraham: "As Christ participated in Abraham and shared his stuff, so Gentiles who come to share the pneuma of Christ in baptism share in this contiguity back to Abraham and are thus seed of Abraham and coheirs as they participate in the stuff of Christ."[42] Being in the seed of Abraham trumps being Jewish or gentile, male or female, slave or free, because the promises which God made to Abraham were to Abraham and to his seed, Christ (3:28). Nonetheless, being in Christ does not obviate Jewish or gentile identity (or, for that matter the categories of male/female, slave/free): "Paul and these gentiles share a common component of their identity, in-Christness, even as they remain otherwise."[43] Being in Christ does not undermine the importance of proper genealogy and ethnicity, as so many scholars assume;[44] rather, Paul's argument demonstrates how important genealogical descent remains for him. Gentiles need to become sons of Abraham. They can do so only through a material incorporation into Christ, Abraham's seed.

## *Abrahamic Descent and the Material Pneuma*

In contrast to the majority of scholarship on Paul, I have avoided translating *pneuma* as "spirit" due to the possibility that readers might misunderstand Paul's argument to mean that gentiles are the spiritual sons of Abraham as opposed to the physical sons of Abraham (i.e., the Jews). As Martin notes, modern interpreters frequently "take Paul's term 'pneumatic' to be equivalent to the modern English term 'spiritual,' which usually designates something that is not 'physical' or 'natural.'"[45] Such a traditional understanding of Christian identity (Christians are spiritual Israel or spiritual Jews) fundamentally misunderstands Paul's arguments about Abrahamic sonship. The spiritual/physical or spiritual/material distinction implies an unreal/real distinction—one that wrongly believes that Paul opposes biological descent (flesh and blood) to a fictive descent (a spiritual kinship based on faith). In contrast, the distinction with which Paul works is not physical versus spiritual (in the sense of non-material), but sarkic—fleshly, as opposed to pneumatic—materially conceived:

> In Romans 8:14–17 and Galatians 4:1–7, Paul seems to be playing on characteristics of pneuma assumed by a range of his contemporaries, especially in his representation of pneuma as a binding agent which unites the gentiles to Christ. That is, the gentiles join Christ by taking his pneuma into their hearts, incorporating his substance into theirs. In this way, this procreative pneuma creates a new kinship, and does so materially. This conception of pneuma as a physical, transformative agent challenges the oppositional relationship between "physical" and "spiritual" kinship which Pauline scholars often assume. Adoption through the spirit is one of a variety of ways to conceive of relatedness; the spirit makes that relation both tangible and material. In Paul the spirit serves as a version of "shared blood" in that it provides a tangible, organic connection between Christ and the gentiles. By the incorporation of Christ's spirit in their bodies, the gentiles inherit his ancestry; they "belong to Christ" (or more literally, they are "of Christ," or "a part of Christ") and are thus descendants of Abraham and adopted sons of God (Gal 3:29).[46]

In the Greco-Roman world, as both Martin and Troels Engberg-Pedersen have stressed, *pneuma* took on a variety of meanings, but, in contrast to modern spiritualizations of the *pneuma*, people almost universally considered *pneuma* to be material stuff. In Stoic thinking, which was the most influential stream of physics and philosophy in the first century CE, "πνεῦμα is one of the basic elements of the universe. It may be thought of as a divine substance, extremely fine but still material, that shapes and holds all reality together, contributing toward the interconnectedness (or 'sympathy,' συμπάθεια) of the entire universe." Thus, "when a Stoic says that God's essence is πνεῦμα, he does *not* mean either that God is immaterial or that the πνεῦμα is a sentient being apart from (or secondary to) God; he means that God is made of matter like everything else that is real, and the matter of which God is made is πνεῦμα."[47] While certain streams of the platonic tradition thought that *pneuma* was immaterial, Martin and Engberg-Pedersen argue that Paul must be understood in light of Stoic thinking on the *pneuma*.

Volker Rabens is critical of this material understanding of *pneuma* in Paul and early Judaism, but suggests that one cannot speak about the portrayals of *pneuma* in Judaism and Christianity as 'merely metaphorical' either.[48] But, given the popularity of Stoic physics in this period, it seems more likely that Paul and many other early Jews conceived of the *pneuma* in materialistic terms: "It is well known that the fundamental corporeality of Stoicism was to a large degree an articulation of a more popular ontology in the ancient world."[49] If Paul originally came from Tarsus, as Luke repeatedly claims (Acts 9:11; 21:39; 22:3), then this likelihood is even greater, since Tarsus produced numerous Stoic philosophers (e.g., Strabo, *Geography* 14.5.14; Lucian, *Octogenarians* 21).[50] Consequently, Stowers rightly decries as unhistorical the metaphorical interpretation of Pauline language of participation: "It is a reinterpretation into the modernist framework to treat the language of participation as fundamentally metaphorical without the referent of a substantial ontology." When Paul talks about believers participating in Christ, he envisages them partaking in his stuff: "Those in Christ participate in him because they share with him the most sublime kind of pneuma, divine pneuma that he received in being resurrected from the dead."[51]

In fact, the role that Aristotle attributes to *pneuma* in the formation of the body fits perfectly Paul's portrayal of the role of the *pneuma* in constructing Christ's body in the assembly of Christ believers: "Now the parts of animals are differentiated by means of *pneuma*" (*Generation of Animals* 2.6.741b.38–40). Just as Aristotle portrays *pneuma* giving rise to the numerous body parts of the embryo of an animal, Paul believes that it is the role of Christ's *pneuma* to apportion different gifts to Christ followers, gifts that make them into different body parts (1 Cor 12:4–11).[52] As Paul states in Rom 8:9, "But if anyone does not have the *pneuma* of Christ, he is not of him" (εἰ δέ τις πνεῦμα Χριστοῦ οὐκ ἔχει, οὗτος οὐκ ἔστιν αὐτοῦ). Most interpreters understand the phrase οὗτος οὐκ ἔστιν αὐτοῦ as referring to possession: those without the *pneuma* do not belong to Christ. But, given the fact that the *pneuma* is material and therefore the *pneuma*'s presence a material presence, one should read this statement materially: those without the *pneuma* are not a part or member of Christ. Those who have the *pneuma* belong to Christ in the same way that a person's arm belongs to his or her body. Michelle V. Lee's work on the body in Paul confirms that this corporeal language is no mere metaphor. According to Lee, the Stoics conceived of three different types of bodies:

1. a body consisting of different and separate parts (διεστώτων), such as a flock of sheep or an army.
2. a body formed out of adjacent parts (συναπτομένων), such as a house or a ship.
3. a unified body (ἡμνωμένα), such as a person, whose unifying force "was the presence of a pervasive πνεῦμα (itself a body) which held all of the parts together."[53]

For the Stoics, this third category of body extends beyond the bodies of persons or animals. In writing to Emperor Nero, for example, Seneca argues for clemency on the basis of his belief that what the Emperor does to his subjects, he does to himself: the Roman Empire is the body and the emperor the *spiritus* holding it all together (*On Clemency* 1.3.1–1.5.3). This argument is not merely metaphorical, for Stoic cosmology insisted that the entire kosmos was a real body, a living organism, held together by the all-pervading *pneuma* that is the Stoic God. According to the first century BCE Stoic philosopher Antipater of Tyre, for instance,

> Reason (*nous*) [=God] pervades every part of the world (*kosmos*), just as does the soul (*psyche*) in us. Only there is a difference of degree; in some parts there is more of it, in others less. For through some parts it passes as a "hold" or containing force, as is the case with our bones and sinews; while through others it passes as intelligence, as in the ruling part of the soul. Thus, then, the whole world is a living being, endowed with soul and reason (*logikon*), and having aether for its ruling principle. (Diogenes Laertius, *Lives of the Philosophers* 7.139; cf. Alexander of Aphrodisias, *Mixtures* 223.25; 224.14; Plutarch, *Against the Stoics* 1085C–D)

This same logic underlies Paul's use of body language in 1 Corinthians and Romans. Infused by Christ's *pneuma*, individual Christ followers become parts of Christ's body.

Through the reception of Christ's material *pneuma*, gentiles receive the very substance—to use a modern conception (and admittedly rough analogy), the very DNA—of Abraham's seed. Significantly, Paul portrays Christ's *pneuma* entering into the hearts of Christ followers: God pours out his love into hearts through the *pneuma* (Rom 5:5), sends the *pneuma* of his son into our hearts (Gal 4:5), and gives the *pneuma* into our hearts as a guarantee (2 Cor 1:22). It is this same *pneuma* that enters the hearts of those in Christ, resulting in the cry, "*Abba*, father" (Gal 4:6; cf. Rom 8:15). Such an understanding of the reception of the *pneuma* may reflect the belief that when *pneuma* enters an embryo, it organizes the process of development of the body, beginning with the heart, before giving shape to the rest of the body (Aristotle, *Generation of Animals* 2.6.741b.15).[54] The reception of Christ's *pneuma* brings about a literal, material rebirth, forming anew the heart that was hard and impenitent and filled with desire (Rom 1:24; 2:5), and working transformation outwards in believers. For this reason, Paul can tell the Galatians that he is in labor pains until Christ is formed in them (ὠδίνω μέχρις οὗ μορφωθῇ Χριστὸς ἐν ὑμῖν, Gal 4:19).

In receiving the *pneuma*, then, gentiles undergo a material transformation—again, to use a modern analogy, they undergo gene therapy—which addresses their genealogical deficiencies as gentiles.[55] Through the *pneuma*, gentiles become

Abraham's sons themselves, albeit sons via a lineage that is distinct from, but related to, Abraham's sarkic sons through Isaac and Jacob: gentiles-in-Christ are children of the promise, like Isaac (Gal 4:28).[56] In Romans 4, Romans 8, and Galatians 3, then, Paul "does not sound as if he were 'spiritualizing' religion, but as if he had a genuine investment in Jewish beliefs about kinship and descent that are central to the Hebrew Bible."[57] Aided by the fundamental tenets of Stoic physics, Paul connects gentiles to Abraham through the *pneuma* of Abraham's seed, Christ.

## *Gentiles as Wild Olive Branches (Rom 11:17–24)*

Romans 11 further demonstrates that Paul envisages the *krasis* of Christ's *pneuma* with gentile flesh. Here, Paul addresses the fact that, while numerous gentiles have responded to his gospel, many of his own compatriots according to the flesh have not believed in the Christ (9:3). He uses the image of the olive tree to make sense of this surprising situation:

> But if some of the branches were cut off, and you a wild olive shoot were grafted among them and share with (συγκοινωνός) the rich root of the olive tree, then do not boast over the branches. But if you boast, [remember that] you do not support the root, but the root supports you. Thus you will say, "The branches were broken off in order that I might be grafted in (Ἐξεκλάσθησαν κλάδοι ἵνα ἐγὼ ἐγκεντρισθῶ)." True. By unfaith they were broken off, but you stand by faith. Do not think proudly, but fear. For if God did not spare the natural branches (τῶν κατὰ φύσιν κλάδων), neither will he spare you. Behold, then, the kindness and severity of God: severity upon the fallen, but the kindness of God upon you. Unless you remain in this kindness, then you also will be cut off. But even the others, if they do not remain in unfaith, they will be grafted in. For God is able again to ingraft them. For if you have been cut off from a naturally wild olive tree and grafted, contrary to nature, into a cultivated olive tree, how much more will those natural branches be grafted back into their own olive tree? (Rom 11:17–24)

Paul likely takes this olive tree imagery from Jer 11:16 and applies it to the unexpected situation in which he finds himself: many Jews have not recognized the Messiah's coming, while many gentiles have and have consequently been grafted into this tree.[58] Similarly, in *On Agriculture*, Philo describes the process of grafting shoots into a stem, claiming that a farmer improves his plants "by inserting grafts into the stem near the roots and joining them with it so that they grow together as one (συμφυεστάτη ἑνώσει)," combining it with the same language that Paul employs in Rom 6:5 to speak of the believer's union with Christ. Strikingly, Philo also compares this arboreal procedure to the adoption of sons: "The same thing happens, I may remark, in the case of men, when adopted sons become by reason of their native good qualities congenial to those who by birth are aliens from them, and so become firmly fitted into the family" (*Agr.* 6). Philo compares the process of adoption, a motif that Paul uses (Rom 8:15, 23; Gal 4:5) in relation to the reception of the *pneuma*, to that of grafting a foreign branch into another tree.[59] Likewise, Tacitus

speaks of Britannicus's ascension to the throne as being fitting since he was both
the engrafted and adopted (*insitus et adoptivus*) son, and consequently the heir to
his father's power (*Annals* 13.14.3–6).

How readers ought to interpret Paul's metaphor here is uncertain. If the
branches are individual Jews, are the roots Abraham, the patriarchs, Israel, or
Christ? What does the trunk represent? For that matter, how does Paul's portrayal
relate to ancient horticultural practices?[60] Regardless of the answers to these questions, there remains much fruit to be gleaned from Paul's olive tree imagery as it
pertains to Paul's views of Jews and gentiles. With regard to Jews, Paul acknowledges that some natural branches have been broken off (Rom 11:17), a claim that
suggests that some fleshly descendants of Abraham no longer enjoy participation
in the life of the olive tree. Importantly, this assertion implies that Paul thinks that
Jews were generally (perhaps even universally) enjoying the benefits of the olive
tree *until* the coming of Christ. Only upon Christ's coming did some Jews fall into
*apistia*, unfaith (11:20; cf. 3:3). In other words, contrary to anti-legalist readings of
Paul, Jews were not alienated or cut off from God and his blessings due to a general human inability to keep the Jewish law. As Paul tells his readers, whereas they
as gentiles were formerly disobedient but have now become obedient, many Jews
have only *now* (νῦν) become disobedient (11:31). The Christ event itself provoked
*apistia* among many Jews and thus led to their being cut off from the olive tree.
Such a shocking and widespread Jewish failure to recognize the Messiah's coming, according to Paul, could only be the result of the divine will, which was using
this failure as a pretext to extend God's mercy to the gentile world (11:11–15, 25).
Nonetheless, even after they have been broken off, unbelieving Jews remain natural olive branches whom God can graft back in with ease (11:24), something Paul
remains confident that God will do.

Part of Paul's confidence arises out of the halakhic position that informs his
thinking here. According to Benjamin D. Gordon, Paul intends to portray the con-
secration of the olive tree when he states: "If the offering is sacred, so too is the
mixture; if the root is sacred, so too are the branches (καὶ εἰ ἡ ῥίζα ἁγία, καὶ οἱ κλάδοι)"
(11:16). Gordon demonstrates that this verse encapsulates a halakhic position regarding agricultural dedications to God (e.g., *m. Meilah* 3.6–8). An important implication
of this thinking, though, is that even as many branches have been cut off, they still
retain their holiness. Having been originally consecrated with the olive tree, such
branches are not merely so much detritus meant for the brush pile; instead, such
cut off branches remain sacred and dedicated to God.[61]

In relation to gentiles, this halakhic principle suggests that God's grafting
of gentiles, wild olive shoots (ἀγριέλαιος), into this cultivated tree, means that
they now participate in the same holiness as the root. They, too, become sacred.
The related genealogical significance of such agricultural imagery is indisputable: "This image of a tree as a lineage works so well because kinship, like plant
growth, is considered organic and contiguous. Each descendant (or new plant) is
literally an elaboration of the 'stuff' of its ancestor. Thus horticultural imagery, like
the language of kinship and ethnicity, assumes an organic connection between
forebears and offspring."[62]

This olive tree imagery may be compared to the words of Rabbi Eleazar, who,
according to *b. Yeb.* 63a, likewise uses grafting language to discuss gentile incorporation into Israel. In explaining the promise of Gen 12:3 (cf. Gal 3:8) that all the families

of the earth would be blessed in Abram, he states, "The Holy One, blessed be He, said to Abraham, 'I have two goodly shoots to engraft on you: Ruth the Moabitess and Naamah the Ammonitess.' All the families of the earth, even the other families who live on the earth are blessed only for Israel's sake." In contrast to the words of Rabbi Eleazar, for Paul gentiles remain wild olive shoots, even as God grafts them into the cultivated tree (11:24).[63] To extend Paul's analogy—with regard to their fiber, gentiles remain wild olive shoots, distinguishable from both the natural olive shoots that remain connected to the tree and the natural olive shoots that have been removed from the tree. Yet, having been grafted into the tree, the tree's life force now courses through wild olive (gentile) wood. While the xylem and phloem, the branches' flesh so to speak, remain wild, the domesticated tree's natural sap flows through wild wood.

The metaphor implies that, while they remain sarkically gentile, gentiles-in-Christ have now become pneumatically connected to Abraham. And just as the sap that flows through a tree is no less material than the cellulose giving the tree its shape, so too being pneumatically connected to Abraham is no less material or real than being sarkically connected to Abraham. While Paul does not explain this analogy thoroughly, it would make sense that Paul envisages Christ's *pneuma* playing the role of the tree's sap. All those who are sarkically descended from Abraham are his children with reference to the flesh. Regardless of whether they trust in Christ Jesus or not, such people remain children of Abraham, Israelites, and Jews. But not all of Abraham's sarkic children have the *pneuma* of Christ. Those fleshly children of Abraham who are in Christ remain connected to the cultivated olive tree and therefore have his *pneuma* indwelling them. On the other hand, those fleshly children of Abraham who are not in Christ have been removed from the tree and do not have his *pneuma* indwelling them. In contrast, since Paul portrays gentiles as being wild olive shoots, this implies that no gentiles, whether they are in Christ or not, are fleshly children of Abraham. But those gentiles who are in Christ also have his *pneuma* flowing through them. In the wake of Christ, Paul divides humanity into four categories:

1. sarkic Jews who have Christ's *pneuma*.
2. sarkic Jews who lack Christ's *pneuma*.
3. sarkic gentiles who have Christ's *pneuma*.
4. sarkic gentiles who lack Christ's *pneuma*.

Here is where the two-track scheme of Franz Mussner, Lloyd Gaston, and John G. Gager, which is so often equated with the radical new perspective, fails to do justice to Paul's thought. Romans 9–11, in addition to Paul's claims that Peter was given the gospel to the circumcision (Galatians 2), demonstrates that Paul thinks Jews need this good news about Christ Jesus as much as gentiles do. Having said this, Paul thinks that Jews need it for somewhat different reasons than gentiles do, a fact that requires two very different sorts of missions. Since his mission is to the gentiles, he spends very little time explicating what problem Jews face that requires this gospel of Christ. Romans 9–11 provides only a partial answer to this problem.[64]

This interpretation of Rom 11:17–24 supports Paul's initial statements about Abrahamic descent in Rom 9:6: not all of those who are out of Israel are Israel (οὐ γὰρ πάντες οἱ ἐξ Ἰσραὴλ οὗτοι Ἰσραήλ). Paul unpacks this cryptic remark by distinguishing between the children of Abraham and the seed of Abraham (οὐδ' ὅτι εἰσὶν σπέρμα Ἀβραὰμ πάντες τέκνα). Unfortunately, the RSV fundamentally misunderstands what Paul says here, translating Rom 9:7 as "not all are children of Abraham because they are his descendants."[65] Paul means to say that not all of Abraham's children are his seed. This becomes clear in Rom 9:8 when Paul quotes God's words to Abraham in Gen 21:12: "In Isaac will your seed be called" (ἐν Ἰσαὰκ κληθήσεταί σοι σπέρμα). Paul proceeds to use the Abraham Narrative to make the uncontroversial observation that not all of Abraham's children, for instance Ishmael and then Abraham's grandson Esau, are reckoned to be his seed. The author of *Jubilees* understands Gen 21:12 in a similar way:

> Through Isaac a name and seed would be named for him. And all of the seed of his sons would become nations. And they would be counted with the nations. But from the sons of Isaac one would become a holy seed and he would not be counted among the nations because he would become the portion of the Most High and all his seed would fall (by lot) into that which God will rule so that he might become a people (belonging) to the LORD, a (special) possession from all people, and so that he might become a kingdom of priests and a holy people. (16.17–18; trans. Wintermute, [*OTP*])

Paul argues that Abraham has two sorts of children, those according to the flesh (τὰ τέκνα τῆς σαρκὸς) and those according to the promise (τὰ τέκνα τῆς ἐπαγγελίας), but only the latter does God consider to be Abraham's seed (λογίζεται εἰς σπέρμα, Rom 9:8). But Paul cannot mean to create a strict dichotomy between those who are Abrahamic children according to the flesh and those who are children according to the promise (a reference to the *pneuma*, as Gal 3:14 makes clear).

In Paul's thinking, gentiles-in-Christ remain flesh-and-blood gentiles (cf. Eph 2:11: τὰ ἔθνη ἐν σαρκί). They cannot change this fact and must not try to do so by adopting the Jewish law. Attempting to become Abrahamic seed via the Jewish law would be on par with undergoing cosmetic surgery, creating the appearance of kinship, without effecting any underlying genealogical change.[66] Yet the evidence of Paul's letters suggests that these gentiles-in-Christ are no longer simply gentiles. Paul portrays them being grafted into Abraham or Israel (Rom 11:17), talks about them as though they are no longer quite gentiles (1 Cor 5:1; 12:2; 1 Thess 4:5; cf. Eph 4:17), and refers to the Israelites in the wilderness as "our" fathers (1 Cor 10:1). At the same time, he continues to refer to gentiles-in-Christ as gentiles.

Joshua D. Garroway has made the fascinating claim, based primarily upon the evidence of Paul's letter to the Romans, that Paul envisages his gentile readers as gentile-Jews. Bringing Homi K. Bhabha's work on hybridity to bear upon Paul's thinking, he argues that gentile believers in Christ are neither gentile, nor Jewish, but both—gentile-Jews.[67] According to Garroway, Paul believes that gentiles become gentile-Jews through faith. Again, while this is essentially correct, Galatians 3–4 (and Romans 8) suggests that it is not faith alone that makes gentiles into these new creatures; rather, it is the *pneuma* which gentiles receive through faith that transforms their genealogical status.

Gentiles-in-Christ are hybrids. In one sense this is true, although this description might mislead, since one could understand hybridity to refer to a mixture in which two entities come together and create a third, new entity—that is, what the Stoics classified as total fusion (σύγχυσις).[68] But, stressing the *hyphen* in the term "gentile-Jews" (although I think "gentile-Abrahamic son" is more accurate), Garroway's argument reflects the fact that gentiles-in-Christ remain fully gentile, even as they have now, through the *pneuma*, become fully Abrahamic sons and seed. The term "gentile-Abrahamic son" functions similarly to the hypostatic union of the divine and human natures of Christ in later Christian theology. Paul's gentile believers do not become a new essence; rather, following Stoic thinking on mixtures, gentiles-in-Christ are characterized by *krasis*: their fleshly gentile identity is thoroughly mixed with, but distinct from, their identity as pneumatic sons of Abraham.[69] The gentile-in-Christ now consists of two natures in one person, not one new composite nature in one person.

## *Christ, the Seed of Abraham*

In the preceding discussion, I have focused on the role that Christ's *pneuma* plays in Paul's argument that gentiles can become Abrahamic seed through his gospel. Because gentiles receive the *pneuma* of Christ Jesus, who was a descendant of Abraham, gentiles receive Abraham's substance. But I have left largely unaddressed the central role that Christ himself plays in Paul's thinking on genealogical descent from Abraham. In Gal 4:6 Paul states that God has sent the *pneuma* of his son into the hearts of those who believe. Since Paul identifies God's son with Christ (e.g., Gal 2:20), his argument about the identity of Christ in Gal 3:15–16 is of considerable importance for clarifying his logic. Christ is not merely a descendant or a seed of Abraham, but *the* promised seed of Abraham. Since Christ is the seed of Abraham, gentile reception of Christ's *pneuma* results in them receiving the very stuff of Abraham's seed.[70]

In Gal 3:16, Paul claims that God spoke the promises to Abraham and to his seed. Although Paul emphasizes the phrase "and to your seed" (καὶ τῷ σπέρματί σου), which occurs in the Abraham Narrative only in Gen 13:15 and 17:8, the fact that he mentions promises, and not merely a promise, suggests that he has the entirety of the Abraham Narrative in mind.[71] Based on these texts, Paul argues that since "seed" (*sperma*) is singular, it refers to one person, not to many, which would require the plural form *spermata*. Again we see Paul's deep concern for Jewish scriptures—even scriptural minutiae, since he focuses on the grammatical number of the noun. Nonetheless, numerous scholars have found Paul's interpretation of the word "seed" rather contrived: after all, *sperma* can and does function as a collective singular, much the same way that the English word "seed" does. How, then, can Paul place such emphasis upon the singularity of the noun? And how can Paul identify Abraham's seed with Christ? According to Ernest de Witt Burton, for instance, Paul "arrived at his thought, not by exegesis of scripture, but from an interpretation of history and then availed himself of the singular noun to express his thought briefly." He concludes that Paul provides no evidence from Jewish scriptures that the Abrahamic seed is the Christ.[72]

But if Paul's exegesis is so indefensible, what hope does he have of convincing the Galatians of his reading? As Christopher D. Stanley argues, "it is Paul's persuasive intent that remains primary at every point, and the modern interpreter must read all that he says in the light of this concern or else risk misunderstanding."[73] In a recent effort to understand Paul's argument, Wright notes that *Christos* appears over forty times within the short letter. By way of comparison, Paul refers to *Christos* more frequently than he refers to *theos* ("God") and *pneuma* combined.[74] Consequently, Wright concludes that Jesus's messiahship is central to Paul's argument in Galatians. When it comes to Paul's claim that Abraham's *sperma* is *Christos*, Wright concludes that Paul means "family" when he uses *sperma*:

> Paul is well aware of, and intends, the collective meaning of *sperma* and lines it up precisely with the incorporative meaning of *Christos*. But if that collective meaning is "family," it can also have its own plural, "families." This offers a straightforward reading of 3:16: the promises did not say "to your families," as though referring to two or more families, but to one, "to your family"—*hos estin Christos*, which is *Christos*.[75]

In other words, Wright understands *Christos* in Gal 3:16 not to refer to Jesus Christ alone, but to Israel (now defined as all those who are in Christ)—a singular family consisting of Jews and gentiles. Problematic for Wright's interpretation is the fact that this equation of the Messiah with Israel is unprecedented, something he himself acknowledges.[76] Interpreting *Christos* to refer to a collective family in Gal 3:16 also requires that Paul shift from using *Christos* to refer to Jesus Christ alone in 3:13–14 to using *Christos* to refer to all those who are in Christ in 3:16, and then back to using *Christos* to refer to Jesus Christ in 3:22–23. To my mind, such exegesis seems even more contrived than Paul's.

Hays offers a different attempt to comprehend Paul's argument, suggesting that Paul's understanding of seed in the Abraham Narrative is connected to 2 Sam 7:12–14. In this oracle, God promises David that he would establish the kingdom of David's seed, and that this seed would build a house for God. Within this context, it is clear that "seed" (LXX: σπέρμα) refers to one person, presumably Solomon (cf. Ps 88:4–5 LXX; 1 Chron 17:11–12; Josephus, *Ant.* 7.93), not to all of David's descendants. As Hays notes, this divine promise to David of a singular seed whose throne God would establish forever lent itself to messianic readings in later Jewish interpretation: the passage uses "*seed* not as a collective term, but as a reference to a specific royal successor to David; thus, it bears evident potential for messianic interpretation—as attested by its inclusion in a florilegium of messianic prophecies discovered among the Dead Sea Scrolls."[77]

Hays refers to *4QFlorilegium*, which understands David's seed in 2 Sam 7:12–14 in messianic terms: "[And] Yнwн [de]clares to you that 'he will build you a house. I will raise up your seed after you and establish the throne of his kingdom [for ev] er. I will be a father to him and he will be a son to me.' This (refers to the) 'branch of David,' who will arise with the Interpreter of the law who [will rise up] in Zi[on in] the [l]ast days" (4Q174 1 I.10–12).[78] The author of *4QFlorilegium* links 2 Sam 7:12–14 to "the branch of David," a reference to the messianic prophecies of Jer 23:5 and 33:15 (cf. Zech 3:8; 6:12). Psalm 17:51 LXX (=2 Sam 22:51 LXX) confirms that David's seed is the Messiah, since it equates the two terms:

[God] magnifies the deliverances of his king,

and does mercy to his *christos*,

to David and to his seed forever.

Additionally, both *Psalm of Solomon* 17 and numerous early believers in Christ identified the prophecy of 2 Sam 7:12–14 with the Messiah (e.g., Luke 1:32–33; Acts 13:23; Heb 1:5; Justin, *Dialogue* 68.5; 118.2).

Although Paul does not cite or allude to 2 Sam 7:12–14, he does identify David's seed as the Messiah or the Christ, specifically Christ Jesus, who was of the seed of David according to the flesh (ἐκ σπέρματος Δαυὶδ κατὰ σάρκα, Rom 1:3).[79] Further, as Dennis C. Duling argues, in 2 Sam 7:12 God states, "I will raise up your seed" (ἀναστήσω τὸ σπέρμα σου), a statement which Paul (or the pre-Pauline formula) might have understood to be a reference to Christ's resurrection from the dead (ἐξ ἀναστάσεως νεκρῶν, Rom 1:4).[80] Finally, Paul understands the reference to David's seed in Ps 17:51 LXX/2 Sam 22:51 LXX messianically, since he cites the preceding verse ("For this reason I will praise you among the gentiles, and I will sing your name," Ps 17:50 LXX/2 Sam 22:50 LXX) within the context of his discussion of Christ's coming to fulfill God's promises to the patriarchs (Rom 15:8–9).

But why does Paul connect the Messiah, the seed of David, to the seed of Abraham in Gal 3:16? The answer, according to Hays, is that the word *sperma* functions as a catchword for Paul: since in 2 Sam 7:12–14 *sperma* refers to the Messiah, Paul believes that it must do so elsewhere. Hays connects Paul's discussion in Gal 3:16 to the use of seed in Gen 13:15 (pointing also to Gen 17:8; 22:18; and 24:7). On the basis of Paul's belief that Christ is the seed of David, then, it becomes apparent how Paul could likewise identify Abraham's seed with Christ. As Hays concludes, the argument of Gal 3:16 "is less perverse than it might appear, depending as it surely does on the linkage of the catchword *seed* to God's promises to David in 2 Sam. 7:12–14."[81]

Agreeing with the exegesis of Hays, Matthew V. Novenson points to another parallel between the Davidic seed and the Abrahamic seed. Both 2 Sam 7:12 and Gen 17:7 use a first-person singular form of the verb "to stand" (ἀναστήσω in 2 Sam 7:12, στήσω in Gen 17:7), to refer to seed, and use the phrase μετὰ σέ ("after you").[82] To be sure, it was common to use a cognate of ἵστημι with a direct object of σπέρμα to refer to the raising of offspring, but the only occurrences of this phrase in which God is the subject are Gen 4:25; 2 Sam 7:12; and 1 Chron 17:11. Although Gen 17:7 does use the verb ἵστημι it does not take σπέρμα as its direct object—God establishes his covenant with Abraham and his seed (cf. Gen 26:3). This difference does not preclude the possibility that Paul or other early Jewish interpreters could have made a connection between these two verses; nonetheless, the verbal parallels between Gen 17:7 and 2 Sam 7:12 do not provide the most convincing account for Paul's connection of the Davidic seed to the Abrahamic seed.

While Hays connects the Davidic seed of 2 Sam 7:12 to the Abrahamic seed through Gen 13:15, and Novenson does so through the parallel terminology of Gen 17:7, I think that Paul finds a different, and stronger, connection between the Davidic seed and the Abrahamic seed in Genesis 15. It is in Genesis 15 that Abraham boldly confronts God with the problem of his continuing childlessness. In response to God's promise ("I am your shield, your wage will be very great" [ὁ μισθός σου πολὺς ἔσται σφόδρα; Gen 15:1]), Abraham names the problem of which the narrator has made readers aware: "Oh Lord, what will you give me, for I remain childless (ἄτεκνος) and the possessor of my house is Eliezer of Damascus?" He goes on to make a stark accusation: "Behold, to me you have not given a seed (σπέρμα) and my house-born slave will inherit me" (15:2–3).

Abraham calls into question God's twice-repeated promise to give the land of Canaan to his seed, since God has yet to provide Abraham with seed. It is at this point in the narrative that God, in response to Abraham's statement that he has no seed in Gen 15:2–3, explicitly promises to give Abraham seed, "The one who comes out of your loins (MT: יצא ממעיך/LXX: ὃς ἐξελεύσεται ἐκ σοῦ) will inherit you." Showing Abraham the heavens, God expands upon this promise: "Look at the heavens and number the stars, if you are able to count them. . . . Thus shall your seed be (οὕτως ἔσται τὸ σπέρμα σου)" (vv. 4–5).

Although Hays does not mention Gen 15:1–5, it also contains a reference to Abraham's seed, thus making it possible for Paul (and other readers) to connect it to 2 Sam 7:12. What is more, there is another significant verbal link between the oracle of 2 Samuel 7 and Gen 15:1–5. As noted, in Gen 15:4 God promises Abraham that his slave would not inherit him; rather, "The one who comes out of your loins (יצא ממעיך/ὃς ἐξελεύσεται ἐκ σοῦ) will inherit you." This expression is rare within Jewish scriptures, occurring only two other times. First, it occurs in 2 Sam 7:12, which states, "I will raise up your seed (זרע/σπέρμα) after you, who shall come forth from your loins (צא ממעיך/ἔσται ἐκ τῆς κοιλίας σου), and I will establish his kingdom."[83] Second, it occurs in 2 Sam 16:11, in reference to David's son Absalom, who was seeking David's life. The latter passage lacks any reference to seed, thus making Gen 15:1–5 and 2 Sam 7:12 the only two passages in Jewish scriptures that refer to a seed coming out of someone.

Admittedly, a problem arises for this suggested connection. While the MT of Gen 15:4 and 2 Sam 7:12 share in common the phrase "out of your loins" the LXX translations of these two books do not. Unlike 2 Sam 7:12 LXX which contains the Greek equivalent to the Hebrew phrase found in both Gen 15:4 MT and 2 Sam 7:12 MT, ἐκ τῆς κοιλίας σου, the LXX translation of Gen 15:4 lacks the phrase "out of your loins," reading instead "out of you" (ἐκ σοῦ). One can account for the reading of LXX Genesis in one of three ways. John William Wevers suggests that the LXX translator intentionally modified the verse from "out of your loins" to "out of you," since the latter is "biologically more appropriate for a male."[84] Two more plausible explanations can be given without ascribing intentionality to this reading. First, it is possible that the LXX translator had a Hebrew *Vorlage* that contained the Hebrew reading ממך ("out of you") due to a scribe mistakenly reading ממך instead of ממעיך. Second, it is possible that while the Hebrew *Vorlage* read ממעיך, the LXX translator misread this phrase as ממך.

Regardless of which explanation one gives for this variant, though, it creates a problem for the suggested explanation for Paul's identification of Christ with Abraham's singular *sperma*. Paul's citations of Genesis 15 demonstrate that he uses the LXX translation. Consequently, his version of Gen 15:4 lacks the phrase "out of your loins" which would help him link it to 2 Sam 7:12. A number of explanations might help to overcome this problem. First, it is possible, although I do not think plausible, that Paul knew of a Greek translation of Gen 15:4 LXX that contained this reading, even though we have no evidence of such a Greek witness to this variant. Second, it is possible that this exegetical connection between the *sperma* of Gen 15:1–5 and the *sperma* of 2 Sam 7:12–14 already existed on the basis of the Hebrew text, an exegetical tradition that Paul inherited and deployed in Galatians, even though the LXX translators had obscured it. In other words, the identification of the Messiah with the seed of Abraham predates Paul's writing of Galatians and perhaps even the Jesus movement. Such a possibility is tantalizing, but we again have no literary evidence to support it. Third, it is possible that Paul was familiar with both Greek and Hebrew manuscripts of Genesis (or, for that matter, Aramaic translations of the Hebrew) and accidentally jumbled the two up in his thinking. This would be akin to a modern English reader who grew up with the King James Bible but has moved on to the New Revised Standard Version who, in quoting a particular verse, conflates both translations. Again, whatever account one gives here, I think this connection between Gen 15:4 and 2 Sam 7:12 provides a particularly helpful explanation for what would otherwise appear to be a contrived argument on Paul's part.

In other words, in light of these verbal parallels, Paul identifies Christ, the Davidic Messiah of 2 Sam 7:12 (cf. Rom 1:4) with the singular seed of Abraham in Gen 15:1–5, and likely, by extension, with other references to Abraham's seed in the Abraham Narrative.[85] This extrapolation is not entirely surprising since a similar phrase to that in Gen 15:4 (ὃς ἐξελεύσεται ἐκ σοῦ) occurs in God's promise to Abraham in 17:6: ". . . and kings will come out of you" (καὶ βασιλεῖς ἐκ σοῦ ἐξελεύσονται).[86] Already in the Abraham Narrative, then, God promises that kings would come out of Abraham, leading the attentive reader of 2 Samuel 7 to recognize that David's seed is the fulfillment of this promise of royal offspring which God made to Abraham.

Incidentally, the construction "one who comes out of" occurs also in Isa 11:1, which states that "a shoot will come out of the root of Jesse" (καὶ ἐξελεύσεται ῥάβδος ἐκ τῆς ῥίζης Ιεσσαι).[87] Thus, a prophetic text that uses a construction virtually unique to 2 Sam 7:12 and Gen 15:4 also contains a messianic hope about one who comes out of another person. Although Paul never cites Isa 11:1, he does quote Isa 11:10, which also refers to the root of Jesse, identifying this root with Christ Jesus in Rom 15:12.[88] As noted above, in Rom 15:9 Paul quotes Ps 17:50 LXX/2 Sam 22:50 LXX: "For this reason I will praise you among the gentiles, and I will sing your name." Since Ps 17:51 LXX/2 Sam 22:51 LXX identifies David's seed as the *Christos*, it seems that Paul connects David's seed in 2 Sam 22:51 (and therefore 2 Sam 7:12–14) to the one who comes forth from Jesse's root in Isa 11:1–10. Paul claims that praise among the gentiles is elicited by the fact that, in Christ, God has confirmed his promises to Israel's patriarchs (15:9). While he does not expand upon which promises he refers to here, it is conceivable that he intends to allude to the promises of Genesis 15. If so, Paul brings together these three texts, 2 Sam 7:12–14, Gen 15:1–5, and Isa 11:1–10, perhaps because they all mention one who comes out of another person.[89] As Novenson argues, Paul connects his own mission of bringing about the obedience of the gentiles (ὑπακοή, Rom 1:5; 15:18) to his belief that Christ is the promised seed of David (Rom 1:3; 15:12). He does so on the basis of two passages from Jewish scriptures that mention the obedience of the gentiles (ὑπακούω; Ps 17:44–45 LXX and Isa 11:14) within a messianic context.[90] Paul's gospel message relates to Israel's long-awaited Messiah who would come to bring about the obedience of gentiles.

Since Christ is the Davidic seed, he is also the Abrahamic seed, as Paul argues in Galatians 3. Gentiles who are born out of faith are placed into Christ and receive the *pneuma* of Christ. Being in Christ, Paul concludes that they are truly in Abraham as well, the precise place where they need to be in order to be blessed, just as Jewish scriptures preached to Abraham long ago: "In you will all the gentiles be blessed" (Gal 3:8). It appears that Paul depends upon a stream of biological understanding that believed that a man's descendants preexist inside him. Such a belief can take two forms: preformation, that is, the belief that living beings develop from basically complete versions of themselves which exist within their ancestors, or pangenesis, in which the seed carries within it all the materials necessary to form a new creature.[91] James Wilberding argues that the *Timaeus* can be understood in terms of either preformation or pangenesis, because Plato claims that men "sow into the womb as if into fertile soil animals not fully formed and too small to be seed" (ὡς εἰς ἄρουραν τὴν μήτραν ἀόρατα ὑπὸ σμικρότητος καὶ ἀδιάπλαστα ζῷα κατοπείραντες, 91d2–3).[92] One could interpret Plato to be saying that a miniature version of the person already existed within one of the parents. On the other hand, a number of Paul's near contemporaries seem to hold to pangenesis. For instance, Seneca claims,

> In the semen there is contained the entire record of the man to be, and the not-yet-born infant has the laws governing a beard and grey hair. The features of the entire body and its successive phases are there, in a tiny and hidden form (*Ut in semine omnis futuri hominis ratio comprehensa est et legem barbae canorumque nondum natus infans habet. Totius enim corporis et sequentis actus in parvo occultoque liniamenta sunt*). (*Natural Questions* 3.29.3; cf. *Moral Letters* 90.29)

Seneca's words suggest that all the essential aspects of a person exist within the semen, or seed, while still within one's ancestors. This belief is even clearer in the first-century BCE philosopher Lucretius, who states, "As soon as the seed comes forth, driven from its retreats, it is withdrawn from the whole body through all the limbs and members, gathering in fixed parts in the loins, and arouses at once the body's genital parts themselves" (*On the Nature of Things* 4.1041–1044). The author of the letter to the Hebrews holds a similar view, arguing that Levi, the founder of one priestly line, paid tithes to Melchizedek, the founder of another priestly line, since Levi was in the loins of his grandfather Abraham (ἐν τῇ ὀσφύϊ τοῦ πατρὸς ἦν) when Abraham paid tithes to Melchizedek (Heb 7:9–10; cf. Gen 14:18–20). What is so interesting about this statement is that Levi is not Abraham's immediate descendant, but his grandson. Multiple future generations, then, can be said to exist within their ancestors. That Paul has something akin to this in mind can be seen in his reference to those who are in Adam (ἐν τῷ Ἀδάμ, 1 Cor 15:22; cf. Romans 5). Since all of Adam's offspring, all humans, were in him when he transgressed God's commandment, they together with Adam are subject to the divine decree of death (cf. Gen 2:17). This ancient understanding of descendants existing within their ancestors helps make sense of how Paul could argue that gentiles are locatively placed in Abraham: by being pneumatically placed in Christ, who is Abraham's seed and who at one time existed in Abraham, gentiles become Abrahamic seed and find themselves to be in Abraham. In discussing Gal 3:8, A. J. M. Wedderburn concedes, "It is hard to conceive of Abraham in 'spatial and ontological' categories, as even figuratively a 'house', a container or the like."[93] The argument that Paul intends readers to understand the preposition ἐν biologically and bodily provides an explanation to this question that is historically situated in the first-century CE Greco-Roman world.

# Conclusion

I have argued in this chapter that although Paul rejects the idea that gentiles need to undergo circumcision and adoption of the Jewish law it is not because he thinks that genealogical descent (or ethnicity, as I am using the term in this book) is unimportant. Paul does not condemn the rite of circumcision and the Jewish law because he finds ethnic reasoning or the common Second Temple Jewish belief in the privilege of Jewish identity to be problematically ethnocentric or exclusivistic. Paul's gospel is just as exclusivistic and ethnocentric as that of his opponents. If contemporary thinkers hope to find in Paul an ancient precursor to modern conceptions of universalism, they will be greatly disappointed. As Jon D. Levenson states, "the apostle's appeal to the Abrahamic promise suggests . . . something very different from the modern universalist's dislike of nationalism, ethnicity, and boundaries."[94] Sirach 45:25 nicely captures the genealogical thinking in which Paul participates: Just as "the king's inheritance passes from son to son alone, so also is the inheritance of Aaron for his seed." Paul applies this same ethnic reasoning to Abraham, concluding that, if gentiles want to receive the promises and inheritance of Abraham, then they need to become genealogically related to him. They need to become his sons. He contrasts circumcision and adoption of the Jewish law to his own gospel proclamation: it is faith that brings gentiles the gift of Christ's *pneuma*. Since Christ is the seed of Abraham, gentiles who have received this *pneuma* become both Abraham's sons and his seed. They are truly descended from Abraham himself now—not sarkically, but pneumatically.

If this argument is correct, it raises two distinct problems. First, while modern interpreters take the promise of Gen 15:5 to assure Abraham that his seed would be as numerous as the stars of heaven, God's reference to one who would come out of Abraham's loins in Gen 15:4 suggests that the seed of Gen 15:3 and 15:5 is singular. How can Abraham's singular seed become like the innumerable stars of heaven? Second, why does Paul think it imperative that gentiles become sons or seed of Abraham? Why can't gentiles, that is, gentiles unrelated to Abraham, enjoy the benefits of Christ's saving action? Why must they become Abraham's seed to do so? In Chapter 5, I address these questions, demonstrating yet again how Paul articulates his gospel in ways that are deeply dependent upon his understanding of the Abraham Narrative.

# 5

# *Abraham, the Promised* Pneuma, *and the Gentile Solution*

*And if you [gentiles] are of Christ, then you are Abraham's seed*
*—heirs with regard to the promise.*

PAUL, Galatians 3:29

ACCORDING TO PAUL, gentiles become sons and seed of Abraham in Christ Jesus. This claim is striking for two reasons. First, Paul's belief that uncircumcised gentiles can be Abraham's heirs is without parallel.[1] The burden of the previous chapter was to show both the way in which such a claim made sense to Paul and the way in which he tried to explain it to other followers of Christ. The indwelling *pneuma* of Abraham's seed, Christ, makes gentiles into seed of Abraham. Pneumatic seed, not fleshly seed, but really, materially, seed of Abraham. Second, as I noted at the end of the preceding chapter, such arguments demonstrate the significant role that Abraham and Abrahamic descent continue to play in Paul's gospel.

Paul believes that Jewish scriptures, the Abraham Narrative in particular, "preached the gospel beforehand to Abraham, saying, 'In you will all the gentiles be blessed'" (Gal 3:8). He repeatedly turns to these scriptures to make sense of his calling to preach the gospel to the gentiles.[2] And, in light of them, Paul concludes that gentiles enter into Abraham through Abraham's seed, Christ, and therefore access the blessing that God promised long ago to Abraham. But what precisely was this blessing that God had promised to give to the gentiles in Abraham and his seed? To answer this question, we must return to Galatians 3–4.

## *The Promise of the Pneuma*

Terence L. Donaldson describes Gal 3:1—4:7 as "a maze of laboured exegesis, puzzling illustrations, and cryptic theological shorthand."[3] One particular point where scholars have almost universally concluded that Paul's exegesis is forced is in his reference to the promise of the *pneuma*. In Gal 3:14, Paul claims that Christ died

> in order that into the gentiles the blessing of Abraham might come in Christ Jesus,
> in order that we might receive the promise of the *pneuma* through faith.

ἵνα εἰς τὰ ἔθνη ἡ εὐλογία τοῦ Ἀβραὰμ γένηται ἐν Χριστῷ Ἰησοῦ,
ἵνα τὴν ἐπαγγελίαν τοῦ πνεύματος λάβωμεν διὰ τῆς πίστεως.

This verse contains a number of exegetical difficulties. First, some early witnesses read "blessing" (εὐλογίαν) in the second purpose clause instead of "promise" (ἐπαγγελίαν), a reading that likely arose because of the presence of εὐλογίαν in v. 14a.[4] A scribe, intentionally or otherwise, thus identified the blessing of the first purpose clause with the promise of the second purpose clause. Although "promise" is likely the better text-critical reading, the scribal intuition of identifying "the blessing of Abraham" with "the promise of the *pneuma*" reflects Paul's intended meaning. That is to say, the second purpose clause functions as an explication of the first purpose clause.[5]

Second, this verse highlights a real difficulty in reading Paul, especially here in Galatians 3–4: the sudden shifts between first- and second-person pronouns and verbs. To whom does Paul refer when he uses the first-person plural "we" or "us"? Most scholars take these first-person plurals to refer to all of those who are in Christ. On the other hand, Bradley K. Trick has recently read the entire argument of Galatians 3–4 in light of his assumption that the first-person plurals refer to Jewish believers in Christ alone.[6] Yet another solution is to read the first-person plurals as referring to gentiles-in-Christ. Lloyd Gaston, for instance, claims that "Paul can so identify with his readers that the first person plural can actually mean 'we Gentiles,' as in 3:14, 'that in Christ the blessing of Abraham might come upon the Gentiles, that we might receive the promise of the Spirit through faith.'"[7] In fact, in spite of his general tendency to universalize Paul's writings, even Augustine concludes that Paul's later claim that "we were slaves to the *stoicheia tou kosmou*" (Gal 4:3) is a reference to gentiles, not Jews: "This is not to be taken as a reference to the Jews from whom Paul was descended, but rather to the Gentiles, at least here, since it is fitting for him to identify himself with the people whom he was sent to evangelize" (*Commentary on Galatians* 29.4; trans. Plumer). Although few scholars find such a use of "we" likely, the two purpose clauses of Gal 3:14 confirm that Paul identifies the gentiles in the first purpose clause with the "we" in the second purpose clause. Since the second purpose clause of v. 14 is in apposition to the first, those gentiles who receive the blessing of Abraham in 14a are the "we" who receive the *pneuma* through faith in 14b. Tertullian provides early support for interpreting the "we" of Gal 3:14a as a reference to gentiles, saying of the verse: "we the gentiles, who once were not sons: and he himself will be a light of the gentiles, and in his name shall the gentiles hope" (*Against Marcion* 5.4.3; trans. Evans).

Third, and this is where the focus of the current chapter lies, scholars have puzzled over Paul's reference to "the promise of the *pneuma*" (ἡ ἐπαγγελία τοῦ πνεύματος). Although one can render this genitive construction in numerous ways, context suggests that one should read it as an explicative genitive—the *pneuma* is what is promised. Three times in his direct address to his readers (Gal 3:1–5), Paul mentions the *pneuma*, once specifically asking them, "Out of works of the law did you receive the *pneuma* or out of the hearing of faith?" (ἐξ ἔργων νόμου τὸ πνεῦμα ἐλάβετε ἢ ἐξ ἀκοῆς πίστεως; 3:2),[8] expecting them to concede that it was out of the hearing of faith. His appeal to the Galatians' experience corresponds closely to his claim in Gal 3:14 that "we receive the promise of the *pneuma* through faith" (τὴν ἐπαγγελίαν τοῦ πνεύματος λάβωμεν διὰ τῆς πίστεως). Further, he claims that God sent the *pneuma* of his son into our hearts (4:6). Each of these passages, then, stresses the reception of the *pneuma*. Additionally, in his reading of Genesis in Gal 4:21–31, Paul argues that the son of the free woman was born through the promise (δι' ἐπαγγελίας, 4:23) and according to the *pneuma* (κατὰ πνεῦμα, 4:29), possibly again identifying the *pneuma* with the promise.[9] Given the context in which the phrase ἡ ἐπαγγελία τοῦ πνεύματος is found, Paul intends the genitive to function epexegetically. The reception of the *pneuma* is what God had promised to Abraham.[10]

Paul's wording in Gal 3:14a confirms that the blessing/promise is the reception of the *pneuma*. Although the majority of translations of 3:14a say that the blessing of Abraham might come to the gentiles, the Greek is better translated as claiming that the blessing might come into the gentiles (εἰς τὰ ἔθνη). Thus Gal 3:14a alludes to the fact that "God sent the *pneuma* of his son into our hearts" (ἐξαπέστειλεν ὁ θεὸς τὸ πνεῦμα τοῦ υἱοῦ αὐτοῦ εἰς τὰς καρδίας ἡμῶν, 4:6).[11]

Luke-Acts provides additional evidence that early believers in Christ identified the reception of the *pneuma* with God's promise. At the end of Luke's gospel, the resurrected Jesus says to his disciples, "And behold I send the promise of my Father upon you (ἀποστέλλω τὴν ἐπαγγελίαν τοῦ πατρός μου ἐφ᾽ ὑμᾶς); but stay in the city until you are clothed in power from on high" (ἐνδύσησθε ἐξ ὕψους δύναμις, 24:49). Luke probably uses the word "power" as a synonym for the *pneuma*, as contemporary Stoic writing suggests.[12] Consequently, the post-resurrection Jesus foretells to his disciples the *pneuma*'s descent upon them at Pentecost (cf. Acts 2). Luke again identifies the *pneuma* as the promise of the Father in the introduction to Acts, here connecting this promise to the imminent baptism of the holy *pneuma* (1:4–5). Finally, after Pentecost and the descent of the *pneuma*, Peter proclaims to the crowds that the post-resurrection Jesus received the promise of the holy *pneuma* (ἐπαγγελίαν τοῦ πνεύματος τοῦ ἁγίου λαβὼν) from the Father (2:32–33). That is, the resurrected Jesus receives the *pneuma* in fulfillment of a promise made long ago and now pours out this *pneuma* upon others. Peter then asserts that those who repent can receive the gift of the holy *pneuma*, once again referring to the *pneuma* as the promise (2:38–39). Although writing well after Paul, Luke demonstrates that other early Christ followers thought that God had promised the *pneuma*, a promise finding fulfillment in his own day. In fact, he too connects the *pneuma* to God's promise to the patriarchs. In his portrayal of Paul, he claims that Paul preached about "the promise to the fathers" (τὴν πρὸς τοὺς πατέρας ἐπαγγελίαν) that has been fulfilled in Jesus's resurrection (13:32–33). Further, he portrays Paul standing trial "for the hope in the promise made by God to our fathers" (ἐπ᾽ ἐλπίδι τῆς εἰς τοὺς πατέρας ἡμῶν ἐπαγγελίας γενομένης ὑπὸ τοῦ θεοῦ, 26:6), which, as the context makes apparent, is the promise of the resurrection. Since he closely associates Jesus's resurrection and exaltation with the promise of the *pneuma*, Luke believes that God promised the *pneuma* to the patriarchs.

To be sure, Jewish scriptures contain numerous references to the giving of the *pneuma* (e.g., Isa 44:3; Ezekiel 36–37). But, reading his claim that the "promises were spoken to Abraham and to his seed" (Gal 3:16) together with 3:14, it is evident that Paul believes that God had promised the *pneuma* to Abraham and to his seed. This assertion leads to a problem, as scholars point out, since the Abraham Narrative (Genesis 12–25) lacks any explicit mention of *pneuma* (or *ruaḥ*). On what scriptural basis, then, does Paul argue that God promised the *pneuma* to Abraham? As Richard B. Hays asks,

> Even if we grant Paul his argument that the promise to Abraham is fulfilled in Christ, what authorizes his further inference that the *Spirit* is the fulfillment of this promise? In Gal 3:14 it is clear that "the blessing of Abraham"

is somehow equated with "the promise of the Spirit." But how can Paul pose this equation? Nowhere in the OT does the promise to Abraham have anything to do with the Spirit. The content of the promise is clear: the land, descendants, and an eternal covenant. There is no reference to the *Spirit* at all. Yet Paul speaks of the presence of the Spirit as an obvious evidence that the promise is now fulfilled. Is this a purely arbitrary assertion?[13]

Since in Genesis God never promises the *pneuma* to Abraham, Nils Dahl concludes that "Paul has, by the standards of Jewish expectations, dissipated the promise's objective content."[14] Hays attempts to avoid this conclusion by arguing that Paul alludes here to Isa 44:3 LXX: "I will give water to the thirsty who walk in a dry land, and I will place my *pneuma* upon your seed and my blessing upon your children." To be sure, Isa 44:3 LXX shares with Galatians 3–4 the vocabulary of *pneuma* (Gal 3:2, 3, 5, 14; 4:6, 29), seed (Gal 3:16, 19, 29), blessing (Gal 3:14), and children (Gal 4:19, 25, 27, 28, 31), but in Isaiah God makes this promise not to Abraham, but to Jacob/Israel (Isa 44:1).[15] Further, if Paul has this passage in mind, he does not clearly intimate it to his readers. Galatians 3 repeatedly signals Paul's interest in the Abraham Narrative, not Isaiah.

In contrast, Sze-Kar Wan contends that Paul's reference to the *pneuma* that God promised to Abraham is understandable in light of the connection Philo makes between Abraham and the divine *pneuma*. According to Philo, God breathed the divine *pneuma* into Abraham, effecting a radical transformation in Abraham's person: "For the divine *pneuma* which was breathed upon him from on high made its lodging in his soul, and invested his body with singular beauty, his voice with persuasiveness, and his hearers with understanding" (*On the Virtues* 217; slightly modified from LCL).[16] As I argued in Chapter 4, Paul and Philo are indebted to a tradition that connected faith to the reception of the *pneuma*. Although they share this connection, the Philonic passage lacks the element of promise: while Abraham himself partakes of the *pneuma*, Philo makes no mention of the *pneuma* coming to his seed or to the gentiles.

Sam K. Williams argues that God's promise of offspring to Abraham implicitly contains within it the promise of the *pneuma*, since Paul later says that Abraham's son-heirs are born according to the *pneuma*.[17] Williams's suggestion points interpreters in the correct direction, but comes up short for two reasons. First, not all of Abraham's offspring are the result of the *pneuma*, as Paul's interpretation of Genesis 16–21 in Gal 4:21–31 indicates. God grants to Hagar and Ishmael numerous offspring, but for Paul such offspring are unrelated to the *pneuma* (Gen 16:10; 21:13; Gal 4:23, 29). Further, while Paul does connect son-heirs to the *pneuma* in Gal 4:29, this later connection leaves those reading Galatians 3 without interpretive help until they arrive at Gal 4:21–31. Consequently, I think that Paul refers to something quite specific in the Abraham Narrative that he and his readers would have understood to be related to the *pneuma*, even if modern readers have failed to make this identification.

## Paul and the Promises of Gen 15:5 and 22:16–18

Attempting to locate which divine statements Paul interprets as the promise of the *pneuma* raises yet another issue: although Paul refers to the promise(s) God made to Abraham and his seed ten times within Galatians 3–4 (3:14, 16, 17, 18[x2], 21, 22, 29; 4:23, 28), the LXX translator of Genesis never once uses either ἐπαγγελία or ἐπαγγέλλομαι. This absence is to be expected since these words are uncommon in the LXX, occurring only seventeen times, the majority of which are found in non-translational LXX books.[18] Exacerbating the issue, Genesis 12–25 is replete with divine declarations to Abraham that the reader could justifiably consider promises. In Genesis 12, for instance, God says that he will bless Abraham, make his name great, and extend a blessing to the nations in him (ἐν σοὶ πᾶσαι αἱ φυλαὶ τῆς γῆς, 12:2–3). Further, he states that he will give the land of Canaan to Abraham's seed (v. 7). In Genesis 13, God repeats his plan to give the land of Canaan to Abraham's seed (13:14–15), adding that he will multiply his seed like the dust of the earth (v. 16). In Genesis 15, God reiterates his intention to give Abraham seed that will be like the stars of heaven (15:5). Again, God claims that Abraham's seed will inherit the land of Canaan (vv. 13–16). When God establishes the covenant of circumcision with Abraham, he repeats that he will multiply him (17:2, 6) and give to his seed the land of Canaan (17:8). When Sarah demands that Abraham cast out Hagar and Ishmael, God informs him that he will make a great nation out of Ishmael (21:13). Finally, after Abraham's near sacrifice of Isaac, God swears an oath that he will bless Abraham, multiply his seed, grant that his seed inherits the gates of his enemies, and bless the gentiles in Abraham's seed (22:16–18). In short, the Abraham Narrative contains numerous promise-like declarations to Abraham. When Paul discusses the promise(s) God made to Abraham and to his seed, to which of these declarations does he refer?

Paul begins his discussion of Abraham by quoting from Gen 15:6: "Abraham trusted God and it was credited to him as righteousness" (Ἀβραὰμ ἐπίστευσεν τῷ θεῷ, καὶ ἐλογίσθη αὐτῷ εἰς δικαιοσύνην, Gal 3:6). Consequently, it is a priori likely that Paul has in view God's promise immediately preceding this statement that caused Abraham to exercise trust in God's faithfulness and ability to do as he says. Although Paul does not make this explicit in Galatians 3–4, he does in Romans 4. There, in his discussion of circumcision, faith, and Abrahamic descent, Paul again quotes Gen 15:6 (Rom 4:3), refers to promises (Rom 4:13, 16, 20, 21), and quotes the promise of Gen 15:5: "So shall your seed be" (Rom 4:18). As Douglas A. Campbell points out, "all of Romans 4 presupposes the argumentative implications of Abraham's trusting God's promises—in context, usually the statements of Genesis 15:1–5." Campbell's observation applies equally well to Galatians 3–4.[19]

In Gen 15:1–5 God answers Abraham's concern that he remains without a son. In response to his distress that he is childless and has no seed (15:2–3), God promises him that "one coming out of him will inherit him" (ὃς ἐξελεύσεται ἐκ σοῦ, οὗτος κληρονομήσει σε, 15:4) and that his seed would be like the stars (15:5). This promise underlines God's commitment to provide Abraham with offspring. As I argued in the preceding chapter, Paul understands the references to seed in Gen 15:1–5 and throughout the Abraham Narrative as an allusion to the messianic seed that God promised David in 2 Sam 7:12. The Davidic Messiah is Abraham's singular seed.[20] When Paul reads the promise that God would make Abraham's seed like the stars, then, he thinks first of Christ being made like the stars, and subsequently of those who are in Christ.

In addition to Gen 15:5, though, a number of scholars have suggested that when Paul refers to God's promise of the *pneuma* he has in mind the Akedah and

God's promises, which immediately follow the near sacrifice of Isaac (Genesis 22). Significantly, God's declaration to Abraham contains the explicit language of oaths. After the sacrifice of Isaac, the angel of the Lord appears to Abraham, saying,

> By myself have I sworn, says YHWH, because you have done this thing, and have not withheld your son, your only begotten, surely I will bless you exceedingly and greatly multiply your seed as the stars of heaven and as the sand that is on the seashore. And your seed will inherit the gate of his enemies. And in your seed all the nations of the earth will be blessed because you listened to my voice. (Gen 22:16–18)

The LXX translator of this oath renders the Hebrew phrase בי נשבעתי as κατ' ἐμαυτοῦ ὤμοσα, reflecting his common translational habit of rendering the verb שבע with the Greek verb ὄμνυμι (cf. Gen 21:23–24, 31; 24:7, 9). It is conceivable that Paul could have referred to this oath as a promise, especially since he does not use the language of oaths in his writings.[21]

Further, Paul's description of Abraham as "faithful" (3:9) might indicate that he has in mind not only Gen 15:1–5, but also Gen 22:16–18. This description of Abraham might allude to God's acknowledgement that Abraham listened to and obeyed (שמע/ὑπήκουσας) the voice of God in offering up Isaac (Gen 22:18). Such a portrayal fits well with other early Jewish interpreters of Genesis, who also connect Abraham's faithfulness to the divine promise of Gen 22:16–18. Sirach, for instance, paraphrases God's oath to Abraham in Genesis 22:16–18 and states that through testing (culminating in the near sacrifice of Isaac), Abraham was found faithful (ἐν πειρασμῷ εὑρέθη πιστός, 44:20). Similarly, in the context of a discussion of the promises of Gen 22:16–18, the author of Hebrews calls his readers to imitate Abraham, who through his πίστις and longsuffering inherited the promises (ἐπαγγελίαι, Heb 6:12; cf. James 2:22). Finally, Josephus claims that, in commanding him to kill his son, God only tested Abraham to see whether he would obey (ὑπακούοι, Ant. 1.233). Thus, Sirach, Hebrews, and Josephus connect God's promises in Gen 22:16–18 to Abraham's faithful obedience to God in offering up Isaac as a sacrifice.

On the basis of Genesis 15, as I argued in the preceding chapter, Paul believes that the one who comes out of Abraham and inherits him is Christ Jesus. And, on the basis of Gen 15:1–5 and Gen 22:16–18, he also believes that Christ is the seed of Abraham. Since those who receive the *pneuma* are in Christ, they too become Abraham's seed and thus are heirs of God's promises.

## *Gen 15:5 and 22:16–18 and the Promise of the Pneuma*

If the promise Paul has in mind comes from Gen 15:5 and 22:16–18, what is it in these two passages that suggests a promise of the reception of the *pneuma*? Again, Gen 15:5 LXX states: "And [God] brought [Abraham] outside and said, 'Look at the heavens, and count the stars, if you are able to count them.' Then [God] said to him, 'So shall your seed be.'" And according to Gen 22:16–18 LXX, the angel of the Lord states, "multiplying I will multiply your seed as the stars of heaven and as the sand that is on the shore of the sea." Both passages hold in common one thing: the promise that Abraham's seed would be like the stars. Although it is one promise, it is repeated twice to Abraham, once before Isaac's birth and once after his near sacrifice, where God ratifies his covenant/promise with an oath (cf. the promise to Isaac in Gen 26:4, in which God says that he will multiply Jacob's seed like the stars of heaven). Paul can therefore refer to the same thing as a singular promise (Gal 3:14, 17, 19, 29; 4:23, 28) and as plural promises (3:16).

To answer the question of why Paul reads these references to the stars as in some way related to the reception of the *pneuma* requires three steps. First, I will establish that a number of early readers of these words took the promise to multiply seed like the stars of heaven not only as a statement of numerical comparison, but also as a statement of qualitative comparison. Second, such a qualitative comparison leads naturally into the question of what people in Paul's day believed stars to be. I will demonstrate that modern interpreters should understand the references to the stars in light of ancient conceptions of the stars, which identified them with divine or angelic beings. Finally, I will show that in Paul's day many people would have thought angels/stars to be pneumatic beings, thus justifying his use of this passage to talk about the promise of the *pneuma*. In other words, Paul, in a way that would have made sense to both Jewish and non-Jewish readers, understood God's repeated promise to bless and multiply Abraham's seed as the stars of heaven to be a statement that God would bless and multiply Abraham's seed so that they would become like the stars/angels, which were thought to be pneumatic. When Paul points to the Galatians' experience of the reception of the *pneuma* on the basis of faith, he reminds them that they have already received the blessing of Abraham apart from works of the law. The reception of the *pneuma* provides gentiles with a source of power that enables them to overcome the problem of sin—something that the Jewish law could not provide. Already in the present, then, believers manifest an angelic existence in terms of a newly empowered moral life. Further, the gift of the *pneuma* serves as a down payment for the resurrection of believers (2 Cor 1:22; 5:5; cf. Eph 1:14), or, as Paul says elsewhere, the *pneuma* functions as the first fruits of the redemption of their bodies (Rom 8:23).

## *Seed Qualitatively Like the Stars*

In Genesis 15, God asks Abraham to number the stars if he is able, promising him that his seed would be like them (οὕτως ἔσται τὸ σπέρμα σου, 15:5). This sounds very much like a numerical promise, one that finds fulfillment, according to Deuteronomy (1:10; 10:22), the Chronicler (1 Chron 27:23), Nehemiah (9:23), and Josephus (*Ant.* 4.116), in Israel's history. Likewise, God's promise in Gen 22:17 to multiply Abraham's seed as the stars of heaven, taken in conjunction with the comparison to the sand of the seashore, appears to imply exponential numerical growth.[22] It is not surprising, therefore, that all modern interpreters have understood these promises to denote the fact that Abraham would have innumerable seed. If numberless seed is all that such comparisons imply, though, one is left to wonder how this blessing differs from the blessing God gives to Hagar (Gen 16:10) and Ishmael (17:20). If Hagar would have innumerable seed through Ishmael, then what is unique about the covenant that God has made with Abraham and

Isaac? Is it important that the Abraham Narrative never compares Ishmael's seed to the stars?

Numerous early interpreters took God's oath to make Abraham's seed like the stars of the heaven to be a promise not of mere numerical likeness, but of qualitative likeness. To understand Paul, then, we must read Galatians 3 in relation to this interpretation, not in relation to what modern scholarship says about the original meaning of these promises in Genesis.[23] Our earliest evidence for this qualitative reading comes from two sources dating to the second century BCE. First, the author of *Jubilees* adds a number of blessings to the patriarchal narratives of Genesis. For instance, when Jacob leaves to find a wife, his mother Rebecca blesses him in the following words:

Blessed are you, O LORD of righteousness and God of Ages;
and may he bless you more than all the generations of man.
May he grant to you the way of righteousness, my son;
and to your seed, may he reveal righteousness.
May he multiply your sons in your life(time);
may they rise up according to the number of the months of the year.
And may their sons be more numerous and greater than the stars of heaven;
and more than the sand of the sea, may their number increase. (25.15–16; trans.
    Wintermute [*OTP*])

The author alludes to the blessing of Gen 22:16–18, with its reference to both stars and sand, taking God's blessing of Abraham and applying it to Jacob and to his seed—Israel. Rebecca's prayer is that God would multiply Jacob's seed in his lifetime to the number of the months of the year, that is, twelve. And she prays that their children would be both more numerous and greater than the stars of the sky. Where the Hebrew of Gen 22:17 uses an imperfect verb with an infinitive absolute (הרבה ארבה) to signify certainty ("I will surely multiply"), the *Ge'ez* of *Jubilees* contains two different verbs—one (*b-z-ḥ*) to signify numerical greatness, and the other (*'-b-y*) to signify the exaltation of Jacob's seed.[24] Consequently, Rebecca's blessing contains the expectation that Jacob's seed would be both quantitatively like the stars of the sky and elevated like them.

Similarly, the Greek translation of Ben Sira, which also dates to the second century BCE, paraphrases God's oath to Abraham in Gen 22:16–18, saying that God assured him that he would

bless the gentiles in his seed (ἐνευλογηθῆναι ἔθνη ἐν σπέρματι αὐτοῦ),
and that he would multiply him as the dust of the earth,
and exalt his seed as the stars (ὡς ἄστρα ἀνυψῶσαι τὸ σπέρμα αὐτοῦ),
and cause them to inherit from sea to sea,
and from the river unto the utmost part of the land. (Sir 44:21)[25]

Instead of preserving the emphatic phrase (πληθύνων πληθυνῶ) of LXX Genesis, which replicates the infinitive absolute in the Hebrew *Vorlage* of Genesis (הרבה ארבה), Sirach's paraphrase modifies Gen 22:17 by linking God's multiplication (πληθῦναι) of Abraham's seed to the sand of the seashore (Sir 44:21), and making no mention of multiplying the seed like the stars.[26] Instead, Sirach claims that

God would exalt (ἀνυψῶσαι) his seed as the stars. Thus, Sirach relates the innumer-ability of Abraham's seed to the sand of the seashore, while relating their exalta-tion to the stars. What this exaltation entails the Greek translator of Sirach does not make clear, although the verb ἀνυψόω suggests elevation from a lowly place to a position of power (e.g., Sir 1:19; 4:11; 11:1; 24:13–14; 47:11). Perhaps, as Bradley C. Gregory argues, this exaltation has to do with an eschatologizing interpretation of Gen 22:16–18, but he fails to note the way in which this interpretation fits into a broader pattern of how other early Jews also understood the verse.[27]

In the first century CE, Philo is expansive in his discussion of Gen 15:5. Quoting God's words to Abraham, he claims that God's promise that Abraham's seed would be like the stars is more than merely numerical:

> When the Lord led [Abraham] outside he said, "Look up into heaven and count the stars, if you can count their sum. So shall your seed be" (οὕτως ἔσται τὸ σπέρμα σου). Well does the text say "so" (οὕτως) not "so many" (τοσοῦτον), that is, "of equal number to the stars" (τοῖς ἄστροις ἰσάριθμον). For He wishes to suggest not number merely, but a multitude of other things, such as tend to happiness perfect and complete. The seed shall be, he says, as the ethereal sight (τὸ ὁρώμενον αἰθέριον) spread out before him, celestial (οὐράνιον) as that is, full of light unshadowed and pure as that is, for night is banished from heaven and darkness from ether. It shall be the very likeness of the stars (ἀστεροειδέστατον). (*Heir* 86–87, slightly modified from LCL)

In his argument that Abraham's seed would be star-like, Philo points to the LXX translator's use of οὕτως, arguing that this adverb conveys something more than mere numerical comparison. Abraham's seed would become ἀστεροειδέστατον, which Philo interprets in this context to mean that he would have virtues of a star-like quality (*Heir* 88).

Similarly, in *Questions and Answers on Genesis*, Philo treats God's promise made to Isaac at Gerar: "I will multiply your seed as the stars of heaven" (καὶ πληθυνῶ τὸ σπέρμα σου ὡς τοὺς ἀστέρας τοῦ οὐρανοῦ, Gen 26:4). He asks:

> What is the meaning of the words, "I will multiply your seed as the stars of the heaven"? Two things are indicated, in which the nature of all things in general consists, (namely) quantity and quality—quantity in "I will multiply," and quality in "as the stars." So may (your seed) be pure and far-shining and always be ranged in order and obey their leader, and may they behave like the luciform (stars) which everywhere with the splendor of ethereal brightness also illumine all other things. (*QG* 4.181, slightly modi-fied from LCL)

As in *Heir* 86–87, Philo interprets the promise to multiply the patriarchs' seed like the stars to be more than a simple numerical claim—to be star-like means to enjoy a certain quality of life. Unlike in his interpretation of Gen 15:5, though, it is not the adverb οὕτως that leads Philo to construe the promise qualitatively, but the reference to the stars themselves: the phrase "as the stars" (ὡς τοὺς ἀστέρας) sug-gests a life of ethereal brightness. In light of this reading of Gen 26:4, it becomes apparent that Philo would have read Gen 22:17, which also contains the phrase "as the stars" (ὡς τοὺς ἀστέρας), in the same way. Confirming the star-like nature of the patriarchs, Philo understands the twelve stones on the priests' garments (Exod 28:21) as representing the patriarchs and the twelve signs of the zodiac, claiming that the stones signify that they do not "go about on the earth like mortals but become heavenly plants and move about in the ether, being established there" (*QE* 2.114). As we shall see below, Philo identifies such star-like existence as an angelic life free from the moral and mortal corruption of earthly elements.

In his rereading of Genesis 15, the author of the first- or second-century CE work entitled the *Apocalypse of Abraham* portrays the angel Iaoel guiding Abraham up to heaven in order to see the angels and stars of the firmament (*Apoc. Abr.* 19). Once there, God commands Abraham, "Look from on high at the stars which are beneath you and count them for me and tell me their number!" Abraham responds, asking "When can I? For I am a man." In the author's interpretive expansion on Gen 15:5, God answers, "As the number of the stars and their power so shall I place for your seed the nations and men, set apart for me in my lot with Azazel" (20.3–5; trans. Rubinkiewicz [*OTP*]). This divine promise that Abraham's seed would be like the stars is both numerical and qualitative: "as the number of the stars and their power."[28] By placing Abraham in the celestial realm, the author depends upon exegetical traditions that interpreted the Hebrew word נבט to signify "looking down." Consequently, when Genesis says that God took Abraham outside and told him to "look down" at the heaven, some interpreters understood this statement to mean that God took Abraham outside the kosmos where he could gaze down upon the stars. We see this tradition preserved much later in the rabbinic compilation of *Numbers Rabbah*: "The expression *habet* (look), said R. Samuel son of R. Isaac, is addressed only to one who is placed above an object" (2.12; cf. *L.A.B.* 18.5). What is more, by raising Abraham above the stars, the author narrates the fulfillment of this promise already in the person of Abraham. In light of this elevation, Abraham's seed would rule over the nations, just as the angel Azazel had before his own rebellion and subsequent fall to earth (14.5). Although the author of the *Apocalypse of Abraham* narrates the events of Genesis 15, he connects the star-like seed of Gen 15:5 to the star-like seed of Gen 22:16–18, since his reference to Abraham's seed taking Azazel's power over the nations narrates his interpretation of Gen 22:17c: "and your seed shall possess the gate of his enemies."[29] The work thus shows that at least one reader close to Paul's time understood both Gen 15:5 and 22:16–18 to refer to the same promise: seed qualitatively like the stars.

Further, a number of early Christian sources interpret the comparison to the stars in this way. For instance, in the late first century, the author of *1 Clement* refers to God's promise to Abraham in Gen 22:17. Like *Jubilees* and Sirach, the author understands the phrase πληθύνων πληθυνῶ to mean both qualitative and quantitative greatness: Abraham's seed would be "glorious and made great" (ἐδοξάσθησαν καὶ ἐμεγαλύνθησαν, 32.3). In the second century CE, Irenaeus states of Gen 15:5, "And, that along with [its] multiplicity, Abraham might also know the glory of his seed, God led him outside at night and said to him, 'look toward heaven and see if you can count the stars of heaven; so shall be your seed'" (*Demonstration of the Apostolic Preaching* 24; trans. Behr). Again, Irenaeus interprets the promise to include both a numerical and a qualitative greatness. A few decades later, in explaining why Jews do not worship the sun, moon, and stars, Origen points to Gen 15:5: "Concerning them the prediction was given to Abraham by the voice of the Lord to him: 'Look up to the heaven and number the stars, if you can count them. And he said to him, So shall your seed be.' A nation which had the hope to become as the stars in heaven would not have worshiped them; for they were to become like them as a result of understanding and keeping the law of God" (*Against Celsus* 5.10; trans. Chadwick). Significantly, Origen proceeds to connect Gen 15:5 to Dan 12:3, showing the way in which one could read the resurrection in Dan 12:3, which depicts resurrection in astral terms, as the fulfillment of Gen 15:5 and 22:17. Likewise, in his *Commentary on Romans*, Origen refers again to Gen 15:5 and claims of Abraham and Sarah, "When they hear of such a hope of posterity and that the glory of their own offspring would be equal to heaven and its stars, when they hear these things, they do not think about their own goods" (4.6.7; trans. Scheck). Here Origen claims that the promise of seed like the stars signifies that Abraham's seed would have a glory equal to the heaven and the stars.[30]

Although rabbinic literature contains no evidence that later rabbis read Gen 15:5 or 22:16–18 to imply a qualitative comparison, it nonetheless demonstrates that some rabbis, like Philo, understood biblical comparisons to the stars in qualitative terms. For instance, according to *Genesis Rabbah*, in response to his brothers' fear that he would take vengeance upon them for their earlier wrongdoing (cf. Gen 50.15), Joseph says, "Ye have been likened to the stars, and who can exterminate the stars?" (*Gen. Rab.* 100.9).[31] Joseph alludes here to his earlier dream about his brothers, portrayed as stars, bowing down before him (Gen 37:9), but a secondary allusion to the divine promise that Abraham's seed would be like the stars remains possible. Regardless, Joseph's claim that his brothers—being like the stars—cannot be exterminated reflects the belief that Genesis alludes to a qualitative likeness, not numerical likeness. This interpretation is likely due to the influence of Dan 12:3, which portrays the resurrected righteous enjoying the indestructible and glorious life of stars. Similarly, *Pesikta Rabbati* reads Dan 12:3,[32] again suggesting that the comparison between Israel and the stars is more than numerical: "Finally, in the time-to-come, Israel will be like the stars. Even as the stars shine in the firmament, so will they shine in the time-to-come. And they that are wise shall shine as the brightness of the firmament . . . as the stars for ever and ever" (11.5; trans. Braude). Extrapolating from such a passage, *Numbers Rabbah* asserts, "When referring to the hereafter, however, [God] compares [Israel] to stars. As the stars sparkle throughout the firmament so will they sparkle in the hereafter; as it is said: And they that are wise shall shine as the brightness of the firmament; and they that turn the many to righteousness as the stars for ever and ever" (2.13). This last statement is of considerable consequence: if such an understanding was both early and widespread, as the above interpretations of Gen 15:5 and 22:17 suggest, then readers of Jewish scriptures would inevitably see references to the world-to-come in every passage that compared Israel to the stars. That is to say, it was some such understanding that led a number of early Jewish and Christian interpreters to read God's promises to Abraham in Gen 15:5 and 22:17 and his promise to Isaac in Gen 26:4 as statements about the quality of life which God had promised Abraham and his seed. In light of this understanding of these promises, Abraham's trust in God was not merely related to having numerous descendants, but also to having descendants who would partake in a beatific life similar to the stars.

The author of *Jubilees*, the Greek translator of Sirach, Philo, the author of the *Apocalypse of Abraham*, and a number of early Christian and rabbinic statements construe the promise that God would make Abraham's seed like the stars in Gen 15:5 and 22:17 to be more than a mere statement of promised fecundity. Such readings occur in works arising out of diverse social contexts, demonstrating that this interpretation was not limited to one or two streams of Jewish thought. To be like the stars is to be exalted like the stars, to have their power, to participate in their ethereal life. It is this interpretation of Gen 15:5 and 22:17 that undergirds Paul's reference to the promised *pneuma* in Galatians 3. God's promise to Abraham and to his seed is that they would be qualitatively like the stars. But what does it mean to be like the stars?

## *The Stars as Angelic Beings in Early Jewish Thinking*

In contrast to modern conceptions, early Jewish writers associated stars with divine beings, sometimes benevolent (or angelic) and sometimes malevolent (or demonic).[33] Numerous passages in Jewish scriptures link or even identify angels and stars. One of the clearest texts identifying stars with divine beings is the Song of Deborah: "From heaven the stars battled, from their courses they battled with Sisera" (Judg 5:20). The author of the Song considers these stars to be powerful heavenly beings fighting on behalf of Israel.[34] Similarly, Ps 148:1–3 connects heavenly bodies and angelic beings:

> Praise YAH!
> Praise YHWH from the heavens,
> praise him in the heights!
> Praise him, all his angels,
> praise him, all his host!
> Praise him, sun and moon, praise him,
> all you shining stars!

While the psalmist may distinguish between angels and heavenly bodies, it is more likely that one should understand these statements to parallel one another. In other words, the psalmist identifies angels, the heavenly host, with the sun, moon, and stars. Likewise, when God appears to Job, he asks him,

> Where were you when I laid the foundation of the earth?
> Tell me, if you have understanding.
> Who determined its measurements—surely you know!
> Or who stretched the line upon it?
> On what were its bases sunk,
> or who laid its cornerstone,
> when the morning stars sang together,
> and all the sons of God (בני אלהים; LXX: ἄγγελοί μου—"my angels")
>   shouted for joy? (38:4–7)

As Othmar Keel and Christoph Uehlinger observe, God "asks Job if he was present when [YHWH] set the cornerstone of the world's foundations, an ancient event celebrated by the divine beings, here specified as stars."[35] The clearest parallels to this verse appear in two Ugaritic texts, one which refers to "the sons of El" as "the assembly of the stars" (*KTU* 1.10.1.3–4 ), and another which refers to a category of gods known as "star-gods" (*KTU* 1.43.2–3). Psalm 89 may also allude to this connection between angels and stars (vv. 5–7):

> Let the heavens praise your wonders, O YHWH,
> your faithfulness in the assembly of the holy ones.
> For who in the skies can be compared to YHWH,
> who among the sons of God (MT: בני אלים; LXX [Ps 88:7]: υἱοὶ θεοῦ)?
> A God feared in the council of the holy ones,
> great and feared above all those who surround him.

The psalmist mentions the sons of God and the holy ones, appellations used of angelic beings, whom he portrays as dwelling, like astral bodies, in the skies.[36] Psalm 103:4 LXX connects God's angels to both *pneuma* and to burning fire. God "makes his angels *pneumata*, and his ministers burning fire (ὁ ποιῶν τοὺς ἀγγέλους αὐτοῦ πνεύματα καὶ τοὺς λειτουργοὺς αὐτοῦ πῦρ φλέγον)." By referring to angels as burning fire, the psalmist portrays angels as fiery bodies, that is, stars. Likewise, Psalm 8 appears to connect the heavenly bodies to angelic beings:

> When I look at your heavens, the work of your fingers,
> the moon and the stars which you have established;
> what is man that you are mindful of him,
> and the son of man that you care for him?
> Yet you have made him a little less than the gods/angels (MT: אלהים;
>     LXX: ἄγγελοι),
> and have crowned him with glory and honor.
> You have given him dominion over the works of your hands;
> you have put all things under his feet. (8:3–7)[37]

Since the psalmist considers the heavenly bodies and then wonders why God takes such account of humanity in comparison to gods, it appears that he has been spurred on to this thought because he has identified the moon and stars with gods, or angelic beings as the LXX translator renders it.

That these various psalms and poetic works closely connect gods/angels and stars should not surprise given the evidence that many, if not all, ancient Israelites thought stars were divine beings. Frequent condemnations of the practice of worshipping the celestial beings demonstrate that the preceding descriptions of the stars, while occurring in poetic literature, are not merely metaphorical. The evidence of these texts confirms that both non-Israelites and some Israelites worshipped the stars of heaven, even if these particular prophets did not. For instance, in Deut 4:19, God commands Israel not to worship the sun, stars, and moon, but says that he has given them for the nations to worship. Likewise, Jeremiah condemns the worship of the sun, moon, and host of heaven (8:20), but, in doing so, acknowledges that they are gods: many in Judah and Israel have offered incense on their roofs "to all the host of heaven" and drink offerings "to other gods."[38] In conjunction with Deut 4:19, it appears that, while he acknowledges the divine nature of the stars, Jeremiah believes it is wrong for Israel to worship them (cf. Deut 17:3–5; 2 Kgs 21:3, 5; 23:4–5; Jer 7:18; 44:17–19, 25; Amos 4:20; and Zeph 1:5).

Numerous passages in Jewish scriptures, then, identify stars with or closely link them to angelic beings. Yet these writers were not alone in identifying stars with angels or divine beings, for one can see this connection in the ancient Near East as well as in Greek thinking.[39] Most important for our discussion of Paul is the fact that Second Temple Jews also frequently identified the stars as angels. For instance, in his rewriting of Gen 6:1–4, the author of the *Animal Apocalypse* portrays the "sons of God" (that is, angelic beings) as heavenly stars that have fallen from heaven (*1 Enoch* 86.1–6; cf. *1 Enoch* 43.1–2). Similarly, the Thanksgiving Scroll states,

> You have stretched out the heavens for your glory.
> You [established] all [their hosts] according to your will,
> and the mighty *ruḥot* according to their statutes,
> before they became [your holy] angels (מלאכי) [. . . ,]
> as eternal *ruḥot* in their dominions,
> luminaries (מאורות) for their mysteries,
> stars (כוכבים) according to [their] paths. (1QHᵃ 9.11b–14a)[40]

Here again we see a close connection between the angels and stars. The author of *Joseph and Aseneth* likewise portrays an angelic visitor to Aseneth as a star:

> When Aseneth finished confessing to the Lord, behold, the morning star arose out of the eastern sky. And Aseneth saw it, and rejoiced and said: "Then the Lord God has indeed heard me—for this star is an angel and herald of the light of the great day." And behold, the heaven was torn open near the morning star and an unspeakable light appeared. And Aseneth fell upon her face in the ashes. And a man from heaven came to her. (14.1–4)

Although it is possible to translate ἄγγελος as "messenger," not "angel," the fact that the star takes on the appearance of a man from heaven suggests that this star is an angelic figure who changes forms in order to address the human Aseneth. Confirming this reading, Ross Shepard Kraemer notes a parallel in a Greek magical papyrus: "[A blazing star] will descend and come to a stop in the middle/of the housetop, and when the star [has dissolved] before your eyes, you will behold the angel whom you have summoned and who has been sent [to you], and you will quickly learn the decisions of the gods" (*PGM* I.74–77; trans. Betz).[41] Similarly, the author of *Ezekiel the Tragedian* portrays Moses's ascension to and enthronement in heaven, where the stars fall to their knees (ἀστέρων πρὸς γούνατα) before him and pass by him "like armed ranks of mortals" (ὡς παρεμβολὴ βροτῶν, 77–81).

Philo—who, as we saw previously, interprets the promises of Gen 15:5 and 26:4 to mean that Abraham's seed would be qualitatively like the stars—also understands stars to be divine or angelic beings. For instance, in commenting on Gen 24:3, he says of the heavenly realms and the stars: "Heaven is the best of the parts of the world, wherefore it has been allotted the highest place, being of the purest substance, and full of stars, each of which is a godlike image" (*QG*

4.87). The stars are godlike images of the purest substance—mind, as Philo says repeatedly elsewhere (e.g., *Special Laws* 1.66; *Giants* 7–8; *Planter* 12), which consists of *aether* (e.g., *Planter* 18) or *pneuma* (e.g., *Dreams* 1.30–33; *Flight and Finding* 133). Significantly, he claims that, upon their deaths, Abraham and his sons "became equal to the angels (ἴσος ἀγγέλοις), for angels—those unbodied and blessed souls—are the host and people of God" (*Sacrifices* 5; cf. *Sacrifices* 6–10). Consequently, Philo portrays Abraham and his sons experiencing the fulfillment of God's promises in Gen 15:5, 22:17, and 26:4.

This connection between stars and angelic beings is found in Jewish expectations of a beatific afterlife. For instance, Dan 12:3 states that in the resurrection the wise shall shine "like the stars" (ככוכבים/ὡσεὶ τὰ ἄστρα τοῦ οὐρανοῦ), signifying that the righteous will go through the process of astralization. If scholars are right in arguing that Daniel 12 depends upon Daniel 8, which portrays angelic beings as stars, then the astral imagery of Daniel 12 conveys the angelification of the righteous at the resurrection.[42] In dependence upon Daniel 12, 2 *Baruch* portrays God's vindicated people in angelic/star-like glory: "They will live in the heights of that world and they will be like the angels and be equal to the stars" (51.10). This expectation of the glorification of the righteous at the eschaton suggests that the righteous become star-like, that is, they become like angels.

This brief survey demonstrates that numerous early readers of Jewish scriptures understood the stars to be angelic or divine beings. With this understanding of the nature of stars in mind, a reader—Jewish or gentile—encountering God's promises to Abraham to make his seed star-like would naturally understand these passages to be claiming that God has promised to make Abraham's seed like the angels, without in any way thinking that he or she has transformed the meaning of God's original promises to the patriarchs. Paul, like many of his contemporaries, read God's promises of star-like seed to signify that Abraham's seed would become like the stars or angels. In light of this evidence, one then needs to ask what Paul and other early Jews would have thought angels to be like, other than astral beings. The answer, at least in part, is that the angels were pneumatic beings.

## *Pneumatic Stars/Angels*

Psalm 104 (Psalm 103 LXX) is one of the earliest writings to depict angelic beings as pneumatic. The psalmist portrays God making his angels/messengers *ruḥot* (מלאכיו רוחות, v. 4). The LXX translator renders this phrase as the one who makes "his angels/messengers *pneumata*" (ὁ ποιῶν τοὺς ἀγγέλους αὐτοῦ πνεύματα). Although one could read this verse impersonally—God makes the winds his messengers— at least one first-century reader of Psalm 103 LXX, the author of Hebrews, took this verse to refer to the pneumatic nature of semi-divine persons: "Of the angels he says, 'Who makes his angels *pneumata*'" (1:7). As David M. Moffitt contends, the author works in Hebrews 1–2 to distinguish between the son and the angels, in part, based on the fact that the son took up human flesh and blood, whereas the angels have only ever been pneumatic beings: "The contrast between the Son and the angels in Heb 1–2 consists in the contrast between blood-and-flesh humanity as the image/glory of God, and the ministering spirits of fire who for a little while hold a place of authority above humanity, but who will be placed under human subjection, along with the rest of the οἰκουμένη, when humanity is fully restored to all the glory and dominion that Adam lost."[43] Thus, the author's argument for the superiority of the son depends here upon his assumption that his readers would agree that angels are pneumatic, demonstrating that both he and they understood Psalm 103 LXX to be claiming that angels were pneumatic beings (cf. *4 Ezra* 8.21–22).

Other early Jews also defined angelic beings as *pneumata*. The author of the book of *Jubilees* apparently saw a close connection between *ruḥot* and angels, at times equating the two. In the prologue, God tells Moses that Israel will be called children of the living God and that "every angel and spirit will know them" (1.25). In his rewriting of Deut 32:8, the author claims that God did not set over Israel any angel or spirit, because he alone was their ruler (*Jub.* 15.31). Both of these passages seem to distinguish between angels and spirits, while nonetheless linking them. Yet in the author's rewriting of the creation narrative of Genesis 1, he states that on the first day God created

> all the spirits who serve before him, namely: the angels of presence; the angels of holiness; the angels of the spirits of fire; the angels of the spirits of the winds; the angels of the spirits of the clouds, of darkness, *snow*, hail, and frost; the angels of the sounds, the thunders, and the lightnings; and the angels of the spirits of cold and heat, of winter, spring, autumn, and summer, and of all the spirits of his creatures which are in the heavens, on earth, and in every (place). (2.2; trans. VanderKam)

Jacques T. A. G. M. van Ruiten argues that the author places the creation of the spirits/angels here on the first day as an interpretation of the phrase *ruaḥ elohim* in Gen 1:2.[44] If this interpretation is correct, it confirms that the author of *Jubilees* identifies angelic beings with *ruaḥ*. Most clearly, the author of *Jubilees* also uses the terms "demon" and "unclean spirit" interchangeably: "And in the third week of this jubilee the unclean spirits began to lead astray the children of the sons of Noah, and to make to err and destroy them. And the sons of Noah came to Noah their father, and they told him concerning the demons which were leading astray and blinding and slaying his sons' sons" (10.1–2; trans. VanderKam).

Similarly, the Book of Watchers portrays the sons of God of Genesis 6 as living and imperishable *pneumata* (πνεύματα ζῶντα αἰώνια, *1 Enoch* 15.4, 6) who defiled themselves by commingling with humans—that is, beings consisting of perishable flesh and blood. According to the Qumran work known as the Community Rule, God created humanity with two *ruḥot*, one of truth and one of deceit.[45] Immediately after making this claim the author talks about the Prince of Light who produces the nature of truth and the Angel of darkness out of whom deceit emerges. Here again we see the identification of *ruḥot* with angelic beings (1QS 3.13—4.26). Similarly, the War Scroll, which portrays the eschatological battle between the forces of God and the forces of Belial, says the following:

> From of old you appointed the Prince of light to assist us, and in [his] ha[nd are all the angels of just]ice, and all the *ruḥot* of truth are under his dominion. You made Belial for the pit, angel of enmity; in dark[ness] is his [dom]ain, his counsel is to bring about wickedness and guilt. All the *ruḥot* of his

lot are angels of destruction, they walk in the laws of darkness; towards it goes their only [de]sire. (1QM 13.10–12)

Both angels and demons, then, are pneumatic beings pitched into battle against one another. This same connection is found in 11QApocryphal Psalms (11Q11), which refers to the *ruḥot* and the demons, and 11QPsalms, which petitions God, stating, "Let not Satan rule over me, nor an impure *ruaḥ*" (11QPsª 19.15).[46] Likewise, in his reading of the angelic guests in Genesis 18, Philo portrays angelic beings consisting of *pneuma*: the angels "changed their pneumatic and soul-like essence, and assumed the appearance of humans" (μεταβαλόντων ἀπὸ πνευματικῆς καὶ ψυχοειδοῦς οὐσίας εἰς ἀνθρωπόμορφον, *On Abraham* 113; slightly modified from LCL; cf. *QG* 1.92).[47]

The gospel writers also frequently refer to impure *pneumata* (e.g., Mark 1:23, 26–27; 3:11, 30; 6:7). Here it is apparent that they mean demons, since they use the words interchangeably, something one can see repeatedly, for instance, in Mark's account of the Gerasene demoniac (Mark 5:1–20).[48] Demons are pneumatic beings who convey some form of impurity to human beings whom they inhabit. At the end of the first century CE, the *Testament of Solomon* depicts Solomon's interrogation of various demonic beings, whom the author refers to as impure *pneumata* (3.6). Another late first-century CE work, the *Testament of Abraham*, portrays Abraham contrasting himself, a being of flesh and blood, to the archangel Michael, a pneumatic being (13.7 [Recension B]). Finally, although considerably later, the sixth-century CE work entitled the *Cave of Treasures* nicely captures the way in which people generally perceived angelic beings. In order to give an explanation as to why the serpent, identified as Satan, brought about the downfall of Adam and Eve, the author suggests that God had commanded all the angels to worship Adam, who was created in his image. But Satan refused to worship Adam, saying to other angels, "Let us not worship and glorify him together with the angels. It is meet that he worships me who am fire and spirit and not that I worship dust formed from dirt" (3.2; trans. Toepel). Satan bases his refusal to worship Adam, the image of God, upon the argument that Adam, being flesh and blood, consists of inferior material compared to the angels, Satan included, who are fiery and pneumatic beings.[49] As in the Letter to the Hebrews, this depiction of Satan's rebellion relies upon the description of angels as being pneumatic in nature found in Psalm 103 LXX.

These texts demonstrate that many Jews believed that the stars/angels were pneumatic beings. As Clement of Alexandria says in the late second or early third century CE, stars are "pneumatic bodies" (σώματα πνεύματικα, *Eclogae Propheticae* 55.1). The reader who understood stars in this way would likely interpret God's promises in Gen 15:5 and 22:17 to make Abraham's seed star-like to be a promise that God would make Abraham's seed like the angels, that is, into pneumatic beings. It is precisely this reading of Gen 15:5 and 22:17 that forms the basis of Paul's claims that God had promised the *pneuma* to Abraham and to his seed.

Strengthening this reading, the predominant physics of the first century CE also identified the stars with semi-divine beings, consisting of a *pneuma*-like substance. Many Greek philosophers, including Plato, Aristotle, and the Stoics, believed that stars were living, sentient, and divine beings. In the *Timaeus*, a highly influential account of the nature of the kosmos, Plato claims that stars were divine living beings (40A–C), an assertion that the *Epinomis*, a pseudepigraphical work written in the name of Plato, also makes (981e1–4).[50] Likewise, Aristotle believes that the stars were ensouled beings (*On the Heavens* 292a18–21; 292b1). In *On Providence and Gods*, the third-century BCE Stoic philosopher Chrysippus claims that the stars were living, divine beings (*SVF* 2.687). After surveying the evidence, Alan Scott concludes that this conception of the stars basically pervaded Hellenistic thought: "Aside from the Epicureans, all the major philosophical schools in the Hellenistic era believed in the divinity of the stars."[51] In light of this common cultural belief, most first-century readers of the promises of star-like seed in the Abraham Narrative would understand these promises to relate to a celestial, semi-divine existence.

What is more, Stoic physics identified the matter of these living stars with *pneuma*.[52] According to Posidonius, who wrote a century before Paul, "a star is a divine body (σῶμα θεῖον) composed of aether, radiant and fire-like, never stationary, but forever moving in a circle" (as preserved in Arius Didymus's *Epitome*, fragment 32; trans. Kidd). Likewise, according to Cicero, the Stoic philosopher Cleanthes thought that stars were divine beings made up of *aether*:

> We must also assign the same divinity to the stars, which are formed from the most mobile and the purest part of the aether, and are not compounded of any other element besides; they are of a fiery heat and translucent throughout. Hence they too have the fullest right to be pronounced to be living beings endowed with sensation and intelligence. That the stars consist entirely of fire Cleanthes holds to be established by the evidence of two of the senses, those of touch and sight. (*On the Nature of Gods* 2.15.39)

The matter of the stars was thought to be *aether*, a substance that some writers compare to *pneuma*. Aristotle, for instance, argues that the element of the stars, *aether*, was *pneuma*-like, placing it above the traditional four elements of earth, water, air, and fire. In *On the Generation of Animals*, he brings together innate heat, *pneuma*, and the material of the stars, *aether*: "the natural substance which is in the *pneuma* . . . is analogous to the element which belongs to the stars" (ἡ ἐν τῷ πνεύματι φύσις, ἀνάλογον οὖσα τῷ τῶν ἄστρων στοιχείῳ, 2.736b38–2.737a1).[53] According to Aristotle, *aether* is "divine, un-ageing, and unchanging, and yet a material element."[54] One can see this same connection in Stobaeus's claim in his *Eclogae* (fifth century CE) that the third-century BCE Stoic philosopher Chrysippus believed *pneuma* to be analogous (ἀνάλογος) to *aether* (*SVF* 2.471). In passing, the first-century CE grammarian Heraclitus avers that "according to the scientists, there are two 'pneumatic' elements [πνευματικῶν στοιχείων], aether and air" (15.3; trans. Russell and Konstan; cf. 22.14). Similarly, in his *Commentary on the Gospel of John*, Origen claims that there are some who "are not ashamed to say that since God is a body he is also subject to corruption, but they say his body is pneumatic and like aether (σῶμα δὲ πνευματικὸν καὶ αἰθερῶδες), especially in the reasoning capacity of his soul" (13.21.128; trans. Heine [=*SVF* 2.1054]).[55] As Samuel Samburksy has argued, the Stoics consistently equated *pneuma* with *aether*, the material of the stars.[56] Consequently, someone who was influenced by Stoic thinking and who therefore connected the stars and *pneuma* could, even apart from knowing Jewish exegetical traditions that connected stars to angels and *pneuma*, take the comparison between Abraham's seed and the stars of the heaven in Gen 15:5 and 22:17 to be a claim that God would multiply Abraham's seed to become pneumatic beings, akin to the stars. In saying this, though, I do not mean to suggest that the *pneuma* that Paul's believers receive is undifferentiated from the pneumatic substance of the stars. For Paul, as I emphasized in the previous chapter, the *pneuma* that Christ followers receive is Christ's *pneuma*. In other words, I do not intend to diminish the christological nature of Paul's pneumatology.[57]

## *The* Pneuma *and Astral Imagery in Paul*

Paul sees the fulfillment of God's promises that Abraham's seed would become star-like or pneumatic beings in the Galatian assemblies' reception of the *pneuma* out of faith, not works of the law (Gal 3:1–5). His claim that this promise is apart from, but not opposed to, the law in no way undermines the law's authority (Gal 3:21). Paul makes the exegetically coherent claim that God's promise to Abraham that his seed would be made like the stars (Gen 15:5; 22:17)—that is, that they would be infused with *pneuma*, the same indestructible matter as the stars—was completely independent of the giving and observance of the Jewish law, which God gave 430 years later (Gal 3:17). As James D. G. Dunn states, for Paul "the law was provided not to give life (only God or his Spirit could do that)."[58] Paul's claim that the law was given some 430 years after the promise is not entirely accurate, since God commanded circumcision, one key component of the law and the matter of dispute in Galatia, to Abraham long before the Sinaitic covenant. Nonetheless, even the promises related to the covenant of circumcision in Genesis 17 make no mention of star-like seed.

   Admittedly, all of this thinking lies beneath the surface of Paul's argument in Galatians 3. Paul believes that stars are angelic beings of pneumatic substance and assumes that his readers know these basic facts. And Paul, like many of his contemporaries, reads the promises of Gen 15:5 and 22:17 to refer to a promise to be like the stars in a qualitative sense. Again, he assumes that his readers would think of these passages when he talks about God's promise of the *pneuma* and equates it with the blessing of Abraham. Perhaps, in his initial preaching of the gospel to the Galatians, Paul explicated the significance of the Abraham Narrative, especially such promises as Gen 15:5 and 22:17, as it pertained to the reception and experience of the *pneuma*. Given the ubiquity of the belief that the stars were divine or semi-divine, pneumatic beings, it is equally possible that Paul merely assumes that his readers, after reflecting upon the Abraham Narrative and the promises of Gen 15:5 and 22:17, would make this connection between star-like seed and their prior reception of the *pneuma*. To modern interpreters this might seem to be an unjustifiable or rather convoluted reading of Gen 15:5 and 22:17—one that Paul would need to explain more fully if he hoped that his readers would follow him. But ancient readers would neither have had trouble following his logic, nor have thought themselves guilty of importing foreign concepts into these texts. In some ways, this is comparable to many modern Christian readers who, without any thought, identify the serpent of Genesis 3 with Satan, despite the fact that Genesis 3 contains no reference to any demonic presence. Consequently, Dahl is wrong to conclude that "Paul has, by the standards of Jewish expectations, dissipated the promise's objective content."[59]

Additionally, Paul elsewhere confirms that he thinks both that stars are pneumatic and that Christ followers take part in a star-like existence in the present, and, would do so more fully in the resurrection. For Paul, then, the reception of Christ's *pneuma* not only forges a new genealogical connection between gentiles and Abraham, it also provides two further benefits to his gentile assemblies: the *pneuma* addresses the problem of morality and the problem of human mortality.

## The *Pneuma* and the Problem of Gentile Morality

In Chapter 2, I argued that Paul depicts the gentile world given over to gross immorality as a consequence of their abandonment of God for the worship of created things (Rom 1:18–32). By exchanging the glory of the immortal God, these people fell short of glory themselves (Rom 1:23; 3:23). This lost glory, as Ben C. Blackwell has shown, relates to incorruption and immortality.[60] Abandoning the immortal God for the worship of mortal beings caused not only immorality, but also mortality. Paul shares this bleak understanding of the gentile world with his literary interlocutor, who was himself a gentile, as I argued in Chapter 2. This gentile, though, sought to escape from this immoral existence through the adoption of the Jewish law, which some Jews, as we saw in Chapter 1, thought disciplined people into a virtuous life. For instance, Philo portrays the gentile convert to Judaism moving "from ignorance to knowledge of things that it is disgraceful not to know, from senselessness to good sense, from lack of self-mastery (*akrateia*) to self-mastery, from injustice to justice, from timidity to boldness" (*On the Virtues* 180, slightly modified from LCL).

In Rom 2:17–29, Paul argues that this gentile's observance of the law, especially as it pertains to circumcision, falls short and leaves him in the same predicament as the non-judaizing gentiles of Rom 1:18–32. Later in Romans 7, Paul attempts to demonstrate to his readers that the judaizing gentile not only fails to keep the Jewish law, but also fails to overcome *akrasia* through adoption of the Jewish law. While the majority of interpreters believe that in Romans 7 Paul portrays either his pre-call or post-call experience of sinfulness, and therefore, by extension all of humanity's (both Jews and gentiles) sinfulness,[61] I am convinced by the argument of Stanley K. Stowers that Paul, through the rhetorical device of speech-in-character (*prosōpopoieia*), portrays a gentile who adopts the Jewish law with the hope of overcoming desire and passion: "Romans 7 plays on a tradition in which Jewish writers held out the law epitomized by the tenth commandment of the decalogue as the solution to Gentile enslavement to passion and desire."[62] Stowers's identification of the "I" with a judaizing gentile is, in fact, the natural extension of my argument in Chapter 2 that Paul engages a gentile who has adopted the Jewish law and now considers himself (wrongly, to Paul's mind) a Jew: the judaizing gentile of Romans 7 is the interlocutor that Paul engages in Romans 1–2. This interpretation fits with both the gentile audience of Romans and Paul's concern to warn his readers of the dangers of this competing gospel that demanded that gentiles observe the Jewish law. For Paul, the Jewish law does not free gentiles from their slavery to sin, and thus it cannot be combined with the gospel to gentiles.

In contrast to this solution, Paul argues that it is the *pneuma* of life in Christ who sets Paul's gentile readers ("you") free from the law of sin and death (Rom 8:2).[63] In Romans 8 Paul outlines the way in which Christ's *pneuma* frees gentiles from the powers of sin and death in order to live in a way that is pleasing to God.[64] As Paula Fredriksen observes, "Given Paul's estimate of the sort of person produced by gentile culture, it would take a miracle for his Gentiles to act the way that he insists they do. And that, in Paul's estimate, is exactly what it was."[65] Paul depicts the miraculous nature of this transformation of gentile morality through his use of astral terminology in Philippians 2.

According to this letter, Christ followers already participate in a star-like existence and glory. Paul calls his readers to imitate Christ, who, being in the form of God, humbled himself, taking on human form, being obedient even to death, only to be exalted (ὑπερύψωσεν) and given a name above all names, in order that celestial, earthly, and chthonic beings would bow to him (Phil 2:8–10). Christ's exaltation above all beings, including those in the heavenly realm, implies that God has raised him over the celestial bodies, angelic beings included. His use of the verb ὑπερυψόω, which occurs only here in his letters (and in the NT), likely alludes either to Ps 96:9 LXX: "For you are Lord, the Most High (σὺ εἶ κύριος ὁ ὕψιστος) over all the earth, greatly exalted (ὑπερυψώθης) over all gods," or to the Hymn of the Three Young Men in the Old Greek of Dan 3:52–90, which repeatedly calls various aspects of the kosmos, from sea creatures to angels, to exalt the Lord forever (ὑπερυψοῦτε αὐτὸν εἰς τοὺς αἰῶνας). Like the Christ-hymn of Philippians 2, these hymns portray heavenly beings submitting to the Lord. In potential support of an allusion to Dan 3:52–90, though, is the fact that the hymn begins by saying to the Lord, "And blessed is your glorious holy name, and to be highly praised and highly exalted forever" (εὐλογημένον τὸ ὄνομα τῆς δόξης σου τὸ ἅγιον καὶ ὑπεραινετὸν καὶ ὑπερυψωμένον εἰς πάντας τοὺς αἰῶνας, 3:52), an emphasis upon the Lord's name that fits nicely with Paul's concern for the name which God gives to Jesus Christ (Phil 2:9–10).[66] Further, he claims that all will confess that Jesus Christ is Lord (κύριος), identifying Christ with the κύριός of either Ps 96:9 LXX or Dan 3:52–90.

As I have argued, numerous early Jewish interpreters of Gen 15:5 and 22:17 understood the promise of star-like seed to be a statement of the angelic exaltation of Abraham's seed, however defined.[67] Just as Christ was obedient (ὑπήκοος) to death, Paul recalls the Philippians' obedience (ὑπηκούσατε, 2:12), exhorting them to do all things without grumbling or questioning in order that they might be blameless and innocent children of God, shining like luminaries in the kosmos (φαίνεσθε ὡς φωστῆρες ἐν κόσμῳ, 2:14–15). While the word φωστήρ can refer to a variety of light-bearing objects, Paul refers here to celestial lights, since he stresses that they shine in the kosmos, that is, in the heavens. The Philippian believers, by participating in the *pneuma* (2:1) and imitating Christ, live a quality of life that makes them star-like in a crooked and perverse generation.[68] Such a portrayal fits well with Philo's reading of Gen 15:5 in *Heir* 86–88, where he argues that Abraham's seed would be qualitatively like the stars—a quality he defines in terms of the virtues. Such behavior is only fitting, given that their citizenship is in heaven (τὸ πολίτευμα ἐν οὐρανοῖς, Phil 3:20). To dwell in heaven, they must take on a nature and pattern of life that is suitable to that realm. To enable this celestial life, God gives them Christ's *pneuma*.

Irenaeus, one of Paul's earliest readers, provides early reception-historical support for my claim that Phil 2:14–15 should be read against the background of God's promise to Abraham to create star-like seed. As noted earlier in this chapter, Irenaeus argues that, by showing Abraham the stars, God promises to make his seed not only as numerous, but also as glorious, as the stars (*Demonstration of the Apostolic Preaching* 24). Later in the same work, he claims that God has fulfilled his promise of star-like seed in Christ, depending upon Paul's argument that the seed mentioned in these divine promises is Christ (Gal 3:15–16). Yet Irenaeus quotes not from Galatians but from Philippians to prove that this promise has been fulfilled: "Thus [Christ] also fulfilled the promise to Abraham, [by] which God promised him to make his seed as the stars of heaven, for Christ accomplished this, being born of the virgin, who was of the seed of Abraham and establishing believers in Him 'as lights in the world,' making the Gentiles righteous by means of the same faith as Abraham" (*Demonstration of the Apostolic Preaching* 35; trans. Behr). By making those gentiles who trust in him "lights in the world," Christ enables them in this present age to participate in a star-like life in fulfillment of Gen 15:5. Significantly, Irenaeus connects this reading of Phil 2:15 to two passages from Jewish scriptures also found in Galatians 3. Like Paul, he quotes both Gen 15:6 ("For Abraham trusted in God and it was reckoned to him as righteousness," cf. Gal 3:6) and Hab 2:4 ("through faith shall the righteous live," cf. Gal 3:11). Elsewhere, he again connects Gen 15:5 to Phil 2:15: "And Abraham believed God, and it was reckoned to him as righteousness: on the one hand that he, the creator of heaven and earth, is God alone, and then that he would make his seed like the stars of heaven (ποιήσει τὸ σπέρμα αὐτοῦ ὡς τὰ ἄστρα τοῦ οὐρανοῦ). This is what was said by Paul: 'As the luminaries in the kosmos'" (ὡς φωστῆρες ἐν κόσμῳ, *Against Heresies* 4.5.3). Twice, then, Irenaeus connects the promise that Paul mentions in Galatians 3 to both the astral imagery of Phil 2:14–15 and the promise of star-like seed in Gen 15:5 and 22:17.

While the astral terminology of Phil 2:14–15 focuses on the newly and pneumatically available moral power of Christ followers, Paul does not intend it to be simply metaphorical. Since Paul, like the majority of his contemporaries, believed that the stars were sentient beings of superior moral capacity, he would find it natural to compare the stars to the moral lives of Christ followers. In both Romans 8 and Galatians 5, Paul makes clear that the reception of Christ's *pneuma* empowers gentiles to address the moral problem inherent to the gentile condition. He therefore rejects the belief of his opponents that the Jewish law provides gentiles with the resources to overcome their morality problem, pointing out how odd it would be to begin with the *pneuma*, but to finish with the flesh, that is, circumcision (Gal 3:1–5). Instead, it is through the *pneuma* that those in Christ wait expectantly for righteousness (Gal 5:5). By walking by and in the *pneuma*, Paul's readers can deny the desire of flesh (5:16), avoid the work of the flesh, and produce the fruit of the *pneuma* (5:17–23). As Paul claims, those who are of Christ—that is, as I argued in Chapter 4, those who are a part of Christ because they have Christ's *pneuma*—have crucified the flesh with its passions and desires (5:24; cf. Romans 6).[69] Enabled by Christ's *pneuma* to participate in the pattern of Christ's life, Paul's gentiles can live a moral life that is comparable to the unblemished life of the stars.

## The *Pneuma* and the Problem of Mortality

Gentile participation in this pneumatically enabled moral life also functions as a foretaste of the solution to their mortality problem. According to Paul, the gift of the *pneuma* in the present guarantees that the gentiles will experience the resurrection in the future (2 Cor 1:22; 5:5; cf. Eph 1:14). Here, too, Paul's description of the resurrection life demonstrates connections to the astral terminology of Gen 15:5 and 22:17.

In his defense of the resurrection of Christ believers in 1 Corinthians 15, Paul distinguishes between the pre-death body and the resurrected body.[70] In attempting to explain the resurrection body, he compares it to the same type of glory shared by the stars, sun, and moon. Arguing that the pre-death body is comparable to a seed of wheat, Paul claims that the resurrected body is no longer a seed of wheat, but instead has a completely different body (σῶμα). He then argues that the different types of animals (humans, land animals, birds, and fish) have different flesh (σάρξ), each pertaining to the environment in which they live (land, sky, water).[71] So too the celestial entities have bodies (σώματα) fit for their domain (15:39–41), with each celestial body having its own glory (δόξα, v. 41). At the resurrection, Christ followers will enter a new environment—the heavens; they require, therefore, a new sort of body (σῶμα). Paul lists different animals existing within different environments: there is one kind of flesh for humanity, another for animals, another for birds, and another for fish, each kind having a flesh that is appropriate for the creature's habitat. This list, in conjunction with a discussion of celestial bodies, suggests that the resurrection involves movement from one habitat, the terrestrial, to another habitat, the celestial, as well as a transformation from one body—fleshly—to another type of body—one that is glorious. Just as human flesh is unsuitable for an aquatic habitat, so too a flesh-and-blood body is incompatible with a celestial habitat. "Flesh and blood are unable to inherit the kingdom of God (σὰρξ καὶ αἷμα βασιλείαν θεοῦ κληρονομῆσαι οὐ δύναται)," precisely because flesh-and-blood bodies are corruptible and "the corruptible [body] cannot inherit the incorruptible [celestial realm] (ἡ φθορὰ τὴν ἀφθαρσίαν κληρονομεῖ)" (15:50).[72] Importantly, this remark fits with the claims of Cicero, who argues that each layer of the kosmos contains animals (including stars) that have bodies appropriate for that layer (*Nature of the Gods* 2.15.42; cf. Plato, *Timaeus* 40A), and is similar to the claims of Philo:

> The air is the abode of incorporeal souls (ψυχῶν ἀσωμάτων), since it seemed good to their Maker to fill all parts of the universe with living beings. He set land-animals on the earth, aquatic creatures in the seas and rivers, and in heaven the stars, each of which is said to be not a living creature only but mind of the purest kind through and through; and therefore in air also, the remaining section of the universe, living creatures exist. . . . For so far is air from being alone of all things untenanted, that like a city it has a goodly population, its citizens being imperishable and immortal souls equal in number to the stars (ἀφθάρτους καὶ ἀθανάτους ψυχὰς ἔχων ἰσαρίθμους ἄστροις). (*Dreams* 1.135–137; cf. *Giants* 7)

Plutarch's writings preserve comparable thinking:

> Yet [the soul] comes from them [the heavens], and to them it returns, not with its body (οὐ μετὰ σώματος), but only when it is most completely separated and set free from the body, and becomes altogether pure, fleshless, and undefiled (καθαρὸν παντάπασι καὶ ἄσαρκον καὶ ἁγνόν). We must not,

therefore, violate nature (παρὰ φύσιν) by sending the bodies of good men with their souls to heaven. (*Life of Romulus* 28.7–8)

Both Plutarch and Philo share in common with Paul the belief that flesh-and-blood bodies cannot inhabit the celestial realm. For Plutarch and Philo, this fact of nature requires that those who ascend to heaven be bodiless. In contrast, Paul believes in a bodily resurrection. Accordingly, he argues that, because flesh and blood are unable inherit heaven, God must transform the bodies of believers into a substance that is well suited to celestial life.[73]

Since Paul has just contrasted terrestrial and celestial bodies, it appears that the resurrection body must have a body similar to the sun, moon, and stars, which, as shown above, both Jews and non-Jews of Paul's day thought consisted of *aether* or *pneuma*. Paul provides a series of contrasts between pre-death bodies and resurrected bodies: pre-death bodies are perishable, dishonorable, and weak (φθορά, ἀτιμία, and ἀσθένεια); resurrected bodies are imperishable and raised in glory and power (ἀφθαρσία, ἐγείρεται ἐν δόξῃ, and ἐγείρεται ἐν δυνάμει; vv. 42–43). Consequently, while the pre-death body consists of the matter of flesh and blood, the resurrected body consists of the matter of *pneuma*.[74] This pneumatic body is a body of glory, just like the celestial bodies. In relation to both Phil 2:15 and 1 Corinthians 15, Troels Engberg-Pedersen draws the following conclusion:

> If the pneuma is already present now among the Philippians—as what is elsewhere called a "down payment"—when they shine *like stars*, then we are very close to the idea we found in 1 Corinthians 15 to the effect that the pneuma will eventually turn those who are resurrected *into* "stars in the world". Then they will no longer shine *like* stars: they will *be* stars—through the operation of the pneuma. Conversely, we may claim, what *makes* them shine like stars already here and now is precisely the actual presence in them of the pneuma as a "down payment."[75]

Engberg-Pedersen's comments rightly highlight the fact that both Phil 2:15 and 1 Corinthians 15 provide evidence within Paul's letters that he thought that Christ followers partake in a pneumatic, star-like existence, in part (or internally, see 2 Cor 4:7, 16–17) now, and most fully in the resurrection, when the internal transformation works its way through the entire body so that it becomes an external transformation as well. In the words of Dale B. Martin, according to Paul, those who are in Christ

> currently partake of two natures: because they possess pneuma, they share something with the heavenly natures; because they are also made up of sarx and psyche, they share something with the earth, Adam, animals, birds, fish, and even dirt (15:39–40, 47–48). The transformation expected at the eschaton will cause the [Christ follower's] body to shed the lower parts of its current nature and be left with the purer, transformed part of the pneuma.[76]

Some scholars, such as N. T. Wright, disagree with the claims of Martin and Engberg-Pedersen that when Paul refers to pneumatic bodies (σῶμα πνευμα-τικόν, vv. 44, 46) he means to signify their substance. After all, Paul contrasts a future pneumatic body to the current *psychic* body (σῶμα ψυχικόν, v. 44), which can hardly mean that Paul thinks humans currently have a body consisting solely of *psyche*—not flesh and blood. Nonetheless, shortly after this remark, Paul claims that the first man (Adam) is χοϊκός—that is, he comes out of and consists of earth (ἐκ γῆς χοϊκός, vv. 47–48). This claim is rooted in the creation narrative of Genesis 2, which depicts God forming the first human out of dirt (χοῦς, Gen 2:7). When Paul describes the second man (Christ) as coming out of heaven (ἐξ οὐρανοῦ, 1 Cor 15:47), the parallelism implies that the second man consists of heavenly stuff: *pneuma* or *aether*. In fact, he makes this claim explicit: Christ became a life-giving *pneuma* (v. 45; cf. 2 Cor 3:17). Paul's belief is that just as those who came out of Adam were also made of dust, so too those who come out of Christ will be made of heavenly stuff—they will bear the image of the heavenly one (1 Cor 15:48–49; cf. Rom 8:29; 2 Cor 3:18). This evidence leads James D. Tabor to conclude: "As Adam was the head of a race of physical [more accurately: flesh and blood] human beings, subject to corruption and death; so Jesus (as a last Adam) is the first of a transformed race or *genus* of heavenly beings, immortal and glorified."[77] In his letter to the Philippians, Paul even contrasts his current life in the flesh (ὁ ζῆν ἐν σαρκί) to his desire to be with Christ: he knows that he needs to remain in the flesh now in order to continue his mission, but he desires to depart and be with Christ—presumably signifying a fleshless existence (Phil 1:22–24). Further, he claims that Christ will one day change the lowly bodies of believers to conform them to the body of his glory (μετασχηματίσει τὸ σῶμα τῆς ταπεινώσεως ἡμῶν σύμμορφον τῷ σώματι τῆς δόξης αὐτοῦ), bodies that will be suitable for the celestial commonwealth in which they will abide (3:20–21). Elsewhere, he argues that the bodies that Christ followers now have are mere terrestrial tents (ἡ ἐπίγειος ἡμῶν οἰκία τοῦ σκήνους), which are destined for destruction. But God will clothe Christ followers in celestial, eternal tents (2 Cor 5:1–5). What can all of these statements mean other than that at the resurrection believers will become pneumatic, celestial beings as well?[78]

The Aristotelian work, *On Pneuma*, attests the fact that people could and did think of *pneuma* in bodily terms: "*pneuma* is a body (*sōma*)" (1.481a9–10). While later than Paul, we see that Tertullian still persists in the belief that *pneuma* is bodily, concluding that God has a body: "For who will deny that God is body, although God is a spirit? For spirit is body, of its own kind, in its own form" (*Against Praxeas* 7; trans. Evans). For that matter, Clement of Alexandria and Origen can use precisely this phrase to speak of the matter of which celestial bodies consist (σώματα πνεύματικα, Clement, *Eclogae Propheticae* 55.1; σῶμα δὲ πνευματικὸν καὶ αἰθερῶδες, Origen, *Commentary on the Gospel of John* 13.21.128 [=*SVF* 2.1054]).

Although Paul does not make explicit that his understanding of an astral-like resurrection is rooted, in part, in the promises of Gen 15:5 and 22:17, we again have reception-historical support for this connection. Alluding to 1 Cor 15:51–52 ("we shall all be changed [ἀλλαγησόμεθα], in a moment, in the blinking of an eye"), Tertullian claims that at the resurrection, "when the destruction of the world and the fire of judgement have been set in motion, we shall be changed in a moment into angelic substance (*angelicam substantiam*), by virtue of that supervesture of incorruption (*incorruptelae superindumentum*), and be translated into that heavenly kingdom." He claims that God had promised the resurrection long ago to Abraham:

[T]he Creator has in fact prophesied that kingdom, and that even without prophecy it had a claim on the belief of such as belong to the Creator. What do you think? When, after that first promise by which it is to be as the sand for multitude, Abraham's seed (*abrahae semen*) is also designed to be as the number of the stars (*ad instar quoque stellarum destinatur*), are not these the intimations of an earthly as well as a heavenly dispensation? (*Against Marcion* 3.24; trans. Evans)

Tertullian connects the promises of Gen 15:5 and 22:17 of seed like the stars of heaven to the resurrection. Significantly, he claims that the resurrection results in the righteous being changed into the very substance of the angels, who, as we have seen, are astral beings. In yet another passage from *Against Marcion*, he brings together Philippians, 1 Corinthians, and God's promise to Abraham of star-like seed: "*Our citizenship*, [Paul] says, *is in heaven*. I recognize here the Creator's very old promise to Abraham: *And I will make thy seed as the stars in heaven*. Consequently also, *One star differeth from another star in glory*" (*Against Marcion* 5.20.7; trans. Evans; cf. 3.24.7; 4.34.14). Here Tertullian connects Paul's claim that believers have a celestial citizenship (Phil 3:20) to God's promise to Abraham that his seed would be like the stars of heaven. Finally, in *On the Incarnation*, he connects Gen 15:5/22:17 directly to 1 Cor 15:41: "*There is one glory of the sun*, which is Christ: *and another of the moon*, the church: *and another of the stars*, the seed of Abraham: for star also differs from star in glory" (52; trans. Evans).[79] In the late fourth century CE, Ambrose too connects Gen 15:5 to 1 Cor 15:41, understanding the promise of star-like seed to be a reference to Abraham's seed, Christ, and to the resurrection of the dead (*On Abraham* 1.1.20). Ambrose describes this resurrection life in the following way: "we are united with the Angels, we are made equal to the stars" (1.1.21; trans. Tomkinson). Since Tertullian, Origen, and Ambrose share in a cosmology that is much closer to Paul's than it is to the cosmology of modern readers, they understand and make explicit Paul's thinking here in ways that most modern readers have failed to do.[81] For Paul, the reception of the *pneuma* signifies that even gentiles will join in the resurrection. Now that they have become Abrahamic seed in Christ, they will become star-like, indestructible seed, according to God's promise to Abraham.

## *Sons of God and Heirs of the Kosmos*

The preceding discussion sheds light on other aspects of Paul's thinking, most notably for the arguments of this book Paul's claim that those who are in Christ, and those who are thus seed and sons of Abraham, are also sons of God (Gal 3:26).[82] Those who receive the *pneuma* of Christ become not only sons of Abraham, but also sons of God, since Christ is both the seed of Abraham and the son of God (Gal 4:6). In contrast to J. Louis Martyn, who contends that Paul stresses divine sonship in Galatians 3–4 in order to minimize the importance of Abrahamic sonship,[83] the preceding interpretation of the promise of the *pneuma* provides an explanation for the way in which Paul's discussion of the seed of Abraham and Abrahamic sonship in Galatians 3–4 turns into a discussion of divine sonship as well. For Paul, genealogical descent from Abraham results in divine descent. Since Paul understands the promises to Abraham and to his seed to mean that they would become like the stars in a qualitative sense, then this promise requires that they become divine or semi-divine beings like the angels. After all, Jewish literature frequently identifies the angels as "sons of God" (e.g., Gen 6:2, Deut 32:8 LXX).[84] Thus, when he avers that Christ followers become sons of God, Paul implies that the reception of the divine *pneuma* divinizes them. This divinization, as Tabor notes, is christologically focused: "The equation of Jesus the Son of God, with the *many* glorified sons of God to follow is God's means of bringing into existence a *family* (i.e., 'many brothers') of cosmic beings, the *Sons of God*, who share his heavenly *doxa*. Or, to put it another way, Jesus already stands at the head of a new *genus* of cosmic 'brothers' who await their full transformation at his arrival from heaven."[85] Like the angels, those in Christ become pneumatic beings—now, in part, at the eschaton, in whole. Through the reception of the *pneuma*, those in Christ now have a share in his same indestructible resurrection life.

For gentiles, the fact that the *pneuma* makes them sons of God means that they no longer exist enslaved to the sons of God or angelic beings under whom God originally placed them (e.g., Deut 32:8; Sir 17:17; *Jub.* 15.30–32). As Paul argues in Gal 4:1–10, the reception of the *pneuma* signifies that they have finally become heirs to God's promises to Abraham and thus are no longer enslaved to the *stoicheia* of the kosmos. Again, while the use of the first-person plural in this passage has led most scholars to conclude that Jews are in view here, Augustine is surely right to conclude that Paul could only have gentiles in mind (Augustine, *Commentary on Galatians* 29.4).[86] Interpreters have long debated the precise nature of these *stoicheia*,[87] but the key to understanding this phrase is Paul's claim that the Galatian gentiles-in-Christ desire to return to their position of slavery under the *stoicheia* precisely by observing "days, months, seasons, and years" (ἡμέρας . . . καὶ μῆνας καὶ καιροὺς καὶ ἐνιαυτούς, 4:10). The observance of these times depends upon submission to the movements of celestial bodies: sun, moon, and stars. Paul alludes here to Gen 1:14 LXX, which states that on the fourth day of creation, God said, "Let there be stars (φωστῆρες) in the firmament of the heaven to give light on the earth, to distinguish between night and day, and let them be for signs and for seasons and for days and for years (ἐστωσαν εἰς σημεῖα καὶ εἰς καιροὺς καὶ εἰς ἡμέρας καὶ εἰς ἐνιαυτοὺς). Although Gen 1:14 does not refer to months, as does Paul, later Jewish interpretations of this verse do. For instance, in *1 Enoch*, Enoch states that the angel Uriel "has revealed to me and breathed over me concerning the luminaries, the months, the festivals, the years, and the days." Uriel has power over the sun, moon, stars, and all the principalities of the heaven, "which set in their (respective) places, seasons, festivals, and months" (82.7–10; trans. Isaac [*OTP*]). Similarly, Philo contends that on the fourth day of creation God made the heavenly bodies to divide seasons (καιρῶν) and days (ἡμερῶν) and nights and months (μηνῶν) and years (ἐνιαυτῶν) (*Creation of the World* 55; cf. 60). The book of *Jubilees* also talks about the sun as a "great sign upon the earth for days, sabbaths, months, feast (days), years, sabbaths of years, jubilees and for all of the (appointed) times of the years" (2.9). Significantly, the Greek manuscripts of *Jubilees* contain a reference to the *stoicheia* just prior to this description of the sun: "And on the fourth [day God made] the sun, the moon, and the stars, and the constellations of the stars, and the *stoicheia*" (2.8). Considerably later than Paul, *Genesis Rabbah* contains this same understanding of Gen 1:14: "AND LET THEM BE FOR SIGNS: this refers to the Sabbaths; AND FOR SEASONS: to the three pilgrimage festivals; AND FOR DAYS: to the beginnings of the months; AND YEARS means the sanctification of the years" (6.1). Such an understanding of the function and power of celestial bodies fits with non-Jewish perceptions as well. For instance, Plato claims that the creation of the heavens coincided with "the production of days and nights and months and years" (*Timaeus* 37E) and that the sun, moon, and stars keep time (38C). Considerably closer to Paul's day, Cicero avers that "Zeno declares that the aether is god. . . . He likewise attributes the same powers to the stars, or at another time to the years, the months and the seasons" (*Nature of the Gods* 1.14.36).

The great irony in Paul's mind is that the formerly "pagan" gentiles, who were at one time under the enslaving power of the *stoicheia*, are in danger of falling under that enslaving power yet again precisely as they adopt Jewish appointed times. The Jewish law, which they thought would provide them freedom from such astral influences, turns out to be *for gentiles* an enslaving force because it places them again under the guidance of the *stoicheia*, not God, since he did not give the Jewish law to them. Paul makes no universal claim about the Jewish law here; rather, he discusses the Jewish law as it pertains to gentiles who want to adopt it. That is to say, Paul does not equate being under the Jewish law as a Jew with being enslaved to the *stoicheia*. If he did, his agreement with the law-observant mission to Jews, which he mentions in Galatians 2, would be hypocritical. Galatians 4:8 confirms that Paul has gentiles in mind—the people he describes neither knew God nor were known by God and worshipped things that were by nature not gods, a description that can only refer to gentiles, not Jews (cf. Wisdom 13:1–3; and Philo, *Contemplative Life* 3–4).

To my knowledge, scholars have failed to connect Paul's discussion of the *stoicheia* of the kosmos, those ruling celestial bodies, which were often thought to be angelic beings, to later rabbinic portrayals of Abraham's own deliverance from enslavement to the stars. Although much later than Paul, a number of rabbinic texts understand Genesis 15 to portray God lifting Abraham above the influence of the celestial bodies. For instance, according to rabbinic tradition, Rabbi Judah claimed in the name of Rab, a third-century rabbi, that the statement that God "brought Abraham out" (Gen 15:5) signified God freeing him from astral influences: "Now Abraham had said unto [God], 'Sovereign of the Universe! I have gazed at the constellation which rules my destiny, and seen that I am not fated to beget children.' To which [God] replied: '*Go forth* from their astrological speculations: Israel is not subject to planetary influences'" (*b. Ned.* 32a [trans. Epstein]; cf. *b. Shabb.* 156a). Similarly, according to *Numbers Rabbah*, Rabbi Joshua said in the name of Rabbi Levi that Gen 15:5 demonstrates that God brought Abraham outside the realm of celestial influence. In light of this heavenly ascent, Rabbi Levi exhorted, "While the sandal is on your foot tread down the thorn; he who is placed below them fears them, but thou [Abraham] art placed above them, so trample them down" (44.12. cf. *Pesikta Rabbati, Piska* 20.2). In this reading, Abraham's trust in God relates also to his confidence that God has liberated him from malevolent astral forces, precisely Paul's concern in Galatians 4.

While these rabbinic traditions postdate Paul's writings, the *Apocalypse of Abraham* provides a much closer parallel. The author of this work portrays an angel who raises Abraham to heaven and thereby demonstrates Abraham's usurpation of the authority and position that the angel Azazel previously held over the gentiles. While Azazel's portion was previously in heaven, and Abraham's on earth, Abraham's ascension portends his inheriting of the heavenly realms, while Azazel's evil choices doom him to the terrestrial realm (13.8). Similarly, in summarizing Genesis 15 and connecting it to Gen 22:17, Pseudo-Philo depicts God's elevation of Abraham above all the stars: "Is it not regarding this people [Israel] that I spoke to Abraham in a vision, saying, '*Your seed will be like the stars in the heaven*,' when I lifted him above the firmament and showed him the arrangements of all the stars?" (*L.A.B.* 18.5). Such ascension scenes visibly depict Abraham's authority over both the gentiles and the heavenly host of angels.

Not only do entrance into Christ and the reception of the *pneuma* free gentiles from slavery to the *stoicheia*, they also guarantee, as Paul makes apparent elsewhere, that Christ followers would one day rule and judge the kosmos and angels: "Do you not know that the saints will judge the kosmos? Now if the kosmos will be judged by you, are you unworthy of trivial judgments? Do you not know that we will judge angels?" (1 Cor 6:2–3). M. David Litwa states of Paul:

> He tells his converts—as if it were common knowledge—that they will someday judge higher, superhuman beings ("angels," 1 Cor 6:3). In promising this, he seems to assume that he and his community will one day have an existence—or at least a status—above those angelic beings (cf. Rom 16:20). Such a cosmic role seems to be part and parcel of transformed Christians judging the whole "cosmos" (1 Cor 6:2). They are those who will be given "all things" by God (Rom 8:32), and who will come into possession of grandiose cosmic realities—including life, death, things present, things to come, and even the world itself (1 Cor 3:21–23).[88]

Paul's assertion that believers in Rome would one day crush Satan under their feet provides a striking parallel to Rabbi Levi's aforementioned statement that, as a result of God's placing Abraham above the malevolent stars, Israel would one day trample them down (*Num. Rab.* 44.12).

Further, Paul's conviction that those in Christ would judge both the kosmos and the angels helps make sense of his claim in Rom 4:13 that Abraham and his seed would inherit the kosmos (cf. 1 Cor 3:22). This understanding of what Abraham's seed would inherit occurs in the context of Paul's only explicit citation of Gen 15:5—"so shall your seed be"—which he quotes in Rom 4:18.[89] Such an eschatological hope contrasts with Paul's claim in Galatians 4 that his readers were formerly slaves under the *stoicheia tou kosmou* (4:3). Previously enslaved to the elements of the kosmos (*stoicheia tou kosmou*), those in Christ are now heirs of the kosmos, which they will one day rule over and judge. Many interpreters take this claim to be a spiritualization of God's promise to give Abraham and his seed the land of Israel (Gen 12:1, 7; 13:15–17; 15:7, 18; 17:8; 24:7; 26:3; 28:4, 12). In other words, they conclude that Paul does not care about the territorial aspect of God's promises to Abraham since he rarely refers to this aspect of Israel's inheritance, and when he does so, for instance in Rom 4:13, he greatly expands the territory from the land of Israel to the kosmos. Yet, as Mark Forman argues, the problem with this assumption "is the deduction that since Paul's inheritance is non-territorial, inasmuch as it is not tied to one specific tract of terrain, it is therefore also necessarily non-material or spiritual in reference."[90]

Additionally, Paul was not the first reader of the patriarchal narratives to greatly expand the boundaries of the promised land. Already in the Greek manuscripts of Sirach, one can see that some Jews thought that God had promised Abraham much more land than the region of Palestine. In his recounting of God's oath to Abraham after the near-sacrifice of Isaac (Gen 22:16–18), the author states, "Therefore [God] assured [Abraham] by an oath, that he would bless the nations in his seed, and that he would multiply him as the dust of the earth, and exalt his seed as the stars, and cause them to inherit from sea to sea, and from the river unto the utmost part of the land" (κατακληρονομῆσαι αὐτοὺς ἀπὸ θαλάσσης ἕως θαλάσσης καὶ ἀπὸ ποταμοῦ ἕως ἄκρου τῆς γῆς, 44:21).[91] Similarly, the book of *Jubilees* universalizes the territory promised to Israel. In his rewriting of Genesis 21, the author says that "[Abraham] remembered the word which was told to him on the day that Lot separated from him [i.e., Gen 13:14–17]. And he rejoiced because the LORD had given him seed upon the earth so that they might inherit the land" (17.3; trans. Wintermute [*OTP*]). Later, he portrays Isaac blessing Jacob: "May you inherit all of the earth" (22.14). Yet again, in his rewriting of God's appearance to Jacob at Bethel, the author expands upon the promise of Gen 26:4–5 ("I will multiply your seed as the stars of heaven, and will give to your seed all these lands; and by your seed all the nations of the earth shall bless themselves, because Abraham listened to my voice and kept my charges, my commandments, my statutes, and my laws"), stating, "I am the LORD who created heaven and earth, and I shall increase you and multiply you very much. And there will be kings from you; they will rule everywhere that the tracks of mankind have been trod. And I shall give to your seed all of the land under heaven and they will rule in all nations as they have desired. And after this all of the earth will be gathered together and they will inherit it forever" (32.18–19; trans. Wintermute [*OTP*]). Perhaps here the author has a Hebrew *Vorlage* of Gen 26:4 similar to the MT, which refers to inheriting "all these lands" (כל הארצת), and interprets it as evidence that Israel will not only inherit its own land, but all lands—the entire earth.[92]

Like *Jubilees*, Philo understands the promises God makes to Jacob at Bethel to include the inheritance of the kosmos (*Dreams* 1.175). Later, the author of *4 Ezra* asks God why, if the world has been created for Israel, Israel has not inherited it (6.59). Finally, according to the *Mekhilta de-Rabbi Shimon bar Yoḥai*, Gen 15:6 demonstrates that Abraham inherited this world and the world-to-come as "a reward for faith" (*Beshallaḥ* 26.6, 8d–h). While these passages extend the boundaries of the promises that God had made to Abraham and his seed, this expansion may not have been intentional. Both the Hebrew word used to refer to the land of Canaan (ארץ) and its Greek counterpart (γῆ) are ambiguous, referring to a specific land or to the entire earth.

Paul's belief that Abraham and his seed were to inherit the kosmos, then, fits with broader trends in early Judaism. Nonetheless, interpreters have wondered why Paul appears to change subjects at this point in Romans 4. How does this reference to inheriting the kosmos relate to the rest of Paul's argument? As Forman notes, most approaches to Romans 4 have "an inability to identify a demonstrable connection between the highly suggestive phrase in verse 13 'inherit the world' and Paul's argument in the verses which follow."[93] Specifically, what does inheriting the kosmos have to do with the theme of God bringing life out of death? As this chapter has indicated, the reception of the *pneuma* raises gentile seed above the powers that have, to this point, ruled them. In this regard, Paul's eschatological expectations parallel the *Apocalypse of Abraham*'s depiction of Abraham's ascent above the heavens where he assumes the place of power over the kosmos that Azazel had enjoyed until his fall. They have now inherited the kosmos and are beginning to rule already as they experience freedom from the cosmic forces of Sin, Satan, and the *stoicheia tou kosmou*, a freedom that enables them to live righteously. At the same time, the *pneuma* guarantees them a share in an indestructible life, and thus Paul's discussion of God raising Christ in Rom 4:25 fits with gentiles ruling the kosmos at the resurrection.

# *Conclusion*

In light of Genesis's apparent silence on the topic, scholars have long been bewildered over Paul's assertion that God had promised the *pneuma* to Abraham and to his seed. When claiming that God had promised the *pneuma* to Abraham and his seed (Gal 3:14–16), Paul intends his readers to recognize that Gen 15:5 and 22:16–18, in promising that Abraham's seed would be like the stars of the heaven, contained the implicit promise of the *pneuma*, the stuff of the stars/angels. To Paul, and to his informed readers, Gen 15:5 and 22:17 were clear references to God's promise of sending the *pneuma* to give birth to seed who were like the stars of heaven. Children like the stars of heaven, by definition, must have the *pneuma*.

Jewish understandings of the stars as pneumatic angelic beings and the Stoic conception of the stars as ethereal or pneumatic celestial bodies explain this longstanding problem for scholars. When Paul read the Abraham Narrative with its promise(s) of seed like the stars of heaven, he heard an obvious reference to the reception of the *pneuma*. The fact that the Galatians had received the *pneuma* upon hearing Paul's gospel proclamation about Jesus Christ, a descendant of Abraham, was proof that Christ was not merely a descendant, a seed, of Abraham, but *the* seed of Abraham, who, through the bestowal of his *pneuma* upon believers, gave birth to a host of pneumatic seed, among even the Galatians—thus bringing the Abrahamic blessing upon and into the gentiles.

Becoming sons of Abraham through Christ's *pneuma* means that gentiles now become Abraham's seed. And it was to Abraham and to this seed, whom Paul identifies as Christ and, by extension, those in Christ, that God gave the promise that they would become like the stars in sharing in an indestructible life. Gentiles who try to become sons of Abraham in any other way do not enter into Christ and therefore do not become the seed and heirs of such wonderful promises. If they become sons of Abraham by adopting the law, they become Ishmaelic sons who have not been promised this inheritance and who thus remain enslaved to the *stoicheia tou kosmou*, instead of being given the power to rule over the entire kosmos as heirs of the father (Rom 4:13; Gal 4:1–6). At best, such sons become connected to the present Jerusalem (Gal 4:25) in a way akin to how the Hasmonean circumcision of the Idumeans brought them into a political alliance with Hasmonean Judea.[94] Gentiles who become Abraham's sons through the *pneuma*, on the other hand, are heirs of the Jerusalem that is above (Gal 4:26), free from the *stoicheia tou kosmou*. It is this inheritance that is not through the law but through the promise, through faith, and through the one seed of Abraham—Christ. To summarize, Paul argues that God promised the *pneuma* to Abraham and his seed. To many Greco-Romans readers, both Jews and gentiles, the promise of star-like seed would have naturally been understood to imply that Abraham's seed would share in the indestructible life of celestial beings. One could call this astralization or angelification or even deification, although Paul never does.[95]

For Paul, then, the gift of the *pneuma* brings about four significant and substantive changes that remedy the gentile problem. First, the gift of the *pneuma*, precisely because it is the *pneuma* of Abraham's seed, Christ, brings gentiles into a genealogical relationship with Abraham himself. Gentiles have now become real, material seed of Abraham (Gal 3:29). Second, this material, pneumatic connection between Abraham and gentiles-in-Christ is also the *pneuma* of the son of God (Gal 4:6), which Paul elsewhere describes as the *pneuma* of God, the *pneuma* of Christ, and the *pneuma* of the one (God) who raised Jesus from the dead (Rom 8:9–11). Thus, those in Christ become sons of God themselves. As a consequence, gentiles have been freed from the malevolent powers—the *stoicheia*—that rule the world. Third, this freedom from the powers of this evil age produces an inner transformation that brings about the solution to the gentile moral problem that Paul caricatures in Rom 1:18–32. The gift of the *pneuma* now results in the moral capacity and ability for self-mastery.[96] Gentiles now can effectively combat the works of the flesh, which keep one from inheriting the kingdom of God (Gal 5:16–21), and produce the fruit of the *pneuma* (5:23–24). Fourth, and finally, through the reception of the *pneuma*, gentiles become seed of Abraham, a virtuous people who have been given the deposit (ἀρραβών) on all the promises of God (2 Cor 1:20; cf. Eph 1:13–14), promises that will result in their mortality being swallowed up by life (2 Cor 5:5) so that they can partake in the indestructible life of the eschaton and rule the kosmos.

# Conclusion

I BEGAN THIS book by arguing that 1 Cor 7:19 both encapsulates the difficulty of and holds the key to understanding Paul's view of the Jewish law: "Circumcision is nothing and uncircumcision is nothing, but (what matters is) keeping the commandments of God." How can Paul make a distinction between the rite of circumcision and the commandments of God, given God's order to Abraham and then to Israel to circumcise their males (Genesis 17; Lev 12:3)? Should one conclude that his view of the law, as evidenced not only by this passage but also by the content of his seven undisputed letters, is fundamentally incoherent?[1] If he has a coherent view of the Jewish law, what was his problem with it? Was it legalism, as so-called Lutheran proponents suggest? Or was it ethnocentrism, as so-called new perspective proponents argue? In contrast to these readings, I have contended in the preceding pages that Paul had no problem with the Jewish law itself: it was, after all, holy, just, and good (Rom 7:12). But even holy things, especially holy things, can be put to misuse.

Scholars have championed Paul's gospel as both freeing and universalistic. Influenced, perhaps, by his call to liberty—"For freedom Christ has freed us! Stand firm, therefore, and do not re-entangle yourselves in a yoke of slavery" (Gal 5:1)—some refer to Paul with such epithets as the "Apostle of the Heart Set Free," and the "Apostle of Liberty." F. C. Baur could even claim that "[Pauline] Christianity is the absolute religion, the religion of the spirit and of freedom, with regard to which Judaism must be looked at from an inferior standpoint, from which it must be classed with Heathenism."[2] Lately, even modern philosophy has taken a shine to Paul.[3] Yet, in contrast to most scholarly reconstructions, Paul's gospel did not free gentiles from needing to keep the Jewish law: according to Paul and many of his contemporary Jews, gentiles never needed to keep it. In fact, he did not argue that gentiles did not need to keep the law; rather, he positively prohibited gentiles who wanted to adopt it from doing so. His own words in such passages as 1 Cor 7:17–24 complicate Christian attempts to portray him as the great preacher of freedom from the suffocating restrictions or narrow-minded ethnocentrism of the Jewish law. Albert Schweitzer perfectly captures this gap between modern Christian depictions of Paul and Paul's own thinking: "Paul's preaching of freedom from the Law is thus by no means conceived in a spirit of freethinking. He compels Jews and non-Jews alike to remain in the state in which they first became believers. The champion of the freedom of Gentile Christianity is at the same time its tyrant. If it desired to become partaker in the blessing of the Law and circumcision, he would not suffer it to do so."[4]

In the first half of this book, I sought to provide a coherent reading of Paul's view of the Jewish law, narrowing the scope of this vexing question by focusing specifically on his statements regarding the rite of circumcision, surely the most central issue that he faced in relation to his gentile mission. His answer to the question of gentiles and the Jewish law was no mere academic exercise; rather, it was formed in the crucible of his mission to preach Christ to the gentiles. Further, I placed this treatment within the broader context of Paul's understanding of the Abraham Narrative (Genesis 12–25). He did not reject the law; rather, he quoted from Jewish scriptures repeatedly, claiming it as the authoritative witness to his gospel. He did not oppose his gospel to the law, the *torah*, in some abstract sense, but he did reject a specific use of the law. Throughout his letters, he resisted the application of the law to gentiles, not because he was the apostle of freedom, but because he believed that the Jewish law did not apply to gentiles. Paul opposed gentile judaizing because it was a misappropriation of the holy law.[5] Indeed, he did not oppose Jews, or Jewish identity, or Jewish behavior and beliefs. He battled any attempt, on the part of Jews or gentiles, to encourage or compel gentiles to adopt the Jewish law. But what precisely did Paul find offensive about gentile observance of the Jewish law? After all, he himself required his gentile assemblies to live in a way that reflected distinctively Jewish beliefs and practices.[6] For Paul, gentile efforts to become sons of Abraham through law observance failed because they sought to overcome a genealogical divide that God had created between Israel and the nations. Again, gentile law observance in Paul's mind, and circumcision most centrally, was little more than cosmetic surgery meant to make gentiles look like Abraham's sons. Here I think that proponents of an anti-ethnocentric reading of Paul are correct to emphasize the importance of understanding the sociological function of the Jewish law, although they are wrong to conclude that Paul did away with the Jewish law in order to overcome this genealogical divide. To the contrary, "Paul's principled resistance to circumcising gentiles-in-Christ . . . *preserves* the distinction *kata sarka* between Jews and the various other ethnic groups within the *ekklêsia*."[7]

Since the genealogical gap between Jew and gentile was divinely created, the only solution to the gentile problem was for God to overcome this gap by rewriting gentile genealogy so that they could become Abrahamic seed. Here I think an anti-legalist reading of Paul, with its emphasis on Paul's contrast between human works and divine action, rightly captures another aspect of Paul's thinking: he did not believe that gentiles could adopt the Jewish law in order to create a kinship bond to Abraham. Instead, since God set Abraham and his descendants apart from the nations, only God could forge a new kinship bond between gentiles and Abraham. Consequently, as Pamela Eisenbaum suggests, we see God's grace and human lineage coinciding: "Paul's argument rests on an implicit assumption underpinning a patrilineal system of kinship. Acquiring membership in a patrilineage is always an act of grace, because a child cannot initiate an adoption or accomplish it for him—or herself. The adopted child is the beneficiary of an act or series of actions that must be performed by the father."[8]

Where both anti-legalist and anti-ethnocentric readings of Paul fall short, though, is in their universalization of Paul's assertions about the Jewish law. To universalize Romans 2 or Galatians 4 so that one interprets Paul's statements to apply to both Jews and gentiles is to misunderstand him. Paul believed that the majority of the Jewish law applied only to the Jewish people. Gentiles, on the other hand, were not to adopt the Jewish law in the hopes of becoming Abrahamic seed. In this regard, he was hardly alone in his day. It has been the burden of this book, particularly Part 1, to demonstrate that Paul's views on the Jewish law did not distinguish him from all of his Jewish contemporaries; rather, his genealogical exclusion of gentiles from Jewishness fit within one broader pattern of Jewish thinking about gentiles. In other words, the uniqueness of Paul's gospel is not to be found in his view of the way in which gentiles related to the Jewish law.[9]

In Part 2, on the other hand, I have tried to show what was in many ways unique to Paul's gospel—his belief that Jesus was the Christ, and that this fact therefore made him the promised seed of Abraham. Even here, as Matthew V. Novenson demonstrates, Paul's thinking was a variant of Jewish messianism.[10] In his death and resurrection, Christ was now bringing about the obedience of the gentiles, which Jewish scriptures foretold (Rom 1:5; 15:18; cf. Ps 17:44–45 LXX and Isa 11:14). Further, in light of his assertion that Jesus was Abraham's seed, Paul made the startling claim that uncircumcised gentiles have become genealogically descended from Abraham through the reception of Christ's *pneuma*. Such a contention was as unprecedented as it was bold: how could one verify it, apart from certain claims about both Christ's identity and the experience of receiving the *pneuma*? No wonder, then, that some of Paul's gentile believers, and the missionaries who competed with him, sought seemingly surer ground for making assertions about Abrahamic descent in the rite of circumcision and the visible practices of the Jewish law. Even Paul saw Abraham's circumcision as a seal of his righteousness (Rom 4:11), after all. Such an outward, although admittedly concealed, sign of righteousness must have appealed to judaizing gentiles who were looking for a more tangible sign of relation to Abraham than the internal down payment of the *pneuma* (1 Cor 1:22; 5:5).

Both anti-legalist and anti-ethnocentric interpreters of Paul fail to do justice to the constitutive nature of ethnic reasoning in Paul's thought. Both, in other words, misunderstand or underestimate the importance of Abraham and Abrahamic descent for Paul's gospel. As I argued in the second half of this book, Paul was convinced that God had rewritten gentile genealogies in order to bring them into Abraham's lineage. Modern scholars might want to describe Paul's ethnic reasoning as the construction of a fictive kinship, but to Paul's mind this new and pneumatic genealogy was no mere legal fiction; rather, the reception of Christ's *pneuma* materially related gentiles-in-Christ to Abraham. In Christ and through the reception of Christ's *pneuma*, gentiles have become Abrahamic seed and sons and now stand to inherit all the promises that God made to Abraham's seed. Such an Abrahamic connection was essential to the way Paul articulated his gospel in both Galatians and Romans. Any interpretation of these letters, therefore, which cannot give an account of the centrality of Abraham and Abrahamic descent for Paul's gospel must be insufficient.

I began this book by comparing the task of interpreting Paul's letters to reading Gautam Malkani's novel, *Londonstani*.[11] Readers of *Londonstani* misunderstand the significance of many details of the narrative because they have mistakenly concluded that Jas, the protagonist of the novel, is Indian, when in fact he is a Caucasian who has adopted the cultural and religious practices of a particular stream of Indian subculture in London. Once one realizes that Jas is not of Indian ethnicity, numerous comments and events take on a considerably different meaning. Similarly, many modern readers of Paul have erroneously assumed that Paul addresses both Jews and gentiles, and have, therefore, mistakenly concluded that his statements about the Jewish law are an indictment of Judaism and its supposedly legalistic or ethnocentric religiosity. Just as the reader of *Londonstani* lacks the knowledge available to characters within the novel's narrative, knowledge that precludes the very interpretations that many readers consider to be most natural and obvious, so too modern readers of Paul's letters lack the knowledge available to Paul's initial readers, knowledge that would again preclude certain modern interpretations of Paul.

Although I argued in the Introduction that there are similarities between readers of *Londonstani* and modern interpreters of Paul's letters, I concede here one important difference: at the very end of the narrative, Malkani provides his readers with the vital hermeneutical key that enables them to see the erroneous nature of their reading. After finishing the novel, the reader can never again misidentify Jas's ethnicity. As the history of interpretation demonstrates, however, interpreters of Paul can read his letters over and over again, yet never receive a key analogous to Malkani's bombshell at the end of *Londonstani* by which they can unlock Paul's statements about the Jewish law. Even the meaning of 1 Cor 7:19, after all, is contested. In this regard, then, we remain at a severe disadvantage in our quest to understand Paul. Our modern interpretations of Paul's letters remain dependent upon our own efforts to create coherence out of them. In the words of Margaret M. Mitchell, "Each reader of Paul's letters, to the present day, formulates a portrait of the soul of the author of these letters in the act of his or her reading." Mitchell proceeds to portray Pauline interpretation as an exercise in necromancy: "Pauline interpretation is fundamentally an artistic exercise in conjuring up and depicting a dead man from his ghostly images in the ancient text, as projected on a background composed from a selection of existing sources. All these portraits are based upon a new configuration of the surviving evidence, set into a particular, chosen, framework."[12] In a field of scholarship so divided over what Paul "really meant," a field characterized by contradictory conjurings, how can we know who has successfully made contact with the dead?

## An Early Reception-Historical Clue to Reading Paul

The preceding chapters serve as my own attempt to conjure up this equally fascinating and troubling dead man in order to make sense of his thinking on circumcision and Abrahamic descent in a way that neither uses Judaism as a foil for Christianity nor denigrates Jewish scriptures and tradition. For those interested in Paul's thinking, I have intended this book to shed new light on Paul's understanding of the Jewish law as it pertains to his mission to the gentiles, providing a reading of some of Paul's most difficult statements about the Jewish law in light of his encoded gentile audience that fits with the concerns of at least some Jews in the Greco-Roman period.

In the remaining pages, I would like to move from Paul's letters themselves to one of the earliest receptions of Paul and his thought. Since his letters do not provide us with an obvious interpretive key to settle our disputes over the way in which to read his statements about the Jewish law correctly, I believe that we can find precisely such a key in the Acts of the Apostles, which functions in a manner akin to Malkani's revelation that his protagonist is Caucasian, not Indian. Luke's portrayal of the apostle Paul purposely excludes certain readings of Paul. Admittedly, the use of Acts in reconstructing Paul's thinking, actions, or biography remains a controversial issue. As F. C. Baur noted long ago, "The unity of the work consists in this idea: its chief tendency is to represent the difference between Peter and Paul as unessential and trifling. To this end Paul is made in the second part to appear as much as possible like Peter, and Peter in the first part as much as possible like Paul."[13] I, too, find the historical reliability of Acts quite problematic, and so have, in the preceding chapters, avoided using it to elucidate Paul's thought. Historians have good reason to question Luke's reliability when it comes to portraying Paul and early Christian history. My appeal to the book of Acts, therefore, functions as corroborating evidence in support of my earlier arguments.[14]

Fundamental to Luke's portrayal of Paul is the way in which, in Acts 21–28, Paul finds himself swept up into a controversy about his views of the Jewish law. When he arrives in Jerusalem and visits the Jerusalem Christ-following assembly, Paul relates one by one the things that God had done among the gentiles through his service (21:19). The Jewish believers in Jerusalem glorify God at the report of the success of his mission, but respond to him by pointing to the things that God has done in their own midst: "You observe, brother, how many myriads there are among the Jews who believe and all of them are zealous for the law" (πόσαι μυριάδες εἰσὶν ἐν τοῖς Ἰουδαίοις τῶν πεπιστευκότων καὶ πάντες ζηλωταὶ τοῦ νόμου ὑπάρχουσιν, 21:20). In light of the success of the gospel among law-observant Jews, the Jerusalem leadership voices a concern to Paul: "[These zealous Jews] have been instructed concerning you that you teach all the Jews among the gentiles apostasy from Moses, telling them neither to circumcise their children nor to observe the customs" (ἀποστασίαν διδάσκεις ἀπὸ Μωϋσέως τοὺς κατὰ τὰ ἔθνη πάντας Ἰουδαίους λέγων μὴ περιτέμνειν αὐτοὺς τὰ τέκνα μηδὲ τοῖς ἔθεσιν περιπατεῖν, 21:21).[15] The leaders in Jerusalem clearly think that this report is wrong and advise Paul on how to go about demonstrating its falsity through an act of temple piety.

This anecdote is axiomatic for what Luke presumes to be the correct understanding of Paul's teaching.[16] First, note the centrality of the question of ethnic identity in this story. While Paul comes to Jerusalem to talk about what God has done through his service among the gentiles, he faces rumors that pertain to what he has been teaching diaspora Jews. Through this episode, Luke directly addresses the question of Paul's view of circumcision. The rumors that swirl accuse Paul of teaching Jews not to circumcise their children, but, according to Luke, the truth is that he teaches only gentiles not to undergo circumcision. Significantly, Luke does not portray the leaders of the Jerusalem assembly arguing with Paul over this facet of his teaching. That is to say, according to Luke, neither Paul nor the Jerusalem assembly believes that gentiles ought to undergo circumcision (so too Acts 15), but both assume that Jewish Christ followers would and ought to continue to circumcise their sons, as the Jewish law prescribes. Acts 21, then, provides external corroboration for the interpretation I have given of 1 Cor 7:19, part of Paul's rule in all of his assemblies. According to Luke, if one takes Paul's message against circumcision and law observance to apply to Jews, then one will inevitably misunderstand Paul. Luke makes it clear that one of the most elementary ways in which

Paul's message could be (and was being) misconstrued was the result of readers misidentifying his intended audience—precisely what proponents of the so-called radical new perspective on Paul have claimed.

Second, Luke depicts these Jewish Christ followers as being extremely zealous for the law (21:20). For Luke, it is praiseworthy that Jewish Christ followers remain committed to the Jewish law. If proponents of anti-legalist or anti-ethnocentric readings of Paul are right, Luke's Paul should respond to this group of law-observant Jews by preaching the gospel of justification by faith—either as a criticism of their works-righteousness (in the anti-legalist perspective) or as a criticism of their misguided ethnocentrism (in the anti-ethnocentric perspective) associated with such Jewish zeal for the law. But he does not. To be sure, Luke's Paul preaches the necessity of trusting in Christ and that such trust brings benefits that the Jewish law cannot provide (Acts 13:38–39). But he does not conclude from this fact that Jewish observance of the law is incompatible with justification by faith. Luke's Paul, once again, fits with the radical new perspective's claim that Paul believed Jewish Christ followers ought to continue in their law observance.[17]

Third, Luke's portrait of Paul requires his readers to conclude not only that such rumors about Paul's preaching were false, but also that Paul himself continued to keep the Jewish law.[18] Luke depicts the Jerusalem leaders suggesting that Paul take part in a rite of purification, with the express intention that "all will know that there is nothing in what they have learned about you [i.e., Paul], but that you yourself live in observance of the law" (21:24). Again, one would expect an anti-legalist or anti-ethnocentric Paul to resist the Jerusalem leaders, accusing them of not being "straightforward with regard to the truth of the gospel" (Gal 2:14). Instead, Luke's Paul agrees to undergo this purification, thereby implicitly affirming the Jerusalem leaders' belief that he continues to keep the Jewish law. In other words, if N. T. Wright and others are correct to argue that "Paul did not himself continue to keep the kosher laws [or other Jewish laws like Sabbath and circumcision]," then either Luke's portrayal of Paul is historically inaccurate and theologically misguided, or Luke accurately depicts Paul's actions, but these actions were themselves fundamentally duplicitous and theologically misguided. Again, the radical new perspective's assertion that Paul continued to observe the Jewish law fits with Luke's narrative.[19]

In fact, Luke continues to address the question of Paul's law observance, for, in the very act of following the advice of the Jerusalem leaders in demonstrating temple piety and concern for ritual purity, Paul finds himself accused of attempting to defile the temple precincts by bringing into it a gentile. Nonetheless, Luke makes apparent that these charges are baseless: Paul did not enter the temple with the intention to profane it (τὸ ἱερὸν ἐπείρασεν βεβηλῶσαι, Acts 24:6); rather, he entered it in order to undergo purification (ἡγνισμένον ἐν τῷ ἱερῷ, 24:18). And, as Bart Koet observes, "The rest of Acts is a defense of Paul's fidelity to the Law."[20] Thus Luke states that when Festus came to Caesarea, the Jews accused Paul of many things that they could not prove. Paul's response to these charges indicates that such accusations pertain, first and foremost, to the Jewish law: "Neither against the law of the Jews, nor against the Temple, nor against Caesar have I sinned" (οὔτε εἰς τὸν νόμον τῶν Ἰουδαίων οὔτε εἰς τὸ ἱερὸν οὔτε εἰς Καίσαρά τι ἥμαρτον, 25:8). Even at the very end of Acts, Luke portrays Paul resolutely defending himself against these charges before the Jewish community in Rome: "Men, brothers, I have done nothing against the people or against the customs of the fathers" (ἐγώ, ἄνδρες ἀδελφοί, οὐδὲν ἐναντίον ποιήσας τῷ λαῷ ἢ τοῖς ἔθεσι τοῖς πατρῴοις, 28:17). Consequently, I find it difficult not to sympathize with David Rudolph's exasperated remark regarding scholarly claims that Luke depicts Paul abandoning observance of the law: "One may ask what more Luke could have included in his narrative to express that Paul was a Torah-observant Jew. Acts is replete with statements that describe Paul as faithful to Jewish law and custom; statements to the contrary are consistently identified as false rumours."[21]

What is so fascinating about the rumor spreading through the Jerusalem assembly, according to Acts 21, is the way in which it perfectly captures the near unanimous assessment of Christian interpreters down through the centuries that Paul taught Jews to abandon Moses, to stop circumcising their sons, and to stop living according to Jewish customs.[22] According to Luke, though, this assessment of Paul's understanding of the Jewish law is simply wrong. As Luke portrays it, the Jerusalem leadership itself knows that these reports are untrue, suggesting that by certain actions Paul can demonstrate the falsity of these claims: "And all will know that what they have been told about you is not [true], but you yourself walk, keeping the law" (21:24).

While both Paul and the Jerusalem assembly believe that Jews ought to continue in their observance of the law, both agree that gentiles should not, a decision of the Jerusalem Council that Luke reiterates here (21:25). On the basis of this decision, Robert W. Wall concludes: "Even as God does not require uncircumcised Gentile converts to follow conventional Jewish practices for fellowship with Jewish believers, neither does God require repentant Jews to forsake their ancestral traditions out of loyalty to the Messiah."[23] I would stress that Luke's point is stronger than Wall suggests: not only does God not require Jewish Christ followers to abandon law observance, he actually requires them to continue in law observance.

## *An Immanent-Critical/Canonical-Critical Postscript*

It is hardly a secret that the vast majority of members in the largest society committed to the academic study of the Bible, the Society of Biblical Literature, are Christian. As natural as it might seem that adherents of a religious tradition would devote themselves to the academic study of their own authoritative texts, the fact goes lamented by some scholars who often perceive an inability of such interpreters to critically distance themselves from their own traditions and theology when they write about biblical texts. In relation to the study of Paul especially, many scholars belong to some tradition of Christianity that is indebted to the Protestant Reformation, which depends heavily upon a certain construal of Paul. My final thoughts, then, primarily address such readers from what a religious-studies perspective calls an immanentist position. An immanentist position in the academic study of religion temporarily inhabits a religious tradition, in order to provide criticism of that tradition from within it. For those readers who are adherents of Christianity, it might be most helpful to think of the way I deploy immanentist criticism here in relation to canonical-critical readings of the Bible.[24]

Contemporary Christian communities encounter Paul's letters in two contexts that differ considerably from Paul's original readers. First, as I noted above, they read Paul's letters separated from the particular historical contingencies that led him to address assemblies of Christ believers. Second, they read his letters within the literary framework of the Christian canon, which introduces readers to Paul first through the narrative of the Acts of the Apostles. As Wall, a canonical critic of the New Testament, observes, "Acts establishes a canonical context within which the [New] Testament letters and the apostolic proclamation they enshrine are interpreted."[25] By placing Acts before Paul's letters, those responsible for the current form of the New Testament canon made Luke's narrative both the introduction and key to Paul's letters. Unlike Malkani's *Londonstani*, then, the New Testament canon gives Christian readers the key to rightly understanding Paul before beginning to read his letters. As Eric W. Scherbenske has helpfully documented, in their efforts to provide a coherent account of Paul's thinking, early Christians provided numerous prefaces to his letters. Scherbenske argues that Marcion's canon, for instance, not only had Galatians first among Paul's letters, but also prefaced them with his *Antitheses* in order to "set out the fundamental rubrics and themes under and through which Marcion interpreted Paul."[26] I suggest that, in response to Marcionite and other readings of Paul, those responsible for the current shape of the New Testament believed that Luke's portrayal of Paul in the Acts of the Apostles best introduced his thought to readers of his letters.[27] To be clear, I do not think that most of the Christians involved in bringing the New Testament into its current shape were aware of (or would have approved of the fact) that Luke portrays a law-observant Paul, so it is unlikely that they would have seen Acts functioning as the kind of key to Paul's letters that I am proposing here. Nonetheless, as C. Kavin Rowe notes, "Hermeneutically, it is crucial to understand that, for Luke, Paul is a 'reliable' character; indeed, he is the human protagonist of much of Acts." Being a reliable character, his statements function as "an interpretive guide" to Luke's narrative. Although others within Luke's narrative world claim that he breaks the Jewish law and teaches Jews to do so, Luke intends the claims of Paul and the Jerusalem leadership to be understood as truthful and trustworthy voices.[28] From an immanent-critical or canonical-critical position, Rowe's claim that Luke's Paul is a reliable character and an interpretive guide to the narrative of Acts should be extended for those readers for whom Acts is Christian Scripture: the Paul of Acts ought to be considered a reliable interpretive guide to the letters of Paul for anyone who considers both Acts and Paul's letters to be scripture.

To put it bluntly, either Luke is wrong or both anti-legalist and anti-ethnocentric understandings of Paul are wrong. Of course, historians should have no qualms about concluding that a source such as Acts may be historically inaccurate. But, to my knowledge, neither proponents of the so-called Lutheran interpretation of Paul nor proponents of the so-called new perspective on Paul read either Luke or Paul as historical evidence alone. Both groups are generally, perhaps universally even, committed to reading Paul and the rest of the New Testament as a theological resource for contemporary Christian appropriation. Surely it is an odd incongruity, then, that, while the shape of the New Testament places Luke's account of Paul in a position where it implicitly functions as the hermeneutical key to Paul's letters, virtually all subsequent Christian interpretations of Paul have chosen to reject Luke's interpretive guide in favor of a position that is equivalent to those voices in Acts that Luke, through the words of the Jerusalem leaders and Paul, claims are incorrect.[29] Ironically, these readings of Paul, both of which originated and largely exist within ecclesial contexts, set him in opposition to the canonical introduction to his writings. From within an immanentist position, I am suggesting that Christian communities and scholars should be troubled by this fact and need to rethink their cherished readings of Paul in light of the tensions such readings create with their own sacred scriptures.[30]

In contrast, the "conjuring" of Paul that I have offered in this book coincides nicely with much of what Luke has to say about Paul. As I noted in the Introduction, my own thinking on Paul is in many ways indebted to what scholars have often referred to as the radical new perspective on Paul, a position particularly associated with the work of Lloyd Gaston, John Gager, and Stanley K. Stowers. What is yet one more irony, though, is that this radical new perspective fails to live up to its name. It is neither new, since Luke had already portrayed Paul in ways that anticipated the work of these scholars,[31] nor is it radical, inasmuch as Christian tradition situated Luke's portrayal of a law-observant Paul within its authoritative canon. This misnomer should, consequently, be abandoned in favor of a new and more accurate name—one that stresses, with Luke and the New Testament canon, that Paul can only be understood *within* Judaism, and not *against* it.[32]

# *Notes*

INTRODUCTION

1. Quotations come from Gautam Malkani, *Londonstani* (London: Fourth Estate, 2006), 5–6.
2. Scholarship continues to argue over the question of how best to translate the Greek word *Ioudaios*: should it be rendered "Jew" or "Judean." I translate *Ioudaios* as "Jew" throughout this book, since, as Daniel R. Schwartz argues ("'Judaean' or 'Jew'? How Should We Translate *Ioudaios* in Josephus?," in *Jewish Identity in the Greco-Roman World/Jüdische Identität in der griechisch-römischen Welt*, ed. Jörg Frey, Daniel R. Schwartz, and Stephanie Gripentrog [AGJU 71; Leiden: Brill, 2007], 3–27), rendering the word in English as "Jew" captures for the modern reader many of the same ambiguities that would have faced those in the Second Temple period when asked what one meant by *Ioudaios*.
3. For minority ethnic identity construction, see Ian S. Moyer, *Egypt and the Limits of Hellenism* (Cambridge, UK: Cambridge University Press, 2011), and Mary T. Boatwright, *Peoples of the Roman World* (Cambridge Introduction to Roman Civilization; Cambridge, UK: Cambridge University Press, 2012). On the construction of Greek and Roman identity, see Jonathan M. Hall, *Ethnic Identity in Greek Antiquity* (Cambridge, UK: Cambridge University Press, 1997); idem, *Hellenicity: Between Ethnicity and Culture* (Chicago: University of Chicago Press, 2002); Ray Laurence and Joanne Berry, eds., *Cultural Identity in the Roman Empire* (London: Routledge, 1998); Irad Malkin, ed., *Ancient Perceptions of Greek Ethnicity* (Center for Hellenic Studies, Colloquia 5; Washington, DC: Center for Hellenic Studies, 2001); David Konstan and Suzanne Saïd, eds., *Greeks on Greekness: Viewing the Greek Past under the Roman Empire* (Cambridge, UK: Cambridge Philological Society, 2006); and Andrew Wallace-Hadrill, *Rome's Cultural Revolution* (Cambridge, UK: Cambridge University Press, 2008).
4. See, for instance, John M. G. Barclay, *Jews in the Mediterranean Diaspora: From Alexander to Trajan (323 BCE–117 CE)* (HCS 33; Berkeley: University of California Press, 1996); Erich S. Gruen, *Heritage and Hellenism: The Reinvention of Jewish Tradition* (HCS 30; Berkeley: University of California Press, 1998); Shaye J. D. Cohen, *The Beginnings of Jewishness: Boundaries, Varieties, Uncertainties* (HCS 31; Berkeley: University of California Press, 1999); John J. Collins, *Between Athens*

*and Jerusalem: Jewish Identity in the Hellenistic Diaspora*, 2d ed. (Biblical Resource Series; Grand Rapids: Eerdmans, 2000); Jörg Frey, Daniel R. Schwartz, and Stephanie Gripentrog, eds., *Jewish Identity in the Greco-Roman World/Jüdische Identität in der griechisch-römischen Welt* (AGJU 71; Leiden: Brill, 2007); Lee I. Levine and Daniel R. Schwartz, eds., *Jewish Identities in Antiquity: Studies in Memory of Menahem Stern* (TSAJ 130; Tübingen: Mohr Siebeck, 2009); and Benedikt Eckhardt, *Ethnos und Herrschaft: Politische Figurationen judäischer Identität von Antiochos III. bis Herodes I* (SJ 72; Berlin: de Gruyter, 2013). Such constructions of Jewishness were part of a broader trend within the Greco-Roman world. For the need to understand Paul within a hellenistic context and, like all Jews of his day, as a hellenized Jew, see the important essays in Troels Engberg-Pedersen, ed., *Paul in His Hellenistic Context* (Minneapolis: Augsburg Fortress, 1995), and idem, ed., *Paul Beyond the Judaism/Hellenism Divide* (Louisville: Westminster John Knox, 2001).

5. Chapter 2 will examine Rom 2:28–29 in more depth, but the interpretation of Gal 6:16 lies outside the main arguments of this book. For a convincing argument that Paul does not redefine Israel as the Christian Church in this verse, see Susan Eastman, "Israel and the Mercy of God: A Re-reading of Galatians 6.16 and Romans 9–11," *NTS* 56 (2010): 367–95.

6. Quotations come from Malkani, *Londonstani*, 340.

7. Iser, *The Act of Reading: A Theory of Aesthetic Response* (Baltimore: Johns Hopkins University Press, 1978), 125. See also idem, *The Implied Reader: Patterns of Communication in Prose Fiction from Bunyan to Beckett* (Baltimore: Johns Hopkins University Press, 1974).

8. My own reading deals almost entirely with the evidence of Romans, Galatians, and 1–2 Corinthians, although I will at times note the evidence of Colossians and Ephesians, since these are among the earliest receptions and interpretations of Paul's thinking.

9. Anders Runesson ("The Question of Terminology: The Architecture of Contemporary Discussions on Paul," in *Paul within Judaism: Restoring the First-Century Context to the Apostle*, ed. Mark D. Nanos and Magnus Zetterholm [Minneapolis: Fortress, 2015], 53–77) has convinced me that we must abandon the common habit of translating the Greek term *ekklēsia* as "church" in Paul's letters. Runesson rightly notes: "When we hear 'church,' we associate the term with a *non-Jewish Christian religious* institution. But this was not what Paul and his contemporaries heard when *ekklēsia* could be a referent to a democratic-like Greek or Roman institution, a Jewish public institution, or a Jewish voluntary association" (71–72). Consequently, I will consistently use "assembly" to translate *ekklēsia*. Cf. Jennifer Eyl, "Semantic Voids, New Testament Translation, and Anachronism: The Case of Paul's Use of *Ekklēsia*," *MTSR* 26 (2014): 315–39.

10. John M. G. Barclay, "Mirror-Reading a Polemical Letter: Galatians as a Test Case," *JSNT* 31 (1987): 73–93. For one ambitious example, see J. Louis Martyn, *Theological Issues in the Letters of Paul* (Nashville: Abingdon, 1997), 7–24.

11. Quotations in this paragraph come from Malkani, *Londonstani*, 175, 197, and 261.

12. See, for instance, Richard B. Hays, *Echoes of Scripture in the Letters of Paul* (New Haven: Yale University Press, 1989), and Francis Watson, *Paul and the Hermeneutics of Faith* (London: T&T Clark, 2004).

13. Another translation problem that confronts Paul's readers is the term τὰ ἔθνη. Outside of Jewish literature, the term just means "the nations." While the term can have this same meaning in Jewish literature, translating the Hebrew phrase

for the nations (הגוים), it frequently is used as a catch-all category for non-Jews. There is no simple solution to its translation into English. Paula Fredriksen ("The Question of Worship: Gods, Pagans, and the Redemption of Israel," in *Paul within Judaism: Restoring the First-Century Context to the Apostle*, ed. Mark D. Nanos and Magnus Zetterholm [Minneapolis: Fortress, 2015], 175–201) prefers the term "pagans," which, although anachronistic, does helpfully convey the fact that these peoples were, from a Jewish perspective, guilty of worshipping false gods. I prefer to render it as "gentiles" instead of "Gentiles," so as to avoid giving the mistaken impression that those referred to by the term constituted a unified ethnicity. See Terence L. Donaldson, " 'Gentile Christianity' as a Category in the Study of Christian Origins," *HTR* 106 (2013): 433–58.

14. Räisänen, *Paul and the Law* (Philadelphia: Fortress, 1983), 10–11. For a criticism of this conclusion, see Douglas A. Campbell, *The Quest for Paul's Gospel: A Suggested Strategy* (London: T&T Clark, 2005), 29–34.

15. Gager, *Reinventing Paul* (Oxford: Oxford University Press, 2000), 11.

16. Because these common titles confuse at least as much as they enlighten, I prefer to call the so-called "Lutheran" reading an "anti-legalistic" reading of Paul and the so-called "new perspective" reading an "anti-ethnocentric" reading of Paul. First, numerous non-Lutherans hold to the "Lutheran" perspective on Paul. As Douglas A. Campbell (*The Deliverance of God: An Apocalyptic Rereading of Justification in Paul* [Grand Rapids: Eerdmans, 2009], 249) argues, "Attacks on the 'Lutheran' reading of Paul are needlessly inflammatory in denominational terms and ought to be abandoned. Lutherans do not have a monopoly on misreading Paul." Second, a number of Lutherans, most notably Krister Stendahl who was the Bishop of Stockholm for the Lutheran Church of Sweden, do not fit into the "Lutheran" camp. In fact, recent Finnish scholarship on Martin Luther has attempted to demonstrate that Luther's own thought does not quite fit what NT scholars call the "Lutheran" perspective. Cf. Carl E. Braaten and Robert W. Jenson, eds., *Union with Christ: The New Finnish Interpretation of Luther* (Grand Rapids: Eerdmans, 1998), and Tuomo Mannermaa, *Christ Present in Faith: Luther's View of Justification* (Minneapolis: Fortress, 2005).

Issues abound with the title "new perspective" as well. For instance, it is becoming increasingly absurd to call the position of this school "new" when its two most prolific authors, James D. G. Dunn and N. T. Wright, first began articulating this perspective in the early 1980s. After all, as novel and popular as the Commodore 64 was in 1982, we neither consider nor call it new. Making matters even worse, their own accounts, which contrast Pauline universalism to Jewish particularlism, have much in common with the early nineteenth-century work of F. C. Baur. For instance, Baur (*Paul the Apostle of Jesus Christ: His Life and Works, His Epistles and Teachings; A Contribution to a Critical History of Primitive Christianity*, trans. A. Menzies, 2 vols. [London: Williams & Norgate, 1873], 1:308–9) can claim that Paul's purpose in Romans was "to remove the last remnants of Jewish particularism."

Finally, some scholarship does not fit into either of these two camps. Well before the rise of the so-called new perspective, some German scholars advocated a mystical account of Paul's theology that opposed traditional Lutheran readings. See, for example, Gustav Adolf Deissmann, *St Paul: A Study in Social and Religious History*, trans. Lionel R. M. Strachan (London: Hodder & Stoughton, 1912); William Wrede, *Paul*, trans. Edward Lummis (London: Philip Green, 1907); and Albert Schweitzer, *The Mysticism of Paul the Apostle*, trans.

William Montgomery (Baltimore: Johns Hopkins University Press, 1953). Most scholars now eschew the use of the word "mysticism" in relation to Paul's thinking, preferring the category of participation. See E. P. Sanders, *Paul and Palestinian Judaism: A Comparison of Patterns of Religion* (Philadelphia: Fortress, 1977), and Campbell, *Deliverance of God*. As Chapters 4 and 5 make clear, my own reading of Paul is greatly indebted to this stream of interpretation. On the variety of contemporary approaches to Paul and the Jewish law, see the helpful introduction of Magnus Zetterholm, *Approaches to Paul: A Student's Guide to Recent Scholarship* (Minneapolis: Fortress, 2009).

17.  For a succinct discussion of Luther's understanding of Paul, see Stephen Westerholm, *Perspectives Old and New on Paul: The "Lutheran" Paul and His Critics* (Grand Rapids: Eerdmans, 2004), 22–41. For recent attempts to defend this interpretation, see, among others, Westerholm, *Perspectives Old and New*; Peter Stuhlmacher, *Revisiting Paul's Doctrine of Justification: A Challenge to the New Perspective* (Downers Grove, IL: InterVarsity Press, 2001); and Donald A. Carson, Peter T. O'Brien, and Mark A. Seifrid, eds., *The Paradoxes of Paul* (vol. 2 of *Justification and Variegated Nomism*; Grand Rapids: Baker Academic, 2004).

18.  A refreshing counter-example within the anti-legalist camp is Stephen Westerholm, "Righteousness, Cosmic and Microcosmic," in *Apocalyptic Paul: Cosmos and Anthropos in Romans 5–8*, ed. Beverly Roberts Gaventa (Waco, TX: Baylor University Press, 2013), 21–38. Westerholm rightly argues that neither Jewish scriptures nor Paul himself thought people needed to keep the Jewish law perfectly. Instead, Westerholm believes that Paul's anthropological pessimism, which arose out of his understanding of the Christ event, led him to conclude that all humans were deeply and incorrigibly sinful and beyond recourse to the Jewish law and the means of atonement it provided. He concludes (32): "even among non-Christ believing Jews, the rites of atonement were thought to apply, not to high-handed sinners, but only to those living basically within the terms of the covenant (cf. Num 15:30–31). For Paul, however, the sinfulness of *all humankind* is radical."

19.  Bultmann, *Primitive Christianity in its Contemporary Setting*, trans. R. H. Fuller (New York: World, 1956), 66. Martin Luther, *A Commentary on St. Paul's Epistle to the Galatians*, trans. Philip S. Watson (Cambridge, UK: James Clarke, 1953), 477. On this tension between boasting and despair see Bultmann, *Theology of the New Testament*, trans. Kendrick Grobel, 2 vols. (London: SCM, 1952), 1:242–44, and the critical discussion of Campbell, *Deliverance of God*, 18–24. Following in Bultmann's footsteps, Richard H. Bell (*The Irrevocable Call of God: An Inquiry into Paul's Theology of Israel* [WUNT 184; Tübingen: Mohr Siebeck, 2005], 146) claims that "if the Jew fulfils the law from A to Z, that is one of the gravest sins he could commit. For the pious Jew then boasts in his performance and feels he has a claim upon God." On this reading, Jews are damned if they do fulfill the law, and damned if they don't.

20.  Hans Joachim Schoeps (*Paul: The Theology of the Apostle in the Light of Jewish Religious History*, trans. Harold Knight [Philadelphia: Westminster, 1961], 28–32), for instance, argues that Paul misunderstands Judaism due to the LXX translators of Jewish scriptures, who wrongly translated *torah* ("instruction") as *nomos* ("law"), thereby importing a foreign legalism into Judaism.

21.  Moore, "Christian Writers on Judaism," *HTR* 14 (1921): 197–254. See also the work of Jewish scholars such as Solomon Schechter, *Some Aspects of Rabbinic Theology* (New York: Macmillan, 1909), and Claude G. Montefiore, *Judaism and St. Paul: Two Essays* (London: Goschen, 1914).

22. See Markus Barth, "Jews and Gentiles: The Social Character of Justification in Paul," *JES* 5 (1968): 241–67, and Krister Stendahl, *Paul Among the Jews and Gentiles, and Other Essays* (Philadelphia: Fortress, 1976).

23. Sanders, *Paul and Palestinian Judaism*, 75. See also Gary A. Anderson, *Sacrifices and Offerings in Ancient Israel: Studies in their Social and Political Importance* (HSM 41; Atlanta: Scholars Press, 1987), and idem, *Sin: A History* (New Haven: Yale University Press, 2009).

24. Howard, *Paul: Crisis in Galatia. A Study in Early Christian Theology*, 2d ed. (SNTSMS 35; Cambridge, UK: Cambridge University Press, 1990), 53.

25. Sanders's own reading of Paul, which stresses "real participation" in Christ, fits more closely with Schweitzer's mystical reading of Paul, than it does with an anti-ethnocentric account of Paul.

26. See, most recently, James D. G. Dunn, *The New Perspective on Paul*, rev. ed. (Grand Rapids: Eerdmans, 2008), and N. T. Wright, *Paul and the Faithfulness of God* (Minneapolis: Fortress, 2013).

27. Dunn, *New Perspective on Paul*, 79. John M. G. Barclay's recent work on grace/gift in Paul underscores this same point. See, for instance, "Under Grace: The Christ-Gift and the Construction of a Christian *Habitus*," in *Apocalyptic Paul: Cosmos and Anthropos in Romans 5–8*, ed. Beverly Roberts Gaventa (Waco, TX: Baylor University Press, 2013), 59–76 (60), in which he concludes: "There is no neutral zone in Paul's cosmos, no pocket of absolute freedom, no no-man's land between the two fronts. The gift of God in Jesus Christ has established not liberation from authority or demand, but a new allegiance, a new responsibility, a new 'slavery' under the rule of grace. Although not itself an imperative, grace is imperatival: it bears within itself the imperative to obey."

28. On Pauline ethics, see John M. G. Barclay, *Obeying the Truth: A Study of Paul's Ethics in Galatians* (SNTW; Edinburgh: T&T Clark, 1988). As Barclay concludes elsewhere ("Paul, the Gift and the Battle over Gentile Circumcision," *ABR* 58 [2010]: 36–56 [54–55]) with regard to works in Galatians, "Against the Lutheran tradition, it is important to insist that these works are not just the after-effect of justifying faith, but integral to it: without these practical expressions of faith, so-called faith is simply hypocrisy (as Paul says regarding Peter, 2:13). The person reconstituted in Christ (2:19–20) is not established 'before and without works,' but is formed precisely in and through works: πίστις in Galatians entails not just faith or trust in Christ but also loyalty or allegiance to the Christ-event."

29. Gager, *Reinventing Paul*, 49, and Dunn's response in *New Perspective on Paul*, 32 n. 122. Likewise, Barclay ("Paul, the Gift," 45) rightly notes that "most of the weight in Dunn's argument in fact rests on a set of Enlightenment and 20th-century social values, concerning universalism, inclusion and diversity, retrojected onto Paul."

30. Dunn, *New Perspective on Paul*, 417 (cf. pages 35, 205). Surely one cannot simply equate the physical violence implied in Dunn's "otherwise" with conversion—not all forms of missionizing are equally violent. Here, I imagine that Dunn is indebted to a healthy sensitivity to the way in which Christian missionizing has historically been complicit in British and European imperialism.

31. Denise Kimber Buell and Caroline Johnson Hodge, "The Politics of Interpretation: The Rhetoric of Race and Ethnicity in Paul," *JBL* 123 (2004): 235–51 (244) and Gregory Tatum, " 'To The Jew First' (Rom 1:16): Paul's Defense of Jewish Privilege in Romans," in *Celebrating Paul: Festschrift in Honor of Jerome Murphy-O'Connor, O.P., and Joseph A. Fitzmyer, S.J.*, ed. Peter Spitaler

(CBQMS 48; Washington, DC: Catholic Biblical Association of America, 2011), 275–86.

32. Rosen-Zvi and Ophir, "Paul and the Invention of the Gentiles," *JQR* 105 (2015): 1–41 (21).

33. Barth, ed., *Ethnic Groups and Boundaries: The Social Organization of Culture Difference* (Boston: Little, Brown, 1969). See also the various essays in John Hutchinson and Anthony D. Smith, eds., *Ethnicity* (Oxford Readers; Oxford: Oxford University Press, 1996), as well as Anthony D. Smith, *Chosen Peoples: Sacred Sources of National Identity* (Oxford: Oxford University Press, 2003), and idem, *The Antiquity of Nations* (Cambridge, UK: Polity, 2004).

34. Matlock, "'Jews by Nature': Paul, Ethnicity, and Galatians," in *Far From Minimal: Celebrating the Work and Influence of Philip R. Davies*, ed. Duncan Burns and J. W. Rogerson (LHB/OTS 484; London: T&T Clark, 2012), 304–15.

35. For this reason, throughout this monograph I use the term "ethnic" (e.g., "ethnic Israel," "ethnic Jews") to refer to genealogical descent. To be clear, this is not because I think genealogical or biological descent is not socially constructed, whereas other ethnic markers are. After all, Jews in Paul's day debated what form of genealogical descent—patrilineal, matrilineal, or bilineal—made one a Jew, as Shaye J. D. Cohen shows in "The Origins of the Matrilineal Principle in Rabbinic Law," *AJSR* 10 (1985): 19–53.

36. See, for instance, Daniel Boyarin, *Border Lines: The Partition of Judaeo-Christianity* (Divinations; Philadelphia: University of Pennsylvania Press, 2004), and Paula Fredriksen and Oded Irshai, "Christian Anti-Judaism: Polemics and Policies," in *The Late Roman-Rabbinic Period*, ed. Steven T. Katz (vol. 4 of *The Cambridge History of Judaism*; Cambridge, UK: Cambridge University Press, 2006), 977–1035. As readers will see, not infrequently I refer to early Christian interpretations of Paul's letters as additional support for my own arguments. My use of this literature is admittedly selective, and motivated in part by the desire to demonstrate that my arguments, while no doubt influenced by my own post-Holocaust sensitivities, at times have pre-Holocaust precedents. These early Christian interpretations, then, serve as one response to Wright's dismissal (*Paul and the Faithfulness of God*, 51) of certain trends within modern Pauline scholarship: "Our moral sensitivities have been so battered by the events of the twentieth century that every time we come within a few paces of such questions [regarding the relationship between Paul's gospel and ethnic Israel] we fear a further bruising, and can hardly bring ourselves to speak the truth about what Paul actually said in case he be accused, even at several removes and only by implication, of complicity in appalling crimes." What is more, I use early Christian writers who are, each in their own way, deeply anti-Jewish and opposed to aspects of the Jewish law, such as circumcision, in order to show that, despite their own theological presuppositions, their readings at times undermine these anti-Jewish presuppositions.

37. See Adam H. Becker and Annette Yoshiko Reed, eds., *The Ways That Never Parted: Jews and Christians in Late Antiquity and the Early Middle Ages* (Minneapolis: Fortress, 2007). On Paul's relationship to Judaism, see Pamela Eisenbaum, *Paul Was Not a Christian: The Original Message of a Misunderstood Apostle* (New York: HarperOne, 2009). Scholars generally recognize that "religion" as a distinct discourse is a significantly later invention. Peter Harrison (*"Religion" and the Religions in the English Enlightenment* [Cambridge, UK: Cambridge University Press, 1990]), Talal Asad (*Genealogies*

*of Religion: Discipline and Reasons of Power in Christianity and Islam*
[Baltimore: Johns Hopkins University Press, 1993]), Tomoko Masuzawa (*The
Invention of World Religions: Or, How European Universalism Was Preserved in
the Language of Pluralism* [Chicago: University of Chicago Press, 2005]), and
Brent Nongbri (*Before Religion: A History of a Modern Concept* [New Haven: Yale
University Press, 2013]), for instance, date the invention of "religion" to
the Enlightenment, although Daniel Boyarin ("The Christian Invention of
Judaism: The Theodosian Empire and the Rabbinic Refusal of Religion,"
*Representations* 85 [2004]: 21–57) has made a strong case for a much earlier date
in the fifth century CE.

38. Cf. Campbell, *Deliverance of God*, 36–95.

39. On epispasm, the process of removing one's circumcision, see 1 Macc 1:14–15,
    *T. Mos.* 8.3, and Josephus, *Ant.* 12.240–241, as well as the discussions of
    Robert G. Hall, "Epispasm and the Dating of Ancient Jewish Writings," *JSP* 1
    (1988): 71–86; idem, "Epispasm: Circumcision in *Reverse*," *BRev* 8 (1992): 52–57;
    and Andreas Blaschke, *Beschneidung: Zeugnisse der Bibel und verwandter Texte*
    (TANZ 28; Tübingen: Francke, 1998), 139–44. David J. Rudolph (*A Jew to the
    Jews: Jewish Contours of Pauline Flexibility in 1 Corinthians 9:19–23* [WUNT 2/304;
    Tübingen: Mohr Siebeck, 2011], 80–81) argues that Paul means "do not put on
    foreskin" (μὴ ἐπισπάσθω) metonymically, signifying his desire that Jews-in-Christ
    would not abandon Jewish practices.

40. Sanders, *Paul, the Law, and the Jewish People* (Minneapolis: Fortress, 1983), 103.

41. Barrett, *A Commentary on the First Epistle to the Corinthians*, 2d ed. (BNTC;
    London: Black, 1971), 169. Reading the verse in a similar way, Wright (*Paul and
    the Faithfulness of God*, 361) concludes that 1 Cor 7:19 is "almost Zen-like in its
    density of redefinition," and demonstrates "that Paul had a sense of humour." I
    doubt that Paul's initial readers would have gotten the joke.

42. See Frank Thielman, "The Coherence of Paul's View of the Law: The Evidence
    of First Corinthians," *NTS* 38 (1992): 235–53.

43. Marcus, "The Circumcision and the Uncircumcision in Rome," *NTS* 35
    (1989): 67–81.

44. In his discussion of Peter's statement that, by giving the Holy Spirit, God made
    no distinction between Jews and gentiles (Acts 15:9), Chrysostom (*Homilies
    on the Acts of the Apostles* 32 [*Nicene and Post-Nicene Fathers*, Series 1, 11:203])
    cites 1 Cor 7:19, demonstrating that he also understands these terms to refer to
    Jewishness and gentileness.

45. Huttunen, *Paul and Epictetus on Law: A Comparison* (LNTS 405; London: T&T
    Clark, 2009), 22–31.

46. Barclay, "Paul, the Gift," 52–53.

47. Huttunen, *Paul and Epictetus on Law*, 28. Regarding the possibility that God
    might have two different sets of commandments, Campbell (*Deliverance of God*,
    42) asserts, "As a matter of strict justice, a prohibition (or a positive command-
    ment) cannot be valid for one group but simultaneously invalid for another. . . .
    There is really no such thing as an *optional* right action prescribed by God." Paul
    and his contemporaries would disagree: the existence of two sets of command-
    ments does not necessarily signify that one set is optional; rather, each set is
    incumbent upon a different group of people.

48. Campbell, "Gentile Identity and Transformation in Christ according to Paul," in
    *The Making of Christianity: Conflicts, Contacts, and Constructions: Essays in Honor
    of Bengt Holmberg*, ed. Magnus Zetterholm and Samuel Byrskog (ConBNT 47;

Winona Lake, IN: Eisenbrauns, 2012), 23–55 (24). Similarly, Peter J. Tomson, *Paul and the Jewish Law: Halakha in the Letters of the Apostle to the Gentiles* (CRINT 1; Assen: Van Gorcum, 1990), 271–72; idem, "Paul's Jewish Background in View of His Law Teaching in 1 Cor 7," in *Paul and the Mosaic Law*, ed. James D. G. Dunn (Grand Rapids: Eerdmans, 2001), 251–70; idem, "Halakhah in the New Testament: A Research Overview," in *The New Testament and Rabbinic Literature*, ed. Reimund Bieringer et al. (JSJSup 136; Leiden: Brill, 2010), 135–206 (204–5); Markus Bockmuehl, *Jewish Law in Gentile Churches: Halakhah and the Beginning of Christian Public Ethics* (Grand Rapids: Baker Academic, 2000), 170–71; Gudrun Holtz, *Damit Gott sei alles in allem: Studien zum paulinischen und frühjüdischen Universalismus* (BZNW 149; Berlin: de Gruyter, 2007), 247–50; Anders Runesson, "Inventing Christian Identity: Paul, Ignatius, and Theodosius I," in *Exploring Early Christian Identity*, ed. Bengt Holmberg (WUNT 226; Tübingen: Mohr Siebeck, 2008), 59–92 (80–81); idem, "Paul's Rule in All the *Ekklēsiai* (1 Cor 7:17–24)," in *Introduction to Messianic Judaism: Its Ecclesial Context and Biblical Foundations*, ed. David Rudolph and Joel Willitts (Grand Rapids: Zondervan, 2013), 214–23; and David J. Rudolph, "Paul's 'Rule in All the Churches' (1 Cor 7:17–24) and Torah-Defined Ecclesiological Variegation," *Studies in Christian-Jewish Relations* 5 (2010): 1–24.

49. Eisenbaum, *Paul Was Not a Christian*, 62–63.

50. Others who belong within this stream of interpretation include Lloyd Gaston, *Paul and the Torah* (Vancouver: University of British Columbia Press, 1987); Gager, *Reinventing Paul*; Stanley K. Stowers, *A Rereading of Romans: Justice, Jews, and Gentiles* (New Haven: Yale University Press, 1994); and Caroline Johnson Hodge, *If Sons, Then Heirs: A Study of Kinship and Ethnicity in the Letters of Paul* (Oxford: Oxford University Press, 2007).

51. Mark D. Nanos and Magnus Zetterholm, eds., *Paul within Judaism: Restoring the First-Century Context to the Apostle* (Minneapolis: Fortress, 2015).

52. For instance, Stowers, *Rereading of Romans*; Runar M. Thorsteinsson, *Paul's Interlocutor in Romans 2: Function and Identity in the Context of Ancient Epistolography* (ConBNT 40; Stockholm: Almqvist & Wiksell, 2003); Paula Fredriksen, "Paul, Purity, and the *Ekklēsia* of the Gentiles," in *The Beginnings of Christianity: A Collection of Articles*, ed. Jack Pastor and Menachem Mor (Jerusalem: Yad Ben-Zvi, 2005), 205–17; and Johnson Hodge, *If Sons, Then Heirs*.

53. Admittedly, Paul does speak in 1 Cor 9:19–23 of becoming a Jew to Jews, which likely signifies that he used different rhetorical tactics when speaking to Jews. Even though Paul believed himself to be the apostle to the gentiles, it is historically implausible that he never had to explain his message and actions to some of his Jewish contemporaries. In such instances, he no doubt defended himself and presented his gospel in ways that would portray it in the best light to his fellow Jews. On understanding this passage to refer to different rhetorical strategies, see Abraham J. Malherbe, "Antisthenes and Odysseus, and Paul at War," *HTR* 76 (1983): 143–73; Clarence E. Glad, *Paul and Philodemus: Adaptability in Epicurean and Early Christian Psychology* (NovTSup 81; Leiden: Brill, 1995); Margaret M. Mitchell, "Pauline Accommodation and 'Condescension' (συγκατάβασις): 1 Cor 9:19–23 and the History of Influence," in *Paul Beyond the Judaism/Hellenism Divide*, ed. Troels Engberg-Pedersen (Louisville: Westminster John Knox, 2001), 197–214; Mark D. Nanos, "Paul's Relationship to Torah in Light of his Strategy 'to Become Everything to Everyone,'" in *Paul and Judaism: Crosscurrents in Pauline Exegesis and the Study*

*of Jewish-Christian Relations*, ed. Reimund Bieringer and Didier Pollefeyt (LNTS 463; London: T&T Clark, 2012), 106–40; and Rudolph, *Jew to the Jews*.

54. Nock, *Conversion: The Old and the New in Religion from Alexander the Great to Augustine of Hippo* (London: Oxford University Press, 1933), 13.

55. Fredriksen, "Judaism, the Circumcision of Gentiles, and Apocalyptic Hope: Another Look at Galatians 1–2," *JTS* 42 (1991): 532–64 (533–34).

56. On Josephus as an historically important witness to the theologies of these three groups, see Jonathan Klawans, *Josephus and the Theologies of Ancient Judaism* (Oxford: Oxford University Press, 2012).

57. E. P. Sanders (*Judaism: Practice and Belief, 63 BCE–66 CE* [London: SCM, 1992]) has argued that enough beliefs and practices were shared to speak of a "Common Judaism," while Jacob Neusner (e.g., *Formative Judaism: Religious, Historical and Literary Studies: Third Series: Torah, Pharisees, and Rabbis* [BJS 46; Chico, CA: Scholars Press, 1983]) prefers to speak of "Judaisms," in order to stress how diffuse early Judaism was. This debate signals the need to understand Jewishness in non-essentialist ways—something of critical importance for thinking about Paul's Jewishness, as Pamela Eisenbaum has argued in "Paul, Polemics, and the Problem of Essentialism," *BibInt* 13 (2005): 224–38.

58. Segal, *Paul the Convert: The Apostolate and Apostasy of Saul the Pharisee* (New Haven: Yale University Press, 1990), 79.

59. Donaldson, *Judaism and the Gentiles: Jewish Patterns of Universalism (to 135 CE)* (Waco, TX: Baylor University Press, 2007). See also David C. Sim and James S. McLaren, eds., *Attitudes to Gentiles in Ancient Judaism and Early Christianity* (LNTS 499; London: T&T Clark, 2014).

60. See Matthew Thiessen, *Contesting Conversion: Genealogy, Circumcision, and Identity in Ancient Judaism and Christianity* (Oxford: Oxford University Press, 2011).

61. See Paula Fredriksen, "Mandatory Retirement: Ideas in the Study of Christian Origins Whose Time Has Come to Go," *SR* 35 (2006): 231–46.

62. For Paul's criticisms of his fellow Jews, see Matthew V. Novenson, "The Self-Styled Jew of Romans 2 and the Actual Jews of Romans 9–11," in *The So-Called Jew in Paul's Letter to the Romans*, ed. Rafael Rodríguez and Matthew Thiessen (Minneapolis: Fortress, 2016) 133–62.

63. Thus, while I agree with the overall arguments of Mark D. Nanos ("The Question of Conceptualization: Qualifying Paul's Position on Circumcision in Dialogue with Josephus's Advisors to King Izates," in *Paul within Judaism: Restoring the First-Century Context to the Apostle*, ed. Mark D. Nanos and Magnus Zetterholm [Minneapolis: Fortress, 2015], 105–52), I differ in arguing that Paul did not merely think that gentiles should not undergo circumcision. Rather, I believe that Paul was convinced that any gentile who underwent circumcision remained a gentile and therefore benefited in no way from the rite. Cavan W. Concannon (*"When You Were Gentiles": Specters of Ethnicity in Roman Corinth and Paul's Corinthian Correspondence* [Synkrisis; New Haven: Yale University Press, 2014], 30–31) makes suggestive comments along these lines, as does Christine Hayes, *What's Divine about Divine Law? Early Perspectives* (Princeton: Princeton University Press, 2015), 141–52.

64. Sanders, *Paul and Palestinian Judaism*, 474–75.

65. Similarly, Westerholm ("Righteousness, Cosmic and Microcosmic," 33): "Paul was no pessimist by nature. But he had come to see that the divine remedy for human sinfulness was the crucifixion of the Messiah. So catastrophic a remedy

demands a catastrophic predicament." My one quibble with Westerholm is that I think that the Christ event caused Paul to rethink the *gentile* predicament, not humanity's predicament. At the same time, as Romans 9–11 shows, the Christ event and subsequent stumbling of many Jews causes a change in the Jewish situation, which Paul found deeply distressing.

66. Of course, there are significant problems with such terms. See Anders Runesson, "Particularistic Judaism and Universalistic Christianity? Some Critical Remarks on Terminology and Theology," *JGRChJ* 1 (2000): 120–44; Denise Kimber Buell, *Why This New Race: Ethnic Reasoning in Early Christianity* (New York: Columbia University Press, 2005); and eadem, "Challenges and Strategies for Speaking about Ethnicity in the New Testament and New Testament Studies," *SEÅ* 79 (2014): 33–51. Recently, Hayes (*What's Divine about Divine Law?*, 151) has characterized Paul's perspective as an "exclusivistic view of Gentile inclusion."

67. Johnson Hodge, *If Sons, Then Heirs.*

68. Paula Fredriksen ("The Question of Worship," 187) rightly states: "*Paul's pagans-in-Christ are neither converts nor god-fearers.* So who and what are they? In the social (thus religious) context of the ancient city, such people were, precisely, nothing. Neither 'Jews' of a special sort (that is, *prosēlytoi*) nor 'normal' pagans (that is, people who showed respect to their own gods), they occupied a social and religious no-man's land. *Eschatologically*, however, they represented a population long anticipated within centuries of Jewish restoration theology; they were pagans-saved-at-the-End." I agree that Paul sees his assemblies as fulfilling the long-expected Jewish hope for gentiles at the eschaton, but nowhere outside of Paul are such gentiles portrayed as becoming Abrahamic sons and seed. Here I agree with Terence L. Donaldson ("Paul within Judaism: A Critical Evaluation from a 'New Perspective' Perspective," in *Paul within Judaism: Restoring the First-Century Context to the Apostle*, ed. Mark D. Nanos and Magnus Zetterholm [Minneapolis: Fortress, 2015], 277–301 [296]), who concludes that "the truly anomalous aspect is Paul['s] insistence that uncircumcised *ethnē*-in-Christ are at the same time full members of Abraham's 'seed' (*sperma*)."

69. Donaldson, "Paul within Judaism," 299 n. 39.

### CHAPTER 1

1. Barclay, "Mirror-Reading a Polemical Letter: Galatians as a Test Case," *JSNT* 31 (1987): 73–93 (81). On the way in which Christian accounts of Judaism have changed in order to confront different theological concerns, see George Foot Moore, "Christian Writers on Judaism," *HTR* 14 (1921): 197–254. Although fitting within the anti-legalist reading of Paul tradition associated with Martin Luther, Peter Stuhlmacher (*Revisiting Paul's Doctrine of Justification: A Challenge to the New Perspective* [Downers Grove, IL: InterVarsity Press, 2001], 35) acknowledges that "Luther saw the Jewish and Jewish-Christian adversaries of Paul as one with the Catholic theologians of his time, while he and his followers appeared in the role of Paul and his pupils. This blurring of the distinction between historical and dogmatic perspectives remains a factor in German Pauline scholarship to this day."

2. For a fine effort to appreciate the logic of Paul's opponents, see Dieter Mitternacht, *Forum für Sprachlose: Eine kommunikationspsychologische und epistolär-rhetorische Untersuchung des Galaterbriefs* (ConBNT 30; Almqvist & Wiksell, 1999).

3.  Donaldson, *Judaism and the Gentiles: Jewish Patterns of Universalism (to 135 CE)* (Waco, TX: Baylor University Press, 2007).

4.  Donaldson, *Judaism and the Gentiles*, 475. According to Augustine (*City of God* 6.11), Seneca claims, in his lost work *On Superstition*, that Jewish customs have spread throughout the Roman Empire. Cf. Seneca, *Moral* 108.22; Plutarch, *Life of Cicero* 7.4–5; and Juvenal, *Satires* 14.96–106. See also the broader discussions of John G. Gager, *Moses in Greco-Roman Paganism* (SBLMS 16; Nashville: Abingdon, 1972), and idem, *The Origins of Anti-Semitism: Attitudes toward Judaism in Pagan and Christian Antiquity* (Oxford: Oxford University Press, 1983).

5.  See Shaye J. D. Cohen, "Respect for Judaism by Gentiles in the Writings of Josephus," *HTR* 80 (1987): 409–30, and Louis H. Feldman, "Proselytes and 'Sympathizers' in the Light of the New Inscriptions from Aphrodisias," *REJ* 148 (1989): 265–305. On the related topic of God-fearers, see Bernd Wander, *Gottesfürchtige und Sympathisanten: Studien zum heidnischen Umfeld von Diasporasynagogen* (WUNT 104; Tübingen: Mohr Siebeck, 1998).

6.  Paula Fredriksen ("Mandatory Retirement: Ideas in the Study of Christian Origins Whose Time Has Come to Go," *SR* 35 [2006]: 231–46 [241]) rightly notes that "ancient 'monotheism' spoke to the imagined architecture of the cosmos, not to its absolute population." Consequently, claims that there is one God in early Judaism should be taken to mean that there is one supreme God, even though there may be numerous divine beings under this one God. For instance, while Philo portrays Abraham coming to worship God instead of the kosmos, he still thinks that the kosmos is divine (e.g., *Eternity of the Kosmos* 46). On non-Jewish and non-Christian monotheism in antiquity, see Polymnia Athanassiadi and Michael Frede, eds., *Pagan Monotheism in Late Antiquity* (Oxford: Oxford University Press, 1999), and Stephen Mitchell and Peter van Nuffelen, eds., *One God: Pagan Monotheism in the Roman Empire* (Cambridge, UK: Cambridge University Press, 2010).

7.  See David Novak, *The Image of the Non-Jew in Judaism: An Historical and Constructive Study of the Noahide Laws* (Toronto Studies in Theology 14; Lewiston, NY: Mellen, 1983), and Klaus Müller, *Tora für die Völker: Die noachidischen Gebote und Ansätze zu ihrer Rezeption im Christentum*, 2d ed. (Studien zu Kirche und Israel 15; Berlin: Institut Kirche und Judentum, 1998).

8.  See Joel Kaminsky, "A Light to the Nations: Was There Mission and or Conversion in the Hebrew Bible?" *JSQ* 16 (2009): 6–22, and, in relation to Paul, Terence L. Donaldson, " 'Proselytes' or 'Righteous Gentiles'? The Status of Gentiles in Eschatological Pilgrimage Patterns of Thought," *JSP* 7 (1990): 3–27.

9.  Scholars debate whether *torah* here refers to the Mosaic law. Joseph Jensen (*The Use of tôrâ by Isaiah: His Debate with the Wisdom Tradition* [CBQMS 3; Washington, DC: Catholic Biblical Association of America, 1973], 124), for instance, believes that *torah* refers to general instruction, not the Mosaic law, while Gerald T. Sheppard ("The 'Scope' of Isaiah as a Book of Jewish and Christian Scriptures," in *New Visions of Isaiah*, ed. Roy F. Melugin and Marvin A. Sweeney [JSOTSup 214; Sheffield: Sheffield Academic, 1996], 257–81) believes that, as the book of Isaiah developed, *torah* came to refer to the Mosaic law.

10. See James M. Scott, "Philo and the Restoration of Israel," in *Society of Biblical Literature 1995 Seminar Papers* (SBLSPS 34; Atlanta: Scholars Press, 1996), 553–75.

11. See Donaldson, *Judaism and the Gentiles*, 89, and Matthew Thiessen, *Contesting Conversion: Genealogy, Circumcision, and Identity in Ancient Judaism and Christianity* (Oxford: Oxford University Press, 2011), 89–94. In contrast, some scholars, such as Michael E. Fuller (*The Restoration of Israel: Israel's Re-gathering and the Fate of the Nations in Early Jewish Literature and Luke-Acts* [BZNW 138; Berlin: de Gruyter, 2006], 74), George W. E. Nickelsburg (*1 Enoch 1: A Commentary on the Book of 1 Enoch, Chapters 1–36; 81–108* [Hermeneia; Minneapolis: Fortress, 2001], 403), and Daniel C. Olson (*A New Reading of the Animal Apocalypse of 1 Enoch: "All Nations Shall be Blessed"* [SVTP 24; Leiden: Brill, 2013], 19–21), see this transformation into bulls including both gentiles and Jews. Regardless of one's position on the issue of whether Jews remain sheep or become bulls, it is clear that gentiles remain gentiles—they do not become sheep, but become, like the righteous Shemite line, bulls.

12. Fredriksen, "Judaism, the Circumcision of Gentiles, and Apocalyptic Hope: Another Look at Galatians 1 and 2," *JTS* 42 (1991): 532–64 (547–48).

13. See Shaye J. D. Cohen, "Conversion to Judaism in Historical Perspective: From Biblical Israel to Postbiblical Judaism," *Conservative Judaism* 36 (1983): 31–45; idem, "Crossing the Boundary and Becoming a Jew," *HTR* 82 (1989): 13–33; and James P. Ware, *The Mission of the Church in Paul's Letter to the Philippians in the Context of Ancient Judaism* (NovTSup 120; Leiden: Brill, 2005), 285–92.

14. See Adolfo D. Roitman, "Achior in the Book of Judith: His Role and Significance," in *"No One Spoke Ill of Her": Essays on Judith*, ed. James C. VanderKam (SBLEJL 02; Atlanta: Scholars Press, 1992), 31–45.

15. For the conversion of the Idumeans, see Josephus, *Ant.* 13.258; *War* 1.63; Strabo, *Geography* 16.2.34; and Ptolemy (cf. Menahem Stern, *Greek and Latin Authors on Jews and Judaism*, 3 vols. [Jerusalem: Israeli Academy of Sciences and Humanities, 1974–84], n. 146). For the conversion of the Itureans, see Josephus, *Ant.* 13.318–319. Scholars disagree over whether these events qualify as conversions, since the Hasmoneans may have forced the Idumeans and Itureans to undergo circumcision and adopt the Jewish law. For instance, Doron Mendels (*The Land of Israel as a Political Concept in Hasmonean Literature: Recourse to History in Second Century B.C. Claims to the Holy Land* [TSAJ 15; Tübingen: Mohr Siebeck, 1987], 57–81) and Martin Goodman (*Mission and Conversion: Proselytizing in the Religious History of the Roman Empire* [Oxford: Clarendon, 1994], 74–76) argue that the Idumeans and Itureans took up Jewish practices out of compulsion, while Aryeh Kasher (*Jews, Idumaeans, and Ancient Arabs: Relations of the Jews in Eretz-Israel with the Nations of the Frontier and the Desert during the Hellenistic and Roman Era [332 BCE–70 CE]* [TSAJ 18; Tübingen: Mohr Siebeck, 1988], 46–77) and Shaye J. D. Cohen (*The Beginnings of Jewishness: Boundaries, Varieties, Uncertainties* [HCS 31; Berkeley: University of California Press, 1999], 116–17) argue that they willingly took up Jewish practices.

16. Donaldson, *Judaism and the Gentiles*, 4–5. Similarly, Nils Alstrup Dahl (*Studies in Paul: Theology for the Early Christian Mission* [Minneapolis: Augsburg, 1977], 191) states, "Jewish monotheism at the time of Paul was universalistic in its way and Christian monotheism remained exclusive. . . . We would come closer to the truth by saying that both Jewish and Christian monotheism are particular as well as universal, specific as well as general." See also Cohen, *Beginnings of Jewishness*, 109–39, and Paula Fredriksen, "What 'Parting of the Ways'? Jews, Gentiles, and the Ancient Mediterranean City," in *The Ways that Never*

*Parted: Jews and Christians in Late Antiquity and the Early Middle Ages*, ed. Adam H. Becker and Annette Yoshiko Reed (Minneapolis: Fortress, 2007), 35–63.

17. But see his brief treatment of exclusion in *Paul and the Gentiles: Remapping the Apostle's Convictional World* (Minneapolis: Fortress, 1997), 52–54.

18. David Janzen, *Witch-hunts, Purity and Social Boundaries: The Expulsion of the Foreign Women in Ezra 9–10* (JSOTSup 350; Sheffield: Sheffield Academic, 2002), 90; Saul M. Olyan, "Purity Ideology in Ezra-Nehemiah as a Tool to Reconstitute the Community," *JSJ* 35 (2004): 1–16; Hannah K. Harrington, "Holiness and Purity in Ezra-Nehemiah," in *Unity and Disunity in Ezra-Nehemiah: Redaction, Rhetoric, and Reader*, ed. Mark J. Boda and Paul L. Redditt (Hebrew Bible Monographs 17; Sheffield: Sheffield Phoenix, 2008), 98–116; and Matthew Thiessen, "The Function of a Conjunction: Inclusivist or Exclusivist Strategies in Ezra 6.19–21 and Nehemiah 10.29–30?" *JSOT* 34 (2009): 63–79.

19. See Christine E. Hayes, *Gentile Impurities and Jewish Identities: Intermarriage and Conversion from the Bible to the Talmud* (Oxford: Oxford University Press, 2002), 73–81, and Thiessen, *Contesting Conversion*, 67–86.

20. Cf. Cana Werman, "*Jubilees* 30: Building a Paradigm for the Ban on Intermarriage," *HTR* 90 (1997): 1–22.

21. Hayes, *Gentile Impurities and Jewish Identities*, 82–89. Although Martha Himmelfarb ("Levi, Phinehas, and the Problem of Intermarriage at the Time of the Maccabean Revolt," *JSQ* 6 [1999]: 1–24) argues that 4QMMT does not deal with intermarriage between Jews and gentiles, she does so, in part, on the assumption that this interpretation requires intermarriage with unconverted gentiles—something that was likely infrequent. But, once one considers the possibility that 4QMMT rejected gentile conversion to Judaism, one can see how the author might have viewed something as intermarriage that other Jews, who believed gentiles could convert to Judaism, did not.

22. On proselyte baptism, see Geza Vermes, "Baptism and Jewish Exegesis: New Light from Ancient Sources," *NTS* 4 (1958): 308–19.

23. Cf. Paula Fredriksen, "From Jesus to Christ: The Contribution of the Apostle Paul," in *Jews and Christians Speak of Jesus*, ed. Arthur Zannoni (Minneapolis: Fortress, 1994), 77–90 (84–85).

24. See the full discussion of David Bryan, *Cosmos, Chaos and the Kosher Mentality* (JSPSup 12; Sheffield: Sheffield Academic, 1995), Donaldson, *Judaism and the Gentiles*, 217–78; and Thiessen, *Contesting Conversion*, 89–94.

25. Again, see the important remarks on the terminology of "particularism" and "universalism" of Anders Runesson, "Particularistic Judaism and Universalistic Christianity? Some Critical Remarks on Terminology and Theology," *JGRChJ* 1 (2000): 120–44.

26. For instance, among those who believe that the opponents are Jews who do not believe in Jesus, see Nikolas Walter, "Hellenistische Diaspora-Juden an der Wiege des Urchristentums," in *The New Testament and Hellenistic Judaism*, ed. Peder Borgen and Søren Giversen (Peabody, MA: Hendrickson, 1997), 37–58, and idem, "Paulus und die Gegner des Christusevangeliums in Galatien," in *L'Apôtre Paul: Personnalité, Style et Conception du Ministère*, ed. Albert Vanhoye et al. (BETL 73; Leuven: Leuven University Press, 1986), 351–56. J. Louis Martyn (*Theological Issues in the Letters of Paul* [Nashville: Abingdon, 1997], 9–14) and the majority of commentators believe the opponents to be Jewish believers in Christ.

27. Johannes Munck, *Paul and the Salvation of Mankind*, trans. Frank Clarke (Richmond, VA: John Knox, 1959), 87–134; Peter Richardson, *Israel in the Apostolic Church* (SNTSMS 10; Cambridge, UK: Cambridge University Press, 1969), 84–96; and Michele Murray, *Playing a Jewish Game: Gentile Christian Judaizing in the First and Second Centuries* CE (Studies in Christianity and Judaism 13; Waterloo, ON: Wilfred Laurier University Press, 2004), 34–36.

28. It is possible that a fear of persecution *by gentiles* did motivate them, as Paula Fredriksen ("How Later Contexts Affect Pauline Content, or: Retrospect is the Mother of Anachronism," in *Jews and Christians in the First and Second Centuries: How to Write Their History*, ed. Peter J. Tomson and Joshua Schwartz [CRINT 13; Leiden: Brill, 2014], 17–51 [45]) explains: "Not requiring complete affiliation with Judaism via circumcision, insisting that family and urban cults nonetheless be renounced, the early apostles walked these Christ-fearing pagans into a social and religious no-man's land . . . the pagan majority in these diaspora cities *was* worried. The gods' anger would affect everyone. In other words, ancestral obligation, not particular beliefs—what people did, not what they thought—was what mattered." For instance, in his second-century CE work entitled *How Should One Behave toward One's Country?* (preserved in Stobaeus, *Anthology* 3.39.36; trans. Ramelli), Hierocles claims that the individual must prefer the safety of his country to his own individual safety and then concludes: "For these reasons I claim that whoever behaves rightly toward his country must rid himself of every passion and illness of the soul. He must also observe the laws of his country as though they were second gods, by living in accord with their guidance and, if anyone should attempt to transgress or change them, by making every effort to prevent him and opposing him in every way."

29. Barclay, "Mirror-Reading."

30. The claim of Walter Schmithals ("Judaisten in Galatien," *ZNW* 74 [1983]: 51–57) that these teachers were gnostics who advocated only circumcision is unlikely.

31. From the time of his calling (Genesis 12) until his circumcision (Genesis 17), Abraham is consistently referred to as "Abram." Only after the covenant of circumcision is he consistently referred to as Abraham. Nonetheless, for clarity's sake, I will call him Abraham throughout.

32. Ben Begleiter, "Imagining a Patriarch: Images of Abraham in Early Jewish and Christian Exegesis" (Ph.D. dissertation, Yale University, 2004), 112.

33. On *Jubilees'* portrayal of Abraham, see Jacques T. A. G. M. van Ruiten, *Abraham in the Book of Jubilees: The Rewriting of Genesis 11:26—25:10 in the Book of Jubilees 11:14—23:8* (JSJSup 161; Leiden: Brill, 2012).

34. Philo's portrayal of Abraham worshipping the kosmos as God coincides with his identification of the Chaldeans with the Stoics. See Harry Austryn Wolfson, *Philo: Foundations of Religious Philosophy in Judaism, Christianity, and Islam*, 2 vols. (Cambridge, MA: Harvard University Press, 1947), 1:176–77, and David T. Runia, *Philo of Alexandria and the Timaeus of Plato* (PhA 44; Leiden: Brill, 1986), 190.

35. The MT reads the second לך as the preposition *lamed* and second-person pronoun: "Take yourself!" Like the midrash, the LXX translator perhaps saw a redundancy here and simplified לך לך to ἔξελθε ("Go out!").

36. All translations of *Midrash Rabbah* come from H. Freedman and Maurice Simon, eds., *Midrash Rabbah*, 10 vols. (London: Soncino, 1939). For a fuller treatment of Abraham and idolatry in rabbinic literature, see Begleiter, "Imagining a Patriarch," 107–47.

37. Ellen Birnbaum (*The Place of Judaism in Philo's Thought: Israel, Jews, and Proselytes* [BJS 290; Atlanta: Scholars Press, 1996], 195) examines Philo's preference for ἐπήλυτος over προσήλυτος, concluding that they are virtually synonymous for Philo and that they "can denote, for example, a person of foreign birth; one who dwells with temporary or inferior status among a foreign population; one who joins a new people, adopting their beliefs and practices; or all the foregoing."

38. Seth Daniel Kunin, *The Logic of Incest: A Structuralist Analysis of Hebrew Mythology* (JSOTSup 185; Sheffield: Sheffield Academic, 1995), 76. Similarly, Scott W. Hahn (*Kinship by Covenant: A Canonical Approach to the Fulfillment of God's Saving Promises* [ABRL; New Haven: Yale University Press, 2009], 105): "The changing of names, for both Abram and Sarai, is a major theme in Genesis 17. Note that in the Abraham cycle the names 'Abram' and 'Sarai' are used consistently by all the hypothetical sources before Genesis 17, and likewise 'Abraham' and 'Sarah' afterward. The name changing in Genesis 17 has been thoroughly integrated into the final form of the text." This thorough integration suggests that the editor intends to portray the covenant of circumcision causing a complete identity change in Abraham and Sarah.

39. On the paradigmatic importance of Abraham in early Jewish thinking, see Samuel Sandmel, *Philo's Place in Judaism: A Study of Conceptions of Abraham in Jewish Literature*, rev. ed. (New York: Ktav, 1971); G. Walter Hansen, *Abraham in Galatians: Epistolary and Rhetorical Contexts* (JSNTSup 29; Sheffield: Sheffield Academic, 1989), 175–99; George W. E. Nickelsburg, "Abraham, the Convert: A Jewish Tradition and Its Use by the Apostle Paul," in *Biblical Figures outside the Bible*, ed. Michael A. Stone and Theodore A. Bergren (Harrisburg, PA: Trinity Press International, 1998), 151–75; and Nancy Calvert-Koyzis, *Paul, Monotheism, and the People of God: The Significance of Abraham Traditions for Early Judaism and Christianity* (JSNTSup 273; London: T&T Clark, 2004).

40. On the question of converts' ability to refer to Israel's patriarchs as their own fathers, see Shaye J. D. Cohen, "Can Converts to Judaism Say 'God of Our Fathers'?" *Judaism* 40 (1991): 419–28.

41. Paul R. Williamson, *Abraham, Israel and the Nations: The Patriarchal Promise and its Covenantal Development in Genesis* (JSOTSup 315; Sheffield: Sheffield Academic, 2000), 183. Similarly, Jean-Noël Aletti (*New Approaches for Interpreting the Letters of Saint Paul: Collected Essays: Rhetoric, Soteriology, Christology, and Ecclesiology*, trans. Peggy Manning Meyer [SubBi 43; Rome: Gregorian and Biblical Press, 2012], 37) claims that "the episode in Gen 17 explicitly states that from now on, in order to be a descendant of the Patriarch and to have access to the blessings that were promised to him, circumcision (which makes one subject to the Law) is necessary."

42. On the concern to master the passions and desire in the Greco-Roman world and the numerous remedies proffered, see Martha C. Nussbaum, *The Therapy of Desire: Theory and Practice in Hellenistic Ethics* (Princeton: Princeton University Press, 1994), and the various essays in John T. Fitzgerald, ed., *Passions and Moral Progress in Greco-Roman Thought* (Routledge Monographs in Classical Studies; New York: Routledge, 2008).

43. See the discussions of, for instance, David C. Aune, "Mastery of the Passions: Philo, 4 Maccabees and Earliest Christianity," in *Hellenization Revisited: Shaping a Christian Response within the Greco-Roman World*, ed. Wendy E. Helleman (Lanham, MD: University Press of America, 1994), 125–58;

Maren Niehoff, *Philo on Jewish Identity and Culture* (TSAJ 86; Tübingen: Mohr Siebeck, 2001), 75–110; Stanley K. Stowers, "Paul and Self-Mastery," in *Paul in the Greco-Roman World*, ed. J. Paul Sampley (Harrisburg, PA: Trinity Press International, 2003), 524–50 (531–34); and Rafael Rodríguez, *If You Call Yourself a Jew: Reappraising Paul's Letter to the Romans* (Eugene, OR: Cascade, 2014), 119–20.

44. Wilson, *Philo of Alexandria: On Virtues* (PACS 3; Leiden: Brill, 2011), 370.

45. On Philo's treatment of circumcision, see Richard D. Hecht, "The Exegetical Contexts of Philo's Interpretation of Circumcision," in *Nourished with Peace: Studies in Hellenistic Judaism in Memory of Samuel Sandmel*, ed. Frederick E. Greenspahn, Earle Hilgert, and Burton L. Mack (Chico, CA: Scholars Press, 1984), 51–79; Andreas Blaschke, *Beschneidung: Zeugnisse der Bibel und verwandter Texte* (TANZ 28; Tübingen: Francke, 1998), 193–223; and Nina E. Livesey, *Circumcision as a Malleable Symbol* (WUNT 2/295; Tübingen: Mohr Siebeck, 2010), 41–76. Some interpreters have argued that Philo inherited the belief that circumcision functioned as a symbol of the excision of the desires from Egyptian perceptions of the ritual, but the earliest evidence of this view, outside of Philo, comes from Ambrose in the fourth century CE: "Egyptians circumcise boys in the fourteenth year, and their girls are said to be circumcised in that same year, inasmuch as the passion of manhood then starts to burn and the menses of the girls take their beginning" (*On Abraham* 2.11.78; trans. Tomkinson). Aetius of Amida (sixth century CE) also views Egyptian female circumcision as a remedy for the problem of female lust (*On Medical Practice* 17.115). This belief surfaces again over a millennium later in the writings of Maimonides. Cf. Shaye J. D. Cohen, *Why Aren't Jewish Women Circumcised? Gender and Covenant in Judaism* (Berkeley: University of California, 2005), 143–73.

46. As I will argue in Chapter 3, Paul's use of the verb ἐπιτελέω in Gal 3:1–5 and the verb τελειόω and the adjective τέλειος in Phil 3:12–15 should be taken as evidence of precisely this use of Genesis 17. Cf. J. Duncan M. Derrett, "Circumcision and Perfection: A Johannine Equation (John 7:22–23)," *EvQ* 63 (1991): 211–24, and Richard B. Hays, "The Letter to the Galatians," in *2 Corinthians-Philemon*, ed. Leander E. Keck (NIB 11; Nashville: Abingdon, 2000), 181–348 (252).

47. Contrary to a number of interpreters, I will attempt to show in Chapters 4 and 5 that Paul did not refer to Abraham in Galatians only in response to his opponents' gospel. Rather, their use of Abraham occasioned his discussion of Abraham, but Paul already believed that both Abraham and the Abraham Narrative were integral to his gospel proclamation.

48. Martyn, *Theological Issues*, 20. For the entirety of Martyn's reconstructed sermon see *Theological Issues*, 20–24. While Martyn's hypothetical sermon arises out of a mirror reading of Galatians, Barclay ("Mirror Reading," 88–89) also concludes that it was highly probable both that these teachers referred to the Abraham Narrative and that they used Genesis 17 in order to convince the Galatians to undergo circumcision.

49. Dunn, *The Epistle to the Galatians* (BNTC; Peabody, MA: Hendrickson, 1993), 104. The majority of interpreters make similar comments. For instance, John M. G. Barclay (*Obeying the Truth: A Study of Paul's Ethics in Galatians* [SNTW; Edinburgh: T&T Clark, 1988], 53) says of Genesis 17: "Armed with such unambiguous texts the agitators could readily demonstrate that, to share in the Abrahamic covenant and the Abrahamic blessing (Gen 12.3; 18.18, etc.), the

Galatians need to be circumcised; indeed, such was the command of God in their Scriptures"; Donaldson (*Paul and the Gentiles*, 120) claims: "The fact that Genesis 17 declares circumcision to be the unconditional prerequisite for membership in Abraham's 'seed' means that the story of Abraham provides much more evident support for the position of the rival teachers than for that of Paul"; and Sam K. Williams (*Galatians* [ANTC; Nashville: Abingdon, 1997], 126) argues that "the agitators found in the Genesis stories indisputable sanction for circumcising all 'sons of Abraham.'"

50. For instance, William G. Braude, *Jewish Proselyting in the First Five Centuries of the Common Era: The Age of the Tannaim and Amoraim* (Providence, RI: Brown University Press, 1940); Bernard J. Bamberger, *Proselytism in the Talmudic Period* (Cincinnati: Hebrew Union College Press, 1939); Louis H. Feldman, "Was Judaism a Missionary Religion in Ancient Times?" in *Jewish Assimilation, Acculturation and Accommodation: Past Traditions, Current Issues and Future Prospects*, ed. Menachem Mor (Studies in Jewish Civilization 2; Lanham, MD: University Press of America, 1992), 24–37; and idem, *Jew and Gentile in the Ancient World: Attitudes and Interactions from Alexander to Justinian* (Princeton: Princeton University Press, 1993), 288–341.

51. Goodman, *Mission and Conversion*, and Scot McKnight, *A Light Among the Gentiles: Jewish Missionary Activity in the Second Temple Period* (Minneapolis: Fortress, 1991). For the most recent treatments of the topic see John Dickson, *Mission-Commitment in Ancient Judaism and in the Pauline Communities: The Shape, Extent and Background of Early Christian Mission* (WUNT 2/159; Tübingen: Mohr Siebeck, 2003), and Michael F. Bird, *Crossing Over Sea and Land: Jewish Missionary Activity in the Second Temple Period* (Peabody, MA: Hendrickson, 2010).

52. On this account see Jacob Neusner, "The Conversion of Adiabene to Judaism: A New Perspective," *JBL* 83 (1964): 60–66; Lawrence H. Schiffman, "The Conversion of the Royal House of Adiabene in Josephus and Rabbinic Sources," in *Josephus, Judaism, and Christianity*, ed. Louis H. Feldman and Gohei Hata (Detroit: Wayne State University Press, 1987), 293–312; Gary Gilbert, "The Making of a Jew: 'God-Fearer' or Convert in the Story of Izates," *USQR* 44 (1991): 299–313; and Daniel R. Schwartz, "God, Gentiles, and Jewish Law: On Acts 15 and Josephus' Adiabene Narrative," in *Geschichte—Tradition—Reflexion: Festschrift für Martin Hengel zum 70. Geburtstag*, ed. Hubert Cancik, Hermann Lichtenberger, and Peter Schäfer, 3 vols. [Tübingen: Mohr Siebeck], 1996), 1:263–82. On important parallels between Paul and the story of Izates, see Mark D. Nanos, "The Question of Conceptualization: Qualifying Paul's Position on Circumcision in Dialogue with Josephus's Advisors to King Izates," in *Paul within Judaism: Restoring the First-Century Context to the Apostle*, ed. Mark D. Nanos and Magnus Zetterholm (Minneapolis: Fortress, 2015), 105–52.

53. The meaning of ἀκριβής is somewhat vague. *A Greek-English Lexicon* (Liddell-Scott-Jones [LSJ]) provides numerous glosses, including "exact," "accurate," "precise," "perfect," "clear," "definite," "strict," and "scrupulous." These are no mere synonyms. Words such as "exact," "accurate," "precise," or "clear," are not necessarily the same as the potentially negative terms "strict," or "scrupulous."

54. Sanders, *Judaism: Practice and Belief, 63 BCE–66 CE* (London: SCM, 1992), 385. See also, Albert I. Baumgarten, "The Name of the Pharisees," *JBL* 102 (1983): 411–28,

and Steve Mason, *Flavius Josephus on the Pharisees: A Composition-Critical Study* (SPB 39; Leiden: Brill, 1991), 89–110.

55. For instance, Alan F. Segal, "The Cost of Proselytism and Conversion," in *Society of Biblical Literature 1988 Seminar Papers* (SBLSPS 27; Atlanta: Scholars Press, 1988), 336–69; James Carleton Paget, "Jewish Proselytism at the Time of Christian Origins: Chimera or Reality?" *JSNT* 62 (1996): 65–103; and David Rokéah, "Ancient Jewish Proselytism in Theory and in Practice," *TZ* 52 (1996): 206–24.

56. E.g., Goodman, *Mission and Conversion*, 70.

57. David M. Moffitt and C. Jacob Butera ("P.Duk. inv. 727r: New Evidence for the Meaning and Provenance of the Word Προσήλυτος," *JBL* 132 [2013]: 159–78) have discovered the earliest extant non-LXX use of the word, where it clearly relates to an alien residing in a foreign community. Further, as I have argued ("Revisiting the προσήλυτος in 'the LXX,' " *JBL* 132 [2013]: 333–50), the widespread belief that the LXX uses the term προσήλυτος to mean "convert" rests upon the methodologically unsound argument of W. C. Allen, "On the Meaning of ΠΡΟΣΗΛΥΤΟΣ in the Septuagint," *The Expositor* 4 (1894): 264–75.

58. See the helpful discussion of the evidence in Shaye J. D. Cohen, "The Significance of Yavneh: Pharisees, Rabbis, and the End of Jewish Sectarianism," *HUCA* 55 (1984): 27–53 (36–43), and Annette Yoshiko Reed, "When Did Rabbis Become Pharisees? Reflections on Christian Evidence for Post-70 Judaism," in *Envisioning Judaism: Studies in Honor of Peter Schäfer on the Occasion of his Seventieth Birthday*, ed. Ra'anan S. Boustan et al., 2 vols. (Tübingen: Mohr Siebeck, 2013), 2:859–96.

59. See, for instance, Vered Noam, "Traces of Sectarian Halakhah in the Rabbinic World," in *Rabbinic Perspectives: Rabbinic Literature and the Dead Sea Scrolls, Proceedings of the Eighth International Symposium of the Orion Center for the Study of the Dead Sea Scrolls and Associated Literature, 7–9 January, 2003*, ed. Steven D. Fraade et al. (STDJ 62; Leiden: Brill, 2006), 67–85, and eadem, "Beit Shammai and the Sectarian Halakhah," *Jewish Studies (World Union of Jewish Studies)* 41 (2002): 45–67 (Hebrew).

60. Goodman, *Mission and Conversion*, 89, Moshe Lavee, "Converting the Missionary Image of Abraham: Rabbinic Traditions Migrating from the Land of Israel to Babylon," in *Abraham, the Nations, and the Hagarites: Jewish, Christian, and Islamic Perspectives on Kinship with Abraham*, ed. George H. van Kooten, Martin Goodman, and Jacques T. A. G. M. van Ruiten (TBN 13; Leiden: Brill, 2010), 203–22.

61. Fredriksen ("Judaism, the Circumcision of Gentiles," 540), who describes gentile conversion as indebted to "the freelance, amateur, non-institutionally based efforts of individuals or the side-effect of unstructured contact through diaspora synagogue communities."

62. For fuller discussions of gentiles and gentile converts in rabbinic literature, see Gary G. Porton, *Goyim: Gentiles and Israelites in Mishnah-Tosefta* (BJS 155; Atlanta: Scholars Press, 1988), and idem, *The Strangers within Your Gates: Converts and Conversion in Rabbinic Judaism* (CSHJ; Chicago: University of Chicago Press, 1994).

63. Moshe Lavee ("'Proselytes are as Hard to Israel as a Scab Is to the Skin': A Babylonian Talmudic Concept," *JJS* 63 [2012]: 22–48) has documented evidence that the Babylonian Talmud contains strong genealogical sentiments that discouraged marriage to gentile converts to Judaism. He argues that

such genealogical concerns developed in the Jewish community in Sassanid Babylonia.

64. Avi Sagi and Zvi Zohar, "The Halakhic Ritual of Giyyur and Its Symbolic Meaning," *JRitSt* 9 (1995): 1–13 (2).

65. Some scholars, such as Carey A. Moore (*Judith: A New Translation with Introduction and Commentary* [AB 40; Garden City, NY: Doubleday, 1985], 70–71), have argued that a Pharisee did in fact compose the book of Judith, but this is no more than mere speculation.

66. See Randall D. Chesnutt, *From Death to Life: Conversion in Joseph and Aseneth* (JSPSup 16; Sheffield: Sheffield Academic, 1995), and Matthew Thiessen, "Aseneth's Eight-Day Transformation as Scriptural Justification for Conversion," *JSJ* 45 (2014): 229–49.

67. Martin Hengel and Roland Deines (*The Pre-Christian Paul*, trans. John Bowden [London: SCM, 1991], 27–28), in keeping with their optimistic view of the historical value of Acts, think it probable that Paul did in fact study with Gamaliel. Against its historicity, see John Knox, *Chapters in a Life of Paul*, rev. ed. (Macon, GA: Mercer University Press, 1987), 21.

68. The first ἔτι is lacking in some Western manuscripts (D*, F, G, 6, 0278, 1739, 1881, a, b, vg^miss, Ambrosiaster), but it is more likely that the word was omitted, perhaps for stylistic purposes, than that it was added.

69. Contrary to Pheme Perkins, *Abraham's Divided Children: Galatians and the Politics of Faith* (The New Testament in Context; Harrisburg, PA: Trinity Press International, 2001), 17. The alternative is that Paul preached that Jews needed to continue to undergo circumcision, yet we know of no reason why Paul, either prior to his calling or after it, would have had to preach that Jews should continue to practice circumcision. Who was saying otherwise?

70. Donaldson, *Paul and the Gentiles*, 275–84, and Hans Hübner, "Gal 3,10 und die Herkunft des Paulus," *KD* 19 (1973): 215–31. But see Douglas A. Campbell ("Galatians 5.11: Evidence of an Early Law-observant Mission by Paul?" *NTS* 57 [2011]: 325–47), who argues that Paul originally preached circumcision after his calling. Justin K. Hardin ("'If I Still Proclaim Circumcision' [Galatians 5:11a]: Paul, the Law, and Gentile Circumcision," *JSPL* 3 [2013]: 145–64) demonstrates that while Campbell's conclusion may be possible, it is improbable.

71. Fredriksen ("Judaism, Circumcision of Gentiles," 552–55) doubts both that Paul would have persecuted early Jewish believers in Christ and that he would then have been persecuted (i.e., disciplined) on the basis of the inclusion of uncircumcised gentiles into their communities, since uncircumcised gentiles could and regularly did attend synagogues. Perhaps—although this suggestion is speculative—such disciplinary actions arose precisely because early Christ followers claimed, as Paul goes on to do in Galatians 3 and Romans 4, that uncircumcised gentiles become sons of Abraham in Christ. Of the patterns of inclusion examined above, only proponents of conversion (and even within this pattern tensions exist) ever had the audacity to claim that gentiles could become sons or children of Abraham. In this sense, Paul's teachings represent a daring and novel claim—gentiles who do not look or act like Jews, Abraham's undisputed children, can claim to be Abraham's descendants and heirs. The subsequent history of Christianity has, I think, adequately demonstrated how dangerous such claims could turn out to be for Jews.

72. On Paul's life as a Pharisee, see J. W. Doeve, "Paulus der Pharisäer und Galater I 13–15," *NovT* 6 (1963): 170–81, and Hengel with Deines, *Pre-Christian*

*Paul.* On the difficulty of translating *ioudaismos* in these verses, see Matthew V. Novenson, "Paul's Former Occupation in *Ioudaismos*," in *Galatians and Christian Theology: Justification, the Gospel, and Ethics in Paul's Letter*, ed. Mark W. Elliott et al. (Grand Rapids: Baker Academic, 2014), 24–39.

73. Quotations come from Betz, *Galatians: A Commentary on Paul's Letter to the Churches in Galatia* (Hermeneia; Philadelphia: Fortress, 1979), 67 n. 105; Martyn, *Galatians: A New Translation with Introduction and Commentary* (AB 33A; New York: Doubleday, 1997), 154; and Sanders, *Paul, the Law, and the Jewish People* (Minneapolis: Fortress, 1983), 175. Cf. F. F. Bruce, *Paul: Apostle of the Free Spirit* (Exeter: Paternoster, 1977), 69; Heikki Räisänen, "Galatians 2.16 and Paul's Break with Judaism," *NTS* 31 (1985): 543–53; Barclay, *Obeying the Truth*, 207; James D. G. Dunn, *The Theology of Paul's Letter to the Galatians* (New Testament Theology; Cambridge, UK: Cambridge University Press, 1993), 37–38; Donaldson, *Paul and the Gentiles*, 263; Bruce W. Longenecker, *The Triumph of Abraham's God: The Transformation of Identity in Galatians* (Nashville: Abingdon, 1998), 75; L. J. Lietaert Peerbolte, *Paul the Missionary* (CBET 34; Leuven: Peeters, 2003), 142; and Stephen Westerholm, *Perspectives Old and New on Paul: The "Lutheran" Paul and His Critics* (Grand Rapids: Eerdmans, 2004), 368. To be fair to Dunn, he elsewhere ("Who Did Paul Think He Was? A Study of Jewish-Christian Identity," *NTS* 45 [1999]: 174–93 [179]) asks a perceptive question: "In Gal 1.13–14 Paul does clearly imply that his life 'in Judaism' belonged to his past. But how does that usage ('Judaism') correlate with the modern categorisation 'Second Temple Judaism'?" Similarly, Timo Laato (*Paul and Judaism: An Anthropological Approach*, trans. T. McElwain [SFSHJ 115; Atlanta: Scholars Press, 1995], 3) helpfully complicates the issue: "Either Paul was able to make explicit no clear distinction between differing Jewish groupings, or he considered Judaism a sufficiently homogenous religion and therefore renounced any further differentiation. If the first case is true we must decide precisely *with which* Judaism Paul had in fact his breach. In the latter case, we must clarify why Paul broke away from the *whole* body of Judaism."

74. Steve Mason, "Jews, Judaeans, Judaizing, Judaism: Problems of Categorization in Ancient History," *JSJ* 38 (2007): 457–512 (461). See also the occurrences of the word *ioudaismos* in a third-century BCE dedicatory inscription of the synagogue at Stobi (in the modern-day Republic of Macedonia) and a funerary inscription from Italy, which Yehoshua Amir discusses in "The Term Ἰουδαϊσμός: A Study in Jewish-Hellenistic Self-Definition," *Immanuel* 14 (1982): 34–41.

75. Quotations come from Cohen, *Beginnings of Jewishness*, 178 and 179. See also Mason ("Jews, Judaeans, Judaizing, Judaism," 462–63), who discusses numerous examples of such derogatory uses of –*izein* verbs. Cohen's reference to Suetonius is based upon the text of Jean Taillardat, *Suétone Peri Blasphēmiōn, Peri Paidiōn: Extraits byzantins* (Paris: Les Belles Lettres, 1967), 62–63.

76. Levenson, *Esther: A Commentary* (OTL; Louisville: Westminster John Knox, 1997), 117. For this reflexive-estimative use of the *hithpael*, see Solomon Zeitlin, "Proselytes and Proselytism during the Second Commonwealth and the Early Tannaitic Period," in *Harry Austryn Wolfson Jubilee Volume: On the Occasion of his Seventy-Fifth Birthday*, 3 vols. (Jerusalem: American Academy for Jewish Research, 1965), 2:871–81 (873), Cohen, *Beginnings of Jewishness*, 181–82, and Ronald J. Williams, *Williams' Hebrew Syntax*, 3d ed. (rev. and exp. by John C. Beckman; Toronto: University of Toronto Press, 2007), 64. For other instances where the *hithpael* form of a Hebrew verb indicates pretension, see 2 Sam 13:5–6 and 1 Kgs 14:5–6.

77. Johnson Hodge, "Apostle to the Gentiles: Constructions of Paul's Identity," *BibInt* 13 (2005): 270–88 (278).
78. Mason, "Jews, Judaeans, Judaizing, Judaism," 469.
79. Cf. Joseph Sievers, *The Hasmoneans and Their Supporters: From Mattathias to the Death of John Hyrcanus I* (SFSHJ 6; Atlanta: Scholars Press, 1990), 35. I follow Codex Alexandrinus here and not Codex Sinaiticus, which reads "among the sons of Israel." See the textual evidence presented in Werner Kappler, *Maccabaeorum Liber I*, 3d ed. (SVTG 9; Göttingen: Vandenhoeck & Ruprecht, 1990).
80. Cf. Terence L. Donaldson, "Zealot and Convert: The Origin of Paul's Christ-Torah Antithesis," *CBQ* 51 (1989): 655–82, and idem, "Israelite, Convert, Apostle to the Gentiles: The Origin of Paul's Gentile Mission," in *The Road from Damascus: The Impact of Paul's Conversion on His Life, Thought, and Ministry*, ed. Richard N. Longenecker (Grand Rapids: Eerdmans, 1997), 62–84.

CHAPTER 2

1. Rudolf Bultmann (*Der Stil der paulinischen Predigt und die kynisch-stoische Diatribe* [FRLANT 13; Göttingen: Vandenhoeck & Ruprecht, 1910]) first argued that Romans contained a diatribe. Stanley K. Stowers (*The Diatribe and Paul's Letter to the Romans* [SBLDS 57; Chico, CA: Scholars Press, 1981]); Thomas Schmeller (*Paulus und die "Diatribe": Eine vergleichende Stilinterpretation* [NTAbh 19; Münser: Aschendorff, 1987]); Neil Elliott (*The Rhetoric of Romans: Argumentative Constraint and Strategy and Paul's Dialogue with Judaism* [JSNTSup 45; Sheffield: JSOT Press, 1990]); and Runar M. Thorsteinsson (*Paul's Interlocutor in Romans 2: Function and Identity in the Context of Ancient Epistolography* [ConBNT 40; Stockholm: Almqvist & Wiksell, 2003]) have expanded upon this argument.
2. F. C. Baur, *Paul the Apostle of Jesus Christ: His Life and Works, His Epistles and Teachings; A Contribution to a Critical History of Primitive Christianity*, trans. A. Menzies, 2 vols. (London: Williams & Norgate, 1873), 1:324. Rudolf Bultmann (*Theology of the New Testament*, trans. Kendrick Grobel, 2 vols. [London: SCM, 1952], 1:108–9) expresses a similar position: "Here debate with Judaism itself was necessary, as Paul's letter to the Romans testifies. For it does not polemize against 'Judaizers,' nor is it occasioned, like Galatians, by the intervention of rival missionaries who want to compel Roman Christians to adopt circumcision. Rather, it develops in purely theoretical fashion the principle of Christian faith in antithesis to the principle of the Jewish Torah-religion." Most recently, see Martinus C. de Boer, "Paul's Mythologizing Program in Romans 5–8," in *Apocalyptic Paul: Cosmos and Anthropos in Romans 5–8*, ed. Beverly Roberts Gaventa (Waco, TX: Baylor University Press, 2013), 1–20 (2).
3. For instance, Wolfgang Wiefel, "Die jüdische Gemeinschaft im antiken Rom und die Anfänge des römischen Christentums: Bemerkungen zu Anlass und Zweck des Römerbriefs," *Judaica* 26 (1970): 65–88; James D. G. Dunn, *Romans 1–8* (WBC 38A; Dallas: Word, 1988), xliv–liv; Joseph A. Fitzmyer, *Romans* (AB 33; New York: Doubleday, 1993), 68–84; Stanley K. Stowers, *A Rereading of Romans: Justice, Jews, and Gentiles* (New Haven: Yale University Press, 1994); and N. T. Wright, "Romans 2:17—3:9: A Hidden Clue to the Meaning of Romans?" *JSPL* 2 (2012): 1–26.
4. As E. P. Sanders (*Paul, the Law, and the Jewish People* [Philadelphia: Fortress, 1983], 123–35) notes, such readings create considerable internal tension

within Paul's letters. Sanders attempts to resolve this tension by claiming that Rom 1:18—2:29 is a synagogue sermon that Paul has inserted into his letter. In light of the apparent tensions between this passage and what Paul says elsewhere, others such as J. C. O'Neill (*Paul's Letter to the Romans* [PNTC; Harmondsworth: Penguin, 1975], 40–56), Winsome Munro (*Authority in Paul and Peter: The Identification of a Pastoral Stratum in the Pauline Corpus and 1 Peter* [SNTSMS 45; Cambridge, UK: Cambridge University Press, 1983], 113) and William O. Walker Jr. ("Romans 1:18—2:29: A Non-Pauline Interpolation?" *NTS* 45 [1999]: 533–52) argue that Rom 1:18—2:29 is a post-Pauline interpolation.

5. Thorsteinsson, *Paul's Interlocutor in Romans 2*, 144.

6. Stowers (*Rereading of Romans*) repeatedly stresses this distinction, although his critics often miss this point. In contrast to this methodology, Richard N. Longenecker (*Introducing Romans: Critical Issues in Paul's Most Famous Letter* [Grand Rapids: Eerdmans, 2011], 55–91) believes one should move from external evidence regarding early Christ followers at Rome to the internal evidence of the letter.

7. On Paul's use of Jewish scriptures in Romans, see, for instance, J. Ross Wagner, *Heralds of the Good News: Isaiah and Paul "In Concert" in the Letter to the Romans* (NovTSup 101; Leiden: Brill, 2002).

8. For instance, see Robert Jewett, *Romans: A Commentary* (Hermeneia; Minneapolis: Fortress, 2007), 70–72; Francis Watson, *Paul, Judaism, and the Gentiles: Beyond the New Perspective* (rev. and exp.; Grand Rapids: Eerdmans, 2007), 179; Peter Lampe, *From Paul to Valentinus: Christians at Rome in the First Two Centuries*, trans. Michael Steinhauser (Minneapolis: Fortress, 2003), 69–79; and Arland J. Hultgren, *Paul's Letter to the Romans: A Commentary* (Grand Rapids: Eerdmans, 2011), 9–11. Steve Mason (" 'For I am Not Ashamed of the Gospel' (Rom. 1.16): The Gospel and the First Readers of Romans," in *Gospel in Paul: Studies on Corinthians, Galatians and Romans for Richard N. Longenecker*, ed. L. Ann Jervis and Peter Richardson [JSNTSup 108; Sheffield: Sheffield Academic, 1994], 254–87), in fact, argues that Paul wrote the letter exclusively to Jewish Christians.

9. While it is possible that "we" refers to Paul and Phoebe (cf. Rom 16:1), Otto Michel (*Der Brief an die Römer*, 14th ed. [KEK 4; Göttingen: Vandenhoeck & Ruprecht, 1978], 75) suggests that here Paul uses the first-person plural pronoun to refer tactfully to himself alone.

10. For others who argue that Paul intends to address only gentiles, see Johannes Munck, *Paul and the Salvation of Mankind*, trans. Frank Clarke (Richmond, VA: John Knox, 1959), 196–209; Stowers, *Rereading of Romans*, 21–33; Mark D. Nanos, *The Mystery of Romans: The Jewish Context of Paul's Letter* (Minneapolis: Fortress, 1996), 78–84; Thorsteinsson, *Paul's Interlocutor in Romans 2*, 87–122; and A. Andrew Das, *Solving the Romans Debate* (Minneapolis: Fortress, 2007), 53–114. In contrast, Theodor Zahn (*Der Brief des Paulus an die Römer* [Kommentar zum Neue Testament 6; Leipzig: Deichert, 1910], 47) argues that ἐν πᾶσιν τοῖς ἔθνεσιν includes Israel. Similarly, C. E. B. Cranfield (*A Critical and Exegetical Commentary on the Epistle to the Romans*, 2 vols., 6th ed. [ICC; Edinburgh: T&T Clark, 1975–79], 1:68) argues that ἐν here signifies geography, not ethnicity, and that Paul's mission is to gentiles and Jews who live outside of Judea. These interpretations fail to take account of the rest of the evidence of Romans.

11. Jewett, *Romans*, 100. More fully, see Jewett, "Romans as an Ambassadorial Letter," *Int* 36 (1982): 5–20. Cf. Paul A. Holloway, "*Commendatio aliqua sui*: Reading Romans with Pierre Bourdieu," *Early Christianity* 2 (2011): 356–83.

12. As Theodoret of Cyrus claims in his *Commentary on Romans* to 1:6: "you too are from these Gentiles, with whose tending I have been entrusted. Do not think I am usurping what belongs to another and seizing pastures allotted to others: the Lord appointed me preacher to all the Gentiles" (trans. Hill).

13. Jewett (*Romans*, 131) argues that this reference to barbarians should be understood in relation to Paul's hope that believers in Rome would support his mission to barbarians in Spain (cf. Rom 15:24, 28). See James R. Harrison ("Paul's 'Indebtedness' to the Barbarian (Rom 1:14) in Latin West Perspective," *NovT* 55 [2013]: 311–48) for the way in which such claims of indebtedness to barbarians would have been heard in Rome and elsewhere.

14. In contrast to Dierk Starnitzke ("'Griechen und Barbaren . . . bin ich verpflichtet' [Röm 1,14]: Die Selbstdefinition der Gesellschaft und die Individualität und Universalität der paulinischen Botschaft," *WD* 24 [1997]: 187–207), who argues that the phrase "Greek and Barbarian" encompasses all of humanity, including Jews. On the punctuation and translation of Rom 1:13–15, see Runar M. Thorsteinsson, "Paul's Missionary Duty towards Gentiles in Rome: A Note on the Punctuation and Syntax of Rom 1,13–15," *NTS* 48 (2002): 531–47.

15. Das, *Solving the Romans Debate*, 57.

16. See Folker Siegert, *Argumentation bei Paulus gezeigt an Röm 9–11* (WUNT 34; Tübingen: Mohr Siebeck, 1985), 166. Contrary to C. K. Barrett, *A Commentary on the Epistle to the Romans* (HNTC; New York: Harpers, 1957), 211–12, and James D. G. Dunn, *Romans 9–16* (WBC 38B; Dallas: Word, 1988), 650–51.

17. See Munck, *Paul and the Salvation of Mankind*, 28 n. 3.

18. Thorsteinsson, *Paul's Interlocutor in Romans 2*, 110–11.

19. On the priestly language of this verse, see Richard J. Gibson, "Paul the Missionary, in Priestly Service of the Servant-Christ (Romans 15.16)," in *Paul as Missionary: Identity, Activity, Theology, and Practice*, ed. Trevor J. Burke and Brian S. Rosner (LNTS 420; London: T&T Clark, 2011), 51–62.

20. Jeffrey A. D. Weima, "Preaching the Gospel in Rome: A Study of the Epistolary Framework of Romans," in *Gospel in Paul: Studies in Corinthians, Galatians and Romans for Richard N. Longenecker*, ed. L. Ann Jervis and Peter Richardson (JSNTSup 108; Sheffield: Sheffield Academic, 1994), 337–66 (355). Cf. idem, "The Reason for Romans: The Evidence of Its Epistolary Framework (1:1–15, 15:14—16:27)," *RevExp* 100 (2003): 17–33, and Matthew V. Novenson, "The Jewish Messiahs, the Pauline Christ, and the Gentile Question," *JBL* 128 (2009): 357–73 (367–72).

21. White, *Remembering Paul: Ancient and Modern Contests over the Image of the Apostle* (Oxford: Oxford University Press, 2014), 102–3.

22. Hays, "The Gospel Is the Power of God for Salvation to Gentiles Only? A Critique of Stanley Stowers's Rereading of Romans," *CRBR* 9 (1996): 27–44 (37). Likewise, on the basis of Romans 16, Sanders (*Paul, the Law, and the Jewish People*, 184) states, "Romans is unique in the Pauline correspondence in containing so many clues to the presence of Jewish Christians among the readership." See also, Anthony J. Guerra, *Romans and the Apologetic Tradition: The Purpose, Genre and Audience of Paul's Letter* (SNTSMS 81; Cambridge, UK: Cambridge University Press, 1995), 166–69.

23. Thorsteinsson, *Paul's Interlocutor in Romans 2*, 99. See Thorsteinsson (*Paul's Interlocutor in Romans 2*, 63–65) for a discussion of second-person addresses (ἀσπάσασθε) in antiquity, as well as Terence Y. Mullins, "Greetings as a New Testament Form," *JBL* 87 (1968): 418–26. Numerous scholars since Baur (*Paul*, 1:381) have argued, based on the evidence of a number of early manuscripts

of Romans that lack this final chapter, that Paul did not write Romans 16, but that it was later appended to the letter. On the text-critical question of Romans 16, see James I. H. McDonald, "Was Romans 16 a Separate Letter?" *NTS* 16 (1970): 369–72; Harry Y. Gamble, *The Textual History of the Letter to the Romans: A Study in Textual and Literary Criticism* (SD 42; Grand Rapids: Eerdmans, 1977); and Norman R. Petersen, "On the Ending(s) to Paul's Letter to Rome," in *The Future of Early Christianity: Essays in Honor of Helmut Koester*, ed. Birger A. Pearson et al. (Minneapolis: Fortress, 1991), 337–47. Although I am convinced that Romans 16 was originally part of Paul's letter, if I were wrong, it would in no way change the substance of the argument that Paul repeatedly signals the gentile identity of his intended readers.

24. Thorsteinsson, *Paul's Interlocutor in Romans 2*, 84 and 5, respectively.

25. For instance, Michel (*Brief an die Römer*, 95–109) argues that Rom 1:18–32 is an example of Paul's missionary preaching. Jean-Noël Aletti ("Rm 1,18—3,20. Incohérence ou cohérence de l'argumentation paulinienne?" *Bib* 69 [1988]: 47–62) argues that Rom 1:18—3:20 demonstrates that all humanity, Jews and gentiles, are in the same situation. See, recently, Richard H. Bell, *No One Seeks for God: An Exegetical and Theological Study of Romans 1.18—3.20* (WUNT 106; Tübingen: Mohr Siebeck, 1998), and Jonathan Linebaugh, "Announcing the Human: Rethinking the Relationship between Wisdom of Solomon 13–15 and Romans 1.18–2.11," *NTS* 57 (2011): 214–37. Other interpreters, such as Cranfield (*Romans*, 1:105) and Jouette Bassler (*Divine Impartiality: Paul and a Theological Axiom* [SBLDS 59; Chico, CA: Scholars Press, 1982], 122), acknowledge that gentiles are Paul's primary target, but claim that he also indicts Jews.

26. Campbell (*The Deliverance of God: An Apocalyptic Rereading of Justification in Paul* [Grand Rapids: Eerdmans, 2009], 357), depending upon the observations of Calvin L. Porter, "Romans 1.18–32: Its Role in the Developing Argument," *NTS* 40 (1994): 210–28 (219).

27. Theodoret of Cyrus makes this same point, connecting Rom 3:2 and 1:19–20: "while the other nations had only the discernment that comes from nature, [Israel] received also the giving of the Law" (*Commentary on Romans* to 3:2; trans. Hill).

28. Cf. Rolf Dabelstein, *Die Beurteilung der "Heiden" bei Paulus* (BBET 14; Bern: Lang, 1981), 82, and Jewett, *Romans*, 160–61. Kathy L. Gaca ("Paul's Uncommon Declaration in Romans 1:18–32 and Its Problematic Legacy for Pagan and Christian Relations," *HTR* 92 [1999]: 165–98 [172]) obscures the differences, unjustifiably translating Ps 105:20 LXX, which refers to "their glory" (τὴν δόξαν αὐτῶν), as "the glory of God." As Stowers (*Rereading of Romans*, 93) says, "This move to include Jews in 'Paul's indictment of idolatry' depends almost entirely on the alleged allusion to Ps 105 together with an inattention to audience, argument, and context."

29. On the connection between idolatry and immorality, see Moshe Halbertal and Avishai Margalit, *Idolatry*, trans. Naomi Goldblum (Cambridge, MA: Harvard University Press, 1992), 9–36.

30. As Diana M. Swancutt ("'The Disease of Effemination': The Charge of Effeminacy and the Verdict of God (Romans 1:18—2:16)," in *New Testament Masculinities*, ed. Stephen D. Moore and Janice Capel Anderson [SemeiaSt 45; Atlanta: SBL Press, 2003], 193–233 [207]) notes, Paul never actually says that these women have sexual relations with other women, only that they exchange natural relations for unnatural ones. Such an accusation, then, may refer

to homoerotic behavior, as most scholars believe, or, as Swancutt argues, to women abandoning the role of the passive sexual partner.

31. So too Stowers, *Rereading of Romans*, 94.

32. Joshua D. Garroway, *Paul's Gentile-Jews: Neither Jew nor Gentile, but Both* (New York: Palgrave Macmillan, 2012), 120. So too Thorsteinsson, *Paul's Interlocutor in Romans 2*, 170.

33. Van Kooten, "Pagan and Jewish Monotheism according to Varro, Plutarch, and St. Paul: The Aniconic, Monotheistic Beginnings of Rome's Pagan Cult—Romans 1:19–25 in a Roman Context," in *Flores Florentino: Dead Sea Scrolls and Other Early Jewish Studies in Honour of Florentino García Martínez*, ed. Anthony Hilhorst et al. (JSJSup 122; Leiden: Brill, 2007), 633–51 (636).

34. Such stereotyped portrayals of others were common in antiquity, as Benjamin Isaac argues in *The Invention of Racism in Classical Antiquity* (Princeton: Princeton University Press, 2002). Cf. Rebecca F. Kennedy, C. Sydnor Roy, and Max L. Goldman, eds. and trans., *Race and Ethnicity in the Classical World: An Anthology of Primary Sources in Translation* (Indianapolis, IN: Hackett, 2013)

35. Van Kooten, "Pagan and Jewish Monotheism."

36. According to Fragment 190, Plutarch claimed that the Egyptians, Babylonians, and the Phrygians "were makers of images and guides to mysteries and initiators into sacred rites, and indeed it was from them that this worship was brought to the Greeks."

37. In contrast, Cicero (*Nature of Gods* 2.3.8) can claim that Roman piety was far superior to the piety of other nations.

38. Cf. Gaca, "Paul's Uncommon Declaration in Romans 1:18–32."

39. For those scholars, such as Douglas A. Campbell (*Framing Paul: An Epistolary Account* [Grand Rapids: Eerdmans, 2014]), who believe that Paul wrote Ephesians, Eph 4:17–19 provides even stronger evidence that Paul intends to portray only the gentile world in Rom 1:18–32.

40. I am indebted to Eric W. Scherbenske (*Canonizing Paul: Ancient Editorial Practice and the Corpus Paulinum* [Oxford: Oxford University Press, 2013], 187) for this reference.

41. Based on the Greek text of Vemund Blomkvist, *Euthalian Traditions: Text, Translation and Commentary* (TUGAL 170; Berlin: de Gruyter, 2012), 73 and 45, respectively.

42. It was Karl Hermann Schelkle (*Paulus, Lehrer der Väter: die altkirchliche Auslegung von Römer 1–11* [Düsseldorf: Patmos, 1956], 71) who noted that Augustine was the first interpreter to identify the judge as a Jew. Nonetheless, one of my doctoral students, Andrew C. Chronister, has demonstrated that, while this reading occurs in both *On the Spirit and Letter* and Augustine's *Letter 194*, his earlier work, *Propositions from the Epistle to the Romans*, understands the judge to be both Jews and gentiles.

43. Barclay, "Paul and Philo on Circumcision: Romans 2:25–9 in Social and Cultural Context," *NTS* 44 (1998): 536–56 (544). Cf. Dunn, *Romans 1–8*, 79, and idem, *The New Perspective on Paul*, rev. ed. (Grand Rapids: Eerdmans, 2005), 217.

44. So too Stowers, *Diatribe and Paul's Letter*, 217, n. 63, Jewett, *Romans*, 196, and Thorsteinsson, *Paul's Interlocutor in Romans 2*, 177–88, contra Michel, *Brief an die Römer*, 113, and Ernst Käsemann, *Commentary on Romans*, trans. and ed. Geoffrey W. Bromiley (Grand Rapids: Eerdmans, 1980), 54. Additionally, as Jouette M. Bassler (*Divine Impartiality*, 131–34) demonstrates, a number of

linguistic connections exist between Rom 1:18–32 and 2:1, most notably, the use of "to do" (ποιέω, 1:28, 32; 2:3) and "to practice" (πράσσω, 1:32; 2:1, 2, 3).

45. Stowers, *Rereading of Romans*, 13.
46. Thorsteinsson, *Paul's Interlocutor in Romans 2*, 169.
47. Stowers, *Rereading of Romans*, 145.
48. This suggestion is similar to, if not quite the same as, the interpretation of Swancutt ("Disease of Effemination," and "Sexy Stoics and the Rereading of Romans 1.18—2.16," in *A Feminist Companion to Paul*, ed. Amy-Jill Levine and Marianne Blickenstaff [Cleveland: Pilgrim Press, 2004], 42–73), who argues that in Rom 2:1–16 Paul addresses a Stoic sage.
49. Stowers, *Rereading of Romans*, 45. Cf. Edith Hall, *Inventing the Barbarian: Greek Self-Definition through Tragedy* (OCM; Oxford: Clarendon, 1989).
50. See Rafael Rodríguez, *If You Call Yourself a Jew: Reappraising Paul's Letter to the Romans* (Eugene, OR: Cascade, 2014).
51. The remainder of this chapter is based upon my article, "Paul's Argument against Gentile Circumcision in Romans 2:17–29," *NovT* 56 (2014): 373–91.
52. Byrne, *Romans* (SP 6; Collegeville, MN: Liturgical Press, 1996), 96. Cf. Käsemann, *Commentary on Romans*, 68–69; Anders Nygren, *Commentary on Romans*, trans. Carl C. Rasmussen (London: SCM, 1952), 130; Cranfield, *Romans*, 1:163–64; Elliott, *Rhetoric of Romans*, 191; Peter Stuhlmacher, *Paul's Letter to the Romans: A Commentary*, trans. Scott J. Hafemann (Louisville: Westminster John Knox, 1994), 48; Dunn, *Romans 1–8*, 109–110; Fitzmyer, *Romans*, 315; Philip F. Esler, *Conflict and Identity in Romans: The Social Setting of Paul's Letter* (Minneapolis: Fortress, 2003), 153; Watson, *Paul, Judaism, and the Gentiles*, 198–99; Nanos, *Mystery of Romans*, 82 n. 138; and Simon J. Gathercole, *Where is Boasting? Early Jewish Soteriology and Paul's Response in Romans 1–5* (Grand Rapids: Eerdmans, 2002), 197–201.
53. Jewett, *Romans*, 220.
54. Stowers, *Rereading of Romans*, 150. So too Ben Witherington with Darlene Hyatt, *Paul's Letter to the Romans: A Socio-Rhetorical Commentary* (Grand Rapids: Eerdmans, 2004), 85, and Wright, "Romans 2:17—3:9."
55. Jewett, *Romans*, 221.
56. Thorsteinsson, *Paul's Interlocutor in Romans 2*, 144.
57. Campbell (*Deliverance of God*, 565) acknowledges the shocking nature of this conclusion, but attempts to obviate the problem by arguing that this redefinition of Jewishness is the unintended "shameful argumentative implication" of the interlocutor's thinking.
58. Wright, *Paul and the Faithfulness of God* (Minneapolis: Fortress, 2013), 921. If this reading of Rom 2:17–29 is correct, one wonders how Wright can justify using the adverb "merely" with regard to such a drastic redefinition. (A similar question arises out of his repeated claims (1243–44) that the phrase "all Israel" in Rom 11:26 is a "polemical redefinition," now referring only to the church, not ethnic Israel.) It is a real irony that elsewhere and in relation to contemporary issues that matter to Wright, he can use rather insidious rhetoric to warn of the dangers of redefinition: "When anybody—pressure groups, governments, civilizations—suddenly change the meaning of key words, you really should watch out. If you go to a German dictionary and just open at random, you may well see several German words which have a little square bracket saying 'N.S.,' meaning National Socialist or Nazi. The Nazis gave those words a certain meaning." (Matthew Schmitz, "N. T. Wright on Gay Marriage: Nature and Narrative

Point to Complementarity," *First Things* [June 11, 2014], n.p. Online: http://www. firstthings.com/blogs/firstthoughts/2014/06/n-t-wrights-argument-against-same-sex-marriage).

59. Further, such redefinition is, as ethnographers have shown, conceivable: ethnicity and identity are always socially constructed. For evidence of such identity construction in early Judaism, see Shaye J. D. Cohen, *The Beginnings of Jewishness: Boundaries, Varieties, Uncertainties* (HCS 31; Berkeley: University of California Press, 1999). On the social construction of ethnicity and how it relates to Paul, see Caroline Johnson Hodge, *If Sons, Then Heirs: A Study of Kinship and Ethnicity in the Letters of Paul* (Oxford: Oxford University Press, 2007).

60. On these allegorists, see D. M. Hay, "Philo's References to Other Allegorists," *SPhilo* 6 (1979–1980): 41–75. It is also possible that the Jewish hellenizers who abandoned circumcision and other Jewish customs in the Antiochan period were attempting to redefine Jewishness in a way that undermined the relevance of such customs for Jewish identity. For instance, Elias Bickerman (*The God of the Maccabees: Studies on the Meaning and Origin of the Maccabean Revolt*, trans. Horst R. Moehring [SJLA 32; Leiden: Brill, 1979], 87) has argued that, at least in their own minds, Jason and Menelaus "wanted to reform Judaism by eliminating the barbaric separatism, which had been introduced only late, and returning to the original form of worship, free of any distortion."

61. Admittedly, scholars generally assign Leviticus 12 to the Priestly writer, and Leviticus 26 to the Holiness Code; nonetheless, physical and metaphorical circumcision can occur within the same work without implying that one or the other is irrelevant. See the helpful discussion of David A. Bernat, *Sign of the Covenant: Circumcision in the Priestly Tradition* (SBLAIL 3; Atlanta: SBL Press, 2009), 97–114.

62. For *Jubilees'* treatment of circumcision, see Matthew Thiessen, *Contesting Conversion: Genealogy, Circumcision and Identity in Ancient Judaism and Christianity* (Oxford: Oxford University Press, 2011), 67–86.

63. See Richard D. Hecht, "The Exegetical Contexts of Philo's Interpretation of Circumcision," in *Nourished in Peace: Studies in Hellenistic Judaism in Memory of Samuel Sandmel*, ed. Frederick E. Greenspahn, Earle Hilgert, and Burton L. Mack (Chico, CA: Scholars Press, 1984), 51–79; Alan Mendelson, *Philo's Jewish Identity* (BJS 161; Atlanta: Scholars Press, 1988), 54–58; and Barclay, "Paul and Philo on Circumcision," 538–43.

64. The phrase "circumcision of the heart" also occurs in Deut 10:16; 30:6; Ezek 44:7–9; and 1QpHab 11:13. See Werner E. Lemke, "Circumcision of the Heart: The Journey of a Biblical Metaphor," in *God So Near: Essays on Old Testament Theology in Honor of Patrick D. Miller*, ed. Brent A. Strawn and Nancy R. Bowen (Winona Lake, IN: Eisenbrauns, 2003), 299–319. Contrary to John Goldingay ("The Significance of Circumcision," *JSOT* 88 [2000]: 3–18), the use of metaphorical circumcision language does not undermine physical circumcision in Jewish scriptures; rather, as Bernat (*Sign of the Covenant*, 104) states, "Only a practice of such moment would be employed to symbolize Israel's transgression and salvation on a communal level." See also the important discussion of the visuality of the language of "heart circumcision" in J. M. F. Heath, *Paul's Visual Piety: The Metamorphosis of the Beholder* (Oxford: Oxford University Press, 2013), 132–37.

65. Quotations come from Barclay, "Paul and Philo on Circumcision," 540, 546.

66. A number of scholars believe that 1 Thess 2:13–16 must be a non-Pauline interpolation. See Birger A. Pearson, "1 Thessalonians 2:13–16: A Deutero-Pauline

Interpolation," *HTR* 64 (1971): 79–94, Hendrikus Boers, "Form Critical Study of Paul's Letters: I Thessalonians as a Case Study," *NTS* 22 (1976): 140–58, and Daryl Schmidt, "1 Thess 2:13–16: Linguistic Evidence for an Interpolation," *JBL* 102 (1983): 269–79. Since the use of *Ioudaios* in 1 Thess 2:14 fits with Paul's use of the word elsewhere, the issue of the authenticity of these verses does not affect my overall argument.

67. Dunn (*Romans 1–8*, 109) likewise notes that Paul "almost always" contrasts the category *Ioudaios* to categories of gentiles. For that matter, as Campbell (*Deliverance of God*, 375) recognizes, "Paul *never* elsewhere in his writings defines a [gentile Christ follower]—whom he would usually call a 'brother'—as a 'Jew,' as v. 29 must suggest on a Christian reading of this figure. This is *unparalleled*. . . . Elsewhere, then, the pagan convert never becomes a 'true' Jew. So the easy claim that this 'true Jew' in Romans 2 is in fact a Christian makes an unparalleled supersessionist assertion—and one without much wider supporting evidence from the rest of Paul." On the basis of this important observation, Campbell believes that these words must come from the mouth of Paul's interlocutor, not Paul. I provide a simpler solution in this chapter.

68. Esler, *Conflict and Identity*, 153, and Cranfield, *Romans*, 1:176.

69. To name but a few interpreters, see Dunn, *Romans 1–8*, 123; Witherington and Hyatt, *Paul's Letter to the Romans*, 91; Stuhlmacher, *Paul's Letter to the Romans*, 48–49; Gathercole, *Where is Boasting?*, 197–98; and Byrne, *Romans*, 96–97. English interpreters are not alone here. For instance, Eduard Lohse (*Der Brief an die Römer*, 15th ed. [KEK 4; Göttingen: Vandenhoeck & Ruprecht, 2003], 113–14) refers to the "rechter Jude" and "wahre Beschneidung"; Ulrich Wilckens (*Der Brief an die Römer*, 3 vols. [EKKNT 6; Neukirchen-Vluyn: Neukirchener Verlag, 1978–1992], 1:156) says that Paul answers the question of "wer in Wahrheit 'Jude' ist," and believes that heart circumcision is "wahre Beschneidung"; and Simon Légasse (*L'Épître de Paul aux Romains* [LD 10; Paris: Cerf, 2002], 211) refers to "le vrai juif."

70. Jewett, *Romans*, 236. Likewise, Fitzmyer (*Romans*, 320–21) concludes: "In effect, he denies the name to those who may outwardly be Jews, but are not so inwardly. The consequences of his indictment would seem to indicate that Paul regards Jews as cut off from the promises to Israel." And Käsemann (*Commentary on Romans*, 74) argues that "the true Jew is an eschatological phenomenon." Byrne (*Romans*, 105) acknowledges the theologically problematic fact that the redefinition "of the Jew (vv. 28–29) does, it is true, appear to annihilate Jewish identity," but then continues to defend this reading.

71. Cranfield, *Romans*, 1:175.

72. Barclay, "Paul and Philo on Circumcision," 545, and Stowers, *Rereading of Romans*, 155. Contrary to Barrett (*Romans*, 59), translations similar to Cranfield's do not merely add "the simplest grammatical supplements."

73. I take the phrase ἐν σαρκί to refer to the foreskin or penis, not to be a broader reference to human efforts or "racial kinship and national identity" (see Dunn, *Romans 1–8*, 124), since the circumcision legislation of Genesis 17 repeatedly uses σάρξ in this way (Gen 17:11, 13, 14, 23, 24, 25; cf. Lev 12:3). As Cranfield (*Romans*, 1:175 n. 2) notes, the rabbis also frequently referred to circumcision in the flesh and meant nothing more than genital circumcision.

74. Arneson, "Revisiting the Sense and Syntax of Romans 2:28–29." I am grateful to Arneson for making available this as yet unpublished research. Witherington (*Paul's Letter to the Romans*, 86) comes closest to this translation: "For [it is] not

the one who is outwardly a Jew, nor the one who is outwardly in the flesh the circumcision, but the one who is inwardly a Jew, and has the circumcision of the heart in the spirit and not the letter, who [seeks] the praise not from humans but from God" (parenthetical additions are Witherington's). Nonetheless, in his comments (91–92), he reverts back to the standard discussion of the "real" or "true" Jew.

75. Barclay, "Paul and Philo on Circumcision," 546, and Jewett, *Romans*, 237.

76. Here I disagree with Fitzmyer (*Romans*, 322), who claims that the statement "one is a Jew in secret, and real circumcision is of the heart" is the climax of Paul's thesis.

77. On whether it is Paul or his interlocutor who asks the question of Rom 3:1, see Campbell, *Deliverance of God*, 574–75; Elliott, *Rhetoric of Romans*, 132–41; Stowers, *Rereading of Romans*, 158–66; and Thorsteinsson, *Paul's Interlocutor in Romans 2*, 236–37. The majority of interpreters believe it is Paul's interlocutor. See also, C. H. Dodd, *The Epistle of Paul to the Romans* (MNTC 6; New York: Harper, 1932), 43; Barrett, *Romans*, 61–62; and Michel, *Brief an die Römer*, 80.

78. For a helpful interpretation of this passage, see Joshua D. Garroway, "Paul's Gentile Interlocutor in Romans 3:1–20," in *The So-Called Jew in Paul's Letter to the Romans*, eds. Rafael Rodríguez and Matthew Thiessen (Minneapolis: Fortress, 2016), 85–100.

79. On this passage, see Michael Cranford, "Election and Ethnicity: Paul's View of Israel in Romans 9.1–13," *JSNT* 50 (1993): 27–41, and Brian J. Abasciano, *Paul's Use of the Old Testament in Romans 9:1–9: An Intertextual and Theological Exegesis* (LNTS 301; London: T&T Clark, 2005).

80. Although it is possible to read ἐπονομάζῃ as a passive ("If you are called a Jew"), it should be rendered in the middle voice ("if you call yourself a Jew") because Paul's emphasis lies heavily upon the interlocutor's perception of himself, not other people's perceptions of him.

81. Likewise, John Chrysostom states, "For he does not say, Behold, thou art a Jew, but 'art called' so" (*Homilies on the Epistle to the Romans*, Homily 6 [*Nicene and Post-Nicene Fathers*, Series 1, 11:368]; cf. *Homilies on the Gospel of Matthew*, Homily 24 [*Nicene and Post-Nicene Fathers*, Series 1, 10:167]). Origen and Chrysostom, of course, go on to state that Christians are the true Jews. As Stowers (*Rereading of Romans*, 148), following Anton Fridrichsen ("Der wahre Jude und sein Lob: Röm. 2,28f," *Symbolae Arctoae* 1 [1922]: 39–49), notes, "Paul uses the popular philosophical motif of name (*onoma*) versus deed/reality (*ergon*), as do Epictetus and Plutarch."

82. Quotations come from Thorsteinsson, *Paul's Interlocutor in Romans 2*, 159, 199 n. 47, and 211, respectively. Paul does use the verb ὀνομάζω in Rom 15:20 without calling into question the veracity of the claim being made. Cf. Eph 1:21; 3:15; 5:3; 2 Tim 2:19. In all of these passages, context makes clear that the claim being made or name being given corresponds to reality.

83. See also, David Frankfurter, "Jews or Not: Reconstructing the 'Other' in Rev 2:9 and 3:9," *HTR* 94 (2001): 403–25 (420); Garroway, *Paul's Gentile-Jews*, 92–95; and Rodríguez, *If You Call Yourself a Jew*.

84. Scholars have debated the meaning of this latter charge of temple robbery/sacrilege and its precise connection to idolatry. For instance, J. Duncan Derrett ("'You Abominate False Gods; but Do You Rob Shrines' Rom 2.22b," *NTS* 40 [1994]: 558–71) lists six different possible translations of this phrase.

85. Cranfield, *Romans*, 1:168. Likewise, Gathercole (*Where is Boasting?*, 212) states, "Israel as a nation is subject to the same defilement [as gentiles] because of these three transgressions: stealing, adultery, and robbery of pagan temples."

86. Dodd, *Epistle of Paul*, 39.

87. Cranfield (*Romans*, 1:168) cites Strack-Billerbeck's *Kommentar zum Neuen Testament aus Talmud und Midrasch* (3:109–111) for evidence of rabbinic accusations against individual teachers who say one thing and do another, but then concedes that these passages do not imply, "as Paul does, that all contemporary Jews are guilty of the evils which are described."

88. Watson, *Paul, Judaism, and the Gentiles*, 203–5. Following Watson, Campbell (*Deliverance of God*, 561) concludes that this story "perfectly" explains this passage. Cf. Dunn, *New Perspective on Paul*, 167 n. 46.

89. Berkley, *From a Broken Covenant to Circumcision of the Heart: Pauline Intertextual Exegesis in Romans 2:17–29* (SBLDS 175; Atlanta: SBL Press, 2000), 133.

90. Tomson, *Paul and the Jewish Law: Halakha in the Letters of the Apostle to the Gentiles* (CRINT 1; Assen: Van Gorcum, 1990), 94.

91. Thorsteinsson (*Paul's Interlocutor in Romans 2*, 217–18) acknowledges that he has "some doubts about the rhetorical effect of such a charge."

92. For example, on the basis of Rom 2:25, Douglas J. Moo (*The Epistle to the Romans* [NICNT; Grand Rapids: Eerdmans, 1996], 156) claims, "Only a *perfect* doing of the law would suffice to justify a person before God." Interpreters sometimes point to remarks found in rabbinic literature. For instance, *t. Demai* 2.5 states: "A proselyte [although Manuscript Erfurt reads *goy* not *ger*] who took upon himself all the obligations of the law except for one item—they do not accept him. R. Yosé the son of R. Judah says, 'Even [if it be] a minor item from among the stipulations of the scribes'" (*t. Demai* 2:5; trans. Neusner). Cf. *b. Bek.* 20b; *b. Shabb.* 31a. But, as Sanders (*Paul, the Law, and the Jewish People*, 28) argues, the stress in rabbinic literature is on the convert's willingness to accept the entire law, not his subsequent ability to keep it perfectly.

93. As Fridrichsen ("Jude," 45) notes, Epictetus frequently accuses so-called Stoics of saying one thing and doing the opposite. For instance, Epictetus, *Discourses* 2.9.19–20: "Why, then, do you call yourself a Stoic, why do you deceive the multitude, why do you act the part of a Jew, when you are a Greek? Do you not see in what sense men are severally called Jew, Syrian, or Egyptian? For example, whenever we see a man halting between two things, we are in the habit of saying, 'He is not a Jew, he is only acting the part (οὐκ ἔστιν Ἰουδαῖος, ἀλλ' ὑποκρίνεται).' But when he adopts the attitude of mind of the man who has been baptized and has made his choice, then he both is a Jew in fact and is also called one" (slightly modified from LCL). Similarly, Epictetus (*Discourses* 3.24.40) says of the self-proclaimed Stoic who does not live like a Stoic, "Why, then, do you call yourself a Stoic? Well, but those who falsely claim Roman citizenship are severely punished, and ought those who falsely claim so great and so dignified a calling and title to get off scot-free?"

94. Hays, *Echoes of Scripture in the Letters of Paul* (New Haven: Yale University Press, 1989), 45.

95. Thorsteinsson, *Paul's Interlocutor in Romans 2*, 219.

96. Campbell, *Deliverance of God*, 564. Here I also disagree with William S. Campbell (*Paul's Gospel in an Intercultural Context: Jew and Gentile in the Letter to the Romans* [New York: Lang, 1992], 167), who states: "In Galatians, as distinct from Romans, the chief function of Paul's argument is to insist that

Gentile Christians do not need to become proselytes to Judaism; whether or not circumcision is obligatory for Christian believers is a crucial issue in the debate, but in Romans circumcision in this sense is not an issue."

97. This interpretation of Rom 2:17–29 also fits well with Stowers's argument ("Romans 7.7–25 as a Speech-in-Character [προσωποποιία]," in *Paul in His Hellenistic Context*, ed. Troels Engberg-Pedersen [Minneapolis: Fortress, 1995], 180–202) that in Rom 7:7–25 Paul depicts a judaizing gentile's anguish over his endeavors to keep the Jewish law, when he finds that he still lacks the self-control he believes it will give him. For a treatment of Romans 7 and how Paul deals with the gentile problem of lack of self-control (*akrasia*), see Chapter 5.

98. Jewett, *Romans*, 232.

99. On *periah*, see Nissan Rubin, "*Brit Milah*: A Study of Change in Custom," in *The Covenant of Circumcision: New Perspectives on an Ancient Jewish Rite*, ed. Elizabeth Wyner Mark (Brandeis Series on Jewish Women; Hanover, NH: Brandeis University Press, 2003), 87–97.

100. Of this uncircumcised person, Stowers (*Rereading of Romans*, 157) asks: "How can Paul say that if an uncircumcised man keeps the just requirements of the law, God will consider him circumcised, when he knows that circumcision is itself a requirement of the law for Jews? The best answer seems to be that Paul, along with many other Jews in antiquity, assumed that the law required different (and fewer) things of gentiles than of Jews. The passage simply assumes that the law requires literal circumcision of Jews but not of gentiles."

101. Jewett, *Romans*, 234. Tellingly, in his brief discussion of this verse, Gathercole (*Where is Boasting?*, 128) omits this phrase.

102. Daniel B. Wallace (*Greek Grammar Beyond the Basics: An Exegetical Syntax of the New Testament* [Grand Rapids: Zondervan, 1996], 368–69) provides no other possible translations of such a construction. Herbert Weir Smyth (*Greek Grammar*, 3d ed., revised by Gordon M. Messing [Cambridge, MA: Harvard University Press, 1984], 1685.1) notes that sometimes this construction refers to a state, feeling, property, or quality, but that such constructions take the verbs εἶναι, γίγνεσθαι, or ἔχειν.

103. E.g., Marie-Joseph Lagrange, *Saint Paul: Épître aux Romains* (EBib; Paris: Gabalda, 1950), 56; Barrett, *Romans*, 59; Otto Kuss, *Der Römerbrief*, 3 vols. (RNT 6; Regensburg: Pustet, 1957–1978), 1:90; Hans Wilhelm Schmidt, *Der Brief des Paulus an die Römer* (THNT 6; Berlin: Evangelische Verlagsanstalt, 1962), 55; Cranfield, *Romans*, 1:174; Moo, *Epistle to the Romans*, 172–73; Fitzmyer, *Romans*, 322; Byrne, *Romans*, 103; Jewett, *Romans*, 219; and Campbell, *Deliverance of God*, 565.

104. Thorsteinsson, *Paul's Interlocutor in Romans 2*, 228 n. 232.

105. Jewett, *Romans*, 867.

106. Schrenk, "γράφω, γραφή, γράμμα, ἐγγράφω, προγράμφω, ὑπογραμμός," *Theological Dictionary of the New Testament*, ed. Gerhard Kittel and Gerhard Friedrich; trans. Geoffrey W. Bromiley, 10 vols. (Grand Rapids: Eerdmans, 1964–1976), 1:742–73 (765); Porter, *Idioms of the Greek New Testament* (Sheffield: Sheffield Academic, 1992), 149; and Dunn, *Romans 1–8*, 123.

107. I have argued elsewhere ("The Text of Genesis 17:14," *JBL* 128 [2009]: 625–42) that the LXX, Samaritan Pentateuch, and *Jubilees* preserve the earliest inferable text of Gen 17:14.

108. For this reading of Genesis 17, see Thiessen, *Contesting Conversion*, 30–42. Even Abraham's (and Israel's) slaves do not enter into the covenant through

circumcision. See Catherine Hezser, *Jewish Slavery in Antiquity* (Oxford: Oxford University Press, 2005), 30–31.

109. Schrenk ("γράφω," *Theological Dictionary of the New Testament* 1:765) also suggests that γράμμα should be rendered as "prescription of the Law." For such a use of γράμμα see, for example, (Ps.-)Plato, *Epinomis* 325D; Aristotle, *Politics* 2.6.16 (1270b.30); Philo, *Special Laws* 3.8; and Thucydides 5.29.3. Thucydides provides a particularly relevant parallel since he uses γράμμα to refer to a single clause within a contract, just as for Paul and the author of *Jubilees* not circumcising at the correct time voids the whole covenant of circumcision in Genesis 17.

110. This reading differs from the MT, which states that "all the gentiles are uncircumcised" (כל הגוים ערלים). Since the LXX reading draws out the contrast with Israel, who is uncircumcised in heart, it is conceivable that the LXX translator added the phrase as an explanatory gloss. On the other hand, it is equally conceivable that scribes purposely omitted the Hebrew phrase "in the flesh" (בבשר) precisely because it appears to contradict the earlier reference to circumcised nations. This latter suggestion becomes more likely in light of the evidence of the Peshitta, Targum, and Arabic versions, which also read "the gentiles are uncircumcised in their flesh."

111. Berkley, *From a Broken Covenant*, 88. Peter C. Craigie et al. (*Jeremiah 1–25* [WBC 26; Dallas: Word, 1991], 153) make this same interpretive mistake with regard to Jeremiah, asserting that the "punishment coming upon all the circumcised included Judah, because all were uncircumcised of heart."

112. Richard C. Steiner, "Incomplete Circumcision in Egypt and Edom: Jeremiah (9:24–25) in the Light of Josephus and Jonckheere," *JBL* 118 (1999): 497–526.

113. Material culture, such as the relief reproduced in *The Ancient Near East in Pictures Relating to the Old Testament* [*ANEP*, figure 629], depicts Egyptian circumcision occurring at a later age. In the corresponding text (reproduced in *Ancient Near Eastern Texts Related to the Old Testament* [*ANET*], 326) the boy speaks to his circumciser, further indicating that infant circumcision is not intended. For Arab circumcision at the age of thirteen, see Gen 17:25 and Josephus, *Ant.* 1.214, as well as Jack M. Sasson, "Circumcision in the Ancient Near East," *JBL* 85 (1966): 473–76, and William H. Propp, "The Origins of Infant Circumcision in Israel," *HAR* 11 (1987): 355–70.

114. Here, see Thiessen, *Contesting Conversion*, as well as the relevant section of Chapter 1 in this work.

115. See the systematic treatments of Stowers, *Rereading of Romans*, Thorsteinsson, *Paul's Interlocutor in Romans 2*, and Rodríguez, *If You Call Yourself a Jew*.

CHAPTER 3

1. Although I translate here the Greek text of Nestle-Aland, 28th edition, it is possible, as Stephen C. Carlson ("'For Sinai is a Mountain in Arabia': A Note on the Text of Galatians 4,25," *ZNW* 105 [2014]: 80–101) argues, that the reference to Hagar is secondary and the statement "for Mount Sinai is in Arabia" (τὸ γὰρ Σινᾶ ὄρος ἐστὶν ἐν τῇ Ἀραβίᾳ) is a marginal scribal gloss that migrated into the text of Galatians. The argument of this chapter does not ultimately depend upon the text-critical decisions one makes at this point.

2. Quotations come from Hays, *Echoes of Scripture in the Letters of Paul* (New Haven: Yale University Press, 1989), 111–12. Christopher D. Stanley (*Arguing*

*with Scripture: The Rhetoric of Quotations in the Letters of Paul* [London: T&T Clark, 2004]) raises the question of how conversant these gentiles would have been with Jewish scriptures. Remarking on this question, Susan Eastman (*Recovering Paul's Mother Tongue: Language and Theology in Galatians* [Grand Rapids: Eerdmans, 2007], 21) states: "Part of the transforming power of a text is precisely in the dynamic relationship between the implied and actual readers: Paul's 'implied reader' challenges his actual readers to become more knowledgeable about Israel's Scriptures in order to understand what he says." One can see this challenge to become better readers explicitly in Gal 4:21, where Paul calls his readers to hear the law fully.

3.  Hanson, *Allegory and Event: A Study of the Sources and Significance of Origen's Interpretation of Scripture* (Richmond, VA: John Knox, 1959), 82; Longenecker, *The Triumph of Abraham's God: The Transformation of Identity in Galatians* (Nashville: Abingdon, 1998), 166; Matera, *Galatians* (SP 9; Collegeville, MN: Liturgical Press, 1992), 172; and Ramsay, *A Historical Commentary on St. Paul's Epistle to the Galatians* (London: Hodder and Stoughton, 1899), 431. For similar sentiments about the unjustifiable nature of Paul's reading of Genesis, see Philip F. Esler, *Galatians* (New Testament Readings; London: Routledge, 1998), 211; Sam K. Williams, *Galatians* (ANTC; Nashville: Abingdon, 1997), 126; and Angela Standhartinger, "Zur 'Freiheit . . . befreit'? Hagar im Galaterbrief," *EvT* 62 (2002): 288–303 (290).

4.  Barrett, "The Allegory of Abraham, Sarah, and Hagar in the Argument of Galatians," in *Essays on Paul* (Philadelphia: Westminster, 1982), 154–70 (162). See also Richard N. Longenecker, *Galatians* (WBC 41; Dallas: Word, 1990), 199.

5.  Matera, *Galatians*, 175.

6.  Such readings of Paul have led not only to theological tensions within Christian thinking, but also to historical tensions between Christians and Jews. Bradley R. Trick's question ("Sons, Seed, and Children of Promise in Galatians: Discerning the Coherence in Paul's Model of Abrahamic Descent" [Ph.D. diss., Duke University, 2010], 6) is germane: "If an arbitrary and admittedly unpersuasive series of arguments represents the best scriptural defense that Christianity has to offer in response to Judaism, then is it any wonder that Christian interactions with Jews have so often substituted unjustified caricature, arbitrary fiat, and violence for reasoned dialogue?"

7.  Watson, *Paul and the Hermeneutics of Faith* (London: T&T Clark, 2004), 207.

8.  For a reconstruction of the missionaries' gospel, see J. Louis Martyn, *Theological Issues in the Letters of Paul* (Nashville: Abingdon, 1997), 7–24; and, more cautiously, John M. G. Barclay, "Mirror-Reading a Polemical Letter: Galatians as a Test Case," *JSNT* 31 (1987): 73–93.

9.  As Eastman (*Recovering Paul's Mother Tongue*, 55) states, "The missionaries' gatekeeping requirement of circumcision, through which they exclude the uncircumcised Gentile believers from fellowship with them, is intended to create intensified zeal and yearning for acceptance into full covenant membership."

10.  Barclay, "Mirror-Reading." See also Franz Mussner, *Der Galaterbrief* (HTKNT 9; Freiburg: Herder, 1974), 27–28.

11.  Segal, *Paul the Convert: The Apostolate and Apostasy of Saul the Pharisee* (New Haven: Yale University Press, 1990), 141.

12.  In this, I disagree with Mark D. Nanos (*The Irony of Galatians: Paul's Letter in First-Century Context* [Minneapolis: Fortress, 2002]), who argues that the missionaries were Jews who did not believe in Christ.

13. Proponents of an anti-ethnocentric Paul often describe Paul's opponents in this way. See, for instance, James D. G. Dunn, *The New Perspective on Paul*, rev. ed. (Grand Rapids: Eerdmans, 2008); N. T. Wright, *The Climax of the Covenant: Christ and the Law in Pauline Theology* (Minneapolis: Fortress, 1992); and idem, *What Saint Paul Really Said: Was Paul of Tarsus the Real Founder of Christianity?* (Grand Rapids: Eerdmans, 1997).

14. Terence L. Donaldson, *Judaism and the Gentiles: Jewish Patterns of Universalism (to 135 CE)* (Waco: Baylor University Press, 2007), 4–5. See also Shaye J. D. Cohen, *The Beginnings of Jewishness: Boundaries, Varieties, Uncertainties* (HCS 31; Berkeley: University of California, 1999), 109–39; Paula Fredriksen, "What 'Parting of the Ways'? Jews, Gentiles, and the Ancient Mediterranean City," in *The Ways that Never Parted: Jews and Christians in Late Antiquity and the Early Middle Ages*, ed. Adam H. Becker and Annette Yoshiko Reed (Minneapolis: Fortress, 2007), 35–63; and John M. G. Barclay, "Paul, the Gift and the Battle over Gentile Circumcision," *ABR* 58 (2010): 36–56 (45).

15. *Jubilees* 15 provides the clearest evidence that some Jews believed that circumcision protected them from malevolent angelic activity (presumably on the basis of Exod 4:24–26), since it connects circumcision to the belief that Israel exists under God's supervision, while the gentiles exist under the influence of angelic beings (15.30–32; cf. Deut 32:8–9).

16. To many modern readers, the rite of circumcision might seem like too painful a requirement to encourage others to convert, but for those living in Anatolia, as Susan Elliott (*Cutting Too Close for Comfort: Paul's Letter to the Galatians in its Anatolian Cultic Context* [JSNTSup 248; London: T&T Clark, 2003]) shows, it would compare favorably to the self-castration that the Cybele cult required of *galli*. See also Stephen Mitchell, *Anatolia: Land, Men, and Gods in Asia Minor*, 2 vols. (Oxford: Clarendon, 1993). Elliott provides an illuminating discussion of the cultural context of Galatia, but I am unconvinced by her claim (14) that "Paul opposed circumcision for pastoral reasons given the Galatians' context. Circumcision was too similar to the ritual castration of the *galli*, the self-castrated servants of the Mother of the Gods. He saw circumcision as a particular threat that would return them to their previous condition. He presented this danger to the Galatians in terms veiled just enough to keep from re-empowering the figure of the Mother of the Gods in their lives." The evidence of Romans, 1 Corinthians, and Philippians suggests that Paul opposed gentile circumcision in diverse cultural settings, not merely in Galatia. For the argument that Paul's gospel was fundamentally Jewish and, therefore, required a degree of judaization on the part of gentiles, see Paula Fredriksen, "Judaizing the Nations: The Ritual Demands of Paul's Gospel," *NTS* 56 (2010): 232–52.

17. So too Richard B. Hays, "The Letter to the Galatians," in *2 Corinthians-Philemon*, ed. Leander E. Keck (NIB 11; Nashville: Abingdon, 2000), 181–348 (252).

18. See John William Wevers, ed., *Genesis* (SVTG 1; Göttingen: Vandenhoeck & Ruprecht, 1974), 176. Similarly, idem, *Notes on the Greek Text of Genesis* (SBLSCS 35; Atlanta: Scholars Press, 1993), 228.

19. Philippians 3 contains this same collocation of words for wholeness and circumcision. Consequently, it is likely that Paul's concern with completeness, as evidenced by words such as ἄμεμπτος, ἄμωμος, and τέλειος, is related to circumcision and reflects the language of competing missionaries who Paul worries will come to preach their gospel to gentiles in Philippi.

20. On the significance of Gen 15:6 in Paul's interpretation of Jewish scriptures, see Maria Neubrand, *Abraham—Vater von Juden und Nichtjuden: Eine exegetische Studie zu Röm 4* (FB 85; Würzburg: Echter, 1997); Pasquale Basta, *Abramo in Romani 4: L'analogia dell'agire divino nella ricerca Esegetica di Paolo* (AnBib 168; Rome: Biblical Pontifical Institute, 2007); and Benjamin Schliesser, *Abraham's Faith in Romans 4: Paul's Concept of Faith in Light of the History of Reception of Genesis 15:6* (WUNT 2/224; Tübingen: Mohr Siebeck, 2007).

21. Sanders, *Paul, the Law, and the Jewish People* (Philadelphia: Fortress, 1983), 68. Similarly, John M. G. Barclay (*Obeying the Truth: A Study of Paul's Ethics in Galatians* [SNTW; Edinburgh: T&T Clark, 1988], 62) argues that "this address and the allegory which follows it would be completely valueless if none of the Galatians was seriously concerned to listen to and submit to the law." Consequently, Hans Hübner (*Law in Paul's Thought: A Contribution to the Development of Pauline Theology*, trans. James C. G. Greig [SNTW; London: T&T Clark, 1984], 21) fundamentally misrepresents Paul, when he claims that "*circumcision is rejected in order to reject the Torah.*" Rightly or wrongly, Paul believes that the Galatians must reject circumcision in order to hear and accept the Torah.

22. Williamson, *Abraham, Israel and the Nations: The Patriarchal Promise and its Covenantal Development in Genesis* (JSOTSup 315; Sheffield: Sheffield Academic, 2000), 182–83, and Löfstedt, "The Allegory of Hagar and Sarah: Gal 4:21–31," *EstBib* 58 (2000): 475–94 (477).

23. Contrary to Joseph Blenkinsopp, "Abraham as Paradigm in the Priestly History in Genesis," *JBL* 128 (2009): 225–41 (237–38), and Konrad Schmid, "Judean Identity and Ecumenicity: The Political Theology of the Priestly Document," in *Judah and the Judeans in the Achaemenid Period: Negotiating Identity in an International Context*, ed. Oded Lipschits, Gary N. Knoppers, and Manfred Oeming (Winona Lake, IN: Eisenbrauns, 2011), 1–26. Despite the fact that God does not include Ishmael in the covenant that he established with Abraham, God does not abandon him (Gen 17:20). As Joel S. Kaminsky (*Yet I Loved Jacob: Reclaiming the Biblical Concept of Election* [Nashville: Abingdon, 2007]) has argued, the opposite of election is not damnation, but non-election. See also, idem, "Did Election Imply the Mistreatment of Non-Israelites?" *HTR* 96 (2003): 397–425.

24. For further problems with viewing circumcision as a process in ancient Israel by which slaves became Israelites, see Matthew Thiessen, *Contesting Conversion: Genealogy, Circumcision and Identity in Ancient Judaism and Christianity* (Oxford: Oxford University Press, 2011), 57–60, and Catherine Hezser, *Jewish Slavery in Antiquity* (Oxford: Oxford University Press, 2005), 30–31.

25. Syrén, *The Forsaken First-born: A Study of a Recurrent Motif in the Patriarchal Narratives* (JSOTSup 133; Sheffield: Sheffield Academic, 1993), 38; Gunkel, *Genesis*, trans. Mark E. Biddle (Macon, GA: Mercer University Press, 1997), 267; and Steuernagel, "Bemerkungen zu Genesis 17," in *Beiträge zur alttestamentlichen Wissenschaft: Karl Budde zum siebzigsten Geburtstag am 13. April 1920 überreicht von Freunden und Schülern*, ed. Karl Marti (BZAW 34; Giessen: Töpelmann, 1920), 172–79.

26. For fuller argumentation, see Thiessen, *Contesting Conversion*, 30–42.

27. Fokkelman, "Time and the Structure of the Abraham Cycle," in *New Avenues in the Study of the Old Testament: A Collection of Old Testament Studies Published*

*on the Occasion of the Fiftieth Anniversary of the Oudtestamentisch Werkgezelschap and the Retirement of Prof. Dr. M. J. Mulder*, ed. A. S. van der Woude (OtSt 25; Leiden: Brill, 1989), 96–109.

28. Matthew Thiessen, "The Text of Genesis 17:14," *JBL* 128 (2009): 625–42.

29. Bernat, *Sign of the Covenant: Circumcision in the Priestly Tradition* (SBLAIL 3; Atlanta: SBL Press, 2009), 55.

30. James C. VanderKam (*Textual and Historical Studies in the Book of Jubilees* [HSM 14; Missoula, MT: Scholars Press, 1977], 283) dates the work to shortly after the Antiochan crisis of 167–164 BCE. He is followed by Klaus Berger, *Das Buch der Jubiläen*, 2d ed. (JSHRZ 3; Gütersloh: Mohn, 1981), 299–300, and Eberhard Schwarz, *Identität durch Abgrenzung: Abgrenzungsprozesse in Israel im 2. vorchristlichen Jahrhundert und ihre traditionsgeschichtlichen Voraussetzungen Zugleich ein Beitrag zur Erforschung des Jubiläenbuches* (Europäische Hochschulschriften 162; Frankfurt: Lang, 1982), 99–129. Nonetheless, a few scholars, such as Doron Mendels (*The Land of Israel as a Political Concept in Hasmonean Literature: Recourse to History in Second Century B.C. Claims to the Holy Land* [TSAJ 15; Tübingen: Mohr Siebeck, 1987], 148–49) and Michael Segal (*The Book of Jubilees: Rewritten Bible, Redaction, Ideology and Theology* [JSJSup 117; Leiden: Brill, 2007]), date it, or at least its final redaction, to the late second century BCE.

31. Millar, "Hagar, Ishmael, Josephus and the Origins of Islam," *JJS* 44 (1993): 23–45 (37). Likewise, Segal, *Paul the Convert*, 196; Michel Testuz, *Les Idées Religieuses du Livre des Jubilés* (Geneva: Droz, 1960), 108; Segal, *Book of Jubilees*, 229–45; Nina E. Livesey, *Circumcision as a Malleable Symbol* (WUNT 2/295; Tübingen: Mohr Siebeck, 2010), 16–21; Jacques T. A. G. M. van Ruiten, "Genesis herschreven en geïnterpreteerd in het boek *Jubileeën*, nader toegelicht met een vergelijking van Genesis 17 en *Jubileeën* 15," *NedTT* 64 (2010): 32–50 (43–44); and Thiessen, *Contesting Conversion*, 67–86.

32. Philo, too, emphasizes that Isaac was the first person to undergo lawful circumcision: "Now the first of our nation who was circumcised by law and was named after the virtue of joy, was called Isaac in Chaldaean" (*QG* 3.38). Rabbinic literature contains similar claims. For instance, according to *Genesis Rabbah*, "R. Joḥanan said: No woman [hitherto] had been intimate for the first time with a man who had been circumcised at eight days save Rebekah" (60.5). Similarly, *Pesikta de Rav Kahana* observes, "Circumcision was inaugurated with Isaac, for when he was eight days old, he was the first to be circumcised, as is said 'Abraham circumcised his son Isaac when he was eight days old'" (12.1). And, finally, *Song of Songs Rabbah* states, "Abraham received the command of circumcision. Isaac inaugurated its performance on the eighth day" (1.2.5).

33. Trick, "Sons, Seed, and Children of Promise in Galatians," 78–79.

34. In Rom 4:1 Paul intends "flesh" (σάρξ) to refer primarily to circumcision, since the only occurrences of σάρξ in the Abraham Narrative refer specifically to the rite of circumcision: God commands Abraham and his descendants to circumcise the flesh of their foreskins (περιτμηθήσεσθε τὴν σάρκα τῆς ἀκροβυστίας ὑμῶν, 17:11), states that the sign of his covenant will be in Abraham's flesh (ἐπὶ τῆς σαρκός, 17:13), and cuts off the infant who is not circumcised in the flesh of his foreskin (τὴν σάρκα τῆς ἀκροβυστίας αὐτοῦ, 17:14). Following God's establishment of the covenant, Abraham circumcises the flesh of his foreskin (τὴν σάρκα τῆς ἀκροβυστίας αὐτοῦ), and the flesh of his entire household (17:24–26). The LXX translator's use of σάρξ to refer to the penis or the foreskin in the Abraham Narrative reflects a wider trend among the Greek translators of Jewish scriptures, as Lev 12:3; 15:2,

3, 19, and Ezek 44:6–9, for instance, make apparent. Likewise, Sirach states that God made a covenant with Abraham in his flesh, a clear reference to circumcision (44:20). In fact, the only references in early Jewish literature to Abraham's σάρξ which do not pertain to circumcision are *T. Abr.* A 20.5, a reference to Abraham's fleshly body failing at the sight of Death; *T. Abr.* B 7.16, a reference to bodily resurrection; and 13.7, where Abraham contrasts his flesh-and-blood body to the angel Michael's pneumatic body. So too Ambrosiaster, as seen in Gerald L. Bray, trans. and ed., *Ambrosiaster: Commentaries on Romans, 1–2 Corinthians* (Ancient Christian Texts; Downers Grove, IL: InterVarsity Press, 2009), 31.

35.  As in Rom 2:25, I take the phrase δι᾽ ἀκροβυστίας as instrumental—its most common usage, not as a purported διά of attendant circumstance. In contrast, most scholars (e.g., Robert Jewett, *Romans: A Commentary* [Hermeneia; Minneapolis: Fortress, 2007], 304; Arland J. Hultgren, *Paul's Letter to the Romans: A Commentary* [Grand Rapids: Eerdmans, 2011], 183) translate διά as "while."

36.  Similarly, N. T. Wright, *Paul and the Faithfulness of God* (Minneapolis: Fortress, 2013), 363.

37.  Although Wright (*Paul and the Faithfulness of God*, 1235) speaks of the "the polychrome people of God" in Paul's thinking (albeit with reference to Ephesians 3), his repeated conclusion that Paul rejects Jewish law observance for Jewish Christ followers leads inevitably to a Paul who demands a monochromatic people of God—gentiles who remain gentiles, and Jews who gentilize. At the end, all those in Christ live like (righteous) gentiles.

38.  Similarly, Theodoret of Cyrus, *Commentary on Romans* to 4:11–12: "Here there is need of distinction: he shows the patriarch as father first of those who believed while uncircumcised, since he himself while still uncircumcised offered God the gift of faith, then of course also of Jews on the grounds of their sharing circumcision with him" (trans. Hill).

39.  Longenecker, *Galatians*, 209.

40.  Ibid.

41.  Schoeps, *Paul: The Theology of the Apostle in the Light of Jewish Religious History*, trans. Harold Knight (Philadelphia: Westminster, 1961), 238 n. 3.

42.  Di Mattei, "Paul's Allegory of the Two Covenants (Gal 4.21–31) in Light of First-Century Hellenistic Rhetoric and Jewish Hermeneutics," *NTS* 52 (2006): 102–22.

43.  Donald A. Russell and David Konstan, eds., (*Heraclitus: Homeric Problems* [WGRW 14; Atlanta: SBL Press, 2005], xiii–xv) outline evidence that this understanding of *allegoria* likely dates back to the sixth century BCE. For recent discussions of *allegoria* in the Greco-Roman world, see Robert Lamberton and John J. Keaney, eds., *Homer's Ancient Readers: The Hermeneutics of Greek Epic's Earliest Exegetes* (Princeton: Princeton University Press, 1992); David Dawson, *Allegorical Readers and Cultural Revision in Ancient Alexandria* (Berkeley: University of California Press, 1992), 23–126; G. R. Boys-Stones, ed., *Metaphor, Allegory, and the Classical Tradition: Ancient Thought and Modern Revisions* (Oxford: Oxford University Press, 2003); and Peter T. Struck, *Birth of the Symbol: Ancient Readers at the Limits of Their Texts* (Princeton: Princeton University Press, 2004).

44.  Di Mattei, "Paul's Allegory," 106. Di Mattei notes that it is difficult to determine which of these two meanings Philo intends. In *Allegorical Interpretation* 2.5, 10; *Drunkenness* 99; *Migration* 131; and *Dreams* 1.67, Moses is the subject of the verb, and so Philo means that Moses speaks allegorically. Elsewhere, according to Philo, scriptures speak allegorically (*Cherubim* 25; *On Joseph* 28;

*Rewards* 125, 159; and *Contemplative Life* 29). Thus, out of the twenty-six occurrences of the verb, only ten times is it possible, but not necessary, to conclude that Philo means to explain something allegorically when the author did not intend it to be (*Allegorical Interpretation* 3.60; *Agriculture* 27, 157; *Migration* 205; *Names* 67; *Dreams* 2.31, 207; *Special Laws* 1.269; *Contemplative Life* 28; and *On Abraham* 99). On Philo's arguments that allegorization was rooted in the intention of the biblical author, see *Confusion of Tongues* 191; *Worse Attacks the Better* 167; *Giants* 34; *Migration* 48; and Maren R. Niehoff, *Jewish Exegesis and Homeric Scholarship in Alexandria* (Cambridge, UK: Cambridge University Press, 2011), 133–51.

45. Dawson, *Allegorical Readers*, 76.
46. Di Mattei, "Paul's Allegory," 122.
47. Di Mattei, "Biblical Narratives," in *As It Is Written: Studying Paul's Use of Scripture*, ed. Stanley E. Porter and Christopher D. Stanley (SBLSymS 50; Atlanta: SBL Press, 2008), 59–93 (86).
48. On this phenomenon, see Kristin de Troyer and Armin Lange, eds., *Reading the Present in the Qumran Library: The Perception of the Contemporary by Means of Scriptural Interpretations* (SBLSymS 30; Atlanta: SBL Press, 2005).
49. Heard, *Dynamics of Diselection: Ambiguity in Genesis 12–36 and Ethnic Boundaries in Post-Exilic Judah* (SemeiaSt 39; Atlanta: SBL Press, 2001), 22. For a similar reading of the historical background of the story of Ishmael in Genesis, see Syrén, *Forsaken First-born*, 54–65, and Danna Nolan Fewell, "The Genesis of Israelite Identity: A Narrative Speculation on Postexilic Interpretation," in *Reading Communities Reading Scripture: Essays in Honor of Daniel Patte*, ed. Gary A. Phillips and Nicole Wilkinson Duran (Harrisburg, PA: Trinity Press International, 2002), 111–18. For Genesis's Persian-period composition, see, most recently, Jonathan Huddleston, *Eschatology in Genesis* (FAT 2/57; Tübingen: Mohr Siebeck, 2012).
50. Hays, *Echoes of Scripture*, 113.
51. This reading has a long and less-than-illustrious history. For instance, in commenting on Gal 4:24–26 in his *Commentary on Galatians*, Jerome can say: "This is the explanation of nearly everyone on this passage: they interpret Hagar the slave woman as the law and the people of the Jews; but Sarah the free woman is the church that is gathered from the Gentiles, which is 'mother' of the saints" (trans. Scheck).
52. Esler, *Galatians*, 209, 210.
53. Hays, *Echoes of Scripture*, 111. See also Dieter Lührmann, *Galatians*, trans. O. C. Dean Jr. (CC; Minneapolis: Fortress, 1992), 89.
54. Westermann, *Genesis 12–36*, trans. John J. Scullion (CC; Minneapolis: Fortress, 1985), 238–39; and von Rad, *Genesis: A Commentary*, rev. ed., trans. John H. Marks (OTL; Philadelphia: Westminster, 1972), 191. See also John Van Seters, "The Problem of Childlessness in Near Eastern Law and the Patriarchs of Israel," *JBL* 87 (1968): 401–8.
55. Berg, "Der Sündenfall Abrahams und Saras nach Gen 16:1–6," *BN* 19 (1982): 7–14.
56. As Adolf Schlatter (*Die Briefe an die Galater, Epheser, Kolosser und Philemon* [Berlin: Evangelische Verlagsanstalt, 1963], 119) concludes, "Isaak war eine Schöpfung der allmächtigen Gnade Gottes." Interestingly, a synagogue prayer claims that God "made Isaac a son of promise" (*Hellenistic Synagogal Prayer* 12.64 [*OTP*]).

57. See Martyn (*Galatians: A New Translation with Introduction and Commentary* [AB 33A; New York: Doubleday, 1997], 451–57), who argues at length for identifying Sarah with Paul's mission and Hagar with his opponents' mission. Building on Martyn's work, Eastman (*Recovering Paul's Mother Tongue*, 131) states, "In 4:21—5:1, by designating Hagar and Sarah as two covenants, and by using the 'missioning' verb γεννάω to describe their respective pregnancies and deliveries, Paul speaks of two distinct Jewish Christian missions to the Gentiles." It should be noted, though, that, in contrast to Paul's depiction of Hagar, the editor of the Abraham Narrative portrays Hagar as entirely passive—a slave whose mistress hands her over to her husband without consultation.

58. Hahn, *Kinship by Covenant: A Canonical Approach to the Fulfillment of God's Saving Promises* (ABRL; New Haven: Yale University Press, 2009), 273.

59. On Paul's use of Isa 54:1, see Karen H. Jobes, "Jerusalem, our Mother: Metalepsis and Intertextuality in Galatians 4:21–31," *WTJ* 55 [1993]: 299–320; Martinus C. de Boer, "Paul's Quotation of Isaiah 54.1 in Galatians 4.27," *NTS* 50 (2004): 370–89; Joel Willitts, "Isa 54,1 in Gal 4,24: Reading Genesis in Light of Isaiah," *ZNW* 96 (2005): 188–210; and Matthew S. Harmon, *She Must and Shall Go Free: Paul's Isaianic Gospel in Galatians* (BZNW 168; Berlin: de Gruyter, 2010), 173–85.

60. Cf. David Novak, *The Election of Israel: The Idea of the Chosen People* (Cambridge, UK: Cambridge University Press, 1995), 188, and Avi Sagi and Zvi Zohar, *Transforming Identity: The Ritual Transition from Gentile to Jew—Structure and Meaning* (Kogod Library of Judaic Studies 3; London: Continuum, 2007).

61. It is possible, as Peder Borgen ("Some Hebrew and Pagan Features in Philo's and Paul's Interpretation of Hagar and Ishmael," in *The New Testament and Hellenistic Judaism*, ed. Peder Borgen and Søren Giversen [Peabody, MA: Hendrickson, 1997], 151–64) and Gerhard Sellin ("Hagar und Sara: Religionsgeschichtliche Hintergründe der Schriftallegorese Gal 4,21–31," in *Das Urchristentum in seiner literarischen Geschichte: Festschrift für Jürgen Becker zum 65. Geburtstag*, ed. Ulrich Mell and Ulrich B. Müller [BZNW 100; Berlin: de Gruyter, 1999], 59–84) suggest, that Paul plays on Hagar's name (הגר), which could be translated as "the *ger*"—that is the resident alien or even proselyte. Philo, for instance, can refer to this Hebrew meaning of Hagar's name (*Preliminary Studies* 20; *Allegorical Interpretation* 3.244; cf. *On Abraham* 251; *Gen. Rab.* 61.4). Nonetheless, even if the entirety of this verse is original (cf. Carlson, "'For Sinai is a Mountain in Arabia'"), I doubt Greek readers in Galatia would have caught such a subtle play on a Hebrew word.

62. Boyarin, *A Radical Jew: Paul and the Politics of Identity* (Contraversions; Berkeley: University of California Press, 1994), 269 n. 44, pointing to Philo, *Worse Attacks the Better* 59–60, and Schoeps, *Paul*, 156. The interpretations of Kimchi and Malbim are summarized by Meir Zlotowitz in *Bereishis/Genesis: A New Translation with a Commentary Anthologized from Talmudic, Midrashic and Rabbinic Sources*, 2 vols. (Brooklyn: Mesorah, 1988), 1:556.

63. Trible, "Ominous Beginnings for a Promise of Blessing," in *Hagar, Sarah, and Their Children: Jewish, Christian, and Muslim Perspectives*, ed. Phyllis Trible and Letty M. Russell (Louisville: Westminster John Knox, 2006), 33–69 (66 n. 32).

64. Kunin, *The Logic of Incest: A Structuralist Analysis of Hebrew Mythology* (JSOTSup 185; Sheffield: Sheffield Academic, 1995), 77.

65. For instance, given the significance that Dunn (*Paul and the New Perspective*, 109) places on the first-century meaning of circumcision, one would expect

greater attention to the LXX version of Genesis 17. In fact, the only Pauline inter-preter I have found who quotes Gen 17:9–14 according to the LXX is Watson, *Paul and the Hermeneutics of Faith*, 212.

66. Segal, *Paul the Convert*, 12.

67. Although the epistolary evidence focuses on a male rite, circumcision, I am not insensitive to the fact that gentile women were equally involved in these discussions and might have felt overshadowed by the focus on a rite that did not directly involve them. Cf. Tatha Wiley, *Paul and the Gentile Women: Reframing Galatians* (New York: Continuum, 2005).

68. See, for instance, Philipp Vielhauer, "Gesetzesdienst und Stoicheiadienst im Galaterbrief," in *Rechtfertigung: Festschrift für Ernst Käsemann zum 70. Geburtstag*, ed. Johannes Friedrich, Wolfgang Pöhlmann, and Peter Stuhlmacher (Tübingen: Mohr Siebeck, 1976), 543–55 (545).

69. Bultmann, *Primitive Christianity in its Contemporary Setting*, trans. R. H. Fuller (New York: World, 1956), 66.

70. As Barclay (*Obeying the Truth*, 64) remarks, "Nothing in this verse indicates that the Galatians' law-observance [or the message of the missionaries] was partial." Here I disagree with Troy W. Martin ("Pagan and Judeo-Christian Time-Keeping Schemes in Gal 4.10 and Col 2.16," *NTS* 42 [1996]: 105–19), and Justin K. Hardin (*Galatians and the Imperial Cult: A Critical Analysis of the First-Century Social Context of Paul's Letter* [WUNT 2/237; Tübingen: Mohr Siebeck, 2008], 118–27), who conclude that Paul refers not to Jewish calendrical observance, but to the Roman imperial cult. Hardin, for instance, argues that if Paul were referring to Jewish law observance here, he would have used terms like "Sabbaths" and "new moons," not generic references to days, months, and years. Nonetheless, Paul seems to allude here to Gen 1:14 (a passage that I will look at in more detail in Chapter 5), which connects the sun, moon, and stars to signs, seasons, days, and years, thereby linking calendrical observances to celestial bodies often thought to be the *stoicheia* of the kosmos. One can see that Jews identified the temporal periods in Gen 1:14 with the Jewish calendar in texts such as *Gen. Rab.* 6.1, which states that signs refer to Sabbaths, seasons to the three pilgrimage festivals, days to the beginning of the months, and years to the sanctification of the years.

71. Dunn, *New Perspective on Paul*, 319.

72. Manuscript Erfurt reads "gentile, "not "proselyte." Jacob Neusner (*The Tosefta: Translated from Hebrew with a New Introduction*, 2 vols. [Peabody, MA: Hendrickson, 2002]) notes that manuscript Vienna Heb. 20 lacks this statement. According to *b. Sanh.* 81a, after reading Ezek 18:9, Rabbi Gamaliel wept, concluding "Only he who does all these things shall live, but not merely one of them." In other words, Gamaliel realized the desperateness of this con-clusion. Nonetheless, Rabbi Akiba consoles him, arguing that "for doing one of these things [shall he live]" (trans. Epstein). Cf. *b. Makk.* 24a.

73. Sanders, *Paul, the Law, and the Jewish People*, 28.

74. Bruce, *The Epistle to the Galatians: A Commentary on the Greek Text* (NIGTC; Grand Rapids: Eerdmans, 1982), 231. Attempting to avoid this reading of Phil 3:5, Thomas R. Schreiner (*The Law and Its Fulfillment: A Pauline Theology of Law* [Grand Rapids: Baker, 1993], 70) makes the indefensible claim that Paul's "pur-pose is to say that his obedience to the law was extraordinary compared to his contemporaries."

75. The Samaritan Pentateuch (ככל התורה אשר יורו) agrees with the LXX reading, but the MT reads: "all which they [i.e., the priests] teach" (ככל אשר יורו). As John P. Meier

puts it (*Law and Love*, vol. 4 of *A Marginal Jew: Rethinking the Historical Jesus* [ABRL; New Haven: Yale University Press, 2009], 28): "Each individual directive from Yahweh qualified as a *tôrâ* in the singular."

76. Similarly, in his *Homilies on Genesis*, Chrysostom summarizes Gen 17:14 in the following way: "Whoever is not circumcised on the prescribed day shall be rooted out for breaking my covenant" (39.13; trans. Hill). Admittedly, in his *Discourses against Judaizing Christians*, Chrysostom understands Paul to be saying that circumcision entails subsequent obedience to the entirety of the Jewish law: "Do not tell me that circumcision is a single command; it is that very command which imposes on you the entire yoke of the Law. When you subject yourself to the rule of the Law in one part, you must obey its commands in all other things" (2.2.4; trans. Harkins). Over a century earlier, Origen provides a similar reading of Gal 5:3, albeit with reference not to circumcision but to Jewish festivals: "If anyone wants to preserve one thing from the observances of the Law, he 'is subject to doing the whole law.' Therefore, let whoever observes these fasts go up 'three times a year' to Jerusalem 'to appear before the Temple of the Lord,' to offer himself to the priest. Let him seek the altar which was turned into dust; let him offer sacrifices, with no high priest standing by. . . . Consequently, all these things must be completed by you who want to observe fasting according to the precept of the Law" (*Homilies on Leviticus* 10; trans. Barkley).

77. See the statements of the early twentieth-century Samaritan high priest, Jacob ben Aaron, in "Circumcision among the Samaritans," *BSac* 65 (1908): 694–710.

78. Similarly, Wright (*Paul and the Faithfulness of God*, 1136): "That, I suggest, is how we should then read Galatians 4.21—5.1: starting with 'Are you prepared to hear what the law says?' in 4.21, it reaches its climax with 'What does the Bible say? Throw out the slave-woman and her son!' "

79. Again, see Thiessen, *Contesting Conversion*, 30–42.

80. In contrast, Hardin (*Galatians and the Imperial Cult*, 85–115) translates Gal 6:13 as, "They are not concerned with the Law, but in order that they may boast in your flesh," arguing that Paul makes no claim about the opponents' own law observance, only that what motivates their preaching of circumcision is avoidance of persecution, not a deep concern that the gentile Galatians observe the Jewish law.

81. Betz, *Galatians: A Commentary on Paul's Letter to the Churches in Galatia* (Hermeneia; Philadelphia: Fortress, 1979), 317. Walter Schmithals (*Paul and the Gnostics*, trans. John E. Steely [Nashville: Abingdon, 1972], 38) thinks that the teachers have abandoned the law apart from circumcision, since this rite "portrayed the liberation of the pneuma-self from the prison of this body." See also Robert Jewett, "The Agitators and the Galatian Congregation," *NTS* 17 (1971): 198–212 (207–8).

82. Critical editions of the Greek text of Galatians agree in reading a present participle, although a number of manuscripts to the letter contain a perfect participle, περιτετμημένοι, instead (P[46], B, F, G, L Ψ, 6, 365, 614, 630, 1175, Ambrosiaster). It is likely that the perfect participle is the result of a scribal modification intended to make clear that these opponents of Paul were Jewish, and therefore had undergone circumcision in the past.

83. Harvey, "Opposition to Paul," in *The Galatians Debate: Contemporary Issues in Rhetorical and Historical Interpretation*, ed. Mark D. Nanos (Peabody, MA: Hendrickson, 2007), 321–33 (326). See also A. Neander, *Geschichte der Pflanzung und Leitung der christlichen Kirche durch die Apostel*, 2 vols., 4th ed.

(Hamburg: Perthes, 1847), 1:366–67; Ernest de Witt Burton, *A Critical and Exegetical Commentary on the Epistle to the Galatians* (ICC; Edinburgh: T&T Clark, 1921), 353; J. H. Ropes, *The Singular Problem of the Epistle to the Galatians* (HTS 14; Cambridge, MA: Harvard University Press, 1929), 44–45; E. Hirsch, "Zwei Fragen zu Galater 6," *ZNW* 29 (1930): 192–97, Johannes Munck, *Paul and the Salvation of Mankind*, trans. Frank Clarke (Richmond, VA: John Knox, 1959), 87–134; Peter Richardson, *Israel in the Apostolic Church* (SNTSMS 10; Cambridge, UK: Cambridge University Press, 1969), 84–97; and Michele Murray, *Playing a Jewish Game: Gentile Christian Judaizing in the First and Second Centuries* CE (Studies in Christianity and Judaism 13; Waterloo, ON: Wilfred Laurier University Press, 2004), 35.

84. Wallace, *Greek Grammar Beyond the Basics: An Exegetical Syntax of the New Testament* (Grand Rapids: Zondervan, 1996), 615, and Buist M. Fanning, *Verbal Aspect in New Testament Greek* (Oxford Theological Monographs; Oxford: Clarendon, 1990), 208.

85. So Betz, *Galatians*, 316.

86. Dunn (*New Perspective on Paul*, 448) argues that Paul's "challenge in 4.21 to those who wanted to be 'under law' (*hupo nomon*) was clearly directed to those of his Galatian converts who were being convinced that they should become full proselytes by accepting the obligations of Israel under the law." On the phrase "under the law," see Joel Marcus, "'Under the Law': The Background of a Pauline Expression," *CBQ* 63 (2001): 72–83.

87. Cohen, *Beginnings of Jewishness*, 175–97, and Murray, *Playing a Jewish Game*, 3–4.

88. Perkins, *Abraham's Divided Children: Galatians and the Politics of Faith* (The New Testament in Context; Harrisburg, PA: Trinity Press International, 2001), 56. Again, though, Paul's gospel itself required a certain degree of judaization of the gentiles, as Fredriksen argues in "Judaizing the Nations."

89. Robert Alter, *The Five Books of Moses: A Translation with Commentary* (New York: Norton, 2004), 103. Similarly, Heard, *Dynamics of Diselection*, 84.

90. Translation taken from Michael Maher, *Targum Pseudo-Jonathan: Genesis: Translated, with Introduction and Notes* (ArBib 1B; Collegeville, MN: Liturgical Press, 1992 [italics removed]). Bruce (*Galatians*, 223) also notes the significance of such interpretive traditions for understanding Gal 4:21–31. On the tradition in *Genesis Rabbah*, see Martha Himmelfarb, "The Ordeals of Abraham: Circumcision and the *Aqedah* in Origen, the *Mekhilta*, and *Genesis Rabbah*," *Hen* 30 (2008): 289–310 (297–99).

91. Lloyd Gaston, *Paul and the Torah* (Vancouver: University of British Columbia Press, 1987), 87 and 90.

92. Betz, *Galatians*, 246, 251. So too Ramsay, *Galatians*, 430–34; Burton, *Galatians*, 261; Marie-Joseph Lagrange, *Saint Paul: Épître aux Galates*, 2d ed. (EBib; Paris: Gabalda, 1950), 121; Schoeps, *Paul*, 234; Jürgen Becker, *Der Brief an Die Galater* (NTD 8; Göttingen: Vandenhoeck & Ruprecht, 1976), 57; Jobes, "Jerusalem, our Mother," 300; James D. G. Dunn, *The Epistle to the Galatians* (BNTC; Peabody, MA: Hendrickson, 1993), 257; and Michael Wolter, "Das Israelproblem nach Gal 4,21–31 und Röm 9–11," *ZThK* 107 (2010): 1–30 (16). Perhaps most offensively, J. B. Lightfoot (*Saint Paul's Epistle to the Galatians* [London: Macmillan, 1905], 184) concludes: "The Apostle thus confidently sounds the death-knell of Judaism at a time when one-half of Christendom clung to the Mosaic law with a jealous affection little short of frenzy, and while the Judaic party seemed to be growing in influence and was strong enough,

even in the Gentile churches of his own founding, to undermine his influence and endanger his life. The truth which to us appears a truism must then have been regarded as a paradox."

93. See, for instance, Daniel Boyarin, *Border Lines: The Partition of Judaeo-Christianity* (Divinations; Philadelphia: University of Pennsylvania, 2004), and Adam H. Becker and Annette Yoshiko Reed, eds., *The Ways That Never Parted: Jews and Christians in Late Antiquity and the Early Middle Ages* (Minneapolis: Fortress, 2007).

94. Apart from Martyn's commentary, see especially his essays entitled "A Law-Observant Mission to Gentiles," and "The Covenants of Hagar and Sarah: Two Covenants and Two Gentile Missions," in *Theological Issues*, as well as Barclay, "Mirror-Reading."

95. Similarly, William S. Campbell (*Paul's Gospel in an Intercultural Context* [New York: Lang, 1992], 127) concludes, "The problem with the traditional Lutheran approach is that, because of the law-gospel debate, Paul's statements to Gentile Christians . . . concerning their (possible) proselytism to Judaism have been frequently interpreted as a blanket criticism of Judaism as such and not merely of the view that required all Gentile Christians to Judaize."

96. Murray, *Playing a Jewish Game*, 29.

97. In this conclusion, Paul's thinking parallels Luke's portrayal of and solution to the gentile problem, which he addresses in Acts 10. See Thiessen, *Contesting Conversion*, 124–40.

98. Boyarin, *Radical Jew*, 32.

CHAPTER 4

1. Although Paul uses the phrase υἱοὶ Ἀβραάμ to refer to both male and female Christ followers, Caroline Johnson Hodge (*If Sons, Then Heirs: A Study of Kinship and Ethnicity in the Letters of Paul* [Oxford: Oxford University Press, 2007], 19–42, 68–72) has convinced me that translating υἱοί as "sons" better captures the fact that for Paul gentiles become υἱοί only as a result of being placed within the one υἱός—Christ. Gentiles become υἱοί of both God and Abraham because they are in Christ—the son of God and son of Abraham. Ultimately, Paul's logic is androcentric because, almost universally, it was sons and not daughters who were adopted (υἱοθεσία) and thus stood to inherit—Paul's precise concern when he speaks of gentiles becoming υἱοί. On adoption and inheritance, see James C. Walters, "Paul, Adoption, and Inheritance," in *Paul in the Greco-Roman World: A Handbook*, ed. J. Paul Sampley (Harrisburg, PA: Trinity Press International, 2003), 42–76. Cf. James M. Scott, *Adoption as Sons of God: An Exegetical Investigation into the Background of ΥΙΟΘΕΣΙΑ in the Pauline Corpus* (WUNT 2/48; Tübingen: Mohr Siebeck, 1992).

2. Eisenbaum, "A Remedy for Having Been Born of Woman: Jesus, Gentiles, and Genealogy in Romans," *JBL* 123 (2004): 671–702 (700).

3. Translating *pistis* presents a number of problems, as Paula Fredriksen ("The Question of Worship: Gods, Pagans, and the Redemption of Israel," in *Paul within Judaism: Restoring the First-Century Context to the Apostle*, ed. Mark D. Nanos and Magnus Zetterholm [Minneapolis: Fortress, 2015], 175–201 [193]) notes: "Here the connotations of our modern English words impede translation of our ancient Greek texts. Our word 'faith,' refracted through the prism

of a long Christian cultural history that runs at least from Tertullian (*credo quia absurdum*) to Kierkegaard, has come to imply all sorts of psychological inner states concerning authenticity or sincerity of 'belief.' In antiquity, *pistis*, and its Latin equivalent, *fides*, connoted, rather, 'steadfastness,' 'conviction,' and 'loyalty.'" On *pistis*, see now the important work of Teresa Morgan, *Roman Faith and Christian Faith: Pistis and Fides in the Early Roman Empire and Early Churches* (Oxford: Oxford University Press, 2015). Here I render *pistis* as "trust," "confidence," or "faith" to signify the relationality that Morgan shows to be inherent in *pistis*.

4. E.g., Daniel Boyarin, *A Radical Jew: Paul and the Politics of Identity* (Contraversions; Berkeley: University of California Press, 1994), 202.

5. Morna D. Hooker, "Heirs of Abraham: The Gentiles' Role in Israel's Story: A Response to Bruce W. Longenecker," in *Narrative Dynamics in Paul: A Critical Assessment*, ed. Bruce W. Longenecker (Louisville: Westminster John Knox, 2002), 85–96 (89).

6. N. T. Wright (*Paul and the Faithfulness of God* [Minneapolis: Fortress, 2013], 969 n. 542) correctly notes that "the point of the passage is still about how 'the blessing of Abraham' comes upon the Gentiles and the promised spirit is outpoured," but fails to apply this insight to his reading of Gal 3:10–14.

7. Richard B. Hays ("The Letter to the Galatians," in *2 Corinthians-Philemon*, ed. Leander E. Keck [NIB 11; Nashville: Abingdon, 2000], 181–348 [257]) acknowledges that this understanding of the Jewish law is "such a ridiculous caricature of Judaism . . . that it could hardly have been taken seriously as a persuasive argument in Paul's time." See also, George Howard, *Paul: Crisis in Galatia: A Study in Early Christian Theology*, 2d ed. (SNTSMS 35; Cambridge, UK: Cambridge University Press, 1990), 53, and Bradley R. Trick, "Sons, Seed, and Children of Promise in Galatians: Discerning the Coherence in Paul's Model of Abrahamic Descent" (Ph.D. diss., Duke University, 2010)," 146–47.

8. Gaston, *Paul and the Torah* (Vancouver: University of British Columbia Press, 1987), 74. Similarly, Stanley K. Stowers (*A Rereading of Romans: Justice, Jews, and Gentiles* [New Haven: Yale University Press, 1994], 246) argues, "The law contains a covenant with Israel but only promises and condemnation for the gentile nations." Cf. Timothy G. Gombis, "Arguing with Scripture in Galatia: Galatians 3:10–14 as a Series of Ad Hoc Arguments," in *Galatians and Christian Theology: Justification, the Gospel, and Ethics in Paul's Letter*, ed. Mark W. Elliott et al. (Grand Rapids: Baker Academic, 2014), 82–90. Although they do not agree with the position of Gaston and Stowers, Christopher D. Stanley ("'Under a Curse': A Fresh Reading of Galatians 3.10–14," *NTS* 36 [1990]: 481–511 [498 n. 52]) and Terence L. Donaldson ("The 'Curse of the Law' and the Inclusion of the Gentiles: Galatians 3.13–14," *NTS* 32 [1986]: 94–112) acknowledge that Paul's concern in this passage focuses solely on gentile inclusion.

9. Wrede, *Paul*, trans. Edward Lummis (London: Philip Green, 1907), 78. Halvor Moxnes (*Theology in Conflict: Studies in Paul's Understanding of God in Romans* [NovTSup 53; Leiden: Brill, 1980], 219), writing on Romans 4, similarly dismisses the importance of the promises of Jewish scriptures for Paul's gospel: "The references to the promise of God have their primary function in Paul's apology for his apostolic preaching and conduct. It was not his intention to describe his gospel as the fulfillment of the promise." In contrast, James D. G. Dunn (*The New Perspective on Paul*, rev. ed. [Grand Rapids: Eerdmans, 2008], 433) states, "The fact, then, that Paul chose to build his theological argument

round the theme of 'promise', despite the term 'covenant' being close to hand and actually in use within the immediate context of his argument, must tell us something about Paul's theology. That theology is better described as 'promise theology' rather than 'covenant theology.'" On the importance of the promise for Paul's gospel, see Gerhard Sass, *Leben aus den Verheißungen: Traditionsgeschichte und biblisch-theologische Untersuchungen zur Rede von Gottes Verheißungen im Frühjudentum und beim Apostel Paulus* (FRLANT 164; Göttingen: Vandenhoeck & Ruprecht, 1995), and Kevin P. Conway, *The Promises of God: The Background of Paul's Exclusive Use of Epangelia for the Divine Pledge* (BZNW 211; Berlin: de Gruyter, 2014).

10. Gaston, *Paul and the Torah*, 47. Similarly, Joshua W. Jipp ("Rereading the Story of Abraham, Isaac, and 'Us' in Romans 4," *JSNT* 32 [2009]: 217–42 [221]): "If Paul's gospel cannot accommodate Abraham by meeting the interlocutor's challenges and if his gospel does not demonstrate continuity with the hero of Israel, then it will by all accounts manifest itself to be untrue to its own stated principles." To Francis Watson's credit, in *Paul and the Hermeneutics of Faith* (London: T&T Clark, 2004) he works to take Paul at his word, although I find unconvincing his argument that Paul sees a fundamental contradiction in Jewish scriptures between faith and works. Again, in the words of Trick ("Sons, Seed, and Children of Promise," 5), "Regardless of the letter's ultimate effectiveness (or lack thereof), Paul clearly intends to present an argument that he believes the Galatians should find compelling." As Wolfgang Iser (*The Act of Reading: A Theory of Aesthetic Response* [Baltimore: Johns Hopkins University Press, 1978], 49) states, "Now it is certainly true that any response to any text is bound to be subjective, but this does not mean that the text disappears into the private world of its individual readers. On the contrary, the subjective processing of a text is generally still accessible to third parties, i.e., available for inter-subjective analysis." With relation to the reception of Paul's letter in Galatia, Paul's reading of Genesis would have experienced considerable pushback from his competitors if they thought it to be indefensible.

11. Trick, "Sons, Seed, and Children of Promise," 69.

12. E. P. Sanders (*Paul, the Law, and the Jewish People* [Minneapolis: Fortress, 1983], 21) believes that Paul has Gen 18:18 in mind, but, as Trick ("Sons, Seed, and Children of Promise," 101) notes, while "only Gen 18:18 incorporates all three elements of Paul's citation: blessing, Abraham, and the nations/gentiles," God does not speak the contents of this verse to Abraham, but about him.

13. Magnus Zetterholm, "Paul within Judaism: The State of the Questions," in *Paul within Judaism: Restoring the First-Century Context to the Apostle*, ed. Mark D. Nanos and Magnus Zetterholm (Minneapolis: Fortress, 2015), 31–51 (50).

14. Hansen, *Abraham in Galatians: Epistolary and Rhetorical Contexts* (JSNTSup 29; Sheffield: Sheffield Academic, 1989), 115.

15. Johnson Hodge, *If Sons, Then Heirs*, 99.

16. I agree with Hans-Joachim Eckstein (*Verheißung und Gesetz: Eine exegetische Untersuchung zu Galater 2,15—4,7* [WUNT 86; Tübingen: Mohr Siebeck, 1996], 119–20) and Trick ("Sons, Seed, and Children of Promise," 122) that the phrase οἱ ἐκ πίστεως in Gal 3:9 refers only to gentiles. As Trick states, "The context limits the scope of the οἱ to the previously mentioned gentiles," but I disagree with Trick's argument that the same phrase in Gal 3:7 refers to Jews. Both occurrences of the phrase οἱ ἐκ πίστεως refer to gentiles, who constitute the subject of Paul's argument.

17. Watson, *Paul and the Hermeneutics of Faith*, 192, and Gaston, *Paul and the Torah*, 29. Cf. Hans Dieter Betz (*Galatians: A Commentary on Paul's Letter to the Churches in Galatia* [Hermeneia; Philadelphia: Fortress, 1979], 152), who notes that 1 Cor 4:6 contains a similar construction of two purpose clauses in apposition to one another.

18. Lambrecht, "Abraham and His Offspring: A Comparison of Galatians 5,1 with 3,13," *Bib* 80 (1999): 525–36 (526).

19. Trick, "Sons, Seed, and Children of Promise in Galatians," 77–78.

20. Martin, "Paul's Pneumatological Statements and Ancient Medical Texts," in *The New Testament and Early Christian Literature in Greco-Roman Context: Studies in Honor of David E. Aune*, ed. John Fotopoulos (NovTSup 122; Leiden: Brill, 2006), 105–26. Perhaps the belief that the *pneuma* enters into people upon hearing the gospel is related to ancient theories of hearing such as is found in Plutarch, who states, "For speech is like a blow—when we converse with one another, the words are forced through our ears and the soul is compelled to take them in" (*Moralia* 588E). This observation would coincide with Timothy Luckritz Marquis's description (*Transient Apostle: Paul, Travel, and the Rhetoric of Empire* [Synkrisis; New Haven: Yale University Press, 2013], 95) of Paul's apostolic self-understanding in 2 Cor 2:14: "Since a letter carrier was authorized to explain the intentions of the letter's author and act as the author's stand-in, Paul depicts himself not simply as a suitable replacement for Christ, but as a courier for Christ's very spirit, transmitting knowledge of Christ (cf. 2:14) in unmediated form."

21. This evidence from Philo's *On the Virtues* and *Mekhilta de-Rabbi Ishmael* suggests that in Gal 3:2, 5, and 14b, at least, the *pistis* Paul has in mind is the trust of Christ followers, not Christ's faith, as Martinus C. de Boer (*Galatians: A Commentary* [NTL; Louisville: Westminster John Knox, 2011], 215), for instance, argues. See also the connection between human trust and the reception of the *pneuma* in John 7:39; Acts 6:5; 11:24; 19:2; Eph 1:13; 2 Thess 2:13. On the broader debate over whether the phrase πιστίς Χριστοῦ means "human faith in Christ" or "Christ's faith(fulness) to God," see James D. G. Dunn, "Once More, ΠΙΣΤΙΣ ΧΡΙΣΤΟΥ," in *Looking Back, Pressing On*, ed. E. Elizabeth Johnson and David M. Hay (vol. 4 of *Pauline Theology*; SBLSymS; Atlanta: Scholars Press, 1997), 61–81; Richard B. Hays, "Πίστις and Pauline Christology: What Is at Stake?" in *Looking Back, Pressing On*, ed. E. Elizabeth Johnson and David M. Hay (vol. 4 of *Pauline Theology*; SBLSymS; Atlanta: Scholars Press, 1997), 35–60; and the collected essays in Michael F. Bird and Preston M. Sprinkle, eds., *The Faith of Jesus Christ: Exegetical, Biblical, and Theological Studies* (Peabody, MA: Hendrickson, 2010).

22. Similar translations include Richard N. Longenecker (*Galatians* [WBC 41; Dallas: Word, 1990], 114): those who "rely on" faith; J. Louis Martyn (*Galatians: A New Translation with Introduction and Commentary* [AB 33A; New York: Doubleday, 1997], 299): "those whose identity is derived from faith"; de Boer (*Galatians*, 191): those who "live on the basis of faith."

23. Hays, *The Faith of Jesus Christ: The Narrative Substructure of Galatians 3:1—4:11*, 2d ed. (Bible Resource Series; Grand Rapids: Eerdmans, 2002), 171. Cf. Trick, "Sons, Seed, and Children of Promise," 60–61.

24. Johnson Hodge, *If Sons, Then Heirs*, 80.

25. Early Christ followers commonly refer to the *pneuma* with the word "power" (*dynamis*). This fits with Stoic language, as Samuel Sambursky (*Physics of the*

*Stoics* [London: Routledge & Kegan Paul, 1959], 36–37) has noted, as well as with Hebrew Bible and ANE conceptions, as Johannes Hehn ("Zum Problem des Geistes im Alten Orient und im Alten Testament," *ZAW* 43 [1925]: 210–25) argues.

26. Lull, *The Spirit in Galatia: Paul's Interpretation of Pneuma as Divine Power* (SBLDS 49; Chico, CA: Scholars Press, 1980), 105.

27. Johnson Hodge, *If Sons, Then Heirs*, 105. P[46] and Marcion omit τοῦ υἱοῦ here. As Gordon D. Fee rightly argues (*God's Empowering Presence: The Holy Spirit in the Letters of Paul* [Peabody, MA: Hendrickson, 1994], 405), Paul's "interest now is to make sure that the Galatians understand who the Spirit is: none other than the Spirit *of Christ*."

28. Sharvy, "Aristotle on Mixtures," *Journal of Philosophy* 80 (1983): 439–57 (440).

29. Samburskyy, *Physics of the Stoics*, 13. See also John Sellars, *Stoicism* (Berkeley: University of California Press, 2006), 88–89.

30. Robert B. Todd, *Alexander of Aphrodisias on Stoic Physics: A Study of the De Mixtione with Preliminary Essays, Text, Translation and Commentary* (Philosophia Antiqua 28; Leiden: Brill, 1976), 34. Cf. Gérard Verbeke, *L'évolution de la doctrine du pneuma, du stoïcisme à s. Augustin: Étude philosophique* (Paris: de Brouwer, 1945), 70–71, and Torstein Theodor Tollefsen, *Activity and Participation in Late Antique and Early Christian Thought* (OECS; Oxford: Oxford University Press, 2012), 136. Sellars (*Stoicism*, 89) argues that the Stoic theory of *krasis* "was proposed precisely to show how it would be possible for the two material principles to be in a total blend with one another. In particular, it was probably proposed in order to offer an explanation for the Stoics' counter-intuitive claim that two bodies, matter [*hylē*] and God [*pneuma*], can both be in the same place at once."

31. On Stoic conceptions of matter, see David Sedley, "Matter in Hellenistic Philosophy," in *Materia: XIII Colloquio Internazionale: Roma, 7–8–9 gennaio 2010*, ed. Delfina Giovannozzi and Marco Veneziani (Lessico intellettuale europeo 113; Rome: Olschki, 2011), 53–66. Modern interpreters of Stoic thinking usually consider the theory of *krasis* to be incoherent, but Daniel Nolan ("Stoic Gunk," *Phronesis* 51 [2006]: 162–83) suggests that the Stoic conception of "atomless gunk" makes this theory comprehensible. Recently, astrophysicists have claimed that dark matter can and does pass through ordinary matter, without any alteration to the two types of matter. That is to say, a body of one type of matter can share the same space as another form of matter in a way that approximates Stoic conceptions of *krasis*.

32. Gitte Buch-Hansen, *"It is the Spirit that Gives Life": A Stoic Understanding of Pneuma in John's Gospel* (BZNW 173; Berlin: de Gruyter, 2010), 77.

33. Johannine literature also contains a pneumatic and mutual interpentration between believer and Christ: "We know that we remain in him and he in us (ἐν αὐτῷ μένομεν καὶ αὐτὸς ἐν ἡμῖν), since he has given of his *pneuma* to us" (1 John 4:13). Cf. 1 John 4:15, John 15:1–7.

34. It is texts such as this one that led later Christian theologians to formulate Trinitarian doctrine. See, for instance, the discussions of Gordon D. Fee, "Christology and Pneumatology in Romans 8:9–11—and Elsewhere: Some Reflections on Paul as a Trinitarian," in *Jesus of Nazareth: Lord and Christ: Essays on the Historical Jesus and New Testament Christology*, ed. Joel B. Green and Max Turner (Grand Rapids: Eerdmans, 1994), 312–31; Friedrich Wilhelm Horn, "Kyrios und Pneuma bei Paulus," in *Paulinische Christologie: exegetische Beiträge: Hans Hübner zum 70. Geburtstag*, ed. Udo Schnelle and Thomas

Söding (Göttingen: Vandenhoeck & Ruprecht, 2000), 59–75 (62–64); and C. Kavin Rowe, "Biblical Pressure and Trinitarian Hermeneutics," *ProEccl* 11 (2002): 295–312 (305–6).

35. Mark Forman (*The Politics of Inheritance in Romans* [SNTSMS 148; Cambridge, UK: Cambridge University Press, 2011], 134) demonstrates that Romans 4 and Romans 8 are connected: "Rom. 4:13 and 8:17 are not isolated ideas but different ways of expressing the concept of God's eschatological renewal of the whole physical cosmos, the entire world. 'Heirs of God' should not be interpreted as the people of God who are God's 'inheritance,' but as the people who inherit God's promise to Abraham." Paul appears to divide his discussion of the *pneuma*, Christ, faith, and Abrahamic sonship/inheritance in Galatians 3 into two discussions in Romans: Romans 4 dealing with faith, inheritance, and Abraham's fatherhood, Romans 8 dealing with inheritance, *pneuma*, and being in Christ. Eisenbaum ("A Remedy for Having Been Born of Woman," 701) also argues for the importance of Abrahamic descent in Romans 5–8, despite the fact that Paul does not explicitly mention Abraham in these chapters. Since Paul's discussion of Abraham (Romans 4 and Romans 9) brackets Romans 5–8, it appears that in Romans Paul links being "in Christ" to Abrahamic descent in the same way we see in Galatians 3–4.

36. Stanley K. Stowers, "What Is 'Pauline Participation in Christ'?" in *Redefining First-Century Jewish and Christian Identities: Essays in Honor of Ed Parish Sanders*, ed. Fabian E. Udoh et al. (Christianity and Judaism in Antiquity 16; Notre Dame: University of Notre Dame Press, 2008), 352–71 (358).

37. As Friedrich Horn (*Das Angeld des Geistes: Studien zur paulinischen Pneumatologie* [FRLANT 154; Göttingen: Vandhoeck & Ruprecht, 1992], 170) and Martin ("Paul's Pneumatological Statments," 117) suggest.

38. Martin, *The Corinthian Body* (New Haven: Yale University Press, 1995), 176. So too Troels Engberg-Pedersen, *Cosmology and Self in the Apostle Paul: The Material Spirit* (Oxford: Oxford University Press, 2010), 174.

39. Wright, *Paul and the Faithfulness of God*, 232. On the *pneuma* in Jewish scriptures and early Judaism, see John R. Levison, *The Spirit in First-Century Judaism* (Leiden: Brill, 2002), and idem, *Filled with the Spirit* (Grand Rapids: Eerdmans, 2009). Cf. Jörg Frey and John R. Levison, eds., *The Holy Spirit, Inspiration, and the Cultures of Antiquity: Multidisciplinary Perspectives* (Ekstasis 5; Berlin: de Gruyter, 2014).

40. Buch-Hansen, *"It is the Spirit that Gives Life"*, 76.

41. It is this tension in Paul's thought that Joshua D. Garroway (*Paul's Gentile-Jews: Neither Jew nor Gentile, but Both* [New York: Palgrave Macmillan, 2012]), and Cavan W. Concannon (*"When You Were Gentiles": Specters of Ethnicity in Roman Corinth and Paul's Corinthian Correspondence* [Synkrisis; New Haven: Yale University Press, 2014]) explore.

42. Stowers, "What Is 'Pauline Participation in Christ'?" 359–60.

43. Johnson Hodge, *If Sons, Then Heirs*, 125.

44. For instance, Martyn (*Galatians*, 374–75) claims that Paul stresses divine sonship in order to minimize the importance of Abrahamic sonship. As I argue in this and the following chapter, Abrahamic sonship and divine sonship are both of considerable importance to Paul, and, in fact, intertwined.

45. Martin, *Corinthian Body*, 127. For a recent example of this confusion in relation to Paul's thinking, see Gil Anidjar, *Blood: A Critique of Christianity* (Religion, Culture, and Public Life; New York: Columbia University Press, 2014), 51.

46. Johnson Hodge, *If Sons, Then Heirs*, 75–76.
47. Quotations come from Terence Paige, "Who Believes in 'Spirit'? Πνεῦμα in Pagan Usage and Implications for the Gentile Christian Mission," *HTR* 95 (2002): 417–36 (425). On Jesus's statement in the Gospel of John that God is *pneuma*, see Buch-Hansen, *"It is the Spirit that Gives Life"*. See the overview of Verbeke, *L'évolution de la doctrine du pneuma*. In relation to Paul, see Horn, *Das Angeld des Geistes*, and Paul Robertson, "De-spiritualizing *Pneuma*: Modernity, Religion, and Anachronism in the Study of Paul," *MTSR* 26 (2014): 365–83.
48. Rabens, *The Holy Spirit and Ethics in Paul: Transformation and Empowering for Religious-Ethical Life* (WUNT 2/283; Tübingen: Mohr Siebeck, 2010).
49. Engberg-Pedersen, *Cosmology and Self*, 19. Based on Plato, *Timaeus* 86D, Martin (*Corinthian Body*, 12) states: "Even in Plato, therefore, the most dualistic of ancient philosophers, we find something quite different from the radical ontological dichotomy between mind and body, matter and nonmatter, familiar from Descartes. We are still dealing with something more like a spectrum of essences than a dichotomy of realms."
50. See David Sedley, "The School, from Zeno to Arius Didymus," in *The Cambridge Companion to the Stoics*, ed. Brad Inwood (Cambridge, UK: Cambridge University Press, 2003), 7–32 (30).
51. Stowers, "What is 'Pauline Participation in Christ'?" 356.
52. Cf. Harold W. Miller, "*Dynamis* and the Seeds," *TAPA* 97 (1966): 281–90.
53. Lee, *Paul, the Stoics, and the Body of Christ* (SNTSMS 137; Cambridge, UK: Cambridge University Press, 2006), 49–50. See the discussions of Achilles, *Isagoge* 14 (*SVF* 2.368) and Chrysippus in Alexander of Aphrodisias, *Mixtures* 216.14–16.
54. See Gad Freudenthal, *Aristotle's Theory of Material Substance: Heat and Pneuma, Form and Soul* (Oxford: Clarendon Press, 1995), 114–15.
55. Michael Boylan (*The Origins of Ancient Greek Science: Blood—A Philosophical Study* [Routledge Monographs in Classical Studies 22; New York: Routledge, 2015], 10) suggests a comparable modern medical analogy: "Since *pneuma* is so powerful and so plastic in its expression, another way to conceptualize it is in the modern example of stem cells. Stem cells are vital and pluripotent so that they can adapt to their environment and repair organs and tissue that are not functioning properly."
56. P⁴⁶ B D*, among others, read "you are" (ὑμεῖς . . . ἐστέ), while ℵ A C Dᶜ K P, among others, read "we are" (ἡμεῖς . . . ἐσμέν). Although the manuscript evidence is rather evenly divided, Martyn (*Galatians*, 443) rightly suggests that the latter variant arose out of the later tendency to read Paul's thinking in terms of a contrast between Christians ("we") and Jews.
57. Stowers, "What is 'Pauline Participation in Christ'?" 358–59.
58. That he chooses an olive tree instead of another tree may also be due to the high esteem given to olive trees and olive oil. For instance, Philo claims that "the ever-virginal olive-tree is of the purest substance which the inerrant sphere attains, for olive-oil is the material of light, and radiant in form is the heaven in which are the light-giving stars" (*QG* 4.1). Further, the *Apocalypse of Sedrach* portrays Sedrach saying to God, "I know that among your own creatures, Master, you loved man first; among the four-footed creatures, the sheep; among trees, the olive; among plants which bear fruit, the vine; among things that fly, the bee; among the rivers, (the) Jordan; among the cities, Jerusalem" (8.2; trans. Agourides [*OTP*]). Interestingly, this portrayal of Israel as a cultivated

olive tree fits with a broader trend of identifying Israel with domesticated animals. See Jonathan Klawans, *Purity, Sacrifice, and the Temple: Symbolism and Supersessionism in the Study of Ancient Judaism* (Oxford: Oxford University Press, 2006), 58–62.

59. In the next chapter, we shall see how this adoption as sons of God relates to God's promises to Abraham.

60. See Myles M. Bourke, *A Study of the Metaphor of the Olive Tree in Romans XI* (Studies in Sacred Theology 2.3; Washington, DC: Catholic University of America Press, 1947), 39–85, and Mark D. Nanos, "'Broken Branches': A Pauline Metaphor Gone Awry? (Romans 11:11–36)," in *Between Gospel and Election: Explorations in the Interpretation of Romans 9–11*, ed. Florian Wilk and J. Ross Wagner (WUNT 257; Tübingen: Mohr Siebeck, 2010), 339–76. On agricultural procedures, specifically, see A. G. Baxter and J. A. Ziesler, "Paul and Arboriculture: Romans 11:17–24," *JSNT* 24 (1985): 25–32, and Philip F. Esler, "Ancient Oleiculture and Ethnic Differentiation: The Meaning of the Olive-Tree Image in Romans 11," *JSNT* 26 (2003): 103–24.

61. Gordon, "On the Sanctity of Mixtures and Branches: Two Halakhic Sayings in Romans 11:16," *JBL* 135 (2016): 355–68.

62. Caroline Johnson Hodge, "Olive Trees and Ethnicities: Judeans and Gentiles in Rom. 11:17–24," in *Christians as a Religious Minority in a Multicultural City: Modes of Interaction and Identity Formation in Early Imperial Rome*, ed. Jürgen Zangenburg and Michael Labahn (JSNTSup 243; London: T&T Clark, 2004), 77–89 (83). Compare to the thinking of Plutarch, who claims that "the principle or force (*dynamis*) emanating from the parent is blended in the progeny, and cohabits its nature, which is a fragment or part of the procreator" (*Moralia* 1001A).

63. So too Johnson Hodge, "Olive Trees and Ethnicities," 88, and Garroway, *Paul's Gentile-Jews*, 11–12.

64. Franz Mussner, "'Christus (ist) des Gesetzes Ende zur Gerechtigkeit für jeden, der glaubt' (Rom 10,4)," in *Paulus—Apostat oder Apostel: Jüdische und christliche Antworten*, ed. Markus Barth et al. (Regensburg: Pustet, 1977), 31–44, Gaston, *Paul and the Torah*, 33, 148, and Gager, *Reinventing Paul* (Oxford: Oxford University Press, 2000), 60. See the helpful discussion of Terence L. Donaldson, "Jewish Christianity, Israel's Stumbling and the *Sonderweg* Reading of Paul," *JSNT* 29 (2006): 27–54. Although many scholars associate Stowers's *Rereading of Romans* with a two-track scheme, this is inaccurate. For instance, Stowers says of Rom 1:16–17: "Paul immediately announces (1:16–17) his confidence that the news about Christ and his faithfulness provides the key to understanding God's plan for dealing justly and successfully with both Jews and Greeks" (36; cf. similar comments on pages 132, 307, 364 n. 5). Stowers is reticent to provide a full account of how the gospel applies to Jews in Paul's thinking: "But what of the Jewish relation to Christ's faithfulness? Here Paul's letters provide only hints. One can understand this lack of clarity because he writes his letters to gentiles, about the gentile situation. Discussions of Israel appear only incidentally. Evidently, however, Israel does have a relation to Christ's faithfulness, although Paul speaks as if it differs from that of the gentiles" (205). No doubt, such circumspection has inadvertently contributed to this confusion about Stowers's argument, but it fits with Paul's own claims that Israel's hardening is a mystery (Rom 11:25). For a treatment of Paul's understanding of Jews who are not Christ followers, see Matthew V. Novenson, "The Self-Styled Jew of Romans

2 and the Actual Jews of Romans 9–11," in *The So-Called Jew in Paul's Letter to the Romans*, ed. Rafael Rodríguez and Matthew Thiessen (Minneapolis: Fortress, 2016), 133–62.

65. Similarly, Joseph A. Fitzmyer, *Romans* (AB 33; New York: Doubleday, 1993), 560–61.

66. For instance, one of Paul's contemporaries, Petronius, mocks the idea of non-Jews undergoing circumcision. The character of Giton exclaims, "Please circumcise us, too, so that we look like (*videamur*) Jews" (*Satyricon* 102.4). For Giton, then, non-Jews who undergo circumcision only look like Jews.

67. Garroway, *Paul's Gentile-Jews*, 8–9. Sze-kar Wan ("Does Diaspora Identity Imply Some Sort of Universality? An Asian-American Reading of Galatians," in *Interpreting Beyond Borders*, ed. Fernando F. Segovia [Bible and Postcolonialism 3; Sheffield: Sheffield Academic, 2000], 107–31 [126]) provides a similar interpretation of Gal 3:28. For this understanding of hybridity, see Homi K. Bhabha, *The Location of Culture* (New York: Routledge, 1994).

68. For a recent effort to read Paul's thinking in this way, see Love L. Sechrest, *A Former Jew: Paul and the Dialectics of Race* (LNTS 410; London: T&T Clark, 2010).

69. So too Caroline Johnson Hodge, "The Question of Identity: Gentiles as Gentiles—but also Not in Pauline Communities," in *Paul within Judaism: Restoring the First-Century Context to the Apostle*, ed. Mark D. Nanos and Magnus Zetterholm (Minneapolis: Fortress, 2015), 153–73.

70. Taking his cue from Troy Martin's work, Jeremy W. Barrier ("Jesus' Breath: A Physiological Analysis of πνεῦμα within Paul's Letter to the Galatians," *JSNT* 37 [2014]: 115–38) helpfully connects Christ the *sperma* to the reception of the *pneuma* using Greco-Roman medical texts. For instance, the second-century CE physician Galen asserts that *sperma* "is full of vital *pneuma*" (πλῆρές ἐστι τοῦ πνεύματος τοῦ ζωτικοῦ, *On Semen* 1.5.18).

71. So too Betz, *Galatians*, 156.

72. Burton, *A Critical and Exegetical Commentary on the Epistle to the Galatians* (ICC; Edinburgh: T&T Clark, 1920), 182. Cf. David Daube, *The New Testament and Rabbinic Judaism* (London: Athlone, 1956), 438–44.

73. Stanley, "Under a Curse," 492.

74. N. T. Wright, "Messiahship in Galatians?," in *Galatians and Christian Theology: Justification, the Gospel, and Ethics in Paul's Letter*, ed. Mark W. Elliott et al. (Grand Rapids: Baker Academic, 2014), 3–23 (8). In Romans, by contrast, Paul uses *theos* 155 times and *Christos* 68 times.

75. Wright, "Messiahship," 17.

76. Wright ("Messiahship," 20): "I would be happy to see indications of fluidity between king and people anywhere in ancient Judaism, but with such evidence either absent or controversial, I would settle for the hypothesis that the resurrection itself generated this link in Paul's mind." Even more problematic and troubling is Wright's continuing insistence that Paul redefines Israel so as to exclude most Jews and include gentiles-in-Christ.

77. Hays, *Echoes of Scripture in the Letters of Paul* (New Haven: Yale University Press, 1989), 85. See also, Max Wilcox, "The Promise of the 'Seed' in the New Testament and the Targumim," *JSNT* 5 (1979): 2–20, and Donald Juel, *Messianic Exegesis: Christological Interpretation of the Old Testament in Early Christianity* (Philadelphia: Fortress, 1988), 82.

78. See George J. Brooke, *Exegesis at Qumran: 4QFlorilegium in Its Jewish Context* (JSOTSup 29; Sheffield: JSOT Press, 1985), 139.

79. Scholars have long debated the meaning of *Christos* in Paul. The majority of scholarship has concluded that the phrase retained little messianic significance for Paul. Dunn's comment (*New Perspective on Paul*, 352) is representative: "As all commentators recognize, 'Christ' had already become a proper name in Paul's writing, having already lost most if not all of its titular force." Recently, however, Matthew V. Novenson (*Christ among the Messiahs: Christ Language in Paul and Messiah Language in Ancient Judaism* [Oxford: Oxford University Press, 2012]) has decisively overturned this conclusion, demonstrating that the term *Christos* functions as an honorific in Paul, one that closely parallels other honorifics used of Hellenistic and Roman rulers. See also, Christopher G. Whitsett, "Son of God, Seed of David: Paul's Messianic Exegesis in Romans 1:3–4," *JBL* 119 (2000): 661–81.

80. Duling, "The Promises to David and Their Entrance into Christianity: Nailing down a likely Hypothesis," *NTS* 20 (1973): 55–77 (73). Scott (*Adoption as Sons of God*, 229–36) provides a strong argument against the conclusion that Rom 1:3–4 is a pre-pauline creed.

81. Hays, *Echoes of Scripture*, 85.

82. Novenson, *Christ among the Messiahs*, 141–42.

83. It also occurs in 1 Chron 17:11 LXX. In contrast, 1 Chron 17:11 MT reads אשר יהיה מבניך ("who will be from your sons").

84. Wevers, *Notes on the Greek Text of Genesis* (SBLSCS 35; Atlanta: Scholars Press, 1993), 205.

85. The fact that Paul refers to Christ's Davidic descent in Rom 1:3–4 and 15:7–13, the bookends of the body of Paul's argument, and connects it to his apostleship to the gentiles undermines Rudolf Bultmann's claim (*Theology of the New Testament*, trans. Kendrick Grobel, 2 vols. [London: SCM, 1952], 1:49) that the title "son of David" in Rom 1:3 is of no significance to Paul. See now the important study of Joshua W. Jipp, *Christ is King: Paul's Royal Ideology* (Minneapolis: Fortress, 2015).

86. Gen 15:4 LXX and Gen 17:6 LXX are considerably closer than the MT here, which raises the possibility that the LXX translator has purposefully modified his translation to bring Gen 15:4 in closer proximity to 17:6. *Targum Neofiti* Gen 17:6 reads "from your loins" (מן חלציך).

87. Additionally, Num 24:7 LXX reads: "A man shall come out of [Jacob's] seed, and he will rule over many gentiles" (ἐξελεύσεται ἄνθρωπος ἐκ τοῦ σπέρματος αὐτοῦ καὶ κυριεύσει ἐθνῶν πολλῶν).

88. See also *Gen. Rab.* 98.9, which states of the root of Jesse mentioned in Isa 11:10: "Israel will not require the teaching of the royal Messiah in the future, for it says, Unto him shall the nations seek (Isa. xi, 10), but not Israel. If so, for what purpose will the royal Messiah come, and what will he do? He will come to assemble the exiles of Israel and to give them [the gentiles] thirty precepts." Cf. the interpretation of this verse in 4QPesher Isaiah[a] (4Q161).

89. On Romans 15, see Matthew V. Novenson, "The Jewish Messiahs, the Pauline Christ, and the Gentile Question," *JBL* 128 (2009): 357–73 (367–72).

90. Novenson, "Jewish Messiahs," 370–71.

91. For a fuller discussion, see Johnson Hodge, *If Sons, Then Heirs*, 93–107. On ancient theories of embryology, see Heinrich Balss, "Praeformation und Epigenese in der griechischen Philosophie," *Archivio di storia della scienza* 4 (1923): 319–25; E. Lesky and J. H. Waszink, "Embryologie," *RAC* (1959): 4:1228–44; and Devin Henry, "Embryological Models in Ancient Philosophy," *Phronesis* 50

(2005): 1–42. On ancient theories of conception, see Anthony Preus, "Galen's Criticism of Aristotle's Conception Theory," *Journal of the History of Biology* 10 (1977): 65–85; Michael Boylan, "The Galenic and Hippocratic Challenges to Aristotle's Conception Theory," *Journal of the History of Biology* 17 (1984): 83–112; and Andrew Coles, "Biomedical Models of Reproduction in the Fifth Century and Aristotle's *Generation of Animals*," *Phronesis* 40 (1995): 48–88.

92. Wilberding, "Porphyry and Plotinus on the Seed," *Phronesis* 53 (2008): 406–32.
93. Wedderburn, "Some Observations on Paul's Use of the Phrases 'in Christ' and 'with Christ,'" *JSNT* 25 (1985): 83–97 (89).
94. Levenson, *Abraham between Torah and Gospel* (Père Marquette Lecture in Theology 2011; Milwaukee: Marquette University Press, 2011), 45.

CHAPTER 5

1. 1 Macc 12:20–21 purports to preserve the letter of the Spartan Areus, who claims that the Spartans and Jews are brothers and that the Spartans are of the *genos* of Abraham. While this letter is surely fictional, as Erich S. Gruen ("The Purported Jewish-Spartan Affiliation," in *Transitions to Empire: Essays in Greco-Roman History, 360–146 B.C., in Honor of E. Badian*, ed. R. W. Wallace and E. M. Harris [Oklahoma Series in Classical Culture 21; Norman: University of Oklahoma Press, 1996], 254–69) argues, it does show that at least one Second Temple Jew could make such a claim. Even so, making claims about gentile Abrahamic descent is one thing (after all, many Jews thought Arabs and Idumeans were of Abrahamic descent), making claims that uncircumcised gentiles were Abraham's rightful heirs is quite another. Terence L. Donaldson ("Paul within Judaism: A Critical Evaluation from a 'New Perspective' Perspective," in *Paul within Judaism: Restoring the First-Century Context to the Apostle*, ed. Mark D. Nanos and Magnus Zetterholm [Minneapolis: Fortress, 2015], 277–301 [296]) concludes similarly: "the truly anomalous aspect is Paul['s] insistence that uncircumcised *ethnē*-in-Christ are at the same time full members of Abraham's 'seed' (*sperma*)."
2. Francis Watson (*Paul and the Hermeneutics of Faith* [London: T&T Clark, 2004]) correctly argues that Paul's thinking moves between the authority of the Christ event and the authority of Jewish scriptures.
3. Donaldson, "The 'Curse of the Law' and the Inclusion of the Gentiles: Galatians 3.13–14," *NTS* 32 (1986): 94–112 (94).
4. E.g., P⁴⁶ D* F G 88* 489, Marcion, and Ambrosiaster. See Bruce M. Metzger, *A Textual Commentary on the Greek New Testament*, 2d ed. (Stuttgart: Deutsche Bibelgesellschaft, 1994), 525.
5. Watson, *Paul and the Hermeneutics of Faith*, 192. For this use of ἵνα, see the Greek grammar of Blass-Debrunner-Funk (BDF) §394, and Daniel B. Wallace, *Greek Grammar Beyond the Basics: An Exegetical Syntax of the New Testament* (Grand Rapids: Zondervan, 1996), 475–76.
6. Trick, "Sons, Seed, and Children of Promise in Galatians: Discerning the Coherence in Paul's Model of Abrahamic Descent" [Ph.D. diss., Duke University, 2010], 196–202. See also Nils Alstrup Dahl, *Studies in Paul: Theology for the Early Christian Mission* (Minneapolis: Augsburg, 1977), 132. On pronominal shifts in Paul's writings, see C. E. B. Cranfield, "Changes in Person and Number in Paul's Epistles," in *Paul and Paulinism: Essays in Honour of C. K. Barrett*, ed.

Morna D. Hooker and Stephen G. Wilson (London: SPCK, 1982), 280–89. For an example of someone who reads the first-person plurals as referring to all believers, see Gordon D. Fee, *God's Empowering Presence: The Holy Spirit in the Letters of Paul* (Peabody, MA: Hendrickson, 1994), 395.

7.  Gaston, *Paul and the Torah* (Vancouver: University of British Columbia Press, 1987), 29. Caroline Johnson Hodge (*If Sons, Then Heirs: A Study of Kinship and Ethnicity in the Letters of Paul* [Oxford: Oxford University Press, 2007], 71) is one of the few to follow Gaston here.

8.  On the meaning of the phrase ἐξ ἀκοῆς πίστεως, see Sam K. Williams, "The Hearing of Faith: ΑΚΟΗ ΠΙΣΤΕΩΣ in Galatians 3," *NTS* 35 (1989): 82–93.

9.  See, for instance, Richard N. Longenecker, *Galatians* (WBC 41; Dallas: Word, 1990), 216, and J. Louis Martyn, *Galatians: A New Translation with Introduction and Commentary* (AB 33A; New York: Doubleday, 1997), 435.

10.  So too the majority of interpreters: Ernest de Witt Burton, *A Critical and Exegetical Commentary on the Epistle to the Galatians* (ICC; Edinburgh: T&T Clark, 1921), 176; Hans Dieter Betz, *Galatians: A Commentary on Paul's Letter to the Churches in Galatia* (Hermeneia; Philadelphia: Fortress, 1979), 153 n. 140; F. F. Bruce, *The Epistle to the Galatians: A Commentary on the Greek Text* (NIGTC; Grand Rapids: Eerdmans, 1982), 168; Joachim Rohde, *Der Brief des Paulus an die Galater* (THKNT 9; Berlin: Evangelische Verlagsanstalt, 1989), 145; James D. G. Dunn, *The Epistle to the Galatians* (BNTC; Peabody, MA: Hendrickson, 1993), 179; Udo Borse, *Der Brief an die Galater* (RNT; Regensburg: Pustet, 1984), 130; Hans-Joachim Eckstein, *Verheißung und Gesetz: Eine exegetische Untersuchung zu Galater 2,15—4,7* (WUNT 86; Tübingen: Mohr Siebeck, 1996), 152; Franz Mussner, *Der Galaterbrief* (HTKNT 9; Freiburg: Herder, 1974), 235; David John Lull, *The Spirit in Galatia: Paul's Interpretation of Pneuma as Divine Power* (SBLDS 49; Chico, CA: Scholars Press, 1980), 163 n. 4; Martyn, *Galatians*, 321; Ulrich Heckel, *Der Segen im Neuen Testament* (WUNT 150; Tübingen: Mohr Siebeck, 2002), 148–49; Scott W. Hahn, *Kinship by Covenant: A Canonical Approach to the Fulfillment of God's Saving Promises* (ABRL; New Haven: Yale University Press, 2009), 122; and Martinus C. de Boer, *Galatians: A Commentary* (NTL; Louisville: Westminster John Knox, 2011), 215.

11.  So too Trick ("Sons, Seed, and Children," 194), who states, "The fronted εἰς τὰ ἔθνη in 3:14a clearly emphasizes that Christ's action in 3:13 enables Abraham's blessing to come 'into the gentiles.'"

12.  See Samuel Sambursky, *Physics of the Stoics* (London: Routledge & Kegan Paul, 1959), 36–37. Thus, while Joseph A. Fitzmyer (*The Gospel according to Luke X–XXIV: A New Translation with Introduction and Commentary* [AB28A; Garden City, NY: Doubleday, 1985], 1585) correctly states that "the Spirit will be the source of the 'power,'" it would be more accurate to say that the *pneuma* is the power.

13.  Hays, *The Faith of Jesus Christ: The Narrative Substructure of Galatians 3:1—4:11*, 2d ed. (Bible Resource Series; Grand Rapids: Eerdmans, 2002), 181. Similarly, Alon Goshen-Gottstein ("The Promise to the Patriarchs in Rabbinic Literature," in *Divine Promises to the Fathers in the Three Monotheistic Religions: Proceedings of a Symposium Held in Jerusalem, March 24–25th, 1993*, ed. Alviero Niccacci [SBFA 40; Jerusalem: Franciscan Printing Press, 1995], 60–97 [62]) states, "When Paul speaks of the promises to the Patriarchs, their content differs from that of the promises in Gen. 17."

14.  Dahl, *Studies in Paul*, 136.

15. As Hays concedes (*Faith of Jesus Christ*, 182–83). Rodrigo J. Morales ("The Words of the Luminaries, the Curse of the Law, and the Outpouring of the Spirit in Gal 3,10–14," *ZNW* 100 [2009]: 269–77) explores the connection that both *Words of the Luminaries* (4Q504) and the *Testament of Judah* 24.2–3, in dependence upon Isa 44:3, make between *ruaḥ/pneuma* and blessing, but this still leaves unexplained the central question about the connection Paul makes between promise and *pneuma*.

16. Sze-Kar Wan, "Abraham and the Promise of the Spirit: Galatians and the Hellenistic-Jewish Mysticism of Philo," in *Society of Biblical Literature 1995 Seminar Papers* (SBLSPS 34; Atlanta: Scholars Press, 1995), 6–22.

17. Williams, "Promise in Galatians: A Reading of Paul's Reading of Scripture," *JBL* 107 (1988): 709–20.

18. Of these seventeen occurrences, nine are found in 1–4 Maccabees (1 Macc 10:15; 11:28; 2 Macc 2:18; 4:8, 27, 45; 3 Macc 1:4; 2:10; 4 Macc 12:9), one in Wisdom of Solomon 2:13, and one in 1 Esdras 1:17, which is a paraphrase of 2 Chron 35:7. Esther 4:7 LXX contains both the noun and the verb, which render the Hebrew אמר. Ps 55:9 LXX, Prov 13:12, and Amos 9:6 contain the noun or the verb, with no synonymous word in the MT. In other words, of the seventeen occurrences of *epangel* in the LXX, only Esther 4:7 LXX corresponds to a Hebrew word in the MT (אמר) that is remotely synonymous. See the discussion of Julius Schniewind and Gerhard Friedrich, "ἐπαγγέλλω, ἐπαγγελλία, ἐπάγγελμα, προεπαγγέλλομαι," *Theological Dictionary of the New Testament*, ed. Gerhard Kittel and Gerhard Friedrich; trans. Geoffrey W. Bromiley, 10 vols. (Grand Rapids: Eerdmans, 1964–1976), 2:576–86. Martyn (*Galatians*, 323) states that the word "promise" appears with regard to Abraham, Isaac, and Jacob in *Ezekiel the Tragedian* 107, but this claim is based on an English translation of the work, since the Greek states, "And remembering them and my gifts . . . (μνησθεὶς δ' ἐκείνων καὶ ἔτ' ἐμῶν δωρημάτων)."

19. Campbell, *The Deliverance of God: An Apocalyptic Rereading of Justification in Paul* (Grand Rapids: Eerdmans, 2009), 742. Cf. N. T. Wright, "Messiahship in Galatians?," in *Galatians and Christian Theology: Justification, the Gospel, and Ethics in Paul's Letter*, ed. Mark W. Elliott et al. (Grand Rapids: Baker Academic, 2014), 3–23.

20. On which, see Matthew V. Novenson, "The Jewish Messiahs, the Pauline Christ, and the Gentile Question," *JBL* 128 (2009): 357–73, and idem, "The Messiah ben Abraham in Galatians: A Response to Joel Willitts," *JSPL* 2 (2012): 163–69.

21. Incidentally, at the end of the first century CE, the author of *1 Clement* appears to conflate Gen 15:5 and Gen 22:17, and refers to them both as a promise: "As was promised by God that 'So shall your seed be as the stars of heaven'" (ὡς ἐπαγγειλαμένου τοῦ θεοῦ, ὅτι ἔσται τὸ σπέρμα σου ὡς οἱ ἀστέρες τοῦ οὐρανοῦ, *1 Clement* 32.2). The first part of the quotation (ἔσται τὸ σπέρμα σου) comes from Gen 15:5, while the latter part of the quotation comes from Gen 22:17 (τὸ σπέρμα σου ὡς οἱ ἀστέρες τοῦ οὐρανοῦ). In other words, like Paul (in both Galatians 3 and Romans 4), one early Christ follower in Rome (a) reads these two passages as referring to the same thing, (b) calls them a promise, and (c) does so in the context of a discussion of Abraham, works, faith, and Christ (31.2—32.3).

22. For examples of this usage, see Plato, *Euthydemus* 294B and also the *Chicago Assyrian Dictionary* 8.47 (b), 48 (g).

23. Admittedly, as Brennan W. Breed (*Nomadic Text: A Theory of Biblical Reception History* [Bloomington: Indiana University Press, 2014]) has argued, questions

of original intention become exceedingly difficult to answer once one acknowledges the composite nature of books like Genesis. Joel S. Baden (*The Promise to
the Patriarchs* [Oxford: Oxford University Press, 2013], 7) has helpfully demonstrated that the disparate materials making up the patriarchal narratives show
that "the promise is a blank theological slate, on which can be inscribed whatever is of significance to the author. It is a means of projecting one's own values
onto the most elemental statement of God's relationship with humanity, shaping the mythical past in the mold of the present."

24. See the entries on these two verbs in Wolf Leslau, *Comparative Dictionary of
Ge'ez* (Wiesbaden: Harrassowitz, 2006), 117 and 55, respectively. I am indebted
to Joel Marcus for help with the *Ge'ez*.

25. The manuscript witnesses to Sir 44:21 differ considerably. The Hebrew MS
B, the only Hebrew witness to the passage, lacks any reference to the dust
of the earth and stars. See Pancratius C. Beentjes, *The Book of Ben Sira in
Hebrew: A Text Edition of All Extant Hebrew Manuscripts and a Synopsis of all
Parallel Hebrew Ben Sira Texts* (VTSup 68; Leiden: Brill, 1997), 78. The Syriac
for v. 21b–d reads "that through his seed all the nations of the earth would be
blessed; that he would make his seed numerous as the sands of the seashore,
and that he would set his seed above all other nations." W. O. E. Oesterley (*The
Wisdom of Ben Sira [Ecclesiasticus]* [London: SPCK, 1916], 127) believed that the
LXX reading was original, but he did not have access to the Hebrew manuscripts of Sirach, which came to light with the discovery of the Dead Sea Scrolls.

26. In his discussion of this passage, Benjamin Schliesser (*Abraham's Faith in
Romans 4: Paul's Concept of Faith in Light of the History of Reception of Genesis
15:6* [WUNT 2/224; Tübingen: Mohr Siebeck, 2007], 172) misses this point.

27. Gregory ("Abraham as the Jewish Ideal: Exegetical Traditions in Sirach
44:19–21," *CBQ* 70 [2008]: 66–81 [80]): "Whereas the imagery of 'stars' is common in statements about God's blessing of Abraham, the use of the image in
the Hebrew Bible is always in a numeric context. Although the star imagery in
Sir 44:21 is qualitative rather than quantitative, the most likely explanation for
this shift in language is that it is simply indicative of the eschatological outlook
of the author."

28. In a note, Rubinkiewicz (*OTP* 1:699) states that the Old Slavonic could also
mean "host."

29. On the theme of Azazel's fall and Abraham's corresponding ascension, see
Andrei A. Orlov, *Heavenly Priesthood in the Apocalypse of Abraham* (Cambridge,
UK: Cambridge University Press, 2013). A similar tradition of star-like ascent
and dominance over Israel's enemies appears in the *Testament of Moses*'s portrayal of Israel's eschatological vindication: "And God will raise you [i.e., Israel]
to the heights. Yea, he will fix you firmly in the heavens, in the place
of their habitations. And you will behold from on high. Yea, you will see your
enemies on the earth" (10.9; trans. Priest [*OTP*]).

30. In his *Homilies on the Song of Songs*, Gregory of Nyssa states that the Lord said
to Abraham: "Look up to heaven and see these stars, if you can measure the
loftiness of their minds" (ἐκμετρῆσαι τῶν νοημάτων τὸ ὕψος, Homily 10; trans.
McCambley). Gregory believes that the command to look at the stars is meant to
draw attention to their elevated intellect and not to their innumerability. Roughly
contemporaneous with Gregory, Ambrose speaks similarly of Gen 15:5: looking
up to the stars, Abraham "perceived the splendor of his posterity as no less lumi-
nous than the radiance of the stars" (*On Abraham* 1.1.20; trans. Tomkinson).

31. Translations of the *Midrash Rabbah* come from H. Freedman and Maurice Simon, eds., *Midrash Rabbah*, 10 vols. (London: Soncino, 1939).

32. Early readers of these texts, such as Paul (1 Cor 15:40–42) or Luke (Acts 13:32–34; 26:6–7), could connect Dan 12:3 to Gen 15:5/22:17, especially if their version of Daniel contained the Prayer of Azariah, which explicitly refers to Gen 22:17 (Greek Dan 3:35–36), and conclude that God had promised Abraham that his seed would be resurrected to a star-like existence.

33. For an extensive discussion, see Dale C. Allison Jr., *Studies in Matthew: Interpretation Past and Present* (Grand Rapids: Baker Academic, 2005), 17–41.

34. Moshe Weinfeld ("Divine Intervention in War in Ancient Israel and in the Ancient Near East," in *History, Historiography and Interpretation: Studies in Biblical and Cuneiform Literatures*, ed. Hayim Tadmor and Moshe Weinfeld [Jerusalem: Magnes, 1983], 121–47 [125–27]) notes both an Egyptian parallel in the Gebel Barkal Stela of Thutmose III, which portrays a star, possibly the god Resheph, fighting on behalf of Egypt, and a Greek parallel in Homer's *Iliad* (4.75), in which Athena descends in the form of a star as a sign of the defeat of the Trojans.

35. Keel and Uehlinger, *Gods, Goddesses, and Images of God in Ancient Israel*, trans. Allan W. Mahnke (Minneapolis: Fortress, 1996), 195.

36. On this passage specifically, see L. Dequeker, "Les Qedôshim du Ps. LXXXIX à la lumière des croyances sémitiques," *ETL* 39 (1963): 469–84. More broadly, see Frank Moore Cross Jr., "The Council of Yahweh in Second Isaiah," *JNES* 12 (1953): 274–77; idem, *Canaanite Myth and Hebrew Epic: Essays in the History of the Religion of Israel* (Cambridge, MA: Harvard University Press, 1973), 12–43; and Theodore Mullen, *The Assembly of the Gods: The Divine Council in Canaanite and Early Hebrew Literature* (HSM 24; Chico, CA; Scholars Press, 1980).

37. On the way in which later rabbis used this passage, among others, to portray a rivalry between angels and humans, see Peter Schäfer, *Rivalität zwischen Engeln und Menschen: Untersuchungen zur rabbinischen Engelvorstellung* (SJ 8; Berlin: de Gruyter, 1975). Schäfer (239–40) argues that Rabbi Akiva was the first to connect this rivalry to Psalm 8, but see Gary A. Anderson, "The Exaltation of Adam and the Fall of Satan," in *Literature on Adam and Eve: Collected Essays*, ed. Gary Anderson, Michael Stone, and Johannes Tromp (SVTP 15; Leiden: Brill, 2000), 83–110 (87 n. 7).

38. For archaeological evidence of astral worship, see Frances Klopper ("Iconographical Evidence for a Theory on Astral Worship in Seventh- and Sixth-Century Judah," in *South African Perspectives on the Pentateuch between Synchrony and Diachrony*, ed. Jurie Le Roux and Eckart Otto [LHB/OTS 463; London: T&T Clark, 2007], 168–84 [174]), who concludes: "Iconographic images show a preference for deities of the night. Their astral forms, especially the crescent moon, the seven stars, or seven sisters, of the Pleiades and the eight-pointed star of Venus appear repeatedly on iconographical images." See also Hans-Peter Stähli, *Solare Elemente im Jahweglauben des alten Testaments* (OBO 66; Freiburg: Universitäts-verlag, 1985), and J. Glen Taylor, *Yahweh and the Sun: Biblical and Archaeological Evidence for Sun Worship in Ancient Israel* (JSOTSup 111; Sheffield: JSOT Press, 1993).

39. For the ancient Near East, see John McKay, *Religion in Judah under the Assyrians* (SBT 2/26; London: SCM, 1973), 45–59, and Francesca Rochberg, " 'The Stars Their Likenesses': Perspectives on the Relation Between Celestial Bodies

and Gods in Ancient Mesopotamia," in *What Is a God? Anthropomorphic and Non-anthropomorphic Aspects of Deity in Ancient Mesopotamia*, ed. Barbara Nevling Porter (Winona Lake, IN: Eisenbrauns, 2009), 41–91. For Greek thinking, see Martin P. Nilsson, "The Origin of Belief among the Greeks in the Divinity of the Heavenly Bodies," *HTR* 33 (1940): 1–8; idem, "Die astrale Unsterblichkeit und die kosmische Mystik," *Numen* 1 (1954): 106–19; and Alan Scott, *Origen and the Life of the Stars: A History of an Idea* (OECS; Oxford: Clarendon, 1991).

40. James R. Davila (*Liturgical Works* [ECDSS 6; Grand Rapids: Eerdmans, 2000], 240) states that "the word 'luminaries' [מאורות] refers to the heavenly bodies that regulate times and seasons (Gen 1:14–18; cf. 1QS x:3), but the Qumran literature also uses the word to mean angels." Cf. the Qumran work known as *Astrological Physiognomies* (4Q186), which connects the angel of darkness and astrology.

41. Kraemer, *When Aseneth Met Joseph: A Late Antique Tale of the Biblical Patriarch and His Egyptian Wife, Reconsidered* (Oxford: Oxford University Press, 1998), 101. While Kraemer and Rivka Nir (*Joseph and Aseneth: A Christian Book* [Hebrew Bible Monographs 42; Sheffield: Sheffield Phoenix, 2012]), among others, have argued that the work is a Christian composition, most scholars believe the work to be Jewish based on its concern about intermarriage between a Jew and a gentile. See, for instance, John J. Collins, "*Joseph and Aseneth*: Jewish or Christian?" *JSP* 14 (2005): 97–112.

42. Cf. Bernhard Hasslberger, *Hoffnung in der Bedrängnis: Eine formkritische Untersuchung zu Daniel 8 und 10–12* (St. Ottilien: Eos, 1977), 190–91, and John E. Goldingay, *Daniel* (WBC 30; Dallas: Word, 1989), 283. On this passage and star-like resurrection, see John J. Collins, "Apocalyptic Eschatology as the Transcendence of Death," *CBQ* 36 (1974): 21–43 (34–37).

43. Moffitt, *Atonement and the Logic of Resurrection in the Epistle to the Hebrews* (NovTSup 151; Leiden: Brill, 2011), 141.

44. Van Ruiten, "Angels and Demons in the Book of *Jubilees*," in *Die Dämonen: Die Dämonologie der israelitisch-jüdischen und frühchristlichen Literatur im Kontext ihrer Umwelt—Demons: The Demonology of Israelite-Jewish and Early Christian Literature in the Context of Their Environment*, ed. Armin Lange, Hermann Lichtenberger, and K. F. Diethard Römheld (Tübingen: Mohr Siebeck, 2003), 585–609 (589). See also Raija Sollamo, "The Creation of Angels and Natural Phenomena Intertwined in the *Book of Jubilees* (4Q Jub$^a$): Angels and Natural Phenomena as Characteristics of the Creation Stories and Hymns in Late Second Temple Judaism," in *Biblical Traditions in Transmission: Essays in Honour of Michael A. Knibb*, ed. Charlotte Hempel and Judith M. Lieu (JSJSup 111; Leiden: Brill, 2006), 273–90.

45. P. Wernberg-Møller ("A Reconsideration of the Two Spirits in the Rule of the Community [1QSerek III,13—IV,26]," *RevQ* 3 [1961]: 413–41) argues that the *ruḥot* here are not cosmic beings but human dispositions, while Arthur E. Sekki (*The Meaning of Ruaḥ at Qumran* [SBLDS 110; Atlanta: Scholars Press, 1989], 211) argues that 1QS refers to both human dispositions and cosmic beings. Sekki (145–71) examines over fifty occurrences of *ruaḥ* in Qumran literature that refer to angelic/demonic beings.

46. On 11Q11, see Hermann Lichtenberger, "Ps 91 und die Exorzismen in 11QPsAp$^a$," in *Die Dämonen: Die Dämonologie der israelitisch-jüdischen und frühchristlichen Literatur im Kontext ihrer Umwelt—Demons: The Demonology of Israelite-Jewish and Early Christian Literature in the Context of Their Environment*, ed. Armin Lange, Hermann Lichtenberger, and K. F. Diethard Römheld (Tübingen: Mohr

Siebeck, 2003), 416–21. On 11QPsᵃ, see David Flusser, "Qumrân and Jewish 'Apotropaic' Prayers," *IEJ* 16 (1966): 194–205. See also 4QIncantation (4Q560) and the related discussion in Douglas L. Penney and Michael O. Wise, "By the Power of Beelzebub: An Aramaic Incantation Formula from Qumran (4Q560)," *JBL* 113 (1994): 627–50.

47. This passage most clearly connects angelic beings to pneumatic beings, but see also John R. Levison, "The Prophetic Spirit as an Angel according to Philo," *HTR* 88 (1995): 189–207.

48. For a lengthy treatment of impure spirits, see Clinton Wahlen, *Jesus and the Impurity of Spirits in the Synoptic Gospels* (WUNT 2/185; Tübingen: Mohr Siebeck, 2004).

49. A similar tradition exists in the Latin text of the first-century CE work known as the *Life of Adam and Eve* 14, although there Satan's reason for refusing to worship Adam has to do with seniority: "Why do you compel me? I will not worship one inferior and subsequent to me. I am prior to him in creation; before he was made, I was already made. He ought to worship me" (trans. Johnson [*OTP*]). Interestingly, this belief persisted into the ninth century CE, when the author of the *Palaea Historica* pronounced an anathema upon anyone who suggested that Satan's downfall was the result of his refusal to worship Adam.

50. For the reception of the *Timaeus*, see Gretchen J. Reydams-Schils, ed., *Plato's Timaeus as Cultural Icon* (Notre Dame: University of Notre Dame Press, 2003).

51. Scott, *Origen and the Life of Stars*, 55.

52. David E. Hahm, *The Origins of Stoic Cosmology* (Columbus: Ohio State University Press, 1977), 70.

53. See Friedrich Solmsen, "The Vital Heat, the Inborn *Pneuma* and the Aether," *JHS* 77 (1957): 119–23; G. E. R. Lloyd, *Aristotle: The Growth and Structure of his Thought* (Cambridge, UK: Cambridge University Press, 1968), 133–39; and Abraham P. Boss and Rein Ferwerda, *Aristotle, On the Life-Bearing Spirit (De Spiritu): A Discussion with Plato and his Predecessors on Pneuma as the Instrumental Body of the Soul* (Leiden: Brill, 2008), 27.

54. Solmsen, "Vital Heat," 119.

55. In *On First Principles* 1.1.1–2, Origen attacks the belief that God is corporeal. From his argument, though, it becomes clear that some early Christians held this belief on the basis of at least two biblical passages: Deut 4:24, which says that God is a "consuming fire" (πῦρ καταναλίσκον), and John 4:24, in which Jesus claims that God is *pneuma*. Clearly such readers of Jewish scriptures, Paul among them, were indebted to Stoic physics, which viewed the divine body as consisting of the material of fiery *aether* or *pneuma*.

56. Sambursky, *Physics of the Stoics*, 1–48.

57. See also Bogdan Gabriel Bucur, *Angelomorphic Pneumatology: Clement of Alexandria and Other Early Christian Witnesses* (VCSup 95; Leiden: Brill, 2009).

58. Dunn, *The New Perspective on Paul*, rev. ed. (Grand Rapids: Eerdmans, 2008), 14.

59. Dahl, *Studies in Paul*, 136.

60. Blackwell, "Immortal Glory and the Problem of Death in Romans 3.23," *JSNT* 32 (2010): 285–308.

61. See, for instance, the discussions of Werner G. Kümmel, *Römer 7 und die Bekehrung des Paulus* (Leipzig: Hinrichs, 1929), and Jan Lambrecht, *The Wretched "I" and Its Liberation: Paul in Romans 7 and 8* (Leuven Theological & Pastoral Monographs 14; Leuven: Peeters, 1992). Watson (*Paul and the Hermeneutics of Faith*, 379) narrows this interpretation: "It is Jewish, not universal human, experience that is rendered here."

62. Stowers, "Romans 7.7–25 as a Speech-in-Character (προσωποποιία)," in *Paul in His Hellenistic Context*, ed. Troels Engberg-Pedersen (Minneapolis: Fortress, 1995), 180–202 (200). See also, Caroline Johnson Hodge, "Apostle to the Gentiles: Constructions of Paul's Identity," *BibInt* 13 (2005): 270–88 (280 n. 31); Emma Wasserman, *The Death of the Soul in Romans 7: Sin, Death, and the Law in Light of Hellenistic Moral Psychology* (WUNT 2/256; Tübingen: Mohr Siebeck, 2008); and Rafael Rodríguez, *If You Call Yourself a Jew: Reappraising Paul's Letter to the Romans* (Eugene, OR: Cascade, 2014), 130–46. Stowers ("Romans 7.7–25," 197, citing PG 79, 1:145) notes that Nilus of Ancyra, a disciple of John Chrysostom, also understood Paul to be using speech-in-character in Romans 7 to depict a gentile who has adopted the law of Moses. Nilus states, "Moreover, the person (τὸ πρόσωπον) is to be understood as belonging to those who have lived outside the law of Moses" (trans. Stowers).

63. Some manuscripts read "me" (με): e.g., A D K L P; others read "us" (ἡμᾶς): e.g., Ψ; and still others "you" (σε): e.g., ℵ B F G. The latter reading is preferable, since the first reading likely arose due to a scribe's intention to harmonize the pronoun in this verse with first-person singular pronouns of Romans 7, and the second reading likely arose in an effort to universalize Paul's statement to apply to all Christians. See the discussion of Metzger, *Textual Commentary*, 456.

64. On this passage, see Troels Engberg-Pedersen, "Galatians in Romans 5–8 and Paul's Construction of the Identity of Christ Believers," in *Texts and Contexts: Biblical Texts in Their Textual and Situational Contexts: Essays in Honor of Lars Hartman*, ed. Tord Fornberg and David Hellholm (Oslo: Scandinavian University Press, 1995), 477–505.

65. Fredriksen, "From Jesus to Christ: The Contribution of the Apostle Paul," in *Jews and Christians Speak of Jesus*, ed. Arthur E. Zannoni (Minneapolis: Fortress, 1994), 77–90 (89).

66. The only other use of this verb in the LXX occurs in Ps 36:35 LXX, which depicts the ungodly person exalting himself.

67. For thorough treatments of the angelic exaltation of Israel, see Mark Stephen Kinzer, "'All Things Under His Feet': Psalm 8 in the New Testament and in Other Jewish Literature of Late Antiquity" (Ph.D. dissertation, University of Michigan, 1995), and Jonah Steinberg, "Angelic Israel: Self-identification with Angels in Rabbinic Agadah and its Jewish Antecedents" (Ph.D. dissertation, Columbia University, 2003).

68. As John Reumann (*Philippians: A New Translation with Introduction and Commentary* [AB 33B; New Haven: Yale University Press, 2008], 393) suggests. See also Gerald F. Hawthorne, *Philippians* (WBC 43; Waco, TX: Word, 1983), 103. Gordon D. Fee (*Paul's Letter to the Philippians* [NICNT; Grand Rapids: Eerdmans, 1995], 246–48) argues that Paul alludes here to Dan 12:1–4. If so, this further confirms that Paul has astral imagery in mind.

69. Peder Borgen (*Paul Preaches Circumcision and Pleases Men: And Other Essays on Christian Origins* [Trondheim: Tapir, 1983], 15–42) notes that many of the fruits of the *pneuma* in Galatians 5 appear among the virtues that, according to Philo, accrue to the proselyte (*On the Virtues* 182). On the way in which Paul contrasts Christ's *pneuma* and circumcision as differing solutions to the gentile moral problem, see Frank J. Matera, "The Culmination of Paul's Argument to the Galatians: Gal. 5.1—6.17," *JSNT* 32 (1988): 79–91. On Paul's christological,

pneumatic ethics in Galatians 5, see Richard B. Hays, "Christology and Ethics in Galatians: The Law of Christ," *CBQ* 49 (1987): 268–90, and John M. G. Barclay, *Obeying the Truth: A Study of Paul's Ethics in Galatians* (SNTW; Edinburgh: T&T Clark, 1988).

70. Most scholarship understands Paul to be laboring to explicate a Jewish understanding of resurrection to a readership that only believes in the immortality of the soul, but this sharp distinction, which authors such as N. T. Wright (*The Resurrection of the Son of God* [Minneapolis: Fortress, 2003]) claim exists between Jewish beliefs in a resurrected body and Greek and Roman beliefs in the immortality of the soul, needs further nuancing in light of the argument of Dag Øistein Endsjø, *Greek Resurrection Beliefs and the Success of Christianity* (New York: Palgrave Macmillan, 2009).

71. Alan G. Padgett ("The Body in Resurrection: Science and Scripture on the 'Spiritual Body' (1 Cor 15:35–58)," *WW* 22 [2002]: 155–63 [159]) notes that Paul's list of animals "is simply the reverse order of Gen 1:20–30," whereas, David A. Burnett ("'So Shall Your Seed Be': Paul's Use of Genesis 15:5 in Romans 4:18 in Light of Early Jewish Deification Traditions," *JSPl* 5 (2015): 211–36) has suggested that Paul structures this list of beings on Deut 4:16–19, which contains the same sequence of terrestrial animals—humans, land animals, birds, [reptiles], fish (Deut 4:16–18), followed by the same sequence of celestial animals—sun, moon, and stars (Deut 4:19).

72. On this polarity, see Jeffrey R. Asher, *Polarity and Change in 1 Corinthians 15: A Study of Metaphysics, Rhetoric, and Resurrection* (HuTH 42; Tübingen: Mohr Siebeck, 2000). Contrary to Wright, *Resurrection of the Son of God*, 355.

73. Paul's thinking is similar to that found in the medieval Jewish work *Gedulat Moshe* ("The Greatness of Moses"): "Metatron said before the Holy One, Blessed be He: 'Moses is not able to ascend [to] the angels, because there are princes of fire among the angels, and he is flesh and blood'. After this, the Holy One, Blessed be He, commanded Metatron, and said to him: 'Go, turn his flesh into flashes of fire so that his strength is like the strength of Gabriel'" (2.3–4; cf. 2.9–11; trans. Spurling).

74. I use "matter" here intentionally. As Dale B. Martin (*The Corinthian Body* [New Haven: Yale University Press, 1995], 106–7) rightly notes, "we should be wary of introducing too quickly into this historical situation a matter/nonmatter dichotomy. It is not at all clear that what we moderns mean by 'matter' (whatever we *do* mean by the term, which is itself not clear in the latter twentieth century) has much relation to what ancient philosophers meant by *hylē*, which is normally translated as 'matter.'" To be sure, though, *hylē* and *pneuma* differ, as made clear by David Sedley, "Matter in Hellenistic Philosophy," in *Materia: XIII Colloquio Internazionale: Roma, 7–8–9 gennaio 2010*, ed. Delfina Giovannozzi and Marco Veneziani (Lessico intellettuale europeo 113; Rome: Olschki, 2011), 53–66.

75. Engberg-Pedersen, *Cosmology and Self in the Apostle Paul: The Material Spirit* (Oxford: Oxford University Press, 2010), 43. See also, Martin, *Corinthian Body*, 117–20.

76. Martin, *Corinthian Body*, 132. Cf. Engberg-Pedersen, *Cosmology and Self*, 32.

77. Tabor, *Things Unutterable: Paul's Ascent to Paradise in its Greco-Roman, Judaic, and Early Christian Contexts* (Studies in Judaism; Lanham, MD: University Press of America, 1986), 17.

78. Cf. M. David Litwa, *"We Are Being Transformed": Deification in Paul's Soteriology* (BZNW 187; Berlin: de Gruyter, 2012), 127. In this regard, it appears that Paul, unlike modern thinkers, does not believe that the type of matter is an essential characteristic of a body. This conclusion coincides with how Sedley ("Matter," 64) describes the Stoics: "the Stoics accept that a thing's *ousia* is not stable enough to constitute its enduring identity."

79. Unlike Paul, though, Tertullian envisages the resurrected having flesh-and-blood bodies that are made angelic. For instance, in *On the Resurrection* 42, Tertullian avers: "For from now on I pronounce that the flesh will certainly rise again, and that, as a result of the change which will supervene, it will take upon it angelic attire" (trans. Evans). Tertullian's use of 1 Corinthians 15 in defense of his belief in the resurrection of the flesh parallels other early Christian rereadings of 1 Corinthians 15. See, for instance, the helpful treatment of Benjamin L. White, "Reclaiming Paul: Reconfiguration as Reclamation in *3 Corinthians*," *JECS* 17 (2009): 497–523 (510–16).

80. For a full discussion of Origen's use of Gen 15:5 and 22:17, see F. Ledegang, *Mysterium Ecclesiae: Images of the Church and its Members in Origen* (BETL 156; Leuven: Peeters, 2001), 630–39.

81. For Stoic influence on the thinking of early Christian writers, see Michel Spanneut, *Le Stoïcisme des Pères de l'Église: de Clément de Rome à Clément d'Alexandrie* (Paris: Éditions du Seuil, 1957).

82. On this terminology, see Tabor, *Things Unutterable*.

83. Martyn, *Galatians*, 374–75.

84. See Brendan Byrne, *"Sons of God"—"Seed of Abraham": A Study of the Idea of the Sonship of God of All Christians in Paul against the Jewish Background* (AnBib 83; Rome: Biblical Institute Press, 1979), 10–13.

85. Tabor, *Things Unutterable*, 11.

86. So too Johnson Hodge (*If Sons, Then Heirs*, 71): "Paul's use of the first-person pronoun 'we' in Galatians 4:3 does not mean he includes [Jews] in this past state, as many commentators assume. Instead, Paul commonly uses the first-person plural 'we' to indicate that he identifies with his gentile audience. Indeed, the whole analogy, in which the 'slaves' become adopted sons of God, makes no sense for Jews, who already enjoy this status (Rom 9:4)."

87. See the full discussion of Andrew John Bandstra, *The Law and the Elements of the World: An Exegetical Study in Aspects of Paul's Teaching* (Kampen: Kok, 1964), and the articles of Eduard Schweizer, "Slaves of the Elements and Worshipers of Angels: Gal 4:3, 9 and Col 2:8, 18, 20," *JBL* 107 (1988): 455–68; idem, "Altes und Neues zu den 'Elementen der Welt' in Kol 2,20; Gal 4,3–9," in *Wissenschaft und Kirche: Festschrift für Eduard Lohse*, ed. Kurt Aland and Siegfried Meurer (Texte und Arbeiten zur Bibel 4; Bielefeld: Luther Verlag, 1989), 111–18; Dietrich Rusam, "Neue Belege zu den στοιχεῖα τοῦ κόσμου (Gal 4,3.9, Kol 2,8.20)," *ZNW* 83 (1992): 119–25; Clinton E. Arnold, "Returning to the Domain of the Powers: *Stoicheia* as Evil Spirits in Galatians 4:3, 9," *NovT* 38 (1996): 55–76; Martinus C. de Boer, "The Meaning of the Phrase τὰ στοιχεῖα τοῦ κόσμου in Galatians," *NTS* 53 (2007): 204–24; and Johannes Woyke, "Nochmals zu den 'schwachen und unfähigen Elementen' (Gal 4.9): Paulus, Philo und die στοιχεῖα τοῦ κόσμου," *NTS* 54 (2008): 221–34.

88. Litwa, *"We Are Being Transformed"*, 11.

89. For more on Gen 15:5 and 22:17 in Romans 4, see Burnett, "'So Shall Your Seed Be.'"

90. Forman, *The Politics of Inheritance in Romans* (SNTSMS 148; Cambridge, UK: Cambridge University Press, 2011), 6. Contrary to the claims of W. D. Davies, *The Gospel and the Land: Early Christianity and Jewish Territorial Doctrine* (Berkeley: University of California Press, 1974), 161–220, and James D. G. Dunn, *Romans 1–8* (WBC 38A; Dallas: Word, 1988), 213.

91. As noted above, the manuscript witnesses to Sir 44:21 differ considerably, but MS B, the only Hebrew witness to the passage, contains the phrase "to give them an inheritance from [s]ea to sea . . . and from the river and to the ends of the earth/land (ארץ)." See Beentjes, *Book of Ben Sira in Hebrew*, 78.

92. In contrast, most LXX witnesses to Gen 26:4 refer to "all this land" (πᾶσαν τὴν γῆν ταύτην).

93. Forman, *Politics of Inheritance*, 60.

94. Cf. Steven Weitzman, "Forced Circumcision and the Shifting Role of Gentiles in Hasmonean Ideology," *HTR* 92 (1999): 37–59.

95. On deification in Paul, see James Tabor, "Paul's Notion of Many 'Sons of God' in its Hellenistic Contexts," *Helios* 13 (1986): 87–97; Michael Gorman, *Cruciformity: Paul's Narrative Spirituality of the Cross* (Grand Rapids: Eerdmans, 2001); idem, *Inhabiting the Cruciform God: Kenosis, Justification, and Theosis in Paul's Narrative Soteriology* (Grand Rapids: Eerdmans, 2009); idem, "Romans: The First Christian Treatise on Theosis," *JTI* 5 (2011): 13–34; Stephen Finlan, "Can We Speak of Theosis in Paul?" in *Partakers of the Divine Nature: The History and Development of Deification in the Christian Traditions*, ed. Michael J. Christensen and Jeffery A. Wittung (Grand Rapids: Baker Academic, 2007), 68–80; Ben C. Blackwell, *Christosis: Pauline Soteriology in Light of Deification in Irenaeus and Cyril of Alexandria* (WUNT 2/314; Tübingen: Mohr Siebeck, 2011); and Litwa, *"We Are Being Transformed"*. Although beyond the scope of this chapter, Paul's concern for the gentile mortality problem fits well within broader Greco-Roman concerns about the afterlife and deification. For instance, on the basis of the reception of Plato's words in *Theaetetus* 176B ("we ought to try to escape from earth to the dwelling of the gods as quickly as we can; and to escape to become like God, so far as this is possible; and to become like God is to become righteous and holy and wise"), Dominic J. O'Meara (*Platonopolis: Platonic Political Philosophy in Late Antiquity* [Oxford: Clarendon, 2003], 34) claims that "divinization describes the goal of the major philosophical schools of the Classical and Hellenistic periods." See also the earlier formulations of this argument in David Sedley, "'Becoming Like God' in the *Timaeus* and Aristotle," in *Interpreting the Timaeus-Critias: Proceedings of the Fourth Symposium Platonicum, Granada. Selected Papers*, ed. Tomás Calvo and Luc Brisson (St. Augustin: Academia Verlag, 1997), 327–39, and idem, "The Ideal of Godlikeness," in *Plato 2: Ethics, Politics, Religion, and the Soul*, ed. Gail Fine (Oxford Readings in Philosophy; Oxford: Oxford University Press, 1999), 309–28, as well as the connection to Paul's thinking in George H. van Kooten, *Paul's Anthropology in Context: The Image of God, Assimilation to God, and Tripartite Man in Ancient Judaism, Ancient Philosophy and Early Christianity* (WUNT 232; Tübingen: Mohr Siebeck, 2008).

96. On self-mastery, see Stanley K. Stowers, "Paul and Self-Mastery," in *Paul in the Greco-Roman World: A Handbook*, ed. J. Paul Sampley (Harrisburg, PA: Trinity Press International, 2003), 524–50.

CONCLUSION

1. Heikki Räisänen, *Paul and the Law* (Philadelphia: Fortress, 1983).

2. Baur, *Paul the Apostle of Jesus Christ: His Life and Works, His Epistles and Teachings,* trans. A. Menzies, 2 vols. (London: Williams & Norgate, 1873), 1:265. See F. F. Bruce, *Paul: Apostle of the Heart Set Free* (Grand Rapids: Eerdmans, 1991 [UK Title: *Paul: Apostle of the Free Spirit*]), and Richard N. Longenecker, *Paul: Apostle of Liberty* (New York: Harper & Row, 1964).

3. See, for instance, Alain Badiou, *Saint Paul: The Foundation of Universalism,* trans. Ray Brassier (Cultural Memory in the Present; Stanford, CA: Stanford University Press, 2003); Jacob Taubes, *The Political Theology of Paul,* trans. Dana Hollander (Cultural Memory in the Present; Stanford, CA: Stanford University Press, 2003); Giorgio Agamben, *The Time that Remains: A Commentary on the Letter to the Romans,* trans. Patricia Dailey (Meridian: Crossing Aesthetics; Stanford, CA: Stanford University Press, 2005); John D. Caputo and Linda Martín Alcoff, eds., *St. Paul among the Philosophers* (Indiana Series in the Philosophy of Religion; Bloomington: Indiana University Press, 2009); and Stanislas Breton, *A Radical Philosophy of Saint Paul,* trans. Joseph N. Ballan (Insurrections; New York: Columbia University Press, 2011).

4. Albert Schweitzer, *The Mysticism of Paul the Apostle,* trans. William Montgomery (Baltimore: Johns Hopkins University Press, 1953), 196. Or, as Pheme Perkins (*Abraham's Divided Children: Galatians and the Politics of Faith* [The New Testament in Context; Harrisburg, PA: Trinity Press International, 2001], 56) says: "Paul is as intolerant of the Gentile who assimilates to Jewish habits and religious practices as the sharp-tongued Roman satirists who make fun of such Judaizing."

5. As Christine Hayes (*What's Divine about Divine Law? Early Perspectives* [Princeton: Princeton University Press, 2015], 151) puts it, "It is not the Torah's inferiority that motivates Paul's rejection of the Torah for Gentiles, but precisely its superiority, its assignation as a privilege to the seed of Israel through Isaac only."

6. See especially Paula Fredriksen, "Judaizing the Nations: The Ritual Demands of Paul's Gospel," *NTS* 56 (2010): 232–52.

7. Paula Fredriksen, "How Later Contexts Affect Pauline Content, or: Retrospect is the Mother of Anachronism," in *Jews and Christians in the First and Second Centuries: How to Write Their History,* ed. Peter J. Tomson and Joshua Schwartz (CRINT 13; Leiden: Brill, 2014), 17–51 (36).

8. Eisenbaum, "A Remedy for Having Been Born of Woman: Jesus, Gentiles, and Genealogy in Romans," *JBL* 123 (2004): 671–702 (694–95).

9. Similarly, Paula Fredriksen ("How Later Contexts Affect Pauline Content," 39), who avers that "to hold that Jewish ancestral traditions were not incumbent upon non-Jews would have been a tautology in antiquity (and remains so today): only Israel is responsible for Israel's law (Rom 9:4)."

10. Novenson, *Christ among the Messiahs: Christ Language in Paul and Messiah Language in Ancient Judaism* (Oxford: Oxford University Press, 2012).

11. Malkani, *Londonstani* (London: Fourth Estate, 2006).

12. Mitchell, *The Heavenly Trumpet: John Chrysostom and the Art of Pauline Interpretation* (Louisville: Westminster John Knox, 2002), 409, 428.

13. Baur, *Paul the Apostle,* 1:6. See also, Philipp Vielhauer, "On the 'Paulinism' of Acts," in *Studies in Luke-Acts,* ed. Leander E. Keck and J. Louis Martyn (Nashville: Abingdon, 1966), 33–50. More recently, see John Knox, *Chapters*

*in a Life of Paul* (New York: Abingdon, 1950); Michael D. Goulder, *A Tale of Two Missions* (London: SCM, 1994); idem, *Paul and the Competing Mission in Corinth* (Library of Pauline Studies; Peabody, MA: Hendrickson, 2001); Gerd Lüdemann, *The Acts of the Apostles: What Really Happened in the Earliest Days of the Church* (Amherst, NY: Prometheus, 2005); and Douglas A. Campbell, *Framing Paul: An Epistolary Account* (Grand Rapids: Eerdmans, 2014). A number of scholars still argue that Acts is historically reliable: e.g., W. Ward Gasque, *A History of the Criticism of the Acts of the Apostles* (BGBE 17; Tübingen: Mohr Siebeck, 1975); Martin Hengel, *Acts and the History of Earliest Christianity*, trans. John Bowden (Philadelphia: Fortress, 1980); and Colin J. Hemer, *The Book of Acts in the Setting of Hellenistic History*, ed. Conrad H. Gempf (WUNT 49; Tübingen: Mohr, 1989).

14. See the similar account of Jacob Jervell, *The Unknown Paul: Essays on Luke-Acts and Early Christian History*, trans. Roy A. Harrisville (Minneapolis: Augsburg, 1984). Admittedly, Paul's writings were appropriated in a whole host of different ways. On Paul's reception, see, for instance, Elaine H. Pagels, *The Gnostic Paul: Gnostic Exegesis of the Pauline Letters* (Philadelphia: Fortress, 1975); Dennis R. MacDonald, *The Legend and the Apostle: The Battle for Paul in Story and Canon* (Philadelphia: Westminster, 1983); Judith Lieu, "'As much My Apostle as Christ Is Mine': The Dispute over Paul between Tertullian and Marcion," *Early Christianity* 1 (2010): 41–59; eadem, "The Battle for Paul in the Second Century," *ITQ* 75 (2010): 3–14; Richard I. Pervo, *The Making of Paul: Constructions of the Apostle in Early Christianity* (Minneapolis: Fortress, 2010); Michael F. Bird and Joseph R. Dodson, eds., *Paul and the Second Century* (LNTS 412; London: T&T Clark, 2012); and Benjamin L. White, *Remembering Paul: Ancient and Modern Contests over the Image of the Apostle* (Oxford: Oxford University Press, 2014). White (104–5) rightly concludes that "the apparent complexity of Paul's own views (regardless of how many letters we now want to attribute to him) and the variety of images that he would have had to self-construct to meet his rhetorical goals . . . meant that he could be idealized by a variety of reputational entrepreneurs. The seven so-called undisputed letters of Paul alone provide a bewildering assortment of perspectives that often defy systematization."

15. On this passage, see Matthew Thiessen, *Contesting Conversion: Genealogy, Circumcision, and Identity in Ancient Judaism and Christianity* (Oxford: Oxford University Press, 2011), 119–20.

16. Contrary to many scholars, I am convinced that Luke knew some, if not all, of Paul's letters. For this position, see the arguments of William O. Walker Jr., "Acts and the Pauline Corpus Reconsidered," *JSNT* 24 (1985): 3–23; Lars Aejmelaeus, *Die Rezeption der Paulusbriefe in der Miletrede (Apg 20:18–35)* (AASF B/232; Helsinki: Suomalainen Tiedeakatemia, 1987); Richard I. Pervo, *Dating Acts: Between the Evangelists and the Apologists* (Santa Rosa, CA: Polebridge, 2006), 51–147; Joseph B. Tyson, *Marcion and Luke-Acts: A Defining Struggle* (Columbia: University of South Carolina, 2006); and, most recently, Ryan S. Schellenberg, "The First Pauline Chronologist? Paul's Itinerary in the Letters and in Acts," *JBL* 134 (2015): 193–213.

17. I would stress yet again that the two-track salvation, one for Jews apart from Christ Jesus and one for gentiles-in-Christ, often associated with the radical new perspective, finds support neither in Acts nor in Paul's writings.

18. I find it surprising, therefore, that John G. Gager ("Did Jewish Christians See the Rise of Islam?," in *The Ways that Never Parted: Jews and Christians in Late Antiquity and the Early Middle Ages*, ed. Adam H. Becker and Annette Yoshiko

Reed [Minneapolis: Fortress, 2007], 361–72 [367]), an early proponent of the radical new perspective, would contrast Luke's portrait of Paul to Paul's own understanding: "Contrary to the portrait of Acts, Paul did not repudiate Judaism—or those whom we call Jewish Christians. . . . The author of Acts has deliberately drafted Paul to serve for his own anti-Jewish and anti-Jewish-Christian message." Contrary to Gager's understanding of Acts, one can see Luke's thoroughgoing commitment to Jewish law observance throughout Luke and Acts. Isaac W. Oliver (*Torah Praxis after 70 CE: Reading Matthew and Luke-Acts as Jewish Texts* [WUNT 2/355; Tübingen: Mohr Siebeck, 2013]) makes the most compelling case for this claim.

19. Wright, *Paul and the Faithfulness of God*, 2 vols. (Minneapolis: Fortress, 2013), 359. Wright makes this claim, explicitly dismissing the evidence of Acts 21, not for a lack of historicity, but because he believes that these actions do not demonstrate that Paul remained Torah observant. Such an interpretation simply cannot be squared with the assertion that Paul himself observes the Jewish law in Acts 21:24.

20. Koet, "Purity and Impurity of the Body in Luke-Acts," in *Purity and Holiness: The Heritage of Leviticus*, ed. Marcel J. H. M. Poorthuis and Joshua Schwartz (Jewish and Christian Perspectives Series 2; Leiden: Brill, 2000), 93–106 (104).

21. Rudolph, *A Jew to the Jews: Jewish Contours of Pauline Flexibility in 1 Corinthians 9:19–23* (WUNT 2/304; Tübingen: Mohr Siebeck, 2011), 57.

22. One notable exception is Augustine, who states in a letter, "Paul was indeed a Jew; and when he had become a Christian, he had not abandoned those Jewish sacraments which that people had received in the right way and for a certain appointed time. Therefore, although he was an apostle of Christ, he took part in observing them; but with this view, that he might show that they were in no wise hurtful to those who, even after they had believed in Christ, desired to retain the ceremonies which by the law they had learned from their fathers; provided only that they did not build on these their hope of salvation, since the salvation which was foreshadowed in these has now been brought in by the Lord Jesus" (*Letter* 40.4 [*Nicene and Post-Nicene Fathers*, Series 1, 1:273]). On Augustine, see Paula Fredriksen, *Augustine and the Jews: A Christian Defense of Jews and Judaism* (New York: Doubleday, 2008).

23. Wall, "Reading Paul with Acts: The Canonical Shaping of a Holy Church," in *Holiness and Ecclesiology in the New Testament*, ed. Kent E. Brower and Andy Johnson (Grand Rapids: Eerdmans, 2007), 129–47 (136).

24. For immanent criticism, see Stephen S. Bush (*Visions of Religion: Experience, Meaning, and Power* [AAR Reflection and Theory in the Study of Religion; Oxford: Oxford University Press, 2014], 200), who states that immanent criticism "looks for incompatibilities and tensions within a social practice instead of appealing to principles external to the practice to criticize it." Canonical criticism is most often associated with the work of Brevard S. Childs. Although Childs wrote a book on the canonical context of Paul's letters entitled *The Church's Guide for Reading Paul: The Canonical Shaping of the Pauline Corpus* (Grand Rapids: Eerdmans, 2008), his argument differs considerably from my own.

25. Wall, "The Acts of the Apostles in Canonical Context," in *The New Testament as Canon: A Reader in Canonical Criticism*, ed. Robert W. Wall and Eugene E. Lemcio (JSNTSup 76; Sheffield: Sheffield Academic, 1992), 110–28 (121).

26. Scherbenske, *Canonizing Paul: Ancient Editorial Practice and the Corpus Paulinum* (Oxford: Oxford University Press, 2013), 114. Nonetheless, Marcion probably inherited a Pauline canon that began with the letter to the Galatians, as John Knox (*Marcion and the New Testament* [New York: AMS Press, 1980], 46–53) argues.

27. In fact, some scholars, such as Tyson (*Marcion and Luke-Acts*), even suggest that Acts was written in the second century CE as a response to Marcionite readings of Paul.

28. C. Kavin Rowe, *World Upside Down: Reading Acts in the Graeco-Roman Age* (Oxford: Oxford University Press, 2009), 80.

29. For instance, Baur (*Paul the Apostle*, 12) avers of Acts: "the Pauline doctrine was so severely repressed that it could only maintain itself through a concession, which modified the hardness and bluffness of its opposition to the law and Judaism, and by this means put itself into a position as far as possible harmonizing the antagonistic views of the powerful Jewish-Christian party opposed to him."

30. On this broader interpretive issue, Markus Bockmuehl (*Seeing the Word: Refocusing New Testament Study* [Studies in Theological Interpretation; Grand Rapids: Baker Academic, 2006], 132) states, "Even the most basic literary reading of the Christian New Testament as a whole cannot fail to notice one obvious but by no means trivial fact, which belongs to the historical footprint—the *effect* of canonizing Paul's relationship with Peter. Despite the undeniable tensions that even the overall narrative itself throws up, the covers of the New Testament bind together, in one formative codex, writings in the name of both Paul and the Jerusalem 'pillars' Peter, James, and John. The implied interpreter of that canonical decision hears the polyphony of its voices as witness to a common subject, which is the gospel." Actually, for Christian readers, this need to create coherence presumably transcends the New Testament and requires that one read the various books of both the Old and New Testaments in a way that coheres. The long and tortuous history of interpretation of the Bible demonstrates the difficulty of this task.

31. For that matter, as John G. Gager has recently shown (*Who Made Early Christianity? The Jewish Lives of the Apostle Paul* [American Lectures on the History of Religions; New York: Columbia University Press, 2015], 37–52), some Jewish thinkers understood Paul similarly. Fascinatingly, as early as the fourteenth century, Profiat Duran made a similarly "immanent-critical" argument about contemporary Christian interpretations of Paul in his work entitled *The Shame of the Gentiles* (*Kelimmat ha-Goyim*), likewise depending upon the evidence of Acts.

32. Cf. Mark D. Nanos and Magnus Zetterholm, eds., *Paul within Judaism: Restoring the First-Century Context to the Apostle* (Minneapolis: Fortress, 2015).

# Bibliography

PRIMARY SOURCES

Abelard, Peter. *Commentary on the Epistle to the Romans*. Translated by Steven R. Cartwright. Fathers of the Church, Mediaeval Continuation 12. Washington, DC: Catholic University of America Press, 2011.

Aland, Barbara, Kurt Aland, Johannes Karavidopoulos, Carlo M. Martini, and Bruce M. Metzger, eds. *Novum Testamentum Graece*. 28th ed. Stuttgart: Deutsche Bibelgesellschaft, 2012.

Ambrose. *On Abraham*. Translated by Theodosia Tomkinson. Etna, CA: Center for Traditionalist Orthodox Studies, 2000.

Ambrosiaster. *Commentaries on Romans and 1–2 Corinthians*. Ancient Christian Texts. Translated and edited by Gerald L. Bray. Downers Grove, IL: InterVarsity Press, 2009.

*The Ante-Nicene Fathers*. Edited by Alexander Roberts and James Donaldson. 1885–1887. 10 vols. Repr. Peabody, MA: Hendrickson, 1994.

Aristotle. *Art of Rhetoric*. Translated by J. H. Freese. Loeb Classical Library. Cambridge, MA: Harvard University Press, 1926.

———. *Politics*. Translated by H. Rackham. Loeb Classical Library. Cambridge, MA: Harvard University Press, 1932.

———. *On the Heavens*. Translated by W. K. C. Guthrie. Loeb Classical Library. Cambridge, MA: Harvard University Press, 1939.

———. *Generation of Animals*. Translated by A. L. Peck. Loeb Classical Library. Cambridge, MA: Harvard University Press, 1953.

———. *On the Life-Bearing Spirit (De Spiritu): A Discussion with Plato and his Predecessors on Pneuma as the Instrumental Body of the Soul*. Translated by Abraham P. Boss and Rein Ferwerda. Leiden: Brill, 2008.

Arnim, Hans Friedrich August von, ed. *Stoicorum Veterum Fragmenta*. 4 vols. Leipzig: B. G. Teubne, 1903–1924.

Athanasius. *Contra Gentes and De Incarnatione*. Edited and translated by Robert W. Thomson. Oxford Early Christian Texts. Oxford: Clarendon Press, 1971.

Augustine. *The City of God against the Pagans*. Edited and translated by R. W. Dyson. Cambridge Texts in the History of Political Thought. Cambridge, UK: Cambridge University Press, 1998.

———. *Commentary on Galatians*. Introduction, Text, Translation, and Notes by Eric Plumer. Oxford Early Christian Studies. Oxford: Oxford University Press, 2003.

Bauckham, Richard, James R. Davila, and Alexander Panayotov, eds. *Old Testament Pseudepigrapha: More Noncanonical Scriptures, Volume One*. Grand Rapids: Eerdmans, 2013.

Beentjes, Pancratius C. *The Book of Ben Sira in Hebrew: A Text Edition of All Extant Hebrew Manuscripts and a Synopsis of all Parallel Hebrew Ben Sira Texts*. Vetus Testamentum Supplements 68. Leiden: Brill, 1997.

Betz, Hans Dieter, ed. *The Greek Magical Papyri in Translation, Including the Demotic Spells*. 2d ed. Chicago: University of Chicago Press, 1992.

Braude, William G. *The Midrash on Psalms*. 2 vols. Yale Judaica Series 13. New Haven: Yale University Press, 1959.

———. *Pesikta Rabbati: Discourses for Feasts, Fasts, and Special Sabbaths*. 2 vols. Yale Judaica Series 18. New Haven: Yale University Press, 1968.

Braude, William G., and Israel J. Kapstein. *Pesikta de-Rab Kahana: R. Kahana's Compilation of Discourses for Sabbaths and Festal Days*. Philadelphia: Jewish Publication Society of America, 2002.

Charlesworth, James H., ed. *The Old Testament Pseudepigrapha*. 2 vols. Garden City, NY: Doubleday, 1983–1985.

Chrysostom. *Discourses against Judaizing Christians*. Translated by Paul W. Harkins. Fathers of the Church 68. Washington, DC: Catholic University of America Press, 1979.

———. *Homilies on Genesis, 18–45*. Translated by Robert C. Hill. Fathers of the Church 82. Washington, DC: Catholic University of America Press, 1990.

Cicero. *On Old Age, On Friendship, On Divination*. Translated by W. A. Falconer. Loeb Classical Library. Cambridge, MA: Harvard University Press, 1923.

———. *On the Nature of the Gods, Academica*. Translated by H. Rackham. Loeb Classical Library. Cambridge, MA: Harvard University Press, 1956.

Danby, Herbert. *The Mishnah: Translated from the Hebrew with Introduction and Brief Explanatory Notes*. Oxford: Oxford University Press, 1933.

Dio Cassius. *Roman History*. Translated by Earnest Cary. 9 vols. Loeb Classical Library. London: Heinemann, 1914–1927.

*Diodorus of Sicily*. Translated by Francis R. Walton et al. 12 vols. Loeb Classical Library. Cambridge, MA: Harvard University Press, 1933–1967.

Diogenes Laertius. *Lives of Eminent Philosophers*. Translated by R. D. Hicks. 2 vols. Loeb Classical Library. London: Heinemann, 1925.

Ehrman, Bart, trans. *The Apostolic Fathers*. 2 vols. Loeb Classical Library. Cambridge, MA: Harvard University Press, 2003.

Elliger, K., and W. Rudolph, eds. *Biblia Hebraica Stuttgartensia*. Stuttgart: Deutsche Bibelgesellschaft, 1967–1977.

Ephrem. *Selected Prose Works: Commentary on Genesis, Commentary on Exodus, Homily on Our Lord, Letter to Publius.* Translated by Edward G. Mathews Jr. and Joseph P. Amar. Fathers of the Church 91. Washington, DC: Catholic University of America Press, 1994.

Epictetus. *The Discourses as Reported by Arrian, the Manual, and Fragments.* Translated by W. A. Oldfather. 2 vols. Loeb Classical Library. London: Heinemann, 1926–1928.

Epstein, Isidore, ed. *The Babylonian Talmud: Translated into English with Notes, Glossary and Indices.* 18 vols. London: Soncino, 1935–1952.

*Euthalian Traditions: Text, Translation and Commentary.* Translated by Vemund Blomkvist. Texte und Untersuchungen zur Geschichte der altchristlichen Literatur 170. Berlin: de Gruyter, 2012.

Fredriksen Landes, Paula. *Augustine on Romans: Propositions from the Epistle to the Romans, Unfinished Commentary on the Epistle to the Romans.* Society of Biblical Literature Texts and Translations 23. Chico, CA: Scholars Press, 1982.

Freedman, H., and Maurice Simon, eds. *Midrash Rabbah.* 10 vols. London: Soncino, 1939.

Friedlander, Gerald. *Pirke de Rabbi Eliezer [The chapters of Rabbi Eliezer the Great] according to the Text of the manuscript belonging to Abraham Epstein of Vienna.* 2d ed. New York: Hermon, 1965.

Galen. *On Semen.* Edition, Translation, and Commentary by Phillip De Lacy. Corpus Medicorum Graecorum 5.3.1. Berlin: Akademie, 1992.

Gall, August Freiherrn von, ed. *Der Hebräische Pentateuch der Samaritaner.* Giessen: Töpelmann, 1914–1918.

Gregory of Nyssa. *Commentary on the Song of Songs.* Translated by Casimir McCambley. Brookline, MA: Hellenic College Press, 1987.

Guggenheimer, Heinrich W., ed. *The Jerusalem Talmud. First Order: Zeraim.* Berlin: de Gruyter, 2003.

Hammer, Reuven. *Sifre: A Tannaitic Commentary on the Book of Deuteronomy.* Yale Judaica Series 24. New Haven: Yale University Press, 1986.

Heraclitus. *Homeric Problems.* Edited and translated by Donald A. Russell and David Konstan. Writings from the Greco-Roman World 14. Atlanta: SBL Press, 2005.

Hierocles the Stoic. *Elements of Ethics, Fragments, and Excerpts.* Edited and translated by Ilaria Ramelli. Translated from the Italian by David Konstan. Society of Biblical Literature Writings from the Greco-Roman World. Atlanta: Society of Biblical Literature, 2009.

Irenaeus of Lyons. *On the Apostolic Preaching.* Translation and Introduction by John Behr. Popular Patristics Series 17. Crestwood, NY: St. Vladimir's Seminary Press, 1997.

Jerome. *Commentaries on Galatians, Titus, and Philemon.* Translated by Thomas P. Scheck. Notre Dame: University of Notre Press, 2010.

*Josephus.* Translated by H. St. J. Thackeray et al. 10 vols. Loeb Classical Library. Cambridge, MA: Harvard University Press, 1926–1965.

———. *Judean Antiquities 1–4.* Translated and edited by Louis H. Feldman. Flavius Josephus: Translation and Commentary 3. Leiden: Brill, 2000.

Justin Martyr. *Dialogue with Trypho.* Translated by Thomas B. Falls. Fathers of the Church 3. Washington, DC: Catholic University of America Press, 2003.

*Juvenal and Persius.* Rev. ed. Translated by G. G. Ramsay. Loeb Classical Library. Cambridge, MA: Harvard University Press, 1969.

Kappler, Werner. *Maccabaeorum Liber I.* 3d ed. Septuaginta: Vetus Testamentum Graecum 9. Göttingen: Vandenhoeck & Ruprecht, 1990.

Lauterbach, Jacob Z. *Mekilta de-Rabbi Ishmael.* 3 vols. Philadelphia: Jewish Publication Society of America, 1933–1935.

*Lucian.* Translated by A. M. Harmon et al. 8 vols. Loeb Classical Library. London: Heinemann, 1913–1961.

Lucretius. *De Rerum Natura.* Translated by W. H. D. Rouse. Revised by Martin Ferguson Smith. 2d ed. Loeb Classical Library. Cambridge, MA: Harvard University Press, 1982.

Maher, Michael, trans. *Targum Pseudo-Jonathan: Genesis: Translated, with Introduction and Notes.* The Aramaic Bible 1B. Collegeville, MN: Liturgical Press, 1992.

Martínez, Florentino García, and Eibert J. C. Tigchelaar, eds. *The Dead Sea Scrolls: Study Edition.* 2 vols. Leiden: Brill, 1997–1998.

McNamara, Martin J., trans. *Targum Neofiti 1: Genesis: Translated with Apparatus and Notes.* The Aramaic Bible 1A. Collegeville, MN: Liturgical Press, 1992.

Nelson, Milward Douglas. *The Syriac Version of the Wisdom of Ben Sira compared to the Greek and Hebrew Materials.* Society of Biblical Literature Dissertation Series 107. Atlanta: Scholars Press, 1988.

Nelson, W. David. *Mekhilta de-Rabbi Shimon bar Yoḥai: Translated into English, with Critical Introduction and Annotation.* Philadelphia: Jewish Publication Society of America, 2006.

Neusner, Jacob. *The Tosefta: Translated from Hebrew with a New Introduction.* 2 vols. Peabody, MA: Hendrickson, 2002.

*The Nicene and Post-Nicene Fathers,* Series 1. Edited by Philip Schaff. 1886–1889. 14 vols. Repr. Peabody, MA: Hendrickson, 1994.

Origen. *Contra Celsum.* Translated by Henry Chadwick. Cambridge, UK: Cambridge University Press, 1953.

———. *On First Principles.* Translated by G. W. Butterworth. New York: Harper & Row, 1966.

———. *Homilies on Genesis and Exodus.* Translated by Ronald E. Heine. Fathers of the Church 71. Washington, DC: Catholic University of America Press, 1982.

———. *Homilies on Leviticus 1–16.* Translated by Gary Wayne Barkley. Fathers of the Church 83. Washington, DC: Catholic University of America Press, 1990.

———. *Commentary on the Gospel according to John, Books 13–32.* Translated by Ronald E. Heine. Fathers of the Church 89. Washington, DC: Catholic University of America Press, 1993.

———. *Commentary on the Epistle to the Romans, Books 1–5.* Translated by Thomas P. Scheck. Fathers of the Church 103. Washington, DC: Catholic University of America Press, 2001.

Pelagius. *Commentary on St Paul's Epistle to the Romans*. Translated with Introduction and Notes by Theodore De Bruyn. Oxford Early Christian Studies. Oxford: Clarendon, 1993.

*Petronius*. Translated by Michael Heseltine. Revised by E. H. Warmington. Seneca. *Apocolocyntosis*. Translated by W. H. D. Rouse. Loeb Classical Library. Cambridge, MA: Harvard University Press, 1975.

*Philo*. Translated by F. H. Colson et al. 12 vols. Loeb Classical Library. Cambridge, MA: Harvard University Press, 1929–1962.

Pietersma, Albert, and Benjamin G. Wright, eds. *A New English Translation of the Septuagint*. Oxford: Oxford University Press, 2007.

Plato. *Theaetetus, Sophist*. Translated by Harold North Fowler. Loeb Classical Library. Cambridge, MA: Harvard University Press, 1921.

———. *Charmides, Alcibiades 1 and 2, Hipparchus, the Lovers, Theages, Minos, Epinomis*. Translated by W. R. M. Lamb. Loeb Classical Library. London: Heinemann, 1927.

———. *Timaeus, Critias, Cleitophon, Menexenus, Epistles*. Translated by R. G. Bury. Loeb Classical Library. London: Heinemann, 1929.

———. *Laches, Protagoras, Meno, Euthydemus*. Translated by W. R. M. Lamb. Loeb Classical Library. Cambridge, MA: Harvard University Press, 1952.

*Plotinus*. Translated by A. H. Armstrong. 7 vols. Loeb Classical Library. Cambridge, MA: Harvard University Press, 1966–1988.

Plutarch. *Lives*. Translated by Bernadotte Perrin. 11 vols. Loeb Classical Library. London: Heinemann, 1914–1926.

———. *Moralia*. Translated by Frank Cole Babbitt et al. 17 vols. Loeb Classical Library. Cambridge, MA: Harvard University Press, 1927–2004.

*Posidonius: The Translation of the Fragments*. Edited and translated by I. G. Kidd. Cambridge Classical Texts and Commentaries 36. Cambridge, UK: Cambridge University Press, 1999.

Pritchard, James B., ed. *The Ancient Near East in Pictures Relating to the Old Testament*. Princeton: Princeton University Press, 1954.

———. *Ancient Near Eastern Texts Relating to the Old Testament*. 3d ed. Princeton: Princeton University Press, 1969.

Rahlfs, Alfred, ed. *Septuaginta: Id est Vetus Testamentum Graece iuxta LXX interpretes*. 9th ed. Stuttgart: Württembergische Bibelanstalt Stuttgart, 1971 [1935].

Seneca. *Ad Lucilium Epistulae Morales*. Translated by Richard M. Gummere. 3 vols. Loeb Classical Library. London: Heinemann, 1917–1925.

———. *Naturales Quaestiones*. Translated by Thomas H. Corcoran. 2 vols. Loeb Classical Library. Cambridge, MA: Harvard University Press, 1971.

Stern, Menahem. *Greek and Latin Authors on Jews and Judaism*. 3 vols. Jerusalem: Israel Academy of Sciences and Humanities, 1974–1984.

Strabo. *The Geography*. Translated by Horace Leonard Jones. 8 vols. Loeb Classical Library. London: Heinemann, 1917–1932.

Suetonius. *Peri Blasphēmiōn, Peri Paidiōn: Extraits byzantins*. Translated by Jean Taillardat. Paris: Les Belles Lettres, 1967.

Tacitus. *The Histories.* Translated by Clifford H. Moore and John Jackson. 4 vols. Loeb Classical Library. Cambridge, MA: Harvard University Press, 1931–1937.

Tatian. *Oratio ad Graecos and Fragments.* Edited and translated by Molly Whittaker. Oxford Early Christian Texts. Oxford: Clarendon, 1982.

Tertullian. *Treatise against Praxeas.* The Text edited, with an Introduction, Translation, and Commentary by Ernest Evans. London: SPCK, 1948.

———. *Treatise on the Resurrection.* The Text edited, with an Introduction, Translation, and Commentary by Ernest Evans. London: SPCK, 1960.

———. *Adversus Marcionem.* Translated by Ernest Evans. 2 vols. Oxford Early Christian Texts. Oxford: Clarendon, 1972.

Theodoret of Cyrus. *Commentary on the Letters of St. Paul.* Translated by Robert Charles Hill. 2 vols. Brookline, MA: Holy Cross Orthodox Press, 2001.

Theophrastus. *Characters. Herodas. Mimes. Sophron and Other Mime Fragments.* Edited and translated by Jeffrey Rusten and I. C. Cunningham. Loeb Classical Library. Cambridge, MA: Harvard University Press, 2002.

Thucydides. *History of the Peloponnesian War.* Translated by Charles Forster Smith. 4 vols. Loeb Classical Library. Cambridge, MA: Harvard University Press, 1919–1923.

Todd, Robert B., ed. *Alexander of Aphrodisias on Stoic Physics: A Study of the De Mixtione with Preliminary Essays, Text, Translation and Commentary.* Philosophia Antiqua 28. Leiden: Brill, 1976.

Townsend, John T. *Midrash Tanhuma: S. Buber Recension.* 3 vols. Hoboken, NJ: Ktav, 1989–2003.

VanderKam, James C. *The Book of Jubilees: A Critical Edition.* Corpus scriptorum christianorum orientalium 511. Leuven: Peeters, 1989.

Wevers, John William, ed. *Genesis.* Septuaginta: Vetus Testamentum Graecum 1. Göttingen: Vandenhoeck & Ruprecht, 1974.

Xenophon. *Cyropaedia.* Translated by Walter Miller. 2 vols. Loeb Classical Library. London: Heinemann, 1914.

SECONDARY SOURCES

Abasciano, Brian J. *Paul's Use of the Old Testament in Romans 9:1–9: An Intertextual and Theological Exegesis.* Library of New Testament Studies 301. London: T&T Clark, 2005.

Aejmelaeus, Lars. *Die Rezeption der Paulusbriefe in der Miletrede (Apg 20:18–35).* Annales Academiae scientiarum fennicae B/232. Helsinki: Suomalainen Tiedeakatemia, 1987.

Agamben, Giorgio. *The Time that Remains: A Commentary on the Letter to the Romans.* Translated by Patricia Dailey. Meridian: Crossing Aesthetics. Stanford, CA: Stanford University Press, 2005.

Aletti, Jean-Noël. "Rm 1,18—3,20. Incohérence ou cohérence de l'argumentation paulinienne?" *Biblica* 69 (1988): 47–62.

————. *New Approaches for Interpreting the Letters of Saint Paul: Collected Essays: Rhetoric, Soteriology, Christology, and Ecclesiology.* Translated by Peggy Manning Meyer. Subsidia Biblica 43. Rome: Gregorian and Biblical Press, 2012.

Allen, W. C. "On the Meaning of ΠΡΟΣΗΛΥΤΟΣ in the Septuagint." *The Expositor* 4 (1894): 264–75.

Allison, Dale C. Jr. *Studies in Matthew: Interpretation Past and Present.* Grand Rapids: Baker Academic, 2005.

Alter, Robert. *The Five Books of Moses: A Translation with Commentary.* New York: Norton, 2004.

Amir, Yehoshua. "The Term Ἰουδαϊσμός: A Study in Jewish-Hellenistic Self-Definition." *Immanuel* 14 (1982): 34–41.

Anderson, Gary A. *Sacrifices and Offerings in Ancient Israel: Studies in their Social and Political Importance.* Harvard Semitic Monographs 41. Atlanta: Scholars Press, 1987.

————. "The Exaltation of Adam and the Fall of Satan." Pages 83–110 in *Literature on Adam and Eve: Collected Essays.* Edited by Gary Anderson, Michael Stone, and Johannes Tromp. Studia in Veteris Testamenti pseudepigrapha 15. Leiden: Brill, 2000.

————. *Sin: A History.* New Haven: Yale University Press, 2009.

Anidjar, Gil. *Blood: A Critique of Christianity.* Religion, Culture, and Public Life. New York: Columbia University Press, 2014.

Arneson, Hans K. "Revisiting the Sense and Syntax of Romans 2:28–29." Unpublished paper.

Arnold, Clinton. "Returning to the Domain of the Powers: *Stoicheia* as Evil Spirits in Galatians 4:3, 9." *Novum Testamentum* 38 (1996): 55–76.

Asad, Talal. *Genealogies of Religion: Discipline and Reasons of Power in Christianity and Islam.* Baltimore: Johns Hopkins University Press, 1993.

Asher, Jeffrey R. *Polarity and Change in 1 Corinthians 15: A Study of Metaphysics, Rhetoric, and Resurrection.* Hermeneutische Untersuchungen zur Theologie 42. Tübingen: Mohr Siebeck, 2000.

Athanassiadi, Polymnia, and Michael Frede, eds. *Pagan Monotheism in Late Antiquity.* Oxford: Oxford University Press, 1999.

Aune, David C. "Mastery of the Passions: Philo, 4 Maccabees and Earliest Christianity." Pages 125–58 in *Hellenization Revisited: Shaping a Christian Response within the Greco-Roman World.* Edited by Wendy E. Helleman. Lanham, MD: University Press of America, 1994.

Baden, Joel S. *The Promise to the Patriarchs.* Oxford: Oxford University Press, 2013.

Badiou, Alain. *Saint Paul: The Foundation of Universalism.* Translated by Ray Brassier. Cultural Memory in the Present. Stanford, CA: Stanford University Press, 2003.

Balss, Heinrich. "Praeformation und Epigenese in der griechischen Philosophie." *Archivio di storia della scienza* 4 (1923): 319–25.

Bamberger, Bernard J. *Proselytism in the Talmudic Period.* Cincinnati: Hebrew Union College Press, 1939.

Bandstra, Andrew John. *The Law and the Elements of the World: An Exegetical Study in Aspects of Paul's Teaching.* Kampen: Kok, 1964.

Barclay, John M. G. "Mirror-Reading a Polemical Letter: Galatians as a Test Case." *Journal for the Study of the New Testament* 31 (1987): 73–93.

———. *Obeying the Truth: A Study of Paul's Ethics in Galatians.* Studies of the New Testament and its World. Edinburgh: T&T Clark, 1988.

———. *Jews in the Mediterranean Diaspora: From Alexander to Trajan (323 BCE–117 CE).* Hellenistic Culture and Society 33. Berkeley: University of California Press, 1996.

———. "Paul and Philo on Circumcision: Romans 2:25–9 in Social and Cultural Context." *New Testament Studies* 44 (1998): 536–56.

———. "Paul, the Gift and the Battle over Gentile Circumcision." *Australian Biblical Review* 58 (2010): 36–56.

———. "Under Grace: The Christ-Gift and the Construction of a Christian *Habitus*." Pages 59–76 in *Apocalyptic Paul: Cosmos and Anthropos in Romans 5–8.* Edited by Beverly Roberts Gaventa. Waco, TX: Baylor University Press, 2013.

Barrett, C. K. *A Commentary on the Epistle to the Romans.* Harper's New Testament Commentaries. New York: Harpers, 1957.

———. *A Commentary on the First Epistle to the Corinthians.* 2d ed. Black's New Testament Commentary. London: Black, 1971.

———. *Essays on Paul.* Philadelphia: Westminster, 1982.

Barrier, Jeremy W. "Jesus' Breath: A Physiological Analysis of πνεῦμα within Paul's Letter to the Galatians." *Journal for the Study of the New Testament* 37 (2014): 115–38.

Barth, Fredrik, ed. *Ethnic Groups and Boundaries: The Social Organization of Culture Difference.* Boston: Little, Brown, 1969.

Barth, Markus. "Jews and Gentiles: The Social Character of Justification in Paul." *Journal of Ecumenical Studies* 5 (1968): 241–67.

Bassler, Jouette M. *Divine Impartiality: Paul and a Theological Axiom.* Society of Biblical Literature Dissertation Series 59. Chico, CA: Scholars Press, 1982.

Basta, Pasquale. *Abramo in Romani 4: L'analogia dell'agire divino nella ricerca Esegetica di Paolo.* Analecta biblica 168. Rome: Biblical Pontifical Institute, 2007.

Baumgarten, Albert I. "The Name of the Pharisees." *Journal of Biblical Literature* 102 (1983): 411–28.

Baur, F. C. *Paul the Apostle of Jesus Christ: His Life and Works, His Epistles and Teachings; A Contribution to a Critical History of Primitive Christianity.* Translated by A. Menzies. 2 vols. London: Williams & Norgate, 1873.

Baxter, A. G., and J. A. Ziesler. "Paul and Arboriculture: Romans 11:17–24." *Journal for the Study of the New Testament* 24 (1985): 25–32.

Becker, Adam H., and Annette Yoshiko Reed, eds. *The Ways That Never Parted: Jews and Christians in Late Antiquity and the Early Middle Ages.* Minneapolis: Fortress, 2007.

Becker, Jürgen. *Der Brief an Die Galater.* Das Neue Testament Deutsch 8. Göttingen: Vandenhoeck & Ruprecht, 1976.

Begleiter, Ben. "Imagining a Patriarch: Images of Abraham in Early Jewish and Christian Exegesis." Ph.D. diss., Yale University, 2004.

Bell, Richard H. *No One Seeks for God: An Exegetical and Theological Study of Romans 1.18—3.20.* Wissenschaftliche Untersuchungen zum Neuen Testament 106. Tübingen: Mohr Siebeck, 1998.

———. *The Irrevocable Call of God: An Inquiry into Paul's Theology of Israel.* Wissenschaftliche Untersuchungen zum Neuen Testament 184. Tübingen: Mohr Siebeck, 2005.

Ben Aaron, Jacob. "Circumcision among the Samaritans." *Bibliotheca Sacra* 65 (1908): 694–710.

Berg, Werner. "Der Sündenfall Abrahams und Saras nach Gen 16:1–6." *Biblische Notizen* 19 (1982): 7–14.

Berger, Klaus. *Das Buch der Jubiläen.* 2d ed. Jüdische Schriften aus hellenistisch-römischer Zeit 3. Gütersloh: Mohn, 1981.

Berkley, Timothy W. *From a Broken Covenant to Circumcision of the Heart: Pauline Intertextual Exegesis in Romans 2:17–29.* Society of Biblical Literature Dissertation Series 175. Atlanta: SBL Press, 2000.

Bernat, David A. *Sign of the Covenant: Circumcision in the Priestly Tradition.* Society of Biblical Literature Ancient Israel and Its Literature 3. Atlanta: SBL Press, 2009.

Betz, Hans Dieter. *Galatians: A Commentary on Paul's Letter to the Churches in Galatia.* Hermeneia. Philadelphia: Fortress, 1979.

Bhabha, Homi K. *The Location of Culture.* New York: Routledge, 1994.

Bickerman, Elias. *The God of the Maccabees: Studies on the Meaning and Origin of the Maccabean Revolt.* Translated by Horst R. Moehring. Studies in Judaism in Late Antiquity 32. Leiden: Brill, 1979.

Bird, Michael F. *Crossing Over Sea and Land: Jewish Missionary Activity in the Second Temple Period.* Peabody, MA: Hendrickson, 2010.

Bird, Michael F., and Preston M. Sprinkle, eds. *The Faith of Jesus Christ: Exegetical, Biblical, and Theological Studies.* Peabody, MA: Hendrickson, 2010.

Bird, Michael F., and Joseph R. Dodson, eds. *Paul and the Second Century.* Library of New Testament Studies 412. London: T&T Clark, 2012.

Birnbaum, Ellen. *The Place of Judaism in Philo's Thought: Israel, Jews, and Proselytes.* Brown Judaic Studies 290. Atlanta: Scholars Press, 1996.

Blackwell, Ben C. "Immortal Glory and the Problem of Death in Romans 3.23." *Journal for the Study of the New Testament* 32 (2010): 285–308.

———. *Christosis: Pauline Soteriology in Light of Deification in Irenaeus and Cyril of Alexandria.* Wissenschaftliche Untersuchungen zum Neuen Testament 2/314. Tübingen: Mohr Siebeck, 2011.

Blaschke, Andreas. *Beschneidung: Zeugnisse der Bibel und verwandter Texte.* Texte und Arbeiten zum neutestamentlichen Zeitalter 28. Tübingen: Francke, 1998.

Blass, F., A. Debrunner, and R. W. Funk. *A Greek Grammar of the New Testament and Other Early Christian Literature.* Chicago: University of Chicago Press, 1961.

Blenkinsopp, Joseph. "Abraham as Paradigm in the Priestly History in Genesis." *Journal of Biblical Literature* 128 (2009): 225–41.

Boatwright, Mary T. *Peoples of the Roman World.* Cambridge Introduction to Roman Civilization. Cambridge, UK: Cambridge University Press, 2012.

Bockmuehl, Markus. *Jewish Law in Gentile Churches: Halakhah and the Beginning of Christian Public Ethics.* Grand Rapids: Baker Academic, 2000.

———. *Seeing the Word: Refocusing New Testament Study.* Studies in Theological Interpretation. Grand Rapids: Baker Academic, 2006.

Boer, Martinus C. de. "Paul's Quotation of Isaiah 54.1 in Galatians 4.27." *New Testament Studies* 50 (2004): 370–89.

———. "The Meaning of the Phrase τὰ στοιχεῖα τοῦ κόσμου in Galatians." *New Testament Studies* 53 (2007): 204–24.

———. *Galatians: A Commentary.* New Testament Library. Louisville: Westminster John Knox, 2011.

———. "Paul's Mythologizing Program in Romans 5–8." Pages 1–20 in *Apocalyptic Paul: Cosmos and Anthropos in Romans 5–8.* Edited by Beverly Roberts Gaventa. Waco, TX: Baylor University Press, 2013.

Boers, Hendrikus. "Form Critical Study of Paul's Letters: I Thessalonians as a Case Study." *New Testament Studies* 22 (1976): 140–58.

Borgen, Peder. *Paul Preaches Circumcision and Pleases Men: And Other Essays on Christian Origins.* Trondheim: Tapir, 1983.

———. "Some Hebrew and Pagan Features in Philo's and Paul's Interpretation of Hagar and Ishmael." Pages 151–64 in *The New Testament and Hellenistic Judaism.* Edited by Peder Borgen and Søren Giversen. Peabody, MA: Hendrickson, 1997.

Borse, Udo. *Der Brief an die Galater.* Regensburger Neues Testament. Regensburg: Pustet, 1984.

Bourke, Myles M. *A Study of the Metaphor of the Olive Tree in Romans XI.* Studies in Sacred Theology 2.3. Washington, DC: Catholic University of America Press, 1947.

Boyarin, Daniel. *A Radical Jew: Paul and the Politics of Identity.* Contraversions. Berkeley: University of California Press, 1994.

———. *Border Lines: The Partition of Judaeo-Christianity.* Divinations. Philadelphia: University of Pennsylvania Press, 2004.

———. "The Christian Invention of Judaism: The Theodosian Empire and the Rabbinic Refusal of Religion." *Representations* 85 (2004): 21–57.

Boylan, Michael. "The Galenic and Hippocratic Challenges to Aristotle's Conception Theory." *Journal of the History of Biology* 17 (1984): 83–112.

———. *The Origins of Ancient Greek Science: Blood—A Philosophical Study.* Routledge Monographs in Classical Studies 22. New York: Routledge, 2015.

Boys-Stones, G. R., ed. *Metaphor, Allegory, and the Classical Tradition: Ancient Thought and Modern Revisions.* Oxford: Oxford University Press, 2003.

Braaten, Carl E., and Robert W. Jenson, eds. *Union with Christ: The New Finnish Interpretation of Luther.* Grand Rapids: Eerdmans, 1998.

Braude, William J. *Jewish Proselyting in the First Five Centuries of the Common Era: The Age of the Tannaim and Amoraim.* Providence, RI: Brown University Press, 1940.

Breed, Brennan W. *Nomadic Text: A Theory of Biblical Reception History.* Bloomington: Indiana University Press, 2014.

Breton, Stanislas. *A Radical Philosophy of Saint Paul.* Translated by Joseph N. Ballan. Insurrections. New York: Columbia University Press, 2011.

Brooke, George. *Exegesis at Qumran: 4QFlorilegium in Its Jewish Context.* Journal for the Study of the Old Testament: Supplement Series 29. Sheffield: JSOT Press, 1985.

Bruce, F. F. *Paul: Apostle of the Free Spirit.* Exeter: Paternoster, 1977 (US title: *Paul, Apostle of the Heart Set Free.* Grand Rapids: Eerdmans, 1991).

———. *The Epistle to the Galatians: A Commentary on the Greek Text.* New International Greek Testament Commentary. Grand Rapids: Eerdmans, 1982.

Bryan, David. *Cosmos, Chaos and the Kosher Mentality.* Journal for the Study of the Pseudepigrapha: Supplement Series 12. Sheffield: Sheffield Academic, 1995.

Buch-Hansen, Gitte. *"It is the Spirit that Gives Life": A Stoic Understanding of Pneuma in John's Gospel.* Beihefte zur Zeitschrift für die neutestamentliche Wissenschaft 173. Berlin: de Gruyter, 2010.

Bucur, Bogdan Gabriel. *Angelomorphic Pneumatology: Clement of Alexandria and Other Early Christian Witnesses.* Supplements to Vigiliae Christianae 95. Leiden: Brill, 2009.

Buell, Denise Kimber. *Why This New Race: Ethnic Reasoning in Early Christianity.* New York: Columbia University Press, 2005.

———. "Challenges and Strategies for Speaking about Ethnicity in the New Testament and New Testament Studies." *Svensk exegetisk årsbok* 79 (2014): 33–51.

Buell, Denise Kimber, and Caroline Johnson Hodge. "The Politics of Interpretation: The Rhetoric of Race and Ethnicity in Paul." *Journal of Biblical Literature* 123 (2004): 235–51.

Bultmann, Rudolf. *Der Stil der paulinischen Predigt und die kynisch-stoische Diatribe.* Forschungen zur Religion und Literatur des Alten und Neuen Testaments 13. Göttingen: Vandenhoeck & Ruprecht, 1910.

———. *Theology of the New Testament.* Translated by Kendrick Grobel. 2 vols. London: SCM, 1952.

———. *Primitive Christianity in its Contemporary Setting.* Translated by R. H. Fuller. New York: World, 1956.

Burnett, David A. "'So Shall Your Seed Be': Paul's Use of Genesis 15:5 in Romans 4:18 in Light of Early Jewish Deification Traditions." *Journal for the Study of Paul and His Letters* 5, (2015): 211–36.

Burton, Ernest de Witt. *A Critical and Exegetical Commentary on the Epistle to the Galatians.* International Critical Commentary. Edinburgh: T&T Clark, 1921.

Bush, Stephen S. *Visions of Religion: Experience, Meaning, and Power.* AAR Reflection and Theory in the Study of Religion. Oxford: Oxford University Press, 2014.

Byrne, Brendan. *"Sons of God"—"Seed of Abraham": A Study of the Idea of the Sonship of God of All Christians in Paul against the Jewish Background.* Analecta Biblica 83. Rome: Biblical Institute Press, 1979.

———. *Romans*. Sacra Pagina 6. Collegeville, MN: Liturgical Press, 1996.

Calvert-Koyzis, Nancy. *Paul, Monotheism, and the People of God: The Significance of Abraham Traditions for Early Judaism and Christianity*. Journal for the Study of the New Testament: Supplement Series 273. London: T&T Clark, 2004.

Campbell, Douglas A. *The Quest for Paul's Gospel: A Suggested Strategy*. London: T&T Clark, 2005.

———. *The Deliverance of God: An Apocalyptic Rereading of Justification in Paul*. Grand Rapids: Eerdmans, 2009.

———. "Galatians 5.11: Evidence of an Early Law-observant Mission by Paul?" *New Testament Studies* 57 (2011): 325–47.

———. *Framing Paul: An Epistolary Account*. Grand Rapids: Eerdmans, 2014.

Campbell, William S. *Paul's Gospel in an Intercultural Context: Jew and Gentile in the Letter to the Romans*. New York: Lang, 1992.

———. "Gentile Identity and Transformation in Christ according to Paul." Pages 23–55 in *The Making of Christianity: Conflicts, Contacts, and Constructions: Essays in Honor of Bengt Holmberg*. Edited by Magnus Zetterholm and Samuel Byrskog. Coniectanea Biblica: New Testament Series 47. Winona Lake, IN: Eisenbrauns, 2012.

Caputo, John D., and Linda Martín Alcoff, eds. *St. Paul among the Philosophers*. Indiana Series in the Philosophy of Religion. Bloomington: Indiana University Press, 2009.

Carlson, Stephen C. "'For Sinai is a Mountain in Arabia': A Note on the Text of Galatians 4,25." *Zeitschrift für die neutestamentliche Wissenschaft und die Kunde der älteren Kirche* 105 (2014): 80–101.

Carson, Donald A., Peter T. O'Brien, and Mark A. Seifrid, eds. *The Paradoxes of Paul*. Vol. 2 of *Justification and Variegated Nomism*. Grand Rapids: Baker Academic, 2004.

Chesnutt, Randall. *From Death to Life: Conversion in Joseph and Aseneth*. Journal for the Study of the Pseudepigrapha: Supplement Series 16. Sheffield: Sheffield Academic, 1995.

Childs, Brevard S. *The Church's Guide for Reading Paul: The Canonical Shaping of the Pauline Corpus*. Grand Rapids: Eerdmans, 2008.

Cohen, Shaye J. D. "Conversion to Judaism in Historical Perspective: From Biblical Israel to Postbiblical Judaism." *Conservative Judaism* 36 (1983): 31–45.

———. "The Significance of Yavneh: Pharisees, Rabbis, and the End of Jewish Sectarianism." *Hebrew Union College Annual* 55 (1984): 27–53.

———. "The Origins of the Matrilineal Principle in Rabbinic Law." *Association for Jewish Studies Review* 10 (1985): 19–53.

———. "Respect for Judaism by Gentiles in the Writings of Josephus." *Harvard Theological Review* 80 (1987): 409–30.

———. "Crossing the Boundary and Becoming a Jew." *Harvard Theological Review* 82 (1989): 13–33.

———. "Can Converts to Judaism Say 'God of Our Fathers'?" *Judaism* 40 (1991): 419–28.

———. *The Beginnings of Jewishness: Boundaries, Varieties, Uncertainties.* Hellenistic Culture and Society 31. Berkeley: University of California Press, 1999.

———. *Why Aren't Jewish Women Circumcised? Gender and Covenant in Judaism.* Berkeley: University of California Press, 2005.

Coles, Andrew. "Biomedical Models of Reproduction in the Fifth Century and Aristotle's *Generation of Animals.*" *Phronesis* 40 (1995): 48–88.

Collins, John J. "Apocalyptic Eschatology as the Transcendence of Death." *Catholic Biblical Quarterly* 36 (1974): 21–43.

———. *Between Athens and Jerusalem: Jewish Identity in the Hellenistic Diaspora.* 2d ed. Biblical Resource Series. Grand Rapids: Eerdmans, 2000.

———. "*Joseph and Aseneth*: Jewish or Christian?" *Journal for the Study of the Pseudepigrapha* 14 (2005): 97–112.

Concannon, Cavan W. *"When You Were Gentiles": Specters of Ethnicity in Roman Corinth and Paul's Corinthian Correspondence.* Synkrisis. New Haven: Yale University Press, 2014.

Conway, Kevin P. *The Promises of God: The Background of Paul's Exclusive Use of Epangelia for the Divine Pledge.* Beihefte zur Zeitschrift für die neutestamentliche Wissenschaft 211. Berlin: de Gruyter, 2014.

Craigie, Peter C., Page H. Kelley, and Joel F. Drinkard Jr. *Jeremiah 1–25.* Word Biblical Commentary 26. Dallas: Word, 1991.

Cranfield, C. E. B. *A Critical and Exegetical Commentary on the Epistle to the Romans.* 2 vols. 6th ed. International Critical Commentary. Edinburgh: T&T Clark, 1975–1979.

———. "Changes in Person and Number in Paul's Epistles." Pages 280–89 in *Paul and Paulinism: Essays in Honour of C. K. Barrett.* Edited by Morna D. Hooker and S. G. Wilson. London: SPCK, 1982.

Cranford, Michael. "Election and Ethnicity: Paul's View of Israel in Romans 9.1–13." *Journal for the Study of the New Testament* 50 (1993): 27–41.

Cross, Frank Moore Jr. "The Council of Yahweh in Second Isaiah." *Journal of Near Eastern Studies* 12 (1953): 274–77.

———. *Canaanite Myth and Hebrew Epic: Essays in the History of the Religion of Israel.* Cambridge, MA: Harvard University Press, 1973.

Dabelstein, Rolf. *Die Beurteilung der "Heiden" bei Paulus.* Beiträge zur biblischen Exegese und Theologie 14. Bern: Lang, 1981.

Dahl, Nils Alstrup. *Studies in Paul: Theology for the Early Christian Mission.* Minneapolis: Augsburg, 1977.

Das, A. Andrew. *Solving the Romans Debate.* Minneapolis: Fortress, 2007.

Daube, David. *The New Testament and Rabbinic Judaism.* London: Athlone, 1956.

Davies, W. D. *The Gospel and the Land: Early Christianity and Jewish Territorial Doctrine.* Berkeley: University of California Press, 1974.

Davila, James R. *Liturgical Works*. Eerdmans Commentaries on the Dead Sea Scrolls 6. Grand Rapids: Eerdmans, 2000.

Dawson, David. *Allegorical Readers and Cultural Revision in Ancient Alexandria*. Berkeley: University of California Press, 1992.

Deissmann, Gustav Adolf. *St Paul: A Study in Social and Religious History*. Translated by Lionel R. M. Strachan. London: Hodder & Stoughton, 1912.

Dequeker, L. "Les Qedôshim du Ps. LXXXIX à la lumière des croyances sémitiques." *Ephemerides theologicae lovanienses* 39 (1963): 469–84.

Derrett, J. Duncan. "Circumcision and Perfection: A Johannine Equation (John 7:22–23)." *Evangelical Quarterly* 63 (1991): 211–24.

———. "'You Abominate False Gods; but Do You Rob Shrines' Rom 2.22b." *New Testament Studies* 40 (1994): 558–71.

Di Mattei, Steven. "Paul's Allegory of the Two Covenants (Gal 4.21–31) in Light of First-Century Hellenistic Rhetoric and Jewish Hermeneutics." *New Testament Studies* 52 (2006): 102–22.

———. "Biblical Narratives." Pages 59–93 in *As It Is Written: Studying Paul's Use of Scripture*. Edited by Stanley E. Porter and Christopher D. Stanley. Society of Biblical Literature Symposium Series 50. Atlanta: SBL Press, 2008.

Dickson, John. *Mission-Commitment in Ancient Judaism and in the Pauline Communities: The Shape, Extent and Background of Early Christian Mission*. Wissenschaftliche Untersuchungen zum Neuen Testament 2/159. Tübingen: Mohr Siebeck, 2003.

Dodd, C. H. *The Epistle of Paul to the Romans*. Moffatt New Testament Commentary 6. New York: Harper, 1932.

Doeve, J. W. "Paulus der Pharisäer und Galater I 13–15." *Novum Testamentum* 6 (1963): 170–81.

Donaldson, Terence L. "The 'Curse of the Law' and the Inclusion of the Gentiles: Galatians 3.13–14." *New Testament Studies* 32 (1986): 94–112.

———. "Zealot and Convert: The Origin of Paul's Christ-Torah Antithesis." *Catholic Biblical Quarterly* 51 (1989): 655–82.

———. "'Proselytes' or 'Righteous Gentiles'? The Status of Gentiles in Eschatological Pilgrimage Patterns of Thought." *Journal for the Study of the Pseudepigrapha* 7 (1990): 3–27.

———. "Israelite, Convert, Apostle to the Gentiles: The Origin of Paul's Gentile Mission." Pages 62–84 in *The Road from Damascus: The Impact of Paul's Conversion on His Life, Thought, and Ministry*. Edited by Richard N. Longenecker. Grand Rapids: Eerdmans, 1997.

———. *Paul and the Gentiles: Remapping the Apostle's Convictional World*. Minneapolis: Fortress, 1997.

———. "Jewish Christianity, Israel's Stumbling and the *Sonderweg* Reading of Paul." *Journal for the Study of the New Testament* 29 (2006): 27–54.

———. *Judaism and the Gentiles: Jewish Patterns of Universalism (to 135 CE)*. Waco, TX: Baylor University Press, 2007.

———. "'Gentile Christianity' as a Category in the Study of Christian Origins." *Harvard Theological Review* 106 (2013): 433–58.

———. "Paul within Judaism: A Critical Evaluation from a 'New Perspective' Perspective." Pages 277–301 in *Paul within Judaism: Restoring the First-Century Context to the Apostle*. Edited by Mark D. Nanos and Magnus Zetterholm. Minneapolis: Fortress, 2015.

Duling, Dennis C. "The Promises to David and Their Entrance into Christianity: Nailing down a likely Hypothesis." *New Testament Studies* 20 (1973): 55–77.

Dunn, James D. G. *Romans 1–8*. Word Biblical Commentary 38A. Dallas: Word, 1988.

———. *Romans 9–16*. Word Biblical Commentary 38B. Dallas: Word, 1988.

———. *The Epistle to the Galatians*. Black's New Testament Commentaries. Peabody, MA: Hendrickson, 1993.

———. *The Theology of Paul's Letter to the Galatians*. New Testament Theology. Cambridge, UK: Cambridge University Press, 1993.

———. "Once More, ΠΙΣΤΙΣ ΧΡΙΣΤΟΥ." Pages 61–81 in *Looking Back, Pressing On*. Edited by E. Elizabeth Johnson and David M. Hay. Vol. 4 of *Pauline Theology*. Society of Biblical Literature Symposium Series 23. Atlanta: Scholars Press, 1997.

———. "Who Did Paul Think He Was? A Study of Jewish-Christian Identity." *New Testament Studies* 45 (1999): 174–93.

———. *The New Perspective on Paul*. Rev. ed. Grand Rapids: Eerdmans, 2008.

Eastman, Susan. *Recovering Paul's Mother Tongue: Language and Theology in Galatians*. Grand Rapids: Eerdmans, 2007.

———. "Israel and the Mercy of God: A Re-reading of Galatians 6.16 and Romans 9–11." *New Testament Studies* 56 (2010): 367–95.

Eckhardt, Benedikt. *Ethnos und Herrschaft: Politische Figurationen judäischer Identität von Antiochos III. bis Herodes I.* Studia Judaica 72. Berlin: de Gruyter, 2013.

Eckstein, Hans-Joachim. *Verheißung und Gesetz: Eine exegetische Untersuchung zu Galater 2,15—4,7.* Wissenschaftliche Untersuchungen zum Neuen Testament 86. Tübingen: Mohr Siebeck, 1996.

Eisenbaum, Pamela. "A Remedy for Having Been Born of Woman: Jesus, Gentiles, and Genealogy in Romans." *Journal of Biblical Literature* 123 (2004): 671–702.

———. "Paul, Polemics, and the Problem of Essentialism." *Biblical Interpretation* 13 (2005): 224–38.

———. *Paul Was Not a Christian: The Original Message of a Misunderstood Apostle*. New York: HarperOne, 2009.

Elliott, Neil. *The Rhetoric of Romans: Argumentative Constraint and Strategy and Paul's Dialogue with Judaism*. Journal for the Study of the New Testament: Supplement Series 45. Sheffield: JSOT Press, 1990.

Elliott, Susan. *Cutting Too Close for Comfort: Paul's Letter to the Galatians in its Anatolian Cultic Context*. Journal for the Study of the New Testament: Supplement Series 248. London: T&T Clark, 2003.

Endsjø, Dag Øistein. *Greek Resurrection Beliefs and the Success of Christianity*. New York: Palgrave Macmillan, 2009.

Engberg-Pedersen, Troels. "Galatians in Romans 5–8 and Paul's Construction of the Identity of Christ Believers." Pages 477–505 in *Texts and Contexts: Biblical Texts in Their Textual and Situational Contexts: Essays in Honor of Lars Hartman*. Edited by Tord Fornberg and David Hellholm. Oslo: Scandinavian University Press, 1995.

———. *Paul in His Hellenistic Context*. Minneapolis: Augsburg Fortress, 1995.

———. *Paul Beyond the Judaism/Hellenism Divide*. Louisville: Westminster John Knox, 2001.

———. *Cosmology and Self in the Apostle Paul: The Material Spirit*. Oxford: Oxford University Press, 2010.

Esler, Philip F. *Galatians*. New Testament Readings. London: Routledge, 1998.

———. "Ancient Oleiculture and Ethnic Differentiation: The Meaning of the Olive-Tree Image in Romans 11." *Journal for the Study of the New Testament* 26 (2003): 103–24.

———. *Conflict and Identity in Romans: The Social Setting of Paul's Letter*. Minneapolis: Fortress, 2003.

Eyl, Jennifer. "Semantic Voids, New Testament Translation, and Anachronism: The Case of Paul's Use of *Ekklēsia*." *Method and Theory in the Study of Religion* 26 (2014): 315–39.

Fanning, Buist M. *Verbal Aspect in New Testament Greek*. Oxford Theological Monographs. Oxford: Clarendon, 1990.

Fee, Gordon D. "Christology and Pneumatology in Romans 8:9–11—and Elsewhere: Some Reflections on Paul as a Trinitarian." Pages 312–31 in *Jesus of Nazareth: Lord and Christ: Essays on the Historical Jesus and New Testament Christology*. Edited by Joel B. Green and Max Turner. Grand Rapids: Eerdmans, 1994.

———. *God's Empowering Presence: The Holy Spirit in the Letters of Paul*. Peabody, MA: Hendrickson, 1994.

———. *Paul's Letter to the Philippians*. New International Commentary on the New Testament. Grand Rapids: Eerdmans, 1995.

Feldman, Louis H. "Proselytes and 'Sympathizers' in the Light of the New Inscriptions from Aphrodisias." *Revue des études juives* 148 (1989): 265–305.

———. "Was Judaism a Missionary Religion in Ancient Times?" Pages 24–37 in *Jewish Assimilation, Acculturation and Accommodation: Past Traditions, Current Issues and Future Prospects*. Edited by Menachem Mor. Studies in Jewish Civilization 2. Lanham, MD: University Press of America, 1992.

———. *Jew and Gentile in the Ancient World: Attitudes and Interactions from Alexander to Justinian*. Princeton: Princeton University Press, 1993.

Fewell, Danna Nolan. "The Genesis of Israelite Identity: A Narrative Speculation on Postexilic Interpretation." Pages 111–18 in *Reading Communities Reading Scripture: Essays in Honor of Daniel Patte*. Edited by Gary A. Phillips and Nicole Wilkinson Duran. Harrisburg, PA: Trinity Press International, 2002.

Finlan, Stephen. "Can We Speak of Theosis in Paul?" Pages 68–80 in *Partakers of the Divine Nature: The History and Development of Deification in the Christian Traditions*. Edited by Michael J. Christensen and Jeffery A. Wittung. Grand Rapids: Baker Academic, 2007.

Fitzgerald, John T., ed. *Passions and Moral Progress in Greco-Roman Thought.* Routledge Monographs in Classical Studies. New York: Routledge, 2008.

Fitzmyer, Joseph A. *The Gospel according to Luke X–XXIV: A New Translation with Introduction and Commentary.* Anchor Bible 28ᴀ. Garden City, NY: Doubleday, 1985.

———. *Romans: A New Translation with Introduction and Commentary.* Anchor Bible 33. New York: Doubleday, 1993.

Flusser, David. "Qumrân and Jewish 'Apotropaic' Prayers." *Israel Exploration Journal* 16 (1966): 194–205.

Fokkelman, J. P. "Time and the Structure of the Abraham Cycle." Pages 96–109 in *New Avenues in the Study of the Old Testament: A Collection of Old Testament Studies Published on the Occasion of the Fiftieth Anniversary of the Oudtestamentisch Werkgezelschap and the Retirement of Prof. Dr. M. J. Mulder.* Edited by A. S. van der Woude. Oudtestamentische Studiën 25. Leiden: Brill, 1989.

Forman, Mark. *The Politics of Inheritance in Romans.* Society for New Testament Studies Monograph Series 148. Cambridge, UK: Cambridge University Press, 2011.

Frankfurter, David. "Jews or Not: Reconstructing the 'Other' in Rev 2:9 and 3:9." *Harvard Theological Review* 94 (2001): 403–25.

Fredriksen, Paula. "Judaism, the Circumcision of Gentiles, and Apocalyptic Hope: Another Look at Galatians 1 and 2." *Journal of Theological Studies* 42 (1991): 532–64.

———. "From Jesus to Christ: The Contribution of the Apostle Paul." Pages 77–90 in *Jews and Christians Speak of Jesus.* Edited by Arthur E. Zannoni. Minneapolis: Fortress, 1994.

———. "Paul, Purity, and the *Ekklēsia* of the Gentiles." Pages 205–17 in *The Beginnings of Christianity: A Collection of Articles.* Edited by Jack Pastor and Menachem Mor. Jerusalem: Yad Ben-Zvi, 2005.

———. "Mandatory Retirement: Ideas in the Study of Christian Origins Whose Time Has Come to Go." *Studies in Religion* 35 (2006): 231–46.

———. "What 'Parting of the Ways'? Jews, Gentiles, and the Ancient Mediterranean City." Pages 35–63 in *The Ways that Never Parted: Jews and Christians in Late Antiquity and the Early Middle Ages.* Edited by Adam H. Becker and Annette Yoshiko Reed. Minneapolis: Fortress, 2007.

———. *Augustine and the Jews: A Christian Defense of Jews and Judaism.* New York: Doubleday, 2008.

———. "Judaizing the Nations: The Ritual Demands of Paul's Gospel." *New Testament Studies* 56 (2010): 232–52.

———. "How Later Contexts Affect Pauline Content, or: Retrospect is the Mother of Anachronism." Pages 17–51 in *Jews and Christians in the First and Second Centuries: How to Write Their History.* Edited by Peter J. Tomson and Joshua Schwartz. Compendia rerum iudaicarum ad Novum Testamentum 13. Leiden: Brill, 2014.

———. "The Question of Worship: Gods, Pagans, and the Redemption of Israel." Pages 175–201 in *Paul within Judaism: Restoring the First-Century Context to the Apostle.* Edited by Mark D. Nanos and Magnus Zetterholm. Minneapolis: Fortress, 2015.

Fredriksen, Paula, and Oded Irshai. "Christian Anti-Judaism: Polemics and Policies." Pages 977–1035 in *The Late Roman-Rabbinic Period.* Edited by Steven T. Katz. Vol. 4 of *The Cambridge History of Judaism.* Cambridge, UK: Cambridge University Press, 2006.

Freudenthal, Gad. *Aristotle's Theory of Material Substance: Heat and Pneuma, Form and Soul.* Oxford: Clarendon Press, 1995.

Frey, Jörg, and John R. Levison, eds. *The Holy Spirit, Inspiration, and the Cultures of Antiquity: Multidisciplinary Perspectives.* Ekstasis 5. Berlin: de Gruyter, 2014.

Frey, Jörg, Daniel R. Schwartz, and Stephanie Gripentrog, eds. *Jewish Identity in the Greco-Roman World/Jüdische Identität in der griechisch-römischen Welt.* Arbeiten zur Geschichte des antiken Judentums und des Urchristentums 71. Leiden: Brill, 2007.

Fridrichsen, Anton. "Der wahre Jude und sein Lob: Röm. 2,28f." *Symbolae Arctoae* 1 (1922): 39–49.

Fuller, Michael E. *The Restoration of Israel: Israel's Re-gathering and the Fate of the Nations in Early Jewish Literature and Luke-Acts.* Beihefte zur Zeitschrift für die neutestamentliche Wissenschaft 138. Berlin: de Gruyter, 2006.

Gaca, Kathy L. "Paul's Uncommon Declaration in Romans 1:18–32 and Its Problematic Legacy for Pagan and Christian Relations." *Harvard Theological Review* 92 (1999): 165–98.

Gager, John G. *Moses in Greco-Roman Paganism.* Society of Biblical Literature Monograph Series 16. Nashville: Abingdon, 1972.

———. *The Origins of Anti-Semitism: Attitudes toward Judaism in Pagan and Christian Antiquity.* Oxford: Oxford University Press, 1983.

———. *Reinventing Paul.* Oxford: Oxford University Press, 2000.

———. "Did Jewish Christians See the Rise of Islam?" Pages 361–72 in *The Ways that Never Parted: Jews and Christians in Late Antiquity and the Early Middle Ages.* Edited by Adam H. Becker and Annette Yoshiko Reed. Minneapolis: Fortress, 2007.

———. *Who Made Early Christianity? The Jewish Lives of the Apostle Paul.* American Lectures on the History of Religions. New York: Columbia University Press, 2015.

Gamble, Harry Y. *The Textual History of the Letter to the Romans: A Study in Textual and Literary Criticism.* Studies and Documents 42. Grand Rapids: Eerdmans, 1977.

Garroway, Joshua D. *Paul's Gentile-Jews: Neither Jew nor Gentile, but Both.* New York: Palgrave Macmillan, 2012.

———. "Paul's Gentile Interlocutor in Romans 3:1–20." Pages 85–100 in *The So-Called Jew in Paul's Letter to the Romans.* Edited by Rafael Rodríguez and Matthew Thiessen. Minneapolis: Fortress, 2016.

Gasque, W. Ward. *A History of the Criticism of the Acts of the Apostles.* Beiträge zur Geschichte der biblischen Exegese 17. Tübingen: Mohr Siebeck, 1975.

Gaston, Lloyd. *Paul and the Torah*. Vancouver: University of British Columbia Press, 1987.

Gathercole, Simon J. *Where is Boasting? Early Jewish Soteriology and Paul's Response in Romans 1–5*. Grand Rapids: Eerdmans, 2002.

Gibson, Richard J. "Paul the Missionary, in Priestly Service of the Servant-Christ (Romans 15.16)." Pages 51–62 in *Paul as Missionary: Identity, Activity, Theology, and Practice*. Edited by Trevor J. Burke and Brian S. Rosner. Library of New Testament Studies 420. London: T&T Clark, 2011.

Gilbert, Gary. "The Making of a Jew: 'God-fearer' or Convert in the Story of Izates." *Union Seminary Quarterly Review* 44 (1991): 299–313.

Glad, Clarence E. *Paul and Philodemus: Adaptability in Epicurean and Early Christian Psychology*. Novum Testamentum Supplements 81. Leiden: Brill, 1995.

Goldingay, John E. *Daniel*. Word Biblical Commentary 30. Dallas: Word, 1989.

———. "The Significance of Circumcision." *Journal for the Study of the Old Testament* 88 (2000): 3–18.

Gombis, Timothy G. "Arguing with Scripture in Galatia: Galatians 3:10–14 as a Series of Ad Hoc Arguments." Pages 82–90 in *Galatians and Christian Theology: Justification, the Gospel, and Ethics in Paul's Letter*. Edited by Mark W. Elliott et al. Grand Rapids: Baker Academic, 2014.

Goodman, Martin. *Mission and Conversion: Proselytizing in the Religious History of the Roman Empire*. Oxford: Clarendon, 1994.

Gordon, Benjamin D. "On the Sanctity of Mixtures and Branches: Two Halakhic Sayings in Romans 11:16." *Journal of Biblical Literature* 135 (2016): 355–68.

Gorman, Michael J. *Cruciformity: Paul's Narrative Spirituality of the Cross*. Grand Rapids: Eerdmans, 2001.

———. *Inhabiting the Cruciform God: Kenosis, Justification, and Theosis in Paul's Narrative Soteriology*. Grand Rapids: Eerdmans, 2009.

———. "Romans: The First Christian Treatise on Theosis." *Journal of Theological Interpretation* 5 (2011): 13–34.

Goshen-Gottstein, Alon. "The Promise to the Patriarchs in Rabbinic Literature." Pages 60–97 in *Divine Promises to the Fathers in the Three Monotheistic Religions: Proceedings of a Symposium Held in Jerusalem, March 24–25th, 1993*. Edited by Alviero Niccacci. Studium Biblicum Franciscanum Analecta 40. Jerusalem: Franciscan Printing Press, 1995.

Goulder, Michael D. *A Tale of Two Missions*. London: SCM, 1994.

———. *Paul and the Competing Mission in Corinth*. Library of Pauline Studies. Peabody, MA: Hendrickson, 2001.

Gregory, Bradley C. "Abraham as the Jewish Ideal: Exegetical Traditions in Sirach 44:19–21." *Catholic Biblical Quarterly* 70 (2008): 66–81.

Gruen, Erich S. "The Purported Jewish-Spartan Affiliation." Pages 254–69 in *Transitions to Empire: Essays in Greco-Roman History, 360–146 B.C., in Honor of E. Badian*. Edited by R. W. Wallace and E. M. Harris. Oklahoma Series in Classical Culture 21. Norman: University of Oklahoma Press, 1996.

————. *Heritage and Hellenism: The Reinvention of Jewish Tradition.* Hellenistic Culture and Society 30. Berkeley: University of California Press, 1998.

Guerra, Anthony J. *Romans and the Apologetic Tradition: The Purpose, Genre and Audience of Paul's Letter.* Society for New Testament Studies Monograph Series 81. Cambridge, UK: Cambridge University Press, 1995.

Gunkel, Hermann. *Genesis.* Translated by Mark E. Biddle. Macon, GA: Mercer University Press, 1997.

Hahm, David E. *The Origins of Stoic Cosmology.* Columbus: Ohio State University Press, 1977.

Hahn, Scott. *Kinship by Covenant: A Canonical Approach to the Fulfillment of God's Saving Promises.* Anchor Bible Reference Library. New Haven: Yale University Press, 2009.

Halbertal, Moshe, and Avishai Margalit. *Idolatry.* Translated by Naomi Goldblum. Cambridge, MA: Harvard University Press, 1992.

Hall, Edith. *Inventing the Barbarian: Greek Self-Definition through Tragedy.* Oxford Classical Monographs. Oxford: Clarendon, 1989.

Hall, Jonathan M. *Ethnic Identity in Greek Antiquity.* Cambridge, UK: Cambridge University Press, 1997.

————. *Hellenicity: Between Ethnicity and Culture.* Chicago: University of Chicago Press, 2002.

Hall, Robert G. "Epispasm and the Dating of Ancient Jewish Writings." *Journal for the Study of the Pseudepigrapha* 1 (1988): 71–86.

————. "Epispasm: Circumcision in *Reverse.*" *Bible Review* 8 (1992): 52–57.

Hansen, G. Walter. *Abraham in Galatians: Epistolary and Rhetorical Contexts.* Journal for the Study of the New Testament: Supplement Series 29. Sheffield: Sheffield Academic, 1989.

Hanson, R. P. C. *Allegory and Event: A Study of the Sources and Significance of Origen's Interpretation of Scripture.* Richmond, VA: John Knox, 1959.

Hardin, Justin K. *Galatians and the Imperial Cult: A Critical Analysis of the First-Century Social Context of Paul's Letter.* Wissenschaftliche Untersuchungen zum Neuen Testament 2/237. Tübingen: Mohr Siebeck, 2008.

————. "'If I Still Proclaim Circumcision' (Galatians 5:11a): Paul, the Law, and Gentile Circumcision." *Journal for the Study of Paul and His Letters* 3 (2013): 145–64.

Harmon, Matthew S. *She Must and Shall Go Free: Paul's Isaianic Gospel in Galatians.* Beihefte zur Zeitschrift für die neutestamentliche Wissenschaft 168. Berlin: de Gruyter, 2010.

Harrington, Hannah K. "Holiness and Purity in Ezra-Nehemiah." Pages 98–116 in *Unity and Disunity in Ezra-Nehemiah: Redaction, Rhetoric, and Reader.* Edited by Mark J. Boda and Paul L. Redditt. Hebrew Bible Monographs 17. Sheffield: Sheffield Phoenix, 2008.

Harrison, James R. "Paul's 'Indebtedness' to the Barbarian (Rom 1:14) in Latin West Perspective." *Novum Testamentum* 55 (2013): 311–48.

Harrison, Peter. *"Religion" and the Religions in the English Enlightenment.* Cambridge, UK: Cambridge University Press, 1990.

Harvey, A. E. "Opposition to Paul." Pages 321–33 in *The Galatians Debate: Contemporary Issues in Rhetorical and Historical Interpretation*. Edited by Mark D. Nanos. Peabody, MA: Hendrickson, 2007.

Hasslberger, Bernhard. *Hoffnung in der Bedrängnis: Eine formkritische Untersuchung zu Daniel 8 und 10–12*. St. Ottilien: Eos, 1977.

Hawthorne, Gerald F. *Philippians*. Word Biblical Commentary 43. Waco, TX: Word, 1983.

Hay, D. M. "Philo's References to Other Allegorists." *Studia Philonica Annual* 6 (1979–1980): 41–75.

Hayes, Christine E. *Gentile Impurities and Jewish Identities: Intermarriage and Conversion from the Bible to the Talmud*. Oxford: Oxford University Press, 2002.

———. *What's Divine about Divine Law? Early Perspectives*. Princeton: Princeton University Press, 2015.

Hays, Richard B. "Christology and Ethics in Galatians: The Law of Christ." *Catholic Biblical Quarterly* 49 (1987): 268–90.

———. *Echoes of Scripture in the Letters of Paul*. New Haven: Yale University Press, 1989.

———. "The Gospel Is the Power of God for Salvation to Gentiles Only? A Critique of Stanley Stowers's Rereading of Romans." *Critical Review of Books in Religion* 9 (1996): 27–44.

———. "Πίστις and Pauline Christology: What Is at Stake?" Pages 35–60 in *Looking Back, Pressing On*. Edited by E. Elizabeth Johnson and David M. Hay. Vol. 4 of *Pauline Theology*. Society of Biblical Literature Symposium Series 23. Atlanta: Scholars Press, 1997.

———. "The Letter to the Galatians." Pages 181–348 in *2 Corinthians-Philemon*. Edited by Leander E. Keck. New Interpreter's Bible 11. Nashville: Abingdon, 2000.

———. *The Faith of Jesus Christ: The Narrative Substructure of Galatians 3:1—4:11*. 2d ed. Bible Resource Series. Grand Rapids: Eerdmans, 2002.

Heard, R. Christopher. *Dynamics of Diselection: Ambiguity in Genesis 12–36 and Ethnic Boundaries in Post-Exilic Judah*. Semeia Studies 39. Atlanta: SBL Press, 2001.

Heath, J. M. F. *Paul's Visual Piety: The Metamorphosis of the Beholder*. Oxford: Oxford University Press, 2013.

Hecht, Richard D. "The Exegetical Contexts of Philo's Interpretation of Circumcision." Pages 51–79 in *Nourished with Peace: Studies in Hellenistic Judaism in Memory of Samuel Sandmel*. Edited by Frederick E. Greenspahn, Earle Hilgert, and Burton L. Mack. Chico, CA: Scholars Press, 1984.

Heckel, Ulrich. *Der Segen im Neuen Testament*. Wissenschaftliche Untersuchungen zum Neuen Testament 150. Tübingen: Mohr Siebeck, 2002.

Hehn, Johannes. "Zum Problem des Geistes im Alten Orient und im Alten Testament." *Zeitschrift für die alttestamentliche Wissenschaft* 43 (1925): 210–25.

Hemer, Colin J. *The Book of Acts in the Setting of Hellenistic History*. Edited by Conrad H. Gempf. Wissenschaftliche Untersuchungen zum Neuen Testament 49. Tübingen: Mohr, 1989.

Hengel, Martin. *Acts and the History of Earliest Christianity*. Translated by John Bowden. Philadelphia: Fortress, 1980.

Hengel, Martin, with Roland Deines. *The Pre-Christian Paul*. Translated by John Bowden. London: SCM, 1991.

Henry, Devin. "Embryological Models in Ancient Philosophy." *Phronesis* 50 (2005): 1–42.

Hezser, Catherine. *Jewish Slavery in Antiquity*. Oxford: Oxford University Press, 2005.

Himmelfarb, Martha. "Levi, Phinehas, and the Problem of Intermarriage at the Time of the Maccabean Revolt." *Jewish Studies Quarterly* 6 (1999): 1–24.

———. "The Ordeals of Abraham: Circumcision and the *Aqedah* in Origen, the *Mekhilta*, and *Genesis Rabbah*." *Henoch* 30 (2008): 289–310.

Hirsch, E. "Zwei Fragen zu Galater 6." *Zeitschrift für die neutestamentliche Wissenschaft und die Kunde der älteren Kirche* 29 (1930): 192–97.

Holloway, Paul A. "*Commendatio aliqua sui*: Reading Romans with Pierre Bourdieu." *Early Christianity* 2 (2011): 356–83.

Holtz, Gudrun. *Damit Gott sei alles in allem: Studien zum paulinischen und früh-jüdischen Universalismus*. Beihefte zur Zeitschrift für die neutestamentliche Wissenschaft 149. Berlin: de Gruyter, 2007.

Hooker, Morna D. "Heirs of Abraham: The Gentiles' Role in Israel's Story: A Response to Bruce W. Longenecker." Pages 85–96 in *Narrative Dynamics in Paul: A Critical Assessment*. Edited by Bruce W. Longenecker. Louisville: Westminster John Knox, 2002.

Horn, Friedrich Wilhelm. *Das Angeld des Geistes: Studien zur paulinischen Pneumatologie*. Forschungen zur Religion und Literatur des Alten und Neuen Testaments 154. Göttingen: Vandhoeck & Ruprecht, 1992.

———. "Kyrios und Pneuma bei Paulus." Pages 59–75 in *Paulinische Christologie: exegetische Beiträge: Hans Hübner zum 70. Geburtstag*. Edited by Udo Schnelle and Thomas Söding. Göttingen: Vandenhoeck & Ruprecht, 2000.

Howard, George. *Paul: Crisis in Galatia: A Study in Early Christian Theology*. 2d ed. Society for New Testament Studies Monograph Series 35. Cambridge, UK: Cambridge University Press, 1990.

Hübner, Hans. "Gal 3,10 und die Herkunft des Paulus." *Kerygma und Dogma* 19 (1973): 215–31.

———. *Law in Paul's Thought: A Contribution to the Development of Pauline Theology*. Translated by James C. G. Greig. Studies of the New Testament and its World. London: T&T Clark, 1984.

Huddleston, Jonathan. *Eschatology in Genesis*. Forschungen zum Alten Testament 2/57. Tübingen: Mohr Siebeck, 2012.

Hultgren, Arland J. *Paul's Letter to the Romans: A Commentary*. Grand Rapids: Eerdmans, 2011.

Hutchinson, John, and Anthony D. Smith, eds. *Ethnicity*. Oxford Readers. Oxford: Oxford University Press, 1996.

Huttunen, Niko. *Paul and Epictetus on Law: A Comparison.* Library of New Testament Studies 405. London: T&T Clark, 2009.

Isaac, Benjamin. *The Invention of Racism in Classical Antiquity.* Princeton: Princeton University Press, 2002.

Iser, Wolfgang. *The Implied Reader: Patterns of Communication in Prose Fiction from Bunyan to Beckett.* Baltimore: Johns Hopkins University Press, 1974.

———. *The Act of Reading: A Theory of Aesthetic Response.* Baltimore: Johns Hopkins University Press, 1978.

Janzen, David. *Witch-hunts, Purity and Social Boundaries: The Expulsion of the Foreign Women in Ezra 9–10.* Journal for the Study of the Old Testament: Supplement Series 350. Sheffield: Sheffield Academic, 2002.

Jensen, Joseph. *The Use of* tôrâ *by Isaiah: His Debate with the Wisdom Tradition.* Catholic Biblical Quarterly Monograph Series 3. Washington, DC: Catholic Biblical Association of America, 1973.

Jervell, Jacob. *The Unknown Paul: Essays on Luke-Acts and Early Christian History.* Translated by Roy A. Harrisville. Minneapolis: Augsburg, 1984.

Jewett, Robert. "The Agitators and the Galatian Congregation." *New Testament Studies* 17 (1971): 198–212.

———. "Romans as an Ambassadorial Letter." *Interpretation* 36 (1982): 5–20.

———. *Romans: A Commentary.* Hermeneia. Minneapolis: Fortress, 2007.

Jipp, Joshua W. "Rereading the Story of Abraham, Isaac, and 'Us' in Romans 4." *Journal for the Study of the New Testament* 32 (2009): 217–42.

———. *Christ is King: Paul's Royal Ideology.* Minneapolis: Fortress, 2015.

Jobes, Karen H. "Jerusalem, our Mother: Metalepsis and Intertextuality in Galatians 4:21–31." *Westminster Theological Journal* 55 (1993): 299–320.

Johnson Hodge, Caroline. "Olive Trees and Ethnicities: Judeans and Gentiles in Rom. 11:17–24." Pages 77–89 in *Christians as a Religious Minority in a Multicultural City: Modes of Interaction and Identity Formation in Early Imperial Rome.* Edited by Jürgen Zangenburg and Michael Labahn. Journal for the Study of the New Testament: Supplement Series 243. London: T&T Clark, 2004.

———. "Apostle to the Gentiles: Constructions of Paul's Identity." *Biblical Interpretation* 13 (2005): 270–88.

———. *If Sons, Then Heirs: A Study of Kinship and Ethnicity in the Letters of Paul.* Oxford: Oxford University Press, 2007.

———. "The Question of Identity: Gentiles as Gentiles—but also Not—in Pauline Communities." Pages 153–73 in *Paul within Judaism: Restoring the First-Century Context to the Apostle.* Edited by Mark D. Nanos and Magnus Zetterholm. Minneapolis: Fortress, 2015.

Juel, Donald. *Messianic Exegesis: Christological Interpretation of the Old Testament in Early Christianity.* Philadelphia: Fortress, 1988.

Kaminsky, Joel. "Did Election Imply the Mistreatment of Non-Israelites?" *Harvard Theological Review* 96 (2003): 397–425.

———. *Yet I Loved Jacob: Reclaiming the Biblical Concept of Election.* Nashville: Abingdon, 2007.

———. "A Light to the Nations: Was There Mission and or Conversion in the Hebrew Bible?" *Jewish Studies Quarterly* 16 (2009): 6–22.

Käsemann, Ernst. *Commentary on Romans.* Translated and edited by Geoffrey W. Bromiley. Grand Rapids: Eerdmans, 1980.

Kasher, Aryeh. *Jews, Idumaeans, and Ancient Arabs: Relations of the Jews in Eretz-Israel with the Nations of the Frontier and the Desert during the Hellenistic and Roman Era (332 BCE–70 CE).* Texte und Studien zum antiken Judentum 18. Tübingen: Mohr (Siebeck), 1988.

Keel, Othmar, and Christoph Uehlinger. *Gods, Goddesses, and Images of God in Ancient Israel.* Translated by Allan W. Mahnke. Minneapolis: Fortress, 1996.

Kennedy, Rebecca F., C. Sydnor Roy, and Max L. Goldman, eds. and trans. *Race and Ethnicity in the Classical World: An Anthology of Primary Sources in Translation.* Indianapolis, IN: Hackett, 2013.

Kinzer, Mark Stephen. "'All Things Under His Feet': Psalm 8 in the New Testament and in Other Jewish Literature of Late Antiquity." Ph.D. diss., University of Michigan, 1995.

Kittel, Gerhard and Gerhard Friedrich, eds. *Theological Dictionary of the New Testament.* Translated by Geoffrey W. Bromiley. 10 vols. Grand Rapids: Eerdmans, 1964–1976.

Klawans, Jonathan. *Purity, Sacrifice, and the Temple: Symbolism and Supersessionism in the Study of Ancient Judaism.* Oxford: Oxford University Press, 2006.

———. *Josephus and the Theologies of Ancient Judaism.* Oxford: Oxford University Press, 2012.

Klopper, Frances. "Iconographical Evidence for a Theory on Astral Worship in Seventh- and Sixth-Century Judah." Pages 168–84 in *South African Perspectives on the Pentateuch between Synchrony and Diachrony.* Edited by Jurie Le Roux and Eckart Otto. Library of Hebrew Bible/Old Testament Studies 463. London: T&T Clark, 2007.

Knox, John. *Marcion and the New Testament.* New York: AMS Press, 1980.

———. *Chapters in a Life of Paul.* Rev. ed. Macon, GA: Mercer University Press, 1987.

Koet, Bart. "Purity and Impurity of the Body in Luke-Acts." Pages 93–106 in *Purity and Holiness: The Heritage of Leviticus.* Edited by Marcel J. H. M. Poorthuis and Joshua Schwartz. Jewish and Christian Perspectives Series 2. Leiden: Brill, 2000.

Konstan, David, and Suzanne Saïd, eds. *Greeks on Greekness: Viewing the Greek Past under the Roman Empire.* Cambridge, UK: Cambridge Philological Society, 2006.

Kooten, George H. van. "Pagan and Jewish Monotheism according to Varro, Plutarch, and St. Paul: The Aniconic, Monotheistic Beginnings of Rome's Pagan Cult—Romans 1:19–25 in a Roman Context." Pages 633–51 in *Flores Florentino: Dead Sea Scrolls and Other Early Jewish Studies in Honour of Florentino García Martínez.* Edited by Anthony Hilhorst, Émile Puech, and Eibert Tigchelaar. Journal for the Study of Judaism: Supplement Series 122. Leiden: Brill, 2007.

———. *Paul's Anthropology in Context: The Image of God, Assimilation to God, and Tripartite Man in Ancient Judaism, Ancient Philosophy and Early Christianity.* Wissenschaftliche Untersuchungen zum Neuen Testament 232. Tübingen: Mohr Siebeck, 2008.

Kraemer, Ross Shephard. *When Aseneth Met Joseph: A Late Antique Tale of the Biblical Patriarch and His Egyptian Wife, Reconsidered.* Oxford: Oxford University Press, 1998.

Kümmel, Werner G. *Römer 7 und die Bekehrung des Paulus.* Leipzig: Hinrichs, 1929.

Kunin, Seth Daniel. *The Logic of Incest: A Structuralist Analysis of Hebrew Mythology.* Journal for the Study of the Old Testament: Supplement Series 185. Sheffield: Sheffield Academic, 1995.

Kuss, Otto. *Der Römerbrief.* 3 vols. Regensburger Neues Testament 6. Regensburg: Pustet, 1957–1978.

Laato, Timo. *Paul and Judaism: An Anthropological Approach.* Translated by T. McElwain. South Florida Studies in the History of Judaism 115. Atlanta: Scholars Press, 1995.

Lagrange, Marie-Joseph. *Saint Paul: Épître aux Galates.* 2d ed. Etudes Biblique. Paris: Gabalda, 1950.

———. *Saint Paul: Épître aux Romains.* Etudes Biblique. Paris: Gabalda, 1950.

Lamberton, Robert, and John J. Keaney, eds. *Homer's Ancient Readers: The Hermeneutics of Greek Epic's Earliest Exegetes.* Princeton: Princeton University Press, 1992.

Lambrecht, Jan. *The Wretched "I" and Its Liberation: Paul in Romans 7 and 8.* Louvain Theological & Pastoral Monographs 14. Leuven: Peeters, 1992.

———. "Abraham and His Offspring: A Comparison of Galatians 5,1 with 3,13." *Biblica* 80 (1999): 525–36.

Lampe, Peter. *From Paul to Valentinus: Christians at Rome in the First Two Centuries.* Translated by Michael Steinhauser. Minneapolis: Fortress, 2003.

Laurence, Ray, and Joanne Berry, eds. *Cultural Identity in the Roman Empire.* London: Routledge, 1998.

Lavee, Moshe. "Converting the Missionary Image of Abraham: Rabbinic Traditions Migrating from the Land of Israel to Babylon." Pages 203–22 in *Abraham, the Nations, and the Hagarites: Jewish, Christian, and Islamic Perspectives on Kinship with Abraham.* Edited by George H. van Kooten, Martin Goodman, and Jacques T. A. G. M. van Ruiten. Themes in Biblical Narrative 13. Leiden: Brill, 2010.

———. "'Proselytes are as Hard to Israel as a Scab Is to the Skin': A Babylonian Talmudic Concept." *Journal of Jewish Studies* 63 (2012): 22–48.

Ledegang, F. *Mysterium Ecclesiae: Images of the Church and its Members in Origen.* Bibliotheca ephemeridum theologicarum lovaniensium 156. Leuven: Peeters, 2001.

Lee, Michelle V. *Paul, the Stoics, and the Body of Christ.* Society for the Study of the New Testament Monograph Series 137. Cambridge, UK: Cambridge University Press, 2006.

Lemke, Werner. "Circumcision of the Heart: The Journey of a Biblical Metaphor." Pages 299–319 in *God So Near: Essays on Old Testament Theology in Honor of Patrick D. Miller*. Edited by Brent A. Strawn and Nancy R. Bowen. Winona Lake, IN: Eisenbrauns, 2003.

Lesky, E., and J. H. Waszink. "Embryologie." *Reallexikon für Antike und Christentum* (1959): 4:1228–44.

Leslau, Wolf. *Comparative Dictionary of Ge'ez*. Wiesbaden: Harrassowitz, 2006.

Levenson, Jon D. *Esther: A Commentary*. Old Testament Library. Louisville: Westminster John Knox, 1997.

———. *Abraham between Torah and Gospel*. Père Marquette Lecture in Theology 2011. Milwaukee: Marquette University Press, 2011.

Levine, Lee I. and Daniel R. Schwartz, eds. *Jewish Identities in Antiquity: Studies in Memory of Menahem Stern*. Texts and Studies in Ancient Judaism 130. Tübingen: Mohr Siebeck, 2009.

Levison, John R. "The Prophetic Spirit as an Angel according to Philo." *Harvard Theological Review* 88 (1995): 189–207.

———. *The Spirit in First-Century Judaism*. Leiden: Brill, 2002.

———. *Filled with the Spirit*. Grand Rapids: Eerdmans, 2009.

Lichtenberger, Hermann. "Ps 91 und die Exorzismen in 11QPsApᵃ." Pages 416–21 in *Die Dämonen: Die Dämonologie der israelitisch-jüdischen und frühchristlichen Literatur im Kontext ihrer Umwelt—Demons: The Demonology of Israelite-Jewish and Early Christian Literature in the Context of Their Environment*. Edited by Armin Lange, Hermann Lichtenberger, and K. F. Diethard Römheld. Tübingen: Mohr Siebeck, 2003.

Liddell, H. G., R. Scott, and H. S. Jones. *A Greek-English Lexicon*. Oxford: Clarendon, 1996.

Lieu, Judith. "'As much My Apostle as Christ Is Mine': The Dispute over Paul between Tertullian and Marcion." *Early Christianity* 1 (2010): 41–59.

———. "The Battle for Paul in the Second Century." *Irish Theological Quarterly* 75 (2010): 3–14.

Lightfoot, J. B. *Saint Paul's Epistle to the Galatians*. London: Macmillan, 1905.

Linebaugh, Jonathan. "Announcing the Human: Rethinking the Relationship between Wisdom of Solomon 13–15 and Romans 1.18—2.11." *New Testament Studies* 57 (2011): 214–37.

Litwa, M. David. *"We Are Being Transformed": Deification in Paul's Soteriology*. Beihefte zur Zeitschrift für die neutestamentliche Wissenschaft 187. Berlin: de Gruyter, 2012.

Livesey, Nina E. *Circumcision as a Malleable Symbol*. Wissenschaftliche Untersuchungen zum Neuen Testament 2/295. Tübingen: Mohr Siebeck, 2010.

Lloyd, G. E. R. *Aristotle: The Growth and Structure of his Thought*. Cambridge, UK: Cambridge University Press, 1968.

Löfstedt, Torsten. "The Allegory of Hagar and Sarah: Gal 4:21–31." *Estudios bíblicos* 58 (2000): 475–94.

Lohse, Eduard. *Der Brief an die Römer*. 15th ed. Kritisch-exegetischer Kommentar über das Neue Testament 4. Göttingen: Vandenhoeck & Ruprecht, 2003.

Longenecker, Bruce W. *The Triumph of Abraham's God: The Transformation of Identity in Galatians*. Nashville: Abingdon, 1998.

Longenecker, Richard N. *Paul: Apostle of Liberty*. New York: Harper & Row, 1964.

———. *Galatians*. Word Biblical Commentary 41. Dallas: Word, 1990.

———. *Introducing Romans: Critical Issues in Paul's Most Famous Letter*. Grand Rapids: Eerdmans, 2011.

Luckritz Marquis, Timothy. *Transient Apostle: Paul, Travel, and the Rhetoric of Empire*. Synkrisis. New Haven: Yale University Press, 2013.

Lüdemann, Gerd. *The Acts of the Apostles: What Really Happened in the Earliest Days of the Church*. Amherst, NY: Prometheus, 2005.

Lührmann, Dieter. *Galatians*. Translated by O. C. Dean Jr. Continental Commentary. Minneapolis: Fortress, 1992.

Lull, David John. *The Spirit in Galatia: Paul's Interpretation of Pneuma as Divine Power*. Society of Biblical Literature Dissertation Series 49. Chico, CA: Scholars Press, 1980.

Luther, Martin. *A Commentary on St. Paul's Epistle to the Galatians*. Translated by Philip S. Watson. Cambridge, UK: James Clarke, 1953.

MacDonald, Dennis R. *The Legend and the Apostle: The Battle for Paul in Story and Canon*. Philadelphia: Westminster, 1983.

Malherbe, Abraham J. "Antisthenes and Odysseus, and Paul at War." *Harvard Theological Review* 76 (1983): 143–73.

Malkani, Gautam. *Londonstani*. London: Fourth Estate, 2006.

Malkin, Irad, ed. *Ancient Perceptions of Greek Ethnicity*. Center for Hellenic Studies, Colloquia 5. Washington, DC: Center for Hellenic Studies, 2001.

Mannermaa, Tuomo. *Christ Present in Faith: Luther's View of Justification*. Minneapolis: Fortress, 2005.

Marcus, Joel. "The Circumcision and the Uncircumcision in Rome." *New Testament Studies* 35 (1989): 67–81.

———. "'Under the Law': The Background of a Pauline Expression." *Catholic Biblical Quarterly* 63 (2001): 72–83.

Martin, Dale B. *The Corinthian Body*. New Haven: Yale University Press, 1995.

Martin, Troy W. "Pagan and Judeo-Christian Time-Keeping Schemes in Gal 4.10 and Col 2.16." *New Testament Studies* 42 (1996): 105–19.

———. "Paul's Pneumatological Statements and Ancient Medical Texts." Pages 105–26 in *The New Testament and Early Christian Literature in Greco-Roman Context: Studies in Honor of David E. Aune*. Edited by John Fotopoulos. Novum Testamentum Supplements 122. Leiden: Brill, 2006.

Martyn, J. Louis. *Galatians: A New Translation with Introduction and Commentary*. Anchor Bible 33A. New York: Doubleday, 1997.

———. *Theological Issues in the Letters of Paul*. Nashville: Abingdon, 1997.

Mason, Steve. *Flavius Josephus on the Pharisees: A Composition-Critical Study.* Studia Post-Biblica 39. Leiden: Brill, 1991.

———. "'For I am Not Ashamed of the Gospel' (Rom. 1.16): The Gospel and the First Readers of Romans." Pages 254–87 in *Gospel in Paul: Studies on Corinthians, Galatians and Romans for Richard N. Longenecker.* Edited by L. Ann Jervis and Peter Richardson. Journal for the Study of the New Testament: Supplement Series 108. Sheffield: Sheffield Academic, 1994.

———. "Jews, Judaeans, Judaizing, Judaism: Problems of Categorization in Ancient History." *Journal for the Study of Judaism in the Persian, Hellenistic, and Roman Periods* 38 (2007): 457–512.

Masuzawa, Tomoko. *The Invention of World Religions: Or, How European Universalism Was Preserved in the Language of Pluralism.* Chicago: University of Chicago Press, 2005.

Matera, Frank J. "The Culmination of Paul's Argument to the Galatians: Gal. 5.1—6.17." *Journal for the Study of the New Testament* 32 (1988): 79–91.

———. *Galatians.* Sacra Pagina 9. Collegeville, MN: Liturgical Press, 1992.

Matlock, R. Barry. "'Jews by Nature': Paul, Ethnicity, and Galatians." Pages 304–15 in *Far From Minimal: Celebrating the Work and Influence of Philip R. Davies.* Edited by Duncan Burns and J. W. Rogerson. Library of Hebrew Bible/Old Testament Studies 484. London: T&T Clark, 2012.

McDonald, James I. H. "Was Romans 16 a Separate Letter?" *New Testament Studies* 16 (1970): 369–72.

McKay, John. *Religion in Judah under the Assyrians.* Studies in Biblical Theology. Second Series 26. London: SCM, 1973.

McKnight, Scot. *A Light Among the Gentiles: Jewish Missionary Activity in the Second Temple Period.* Minneapolis: Fortress, 1991.

Meier, John P. *Law and Love.* Vol. 4 of *A Marginal Jew: Rethinking the Historical Jesus.* Anchor Yale Bible Reference Library. New Haven: Yale University Press, 2009.

Mendels, Doron. *The Land of Israel as a Political Concept in Hasmonean Literature: Recourse to History in Second Century B.C. Claims to the Holy Land.* Texte und Studien zum antiken Judentum 15. Tübingen: Mohr Siebeck, 1987.

Mendelson, Alan. *Philo's Jewish Identity.* Brown Jewish Studies 161. Atlanta: Scholars Press, 1988.

Metzger, Bruce D. *A Textual Commentary on the Greek New Testament.* 2d ed. Stuttgart: Deutsche Bibelgesellschaft, 1994.

Michel, Otto. *Der Brief an die Römer.* 14th ed. Kritisch-exegetischer Kommentar über das Neue Testament 4. Göttingen: Vandenhoeck & Ruprecht, 1978.

Millar, Fergus. "Hagar, Ishmael, Josephus and the Origins of Islam." *Journal of Jewish Studies* 44 (1993): 23–45.

Miller, Harold W. "*Dynamis* and the Seeds." *Transactions and Proceedings of the American Philological Association* 97 (1966): 281–90.

Mitchell, Margaret M. "Pauline Accommodation and 'Condescension' (συγκατάβασις): 1 Cor 9:19–23 and the History of Influence." Pages 197–214 in

*Paul Beyond the Judaism/Hellenism Divide*. Edited by Troels Engberg-Pedersen. Louisville: Westminster John Knox, 2001.

———. *The Heavenly Trumpet: John Chrysostom and the Art of Pauline Interpretation*. Louisville: Westminster John Knox, 2002.

Mitchell, Stephen. *Anatolia: Land, Men, and Gods in Asia Minor*. 2 vols. Oxford: Clarendon, 1993.

Mitchell, Stephen, and Peter van Nuffelen, eds. *One God: Pagan Monotheism in the Roman Empire*. Cambridge, UK: Cambridge University Press, 2010.

Mitternacht, Dieter. *Forum für Sprachlose: Eine kommunikationspsychologische und epistolär-rhetorische Untersuchung des Galaterbriefs*. Coniectanea neotestamentica or Coniectanea biblica: New Testament Series 30. Almqvist & Wiksell, 1999.

Moffitt, David M. *Atonement and the Logic of Resurrection in the Epistle to the Hebrews*. Novum Testamentum Supplements 151. Leiden: Brill, 2011.

Moffitt, David M., and C. Jacob Butera. "P.Duk. inv. 727r: New Evidence for the Meaning and Provenance of the Word Προσήλυτος." *Journal of Biblical Literature* 132 (2013): 159–78.

Montefiore, Claude G. *Judaism and St. Paul: Two Essays*. London: Goschen, 1914.

Moo, Douglas J. *The Epistle to the Romans*. New International Commentary on the New Testament. Grand Rapids: Eerdmans, 1996.

Moore, Cary A. *Judith: A New Translation with Introduction and Commentary*. Anchor Bible 40. Garden City, NY: Doubleday, 1985.

Moore, George Foot. "Christian Writers on Judaism." *Harvard Theological Review* 14 (1921): 197–254.

Morales, Rodrigo J. "The Words of the Luminaries, the Curse of the Law, and the Outpouring of the Spirit in Gal 3,10–14." *Zeitschrift für die neutestamentliche Wissenschaft und die Kunde der älteren Kirche* 100 (2009): 269–77.

Morgan, Teresa. *Roman Faith and Christian Faith: Pistis and Fides in the Early Roman Empire and Early Churches*. Oxford: Oxford University Press, 2015.

Moxnes, Halvor. *Theology in Conflict: Studies in Paul's Understanding of God in Romans*. Novum Testamentum Supplements 53. Leiden: Brill, 1980.

Moyer, Ian S. *Egypt and the Limits of Hellenism*. Cambridge, UK: Cambridge University Press, 2011.

Mullen, Theodore. *The Assembly of the Gods: The Divine Council in Canaanite and Early Hebrew Literature*. Harvard Semitic Monographs 24. Chico, CA: Scholars Press, 1980.

Müller, Klaus. *Tora für die Völker: Die noachidischen Gebote und Ansätze zu ihrer Rezeption im Christentum*. 2d ed. Studien zu Kirche und Israel 15. Berlin: Institut Kirche und Judentum, 1998.

Mullins, Terence Y. "Greetings as a New Testament Form." *Journal of Biblical Literature* 87 (1968): 418–26.

Munck, Johannes. *Paul and the Salvation of Mankind*. Translated by Frank Clarke. Richmond, VA: John Knox, 1959.

Munro, Winsome. *Authority in Paul and Peter: The Identification of a Pastoral Stratum in the Pauline Corpus and 1 Peter.* Society for New Testament Studies Monograph Series 45. Cambridge, UK: Cambridge University Press, 1983.

Murray, Michele. *Playing a Jewish Game: Gentile Christian Judaizing in the First and Second Centuries CE.* Studies in Christianity and Judaism 13. Waterloo, ON: Wilfred Laurier University Press, 2004.

Mussner, Franz. *Der Galaterbrief.* Herders theologischer Kommentar zum Neuen Testament 9. Freiburg: Herder, 1974.

———. "'Christus (ist) des Gesetzes Ende zur Gerechtigkeit für jeden, der glaubt' (Rom 10,4)." Pages 31–44 in *Paulus—Apostat oder Apostel? Jüdische und christliche Antworten.* Edited by Markus Barth et al. Regensburg: Pustet, 1977.

Nanos, Mark D. *The Mystery of Romans: The Jewish Context of Paul's Letter.* Minneapolis: Fortress, 1996.

———. *The Irony of Galatians: Paul's Letter in First-Century Context.* Minneapolis: Fortress, 2002.

———. "'Broken Branches': A Pauline Metaphor Gone Awry? (Romans 11:11–36)." Pages 339–76 in *Between Gospel and Election: Explorations in the Interpretation of Romans 9–11.* Edited by Florian Wilk and J. Ross Wagner. Wissenschaftliche Untersuchungen zum Neuen Testament 257. Tübingen: Mohr Siebeck, 2010.

———. "Paul's Relationship to Torah in Light of His Strategy 'to Become Everything to Everyone' (1 Corinthians 9:19–22)." Pages 106–40 in *Paul and Judaism: Crosscurrents in Pauline Exegesis and the Study of Jewish-Christian Relations.* Edited by Reimund Bieringer and Didier Pollefeyt. Library of New Testament Studies 463. London: T&T Clark: 2012.

———. "The Question of Conceptualization: Qualifying Paul's Position on Circumcision in Dialogue with Josephus's Advisors to King Izates." Pages 105–52 in *Paul within Judaism: Restoring the First-Century Context to the Apostle.* Edited by Mark D. Nanos and Magnus Zetterholm. Minneapolis: Fortress, 2015.

Nanos, Mark D. and Magnus Zetterholm, eds. *Paul within Judaism: Restoring the First-Century Context to the Apostle.* Minneapolis: Fortress, 2015.

Neander, A. *Geschichte der Pflanzung und Leitung der christlichen Kirche durch die Apostel.* 2 vols. 4th ed. Hamburg: Perthes, 1847.

Neubrand, Maria. *Abraham—Vater von Juden und Nichtjuden: Eine exegetische Studie zu Röm 4.* Forschung zur Bibel 85. Würzburg: Echter, 1997.

Neusner, Jacob. "The Conversion of Adiabene to Judaism: A New Perspective." *Journal of Biblical Literature* 83 (1964): 60–66.

———. *Formative Judaism: Religious, Historical and Literary Studies: Third Series: Torah, Pharisees, and Rabbis.* Brown Judaic Studies 46. Chico, CA: Scholars Press, 1983.

Nickelsburg, George W. E. *1 Enoch 1: A Commentary on the Book of 1 Enoch, Chapters 1–36; 81–108.* Hermeneia. Minneapolis: Fortress, 2001.

———. "Abraham, the Convert: A Jewish Tradition and Its Use by the Apostle Paul." Pages 151–75 in *Biblical Figures outside the Bible.* Edited by Michael A. Stone and Theodore A. Bergren. Harrisburg, PA: Trinity Press International, 1998.

Niehoff, Maren R. *Philo on Jewish Identity and Culture.* Texte und Studien zum antiken Judentum 86. Tübingen: Mohr Siebeck, 2001.

———. *Jewish Exegesis and Homeric Scholarship in Alexandria.* Cambridge,
UK: Cambridge University Press, 2011.

Nilsson, Martin P. "The Origin of Belief among the Greeks in the Divinity of the
Heavenly Bodies." *Harvard Theological Review* 33 (1940): 1–8.

———. "Die astrale Unsterblichkeit und die kosmische Mystik." *Numen* 1 (1954): 106–19.

Nir, Rivka. *Joseph and Aseneth: A Christian Book.* Hebrew Bible Monographs 42.
Sheffield: Sheffield Phoenix, 2012.

Noam, Vered. "Beit Shammai and the Sectarian Halakhah." *Jewish Studies (World
Union of Jewish Studies)* 41 (2002): 45–67 (Hebrew).

———. "Traces of Sectarian Halakhah in the Rabbinic World." Pages 67–85 in
*Rabbinic Perspectives: Rabbinic Literature and the Dead Sea Scrolls, Proceedings of
the Eighth International Symposium of the Orion Center for the Study of the Dead Sea
Scrolls and Associated Literature, 7–9 January, 2003.* Edited by Steven D. Fraade,
Aharon Shemesh, and Ruth A. Clements. Studies on the Texts of the Desert of
Judah 62. Leiden: Brill, 2006.

Nock, A. D. *Conversion: The Old and the New in Religion from Alexander the Great to
Augustine of Hippo.* London: Oxford University Press, 1933.

Nolan, Daniel. "Stoic Gunk." *Phronesis* 51 (2006): 162–83.

Nongbri, Brent. *Before Religion: A History of a Modern Concept.* New Haven: Yale
University Press, 2013.

Novak, David. *The Image of the Non-Jew in Judaism: An Historical and Constructive Study
of the Noahide Laws.* Toronto Studies in Theology 14. Lewiston, NY: Mellen, 1983.

———. *The Election of Israel: The Idea of the Chosen People.* Cambridge,
UK: Cambridge University Press, 1995.

Novenson, Matthew V. "The Jewish Messiahs, the Pauline Christ, and the Gentile
Question." *Journal of Biblical Literature* 128 (2009): 357–73.

———. *Christ among the Messiahs: Christ Language in Paul and Messiah Language in
Ancient Judaism.* Oxford: Oxford University Press, 2012.

———. "The Messiah ben Abraham in Galatians: A Response to Joel Willitts."
*Journal for the Study of Paul and His Letters* 2 (2012): 163–69.

———. "Paul's Former Occupation in *Ioudaismos.*" Pages 24–39 in *Galatians and
Christian Theology: Justification, the Gospel, and Ethics in Paul's Letter.* Edited by
Mark W. Elliott et al. Grand Rapids: Baker Academic, 2014.

———. "The Self-Styled Jew of Romans 2 and the Actual Jews of Romans 9–11."
Pages 133–62 in *The So-Called Jew in Paul's Letter to the Romans.* Edited by Rafael
Rodríguez and Matthew Thiessen. Minneapolis: Fortress, 2016.

Nussbaum, Martha C. *The Therapy of Desire: Theory and Practice in Hellenistic Ethics.*
Princeton: Princeton University Press, 1994.

Nygren, Anders. *Commentary on Romans.* Translated by Carl C. Rasmussen.
London: SCM, 1952.

O'Meara, Dominic J. *Platonopolis: Platonic Political Philosophy in Late Antiquity.*
Oxford: Clarendon, 2003.

O'Neill, J. C. *Paul's Letter to the Romans*. Pelican New Testament Commentaries. Harmondsworth: Penguin, 1975.

Oesterley, W. O. E. *The Wisdom of Ben Sira (Ecclesiasticus)*. London: SPCK, 1916.

Oliver, Isaac W. *Torah Praxis after 70 CE: Reading Matthew and Luke-Acts as Jewish Texts*. Wissenschaftliche Untersuchungen zum Neuen Testament 2/355. Tübingen: Mohr Siebeck, 2013.

Olson, Daniel C. *A New Reading of the Animal Apocalypse of 1 Enoch: "All Nations Shall be Blessed."* Studia in Veteris Testamenti Pseudepigrapha 24. Leiden: Brill, 2013.

Olyan, Saul M. "Purity Ideology in Ezra-Nehemiah as a Tool to Reconstitute the Community." *Journal for the Study of Judaism in the Persian, Hellenistic, and Roman Periods* 35 (2004): 1–16.

Oppenheim, A. L. et al., eds. *The Assyrian Dictionary of the Oriental Institute of the University of Chicago*. Chicago: The Oriental Institute, 1956–.

Orlov, Andrei A. *Heavenly Priesthood in the Apocalypse of Abraham*. Cambridge, UK: Cambridge University Press, 2013.

Padgett, Alan G. "The Body in Resurrection: Science and Scripture on the 'Spiritual Body' (1 Cor 15:35–58)." *Word and World* 22 (2002): 155–63.

Pagels, Elaine H. *The Gnostic Paul: Gnostic Exegesis of the Pauline Letters*. Philadelphia: Fortress, 1975.

Paget, James Carleton. "Jewish Proselytism at the Time of Christian Origins: Chimera or Reality?" *Journal for the Study of the New Testament* 62 (1996): 65–103.

Paige, Terence. "Who Believes in 'Spirit'? Πνεῦμα in Pagan Usage and Implications for the Gentile Christian Mission." *Harvard Theological Review* 95 (2002): 417–36.

Pearson, Birger A. "1 Thessalonians 2:13–16: A Deutero-Pauline Interpolation." *Harvard Theological Review* 64 (1971): 79–94.

Peerbolte, L. J. Lietaert. *Paul the Missionary*. Contributions to Biblical Exegesis and Theology 34. Leuven: Peeters, 2003.

Penney, Douglas L., and Michael O. Wise. "By the Power of Beelzebub: An Aramaic Incantation Formula from Qumran (4Q560)." *Journal of Biblical Literature* 113 (1994): 627–50.

Perkins, Pheme. *Abraham's Divided Children: Galatians and the Politics of Faith*. The New Testament in Context. Harrisburg, PA: Trinity Press International, 2001.

Pervo, Richard I. *Dating Acts: Between the Evangelists and the Apologists*. Santa Rosa, CA: Polebridge, 2006.

———. *The Making of Paul: Constructions of the Apostle in Early Christianity*. Minneapolis: Fortress, 2010.

Petersen, Norman R. "On the Ending(s) to Paul's Letter to Rome." Pages 337–47 in *The Future of Early Christianity: Essays in Honor of Helmut Koester*. Edited by Birger A. Pearson et al. Minneapolis: Fortress, 1991.

Porter, Calvin L. "Romans 1.18–32: Its Role in the Developing Argument." *New Testament Studies* 40 (1994): 210–28.

Porter, Stanley E. *Idioms of the Greek New Testament*. Sheffield: Sheffield Academic, 1992.

Porton, Gary G. *Goyim: Gentiles and Israelites in Mishnah–Tosefta*. Brown Judaic Studies 155. Atlanta: Scholars Press, 1988.

———. *The Strangers within Your Gates: Converts and Conversion in Rabbinic Judaism*. Chicago Studies in the History of Judaism. Chicago: University of Chicago Press, 1994.

Preus, Anthony. "Galen's Criticism of Aristotle's Conception Theory." *Journal of the History of Biology* 10 (1977): 65–85.

Propp, William H. "The Origins of Infant Circumcision in Israel." *Hebrew Annual Review* 11 (1987): 355–70.

Rabens, Volker. *The Holy Spirit and Ethics in Paul: Transformation and Empowering for Religious-Ethical Life*. Wissenschaftliche Untersuchungen zum Neuen Testament 2/283. Tübingen: Mohr Siebeck, 2010.

Rad, Gerhard von. *Genesis: A Commentary*. Rev. ed. Translated by John H. Marks. Old Testament Library. Philadelphia: Westminster, 1972.

Räisänen, Heikki. *Paul and the Law*. Philadelphia: Fortress, 1983.

———. "Galatians 2.16 and Paul's Break with Judaism." *New Testament Studies* 31 (1985): 543–53.

Ramsay, W. M. *A Historical Commentary on St. Paul's Epistle to the Galatians*. London: Hodder and Stoughton, 1899.

Reumann, John. *Philippians: A New Translation with Introduction and Commentary*. Anchor Bible 33B. New Haven: Yale University Press, 2008.

Reydams-Schils, Gretchen J., ed. *Plato's Timaeus as Cultural Icon*. Notre Dame: University of Notre Dame Press, 2003.

Richardson, Peter. *Israel in the Apostolic Church*. Society for New Testament Studies Monograph Series 10. Cambridge, UK: Cambridge University Press, 1969.

Robertson, Paul. "De-spiritualizing *Pneuma*: Modernity, Religion, and Anachronism in the Study of Paul." *Method and Theory in the Study of Religion* 26 (2014): 365–83.

Rochberg, Francesca. "'The Stars Their Likenesses': Perspectives on the Relation Between Celestial Bodies and Gods in Ancient Mesopotamia." Pages 41–91 in *What Is a God? Anthropomorphic and Non-anthropomorphic Aspects of Deity in Ancient Mesopotamia*. Edited by Barbara Nevling Porter. Winona Lake, IN: Eisenbrauns, 2009.

Rodríguez, Rafael. *If You Call Yourself a Jew: Reappraising Paul's Letter to the Romans*. Eugene, OR: Cascade, 2014.

Rohde, Joachim. *Der Brief des Paulus an die Galater*. Theologischer Handkommentar zum Neuen Testament 9. Berlin: Evangelische Verlagsanstalt, 1989.

Roitman, Adolfo D. "Achior in the Book of Judith: His Role and Significance." Pages 31–45 in *"No One Spoke Ill of Her": Essays on Judith*. Edited by James C. VanderKam. Society of Biblical Literature Early Judaism and Its Literature 02. Atlanta: Scholars Press, 1992.

Rokéah, David. "Ancient Jewish Proselytism in Theory and in Practice." *Theologische Zeitschrift* 52 (1996): 206–24.

Ropes, J. H. *The Singular Problem of the Epistle to the Galatians*. Harvard Theological Studies 14. Cambridge, MA: Harvard University Press, 1929.

Rosen-Zvi, Ishay, and Adi Ophir. "Paul and the Invention of the Gentiles." *Jewish Quarterly Review* 105 (2015): 1–41.

Rowe, C. Kavin. "Biblical Pressure and Trinitarian Hermeneutics." *Pro Ecclesia* 11 (2002): 295–312.

———. *World Upside Down: Reading Acts in the Graeco-Roman Age.* Oxford: Oxford University Press, 2009.

Rubin, Nissan. "*Brit Milah*: A Study of Change in Custom." Pages 87–97 in *The Covenant of Circumcision: New Perspectives on an Ancient Jewish Rite.* Edited by Elizabeth Wyner Mark. Brandeis Series on Jewish Women. Hanover, NH: Brandeis University Press, 2003.

Rudolph, David J. "Paul's 'Rule in All the Churches' (1 Cor 7:17–24) and Torah-Defined Ecclesiological Variegation." *Studies in Christian-Jewish Relations* 5 (2010): 1–24.

———. *A Jew to the Jews: Jewish Contours of Pauline Flexibility in 1 Corinthians 9:19–23.* Wissenschaftliche Untersuchungen zum Neuen Testament 2/304. Tübingen: Mohr Siebeck, 2011.

Ruiten, Jacques T. A. G. M. van. "Angels and Demons in the Book of *Jubilees*." Pages 585–609 in *Die Dämonen: Die Dämonologie der israelitisch-jüdischen und frühchristlichen Literatur im Kontext ihrer Umwelt—Demons: The Demonology of Israelite-Jewish and Early Christian Literature in the Context of Their Environment.* Edited by Armin Lange, Hermann Lichtenberger, and K. F. Diethard Römheld. Tübingen: Mohr Siebeck, 2003.

———. "Genesis herschreven en geïnterpreteerd in het boek *Jubileeën*, nader toegelicht met een vergelijking van Genesis 17 en *Jubileeën* 15." *Nederlands theologisch tijdschrift* 64 (2010): 32–50.

———. *Abraham in the Book of Jubilees: The Rewriting of Genesis 11:26—25:10 in the Book of Jubilees 11:14—23:8.* Journal for the Study of Judaism: Supplement Series 161. Leiden: Brill, 2012.

Runesson, Anders. "Particularistic Judaism and Universalistic Christianity? Some Critical Remarks on Terminology and Theology." *Journal of Greco-Roman Christianity and Judaism* 1 (2000): 120–44.

———. "Inventing Christian Identity: Paul, Ignatius, and Theodosius I." Pages 59–92 in *Exploring Early Christian Identity.* Edited by Bengt Holmberg. Wissenschaftliche Untersuchungen zum Neuen Testament 226. Tübingen: Mohr Siebeck, 2008.

———. "Paul's Rule in All the *Ekklēsiai* (1 Cor 7:17–24)." Pages 214–23 in *Introduction to Messianic Judaism: Its Ecclesial Context and Biblical Foundations.* Edited by David Rudolph and Joel Willitts. Grand Rapids: Zondervan, 2013.

———. "The Question of Terminology: The Architecture of Contemporary Discussions on Paul." Pages 53–77 in *Paul within Judaism: Restoring the First-Century Context to the Apostle.* Edited by Mark D. Nanos and Magnus Zetterholm. Minneapolis: Fortress, 2015.

Runia, David T. *Philo of Alexandria and the Timaeus of Plato.* Philosophia Antiqua 44. Leiden: Brill, 1986.

Rusam, Dietrich. "Neue Belege zu den στοιχεῖα τοῦ κόσμου (Gal 4,3.9, Kol 2,8.20)." *Zeitschrift für die neutestamentliche Wissenschaft und die Kunde der älteren Kirche* 83 (1992): 119–25.

Sagi, Avi, and Zvi Zohar. "The Halakhic Ritual of Giyyur and Its Symbolic Meaning." *Journal of Ritual Studies* 9 (1995): 1–13.

———. *Transforming Identity: The Ritual Transition from Gentile to Jew—Structure and Meaning.* Kogod Library of Judaic Studies 3. London: Continuum, 2007.

Sambursky, Samuel. *Physics of the Stoics.* London: Routledge & Kegan Paul, 1959.

Sanders, E. P. *Paul and Palestinian Judaism: A Comparison of Patterns of Religion.* Philadelphia: Fortress, 1977.

———. *Paul, the Law, and the Jewish People.* Philadelphia: Fortress, 1983.

———. *Judaism: Practice and Belief, 63 BCE–66 CE.* London: SCM, 1992.

Sandmel, Samuel. *Philo's Place in Judaism: A Study of Conceptions of Abraham in Jewish Literature.* Augmented ed. New York: Ktav, 1971.

Sass, Gerhard. *Leben aus den Verheißungen: Traditionsgeschichtliche und biblisch-theologische Untersuchungen zur Rede von Gottes Verheißungen im Frühjudentum und beim Apostel Paulus.* Forschungen zur Religion und Literatur des Alten und Neuen Testaments 164. Göttingen: Vandenhoeck & Ruprecht, 1995.

Sasson, Jack M. "Circumcision in the Ancient Near East." *Journal of Biblical Literature* 85 (1966): 473–76.

Schäfer, Peter. *Rivalität zwischen Engeln und Menschen: Untersuchungen zur rabbinischen Engelvorstellung.* Studia Judaica 8. Berlin: de Gruyter, 1975.

Schechter, Solomon. *Some Aspects of Rabbinic Theology.* New York: Macmillan, 1909.

Schelkle, Karl Hermann. *Paulus, Lehrer der Väter: die altkirchliche Auslegung von Römer 1–11.* Düsseldorf: Patmos, 1956.

Schellenberg, Ryan S. "The First Pauline Chronologist? Paul's Itinerary in the Letters and in Acts." *Journal of Biblical Literature* 134 (2015): 193–213.

Scherbenske, Eric W. *Canonizing Paul: Ancient Editorial Practice and the Corpus Paulinum.* Oxford: Oxford University Press, 2013.

Schiffman, Lawrence H. "The Conversion of the Royal House of Adiabene in Josephus and Rabbinic Sources." Pages 293–312 in *Josephus, Judaism, and Christianity.* Edited by Louis H. Feldman and Gohei Hata. Detroit: Wayne State University Press, 1987.

Schlatter, Adolf. *Die Briefe an die Galater, Epheser, Kolosser und Philemon.* Berlin: Evangelische Verlagsanstalt, 1963.

Schliesser, Benjamin. *Abraham's Faith in Romans 4: Paul's Concept of Faith in Light of the History of Reception of Genesis 15:6.* Wissenschaftliche Untersuchungen zum Neuen Testament 2/224. Tübingen: Mohr Siebeck, 2007.

Schmeller, Thomas. *Paulus und die "Diatribe": Eine vergleichende Stilinterpretation.* Neutestamentliche Abhandlungen 19. Münster: Aschendorff, 1987.

Schmid, Konrad. "Judean Identity and Ecumenicity: The Political Theology of the Priestly Document." Pages 1–26 in *Judah and the Judeans in the Achaemenid Period: Negotiating Identity in an International Context*. Edited by Oded Lipschits, Gary N. Knoppers, and Manfred Oeming. Winona Lake, IN: Eisenbrauns, 2011.

Schmidt, Daryl. "1 Thess 2:13–16: Linguistic Evidence for an Interpolation." *Journal of Biblical Literature* 102 (1983): 269–79.

Schmidt, Hans Wilhelm. *Der Brief des Paulus an die Römer*. Theologischer Handkommentar zum Neuen Testament 6. Berlin: Evangelische Verlagsanstalt, 1962.

Schmithals, Walter. *Paul and the Gnostics*. Translated by John E. Steely. Nashville: Abingdon, 1972.

———. "Judaisten in Galatien." *Zeitschrift für die neutestamentliche Wissenschaft und die Kunde der älteren Kirche* 74 (1983): 51–57.

Schmitz, Matthew. "N. T. Wright on Gay Marriage: Nature and Narrative Point to Complementarity." *First Things* (June 11, 2014). No pages. Online: http://www.firstthings.com/blogs/firstthoughts/2014/06/n-t-wrights-argument-against-same-sex-marriage.

Schoeps, Hans Joachim. *Paul: The Theology of the Apostle in the Light of Jewish Religious History*. Translated by Harold Knight. Philadelphia: Westminster, 1961.

Schreiner, Thomas R. *The Law and Its Fulfillment: A Pauline Theology of Law*. Grand Rapids: Baker, 1993.

Schwartz, Daniel R. "God, Gentiles, and Jewish Law: On Acts 15 and Josephus' Adiabene Narrative." Pages 263–82 in vol. 1 of *Geschichte—Tradition—Reflexion: Festschrift für Martin Hengel zum 70. Geburtstag*. Edited by Hubert Cancik, Hermann Lichtenberger, and Peter Schäfer. 3 vols. Tübingen: Mohr [Siebeck], 1996.

———. "'Judaean' or 'Jew'? How Should We Translate *Ioudaios* in Josephus?" Pages 3–27 in *Jewish Identity in the Greco-Roman World/Jüdische Identität in der griechisch-römischen Welt*. Edited by Jörg Frey, Daniel R. Schwartz, and Stephanie Gripentrog. Arbeiten zur Geschichte des antiken Judentums und des Urchristentums 71. Leiden: Brill, 2007.

Schwarz, Eberhard. *Identität durch Abgrenzung: Abgrenzungsprozesse in Israel im 2. vorchristlichen Jahrhundert und ihre traditionsgeschichtlichen Voraussetzungen Zugleich ein Beitrag zur Erforschung des Jubiläenbuches*. Europäische Hochschulschriften 162. Frankfurt: Lang, 1982.

Schweitzer, Albert. *The Mysticism of Paul the Apostle*. Translated by William Montgomery. Baltimore: Johns Hopkins University Press, 1953.

Schweizer, Eduard. "Slaves of the Elements and Worshipers of Angels: Gal 4:3, 9 and Col 2:8, 18, 20." *Journal of Biblical Literature* 107 (1988): 455–68.

———. "Altes und Neues zu den 'Elementen der Welt' in Kol 2,20; Gal 4,3–9." Pages 111–18 in *Wissenschaft und Kirche: Festschrift für Eduard Lohse*. Edited by Kurt Aland and Siegfried Meurer. Texte und Arbeiten zur Bibel 4. Bielefeld: Luther Verlag, 1989.

Scott, Alan. *Origen and the Life of the Stars: A History of an Idea.* Oxford Early Christian Studies. Oxford: Clarendon, 1991.

Scott, James M. *Adoption as Sons of God: An Exegetical Investigation into the Background of ΥΙΟΘΕΣΙΑ in the Pauline Corpus.* Wissenschaftliche Untersuchungen zum Neuen Testament 2/48. Tübingen: Mohr Siebeck, 1992.

———. "Philo and the Restoration of Israel." Pages 553–75 in *Society of Biblical Literature 1995 Seminar Papers.* Society of Biblical Literature Seminar Papers 34. Atlanta: Scholars Press, 1996.

Sechrest, Love L. *A Former Jew: Paul and the Dialectics of Race.* Library of New Testament Studies 410. London: T&T Clark, 2010.

Sedley, David. "'Becoming Like God' in the *Timaeus* and Aristotle." Pages 327–39 in *Interpreting the Timaeus-Critias: Proceedings of the Fourth Symposium Platonicum, Granada. Selected Papers.* Edited by Tomás Calvo and Luc Brisson. St. Augustin: Academia Verlag, 1997.

———. "The Ideal of Godlikeness." Pages 309–28 in *Plato 2: Ethics, Politics, Religion, and the Soul.* Edited by Gail Fine. Oxford Readings in Philosophy. Oxford: Oxford University Press, 1999.

———. "The School, from Zeno to Arius Didymus." Pages 7–32 in *The Cambridge Companion to the Stoics.* Edited by Brad Inwood. Cambridge, UK: Cambridge University Press, 2003.

———. "Matter in Hellenistic Philosophy." Pages 53–66 in *Materia: XIII Colloquio Internazionale: Roma, 7–8–9 gennaio 2010.* Edited by Delfina Giovannozzi and Marco Veneziani. Lessico intellettuale europeo 113. Rome: Olschki, 2011.

Segal, Alan F. "The Cost of Proselytism and Conversion." Pages 336–69 in *Society of Biblical Literature 1988 Seminar Papers.* Society of Biblical Literature Seminar Papers 27. Atlanta: Scholars Press, 1988.

———. *Paul the Convert: The Apostolate and Apostasy of Saul the Pharisee.* New Haven: Yale University Press, 1990.

Segal, Michael. *The Book of Jubilees: Rewritten Bible, Redaction, Ideology and Theology.* Journal for the Study of Judaism: Supplement Series 117. Leiden: Brill, 2007.

Sekki, Arthur E. *The Meaning of Ruaḥ at Qumran.* Society of Biblical Literature Dissertation Series 110. Atlanta: Scholars Press, 1989.

Sellars, John. *Stoicism.* Berkeley: University of California Press, 2006.

Sellin, Gerhard. "Hagar und Sara: Religionsgeschichtliche Hintergründe der Schriftallegorese Gal 4,21–31." Pages 59–84 in *Das Urchristentum in seiner literarischen Geschichte: Festschrift für Jürgen Becker zum 65. Geburtstag.* Edited by Ulrich Mell and Ulrich B. Müller. Beihefte zur Zeitschrift für die neutestamentliche Wissenschaft 100. Berlin: de Gruyter, 1999.

Sharvy, Richard. "Aristotle on Mixtures." *Journal of Philosophy* 80 (1983): 439–57.

Sheppard, Gerald T. "The 'Scope' of Isaiah as a Book of Jewish and Christian Scriptures." Pages 257–81 in *New Visions of Isaiah.* Edited by Roy F. Melugin and Marvin A. Sweeney. Journal for the Study of the Old Testament: Supplement Series 214. Sheffield: Sheffield Academic, 1996.

Siegert, Folker. *Argumentation bei Paulus gezeigt an Röm 9–11*. Wissenschaftliche Untersuchungen zum Neuen Testament 34. Tübingen: Mohr Siebeck, 1985.

Sievers, Joseph. *The Hasmoneans and Their Supporters: From Mattathias to the Death of John Hyrcanus I*. South Florida Studies in the History of Judaism 6. Atlanta: Scholars Press, 1990.

Sim, David C., and James S. McLaren, eds. *Attitudes to Gentiles in Ancient Judaism and Early Christianity*. Library of New Testament Studies 499. London: T&T Clark, 2014.

Smith, Anthony D. *Chosen Peoples: Sacred Sources of National Identity*. Oxford: Oxford University Press, 2003.

———. *The Antiquity of Nations*. Cambridge, UK: Polity, 2004.

Smyth, Herbert Weir. *Greek Grammar*. 3d ed. Revised by Gordon M. Messing. Cambridge, MA: Harvard University Press, 1984.

Sollamo, Raija. "The Creation of Angels and Natural Phenomena Intertwined in the *Book of Jubilees* (4Q Jubᵃ): Angels and Natural Phenomena as Characteristics of the Creation Stories and Hymns in Late Second Temple Judaism." Pages 273–90 in *Biblical Traditions in Transmission: Essays in Honour of Michael A. Knibb*. Edited by Charlotte Hempel and Judith M. Lieu. Journal for the Study of Judaism: Supplement Series 111. Leiden: Brill, 2006.

Solmsen, Friedrich. "The Vital Heat, the Inborn *Pneuma* and the Aether." *Journal of Hellenic Studies* 77 (1957): 119–23.

Spanneut, Michel. *Le Stoïcisme des Pères de l'Église: de Clément de Rome à Clément d'Alexandrie*. Paris: Éditions du Seuil, 1957.

Stähli, Hans-Peter. *Solare Elemente im Jahweglauben des alten Testaments*. Orbis biblicus et orientalis 66. Freiburg: Universitäts-verlag, 1985.

Standhartinger, Angela. "'Zur Freiheit . . . befreit'? Hagar im Galaterbrief." *Evangelische Theologie* 62 (2002): 288–303.

Stanley, Christopher D. "'Under a Curse': A Fresh Reading of Galatians 3.10–14." *New Testament Studies* 36 (1990): 481–511.

———. *Arguing with Scripture: The Rhetoric of Quotations in the Letters of Paul*. London: T&T Clark, 2004.

Starnitzke, Dierk. "'Griechen und Barbaren . . . bin ich verpflichtet' (Röm 1,14): Die Selbstdefinition der Gesellschaft und die Individualität und Universalität der paulinischen Botschaft." *Wort und Dienst* 24 (1997): 187–207.

Steinberg, Jonah. "Angelic Israel: Self-identification with Angels in Rabbinic Agadah and its Jewish Antecedents." Ph.D. diss., Columbia University, 2003.

Steiner, Richard C. "Incomplete Circumcision in Egypt and Edom: Jeremiah (9:24–25) in the Light of Josephus and Jonckheere." *Journal of Biblical Literature* 118 (1999): 497–526.

Stendahl, Krister. *Paul Among the Jews and Gentiles, and Other Essays*. Philadelphia: Fortress, 1976.

Steuernagel, Carl. "Bemerkungen zu Genesis 17." Pages 172–79 in *Beiträge zur alt-testamentlichen Wissenschaft: Karl Budde zum siebzigsten Geburtstag am 13. April*

*1920 überreicht von Freunden und Schülern.* Edited by Karl Marti. Beihefte zur Zeitschrift für die alttestamentliche Wissenschaft 34. Giessen: Töpelmann, 1920.

Stowers, Stanley K. *The Diatribe and Paul's Letter to the Romans.* Society of Biblical Literature Dissertation Series 57. Chico, CA: Scholars Press, 1981.

———. *A Rereading of Romans: Justice, Jews, and Gentiles.* New Haven: Yale University Press, 1994.

———. "Romans 7.7–25 as a Speech-in-Character (προσωποποιία)." Pages 180–202 in *Paul in His Hellenistic Context.* Edited by Troels Engberg-Pedersen. Minneapolis: Fortress, 1995.

———. "Paul and Self-Mastery." Pages 524–50 in *Paul in the Greco-Roman World: A Handbook.* Edited by J. Paul Sampley. Harrisburg, PA: Trinity Press International, 2003.

———. "What Is 'Pauline Participation in Christ'?" Pages 352–71 in *Redefining First-Century Jewish and Christian Identities: Essays in Honor of Ed Parish Sanders.* Edited by Fabian E. Udoh et al. Christianity and Judaism in Antiquity 16. Notre Dame: University of Notre Dame Press, 2008.

Strack, Hermann L., and Paul Billerbeck. *Kommentar zum Neuen Testament aus Talmud und Midrasch.* 6 vols. Munich: Beck, 1922–1961.

Struck, Peter T. *Birth of the Symbol: Ancient Readers at the Limits of Their Texts.* Princeton: Princeton University Press, 2004.

Stuhlmacher, Peter. *Paul's Letter to the Romans: A Commentary.* Translated by Scott J. Hafemann. Louisville: Westminster John Knox, 1994.

———. *Revisiting Paul's Doctrine of Justification: A Challenge to the New Perspective.* Downers Grove, IL: InterVarsity Press, 2001.

Swancutt, Diana M. "'The Disease of Effemination': The Charge of Effeminacy and the Verdict of God (Romans 1:18—2:16)." Pages 193–233 in *New Testament Masculinities.* Edited by Stephen D. Moore and Janice Capel Anderson. Semeia Studies 45. Atlanta: SBL Press, 2003.

———. "Sexy Stoics and the Rereading of Romans 1.18—2.16." Pages 42–73 in *A Feminist Companion to Paul.* Edited by Amy-Jill Levine and Marianne Blickenstaff. Cleveland: Pilgrim Press, 2004.

Syrén, Roger. *The Forsaken First-born: A Study of a Recurrent Motif in the Patriarchal Narratives.* Journal for the Study of the Old Testament: Supplement Series 133. Sheffield: Sheffield Academic, 1993.

Tabor, James. "Paul's Notion of Many 'Sons of God' in its Hellenistic Contexts." *Helios* 13 (1986): 87–97.

———. *Things Unutterable: Paul's Ascent to Paradise in its Greco-Roman, Judaic, and Early Christian Contexts.* Studies in Judaism. Lanham, MD: University Press of America, 1986.

Tatum, Gregory. "'To The Jew First' (Romans 1:16): Paul's Defense of Jewish Privilege in Romans." Pages 275–86 in *Celebrating Paul: Festschrift in Honor of Jerome Murphy-O'Connor, O.P., and Joseph A. Fitzmyer, S.J.* Edited by Peter Spitaler.

Catholic Biblical Quarterly Monograph Series 48. Washington, DC: Catholic Biblical Association of America, 2011.

Taubes, Jacob. *The Political Theology of Paul*. Translated by Dana Hollander. Cultural Memory in the Present. Stanford, CA: Stanford University Press, 2003.

Taylor, J. Glen. *Yahweh and the Sun: Biblical and Archaeological Evidence for Sun Worship in Ancient Israel*. Journal for the Study of the Old Testament: Supplement Series 111. Sheffield: JSOT Press, 1993.

Testuz, Michel. *Les Idées Religieuses du Livre des Jubilés*. Geneva: Droz, 1960.

Thielman, Frank. "The Coherence of Paul's View of the Law: The Evidence of First Corinthians." *New Testament Studies* 38 (1992): 235–53.

Thiessen, Matthew. "The Function of a Conjunction: Inclusivist or Exclusivist Strategies in Ezra 6.19–21 and Nehemiah 10.29–30?" *Journal for the Study of the Old Testament* 34 (2009): 63–79.

———. "The Text of Genesis 17:14." *Journal of Biblical Literature* 128 (2009): 625–42.

———. *Contesting Conversion: Genealogy, Circumcision and Identity in Ancient Judaism and Christianity*. Oxford: Oxford University Press, 2011.

———. "Revisiting the προσήλυτος in 'the LXX.'" *Journal of Biblical Literature* 132 (2013): 333–50.

———. "Aseneth's Eight-Day Transformation as Scriptural Justification for Conversion." *Journal for the Study of Judaism in the Persian, Hellenistic, and Roman Periods* 45 (2014): 229–49.

———. "Paul's Argument against Gentile Circumcision in Romans 2:17–29." *Novum Testamentum* 56 (2014): 373–91.

Thorsteinsson, Runar M. "Paul's Missionary Duty towards Gentiles in Rome: A Note on the Punctuation and Syntax of Rom 1.13–15." *New Testament Studies* 48 (2002): 531–47.

———. *Paul's Interlocutor in Romans 2: Function and Identity in the Context of Ancient Epistolography*. Coniectanea neotestamentica or Coniectanea biblica: New Testament Series 40. Stockholm: Almqvist & Wiksell, 2003.

Tollefsen, Torstein Theodor. *Activity and Participation in Late Antique and Early Christian Thought*. Oxford Early Christian Studies. Oxford: Oxford University Press, 2012.

Tomson, Peter J. *Paul and the Jewish Law: Halakha in the Letters of the Apostle to the Gentiles*. Compendia rerum iudaicarum ad Novum Testamentum 1. Assen: Van Gorcum, 1990.

———. "Paul's Jewish Background in View of His Law Teaching in 1 Cor 7." Pages 251–70 in *Paul and the Mosaic Law*. Edited by James D. G. Dunn. Grand Rapids: Eerdmans, 2001.

———. "Halakhah in the New Testament: A Research Overview." Pages 135–206 in *The New Testament and Rabbinic Literature*. Edited by Reimund Bieringer et al. Journal for the Study of Judaism: Supplement Series 136. Leiden: Brill, 2010.

Trible, Phyllis. "Ominous Beginnings for a Promise of Blessing." Pages 33–69 in *Hagar, Sarah, and Their Children: Jewish, Christian, and Muslim Perspectives*. Edited by Phyllis Trible and Letty M. Russell. Louisville: Westminster John Knox, 2006.

Trick, Bradley K. "Sons, Seed, and Children of Promise in Galatians: Discerning the Coherence in Paul's Model of Abrahamic Descent." Ph.D. diss., Duke University, 2010.

Troyer, Kristin de, and Armin Lange, eds. *Reading the Present in the Qumran Library: The Perception of the Contemporary by Means of Scriptural Interpretations.* Society of Biblical Literature Symposium Series 30. Atlanta: SBL Press, 2005.

Tyson, Joseph B. *Marcion and Luke-Acts: A Defining Struggle.* Columbia: University of South Carolina, 2006.

Van Seters, John. "The Problem of Childlessness in Near Eastern Law and the Patriarchs of Israel." *Journal of Biblical Literature* 87 (1968): 401–8.

VanderKam, James C. *Textual and Historical Studies in the Book of Jubilees.* Harvard Semitic Monographs 14. Missoula, MT: Scholars Press, 1977.

Verbeke, Gérard. *L'évolution de la doctrine du pneuma, du Stoicisme à s. Augustin: Étude philosophique.* Paris: de Brouwer, 1945.

Vermes, Geza. "Baptism and Jewish Exegesis: New Light from Ancient Sources." *New Testament Studies* 4 (1958): 308–19.

Vielhauer, Philipp. "On the 'Paulinism' of Acts." Pages 33–50 in *Studies in Luke-Acts.* Edited by Leander E. Keck and J. Louis Martyn. Nashville: Abingdon, 1966.

———. "Gesetzesdienst und Stoicheiadienst im Galaterbrief." Pages 543–55 in *Rechtfertigung: Festschrift für Ernst Käsemann zum 70. Geburtstag.* Edited by Johannes Friedrich, Wolfgang Pöhlmann, and Peter Stuhlmacher. Tübingen: Mohr, 1976.

Wagner, J. Ross. *Heralds of the Good News: Isaiah and Paul "In Concert" in the Letter to the Romans.* Novum Testamentum Supplements 101. Leiden: Brill, 2002.

Wahlen, Clinton. *Jesus and the Impurity of Spirits in the Synoptic Gospels.* Wissenschaftliche Untersuchungen zum Neuen Testament 2/185. Tübingen: Mohr Siebeck, 2004.

Walker, William O. Jr. "Acts and the Pauline Corpus Reconsidered." *Journal for the Study of the New Testament* 24 (1985): 3–23.

———. "Romans 1:18—2:29: A Non-Pauline Interpolation?" *New Testament Studies* 45 (1999): 533–52.

Wall, Robert W. "The Acts of the Apostles in Canonical Context." Pages 110–28 in *The New Testament as Canon: A Reader in Canonical Criticism.* Edited by Robert W. Wall and Eugene E. Lemcio. Journal for the Study of the New Testament: Supplement Series 76. Sheffield: Sheffield Academic, 1992.

———. "Reading Paul with Acts: The Canonical Shaping of a Holy Church." Pages 129–47 in *Holiness and Ecclesiology in the New Testament.* Edited by Kent E. Brower and Andy Johnson. Grand Rapids: Eerdmans, 2007.

Wallace, Daniel B. *Greek Grammar Beyond the Basics: An Exegetical Syntax of the New Testament.* Grand Rapids: Zondervan, 1996.

Wallace-Hadrill, Andrew. *Rome's Cultural Revolution.* Cambridge, UK: Cambridge University Press, 2008.

Walter, Nikolas. "Paulus und die Gegner des Christusevangeliums in Galatien." Pages 351–56 in *L'Apôtre Paul: Personnalité, Style et Conception du Ministère.* Edited by Albert Vanhoye et al. Bibliotheca ephemeridum theologicarum lovaniensium 73. Leuven: Leuven University Press, 1986.

————. "Hellenistische Diaspora-Juden an der Wiege des Urchristentums." Pages 37–58 in *The New Testament and Hellenistic Judaism*. Edited by Peder Borgen and Søren Giversen. Peabody, MA: Hendrickson, 1997.

Walters, James C. "Paul, Adoption, and Inheritance." Pages 42–76 in *Paul in the Greco-Roman World: A Handbook*. Edited by J. Paul Sampley. Harrisburg, PA: Trinity Press International, 2003.

Wan, Sze-Kar. "Abraham and the Promise of the Spirit: Galatians and the Hellenistic-Jewish Mysticism of Philo." Pages 6–22 in *Society of Biblical Literature 1995 Seminar Papers*. Society of Biblical Literature Seminar Papers 34. Atlanta: Scholars Press, 1995.

————. "Does Diaspora Identity Imply Some Sort of Universality? An Asian-American Reading of Galatians." Pages 107–31 in *Interpreting Beyond Borders*. Edited by Fernando F. Segovia. Bible and Postcolonialism 3. Sheffield: Sheffield Academic, 2000.

Wander, Bernd. *Gottesfürchtige und Sympathisanten: Studien zum heidnischen Umfeld von Diasporasynagogen*. Wissenschaftliche Untersuchungen zum Neuen Testament 104. Tübingen: Mohr Siebeck, 1998.

Ware, James P. *The Mission of the Church in Paul's Letter to the Philippians in the Context of Ancient Judaism*. Novum Testamentum Supplements 120. Leiden: Brill, 2005.

Wasserman, Emma. *The Death of the Soul in Romans 7: Sin, Death, and the Law in Light of Hellenistic Moral Psychology*. Wissenschaftliche Untersuchungen zum Neuen Testament 2/256. Tübingen: Mohr Siebeck, 2008.

Watson, Francis. *Paul and the Hermeneutics of Faith*. London: T&T Clark, 2004.

————. *Paul, Judaism, and the Gentiles: Beyond the New Perspective*. Rev. ed. Grand Rapids: Eerdmans, 2007.

Wedderburn, A. J. M. "Some Observations on Paul's Use of the Phrases 'in Christ' and 'with Christ.'" *Journal for the Study of the New Testament* 25 (1985): 83–97.

Weima, Jeffrey A. D. "Preaching the Gospel in Rome: A Study of the Epistolary Framework of Romans." Pages 337–66 in *Gospel in Paul: Studies in Corinthians, Galatians and Romans for Richard N. Longenecker*. Edited by L. Ann Jervis and Peter Richardson. Journal for the Study of the New Testament: Supplement Series 108. Sheffield: Sheffield Academic, 1994.

————. "The Reason for Romans: The Evidence of Its Epistolary Framework (1:1–15, 15:14—16:27)." *Review and Expositor* 100 (2003): 17–33.

Weinfeld, Moshe. "Divine Intervention in War in Ancient Israel and in the Ancient Near East." Pages 121–47 in *History, Historiography and Interpretation: Studies in Biblical and Cuneiform Literatures*. Edited by Hayim Tadmor and Moshe Weinfeld. Jerusalem: Magnes, 1983.

Weitzman, Steven. "Forced Circumcision and the Shifting Role of Gentiles in Hasmonean Ideology." *Harvard Theological Review* 92 (1999): 37–59.

Werman, Cana. "*Jubilees* 30: Building a Paradigm for the Ban on Intermarriage." *Harvard Theological Review* 90 (1997): 1–22.

Wernberg-Møller, P. "A Reconsideration of the Two Spirits in the Rule of the Community [IQSerek III,13—IV,26]." *Revue de Qumran* 3 (1961): 413–41.

Westerholm, Stephen. *Perspectives Old and New on Paul: The "Lutheran" Paul and His Critics.* Grand Rapids: Eerdmans, 2004.

———. "Righteousness, Cosmic and Microcosmic." Pages 21–38 in *Apocalyptic Paul: Cosmos and Anthropos in Romans 5–8.* Edited by Beverly Roberts Gaventa. Waco, TX: Baylor University Press, 2013.

Westermann, Claus. *Genesis 12–36.* Translated by John J. Scullion. Continental Commentary. Minneapolis: Fortress, 1985.

Wevers, John William. *Notes on the Greek Text of Genesis.* Society of Biblical Literature Septuagint and Cognate Studies 35. Atlanta: Scholars Press, 1993.

White, Benjamin L. "Reclaiming Paul: Reconfiguration as Reclamation in *3 Corinthians*." *Journal of Early Christian Studies* 17 (2009): 497–523.

———. *Remembering Paul: Ancient and Modern Contests over the Image of the Apostle.* Oxford: Oxford University Press, 2014.

Whitsett, Christopher G. "Son of God, Seed of David: Paul's Messianic Exegesis in Romans 1:3–4." *Journal of Biblical Literature* 119 (2000): 661–81.

Wiefel, Wolfgang. "Die jüdische Gemeinschaft im antiken Rom und die Anfänge des römischen Christentums: Bemerkungen zu Anlass und Zweck des Römerbriefs." *Judaica* 26 (1970): 65–88.

Wilberding, James. "Porphyry and Plotinus on the Seed." *Phronesis* 53 (2008): 406–32.

Wilckens, Ulrich. *Der Brief an die Römer.* 3 vols. Evangelisch-katholischer Kommentar zum Neuen Testament 6. Neukirchen-Vluyn: Neukirchener Verlag, 1978–1992.

Wilcox, Max. "The Promise of the 'Seed' in the New Testament and the Targumim." *Journal for the Study of the New Testament* 5 (1979): 2–20.

Wiley, Tatha. *Paul and the Gentile Women: Reframing Galatians.* New York: Continuum, 2005.

Williams, Ronald J. *Williams' Hebrew Syntax.* 3d ed. Revised and expanded by John C. Beckman. Toronto: University of Toronto Press, 2007.

Williams, Sam K. "*Promise* in Galatians: A Reading of Paul's Reading of Scripture." *Journal of Biblical Literature* 107 (1988): 709–20.

———. "The Hearing of Faith: ΑΚΟΗ ΠΙΣΤΕΩΣ in Galatians 3." *New Testament Studies* 35 (1989): 82–93.

———. *Galatians.* Abingdon New Testament Commentary. Nashville: Abingdon, 1997.

Williamson, Paul R. *Abraham, Israel and the Nations: The Patriarchal Promise and its Covenantal Development in Genesis.* Journal for the Study of the Old Testament: Supplement Series 315. Sheffield: Sheffield Academic, 2000.

Willitts, Joel. "Isa 54,1 in Gal 4,24: Reading Genesis in Light of Isaiah." *Zeitschrift für die neutestamentliche Wissenschaft und die Kunde der älteren Kirche* 96 (2005): 188–210.

Wilson, Walter T. *Philo of Alexandria: On Virtues.* Philo of Alexandria Commentary Series 3. Leiden: Brill, 2011.

Witherington, Ben, with Darlene Hyatt. *Paul's Letter to the Romans: A Socio-Rhetorical Commentary*. Grand Rapids: Eerdmans, 2004.

Wolfson, Harry Austryn. *Philo: Foundations of Religious Philosophy in Judaism, Christianity, and Islam*. 2 vols. Cambridge, MA: Harvard University Press, 1947.

Wolter, Michael. "Das Israelproblem nach Gal 4,21–31 und Röm 9–11." *Zeitschrift für Theologie und Kirche* 107 (2010): 1–30.

Woyke, Johannes. "Nochmals zu den 'schwachen und unfähigen Elementen' (Gal 4.9): Paulus, Philo und die στοιχεῖα τοῦ κόσμου." *New Testament Studies* 54 (2008): 221–34.

Wrede, William. *Paul*. Translated by Edward Lummis. London: Philip Green, 1907.

Wright, N. T. *The Climax of the Covenant: Christ and the Law in Pauline Theology*. Minneapolis: Fortress, 1992.

———. *What Saint Paul Really Said: Was Paul of Tarsus the Real Founder of Christianity?* Grand Rapids: Eerdmans, 1997.

———. *The Resurrection of the Son of God*. Minneapolis: Fortress, 2003.

———. "Romans 2:17—3:9: A Hidden Clue to the Meaning of Romans?" *Journal for the Study of Paul and His Letters* 2 (2012): 1–26.

———. *Paul and the Faithfulness of God*. 2 vols. Minneapolis: Fortress, 2013.

———. "Messiahship in Galatians?" Pages 3–23 in *Galatians and Christian Theology: Justification, the Gospel, and Ethics in Paul's Letter*. Edited by Mark W. Elliott et al. Grand Rapids: Baker Academic, 2014.

Yoshiko Reed, Annette. "When Did Rabbis Become Pharisees? Reflections on Christian Evidence for Post-70 Judaism." Pages 859–96 in vol. 2 of *Envisioning Judaism: Studies in Honor of Peter Schäfer on the Occasion of his Seventieth Birthday*. 2 vols. Edited by Ra'anan S. Boustan et al. Tübingen: Mohr Siebeck, 2013.

Zahn, Theodor. *Der Brief des Paulus an die Römer*. Kommentar zum Neue Testament 6. Leipzig: Deichert, 1910.

Zeitlin, Solomon. "Proselytes and Proselytism during the Second Commonwealth and the Early Tannaitic Period." Pages 871–81 in vol. 2 of *Harry Austryn Wolfson Jubilee Volume: On the Occasion of his Seventy-Fifth Birthday*. 3 vols. Jerusalem: American Academy for Jewish Research, 1965.

Zetterholm, Magnus. *Approaches to Paul: A Student's Guide to Recent Scholarship*. Minneapolis: Fortress, 2009.

———. "Paul within Judaism: The State of the Questions." Pages 31–51 in *Paul within Judaism: Restoring the First-Century Context to the Apostle*. Edited by Mark D. Nanos and Magnus Zetterholm. Minneapolis: Fortress, 2015.

Zlotowitz, Meir. *Bereishis/Genesis: A New Translation with a Commentary Anthologized from Talmudic, Midrashic and Rabbinic Sources*. 2 vols. Brooklyn: Mesorah, 1988.

# Index of Ancient Sources

ANCIENT NEAR EASTERN WRITINGS

# Index of Modern Authors

# Index of Subjects

Printed in the USA
CPSIA information can be obtained
at www.ICGtesting.com
CBHW021753150224
4376CB00004B/372